THE
NEW BOOK
OF
KNOWLEDGE

The New Book of Knowledge

Scholastic Library Publishing, Inc.
Danbury, Connecticut

VOLUME 11

L

L, the twelfth letter in the English alphabet, was also the twelfth letter in the ancient Hebrew and Phoenician alphabets, and it was the eleventh letter in the classical Greek alphabet. The Hebrews and Phoenicians called it *lamed*. The Greeks called it *lambda*.

Many language scholars believe that the Phoenician word *lamed* meant "goad," or "crooked staff," and that the letter was a picture of a goad. The letter *lamed* looked like this: *l*.

The classical Greek *lambda* was used in eastern Greece. Different versions of the letter existed in other parts of the country. The form first used by the Romans when they adapted the Greek alphabet was the western Greek form of the letter. The Etruscans, who played an important role in the shaping of the Roman alphabet, also used this form of the letter. It looked like this: *l*. The Romans later made their letters more regular and gave the letter L the shape it has today.

The two main sounds of the letter in English are called the "clear" and the "dark" L. When the back of the tongue curves downward, as in the words *lumber, lake,* and *laugh,* the sound of the clear L is produced. The back of the tongue is raised toward the soft palate to produce the dark sound of the letter. Examples of words with the dark sound of the letter are *field, full,* and *cattle.* There are also some English words, such as *should* or *calf,* in which the L is silent.

The letter L is found in many abbreviations. In Roman numerals L stands for 50, and an L with a line above it ($\overline{L}$) denotes 50,000. In English money an L with a crossbar (£) stands for pound (from the Latin *libra,* or "pound"). LL.B. (for the Latin *Legum Baccalaureus,* meaning "Bachelor of Laws") is a degree held by lawyers. In dictionaries, L is usually the abbreviation for Latin, and in measurement it is the symbol for liter, a unit of volume.

Reviewed by MARIO PEI
Author, *The Story of Language*

See also ALPHABET.

SOME WAYS TO REPRESENT L:

The **manuscript** or printed forms of the letter (left) are highly readable. The **cursive** letters (right) are formed from slanted flowing strokes joining one letter to the next.

The **Manual Alphabet** (left) enables a deaf person to communicate by forming letters with the fingers of one hand. **Braille** (right) is a system by which a blind person can use fingertips to "read" raised dots that stand for letters.

The **International Code of Signals** is a special group of flags used to send and receive messages at sea. Each letter is represented by a different flag.

International Morse Code is used to send messages by radio signals. Each letter is expressed as a combination of dots (•) and dashes (--).

LABOR, UNITED STATES DEPARTMENT OF

The U.S. Department of Labor (DOL) was created in 1913 to promote the welfare of working Americans. At that time, most people worked about 50 hours a week for about 22 cents an hour. Hazardous working conditions were common.

Today, most Americans are employed in steady, decent jobs and are protected by safety and health legislation. Laws guarantee most of them a minimum wage, unemployment insurance, and workers' compensation if they are injured on the job. Employers cannot turn down a person for a job or refuse a promotion because of race, sex, religion, age, country of birth, veteran's status, or disability.

The Labor Department enforces laws that protect the pension rights of workers. It also upholds laws requiring safe and healthy workplaces, and it helps people find jobs and sponsors training programs for those who need it. The department also oversees an unemployment insurance system that provides an emergency financial cushion for people who are temporarily out of work. In addition, it keeps track of wages, prices, and employment and other labor statistics.

The Department of Labor is one of the 15 executive departments of the United States government. It is headed by a secretary, who is nominated by the president and confirmed by the Senate. The secretary of Labor is a member of the president's cabinet.

Organization

The **Employment Standards Administration** (ESA) has four programs: the Wage and Hour Division, the Office of Federal Contract Compliance Programs, the Office of Labor-Management Standards, and the Office of Workers' Compensation Programs. The ESA administers laws that regulate minimum wages, overtime pay, and child labor. This agency also enforces laws requiring federal contractors and subcontractors to provide equal opportunities to their workers and to pay locally acceptable wages. And it creates standards for the operation of unions to protect the rights of union members.

The **Employment and Training Administration** (ETA) provides training, job placement, and financial assistance to millions of people who need help getting and keeping jobs. There are special training programs for older workers, seasonal farmworkers, Native Americans, and others. The ETA also administers the Job Corps, a nationwide network of employment and job training centers for disadvantaged youths.

The **Occupational Safety and Health Administration** (OSHA) was established in 1971 by an act of Congress. It develops standards to assure safe and healthful workplaces and conducts periodic inspections.

The **Mine Safety and Health Administration** (MSHA) monitors the safety of working conditions. Training and technical assistance are provided to miners and owners of mining and milling operations.

The **Employee Benefits Security Administration** (EBSA) helps regulate about 700,000 private sector pension plans under the guidelines of the Employment Retirement Income Security Act (ERISA). ERISA handles nearly $5 trillion in assets and about 6 million welfare plans that provide medical, disability, severance, training, and other benefits.

The **Veterans' Employment and Training Service** (VETS) works with state employment services to make sure that any veteran who wants a job can find one or obtain the training necessary to get one.

Secretaries of Labor		
Name	**Took Office**	**Under President**
William B. Wilson	1913	Wilson
James J. Davis	1921	Harding, Coolidge, Hoover
William N. Doak	1930	Hoover
Frances Perkins	1933	F. D. Roosevelt, Truman
Lewis B. Schwellenbach	1945	Truman
Maurice J. Tobin	1948	Truman
Martin P. Durkin	1953	Eisenhower
James P. Mitchell	1953	Eisenhower
Arthur J. Goldberg	1961	Kennedy
W. Willard Wirtz	1962	Kennedy, L. B. Johnson
George P. Shultz	1969	Nixon
James D. Hodgson	1970	Nixon
Peter J. Brennan	1973	Nixon, Ford
John T. Dunlop	1975	Ford
W. J. Usery, Jr.	1976	Ford
Ray Marshall	1977	Carter
Raymond J. Donovan	1981	Reagan
William E. Brock III	1985	Reagan
Ann Dore McLaughlin	1987	Reagan
*Elizabeth Dole	1989	G. Bush
Lynn Martin	1991	G. Bush
Robert B. Reich	1993	Clinton
Alexis M. Herman	1997	Clinton
Elaine Chao	2001	G. W. Bush

*Subject of a separate profile. Consult the Index.

The **Bureau of Labor Statistics** collects, analyzes, and publishes information on the American work force. It tracks the number of people working, the wages they earn, the hours they work, and the prices they pay for food, housing, and clothing.

The **Women's Bureau** strives to raise the economic status of working women by seeking fair employment policies and to improve working conditions. Agency programs provide job training and placement, support services, and technical assistance.

The **Bureau of International Labor Affairs** helps formulate international economic and immigration policies that affect American workers. It also represents the Labor Department in international trade negotiations.

Among the other agencies of the Labor Department are the Office of the Inspector General, which checks for fraud, waste, and abuse; the Solicitor's Office, which provides legal services; and the Office of Policy, which coordinates evaluation, research, and policy.

The Department of Labor also promotes employment and business opportunities through the **21st Century Workforce Initiative**, the **Center for Faith-Based and Community Initiatives**, and the **Office of Small Business Programs**.

The U.S. Department of Labor has regional offices in 15 cities. Its headquarters are located at 200 Constitution Avenue, N.W., Washington, D.C. 20210.

United States Department of Labor

LABOR DAY. See HOLIDAYS.

LABOR-MANAGEMENT RELATIONS

The **labor force** is made up of individuals who make their living by working for someone else and who are paid for their services in the form of wages or salaries. Because the workers in the labor force are employed by other people, they are called **employees**. Not included are the self-employed—those who make their living from the fees they receive from their clients or patients.

In the early days of industry most business and industrial organizations were run and managed by the people who owned them. As organizations grew larger, corporations were formed. A **corporation** is an organization in which a group of persons is permitted by law to act as one person. A corporation is permitted to sell shares of stock—representing ownership—in a business. In this way, many people outside an organization may actually own it.

As corporations grow, it becomes necessary to hire people to manage them. These people

Collective bargaining is a process through which management and labor may settle their differences. If the two groups cannot reach an agreement, an outside mediator may be brought in to ease negotiations. For example, to end a nine-month-long mining strike, William Usery (far right), a federal mediator appointed by then Secretary of Labor Elizabeth Dole (center), successfully negotiated an agreement between Pittston Coal Company chairman Paul Douglas (left) and the president of the United Mine Workers union, Richard Trumka (right).

work for salary, but their responsibilities are very much like those of the owner-manager. Their job is to represent the owner in running the business. They belong to management.

Management, then, is the group of individuals within an organization that is responsible for setting goals and directing the production of goods or services. This group includes managers who are also owners of the company, as well as managers who are employed by the company. The owner or president and the top officials clearly belong to management, as do managers who represent the owner or those who run the organization.

▶THEY AGREE AND DISAGREE

Labor and management agree in some areas and disagree in others. Both have a common interest in a healthy economy. Both wish to see the economy grow, so that more goods and services are bought. This in turn means that more jobs are provided, bringing increased wages and salaries to the workers and increased profits to the owners.

In an industry or business firm, labor and management have a common interest in producing goods or services that will sell. This means that they must be able to compete in quality, quantity, and price.

Some countries—the United States is an example—have a competitive economic system. In this kind of system a product must be able to compete successfully and efficiently against the products of other companies. A company will be successful if enough of the product is sold to pay the necessary expenses and to provide a profit as well. If a business or industry is not able to compete—its product may not fill the needs or expectations of its market, it may be poor in quality, or its production may be particularly inefficient—it will fail. When a business or industry fails, its owners lose their money (investment), and its employees lose their jobs.

Goods and services are produced by owners and the employees working together. How much of the money (income) made by a business or industry should go to the owner and how much to the employee? Today it is harder than ever to find an answer because most business organizations are much larger than they used to be. It is on this question of how to divide up the income of a company that management and labor often disagree.

▶GROWTH AFFECTS LABOR-MANAGEMENT RELATIONS

Suppose that a person who owns tools, a building, and materials hires another person to make chairs. Both people are interested in producing chairs that other people will want to buy. Both hope the business can sell enough chairs to make the money needed for it to stay in business.

The owner-manager and the employee will share the income. The owner-manager must get back the cost of the tools, the building, and the materials and must also put aside money to replace tools, repair buildings, and buy new materials. He or she may also hope to save money or to be able to borrow money (which can be paid back with interest from the income of the business) so the business can expand. In return for the use of the owner's money and services as manager, the owner wants income in the form of profit—money left over after necessary expenses have been paid. Another part of the income must be paid as wages to the person who works for the owner.

Although the owner-manager and employees share a common interest in the business and are dependent on each other, both want to get as much money as possible for their respective services. They will reach an agreement as to how much the worker is to receive. This agreement is reached when the worker consents to work for the owner-manager at a certain wage.

The agreement will depend on many things —the availability of workers (**labor supply**) and how many other jobs are open to the worker (**labor demand**). The wages being paid to other workers (**wage level**) must be taken into account, as well as the demand for the product (**product market**). Other considerations are the amount of profit coming to the owner versus the amount that could be earned if the time and money were used in some other way. Changes in any of these factors may cause the owner-manager or the employee to try to change the original wage agreement.

The basic elements of labor-management relations are contained in this example of a single owner-manager and single employee. But when a business is successful and grows, its organization becomes more complicated.

The original owner may hire others to help manage the business. These members of man-

Workers in the labor force agree to fulfill specific job requirements in exchange for wages and other benefits, such as health insurance and retirement pensions.

agement will share the owner's goals and interests. More workers may be hired to make chairs. They, like the original employee, will want to get as much money as they can for their services.

The job of making the chairs may become specialized—each worker doing only part of the job. One may make chair legs, one may make seats, one may make chair backs, one may put the parts together. The company may even start to make other products, such as tables and beds, that require workers with different skills. These changes would make it necessary for management to decide on several wage rates, not just one. The rates could depend on the skills that are needed.

Labor-management relations in a large business are more complicated than in a small business, but their basic elements do not change. In the one-owner, one-employee business, labor and management can talk directly with each other and discuss their problems. In the larger business there is apt to be less contact between labor and management, and it is harder to solve problems between them.

Labor's Position. Sometimes labor may have a strong position in bargaining with management. This may happen when the supply of labor is short, as in wartime, or when a particular skill is scarce. But the individual worker has little bargaining power, because an employee can only give or refuse to give services. Only when other job opportunities exist do workers have much influence in bargaining with management.

Management's Position. Management is in a stronger position in bargaining over wages and terms of employment because usually there are more people looking for work than there are jobs. It is also management that decides when to expand or hire more labor and when to cut production and lay off or fire certain workers. Management may also decide to introduce new tools or machines, such as computers, that take the place of human labor or that allow the same amount of labor to produce more goods or services.

▶**THE GOVERNMENT STEPS IN TO PROTECT LABOR**

The basic conflict between labor and management and the natural weakness in labor's bargaining position appeared early in the development of industrial society. Labor was plentiful, so wages were low and work hours were long. Women and children could be more easily exploited (underpaid or unjustly used) than men, and so suffered most. Of course, not all owners and managers were unkind. But if they did not do what other owners and managers did, their labor costs became too high. They could not compete with others

Managers make decisions to make their business profitable. They must also supervise their employees so that work is done in an efficient and cost-effective manner.

and were forced out of business. These conditions led to many problems—exploitation of women and children, low wages, long hours, unsafe conditions, and unemployment.

Management says that it must be free to decide how best to use labor in the business organization. Labor, which depends on continued employment to make a living, tries to limit the decisions management can make. Many managers look out for the well-being of their employees, but others think of labor as a resource to be used and paid as little as possible. In order to protect labor and to make the balance of bargaining power more equal, governments have passed certain laws.

The Workers' Rights and Safety

All industrial nations have laws to prevent labor from being exploited. The earliest laws of this kind had to do with the employment of women and children. These laws regulated working hours, wages, the age at which children could start work, and other similar matters. Some governments passed laws requiring health and safety standards.

Social Insurance

For most people any interruption of their income due to injury, sickness, unemployment, or old age can cause economic disaster.

Not all employers can afford programs that offer protection to their workers, so governments have had to provide protection to some degree. The earliest social insurance laws in the United States had to do with workers' compensation, providing medical care and limited income payments to workers who became sick or were injured or died as a result of conditions or an accident on the job. Federal laws later provided payments to workers during periods of temporary unemployment, permanent disability, or upon reaching retirement age.

Social security benefits have greatly increased since Congress first passed the Social Security Act in 1935. Today almost all wage and salary earners are entitled to such benefits.

In 1974, in an effort to guarantee pension plans in privately owned businesses, Congress passed the Employee Retirement Income Security Act (ERISA). This means that if a company cannot pay the retirement benefits it has promised a worker, the government will cover the payments, up to a certain amount.

Several years before ERISA was enacted, Congress passed the Occupational Safety and Health Act (OSHA) to protect workers against job-related injuries and illnesses. All of these benefits and protections combined are called the "social wage."

Labor-Management Relations

Another type of government legislation aims to provide more balance to the labor-management bargaining relationship. When all the workers of an employer or entire industry act together, they have a stronger bargaining position than does the individual worker. That is why labor unions developed.

The Wagner Act. The first permanent federal law governing labor-management relations in the United States (outside the railroad industry) was the National Labor Relations Act, also called the Wagner Act, of 1935.

The basic aims of the Wagner Act were to:

(1) prevent certain actions by management to make the development of unions difficult;

(2) guarantee the right of any group of employees to form a union and bargain collectively (together) with management; and

(3) set up a federal agency, the National Labor Relations Board (NLRB).

The purpose of the NLRB was to provide employees with the means of deciding whether they wanted a union to represent them and to enforce other conditions of the act. These included preventing employers from using "unfair labor practices"—doing things the law forbids. An example of an unfair labor practice is interfering with union organization by firing or refusing to hire a person because of union membership or activity. Several states adopted similar laws.

The Wagner Act and the NLRB speeded the growth of union activity and made the collective-bargaining process more important. They made the balance between labor and management more equal. Some people believed that they gave the unions too much power. They thought certain changes were needed to protect the rights of management and of individual union members. So two new laws were passed.

The Taft-Hartley Act. Due to labor unrest, the Labor-Management Act (or Taft-Hartley Act) of 1947 was passed following a wave of strikes in 1946 and 1947. It was an amendment to the Wagner Act. The purposes of the Taft-Hartley Act were to:

(1) prevent major strikes that would cause public emergencies and look for ways of settling them;

(2) forbid some union practices that had been found to be unfair and check the use of some union tactics;

(3) permit labor and management to sue each other in federal courts for damages suffered as a result of breaking a collective-bargaining contract; and

(4) require unions to file certain financial and organizational data with the United States Department of Labor if unions wished to use the administrative safeguards available in the act.

The Labor-Management Reporting and Disclosure Act. In 1959 the Labor-Management Reporting and Disclosure (or Landrum-Griffin) Act was passed. The purposes of this act were to:

(1) report more complete financial and organizational data;

(2) deal more effectively with corrupt practices of employers or unions and with undemocratic union procedures;

(3) change some of the curbs on unfair labor practices contained in the Taft-Hartley Act; and

(4) make clear what authority the state and federal governments have over matters involved in labor-management relations.

These laws did not change the basic right of the worker to engage in union activities and to bargain collectively with management.

▶ UNION ORGANIZATIONS IN THE UNITED STATES

A labor, or trade, union is an association of wage earners in a trade or closely related trades. Its purpose is to protect and advance its members' interests with regard to wages and hours and conditions of employment. This may mean providing legal advice, taking political action, or influencing government representatives. Union members pay monthly dues to cover union operating and administration expenses. The money is also used to aid members during illness, old age, strikes, and periods of unemployment.

Issues In Collective Bargaining

In collective bargaining, management deals with its workers as a group rather than as individuals. It negotiates terms of wages and hours and conditions of employment with unions representing the workers, not with the workers themselves. Conditions of employment and of settling disputes that may arise are determined for the workers through the union and the collective-bargaining process.

Union Security. Keeping their unions secure is an important issue to union members. Sections in collective-bargaining agreements

SOME LABOR TERMS

Affirmative action—Policies or programs designed to eliminate discrimination against minorities in the workplace and in other institutions and overcome the effects of past discrimination.

Arbitration—An arrangement under which labor and management agree to refer disputes to an outside third party and to obey its decisions. The government orders **compulsory arbitration** for disputes that affect the public interest.

Benefits—Vacation time, pension plans, health insurance, and other extras provided for employees and paid for, in part or in full, by the company.

Checkoff—That part of a worker's wages that is deducted by the employer and paid directly to the union as dues.

Equal Employment Opportunity Commission (EEOC)—An independent federal agency that may take legal action against businesses on behalf of job applicants who feel they have been discriminated against because of their race, religion, sex, or national origin.

Featherbedding—Union practice of requiring management to continue to employ workers who are no longer necessary. (A management term).

Grievance—A complaint about wages, or similar matters, directed by labor against management.

Lockout—An employer's refusal to let his or her employees enter their place of work unless they accept the employer's terms.

Minimum wage—The lowest hourly wage a business can legally pay an adult worker. In 1991 the minimum wage was raised to $4.25.

Open shop—A company's freedom to hire workers who have not joined a union and are not required to.

Pickets—People posted at a place of work or business by a labor union to discourage nonunion workers from entering and to discourage the public from trading.

Seniority—Worker's rank according to the length of service. The longer a worker is employed, the greater are his or her rights to job security, promotion, and favored treatment.

Strike or walkout—Workers' refusal to work in order to obtain certain benefits or concessions from their employer.

Strikebreaker—Person hired by an employer to do the work of an employee who is on strike.

Union shop—A requirement that a company hire workers who, if not union members already, must join a union within a certain time.

are included to protect the union as an institution. Management has always fought for an **open shop**. An open shop exists when management may hire a person who is not a union member, and the employee need not join a union. Unions have always felt that their greatest security rested in the **closed shop**—that is, an agreement that management will hire and keep only union members. The Taft-Hartley Act, however, declared that the closed shop was not legal.

Most collective-bargaining contracts provide for either a **union shop** or for **maintenance of membership**. Under a union-shop agreement, management may hire anyone. However, all workers who are hired must join the union within a certain period of time, usually thirty days. They must also remain in the union as long as they are employed.

Job Security. Employees naturally are concerned about keeping their jobs. The union generally tries to make sure that the contract limits management's right to fire or lay off an employee. A worker can be fired or laid off temporarily only under special circumstances. The firing or layoff, furthermore, is subject to review under the **grievance procedure**.

The grievance procedure is an important part of a union-management agreement. It is designed to permit settlement of disputed issues during the contract without interrupting work. Sometimes the representatives cannot arrive at an agreement themselves. Many labor contracts state that when this happens, the issue will be referred to an outside third party who will not favor one side over the other. This third-party settlement is called **arbitration**. Both union and management must obey its decisions.

Seniority. Related to a worker's job security is the length of time a worker has been employed compared with other workers. Seniority governs the order in which workers are laid off—those who have been employed the shortest time are laid off first. When the firm begins to recall (bring back) workers, those with the longest term of employment are recalled first. Seniority also counts in such matters as length of vacation, wages, and preference in promotion to better jobs. It is based on the idea that the longer a worker is employed by an organization, the greater right he or she has to continued employment and favorable treatment in other matters.

Before collective-bargaining procedures with management can begin, labor union members must come together to reach an agreement regarding their demands.

Benefits. Another important part of wage settlements are the benefits given to workers in addition to their wages. The term "benefits" describes such extras as holidays and vacations with pay, retirement pensions, health care insurance, life insurance, and other related benefits, such as 401(k) income savings and other investment plans.

Unemployment. Workers and their unions are always fearful of unemployment. Job losses may result from a drop in the general economy or the lack of demand for a certain product. This type of unemployment generally is considered to be temporary. Unions have tried to provide seniority guarantees in labor contracts to protect workers with the longest terms of service. They have also tried to negotiate labor contracts that will guarantee a certain minimum period of employment or a minimum amount of income.

Unions also have tried to develop contract provisions that oblige management to make some final payment to workers who have been permanently discharged. This money can provide critical support to workers as they look for other jobs.

Technological Changes

With increasing speed since the 1950's, technological changes have eliminated many jobs. A combination of automation (the automatic operation of machines by other machines) and computers has changed the way work is done in factories and offices. In many circumstances, fewer workers have been needed to produce similar amounts of goods and other output. As a result, unions and management have had to develop programs to train workers in new skills and place them in different jobs.

Overall, however, unions have been unable to resist technological changes. New methods of production and clerical work have weakened the bargaining power of workers and their unions. By the 1980's, more employers managed their workers without the presence of unions. In fact, technological change is the primary reason unions today try to settle disputes without interrupting work. Legislation and legal rulings have also curbed labor's power to stop production.

Negotiating health benefits for workers is a high priority for labor unions. It is especially important to those whose work conditions can lead to illness, such as this coal miner who now suffers from black-lung disease.

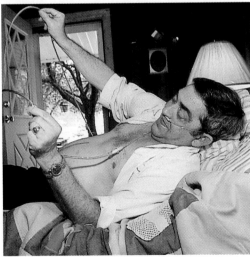

METHODS UNIONS USE TO ACHIEVE THEIR GOALS

Both unions and management today realize the importance of settling disputes without interrupting work. Today unions seldom use the **strike** (stopping work) to force an agreement by management. Similarly, management seldom uses the **lockout** (shutting down the workplace) to force an agreement by the union or the workers.

Strikes or lockouts may occur when a union is trying to get management to accept it as the bargaining agent for a firm's workers. They may also occur when a new contract is being negotiated and disputes that cannot be settled by bargaining arise over its provisions. But even here, laws affecting labor make it difficult to take such action. The government also provides the services of skilled labor mediators to help both parties arrive at a settlement.

Unions put pressure on management in another way—by **picketing**. This means patrol-ling near the plant or place of business with a sign advising workers and the public that a dispute exists between union and management. One purpose is to force management to settle with the union through the use of public opinion. Another purpose is to prevent workers from continuing to work—a union member is not supposed to cross a picket line. Usually the use of picketing is regulated by federal law.

UNIONS AND INDUSTRIAL RELATIONS

Unions also exercise an indirect influence on labor-management relations. They speak on issues or work for laws of economic, social, and political importance. As a consequence, unions influence industrial relations through governmental legislation setting minimum wages, retirement procedures, and health and safety conditions.

Unions, however, have a smaller influence on industrial relations than in the recent past. Today, they represent less than 18 percent of all workers. Some of the nation's largest corporations practice what are called alternative industrial-relations systems. At such firms, employers grant workers special conditions and protections without negotiating with unions. They insist that employers and workers are partners in a common enterprise in which voluntary cooperation produces the best results. As a result, unions now try to negotiate agreements in a more cooperative fashion.

Despite its shrinking influence in the United States, organized labor continues to have a considerable impact on industrial relations. In Europe, where unions are linked to political parties and represent a larger proportion of workers, labor has had an even greater impact on the society and economy. In the newly democratic nations of Eastern Europe and Russia, a new generation of independent unions is claiming for itself a similar role in a modern industrial economy.

ROBERT F. RISLEY
New York State School of
Industrial and Labor Relations
Cornell University

Reviewed by MELVYN DUBOFSKY
Chairperson, Department of History
State University of New York at Binghamton

See also LABOR, U.S. DEPARTMENT OF; LABOR MOVEMENT; SOCIAL SECURITY; UNEMPLOYMENT AND UNEMPLOYMENT INSURANCE, WORKERS' COMPENSATION.

Union members may go on strike to demonstrate their dissatisfaction with management's decisions. By refusing to work, labor hopes to force management to make concessions. Most strikes end when both sides agree to compromise. In 1990 a five-month strike against the *New York Daily News* (*below*) ended when the paper was sold, and the unions were able to negotiate acceptable terms with the new owner.

LABOR MOVEMENT

Labor is a word that generally describes the work people are hired to perform for others. Workers, or laborers, are paid for their labor in the form of salaries and wages, which they use to pay for food, clothing, shelter, and other necessities of life.

The word labor also is used to describe the workers themselves taken together as a group. So when we speak of "labor's goals," we actually mean the goals of the workers. Likewise, when we speak of the labor movement, we refer to the sequence of historical events and efforts through which labor has sought to improve overall working conditions. The most significant outcome of the modern labor movement has been the development and evolution of labor unions.

▶ THE PURPOSE OF LABOR UNIONS

Before labor unions existed, employers had a great deal of power. Some employers, in order to increase their profits, took advantage of their workers, paying them extremely low wages and working them long hours. There were no laws to protect workers from unsafe work environments; if they got sick or were injured on the job, no insurance programs existed to help support them or their families while they recovered. To gain more control over their work environments, workers began grouping together to form unions.

A labor union is an organization of workers, who work in a specific trade or closely related trades. Membership dues pay for operating expenses and aid members during illness, old age, strikes, and periods of unemployment.

The primary purpose of a union is to prevent employers from taking unfair advantage of their employees. Through a process called **collective bargaining**, union representatives protect workers' rights by negotiating contracts with employers that are favorable to the workers. (For more information, see LABOR-MANAGEMENT RELATIONS in this volume.)

▶ HOW THE LABOR MOVEMENT BEGAN

Prior to the modern era, most people did not work for wages. In ancient Greece and Rome, slaves performed much of the labor. Food and shelter were provided by their masters in return. Later, during the Middle Ages, serfs were required to do agricultural work for lords

By joining together to voice their demands, union members hope to persuade employers to increase wages and improve working conditions.

in return for protection against enemy invaders. These serfs did not earn wages.

As trade slowly began to develop, people began moving into towns, where they produced food, clothing, and utensils by hand. Artisans and other crafts people worked at home or in small shops that became known as cottage industries. Artisans who made similar crafts organized themselves into associations called guilds. Guilds existed for almost every type of crafts people, such as blacksmiths (ironworkers) and cordwainers (shoemakers).

The Industrial Revolution

Many centuries later in England, toward the end of the 1700's, methods of production changed dramatically with the invention of several crude machines. These machines, used chiefly for spinning and weaving, revolutionized England's textile industry.

Machinery soon began to appear in other industries. Much of it was powered by steam engines, which had been developed by a Scottish instrument maker named James Watt (1736–1819). Machinery could produce more goods in less time than could an individual person working by hand. New methods of transportation and distribution also created a wider demand for goods.

This economic and industrial upheaval became known as the Industrial Revolution. It soon spread to the rest of western Europe and to the United States. By the beginning of the 1800's, it had almost completely changed the way in which people in the Western world lived. Small shops gave way to factories, which were required to house the large machines. Both the factories and the machines were expensive, and only people with sufficient capital—wealth in money or goods—could afford to own them. These owners became known as capitalists.

The Industrial Revolution divided society into two new classes—the capitalists (owners) and the workers (wage earners). Factory workers were dependent on the owners who paid them wages. The owners rarely worked alongside the workers as they had once done in the days of cottage industries. As a result, workers did not feel close to their employers, and when their work caused them problems, they felt that there was no one to whom they could turn.

In the early factory days, job conditions were often bad, particularly in the early English cotton mills. Before the Industrial Revolution, workers had craft guilds to aid them, but no agencies now existed to protect factory workers. So they began grouping together to form unions. By acting together, they hoped

to place themselves in a stronger position to deal with their grievances and complaints.

These trade unions were mostly founded in the workers' social clubs. However, the British Parliament soon passed laws making trade unions illegal. The workers' status did not improve until 1868 when Parliament passed the Trade Union Act and the workers formed the Trade Unions Congress (TUC).

▶ **THE LABOR MOVEMENT GROWS IN THE UNITED STATES**

One of the greatest difficulties that early American unions had to overcome was the public's unfavorable opinion of them. American society generally stressed individualism and scorned the actions of organized labor groups. Workers were thought of as servants, meant only to obey the orders of their employers. Many workers who formed unions and made demands on their employers were arrested and tried for the "crime" of trying to improve their conditions. In 1806, for example, a group of Philadelphia cordwainers was found guilty of a "conspiracy to raise their own wages." Despite the cultural and legal obstacles to organized labor, by the 1820's American workers began to form citywide trade associations, such as the Mechanics' Union of Trade Associations, founded in 1828.

The Rise of National Federations of Labor Unions

In the 1850's the number of union organizations began to grow. Craft unions were formed by printers, stonecutters, and others. During and immediately following the Civil War (1861–65), business boomed. With labor in such high demand, more unions flourished.

The first important national labor federation—or group of labor unions—was formed in 1866 to give a more powerful voice to the individual labor unions. This federation,

The Industrial Revolution gave rise to "sweatshops." Workers, desperate to earn a living, were crowded into unsafe factories, where they labored for insignificant wages and received no benefits.

Child labor was the cruelest consequence of unchecked employment practices. These "breaker boys" sorted lumps of coal in the mines ten hours a day.

called National Labor Unions (NLU), favored an eight-hour workday and putting an end to child labor. By 1872, however, the NLU had ceased to exist.

In the 1870's, strikes among the anthracite coal miners of Pennsylvania and eastern railway workers resulted in violence, and in the latter case federal troops were sent to maintain law and order. The violence made labor organizations very unpopular with the public at large and limited their credibility.

The Knights of Labor

In 1869 several Philadelphia garment cutters under the leadership of Uriah S. Stephens founded the Noble Order of the Knights of Labor. Employers at that time were very unfriendly toward unions, so the Knights began as a secret organization. In 1878 it became a national federation. The Knights favored farmers' and producers' co-operatives, public ownership of utilities, and other reform measures. Membership skyrocketed to more than 700,000 by 1886.

The Knights then became involved in quarrels, strikes, and other difficulties with the national craft unions. On May 4, 1886, strikers from the McCormick Harvester Works in Chicago held a meeting at Haymarket Square. One group, not related to the Knights, exploded a bomb, killing a number of people, including several policemen. Again there was a sharp public reaction against labor, even though the unions played no part in the riot. Terence V. Powderly, Grand Master Work-

The Great Railroad Strike of 1877 was among the first of many strikes against the powerful railroad industry. Angry workers, dissatisfied with the corrupt business practices of the railroad tycoons, vandalized railroad property (*above*) from Pittsburgh to Chicago. In Baltimore, U.S. troops were called in to control violent street rioters (*right*).

The International Ladies' Garment Workers' Union (*top*) **and the Women's Trade Union League** (*above*) **protested on behalf of immigrants, women, and children—the three most oppressed segments of the work force.**

man of the Knights, was a reformer rather than an organizer. He was not able to hold the Knights together, and it finally went out of existence.

American Federation of Labor (AFL)

A rival organization to the Knights of Labor was launched in Pittsburgh in 1881. Called the Federation of Organized Trades and Labor Unions (FOOTALU), its purpose was to promote the interests of the craft unions. The group was reorganized in 1886 and renamed the American Federation of Labor (AFL). One of the group's founders and its first president was Samuel Gompers, the leader of the Cigarmakers' Union.

The federation was weakened by two violent strikes. In 1892, steelworkers went on strike at the Carnegie Company plant in Homestead, Pennslyvania. Several hundred private police from the Pinkerton Detective Agency battled them. Plant manager Henry C. Frick was determined to crush the union—"If it takes all summer . . . Yes, even my life itself." The strike collapsed. In 1894, federal troops put down another strike, this time by workers against the Pullman Company in Chicago. This strike was led by Eugene V. Debs, leader of American Railway Union.

The function of the AFL was to charter national unions. Its leaders, believing that the federation should not become too involved in politics, devoted their energies to achieving results through collective bargaining.

Profiles

David Dubinsky (Dobnievski) (1892–1982), born Brest-Litovsk, Russia. After immigrating to the United States in 1911, Dubinsky became a skilled cutter and joined the International Ladies' Garment Workers' Union. He served as

Eugene V. Debs

president of that union for more than three decades (1932–66) and was one of the original founders of the Committee for Industrial Organization. Although an early dedicated Communist, Dubinsky later helped found Americans for Democratic Action in 1947. He received many citations and awards for his work.

Eugene V. Debs (1855–1926), born Terre Haute, Ind. Debs helped organize the American Railway Union in 1893 and was sent to prison for organizing a strike against the Pullman Company in 1894. In 1898 he helped found the Social Democratic Party, later known as the Socialist Party of America. Debs was the Socialist Party candidate for president of the United States in 1900, 1904, 1908, 1912, and 1920. He was imprisoned for opposing government policies during World War I and ran his last campaign from prison. His sentence was lifted in 1921.

Samuel Gompers (1850–1924), born London. Gompers is considered the father of the modern American labor move-

Samuel Gompers

Industrial Workers of the World

Some labor groups felt that the AFL was too conservative. Among those dissatisfied were Eugene Debs, William D. (Big Bill) Haywood, and Daniel De Leon. In 1905, these men founded a revolutionary group called the Industrial Workers of the World (IWW), whose members were nicknamed Wobblies. Their ultimate goal was to force an overthrow of the capitalist system. They believed that the workers should own the means of production, not a handful of wealthy capitalists. The Wobblies were thus associated politically with the Socialist Party.

The Wobblies favored strikes and sabotage instead of collective bargaining. To their ranks they drew mainly unskilled labor from the West and political radicals from eastern textile mills. After 1920, the IWW lost members to the Communist Party and other left-wing political groups. Other organized labor groups opposed the Wobblies, and the IWW gradually lost its influence.

The Industrial Workers of the World organized unskilled laborers into a revolutionary union of industries. Known as Wobblies, the group's members were feared political radicals, who preached permanent class warfare against employers and sought to replace capitalism with industrial democracy.

---

ment. In 1886 he was elected the first president of the American Federation of Labor (AFL), and, except for one year (1895), he served in that position until his death. For more information, see the article GOMPERS, SAMUEL, in Volume G.

William Dudley (Big Bill) Haywood (1869–1928), born Salt Lake City, Utah. Haywood was one of the most feared labor leaders in U.S. history. He left school at an early age, became a miner to help support his family, and later joined a union called the Western Federation of Miners. In 1905 Haywood chaired the founding convention of the Industrial Workers of the World (IWW). The following year he was

William D. (Big Bill) Haywood

arrested and charged with conspiracy in the murder of Frank Steunenberg, a former governor of Idaho. Haywood was acquitted of the charge and went on to become the top official of the IWW (1915–17), at which time he was labeled "the most dangerous man in America." In 1918 he was convicted of spying under wartime espionage laws along with 100 other IWW leaders. Haywood jumped bail and fled to the Soviet Union. For more information, see the article IDAHO (History) in Volume I.

Sidney Hillman (1887–1946), born Zagare, Lithuania. During his career as a union official, Hillman promoted labor-management cooperation. He served as president (1915–46) of the Amalgamated

Clothing Workers of America and as vice president (1938–46) of the Congress of Industrial Organizations (CIO). He was one of President Franklin D. Roosevelt's key labor advisers and helped develop New Deal policies during the Great Depression of the 1930's. As chairman (1943–46) of the CIO's Political Action Committee, he established close ties between the CIO and the Democratic Party. In 1946 he helped found the World Federation of Trade Unions (WFTU).

James R. (Jimmy) Hoffa (1913–75?), born Brazil, Ind. The son of a coal miner, Hoffa left school after the ninth grade and became a stockboy and freight handler in Detroit. In 1931 he founded a local union, which he later brought into the International Brotherhood of Teamsters

Profiles

Congress of Industrial Organizations (CIO)

By the 1930's the American economy was dominated by mass-production industries. The AFL, which organized primarily on a craft basis, failed to organize the mass-production industries because the industries used unskilled labor—workers who were not indentified with a particular craft. Some leaders in the AFL, including John L. Lewis of the United Mine Workers (UMW), thought that a new kind of organization was required to represent all of the workers in an entire industry. Lewis created such a union in 1935, called the Committee for Industrial Organization, but it was soon forced out of the AFL.

In 1937 the Committee for Industrial Organization launched a successful sit-down strike against General Motors and organized the automobile industry. That same year, under the leadership of Philip Murray, it also organized the steel industry. In 1938 the group changed its name to Congress of Industrial Organizations (CIO).

Many workers flocked to join the AFL and the CIO during the 1940's. At the end of World War II, the government lifted the wage and price controls that had benefited the workers. The removal of this safeguard resulted in many strikes. This, in turn, led to the passage of the Labor-Management Relations Act (or Taft-Hartley Act) of 1947, which placed restrictions on strikes that were considered by the government to endanger the nation's safety, health, or welfare.

John L. Lewis, "the roaring lion of labor," led the United Mine Workers (UMW) for forty years. This 1940's caricature pictures him addressing his union members.

The AFL-CIO

The Taft-Hartley Act was a setback for labor, and some people believed that the AFL and CIO should join forces to strengthen labor's position and influence. The two organizations finally merged in 1955, and George Meany became the first president of the combined AFL-CIO. In addition to negotiating contracts for labor, the AFL-CIO established

Profiles

(IBT). As president (1957–71) of the IBT, Hoffa built the truckers' union into one of the largest and most powerful in the country. However, during federal investigations of union corruption by organized crime in the 1950's, Hoffa and the Teamsters figured prominently. In 1964 he was convicted on several different criminal charges, including misuse of union funds, and in 1967 he began serving a 13-year prison term. President Richard Nixon lifted Hoffa's prison term in 1971 under the condition that he not participate in union affairs until 1980. Hoffa disappeared, however, in 1975. It is presumed that he was the victim of a gangland murder.

Joseph Lane Kirkland (1922–99), born Camden, S.C. Kirkland joined the AFL staff in 1948 and for many years was chief assistant to AFL-CIO president George Meany, whom he succeeded as president (1979–95). Kirkland vigorously criticized the economic policies of President Ronald Reagan's administration and led union support for Democratic presidential candidates.

John L. Lewis (1880–1969), born Lucas, Ia. Lewis had a fifty-year career as a union official. In 1920, he became president of the United Mine Workers (UMW), a position he held until his retirement in 1960. In 1935 he formed the Committee for Industrial Organization. As president of the CIO (1935–40), Lewis became the most powerful labor leader in the United States and a force in national politics. During World War II and afterward, Lewis led the miners in a series of controversial strikes that won them substantial medical and retirement benefits. For more information, see the article LEWIS, JOHN L. in this volume.

George Meany (1894–1980), born Bronx, N.Y. A plumber by trade, Meany was a union official most of his life. He served as vice president of the New York State Federation of Labor (1934–39). Later he was elected secretary-treasurer of the American Federation of Labor (AFL) and became its president in 1952. Meany successfully engineered the merger of the AFL and CIO in 1955 and served as president of the combined AFL-CIO until his retirement in 1979. A dedicated anti-Communist, Meany played an active role in politics and was a strong influence in the Democratic Party.

Philip Murray (1886–1952), born Blantyre, Scotland. In 1902 he immigrated to western Pennsylvania, where he began working in the coal mines. In 1919 he was elected vice president of the United Mine Workers (UMW). He held that position for twenty years, working closely with UMW president John L. Lewis. In 1935 he

The 1955 merger of the American Federation of Labor (AFL) and the Congress of Industrial Organizations (CIO) strengthened labor's political and economic influence.

Today the AFL-CIO is recognized as the voice of organized labor in the United States, but not all union members are associated with it. Some belong to two minor organizations—the Confederated Unions of America and the National Independent Union Council. Still others, such as the National Education Association (NEA), operate entirely independently. However, three major unions that had long been independent rejoined the AFL-CIO in the 1980's—the United Auto Workers (UAW); the International Brotherhood of Teamsters, Chauffeurs, Warehousemen, and Helpers of America (truck drivers and others); and the United Mine Workers (UMW).

▶ **POLITICS AND LABOR IN THE UNITED STATES**

Unions usually work for reforms through established political parties, although they have occasionally tried to develop parties of their own. The first labor party, the Workingmen's Party, appeared in 1828. The ten-hour day and free public schools were major issues in its political campaigns.

After the Civil War, labor continued to feel that the government was unfriendly to its aims. Workers and farmers joined to form the Greenback-Labor Party in 1878. They supported wider use of paper currency, the eight-hour day, and votes for women.

Many leaders of the various socialist groups supported the economic aims of the unions. But they hoped eventually to transform America's capitalist society into a socialist workers'

departments to handle government legislation and legal matters; to fight for civil rights, social security benefits, occupational safety and health, veterans' benefits, and full-time employment; and to promote projects to improve education, housing, and community services. However, in spite of all of its efforts, union membership continued to decline over the next three decades.

Lane Kirkland

George Meany

helped Lewis form the Committee for Industrial Organization. He served as chairman (1936–42) of the Steelworkers Organizing Committee and later as president (1942–52) of the United Steelworkers of America. Murray replaced Lewis as president of the CIO in 1940, serving until his death in 1952.

A. Philip Randolph (1889–1979) was born Asa Philip Randolph in Crescent City, Fla. In 1925, at a time when blacks were excluded from unions, Randolph organized the Brotherhood of Sleeping Car Porters, which helped African Americans gain entry into the American labor movement in the 1930's. During World War II, he won jobs for blacks in the defense industries by threatening a protest march on the nation's capital. In 1955, Randolph was named vice president of the newly merged AFL-CIO. A leader in the movement for civil rights, he actively fought to end discrimination in employment. He also directed the August 1963 civil rights March on Washington.

Walter P. Reuther (1907–70), born Wheeling, W. Va. As a young man, Reuther went to Detroit to work in the automobile factories. He played a prominent role in the sit-down strikes of the 1930's that led to the establishment of the United Automobile Workers (UAW). As president (1946–70) of the UAW, he succeeded in obtaining for union members such benefits as cost-of-living wage increases and health and pension benefits. In 1952, Reuther succeeded Philip Murray as president of the CIO and helped plan its 1955 merger with the AFL. As vice president (1955–68) of the AFL-CIO, he ran the Industrial Union Department. Reuther was a founding member of Americans for Democratic Action (ADA). He played a prominent role in Democratic Party politics and was a staunch supporter of the civil rights movement.

Profiles

Solidarity, a federation of Polish trade unions led by Lech Walesa (right), was the first independent labor union permitted by a Communist government.

society, wherein the means of production would be owned by workers instead of by a private individual or corporation.

Several small labor parties sprang up in the 1930's. Most important of these was the American Labor Party. It supported progressive candidates of the major parties and in some cases nominated its own.

Today the AFL-CIO is closely linked with the Democratic Party, although no formal relationship exists. The voting power of union members is strongest in largely industrial areas, and the "labor vote" is highly prized, especially in U.S. presidential elections.

▶ ORGANIZED LABOR AROUND THE WORLD

In many parts of the world there are more agricultural than industrial workers in the labor force. Because unions usually form around industries, the labor movement is strongest in industrialized nations.

In Canada the labor movement is closely associated with labor in the United States. Most union members belong to the Canadian Labour Congress (CLC), which was formed in 1956. In the province of Quebec there are Roman Catholic labor syndicates, which are similar to unions. These syndicates belong to the Confederation of National Trade Unions (CNTU).

Outside North America

In most countries outside North America the labor movement is associated with a political party. The Trades Union Congress (TUC) in Great Britain, for example, is politically allied with the Labour Party. Japan and Mexico have several large federations of unions, each representing a different opinion. Various unions in France and Italy represent Roman Catholic concerns as well as Socialist and Communist viewpoints.

The Communist labor unions in the Soviet-controlled nations of Eastern Europe were very different from those in Western industrial nations because their right to strike or bargain with management was limited. However, when the Communist structure began to crumble in the late 1980's, independent labor unions began to emerge throughout the newly formed Russian Federation.

Labor movements in Africa, Asia, and Latin America have existed since the early 1900's, but as the economies of these areas are largely based on agriculture, the power of organized labor is limited in these regions. After World War II, industry made rapid gains in such countries as Japan, India, South Korea, Taiwan, Singapore, South Africa, Brazil, and Mexico. Today union activities in these countries are a part of everyday life.

▶ INTERNATIONAL ORGANIZATIONS

Internationally there are two dominant labor organizations—the World Federation of Trade Unions (WFTU) and the International Confederation of Free Trade Unions (ICFTU). Rivalry between these two groups has encouraged the growth of unions in less-developed countries. The International Labor Organization (ILO), founded in 1919, became a specialized agency of the United Nations in 1945. Its aims are to promote collective bargaining and improve working conditions around the world.

LOUIS HOLLANDER
Former Vice President
Amalgamated Clothing Workers of America

Reviewed by MELVYN DUBOFSKY
State University of New York, Binghamton

See also CHILD LABOR; DEBS, EUGENE V.; GOMPERS, SAMUEL; GUILDS; INDUSTRIAL REVOLUTION; INDUSTRY; LABOR-MANAGEMENT RELATIONS; LEWIS, JOHN L.; SOCIALISM.

LABRADOR. See NEWFOUNDLAND AND LABRADOR.

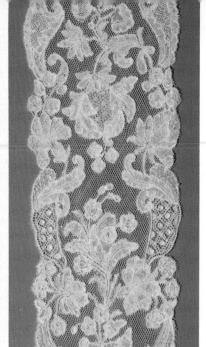

Left: Bobbin lace is made with numerous threads, each attached to a bobbin, or spool. The lacemaker follows a pattern, interlacing the threads to create the design. Right: A piece of 18-century Flemish bobbin lace reveals an intricate and lovely design.

LACE

Lace is an airy and delicate fabric made of fine threads worked into lovely patterns. Lace adorns many things we wear and use. It may be made by hand or by machine.

Handmade lace is usually made by one of two methods: the needle method or the bobbin method. **Needle lace** is made by drawing the pattern on a thick piece of paper backed by linen. The outline of the pattern is stitched onto the paper. The stitching is used as a framework. On it the lacemaker works with a needle and a single thread, building up the pattern with looped stitches. When the work is completed, the framework stitches are clipped from the linen and the paper, and the lace is lifted off.

Needle lace is considered to be the older of the two types of handmade lace. Many samples of needle lace dating from the 1500's are in existence today.

Among the most well-known needle laces are Venetian and Alençon. **Venetian lace** may have heavy, sculptured-looking floral designs or tiny, delicate designs of rose petals. In either type the design can be raised. **Alençon lace** often has floral designs outlined by a slightly heavier thread.

Bobbin lace can be made with a large number of threads, each fastened to a bobbin (spool). The pattern is drawn on paper, and the paper is fastened onto a cushion. The end of each bobbin thread is attached to the cushion. Pins are stuck into the cushion to keep the threads in position while the lace is being made. The lacemaker moves pairs of bobbins from side to side, twisting and interlacing the threads.

The first bobbin laces were made in Italy, but the finest and most treasured bobbin laces are Belgian in origin. Most lace is made of white linen thread, but the French **Chantilly lace,** a bobbin lace, was often made of black silk thread. It has vine or spray patterns on a mesh ground, and was favored for evening dresses and bridal veils.

Machine-made lace usually copies the designs of handmade lace. A machine often used today is the Leavers machine, first patented in Britain in 1813. It is a very large machine, weighing about 17 metric tons and covering a floor space about 3 meters (10 feet) wide and 45 meters (150 feet) long.

Different laces may have Italian, Belgian, French, or English names because they were named for their towns of origin. Today handmade lace is made chiefly in Italy and Belgium. Machine-made lace is produced in England, France, and the United States.

Reviewed by CHRISTA C. MAYER THURMAN
Art Institute of Chicago

LACROSSE

Lacrosse is a game that was developed by the North American Indians. It is the oldest organized sport in America.

When the French settlers of Canada saw it played, they called it lacrosse. The stick and net used in the game looked to them like a *crosse,* or crosier—the curved staff carried by a bishop. The modern stick has a handle and a triangular webbed net. Two sides of the net are attached to wooden side walls.

▶ PLAYING THE GAME

Lacrosse is played by two teams of ten players each—three attack, three midfield, three defense, and one goalkeeper. The length of the collegiate game is 60 minutes, divided into 4 periods, each 15 minutes long. The high-school game is 40 minutes long.

Each team tries to control the ball, which is about 8 inches in circumference, and to score by putting the ball into the opponents' goal. The ball is kept in play by being carried in a player's stick and eventually passed to a teammate who will shoot it at the goal. When the ball falls to the ground, a player can pick it up with a scooping motion of his stick. Any player may kick the ball, but only the defending goalie can bat the ball with his hand.

When throwing, a player does not usually face his target; his body is turned to the side. Passes are made in several ways. The long pass requires different motions from the short pass. The easily-blocked shovel pass is used for very short distances.

In catching, the head of the stick is turned

so the entire net, or pocket, is prepared to receive the ball. While the player is running, the stick is turned upward and the ball is cradled in the pocket. Scooping—that is, picking the ball off the ground with the stick—is very important, since the ball is often loose on the field.

▶ TEAM OFFENSE AND DEFENSE

The three attackmen and three midfielders make up the attacking team. Their job is to carry out a play that will score a goal.

To get a man free for a shot, the three midfielders can use a weaving pattern. The opposing defensemen change position to cover them. To increase pressure on the defense, two attackmen behind the goal can also begin weaving. The other attackman remains near the crease, the 9-foot-radius circle around the goal (the goal is 6 feet wide).

The pass and cut is an effective play. An offensive player passes the ball to a teammate and fakes in one direction. Then he breaks for the goal and receives a return pass.

A screen, or pick, occurs when an offensive player blocks out the defenseman guarding another offensive player of the first man's team. This allows the latter to get free to take a close shot at the goal or to receive a pass in shooting territory.

The two attackmen who play behind the goal must control the ball when it is in their area. And they must look for chances to pass the ball to an open man. This is called feeding. They may feed the crease attackman, who might try for a goal. Or they may cut, or feed, a midfielder who is in a position for a shot.

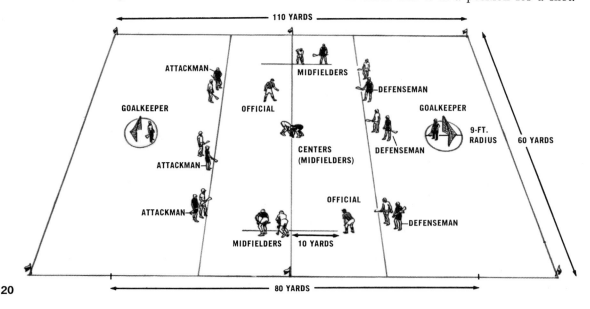

The attackmen must be able to dodge by their defensemen and come around to the front of the goal for a shot. They must also "back up" the goal. This means they must cover stray shots, missed passes, or any other balls that go past the goal.

The crease attackman usually plays several yards outside the crease. He tries to screen the goalie's vision on shots taken more than 10 yards from the goal. He must be ready to play rebounds off the goalie or loose balls in the crease area. Whatever feeds he receives should give him point-blank shots, because he plays so close to the other team's goal.

When the attack loses the ball, it begins riding the other team's defense—covering very closely to keep the defense from passing the ball or from clearing, or getting the ball out of their defensive territory to their attack.

The goalkeeper, three defensemen, and three midfielders make up the defensive unit of a team. (The three attackmen must remain on their side of the center line.) A team's defense must be unified and well co-ordinated to keep its opponent's attack from scoring.

Most teams use a man-to-man defense, in which each defensive player—with the exception of the goalie—guards one attacking player. In the zone defense, each man has an area to cover. He guards any offensive player who comes into this zone.

A defenseman should have quick reactions and good balance and must be fast and aggressive. He should play between his man and the goal and be in a position to see both his man and the ball. He should never rush or step into his opponent, thus allowing the man to dodge and break away from him.

When his opponent has the ball, the defenseman tries to dislodge it by "checking," or striking, the attackman's stick with his own, or he can use his stick to block the passes or shots his attackman may try.

Basic Rules

Length of Game. The game lasts for 4 periods—each 10 or 15 minutes—with a 2-minute rest between quarters and 10 minutes between halves. At each intermission the teams change goals. If the score is tied at the end of a regulation game, there is a 5-minute intermission, then play is continued. There are 2 overtime periods of 5 minutes each. If the score is tied at the end of the overtime, the game ends and is declared a tie.

Time-outs. Each team is allowed 1 time-out—2 minutes long—per period. The clock is also stopped under the following conditions:

(a) When the ball goes out of bounds.
(b) After a team scores.
(c) When a player is injured.
(d) When a penalty is being enforced.
(e) At the end of each period.

Scoring. A goal counts 1 point.

Face-offs. At the beginning of each period or after a goal has been scored, play is started by a face-off. The two center midfielders line up at the center of the field, each facing the goal his team will be attacking. They go into a crouch with their sticks on the ground. The heads of the sticks should be placed back to back. The players rest their gloved hands on the ground. The referee then puts the ball between the sticks. When he blows the whistle, the centers battle for possession of the ball, each trying to control it with his stick.

Ball Out of Bounds. A ball that goes out of bounds past a sideline or end line is not given to the team whose player touched it last, but to the opposite team. The only exception is a ball that goes out of bounds after a shot at the goal. It is given to the player who—when play is suspended—is nearest to the point where the ball goes out of bounds. This player's team is then in possession of the ball.

Offside. Each team must have at least three men on the attack half of the field and four men on the defensive half. If a team does not have enough men in either half of the field, an offside penalty is called. It is considered a technical foul.

Personal and Technical Fouls. A player who commits a personal foul is suspended from the game for 1 to 3 minutes, and the ball is given to the team that was fouled. Body checking from the rear, slashing an opponent with the stick, tripping, pushing, holding, unnecessary roughness, and unsportsmanlike conduct—all are personal fouls. Technical fouls include interference, touching the ball with the hand, and going offside. The player who commits a technical foul is suspended for 30 seconds or his team loses the ball.

ROBERT H. SCOTT
Lacrosse Coach, Johns Hopkins University

The young Marquis de Layafette began the brilliant career that made him an American hero when he joined George Washington to fight in the Revolutionary War.

LAFAYETTE, MARQUIS DE (1757–1834)

The Marquis de Lafayette, who fought for the freedom of the American colonies, devoted himself to the cause of human liberty perhaps more unselfishly than any other individual of his time.

Marie Joseph Paul Yves Roch Gilbert du Motier, Marquis de Lafayette, was born on September 6, 1757, in the family château of Chavaniac in the Auvergne region of France. At the age of 11 he was sent to military school in Paris. At 16 the Marquis was married to 14-year-old Adrienne de Noailles.

In 1776 the tall, red-haired Lafayette, now a captain of dragoons, decided to go to America to fight for the freedom of the colonies. He was impelled by curiosity, a hunger for glory, and sympathy for the American cause.

He first saw action at the Battle of Brandywine. After enduring the winter hardships of Valley Forge, he distinguished himself at the Battle of Monmouth. Entrusted by George Washington with the defense of Virginia, he was at Yorktown on October 19, 1781, for the surrender of the British under Lord Cornwallis. With American independence assured, Lafayette, then barely 24, returned to France.

But the clouds of a far bloodier revolution hung over his homeland. Throughout France's terrible struggle, Lafayette tried to achieve a constitutional government. This alone, he thought, could bring real liberty.

Lafayette was elected to the Estates General, the French assembly, as a representative of the nobility. Three days before the Bastille prison fell on July 14, 1789, he proposed a declaration of the rights of man, patterned after Thomas Jefferson's.

Lafayette was elected commander of the National Guard, the people's militia. Yet he and his guardsmen repeatedly protected the royal family from the people during the stormy months that followed. Lafayette wanted a constitution, not assassination.

In September, 1791, Louis XVI signed the constitution limiting his powers. Lafayette then went home happily to Chavaniac.

But Louis had not learned that his absolute power existed no longer. When he started a highly unpopular war with Austria, the radical Jacobin party, backed by the Paris masses, made him a virtual prisoner. Lafayette was away fighting against the Austrians. He wanted to lead his troops to Paris to restore the King to the power the constitution guaranteed him. But his men refused to follow. Lafayette was denounced as a traitor to the revolution, and he fled to Belgium. There he was captured and spent the next five years in prison.

Back in France in 1797, Lafayette soon found himself at odds with Napoleon Bonaparte, whom he considered a tyrant. Lafayette retired with Adrienne to farm her estate of La Grange, practically all that was left to them, until Napoleon's downfall in 1814 and the restoration of the Bourbons under Louis XVIII. In 1819, Lafayette was elected to the Chamber of Deputies. But his liberal stand made him hated by the Royalists, who defeated him for re-election in 1824. That year, Lafayette, with his son, whom he had named for George Washington, returned for a visit to the United States. He was greeted everywhere with an emotional and loving welcome.

Lafayette died in Paris on May 20, 1834. Royalist France would permit no demonstrations in his honor. But in the United States, flags flew at half-mast, and the army went into mourning for six months, as it had after George Washington's death.

HODDING CARTER
Author, *Marquis de Lafayette:
Bright Sword for Freedom*

LAFFITE, JEAN (1780?–1826?)

Legend and mystery surround the life of the pirate Jean Laffite (or Lafitte). He was born in southwestern France about the year 1780. He emigrated to the West Indies and then to the United States. By 1809 he was the owner, with his brother Pierre, of a blacksmith shop in New Orleans.

Jean Laffite soon set up headquarters on an island in Barataria Bay southwest of New Orleans. He became the leader of a daring band of pirates who attacked British, Spanish, and American ships. Their booty was smuggled into New Orleans, where Pierre sold the stolen goods.

In 1814 the United States government sent an expedition to destroy the Baratarian settlement. Among the prisoners taken was Pierre Laffite. At the time, the United States and Great Britain were fighting the War of 1812. The British were preparing to attack New Orleans, and they offered Jean Laffite $30,000 to aid them in taking the city. Despite the attack on Barataria, Laffite remained loyal to the United States. Under the direction of General Andrew Jackson, the Baratarians took part in the Battle of New Orleans in January 1815. The Americans were victorious, but without the help of Laffite's pirates, the battle might have been lost. The payment Jean Laffite asked was a pardon for his men, which the United States granted.

But soon, Laffite, who had become a hero in New Orleans, was again involved in piracy. He attacked all ships, regardless of the flags they flew. By 1817 the Lafittes had established themselves on an island at the site of present-day Galveston, Texas. They attracted a band of about 1,000 men.

In 1820 the United States sent an expedition to wipe out the colony. According to legend, Jean Laffite loaded his valuables aboard his ship, set fire to his buildings, and escaped before the attack force arrived. Little is known of him after that, but it is believed that his next headquarters were in Yucatan, Mexico, and that he died in 1826.

Reviewed by EDITH McCALL
Author, *Pirates and Privateers*

LA FOLLETTE, ROBERT M. See UNITED STATES, CONGRESS OF THE (Profiles: Senators).

LA FONTAINE, JEAN DE. See FABLES.

LA GUARDIA, FIORELLO (1882–1947)

Fiorello Henry La Guardia was a U.S. congressman and an enormously popular three-term mayor of New York City.

La Guardia was born in New York City on December 11, 1882. His boyhood was spent in Prescott, Arizona. In 1898, Fiorello's father died shortly after returning with his family to Italy. Fiorello then worked in various U.S. consulates in Europe. He returned to the United States in 1906 and became an interpreter while studying law at night. In 1914 the young lawyer ran for Congress as a Republican in a Democratic district in New York. He was defeated but in 1916 he ran again and this time was elected.

In 1917, La Guardia left Washington to serve as an aviator in World War I. He returned to Congress and was re-elected in 1918. In 1919 he became president of the Board of Aldermen of New York City. In 1922 he won a third term in Congress, where his liberal views and strong personality antagonized both Republicans and Democrats. Nevertheless, the voters re-elected him to four more terms.

In 1933 the Fusion Party, a reform party, nominated La Guardia for the office of mayor of New York City. He was elected and, with boundless energy, set to work to reform the city. He balanced the budget, fought graft, and cleared slums. He built new parks, low-cost housing projects, roads, and an airport. He won the admiration of the people of New York, who called him "The Little Flower" (the translation of his Italian first name). His voice became well known to city children when, during a newspaper strike, he went on the radio to read the comics to them.

La Guardia retired as mayor in 1945. The next year, he was appointed director general of the United Nations Relief and Rehabilitation Administration (UNRRA). He died in New York City on September 20, 1947.

Reviewed by STUART ROCHESTER
Historian, U.S. Department of Defense

LAKE CHARLES. See LOUISIANA (Cities).

LAKES

Lakes are inland bodies of water that occupy depressions in the surface of the land. They result wherever the natural drainage is blocked or impeded. Water falling on the land in the form of rain or snow runs downhill toward the oceans as rivers and streams. But where the surface is uneven or irregular, it collects in low places, or depressions, called basins.

Where the climate is humid, more water flows into a lake basin than is lost through evaporation. In this way lake basins tend to fill up, and the water remains fresh. As the water rises, it overflows the basin and runs out at the lowest point. In most regions of the world, this means that the water eventually flows down into an ocean or sea.

But if the basin lacks an outlet to the sea, the water will end up in a landlocked basin in the interior of a landmass instead. In such areas, the climate tends to be dry, so lakes that form in these interior basins gradually lose their water by evaporation. As a result, the water in such lakes is usually saline (salty), because as the water evaporates into the air, the dissolved mineral salts are left behind in the lake. Many landlocked lakes are seasonal in nature. They exist for a short time after heavy rains, but shrink or disappear completely during dry weather.

▶ HOW LAKE BASINS ARE FORMED

Lake basins are formed in several ways: by glaciers gouging out the land as they move or dropping sand and gravel as they melt and waste away; by movements of the Earth's crust; by volcanic action; by waves and currents along coasts; by changes in a river's course on land; by groundwater dissolving away bedrock-like limestone; and by humans,

Clockwise from left: Loch Lomond, the largest lake in Great Britain, was formed by glaciers. The high salt content of the Dead Sea makes it very buoyant. Lake Mead, the largest artificial lake in the United States, was created when Hoover Dam was built. Fishing boats sail on Lake Victoria, Africa's largest lake.

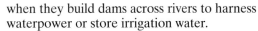

when they build dams across rivers to harness waterpower or store irrigation water.

Glacial Lakes. The most numerous lakes are found in regions that were previously glaciated. For example, the northern parts of North America and Eurasia that were once covered by continental glaciers have literally thousands of lakes, ponds, swamps, and marshes. But even farther south, in mountainous regions where temperatures were below freezing, smaller tongues of ice gouged out deep basins, many of which are occupied by picturesque lakes today.

Many of the lakes formed by continental glaciers are of considerable size, such as the four lower Great Lakes of North America (apart from Lake Superior); Lake Winnipeg, Great Slave Lake and Great Bear Lake in Canada; Lakes Ladoga and Onega in Russia; and Lake Vänern in Sweden.

In Central Asia, two of the largest present-day lakes, the Aral Sea and the Caspian Sea, are remnants of once-greater lakes originally formed at the end of the Ice Age. Similarly, Great Salt Lake, in Utah, is but a small remainder of a vast glacial lake of the past, Lake Bonneville.

Fault Lakes. Many of the world's most beautiful lakes have been produced by movements of the Earth's crust, or **faulting**. Where the Earth has cracked open as its surface has been pulled apart, blocks of its crust drop down to form deep fault valleys. Water draining into such basins has given rise to some of the deepest lakes on our planet, including Lake Baikal in Russian Asia and Lake Superior between the United States and Canada.

Because the continent of Africa is broken by a great fault several thousand miles in length, it is the home of many of the largest and deepest fault lakes in the world. This immense crack in the Earth is known as the Great Rift Valley, and it runs from Mozambique in the south to Ethiopia and Eritrea in the north. It continues northward as the Red Sea, an arm of which extends into the Gulf of Aqaba in Saudi Arabia, ending as a deep trench between Jordan and Israel, home of another fault lake, the Dead Sea. Near the southern end of the Great Rift Valley are Lake Malawi and Lake Tanganyika, while farther north are Lakes Kivu, Edward, and Albert. Lake Turkana (or Rudolf) lies in a fault valley on the border between Kenya and Ethiopia.

Volcanic Action. Sometimes lakes are created by volcanoes. A volcano may send a lava flow cascading down a mountainside, damming up a river and creating a lake in the valley behind it. Often, after a volcano becomes extinct or inactive, its crater fills with water, forming a small lake in the throat of the volcano itself. On occasion, a volcano will erupt so violently that a major part of the volcano will also be blown away, leaving a gaping hole that geologists call a **caldera**. Crater Lake in southern Oregon is actually the caldera of an ancient volcano called Mount Mazama. Other examples of lakes produced in this manner are Lake Atitlán in Guatemala, Lake Ilopango in El Salvador, and Lake Taupo in New Zealand.

Waves and Currents. Along coastal areas, waves and shore currents sometimes close inlets and temporarily create lakes out of bays and estuaries. One such place is Lake Maracaibo in Venezuela, an inlet of the Caribbean Sea. A sand bar only 13 feet (4 meters) deep separates the two water bodies. Because the lake basin is a major source of oil, a channel has been cut through the bar, making it possible for large ships to enter the lake.

WONDER QUESTION

What seas are actually lakes?

If you look at a map of the world, you will notice that many bodies of water located in the interior of continents are called seas, when they are actually lakes. Notable examples are the Salton Sea in southern California and the Caspian Sea, the Aral Sea, the Dead Sea, and the Sea of Galilee in Asia. The word "sea" is usually reserved for a partially enclosed portion of the open ocean. The word "lake," on the other hand, is used to describe a water body that is surrounded by land.

Rivers. Most rivers carry a lot of soil material along with them as they flow, ranging from small pebbles and coarse sands to silt (fine soil particles) and mud, depending on the speed of their current. In periods of high water when the river overflows its banks, much of this material is spread over the river's floodplain. As a result, the river often changes course, digging a new channel where the water is flowing faster and filling an older one with silt where it is meandering (winding) more slowly back and forth. As it straightens itself out by cutting off big looping turns, it leaves a number of curved stretches of water along the sides of its valley. These are called **oxbow lakes** and are very numerous along large rivers like the Mississippi, Missouri, and Ohio. Of course, they seldom last very long because they are usually

Oregon's Crater Lake is actually a caldera, left after the violent eruption of an ancient volcano. A cinder cone, known as Wizard Island (center), rises up from the bottom of the caldera.

Florida's Lake Okeechobee formed as groundwater dissolved limestone bedrock, producing sinkholes.

filled in or reshaped the next time the river floods.

Groundwater. In places where limestone bedrock is found, groundwater may dissolve enough of the limestone so that the surface caves in, producing what are called **sinkholes**. Such water-filled basins are really small lakes which, as time goes on, may continue dissolving into larger and larger depressions. Florida in the southern United States contains many lakes of this type, of which the largest example is Lake Okeechobee.

Dams. Each time a dam is constructed across a major river to generate electricity or store water for irrigation, an artificial lake or reservoir is created. For example, when Hoover Dam was built across the Colorado River between Arizona and Nevada, Lake Mead was created.

Lake Victoria in East Africa occupies a shallow basin on a plateau between two rift valleys. Its outlet, at Jinja, Uganda, is the main source of the Nile River. When the Owens Falls Dam was built across the river there in 1954, the water level of the lake was raised several feet, turning it into a giant reservoir. The Itaipu Dam, on the Paraná River between Brazil and Paraguay, is the world's largest hydroelectric dam, forming a lake more than 100 miles (161 kilometers) long.

▶ **WHY LAKES DISAPPEAR**

Natural lakes are temporary features of the landscape. In time, as a lake's outlet river cuts downward, it may eventually drain the lake. On the other hand, its inlet river may bring in so much sediment that it will gradually fill up the lake. As it becomes shallower and shallower, the lake may overgrow with vegetation and become a marsh or a swamp. Or the climate may change, and more water may be lost to evaporation than is contributed by precipitation. However, very large and deep lakes such as the Great Lakes are in no danger of being drained or filled.

▶ **EFFECT OF LAKES**

Freshwater lakes, whether natural or artificial, supply water to cities and industries. Large lakes modify and temper the local climate. Areas downwind of lakes stay cooler longer in the spring because the lake water warms more slowly than the land. These same areas also stay warmer longer in the autumn because they lose their warmth more slowly than the land. For this reason, many such areas are devoted to orchard and vineyard crops. Lakes are also a source of fish and offer recreational opportunities such as fishing, boating, swimming, and ice-skating.

▶ **ENVIRONMENTAL CONCERNS**

Lakes face two kinds of environmental problems: threats to water quality and the deterioration of shoreland. Pollution by cities and towns, industrial waste, the impact of

Lake Baikal in Russian Asia is the deepest lake in the world. Its long, narrow shape, mountainous sides, and great depth are evidence of its fault-valley origins.

shipping, and poor agricultural practices have led to poisoning of water and changes in its temperature. This presents a serious threat to the ecology.

Many lakes lose fish and other aquatic life because of the growth of too many aquatic weeds and algae, which use up too much of the oxygen in the water. Certain chemicals act as nutrients (food) for undesirable plants and cause them to grow rapidly. Eventually they use up all the oxygen in the water, and the fish and other aquatic life die by suffocation. When the water is completely filled with algae and there is no oxygen left, the algae die, and what is left is a pool of rotting and decayed plants. (See the article WATER POLLUTION in Volume WXYZ for more information on the specific causes of pollution of lakes and other bodies of water.)

In order to conserve the world's water resources, many governments have taken steps not only to protect their lakes but also to reverse some of the damage already done. In the United States, the Environmental Protection Agency (EPA) is charged with preventing water pollution, ensuring clean and safe water, and protecting aquatic ecosystems.

▶ **SELECTED LAKES OF THE WORLD**

Lake Albert, located on the border between Uganda and the Democratic Republic of Congo, is a source of the Nile River. The lake is 100 miles (161 kilometers) long and 20 miles (32 kilometers) wide; its area is 2,075 square miles (5,374 square kilometers).

The Aral Sea lies between Kazakhstan and Uzbekistan and has an area of more than 11,000 square miles (28,500 square kilometers). Because the water losses from evaporation and irrigation are so great, the lake has an average salinity of 10 percent, making it about three times saltier than the ocean.

Lake Atitlán is located in the mountains west of Guatemala City, the capital of Guatemala. The lake occupies a vast caldera that is 12 miles (19 kilometers) long, 6 miles (10 kilometers) wide, and 1,000 feet (305 meters) deep.

Lake Baikal is the deepest lake in the world, reaching a depth of 5,715 feet (1,742 meters). Located in Russian Asia, it has the greatest volume of fresh water of any lake in the world, amounting to one-fifth of the global total. Measuring 395 miles (636 kilometers) in length, it has an area of 11,780 square miles (30,510 square kilometers).

Lake Balaton, the largest lake in central Europe, is located in western Hungary about 55 miles (89 kilometers) southwest of Budapest. Measuring 232 square miles (601 square kilometers) with a maximum depth of 35 feet (11 meters), the lake occupies a fault valley whose rolling hillsides are covered with vineyards. Because lakes are so rare in this part of Europe, Balaton has become one of the great inland resorts of the region.

Lake Balkhash lies 600 miles (966 kilometers) east of the Aral Sea, in southeast Kazakhstan. With an area of 7,115 square miles (18,428 square kilometers), most of its water comes from the Ili River, which enters near the south end of the lake. The western half of the lake is composed of fairly fresh water. On the other hand, the region is dry and evaporation is so intense that the northeastern arm of the lake, far from the inflowing river water, is quite salty.

The Caspian Sea, the world's largest inland body of water, forms part of the traditional boundary line between Europe and Asia. It measures 746 miles (1,200 kilometers) from north to south and 270 miles (434 kilometers) from west to east; it has an area of 143,550 square miles (371,795 square kilometers). However, because more and more water has been used for irrigation in surrounding subhumid regions, the lake level has been dropping noticeably in recent decades.

Lake Chad is located on the Sahara desert's southern border, where the four African countries of Chad, Niger, Nigeria, and Cameroon meet. Although it is fed by the Chari and Logone rivers from the south, the rainfall is so undependable and the evaporation is so great that the lake is constantly changing in size. Its area ranges from about 3,800 square miles to 9,900 square miles (9,842 to 25,641 square kilometers) in area and varies in depth from about 13 to 23 feet (4 to 7 meters) in the south to only about 13 feet (4 meters) in the northwest.

Lake Champlain, located near the southeastern edge of the Canadian Shield, lies between the Adirondack Mountains of New York and the Green Mountains of Vermont. It is about 125 miles (201 kilometers) long and has an area of 430 square miles (1,114 square kilometers). It was named for the French explorer Samuel de Champlain, who discovered it in 1609.

Lake Chapala, the largest lake in Mexico, is located in the west central part of the country near the city of Guadalajara. With a length of 50 miles (81 kilometers), it is a typical example of a lake basin formed by faulting, for it is long and narrow and has steep sides.

Lake Como, located in northern Italy, is one of the largest and most beautiful lakes in the country. The lake is 37 miles (60 kilometers) in length and has an area of 56 square miles (145 square kilometers). It is surrounded by the southern foothills of the Alps in Italy, and many tourist resorts are located nearby.

Lake Como, in the foothills of the southern Alps, is one of Italy's loveliest lakes. Its scenic location makes it a popular tourist spot.

Lake Constance lies on the borders of Switzerland, Germany, and Austria, in the northwestern foothills of the Alps in Switzerland. It is 46 miles (74 kilometers) in length and 210 square miles (544 square kilometers) in area, and it has a maximum depth of 827 feet (252 meters).

Crater Lake, located in the Cascade Mountains in Oregon, is also a national park. The lake lies in a caldera that is about 6 miles (10 kilometers) long, 5 miles (8 kilometers) wide, and 1,932 feet (589 meters) deep at its deepest point. The lake contains a cinder cone that grew out from the bottom of the caldera to form what is known as Wizard Island.

The Dead Sea, located on the boundary between Jordan and Israel, measures 1,312 feet (400 meters) below sea level—the lowest point on the surface of the Earth. The lake is 51 miles (82 kilometers) long and, at the

Lake Geneva in Switzerland is famous for its scenic beauty. The historic castle of Chillon rises at its eastern end.

most, 11 miles (18 kilometers) wide; its area is 394 square miles (1,020 square kilometers). Because the rate of evaporation is so high and the inflow is so small, the Dead Sea is extremely salty and totally lacking in fish or wildlife—hence its name.

Dongting Hu, in central China, is a product of east Asia's frequent monsoons. The lake receives the spillover from the Yangtze (Chang) River and varies greatly in size from the dry winter season, when its area is 1,430 square miles (3,704 square kilometers), to the rainy summer season, when it ranges from 3,500 to 4,000 square miles (9,065 to 10,360 square kilometers).

Lake Erie is the fourth largest of the five Great Lakes of North America. It is also the shallowest, measuring 210 feet (64 meters) at its greatest depth. See the article GREAT LAKES in Volume G.

Lake Eyre is the largest salt lake in Australia. Located in South Australia, it covers at its maximum more than 3,600 square miles (9,324 square kilometers), but due to its uneven inflow and high evaporation, it is usually much smaller. Lake Eyre also contains the lowest point in Australia, about 52 feet (16 meters) below sea level.

Sea of Galilee, also known as Lake Tiberias, is a freshwater lake in northern Israel. It is 13 miles (21 kilometers) long, 7 miles (11 kilometers) wide, and about 700 feet (212 meters) below sea level. The lake is the northernmost water body in the Great Rift Valley.

Lake Garda, the largest lake in Italy, is located in the north of the country. It is 32 miles (52 kilometers) long, has a maximum width of 11 miles (18 kilometers), and an area of 143 square miles (370 square kilometers). The lake is noted for its scenic beauty and attracts many tourists.

Lake Geneva lies in the northwestern foothills of the Swiss Alps. The lake is 45 miles (72 kilometers) long and 1½ to 9 miles (2.4 to 14 kilometers) wide and has an area of 224 square miles (580 square kilometers). The lake was formed by the glacial damming of the Rhône River as it flowed out of the Alps on its way to the Mediterranean Sea.

THE WORLD'S LARGEST LAKES

Name	Location	Area	
		square miles	square kilometers
Caspian Sea	Borders Kazakhstan, Turkmenistan, Iran, Azerbaijan, Russia	143,550	371,795
Lake Superior	Canada and United States	31,800	82,362
Lake Victoria	Borders Kenya, Tanzania, Uganda	26,828	69,485
Lake Huron	Canada and United States	23,000	59,570
Lake Michigan	United States	22,400	58,000
Lake Tanganyika	Borders Burundi, Tanzania, Zambia, Democratic Republic of Congo	12,700	32,893
Great Bear Lake	Canada	12,275	31,792
Lake Baikal	Russia	11,780	30,510
Lake Malawi (also called Lake Nyasa)	Borders Tanzania, Mozambique, Malawi	11,430	29,604
Aral Sea	Borders Kazakhstan, Uzbekistan	11,000	28,500

Source: Webster's Geographical Dictionary

Great Bear Lake, located in the Northwest Territories of Canada, is the largest lake entirely within the country. Its area is 12,275 square miles (31,792 square kilometers) and greatest depth is 1,356 feet (413 meters). Important deposits of radium and uranium are found on the northeastern shores of the lake.

Great Salt Lake, in northern Utah, is the largest natural body of water between the Great Lakes and the Pacific Ocean. About 80 miles (130 kilometers) long and 35 miles (55 kilometers) wide, it has a total area of about 2,000 square miles (5,180 square kilometers). However, at the end of the Ice Age, its predecessor, Lake Bonneville, covered over 20,000 square miles (51,800 square kilometers). But as the climate grew warmer and drier, it gradually evaporated. In the process, the soluble salts carried down by the rivers became more concentrated, until today the Great Salt Lake is far saltier than the ocean.

Great Slave Lake, in the south central mainland of Canada's Northwest Territories, has an area of 10,980 square miles (28,438 square kilometers) and is 298 miles (479 kilometers) long. Its maximum depth is 2,015 feet (614 meters). Yellowknife, the capital and largest city of the Northwest Territories, is located on its northern shore, and its outlet forms the headwaters of the Mackenzie River.

Lake Huron is the second largest of the five Great Lakes of North America. See the article GREAT LAKES in Volume G.

Lake Kariba, one of the world's largest artificial lakes, forms part of the border between Zambia and Zimbabwe. Located on the Zambezi River and created by the Kariba Dam, it lies downstream from Victoria Falls. It is 175 miles (282 kilometers) long and 2,050 square miles (5,310 square kilometers) in area; its depth is 390 feet (119 meters).

Lake Ladoga, located in northwest Russia, is the largest freshwater lake in Europe and the second largest in Russia. With an area of 6,835 square miles (17,703 square kilometers), it is 124 miles (200 kilometers) long and 75 miles (121 kilometers) wide and has a maximum depth of 738 feet (255 meters).

Loch Lomond, located in the Scottish Highlands, is the largest lake in Great Britain. Its area measures 27 square miles (70 square kilometers), and it is 24 miles (39 kilometers) long, with a maximum width of 5 miles (8 kilometers). It is also an important tourist attraction, famed for its lovely natural setting.

Lake Louise, located in southwest Alberta, Canada, in Banff National Park, is noted for

The Great Salt Lake in northern Utah is a remnant of its Ice Age predecessor, Lake Bonneville. It is far saltier than the ocean.

its beautiful scenery. Measuring $1\frac{1}{2}$ miles (2.4 kilometers) by $\frac{3}{4}$ mile (1.2 kilometers), it has an altitude of 5,670 feet (1,728 meters).

Lake of Lucerne lies in the northwestern foothills of the Alps in Switzerland. It has a area of 44 square miles (114 square kilometers). Also known as Vierwaldstätter See, or the Lake of the Four Forest Cantons, it was the setting for a play about William Tell, a legendary hero of Switzerland.

Lake Maggiore, the second largest lake in Italy, is located in the southern flanks of the Alps on the border with Switzerland. The lake is about 40 miles (64 kilometers) long and about 2 miles (3 kilometers) wide, and it has an area of 81 square miles (210 square kilometers). Its mild climate and beautiful scenery make it a center of both agriculture and tourism.

Lake Maracaibo in Venezuela lies in one of the world's richest petroleum-producing regions, and many natural gas plants and oil wells operate there. It is also the largest lake in South America.

Lake Malawi (also called Lake Nyasa) in Southeast Africa has an area of 11,430 square miles (29,604 square kilometers). The lake empties through the Shire River into the Zambezi River, which flows into the Indian Ocean. Malawi has more different species of fish than any other lake in the world.

Lake Manitoba is located in southern Manitoba, Canada. With an area of about 1,800 square miles (4,660 square kilometers), the lake is about 140 miles (225 kilometers) long and connects to **Lake Winnipegosis** and **Lake Winnipeg**. All three of these lakes are remnants of the largest post-glacial lake in North America known as Lake Agassiz, which covered an extensive area of the provinces of Manitoba and Saskatchewan as well as parts of the states of North Dakota and Minnesota.

Lake Maracaibo, the largest lake in South America, is located in the western part of Venezuela. Its area is 5,217 square miles (13,512 square kilometers). A relatively shallow arm of the Caribbean Sea—its maximum depth is 115 feet (35 meters)—the lake receives most of its water from the Catatumbo River, which enters from the southwest.

Lake Mead, the largest artificial lake in the United States, is located on the Colorado River between Arizona and Nevada. A reservoir, Mead was formed by Hoover Dam. It has an area of 227 square miles (588 square kilometers), a length of 115 miles (185 kilometers), and, near the dam, a depth of over 500 feet (150 meters).

Lake Michigan is the third largest of the five Great Lakes of North America and the largest body of fresh water located entirely within the United States. See the article GREAT LAKES in Volume G.

Lake Nasser, one of the world's largest artificial lakes, is about 300 miles (483 kilometers) long. The lake was formed after the Aswan High Dam was built across the Nile River near the border of Egypt and Sudan, in order to store surplus floodwater for use throughout the year.

Loch Ness is a freshwater lake located in the Scottish Highlands of northern Scotland. Part of the Caledonian Canal waterway system, the lake is 23 miles (37 kilometers) long. Loch Ness is said to be the home of a sea monster, but no one has been able to prove its existence. See the article LOCH NESS MONSTER in this volume.

Lake Neuchâtel is the largest lake lying entirely within Switzerland. Located in the northwestern foothills of the Alps in Switzerland, it has an area of 84 square miles (218 square kilometers) and a maximum depth of 502 feet (153 meters).

Lake Nicaragua is the largest lake in Central America and the only lake in the world that contains freshwater sharks, swordfish, and tarpon. Although all these species were originally native to the ocean, when volcanic action cut the lake off from the open sea, these marine animals were trapped and had to adapt to their new environment. Located in southern Nicaragua, the lake has an area of 3,100 square miles (8,000 square kilometers).

Lake Okeechobee, the largest lake in the southern United States, is located on the edge of the Everglades near the southern end of Florida. It is about 40 miles (65 kilometers) long by 25 miles (40 kilometers) wide and has a maximum depth of about 20 feet (6 meters).

Lake Onega, located in northwest Russia, is the second largest freshwater lake in Europe. It has an area of 3,710 square miles (9,609 square kilometers) and is frozen over half of the year.

Lake Ontario is the smallest and easternmost of the five Great Lakes of North America. See GREAT LAKES in Volume G.

Lake Peipus, located on the boundary between Estonia and Russia, is one of the largest lakes in Europe. With an area of 1,390 square miles (3,600 square kilometers), it is 60 miles (97 kilometers) long and 31 miles (50 kilometers) wide.

Lake Placid, located in the Adirondack Mountains in northeastern New York, is about 5 miles (8 kilometers) long and a maximum of 1½ miles (2 kilometers) wide; its elevation is 1,860 feet (567 meters). A winter resort area, it was the site of the 1932 and 1980 Winter Olympic Games.

Lake Pontchartrain, located in southeastern Louisiana, is about 40 miles (64 kilometers) long and has an area of 630 square miles (1,632 square kilometers); New Orleans lies between the lake and the Mississippi River. Pontchartrain Causeway—the largest causeway in the world—is 29 miles (47 kilometers) long and crosses 23 miles (37 kilometers) of open water in the lake.

Lake Powell, an artificial lake, is located on the Colorado River between Arizona and Utah. Created by the Glen Canyon Dam in 1964, the lake's area is 252 square miles (653 square kilometers), and its altitude is 3,700 feet (1,128 meters).

Lake St. Clair is located between Michigan and Ontario, Canada; the

U.S.-Canadian boundary passes through the lake. Its area is about 450 square miles (1,150 square kilometers), and it is about 30 miles (48 kilometers) long. The lake connects with Lake Erie by the Detroit River, and Lake Huron by the St. Clair River.

The Salton Sea, actually a saline lake, is located in the interior of the Imperial Valley of southern California. Its area is 360 square miles (932 square kilometers), and it is about 235 feet (70 meters) below sea level.

Lake Superior has the largest area of any freshwater lake in the world and is the deepest of the five Great Lakes of North America. See the article GREAT LAKES in Volume G.

Lake Tana, the largest lake in Ethiopia, has an area of about 1,100 square miles (2,849 square kilometers). Located on the Ethiopian plateau in the north of the country at an elevation of 6,000 feet (1,829 meters), Tana is the principal source of the Blue Nile.

Lake Tanganyika in Southeast Africa is the world's longest freshwater lake. Its maximum depth is 4,710 feet (1,436 meters), making it the second-deepest lake in the world. It measures some 410 miles (660 kilometers) from north to south and between 10 to 45 miles (16 to 72 kilometers) in width.

Lake Titicaca, one of the largest inland water bodies in South America, forms part of the border between Peru and Bolivia. A remnant of a post-glacial lake, it is 122 miles (196 kilometers) long and 45 miles (72 kilometers) wide and covers an area of more than 3,200 square miles (8,288 square kilometers). Lo-

A man paddles a balsa (small reed boat) on Lake Titicaca. The lake forms part of the boundary between Bolivia and Peru and is the world's highest navigable body of water.

cated at an elevation of 12,500 feet (3,810 meters), this vast freshwater lake is the highest navigable body of water in the world.

Tonle Sap, located in western Cambodia, varies greatly in size from the dry winter season to the rainy summer season, ranging in area from 1,000 to 9,500 square miles (2,590 to 24,605 square kilometers). The lake receives water from the Mekong River when it is in flood stage.

Lake Turkana is located in the Great Rift Valley in northern Kenya. The lake is 154 miles (248 kilometers) long and 10 to 20 miles (16 to 32 kilometers) wide. Its area is 2,473 square miles (6,405 square kilometers). The region surrounding the lake has yielded some of the earliest evidence of the human race.

Lake Victoria is the largest lake in Africa, the Nile River's largest source, and the second largest freshwater lake in the world. Its area is 26,828 square miles (69,485 square kilometers) and it is about 250 miles (400 kilometers) long and 200 miles (320 kilometers) wide. It is situated just south of the equator, at an elevation of about 3,720 feet (1,135 meters).

Lake Volta is a reservoir located in southeastern Ghana, on the Volta River; its area is 3,275 square miles (8,482 square kilometers). The lake was produced by the construction of a great hydroelectric power dam.

Lake of the Woods is located on the borders of southwestern Ontario, southeastern Manitoba, and northern Minnesota. It has an area of 1,695 square miles (4,390 square kilometers) and was an early way station for fur traders in interior North America.

Reviewed by VINCENT H. MALMSTRÖM
Dartmouth College

See also DAMS; HAZARDOUS WASTES; RIVERS; WATER; WATER POLLUTION.

LAMAR, MIRABEAU BUONAPARTE. See TEXAS (Famous People).

LAMB, CHARLES (1775–1834) AND MARY (1764–1847)

Charles Lamb, critic and essayist, was born in London on February 10, 1775, eleven years after his sister Mary, born December 3, 1764. Their father, the clerk of a successful lawyer, sent Charles at age 7 to Christ's Hospital, a famous school for underprivileged children. There he formed his lifelong friendship with the poet Samuel Taylor Coleridge.

When Charles left school in 1789, he went to work in South Sea House, a financial organization. In 1792, Charles won an appointment in the accounting office of East India House, where he remained until 1825.

The decisive event in the lives of Charles and Mary Lamb occurred in 1796, when Mary, who had become mentally ill, stabbed their mother to death. To save his sister from years in an asylum, Charles became her guardian. In later years her attacks of insanity were only occasional. With quiet heroism, Lamb devoted his life to caring for his sister.

When she was healthy, Mary shared her brother's love of literature. They worked together on their first great success, *Tales from Shakespear* (1807), a retelling of the plays for children. Charles recounted the tragedies, and Mary the comedies. Lamb also wrote a child's version of Homer's *Odyssey*. His *Specimens of English Dramatic Poets Who Lived About the Time of Shakespear* (1808) showed Lamb to be an outstanding critic.

In 1796 four sonnets that Lamb had written were included in a volume of Coleridge's poems. More of his poems appeared in other collections. But Charles Lamb is best known for his essays. When *The London Magazine* was founded in 1820, he began writing essays for it, signing himself "Elia." The essays were a great success and were first published in book form in 1823 as *Essays of Elia*.

The year 1823 found Mary well enough for the Lambs to adopt a child, Emma Isola, who brought great happiness to them in their last years. Charles Lamb died on December 27, 1834, in Edmonton. Mary Lamb died on May 20, 1847, in St. John's Wood and was buried with her brother.

RANDEL HELMS
Arizona State University

LA METTRIE, JULIEN OFFROY DE. See ENLIGHTENMENT, AGE OF (Profiles).

L'AMOUR, LOUIS. See NORTH DAKOTA (Famous People).

LAMPS. See LIGHTING.

LANDSCAPE GARDENING. See GARDENS AND GARDENING.

LANGMUIR, IRVING (1881–1957)

Irving Langmuir was an American scientist and engineer. When asked why he worked so hard in science, Langmuir replied: "Whatever work I've done, I've done for the fun of it." He must have had a great deal of fun. His discoveries and inventions have added a great deal to our knowledge of the natural world and have affected all of us.

Irving was born in Brooklyn, New York, on January 31, 1881. His father was a businessman. His older brother, Arthur, was interested in chemistry, which attracted Irving's interest too. When he was 12, the family went to Europe for 3 years. Irving attended school in Paris. Irving—not yet a teen-ager—began to climb mountains in the Alps. This became a lifelong hobby, which he later combined with a scientific interest in meteorology, the science of weather.

Irving went to college at Pratt Institute in Brooklyn and the Columbia School of Mines in Manhattan. He studied metallurgy, the science and technology of metals. After obtaining his degree in 1903, Irving went to Germany and continued his studies at Göttingen University. His major professor was Walther Hermann Nernst (1864–1941), an outstanding chemist of the early 20th century.

In 1906, when Langmuir returned to the United States, about the only type of work open to a scientist was teaching. A few large industrial companies, however, were beginning to establish research laboratories. After 3 years of teaching, Langmuir took a position in the General Electric Company Research Laboratory at Schenectady, New York. He spent most of the rest of his life there.

At the time that Langmuir began his research for the General Electric Laboratory, the incandescent (glowing) light bulb had come into widespread use as the principal artificial light. The filaments of these light bulbs were tungsten wires, which were heated electrically until they became white-hot. These filaments did not last very long. In 1912 Langmuir discovered that their lifetime could be greatly increased by filling the light bulb with an inert gas, such as argon. (An inert gas does not usually react with other chemical elements.) This discovery decreased the cost

of lighting America by hundreds of millions of dollars a year.

From this spectacular discovery, made only 3 years after he began his research, Langmuir went on to make many others. He invented the atomic hydrogen welding torch. He developed a new kind of vacuum pump that made possible a whole new set of industries and greatly aided the development of radio and television. He and his fellow workers did much of the early work in rainmaking.

Throughout Langmuir's life he combined scientific studies with engineering applications. He believed strongly that if industry would support scientific research, it would profit greatly from the results.

In 1932 Langmuir received the Nobel prize in chemistry "for his discoveries and investigations in surface chemistry." The research that had led to this award had come out of his earliest studies on what happens to the surface of a tungsten light-bulb filament when it is heated. Langmuir died August 16, 1957.

DUANE H. D. ROLLER
The University of Oklahoma

LANGUAGE ARTS

In the United States the term "language arts" describes generally the English program at the elementary-school level. Most secondary schools simply use the more familiar term "English."

The language arts consist of all the forms of communication in which words are used. There are four language arts: listening, speaking, reading, and writing. Speaking involves the skills of speech. Both silent and oral reading are language arts. Writing includes handwriting and spelling.

Most of our communication today is oral. We talk and listen to one another much more frequently than we write. It is important, therefore, that students develop the habits and skills of effective oral communication.

Listening. Listening involves attentive, accurate hearing and interpretation of what is heard. A person gains both information and pleasure from listening. Like reading, listening requires the listener to identify main ideas and related details, to make inferences, and to draw conclusions. Practice in directed listening develops critical and appreciative listeners and, in turn, it also develops more effective speakers.

Speaking. Speaking involves the selection and organization of ideas, and the ability to communicate these ideas orally. Effective speaking requires clear enunciation, correct pronunciation, and an audible voice. Speaking usually takes the form of conversation or discussion. It is not easy to tell one from the other in social situations. Most conversations tend to develop into discussions of a particular topic of interest to the listeners. The ability to express oneself clearly, make suitable comments, identify fact and opinion, and differ from others in socially acceptable ways is characteristic of a good speaker or conversationalist.

Oral communication also includes oral reading of prose and poetry, giving directions, making reports, reciting poetry, telling stories, and dramatics in one form or another.

Reading. Reading takes its place with listening as a major source of information and pleasure. In the process of learning to read, one masters the symbols of written language —letters of the alphabet and the sounds they represent. One also learns word meanings and sentence patterns. Understanding main ideas, recognizing and relating details, making inferences, drawing conclusions, and predicting outcomes are reading skills that students learn and practice in a language-arts reading program. Such a program has two main aims. First, it teaches the student to read critically and at the proper speed. Second, it produces students who like to read and who read on their own as a form of recreation.

A student's fondness for reading is developed mainly through a literature program. Getting to know stories, poems, and plays of literary worth is the reward for learning to read. Literary appreciation develops slowly over the years. As the reader grows older and experiences more of life, a background for appreciating the varied experiences of others is gained. Character study and plot interpretation also help students understand themselves and others.

Writing. Written expression involves the art of composition and the skill of recording the composition for another's reading. Writing letters; expressing one's ideas, opinions, emotions, and reactions; and writing original poems, stories, or plays are the usual forms of creative composition, or expressive or narrative writing. Giving directions, explaining or documenting a position or opinion, and sharing information are referred to as factual or expository writing.

Ideas, words, and sentence patterns must be recorded legibly and correctly. Manuscript writing, a form of handwriting using unjoined printed letters, is generally taught in the primary grades, with a later switch to cursive, or script, writing. In both forms the emphasis is on easily legible writing. Clear writing is a courtesy to the reader and essential to good communication. The proper use of capital letters and punctuation marks is another aid to effective communication.

The language arts are interwoven. For example, a good understanding of listening and speaking skills and being able to use them effectively improves one's ability to read. In turn, good listening, speaking, and reading skills are reflected in one's writing.

MILDRED A. DAWSON
Co-author, *Children Learn the Language Arts*
See also HANDWRITING; READING; SPELLING.

LANGUAGES

Language is something taken for granted. Yet without it governments could not operate, businesses would close, trade could not be carried on, and science and industry would be a hopeless tangle. In fact, without language most human activity would cease.

The word "language" comes from the Latin word *lingua*, which means "tongue." The tongue is used in more sound combinations than any other organ of speech. A broader interpretation of "language" is that it is any form of expression. This includes writing, sign language, dance, music, painting, and mathematics. But the basic form of language is speech. Speech makes human beings different from all other animals. No human group is without a form of speech, while no animal group has ever succeeded in combining sound and meaning into the complex code that humans use. An animal can show joy, fear, dislike, or alarm through its voice, but it cannot carry the message beyond the immediate situation. People can refer to the present, past, or future. They can deal with what is out of sight and millions of miles away. Their speech becomes a particular language when two or more human beings decide that a certain sound or set of sounds shall have the same meaning for them.

▶ **ORIGIN OF LANGUAGE**

Where, when, and how language began is still a mystery, though there are many theories on the subject. One favorite theory is that early humans imitated the sounds they heard in nature, such as the barking of a dog or the gurgling of a brook. Those who favor this theory believe that it explains why there are so many languages in the world. A rooster's crow may have struck the ear of one person in one way, but it may have sounded slightly different to another person. Both people were probably able to convince others that their own imitation of the sound was the only correct one. Thus, they say, the sound a rooster made came to be "cock-a-doodle-doo" in English, *cocorico* in French, *cucuricu* in Romanian, and *chicchirichi* in Italian.

Today there are nearly 3,000 separate spoken tongues. Some, such as English and Chinese, are spoken by hundreds of millions of people. Others, such as some of the native tongues of the American Indians, are spoken by only a few thousand or a few hundred people.

All languages have certain things in common, though their differences are enormous. They all consist of sounds produced by the vocal organs (the throat, nose, tongue, palate, teeth, and lips) and received by the ear. The vocal organs are capable of producing hundreds or perhaps thousands of different sounds. Each language group selects and uses only a small number of these—usually between 10 and 60. Different languages use different sets of sounds. People grow accustomed to the sounds of their own language. When they need to learn a new set of sounds, they find that their old language habits get in their way.

The sounds used by any language are arranged so that they produce words that have certain meanings. When the sounds of D, O, and G are lined up, they produce the word "dog." English-speakers agree that the spoken word "dog" represents a particular animal. If one English-speaker says "dog," another English-speaker will automatically see the image of a dog. But the same word will be meaningless to a Russian, who uses the word *sobaka* for the dog image, or to an Italian, who uses the word *cane*.

Words also have to follow certain rules. These are by no means the same in all languages. In English if you want to speak about more than one dog, you add the letter *s* and get "dogs." In Italian you change the last letter of *cane* to *i* and get *cani*. In English "I see her" has a certain meaning, and it is normal for English-speakers to arrange the words in that order. In Italian, however, it is just as normal to arrange the words so that they equal "I her see."

Despite their many differences, then, all languages have three things in common: a set of individual sounds, a particular way of ordering sounds into words or word units, and rules for such things as word endings and the arrangement of words in a certain order. To learn a new language, you must first learn to produce a new set of sounds. Then you must learn to accept new words for given meanings. Finally, you must learn new rules for how to use your new words. This is not really as difficult as it sounds. In fact, you have done it all before. As a baby, you began to imitate the sounds produced by your parents and other people around you. You connected the sounds with certain objects, actions, or ideas. You learned to string your words along in a certain way and to make changes in them when necessary for their meaning.

▶WRITING

The invention of writing gave people a way to keep a permanent record of their thoughts. The oldest writing that we have any record of is that of the ancient Sumerians. The records go back at least to 3500 B.C. Sumerian writing was in the form of pictures that told a story or gave a message. Something similar is still used today in comic strips and in certain traffic signs. Modern picture writing, however, is usually helped along by written words—such as the captions in the comic strips and the words "School—Slow" written on the traffic sign that pictures a schoolhouse.

The original word pictures had no captions or any explanation based on speech. Nevertheless, the art of picture writing became so highly developed that even very abstract ideas could be expressed by it. The present-day Chinese system of writing has word pictures of this kind. The Chinese word "bright," for example, is a combination of the symbol for sun and the symbol for moon.

SUN 明月 MOON

The Alphabet

An important advance in the development of language was made by the Phoenicians. They decided to let some of their picture letters stand for the sounds they used in their speech. This led to the first alphabet, a series of symbols that stood for the language's speech sounds. The oldest example of Phoenician alphabetic writing seems to be the one found on the stone coffin of the Phoenician king Ahiram, who ruled in the 11th century B.C.

An alphabetic system of writing, once it is put into operation, tends to change very little. Spoken language, on the other hand, is always changing. The result is that there is often a great difference between the way words are written and the way they are spoken. The English spelling of the word "knight," for example, reflects the pronunciation of a thousand years ago. In those days the K was pronounced, the I sound was similar to the I in "it," and the GH represented a sound that has disappeared from English. The word is still spelled the old way, however, because writing habits change much more slowly than speech habits.

Language specialists have tried to overcome this problem with the International Phonetic Alphabet (IPA), in which each symbol stands for just one speech sound. In the IPA both "knight" and "night" appear as [najt].

English is far from being one of the oldest languages, yet even in its comparatively short life it has changed drastically. The opening words of the Lord's Prayer in Anglo-Saxon, the English spoken in the 6th or 7th century, are as follows: "Fæder ūre, thū the eart on heofonum, sī thīn nama gehālgod. Tōbecume thīn rīce. Gewurthe thīn willa on eorthan swā swā on heofonum." The Norman conquest of England in 1066 changed the whole course of the English language. French became the language of the upper classes until the beginning of the 14th century. Even then English was not used in writing. Only in the 15th century did English take the place of French and Latin in official documents. By then English had undergone tremendous changes in its grammar and vocabulary. Today the same lines of the Lord's Prayer look like this: "Our Father which art in heaven, Hallowed be thy name. Thy kingdom come. Thy will be done on earth, as it is in heaven."

All languages change. French, Spanish, and Italian were the Latin of Caesar and Cicero 2,000 years ago. English, German, Dutch, and the Scandinavian tongues were once the same language.

▶THE INDO-EUROPEAN FAMILY

More than half the world's population speak languages that are definitely related. This vast family of languages is called Indo-European because it includes tongues spoken by people from northern India all the way across Europe. The major languages of the

PRESENT-DAY INDO-EUROPEAN LANGUAGES

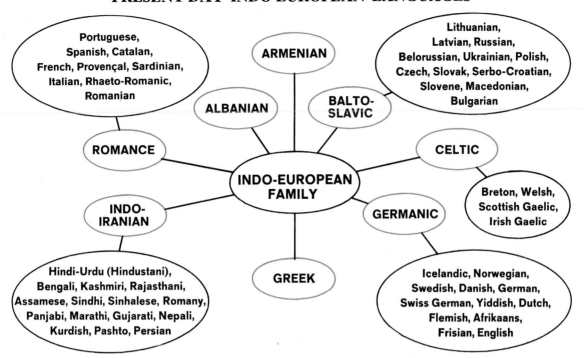

Americas, Australia, and New Zealand are also Indo-European, since they all came from European countries. The Indo-European group includes such different languages as Russian, Hindi, Persian, Armenian, Albanian, Greek, and Welsh.

There is no written record of an Indo-European language, but scholars have pieced together a language that they think must be very much like it. The Indo-European people may have lived in northern Europe around the shores of the Baltic. They were probably nomadic—that is, they wandered about a great deal in search of food. Some of them wandered to the south, others to the east and west. Eventually some went north and crossed the English Channel to what is now Britain. Wherever they went, a new language, based on the original Indo-European tongue, developed in its own way.

A Danish language scholar, Rasmus Rask (1787–1832), was the first to prove that all these languages were related. All the Indo-European languages are similar in three ways: in grammatical structure; in vocabulary, especially in certain key words, such as "father," "mother," "sister," and "brother"; and in sound patterns. One of the most important ways of showing that two languages are related is to show that certain sounds in

one language are matched with certain sounds in another. For example, the relationship between English and Latin is shown in words that begin with P in Latin and F in English—compare the Latin *pater, pes, piscis* with the English *father, foot, fish.*

▶ OTHER LANGUAGE FAMILIES

The rest of the world's people speak languages that seem to be unconnected with Indo-European tongues. These fall into separate families. Chief among them are the **Semitic** and **Cushitic** families of North Africa and the Near East. The two most widely spoken Semitic languages are Hebrew and Arabic. Hebrew is the official tongue of Israel and the prayer tongue of Jews throughout the world. Various forms of Arabic are spoken in Morocco, Algeria, Tunisia, Libya, Egypt, Syria, Lebanon, Saudi Arabia, Yemen, Jordan, and Iraq. It is the sacred tongue of Islam.

The Cushitic family appears in parts of northeastern Africa. Cushitic languages are spoken by various groups in southern Egypt and the Sudan. However, the languages of Ethiopia belong to the Semitic family. Today there are probably about 150 million people who speak Semitic and Cushitic languages.

A **Hamitic** group of languages was represented in ancient times by the Egyptian of the pharaohs. Other Hamitic tongues were spoken by the ancient Numidians and Libyans and throughout North Africa. Present-day Berber dialects, ranging from Morocco to Egypt and the Sahara, are Hamitic.

The **Uralic** family includes Finnish, Estonian, Sami (formerly called Lapp), and Hungarian. Some language scholars connect these languages with the **Altaic** languages (which include Turkish) in a **Ural-Altaic** classification. Other scholars prefer to keep the two families separate.

The **Sino-Tibetan** group includes all variations of Chinese, with about 1 billion speakers, and Thai, Burmese, and Tibetan. **Japanese** and **Korean** are separate languages. The **Dravidian** languages, such as Tamil, Telugu, Malayalam, Toda, and Kota, are spoken in southern India. The **Malayo-Polynesian** family includes Malay, Indonesian, Javanese, Balinese, languages of the Philippines, and most of the languages spoken on the islands of the Pacific Ocean.

African and Native American languages are divided into many groups. Other small, separate families are **Caucasian**, which includes languages spoken in the Caucasus Mountain region; **Basque**, spoken by the people of the Pyrenees Mountains; and the native languages of Australia, Tasmania, and New Guinea. Some experts think that Basque is the sole survivor of a once widespread family of pre-Indo-European tongues.

▶ **HOW LANGUAGES CHANGE**

Languages are shaped and changed in many ways. New words are brought to a country through trade, war, or settlers from a foreign land. When the Romans conquered the nations of western and southern Europe, the languages of the conquered lands were replaced by the Latin of the Romans. Spanish became the major language of South America because most of the original conquerors and settlers came from Spain. In Brazil, where the Portuguese settled, Portuguese is the national tongue. Colonists from Great Britain made the United States an English-speaking nation.

To fit changing times, it is sometimes necessary to invent new words. The words "astronaut" and "television" did not exist before the 1900's. Words are also dropped from a language, because they are no longer needed or because their meaning has been forgotten.

Many words that were well-known in Shakespeare's time, such as "trow," which means "believe," are today unfamiliar to many people. Words also drop old meanings and take on new ones. "Meat," for example, used to mean any kind of food. Today it generally means only animal flesh.

Languages often borrow words from other languages. Many food names used in English, such as "omelet" and "crepe suzette," were borrowed directly from the French.

Occasionally new words are made by joining two old words together. "Brunch" is made up of "breakfast" and "lunch"; "smog," of "smoke" and "fog." Lewis Carroll invented many words of this kind. He called them portmanteau words. A portmanteau is a suitcase with two uses. It travels as an ordinary suitcase and opens up to be a clothes wardrobe. Portmanteau words carry two meanings in a single word. One of Carroll's best-known portmanteau words is "slithy" for "slimy" and "lithe."

Slang changes a language, too. Sometimes slang words or expressions are popular for a while and then are forgotten or fall into disuse, like "twenty-three skiddoo" or "the cat's whiskers." Sometimes they become a permanent part of the language, such as "okay" or "corny." Some language scholars think that all slang is acceptable. They argue that proper language is the language people are actually speaking, not the language they should be speaking. Others believe it is important to limit the use of slang in order to keep high standards of good speech.

Some languages have not developed naturally over time. Instead, these artificial, or universal, languages have been purposely created in an attempt to establish a single language that could be understood by anyone in a particular field (such as mathematics or computer science) or anyone in the world. The most widely accepted artificial language has been Esperanto, introduced in 1887 and based on many Indo-European languages. Another artificial language, Lingua Cosmica, was created to communicate with possible extraterrestrial beings.

MARIO PEI
Columbia University

See also GRAMMAR; WRITING; articles on individual languages.

LANSING. See MICHIGAN (Cities).

LAOS

Laos is a small nation of Southeast Asia. Centuries ago its people ruled a great kingdom that was known as the kingdom of a million elephants. Eventually the kingdom declined under the pressure of more powerful neighbors. Near the end of the 1800's, Laos became a French protectorate. Its modern history dates from 1953, when it regained its independence. In the years following independence, Laos was torn by civil war. A Communist government took power in 1975 and continues to rule Laos today.

▶THE PEOPLE

Ethnic Groups. The dominant people of Laos are the Lao, who make up almost half the population. The Lao, who are related to the Thai of neighboring Thailand, live on the plains bordering the Mekong River and its tributaries. The mountains of Laos are inhabited by varied ethnic groups, including the Meo (Hmong), Yao, and Kha (or Lao Theung).

The Lao are mainly farmers, who grow rice on the irrigated lands of the Mekong Valley. This is the most fertile region of the country and the most densely populated. The moun-

tainous areas are more sparsely populated. The mountain peoples live in widely scattered villages, growing crops on small plots of land.

Language and Religion. Lao, a language closely related to Thai, is the official language of the country. The mountain peoples speak various languages and dialects. The Kha speak a dialect of the Mon-Khmer language of neighboring Cambodia.

The Mekong River is the dominant geographical feature of Laos. It is an important source of transportation and supplies fish and water for irrigating rice fields.

41

Even under Communist rule, religion remains an important part of Lao life. Most Lao practice Theravada Buddhism.

Almost all the people are Buddhists. The Lao belong to the Theravada school, one of the two branches of Buddhism. Some of the people, especially among the mountain tribes, also observe older religious beliefs involving spirits (or *phi*). A few of the mountain peoples are Christians.

Festivals and Music. Many religious festivals are observed during the year. The Lao New Year is celebrated in April. *Vixakha Bouxa*, or *Boun Bang-Fay*, the festival that honors the birth, enlightenment, and death of Buddha, comes at the time of the full moon in May. In July, *Khao Vassa*, the beginning of fasting, is celebrated. *Ho Khao Slak*, which comes in the autumn, is to the children of Laos what Christmas is to American children.

The Lao love music, especially singing. The most popular musical instruments are the flute and a bamboo harmonica called a *khene*. The Lao also enjoy watching professional dancing troupes perform.

▶ **THE LAND**

Laos is a landlocked country, bordered by five other nations—China, Vietnam, Myanmar, Thailand, and Cambodia. Most of the land is hilly or mountainous. The northern third of the country has a rugged, mountain-

ous landscape. A mountain range called the Annamese Cordillera runs through central and southern Laos and along its border with Vietnam in the east.

The Mekong River marks the western boundary between Laos and Thailand. The first bridge across the river linking the two countries opened in 1994. Most of Laos' cities and large towns are located on or near the river. Its tributaries help irrigate the surrounding rice fields. It is also Laos' main transportation system and a hydroelectric power source. Its waters teem with fish, which are an important part of the people's diet.

More than half of Laos' land is covered with forests, which are one of its chief natural resources, providing timber for export. However, in order to prevent deforestation, or the loss of forested areas, the government has set limits on timber cutting.

Climate. Laos has two distinct seasons—dry and wet. Between November and April the weather is dry and cool, with temperatures ranging from about 40 to 70°F (4 to 21°C). The wet season begins in May, bringing heavy rainfall and high temperatures.

Cities. Laos has few large cities. The two most important are Vientiane and Luang Prabang, both located on the Mekong River. Vientiane is the capital and largest city and the country's commercial center. Luang Prabang is the former royal capital.

FACTS and figures

LAO PEOPLE'S DEMOCRATIC REPUBLIC is the official name of the country.

LOCATION: Southeast Asia.

AREA: 91,429 sq mi (236,800 km²).

POPULATION: 5,600,000 (estimate).

CAPITAL AND LARGEST CITY: Vientiane.

MAJOR LANGUAGE: Lao (official).

MAJOR RELIGIOUS GROUP: Buddhist.

GOVERNMENT: Communist Republic. **Head of state**—president. **Head of government**—prime minister. **Legislature**—National Assembly.

CHIEF PRODUCTS: Agricultural—rice, coffee, cotton, tobacco, livestock. **Manufactured**—forest products (including timber), textiles, processed agricultural products. **Mineral**—tin, salt (also undeveloped deposits of iron ore, coal, copper, and other minerals).

MONETARY UNIT: New kip (1 new kip = 100 at).

Nearly 80 percent of Laos' population must grow its own food to survive. Mountain villagers, such as these Meo tribeswomen, plant rice, the country's chief food crop. Corn, wheat, vegetables, and fruit are also grown, and fish provide a major source of protein. The country must still import additional food to feed its people.

▶ **THE ECONOMY**

Laos is one of the world's poorest countries. Most of the people are subsistence farmers, growing food for their own use. The most important crop is rice, which is the staple food.

There is little industry. Some of the people are engaged in mining, forestry, and fishing. Textiles are among the chief manufactured goods. Tin and salt are mined in commercial quantities. Laos is known to have deposits of other valuable minerals, including iron ore, coal, and copper, but has not been able to develop them. Textiles, clothing, wood, and wood products are the leading exports. Hydroelectric power is also sold to Thailand, which borders Laos on the west.

Although Laos has a Communist form of government, private ownership of land and businesses and foreign investment are permitted under the constitution.

▶ **HISTORY AND GOVERNMENT**

Early History. The early ancestors of the Lao migrated to what is now Laos from southern China. In 1353 the first historic Lao ruler, Fa Ngoun, united the Lao states into a kingdom called Lan Chang (Lan Xang), or the kingdom of "a million elephants." The large kingdom lasted until the 1700's, when it again was divided.

During the 1800's, most of Laos was ruled by Siam (modern-day Thailand). France gained control of Laos in 1893 and governed it, under the Lao kings, as part of French Indochina, which also included present-day Vietnam and Cambodia.

Independence and Civil War. Laos gained complete independence from France in 1953. The 1954 Geneva agreements, which ended the war for independence in Indochina, recognized Laos as a unified, independent, and neutral country. The years following independence, however, were marked by civil war between forces loyal to the royal government and Communist guerrillas known as the Pathet Lao.

In 1961–62 a second Geneva conference was held to try to resolve Laos' political problems. A coalition Lao government was formed from the three political factions—conservatives, neutralists, and Communists.

In spite of its neutrality, Laos, because of its border with Vietnam, was drawn into the Vietnam War. Within the country itself, the civil war between Communist and non-Communist forces continued.

Recent History. The Communists gradually won control of the countryside and in 1975 gained complete control of Laos. King Savang Vatthana was forced to give up the throne, ending the centuries-old Lao monarchy.

Laos' present government is based on a constitution adopted in 1991, which provides for only one legal political party, the Lao People's Revolutionary Party. The legislative body is the National Assembly, elected for five years. The National Assembly elects the president, who, in turn, appoints a prime minister to head the Council of Ministers.

THOMAS F. BARTON
Indiana University

See also VIETNAM WAR.

LAPLAND

Lapland is a vast region, covering approximately 150,000 square miles (388,500 square kilometers) of the northernmost parts of Norway, Sweden, Finland, and the Kola Peninsula in Russia. It extends from the Norwegian Sea in the west to the White Sea in the east and from the Barents Sea of the Arctic Ocean in the north to the Gulf of Bothnia in the south. Increasingly, the name "Samiland" is used to refer to this region. But many, especially outsiders, still call it Lapland.

▶ PEOPLE

Lapland is the home of the Sami, the indigenous (native) people of far northern Europe. Swedes, Norwegians, Finns, and Russians who now also live in the region once called these indigenous people Lapps. But "Sami" has become the preferred name for the people, as the Sami themselves consider the word "Lapp" offensive.

The Sami—about 65,000 in number today—once roamed through a broad territory in south and central Finland and along the Scandinavian Peninsula as far south as central Norway and Sweden. Then southern Norwegians, Swedes, and Finns, looking for new settlements, pushed the Sami northward. The majority settled north of the Arctic Circle. Smaller numbers of Sami established themselves farther south, however, blending in with the surrounding majority cultures.

In the past, the Sami were categorized by where they lived and by the source of their livelihood. Traditional occupations were fishing and reindeer herding. For the latter, the Sami adopted a nomadic lifestyle. They moved with the reindeer herds, traveling in lightweight sleds and living in tents that could be taken down and transported easily. They dressed in traditional colorful clothes or in fur. But this image of the Sami is outdated. Today's Sami still wear their traditional clothing on festive occasions, but they usually wear modern dress. They still herd reindeer, but often by snowmobile and with the help of technological advances such as radar. These modern conveniences make a nomadic lifestyle unnecessary.

The Sami language is different from the other Nordic languages, although it is distantly related to Finnish. Of its three dialects, North-Sami is the most widely spoken. For centuries, the Sami were discouraged—and sometimes forbidden—from using their own language by the majority population.

Since the 1970's, efforts have been made to preserve the Sami heritage. The Sami language has become the language of choice in many schools that cater to a large Sami population. Several universities in Norway, Sweden, and Finland offer Sami studies programs. In addition, several Sami centers promote awareness and help educate people about the Sami as an indigenous ethnic group. The Nordic governments and the Euro-

A Sami couple in traditional dress guide tourists on a reindeer-drawn sleigh ride in Lapland. The Sami, native inhabitants of this vast region in Europe's far north, have adopted a more modern lifestyle but strive to preserve their cultural heritage.

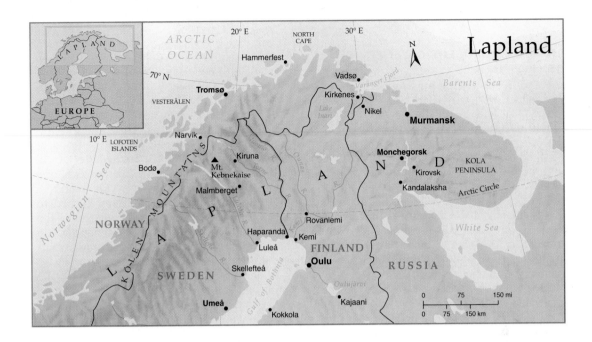

pean Union now sponsor and subsidize similar Sami educational projects.

▶ LAND

Lapland is a region of snowcapped mountains, rolling tundra (treeless plains), rushing rivers, and sparkling lakes. The region's highest point is Mount Kebnekaise, which rises to a height of 6,965 feet (2,123 meters) in Swedish Lapland's Kjølen Mountains. Temperatures average between 50 and 70°F (10 and 21°C) in summer, while in winter they may drop below 0°F (–18°C). Precipitation varies, but much of it falls as snow, which stays on the ground for as long as six to seven months of the year.

Because much of Lapland lies north of the Arctic Circle, the sun shines continuously there for two months during the summer; the region is sometimes called the Land of the Midnight Sun. In midwinter the conditions are reversed. Although there are a few hours of twilight at midday, the sun does not rise at all. During this season the darkness is driven away by the light of the moon and stars and by the brightness of the snow that blankets the ground.

▶ ECONOMY

The reindeer has traditionally been important in the economy of the Sami. It once supplied them with everything they needed—milk, meat, clothing, and even knife handles from the antlers and thread from the sinews. It also served as a work animal. Today the reindeer is raised mainly for meat.

The way of life in Lapland has changed dramatically during recent decades. Although reindeer herding is still important in some areas, the Sami have made use of the region's other resources to earn their livelihoods. One of the largest deposits of high-grade iron ore in the world is located near the mining town of Kiruna in Swedish Lapland. In northern Norway, the fishing industry is significant. Timber is a major resource of the Swedish and Finnish sections of Lapland. The region's rushing rivers are a chief source of hydroelectric power. The exploitation of Lapland's natural resources has sometimes caused conflict between the traditional Sami, who would like humans to live in close harmony with nature, and those who would profit from development.

VINCENT MALMSTROM
Dartmouth College
Reviewed by ROLAND THORSTENSSON
Department of Scandinavian Studies
Gustavus Adolphus College

See also FINLAND; NORWAY; RUSSIA; SWEDEN.

LARDNER, RING. See MICHIGAN (Famous People).

LARVA. See METAMORPHOSIS.

LARYNGITIS. See DISEASES (Descriptions of Some Diseases).

LA SALLE, ROBERT CAVELIER, SIEUR DE (1643–1687)

Robert Cavelier, Sieur de La Salle, was one of the most famous fur traders and explorers in the history of North America. He was the first European to descend the Mississippi River to its mouth in the Gulf of Mexico.

Robert Cavelier was born in Rouen, France, in 1643. He was educated as a Jesuit missionary but left the religious life and went to Canada in 1666 or 1667. He received a grant of land near Montreal that as a joke was called La Chine (China) because of his great interest in finding a route across North America to the riches of Asia.

Like other fur traders of his day, Cavelier combined exploration with fur trading. From 1669 to 1671 he traveled with French missionaries among the Iroquois Indians south of Lake Ontario.

According to his own account, Cavelier was the first European to explore the Ohio River. He dreamed of building a great French fur empire in the Mississippi basin. Count Frontenac, who arrived in 1672 to become governor of New France, encouraged La Salle to pursue his dream.

In 1673 Frontenac sent Cavelier to invite the neighboring Iroquois tribes to a historic meeting at Cataraqui (now Kingston, Ontario). There peace was made between the Iroquois and the French. At Cataraqui, Cavelier built Fort Frontenac. This post was important to the fur trade because it stood at the east end of Lake Ontario, where the St. Lawrence River begins. When the fort was completed, Cavelier was put in command.

The next year, 1674, Cavelier returned to France. He was made a noble and given the title Sieur de La Salle. Fort Frontenac and the surrounding lands were given to him as his seigneury, or estate.

When La Salle returned to New France, he built two ships to carry on the fur trade. La Salle and Count Frontenac were eager to gain control of the whole fur trade. They extended their enterprise into the upper Mississippi Valley by building Fort Crèvecoeur on the Illinois River. This was the first establishment of Europeans in the Mississippi Valley.

King Louis XIV had given La Salle permission to settle the Mississippi Valley. But he did not begin his search for the mouth of the Mississippi River until 1682, after the French government complained that he was neglecting exploration. In that year he made his famous trip down the great river that Jolliet and Marquette had explored in 1673. La Salle named the vast, newly discovered land Louisiana, after King Louis.

La Salle returned to France with news of his discovery. In 1684 he was sent out again with a party of settlers and four ships to start a colony on the Mississippi. The ships missed the mouth of the river and landed instead at Matagorda Bay on the coast of Texas— more than 300 miles (480 kilometers) west of the Mississippi. Some of their supplies were lost in the landing. Indian attacks and accidents killed many of the settlers. With most of the survivors, La Salle began a march to reach the Mississippi. But on the way, some of the men mutinied, and on March 19, 1687, La Salle was murdered.

JOHN MOIR
University of Toronto

See also JOLLIET, LOUIS, AND JACQUES MARQUETTE.

THE EXPLORATIONS OF ROBERT CAVELIER, SIEUR DE LA SALLE

LASERS

Lasers produce light of a very special—and useful—kind. Surgeons use beams of laser light to correct vision defects. Geologists use laser instruments for predicting earthquakes. And astronomers use laser-aided telescopes to see distant stars more clearly. Lasers also let us hear noise-free music on compact discs and see spectacular displays of colorful beams during rock concerts.

The word "laser" stands for *l*ight *a*mplification by *s*timulated *e*mission of *ra*diation. To understand this term, we first need to know some things about ordinary light—the kind of light produced by the sun or by an electric lightbulb.

A laser projection system creates a spectacular display of colorful beams around a dancer on a stage.

▶ WHAT IS A LASER?

Both ordinary light and laser light are forms of energy called **radiation**, and they begin inside atoms, the particles that make up all matter. Around the center of each atom orbit smaller particles called **electrons**. These electrons exist at specific energy levels, or states.

Atoms usually exist in the lowest possible energy level, or **ground state**. An electron in the ground state can be raised to a higher energy level, or **excited state**, by absorbing energy—for example, from a flash of light, an electrical current, or another electron. Electrons in an excited state fall back to a ground state by themselves, or spontaneously. When this happens, the electrons give off, or **emit**, radiation in the form of tiny particles of light called **photons**. This process—the spontaneous emission of radiation—produces the photons you see as ordinary light when you turn on a lightbulb.

Laser light occurs when a group of similar atoms exist in an excited state. The atoms' high-energy electrons continually emit photons. These photons then collide with other high-energy electrons and cause, or stimulate, them to emit more photons in a chainlike reaction. This process—the stimulated emission of radiation—greatly increases the number of photons and amplifies the light, or makes it more intense. The result is light amplification by stimulated emission of radiation: laser light.

Ordinary Light

Scientists think of light rays as swarms of photons that travel in waves, rather like the water waves you see in oceans or lakes. The distance between the **crest**, or top, of one wave and the crest of the next wave is called a **wavelength**. Light waves are extremely short. The wavelengths of even the longest light waves are only a few millionths of a centimeter.

Although light from the sun or an electric bulb is often called "white light," it is really a mixture of many colors of light, each having a different wavelength.

Ordinary light rays also travel in many different directions. Even when we aim the rays, as with a flashlight, they still do not travel in exactly the same direction. The rays spread out, and the beam weakens as it gets farther from the flashlight.

Ordinary light from a flashlight spreads out in many different colors.

A laser produces an intense beam of light in one color that does not spread out from its source.

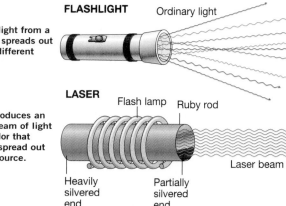

FLASHLIGHT Ordinary light

LASER Flash lamp Ruby rod

Laser beam

Heavily silvered end

Partially silvered end

A laser's energy can be focused on a spot, heating it to thousands of degrees. This makes lasers ideal for cutting metal parts, such as these saw blades.

Laser Light

A laser produces a very different type of light. Unlike ordinary light, laser light is only one color. Its rays all have exactly the same wavelength.

This makes it possible for all the waves to travel **in phase** (in step). That is, the crests of all the waves are lined up. When light waves are in phase, they strengthen one another. The waves all move together in the same direction, without spreading. The light is said to be **coherent**.

Because rays of laser light do not spread, they can be focused by a lens or curved mirror as an intense, powerful beam on a very small spot. They can also be sent long distances into space with little weakening.

▶ HOW LASERS WORK

Most lasers have three common components: a light-emitting medium, an energy source that will stimulate the medium to emit light, and a way of controlling the direction of the resulting laser beam. To understand these components, let us consider a common kind of laser called the ruby laser.

The light-emitting medium is a synthetic ruby, much like the gemstone but made in a laboratory. The ruby is a transparent crystal of aluminum oxide scattered with atoms of chromium, which give it a reddish color. The ruby is in the shape of a rod with two reflective ends, one heavily silvered and the other partially silvered. These ends act as mirrors that control the direction of the laser beam. The energy source is a tube-shaped lamp, wrapped around the ruby rod.

When the lamp flashes its bright white light, it provides a brief jolt of energy to the chromium atoms in the rod. This energy excites the atoms, which emit photons that collide with other excited atoms and stimulate the emission of more photons. As they bounce back and forth between the rod's reflective ends, the photons rapidly build in intensity and burst out of the rod's partially silvered end as a powerful pulse of coherent red laser light.

Other Kinds of Lasers

Lasers come in all sizes and shapes. Each type of laser is based on its light-emitting medium, which can be a solid, liquid, or gas.

In addition to ruby crystals, there are other solids that can act as a light-emitting medium. For example, **semiconductor lasers** (also called **diode lasers**) use the same kind of solid-state material found in the transistors of calculators and other electronic devices. A small electrical current is passed through the semiconductor, exciting carriers of positive and negative electrical charges. These charges combine and cancel out each other, emitting energy in the process. This energy appears as laser light. Semiconductors are not much bigger than the tip of a ballpoint pen. They have relatively low power output. But because of their tiny size, they are ideal for small devices such as laser pointers, laser printers, and compact disc players.

Gas lasers use a light-emitting medium based on a pure gas, such as carbon dioxide, or a mixture of gases, such as helium and neon. These lasers usually consist of a gas-filled tube with electrical connectors at each end. The connectors are attached to a power supply. When the power is turned on, electricity raises the electrons to excited levels, producing laser light. Different gases produce different colors of light. Most gas lasers give off a continuous beam of light, rather than the pulses of light produced by a ruby laser.

Liquid lasers are sometimes called dye lasers because their light-emitting medium is typically an organic dye in a liquid solution. Dye lasers are special because the excited states corresponding to different energy levels are so numerous. As a result, dyes can produce a range of laser-light colors, most of them visible. It is also possible to "tune" dye lasers to produce a particular color.

► HOW LASERS ARE USED

Once considered a scientific curiosity, the laser has proven to be a practical tool with hundreds of applications in industry, electronics, medicine, science, and other fields.

Industry and Commerce

A laser can aim an immensely powerful beam of light onto a very small spot, heating it to thousands of degrees. This makes the laser valuable for many industrial uses. Examples include cutting out saw blades; cutting many layers of fabrics into patterns for making clothing; drilling holes through industrial diamonds; welding small components such as battery cases for heart pacemakers; and treating engine parts with heat so that they become more resistant to wear.

The straightness of a laser beam makes it an excellent tool for surveying, construction, and quality control. Surveyors aim laser beams over long distances to help them plot the boundaries between properties of land. Construction crews use lasers to align long pipes precisely and guide machines during the drilling of tunnels and building of bridges. Factories use lasers in quality control, such as detecting surface defects in manufactured products.

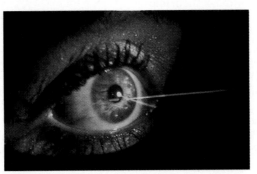

A surgeon carefully aims laser light into this patient's eye in order to diagnose a vision problem known as glaucoma.

Lasers are also widely used in commerce. Checkout clerks in supermarkets use laser scanners that "read" the price of each item by reflecting laser light off a pattern of lines, called a Universal Product Code (UPC), printed on the package. When the customer pays, it is often with a credit card that has a small laser-made **hologram**, or three-dimensional image, stamped on it. Holograms are very difficult to reproduce and are therefore used to deter counterfeiters.

Electronics

Many modern electronic devices have small semiconductor lasers inside them. For example, a compact disc (CD) player has a laser that bounces light off tiny pits (coated by a reflective metal film) in a CD's plastic surface. A device inside the CD player then detects the reflected light and converts it into electronic signals that can be heard as sound over speakers. Computers use similar disks called CD-ROM's to store large amounts of information. Digital video disc (DVD) machines also use lasers to play recorded movies.

Lasers can be used to transmit information very quickly. Most long-distance phone calls today are routed through a **fiber-optic cable**, which is made of glass fibers about as thick as a human hair. A fiber-optic cable carries information from light pulses sent from a laser. Fiber-optic cables are also used to send data shared by millions of computers on the global network known as the Internet. Large volumes of data can be transmitted at nearly the speed of light!

Medicine

A surgeon can aim a laser beam into the eye to diagnose and treat some vision problems without having to cut into the eye. For instance, lasers are used to alter the shape of the eye's cornea with microscopic incisions, reducing or eliminating nearsightedness.

However, laser light can also severely damage a person's eyes. Even low-power lasers can be hazardous if looked at directly for several seconds at close range. Because of this danger, most lasers carry warning labels indicating that they should be operated by only properly trained technicians or other adults who carefully follow safety procedures.

Lasers can remove tumors quickly and painlessly without damaging surrounding tissue. Lasers can also remove skin blemishes, such as port-wine stains, and even "permanent" tattoos. And lasers can remove tartar (a chalky material that can bring about infection) from teeth before gum disease occurs.

Science

Astronomers use laser instruments to measure the distances between Earth and the

LASERS • 46c

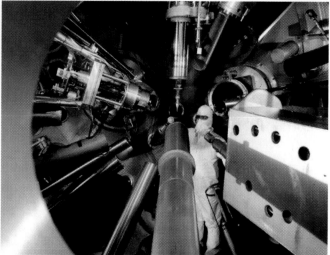

Left: A laser guide star, which helps astronomers focus telescopes, shoots out of an observatory. *Above:* A scientist inspects Nova, the world's most powerful laser, used in research on fusion energy.

moon, and the distances to orbiting satellites, with great accuracy. Astronomers also use **laser guide stars**—laser beams pointing toward the sky—to help them focus their telescopes better so they can see stars and planets in greater detail.

Geologists can predict earthquakes using lasers to detect very slight movements of Earth's crust. Chemists often use lasers to detect small amounts of impurities in samples of air and water.

Lasers are also being used in the quest for a powerful source of energy called **fusion**. Scientists in California are constructing the National Ignition Facility, which will contain a very powerful solid-state laser. They will use the facility to gain a better understanding of fusion, the process that generates the sun's energy. They also hope such studies will determine whether fusion can be harnessed as a long-term energy source on Earth.

▶ DEVELOPMENTS IN LASERS

The laser is descended from the **maser**, which stands for *m*icrowave *a*mplification by *s*timulated *e*mission of *r*adiation. Just as lasers amplify light, masers amplify microwaves. These are radio waves thousands of times longer than light waves. Masers were developed in the 1950's by scientists in the United States and the Soviet Union.

Microwaves from masers made it possible to design atomic clocks—time-keeping devices accurate to within one second in thousands of years. Astronomers also use masers to detect and amplify the weak radio signals generated by stars and galaxies.

In 1960, the first **optical laser** was invented. Theodore H. Maiman, a U.S. scientist, used a ruby rod to produce the optical laser's beam of visible light. More types of lasers—gas, liquid, and semiconductor—soon followed.

Still other types of lasers are being developed. For example, scientists expect that blue-light lasers will eventually replace red-light lasers commonly used in compact-disc devices. Blue-light lasers produce a shorter wavelength, making it possible to store two to four times more data on future disks.

Some day, lasers may even enable astronauts to voyage farther into space at speeds greater than ever before. Future spacecraft could use laser-generated fusion to propel them to Mars and other planets. Lasers may also help clean up **space debris**—material left over from old satellites and other objects sent into orbit around Earth. Laser pulses would knock the debris out of orbit, causing it to burn up in the atmosphere.

Lasers will no doubt continue to broaden our knowledge of light and matter, the fundamental building blocks of nature. It will be this knowledge that will help us further understand nature and explore our solar system, the stars, and beyond.

DON CORRELL
TOM SPAFFORD
Laser Programs
Lawrence Livermore National Laboratory

See also ATOMS; ELECTRONICS; LIGHT; RADIATION.

LATIN AMERICA

The term "Latin America" refers to Mexico and all countries and political units in Central and South America. The area includes 33 independent nations, along with French Guiana and some island possessions of the United States, Great Britain, France, and the Netherlands. Landforms, climate, and lifestyles in Latin America vary greatly. But common experience and historical developments unite its peoples in many ways.

Latin America is a region of extreme contrasts. It is characterized by the magnificent high Andes mountains and the massive Amazon River. There are lush rain forests in the Amazon Basin, while Chile's Atacama Desert is considered the driest area in the world.

Latin America is both rich and poor. Natural resources are many and varied, but they are unevenly distributed. The region is a major exporter of bauxite, iron ore, copper, and lead, for example. But it has very little coal, and only five or six nations are self-sufficient in petroleum. Much of the world's coffee, bananas, and sugarcane is produced there, but basic foodstuffs like wheat must be imported. Latin America contains the oldest universities in the Western Hemisphere, but many of its people today cannot read or write. Regional incomes are near the world average but are far below those of the more industrialized nations. Rapid population growth and increasing urbanization have created many demands that are difficult to meet.

▶ ORIGIN OF THE NAME

The name "Latin America" was first used in the early 1800's to differentiate American countries with populations of southern European (Latin) origin from those of northern European origin. For this reason the English-speaking nations in the area—and the overseas possessions of the United States, Great Britain, France, and the Netherlands—are sometimes not considered part of Latin America.

But there was another reason for the use of the term. The first republic in the world was the ancient Roman republic of the

From top to bottom: Couples on a street in Buenos Aires, Argentina, demonstrate the tango, a dance that developed there in the late 1800's. Most Latin Americans living on the islands of the Caribbean are of African ancestry. Native Indians make up more than half the population of Bolivia.

Above: Montevideo, the capital of Uruguay, is situated on the South Atlantic coast.
Below: People of strictly European ancestry are a minority in Latin American countries.

Latins. This Latin republic—its laws, its organization, even its architecture—served as an inspiration to the Latin Americans in their struggle for independence. To this day the legal systems of many of the Latin American republics are based on Roman law.

▶ PEOPLE

The people of Latin America are as varied as the landscape in which they live. The major groups are Indians, whites, blacks, mestizos (people of both Indian and white ancestry), and mulattoes (people of both black and white ancestry).

Indians—Latin America's first inhabitants—settled in Latin America thousands of years before the European explorer Christopher Columbus claimed the New World for Spain in 1492. The world's earliest known settlement, in Monte Verde, Chile, was established about 12,000 years ago. Great Indian civilizations—the Aztecs, Maya, Chibchas, and Incas—later developed on the plateaus and high mountain valleys in Mexico, Guatemala, Colombia, Ecuador, Peru, and Bolivia. In the West Indies and in the coastal plains and rain forests

of South America, the Indian population was smaller, more scattered, and less developed culturally.

Today Indian populations differ from place to place. Few Indians have lived in Uruguay since the European conquest. Fewer than 1 percent of the people of Costa Rica and Argentina are Indian. But in Guatemala, Peru, Bolivia, and Ecuador, nearly 50 percent of the people are Indian. A strong presence is also evident in Mexico.

Soon after Columbus discovered the Americas while searching for a sea route to Asia, the Spanish and Portuguese sent soldiers, known as conquistadores, to conquer the native peoples and establish colonies. With their superior weapons and firepower, the Europeans soon established dominance throughout the region.

Until the 1800's, white people of European ancestry who were born in Latin America called themselves *criollos*, meaning "well-born." The *criollos* felt more attached to the countries from which their ancestors came than they did to their own place of birth. Their homes, dress, food, and customs were modeled after those of their mother countries, and many sent their children to school in Europe. But in the 1800's, the Latin American republics gained their independence from Spain and Portugal, and the *criollos* assumed leadership. At that time, most *criollos* established a new loyalty to their American homeland. Today, the term *criollo* has little significance, except perhaps in Ecuador and Colombia, where a tradition of a colonial aristocracy has been maintained.

In the 1900's, foreigners from other lands immigrated to Latin America, particularly to Argentina, Costa Rica, Chile, and Uruguay. Italians and Germans arrived at the turn of the century, and many Chinese and Japanese after 1945, at the end of World War II.

Mestizos make up the largest segment of the populations of Mexico; the Central American republics of El Salvador, Honduras, Nicaragua, and Panama; and the South American republics of Colombia, Venezuela, Chile, and Paraguay. They also make up the largest element in Latin America's growing middle-income group. Many mestizos are lawyers, political leaders, business people, teachers, doctors, scientists, and artists.

Africans were brought to Latin America as early as the 1500's and as late as the mid-1800's. They worked as slaves on plantations in the West Indies of the Caribbean, in the coastal lowlands of Central America, in Brazil, and on the northeastern coast of South America. Some became legally free. But like the Indians, they were subject to harsh social and economic inequalities. Haitians are mainly of African ancestry. Blacks and mulattoes also make up significant portions of the populations of Cuba, Barbados, Puerto Rico, the Dominican Republic, Panama, Jamaica, Trinidad and Tobago, Guyana, Suriname, French Guiana, and Brazil.

Language

Latin America's languages are as varied as its ethnic groups. Spanish and Portuguese are the major languages, but many others are also spoken.

Spanish and Portuguese. Nearly two-thirds of the people of Latin America speak Spanish, and about one-third speak Portuguese. The Spanish once ruled more than half of the now-independent countries of Latin America, while Portugal held power in Brazil, the single largest country. Language is therefore one of the cultural elements many Latin Americans have in common. A Puerto Rican poet or an Argentinian novelist can be read by a Panamanian, a Honduran, or a Mexican.

An Argentinian or a Peruvian can understand the Spanish of a Spaniard. A Brazilian can understand a native Portuguese. But Spanish and Portuguese as spoken in Latin America differ somewhat in speech pattern, rhythm, and accent from the languages spoken in Spain and Portugal. These differences are much like those among English-speaking people from the United States and Great Britain or Australia.

Other Languages. Millions of people of Indian ancestry speak their own traditional languages as well as their country's official language. Several countries with large Indian populations take pride in remembering and maintaining their Indian heritage. The most important example of this is in Paraguay, which is effectively bilingual, using both Guaraní and Spanish. Peru is also bilingual: Quechua as well as Spanish is taught in the schools. The most widely spoken Indian languages are Nahuatl, Mixtec, Tarascan, and Zapotec (in Mexico); Aymará (in Bolivia and Peru); Guaraní (in Paraguay); Maya (in Mexico and Guatemala); and Quechua (in Peru and Ecuador).

Many of the Indians in Mexico, Guatemala, Bolivia, Peru, and Ecuador do not read or

INDEPENDENT COUNTRIES OF LATIN AMERICA

Antigua and Barbuda*	Guyana*
Argentina	Haiti
Bahamas*	Honduras
Barbados*	Jamaica*
Belize*	Mexico
Bolivia	Nicaragua
Brazil	Panama
Chile	Paraguay
Colombia	Peru
Costa Rica	Saint Kitts–Nevis*
Cuba	Saint Lucia*
Dominica*	Saint Vincent and the
Dominican Republic	Grenadines*
Ecuador	Suriname*
El Salvador	Trinidad and Tobago*
Grenada*	Uruguay
Guatemala	Venezuela

*Countries sometimes included in Latin America.

write Spanish, but most speak and understand it. However, because a common written and spoken language is necessary to unify a modern nation, great efforts are being made in the schools to teach people how to communicate in their nation's official language.

English is the most important of Latin America's other languages. It is the official language of Belize and Guyana, as well as of a number of the Caribbean islands, such as Trinidad and Tobago, Jamaica, Dominica, Grenada, and Barbados. It is also a major second language throughout Latin America.

French is the official language of Haiti, French Guiana, and the Caribbean islands of Martinique and Guadeloupe. The French spoken in Haiti, known as Creole, differs considerably from the language spoken in France. Blacks have added words and even elements of grammar of their own. Dutch is the official language of Suriname and is spoken on such Caribbean islands as Aruba and Curaçao.

Many other ethnic groups can be found in Latin America, chiefly in urban centers. Many of them—such as the Chinese, Japanese, Germans, Italians, and Arabs—still speak their ancestral language while at home.

Language and Environment. Many words for foods, everyday things, and customs in Latin America come from Indian or African languages. "Chocolate," for example, comes from the ancient Aztec word *chocolatl.*

The Spanish, Portuguese, and French languages spoken in Latin America contain many new words that originated in America. Words that mean the same thing may differ from country to country. A Chilean says *huaso* for "cowboy," but an Argentinian says *gaucho*; a Costa Rican, *sabanero*; a Colombian, *llanero*; and a Brazilian, both *gaucho* and *vaquero*. A Bolivian and a Peruvian say *oriente* ("east") when speaking of the frontier or last-settled part of a country, but a Cuban speaks of *la manigua* ("the bush"). A public bus is called a *guagua* in many parts of the Spanish Caribbean. But *camión* and *autobus* are common elsewhere in Latin America. A Venezuelan says *cambur* when speaking of a banana, but a Mexican says *plátano*.

Religion

Many of the world's religions are practiced in Latin America. But most Latin Americans are Roman Catholic. The Spanish and Portuguese conquistadores, who were devout Roman Catholics, converted many Indians to their faith. Today in countries with large Indian populations, such as Mexico, Guatemala, Bolivia, and Peru, religious practices reflect a heavy mingling of Indian and Catholic traditions. Local saints' days and celebrations of miracles are included in the calendar of regular church observances. Religious and civic holidays often contain combined elements of ancient Indian and Catholic religions.

Africans brought their religious traditions to Latin America and combined them with Christian beliefs and practices. Many blacks and mulattoes in rural Cuba, the Dominican Republic, Haiti, and Brazil practice Catholicism, which has been modified greatly by the belief systems of African-based religions. These include *candomblé* (in Brazil), Santería (in Cuba and Puerto Rico), and voodoo (in Haiti).

Curaçao, a possession of the Netherlands, has the oldest Jewish synagogue in the New World. Buenos Aires, Mexico City, and Rio de Janeiro also have significant Jewish com-

Religious observances during the Holy Week before Easter include commemorating the crucifixion of Jesus Christ. Most Latin Americans are Roman Catholic.

Above: A Peruvian farmer plows a field in a valley in the Andean Highlands. *Right:* Guatemalans and other Latin Americans are renowned for their handmade pottery.

munities. There are Hindus and Muslims in Trinidad and in Guyana. Many people in Argentina and Brazil practice Shinto and Buddhism, the major religions of Japan and China. Protestant minorities exist in every country, and in some, such as Guatemala, they are fast becoming the majority.

Way of Life

Traditionally, Latin Americans are early risers. Around seven o'clock, they have a breakfast of coffee and milk, hot chocolate with buns, or, in Central America and Mexico, tortillas and beans. If they can afford it, they have eggs and bacon. They work until noon or one o'clock, when they go home to eat the big meal of the day. After the meal, many people take a siesta, or afternoon nap. It is still common for many shops and businesses, as well as farms, to stop work for two or three hours in the middle of the day. Intense heat and high altitudes make this habit necessary and desirable. This results in a work day that begins earlier and ends later than it does in the United States.

In many regions, however, the traditional siesta is disappearing. Many urban businesses are changing to lunch breaks of an hour or less. As working hours change, so does the character of the midday meal. At six or seven

o'clock, the Latin American eats a snack called a *merienda.* Dinner is eaten quite late in Latin America—nine o'clock or even later.

A large part of Latin America remains rural and agricultural. Many Latin Americans live in villages that are shut in by great mountains or rivers. These people are likely to be Indians whose way of life is strongly influenced by that of their ancestors. But the huge migration of large numbers of people—particularly young people—from rural to urban areas is an important recent trend.

As cities have grown larger, the differences between rural and urban ways of life have begun to disappear. The construction of highways and roads connecting cities and the countryside has increased travel and interaction. Better communication systems also help to bridge distances. Transistor radios, cell phones, and satellite television are now found even in the most rural areas and serve better than the written word to spread information and ideas.

Rural Life. In the rural areas, the materials and methods of building a home have changed little over the centuries. The rural home normally contains one or two rooms and is made of available materials—logs, boards, or adobe.

Many things used in Latin American homes go back to pre-Columbian days (the era before Columbus discovered the New World). The *petate*, a straw mat common in Latin America, is a bed which the Latin American peasant uses throughout his or her life. (The well-to-do Latin American uses a handwoven *petate* as a floor or wall decoration.) Every rural home has a hearth, or a *brasero* or *fogón*. This is an iron stand or a raised stone platform on which charcoal or wood is burned for cooking. Rural homes in Mexico and parts of Central America still use a three-legged stone mortar (*metate*) to grind corn. Smaller mortars are used for mashing vegetables and spices.

City Life. Latin America has more than 30 cities with populations exceeding 1 million. Mexico City, São Paulo, Rio de Janeiro, Santiago, Lima, Buenos Aires, Caracas, and Bogotá are the largest.

New World cities are laid out typically in simple, straight lines radiating from a central square, called a plaza. Surrounding the plaza are buildings that give form and authority to the city. On one side is the church. On another are the government buildings. Homes of the wealthy and important businesses may occupy the rest of the plaza. Most plazas have covered arcades for the convenience of shoppers. The main plaza usually contains a covered bandstand where music is played several times a week. Monasteries, convent schools,

hospitals, and private homes are built on the streets leading away from the square.

The average city home is chiefly Spanish in origin. Thick stone or adobe walls insulate from the heat or cold. A central patio is a common feature, and the front door usually opens directly to the street. The patio is the center of the home. There the children play, household tasks are performed, and family and friends sit and talk. Plants and birdcages often decorate the patio. The kitchen, bedrooms, and living room open onto the central patio to receive the maximum amount of air and sunshine. The Latin American home, no matter how modest, combines the outdoors and the indoors.

Homes of the wealthy are more elaborate and have all the newest conveniences of modern living. A typical home has a doorway that leads into an open hall. This hall, in turn, leads onto the patio, which is bounded on all sides by columns and arches. Sometimes there is a second patio, used as an orchard and for the servants' quarters. Ceilings in bedrooms are high. Walls are usually painted white, but doorways and floors are often decorated with colored tiles. Balconies and gates are made of wrought iron. The modern Latin American home may use new materials—glass, marble, brick, concrete, and steel. But

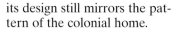

its design still mirrors the pattern of the colonial home.

People with low incomes sometimes live near the city center in a type of apartment house called a *vecindad* (tenement). These houses are often two stories high, with a long patio. Families live around the patio. Sometimes four or five people occupy one room. Clotheslines and washing and bathing facilities, all found on the patio, are used in common by all residents.

The poorest people live in squatter settlements found on the outskirts of the cities. Here the people live in shanties and the streets are not paved. There are no sewers, and there is little running water. The slums have various Spanish names, including *barriadas*, *miserias*, and *callampas*. In Portuguese they are called *favelas*. These sections contrast with the beauty and wealth of colonial houses, modern mansions, and hotels. Most countries have attempted some forms of urban slum clearance. But recent community efforts to improve shantytowns have been recognized. Social organization, neighborhood pride, and self-help projects can often

Above left: Mexico City is the second largest city in Latin America, after Saõ Paulo, Brazil. **Above:** Buenos Aires, the capital and largest city of Argentina, is known for its broad tree-lined boulevards. **Left:** University students discuss their studies in Caracas, Venezuela.

transform shantytowns into more livable communities.

Food and Drink. The food of the average Latin American is simple, robust, and appetizing. Often, but not always, it is highly spiced with hot peppers. Hot sauce is usually found on the table. The staple foods are rice, beans, eggs, beef, pork, lamb, fish, and squash and other vegetables. Corn (maize), avocados, potatoes, cassava (a starchy root), tomatoes, cocoa, and many varieties of nuts and fruits are just some of the foods native to Latin America. The plantain, a large cooking banana, is as widely eaten in the Caribbean as corn is in Mexico and Central America or as potatoes are in South America. Fruit is abundant. Some kinds are known only in tropical Latin America. Mangoes, breadfruit, and papayas are among the many fruits eaten in tropical regions.

Each country has developed its own national dishes. Argentina is noted for fine steaks. Chile is known for its *empanadas*, or flour dumplings filled with fish or meat, olives, and spices. In Venezuela, corn dumplings stuffed with meat and fish are called *hallacas*. *Mole*, a meat dish in a spicy sauce made with chiles and often chocolate, is popular in Mexico. *Cebiche* is a fine Peruvian fish platter, and the *llapingachos* of Ecuador are potatoes stuffed with cream cheese and eggs. Brazil's national dish is *feijoada*, black beans cooked with various meats and served with rice and a mixture of cassava, oranges, and other fruit. Soups and desserts are equally varied. The type of cooking varies, depending on local resources. The tequila of Mexico (a strong drink distilled from a variety of the century plant), the *aguardiente* of Colombia and Ecuador, the *tiste* of Bolivia, and the wines of Chile are among the national drinks. Maté, a tea-like beverage, is also popular throughout Latin America.

Dress. Modern dress is common throughout Latin America. People in towns and cities dress the same way as city people in Europe or the United States. The business world is particularly formal. But in a great many regions of Latin America, garments of Indian style and design are still worn. Traditional folk dress is ornamented and brightly colored but dignified and tasteful. The *huipil*, worn by the Indian women of Mexico and Guatemala, is made of two long pieces of cloth sewn together, with an opening for the head. This garment is worn over the shoulders like a cape. Short trousers and embroidered shirts tied at the waist are worn by the Indians in southern Mexico and Guatemala.

Every country has its distinctive regional dress. The man's straw hat, varied in size and shape, is seen everywhere in tropical Latin America. Woolen caps for the men and derby hats for the women are commonly worn by the Indians in the cold, windswept Andes of Bolivia and Peru. Jewelry varies from modest strings of colored beads, shells, and coral to elaborate silver and gold earrings and bracelets.

Sports. Soccer is the national sport of most countries. But basketball, baseball, boxing, rugby, and tennis have become increasingly popular. Bullfights are enjoyed in Mexico, Central America, and most of Andean South America.

Holidays. Each country has its own holidays to celebrate—independence day, the birth or death of a national hero, or the anniversary of an event in the nation's history. But most of Latin America's holidays are religious in nature. Every village, town, and city has its patron saint. Religious pilgrimages, folk dances, songs, and fireworks are familiar ways of celebration. New Year's Day, Carnival, Easter Sunday, All Souls' Day, and Christmas are some of the major holidays observed by most Latin Americans.

Honduran schoolboys, dressed in uniform, enjoy a field trip. Most Latin Americans, especially in urban areas, wear modern-style clothing.

Carnival, or Mardi Gras, is a celebration introduced by the Spanish and Portuguese. People wearing masks and elaborate costumes parade through the streets. Festive parties are held in most homes. Carnival is a burst of joy and freedom before Lent, a 40-day period of self-denial practiced by most Christians. The carnivals of Trinidad and Tobago, Haiti, and Brazil in particular are internationally famous.

Easter Sunday is a high point in religious celebration. The day may begin with the burning of a papier-mâché Judas in the streets. It may close with an evening stroll in the plaza as a band plays. Young men break colored eggshells filled with confetti or perfume and shower the contents on young women as they stroll in opposite directions around the square.

All Souls' Day is observed by visits to cemeteries. People bring flowers, foods, and pictures of the dead. In some places there are all-night vigils and prayers. Respect for the dead makes this one of Latin America's most solemn days.

Christmas is observed, with slight variations, throughout Latin America. In Brazil, dancing and carols often precede midnight mass. In Costa Rican homes, an entire room is set aside for a nativity scene. In Chile, thousands of people gather at the little town of

Iglesia San Francisco, located in Quito, Ecuador, was one of the first churches built by the Spanish in Latin America.

Andacollo to pay homage to the Virgin Mary. Many Colombians put up Christmas trees.

Nowhere does Christmastime last longer or have more magic than in Mexico. There the season, called *La Posada*, begins on December 16. Each night, families and their guests act out Mary and Joseph's search for lodging. There are prayers and songs. Candies, fruits, other food, and punch are available for all.

The children enjoy breaking a piñata each evening. The piñata is a clay pot covered with papier-mâché and colored tissue paper and filled with candies, fruits, and coins. It may take one of many shapes, such as a head of lettuce, a donkey, a fish, a ship, or a stork.

When it is broken, children scramble for the contents. It is the cheerful end to each evening from December 16 through December 24 (Christmas Eve), when the family attends midnight Mass.

Santa Claus, a relatively recent figure in Latin American celebrations, has been received enthusiastically. Gifts may also be received on January 6, celebrating the visit of the three Magi (kings) to the infant Jesus. Children may leave a bundle of hay or a pot of water for the Magi's camels.

Customs and Traditions. Throughout Latin America, the extended family is held dear. Loyalty and responsibility to one's family is extremely important. Parents teach their children obedience and respect for authority. Piety, gallantry, and courtesy are also carefully cultivated in the Latin American child. These qualities are also emphasized in courtship. Customs are rapidly changing. But prior to marriage, couples are typically chaperoned.

In Latin America, a girl does not lose her own family name when she marries. If Cecilia López marries Juan Díaz, she becomes Cecilia López de (of) Díaz. Her family name also lives on in her children. Her son Pablo, for example, would be known as Pablo Díaz López; her daughter Catalina, as Catalina Díaz López. All legal documents—baptismal records, school certificates, passports—bear in sequence the given name, father's family name, and mother's family name.

Catholic children—rich or poor, urban or rural—are baptized and named for the saint on whose day they were born. Frequently the names of other close members of the family are added, so that a child sometimes has five or six names.

In cities and in the country, the choice of a godfather and godmother (*compadres*) is of very great importance. Nothing brings two Catholic Latin Americans closer together than for one to be the godparent of the other's child. The child's religious upbringing,

Archaeologists in Monte Verde, Chile, study the remains of the oldest inhabited site yet discovered in Latin America.

welfare, education, and even support are sometimes entrusted to the godparents. Baptism takes place in the church and is followed by a party. In the country, this party includes a feast, dances, and songs. In the city it is customary to dance to popular music and eat sandwiches and cakes.

Wedding ceremonies usually take place in church. But the preparations and the celebrations that follow a wedding vary from country to country, from religion to religion, and from region to region. A civil ceremony is considered as binding as a religious one. But most Catholic couples do not feel properly married without a church ceremony.

The status of women is improving throughout Latin America. Professional opportunities vary from country to country and group to group. But more women have careers in government, science, diplomacy, and business than ever before.

▶ CULTURAL HERITAGE

In most Latin American countries, the Indians' contributions are old and many-sided. For this reason, some people prefer to call the

Mexican artist Frida Kahlo (shown in a self-portrait, *near right*) and the Chilean poet Pablo Neruda (*far right*) were among the most notable Latin American cultural figures of the 1900's.

region Indo-America. But this term is not entirely accurate. Costa Rica, Argentina, and Uruguay are largely European in origin. In most of the Caribbean, Brazil, Suriname, Guyana, and French Guiana, the African rather than the Indian has been the dominant influence on life and culture.

Latin Americans are fine artisans and still make many things by hand. Although mass-produced goods are now very common, unique handcrafted items can still be found. Latin American designs are original and colors are bold, so that the simplest dish has individual beauty. The pottery and ceramics of Latin America are unique and varied. Each region uses its own designs.

For more information on Latin American culture, see the articles LATIN AMERICA, ART AND ARCHITECTURE OF, LATIN AMERICA, LITERATURE OF, and LATIN AMERICA, MUSIC OF following this article.

▶ HISTORY AND GOVERNMENT

An ever-changing mix of "protected" democracies (those that are controlled by the military) and dictatorships characterizes the political climate of Latin America. Many of the reasons for this constant political turmoil may be understood by examining the history of the region.

Colonial Times

The colonial history of Latin America is very different from the much shorter colonial periods of the United States and Canada. Three centuries of Spanish and Portuguese rule gave Latin Americans little experience in self-government.

In the Spanish and Portuguese colonies, the king was supreme. The Spanish king ruled through the Council of the Indies and through the viceroys (governors who represented the king in the colonies). The Portuguese king governed through the Transmarine Council. The members of both councils were appointed by their king and lived in Spain and Portugal. The councils issued laws, supervised the church, and regulated trade and trade routes.

This system of government meant that people born in the New World had little op-

portunity to govern themselves. A few *criollos* were appointed to the *cabildos* or *senados da camara* (town councils), as *regidores* (town councillors). The mestizos had even fewer social and political rights. They were even less prepared for self-government. The Indians who worked for the landowners and mine owners were treated like slaves. The blacks, who worked on the plantations, actually were slaves. Thus, only the *criollos* gained some experience in government.

In the 1800's, most Latin American countries revolted and became independent republics. It was not surprising that the wars for independence were led by *criollos*, like Simón Bolívar, José de San Martín, Miguel Hidalgo y Costilla, and Francisco de Miranda, or by exceptional mestizos, like José María Morelos y Pavón. Only Brazil made a peaceful transition from colony to independent monarchy and, later, from monarchy to republic.

The *criollo* group included the higher clergy, the wealthy landowners and mine owners, and the merchants. These leaders were overwhelmingly conservative and sought to maintain the social, economic, and political systems of the colonial period, but without the Spanish rulers. They firmly believed that the people were not ready for self-government due to lack of education, perceived racial inferiority, and great geographic barriers of mountains, jungles, and deserts.

Independence was followed by quarrels between liberals and conservatives. These two groups were divided on economic policy and on the question of the relationship between the government and the Roman Catholic Church. They also disagreed about whether the provinces or the federal government should exercise the greater power. The liberals opposed the Church's ownership of land and its control of education and marriage, but the conservatives supported the Church. The liberals opposed government control of the economy, but the conservatives (who usually controlled the government) favored governmental control of financial investments and tariffs. Finally, liberals wanted less centralization of government, while conservatives favored more centralization.

Coups d'état and dictatorships were common throughout the 1800's. Strong leaders,

While on an expedition to India in 1500, Portuguese explorer Pedro Cabral was swept off course across the Atlantic. He landed in Brazil and claimed an enormous territory for Portugal.

known as *caudillos*, ruled in many countries. To this day many Latin Americans tend to admire the strong individual who takes control of a nation. Most changes in government, however, have simply replaced the leaders at the top. They have usually had little effect on the common people.

Politics and Government Today

Unstable governments in modern times have often swung back and forth between civilian and military rule. Authoritarian governments, in which people have no control over the actions of their leaders, have been more common under the military. In some countries, military rulers brought about reforms and pushed for more social equality. By contrast, democratically elected presidents have sometimes behaved like dictators.

Today most nations in Latin America are multiparty democracies in which power changes hands in an orderly fashion. In some countries, however, although elections may be held and a civilian president installed, the real power remains with the leaders of the military. Reducing military control remains one of Latin America's greatest challenges.

▶ A WORLD OF CHANGE

Latin America is a region undergoing tremendous changes, challenges, and crises. As civilians struggle to establish genuine democracies, ongoing problems such as racial division and discrimination must be recognized and confronted. Another concern is the rapid population growth that is profoundly widening the gap between rich and poor. Most of the land and wealth is still controlled by an elite few. There are few jobs for those flocking to the cities in search of a better life. Too many people are still unable to read and write, and even more lack adequate housing and health care.

By 2002 there was growing dissatisfaction with the democratic and free-market economic reforms that had been adopted so enthusiastically in the 1990's. The new democratic governments were often weak and corrupt, and opening up the economy to private investment had not made life better for most of the poor. With 44 percent of Latin Americans still living in poverty, job layoffs and cutbacks in government programs for the poor led to widespread protests.

Eva Perón, popularly known as Evita, was the second wife of former Argentine president and dictator Juan Perón. Her concern for social welfare made her an idol of the poor and laboring classes.

International Relations

Latin Americans are taking an increasingly active role in their own and world affairs. Belize and several island nations in the Caribbean became independent in the late 1970's and early 1980's. The United States transferred control of the Panama Canal to Panama on December 31, 1999.

All independent Latin American countries are members of the United Nations, and the Organization of American States (OAS) provides a forum for nations in the region to discuss their common concerns. The Central American Common Market has been revived; the Common Market of the South (Mercosur) was founded in 1989; and the Andean Common Market was established in 1992. All trade barriers between Mexico, Colombia, and Venezuela ended in 1994. These and other developments have resulted in a dramatic increase in interregional trade that Latin Americans hope will bring economic growth and social progress.

DAVID M. JONES
University of South Carolina
Reviewed by THOMAS M. DAVIES, JR.
Director, Center for Latin American Studies
San Diego State University

See also CARIBBEAN SEA AND ISLANDS; CENTRAL AMERICA; NORTH AMERICA; ORGANIZATION OF AMERICAN STATES (OAS); SOUTH AMERICA; and articles on individual Latin American countries.

The ruins of Machu Picchu, an ancient Inca city, still stand in Peru. The cultures of native peoples are a key element of Latin American art and architecture.

LATIN AMERICA, ART AND ARCHITECTURE OF

The art of Latin America is remarkably varied due to the many different kinds of populations and traditions found in its main regions: Mexico and Central America, the Caribbean, and South America. In fact, Latin America consists of more than thirty countries, each of which has its own historical and cultural experiences.

Although this diversity makes Latin American art difficult to define, one common trait that can be identified is the presence of three distinct cultural heritages: Indian, European, and African. Before colonization, Mexico, Central America, and the Andean region of South America contained large numbers of native Indian peoples whose sophisticated cultures were later blended with the traditions brought by the Europeans. On the other hand, in the Caribbean and eastern South America, where native populations were small or destroyed by the invaders and colonizers, European traditions were imposed with little resistance. The culture of these two areas was also greatly affected by Africans brought there as slaves by the Europeans.

This blending of cultures is an important characteristic of Latin American art. To the initial mix of Indian, African, and European traditions, other elements were added during the 1800's and 1900's. European immigrants and Latin American artists studying abroad brought in newer international artistic trends. These were combined with the arts of the various nations and transformed at the local level into something new and original. Difficult economic and political conditions have often limited the work of Latin American artists; nevertheless, they have continuously made significant contributions to world art.

▶COLONIAL ART AND ARCHITECTURE

The occupation of present-day Latin America by the Spanish and Portuguese began at the end of the 1400's. After the Spanish subdued the native peoples, they divided the conquered lands into four colonies, or viceroyalties: New Spain (present-day Mexico and Central America) and the viceroyalties of New Granada, Peru, and Río de la Plata (Spanish territories south of Panama). At the same time, the Portuguese founded the viceroyalty of Brazil. All the Spanish and Portuguese colonies became independent during the 1800's.

In order to control the native populations and convert them to Christianity, the Spanish destroyed many of the Indians' cultural landmarks. Churches were built on the ruins of native temples, taking advantage of the spiritual importance of these sites for the Indians. This led to associations between Christian saints and native gods; churches were often decorated with figures that combine pagan and Christian characteristics.

The Plateresque Style. The forced conversions of large numbers of native peoples led to a need for bigger churches. A solution was found in a Latin American version of the Spanish Renaissance style called plateresque. This style has elegant exterior decoration that looks like the work of silversmiths (*plateros*).

Plateresque forms were combined with Gothic vaults—high arched ceilings suitable for large buildings—and open chapels facing on spacious courtyards, from which large congregations could hear mass.

One of the best examples of this style is the Church of San Augustín in Acolman, Mexico, built about 1560. The inside walls are decorated with a series of magnificent frescoes (paintings done on wet plaster) of religious subjects. The themes and styles of the frescoes followed European models.

Baroque Architecture. During the 1600's and 1700's, the baroque, a new style brought from Europe, was successfully adopted throughout Latin America. The baroque style, with its lavish decoration and dramatic effects, inspired new ways of expressing the blend of the native and European heritages.

Latin American builders modified the baroque style to suit the environment of the New World: Areas plagued by earthquakes needed thicker walls, and tropical regions required wood ceilings to provide better ventilation. Other regional traits were painted plaster and tile work, as well as lavishly decorated facades (fronts) and interiors. In coastal areas, European baroque models were followed more closely, while Indian and local influences grew stronger in the more isolated inland cities. Similarly, cathedrals and parish churches tended to be more plain, while churches built by religious orders reflected in their splendor the monks' efforts to capture the imagination of the native peoples.

In New Spain, the somber European style of the Cathedral of Mexico City was abandoned in smaller urban centers in favor of more expressive styles. For example, the interior of the magnificent Rosary Chapel in the Monastery Church of Santo Domingo in Puebla, Mexico, is covered with brightly painted plasterwork. In New Granada, where native influence was weaker, baroque building styles were more closely linked with those of Europe. The Church of the Jesuits in Quito, Ecuador, was built following Italian models for the plan and facade. But the interior shows a strong Arabic influence in the geometric patterns of its stucco decoration. This decoration is also an example of the use of gold ornamentation on red background, characteristic of Quito artists.

Baroque architecture of the viceroyalty of Peru had special modifications designed to withstand earthquakes, such as the cane-and-wood roofing known as *quincha* and the use of thick old Inca walls for the foundations of buildings. In the Church of the Jesuits in Cuzco, the facade is protected from tremors by two flanking bell towers, whose massiveness is balanced by elegant decoration.

Above: Santo Domingo Cathedral (1512–41), on the island of Hispaniola, was the first cathedral built in the New World. *Left:* The Church of the Jesuits (1651–68) in Cuzco, Peru, features two massive bell towers.

Far left: The Prophet Daniel is one of the statues of the twelve prophets made (1800–1805) by the Brazilian sculptor and architect O Aleijadinho, whose powerfully expressive works mark the peak of baroque sculpture in Brazil.

Near left: A crucifixion scene by Capiscara in the Jesuit Church in Quito, Ecuador, features painted figures clothed in rich costumes. The dazzling gold decoration is typical of the baroque style.

Opposite page: Prilidiano Pueyrredón, a Latin American painter of the 1800's, depicted scenes on the pampas (plains) of his native Argentina in such works as *A Stop in the Country.*

Unlike Peru, Brazil is not threatened by earthquakes. Baroque architects there did not have to design quake-proof buildings and thus were free to experiment with more inventive forms. An interesting regional style developed in Minas Gerais, a wealthy gold-mining area. Several churches were built in Ouro Preto, a city in the region. One, the church of Nossa Senhora do Rosário (1785), shows the typical tendency of that region toward curving forms. In Bahia, the capital of the viceroyalty of Brazil, facades were patterned after Portuguese models, but interiors, such as that of Bahia's cathedral, exploded in dazzling displays of gold decoration.

Baroque Painting and Sculpture. With the exception of the School of Cuzco in Peru, which developed a more unique style, colonial painters of the baroque era closely followed European models. Portraits were popular among wealthy members of the colonial nobility, who posed for formal likenesses dressed in their best finery. Important painters included Cristóbal de Villalpando of Mexico, Miguel de Santiago of Ecuador, and Melchor Pérez de Holguín of Peru.

Sculptors, on the other hand, worked in more independent styles. Most of them carved images in wood and either gilded them (coated them with a layer of gold) or covered them with plaster, which was later painted. Often, the figures were designed to be dressed in rich cloth costumes. Among the most important baroque sculptors were Jerónimo Balbás, who created many monumental altarpieces in Mexico; Alonso de la Paz, a Guatemalan who made high-quality painted sculptures; and Manuel Chili (called Capiscara) of the School of Quito, who based his sculptural groups on Spanish and Italian models. Sculptors in inland regions, rather than imitating European works, emphasized flattened forms. A notable example is the Virgin of Guadalupe in the Cathedral of Sucre, Bolivia.

An outstanding colonial sculptor was Brazil's Antonio Francisco Lisboa, known as O Aleijadinho ("The Little Cripple"). His painted-wood figures (1797–99) in the church of Bom Jesus, Congonhas do Campo, and his dramatic stone statues of the twelve prophets (1800–1805) outside the same church mark the peak of Brazilian baroque sculpture.

1800'S

During the first half of the 1800's, most Spanish-American colonies gained independence and formed into separate republics. Brazil became independent from Portugal in 1822, but it was ruled by the Portuguese royal family until the late 1800's. With indepen-

In addition to native artists, many European and North American artists traveled through Latin America painting scenes of everyday life. Styles and techniques were learned from them, as well as from foreign artists and architects hired to teach at newly founded academies and schools of fine arts. Soon, local

dence came a rejection of Spanish and Portuguese traditions in favor of French cultural models.

Architecture. The most important trend in architecture of the early 1800's was **neoclassicism.** This style, which originated in France, used columned facades and other forms inspired by the classical architecture of ancient Greece and Rome. In Brazil, the French architect Grandjean de Montigny designed the Imperial Academy of Fine Arts and other official buildings in the neoclassic style.

Painting. The 1800's produced few sculptors in Latin America. Painting was the most important of the arts. Many young republics defined their national identities through images of heroes and battles, landscapes, and portraits, painted in the styles of French artists. The Mexican landscape painter José Maria Velasco specialized in views of the Valley of Mexico, while the Venezuelan Arturo Michelena portrayed the national heroes of his country's war of independence. Juan Manuel Blanes of Uruguay and Prilidiano Pueyrredón of Argentina worked on portraits of important people as well as of gauchos (cowboys).

artists began to travel to European cities for training. By the turn of the century, there had emerged in Latin America a wealthy cultural elite, who showed a strong preference for French styles in art and architecture.

1900'S

The first two decades of the 1900's saw the rise of three important modern art movements in Latin America: muralism, modernism, and martinfierrism. The **muralists**, centered in Mexico, included Diego Rivera, David Alfaro Siqueiros, and José Clemente Orozco. Brazil's **modernists** included Anita Malfatti, Lasar Segal, and Tarsila do Amaral. The **martinfierrists**, based in Argentina, took their name from the famous Argentine epic poem *Martín Fierro*. They included Norah Borges, Emilio Pettoruti, and Xul Solar. All these artists, except Orozco, had been active in various European modern art movements. When they returned to their native countries, they rejected the styles of the late 1800's, still popular in Latin America, in favor of modern trends.

Artists like Rivera and Amaral turned to the native and popular cultures of their own countries as a source of artistic inspiration. Pettoruti and Xul Solar used the modern styles of cubism and futurism to express the urban experience of the rapidly growing Latin American cities.

The Mexican muralists painted large-scale frescoes that commented on contemporary events. Their realistic style was well suited to their purpose of conveying the ideals of the Mexican Revolution. Muralism had a major impact in both North and South America. During the 1930's, it inspired the work of socially active artists such as Candido Portinari in Brazil and Antonio Berni in Argentina. The muralists' dignified representations of native peoples also influenced many artists in the Andean region.

Surrealism. During the 1930's and 1940's, the modern art movement known as surrealism became popular in many Latin American countries. Surrealist artists tried to portray the world of dreams and the unconscious by painting images from their imagination. The Chilean painter Roberto Matta developed a highly personal version of surrealism, and his work had a significant influence on the art of the United States. In Mexico, artists such as Rufino Tamayo, Leonora Carrington, Juan O'Gorman, and Frida Kahlo favored themes that ranged from the dreamlike to the personal and autobiographical. Another surrealist, Wilfredo Lam, successfully combined European styles with cultural elements from his Afro-Cuban background.

Above: The murals of Diego Rivera comment on Mexican history. *Below: Mundo* (1925), by Argentine painter Xul Solar. *Below left:* Works by Colombian artist Fernando Botero often feature comically plump figures.

The Foreign Ministry Building is one of many structures designed by architect Oscar Niemeyer for Brasília, the capital of Brazil. The plan for the capital and its buildings was one of the most ambitious architectural projects of modern Latin America.

Abstract Movements. The abstract art movement began to grow in Latin America during the 1930's. Abstract art usually consists of lines, colors, and shapes that do not represent any real object. An early figure in the abstract movement was Uruguayan artist Joaquín Torres-García. His paintings and sculptures, although not completely abstract, combined simplified figures with geometric shapes. His art and teachings were highly influential throughout Latin America, particularly in Uruguay and Argentina.

Torres-García paved the way for younger artists who developed purely geometric and abstract styles. In Argentina in the 1940's, artists of the Concrete Invention and Madi groups, such as Tomás Maldonado and Gyula Kosice, made irregularly shaped paintings of basic geometric forms and color planes, as well as mobile abstract sculptures. In Brazil, the Neo-Concrete artists of São Paulo, such as Helio Oiticica and Lygia Clark, transformed simple geometric shapes and color planes into playful sculptures and intensely colored installations.

Many Latin American artists worked in abstract styles after the 1950's. Among them were the painters Fernando de Szyszlo (Peru), María Luisa Pacheco (Bolivia), and Gunther Gerzso (Mexico) and the sculptors Jesús Rafael Soto (Venezuela), Edgar Negret (Colombia), and Julio LeParc (Argentina).

Figure Painting. After the 1960's, many Latin American artists turned to the human figure as a way to express the widespread suffering of contemporary life. In the following decades, different styles of figure painting existed side by side. For example, Brazil's Antonio H. Amaral painted realistic images with hidden political commentaries, and Colombia's Fernando Botero painted satirical works featuring comically plump figures, while the paintings of Puerto Rico's Rafael Ferrer have an expressionistic quality.

Conceptual Art. Latin American artists such as Luis Camnitzer (Uruguay) and Catalina Parra (Chile) began to work with conceptual art in the 1960's. Conceptual artworks have two parts: an idea or concept, and a written or visual explanation of that concept. Photographs, texts, sound and video recordings, maps, and diagrams are among the techniques used to explain or document the concept.

Architecture. Several large building projects were undertaken in different parts of Latin America during the 1900's. The University of Mexico was designed in 1950–53 by a group of more than 150 architects, including Juan O'Gorman and Félix Candela. It combines modern architecture with the work of Mexican muralists. Similarly, the University City in Caracas, Venezuela, built in 1950–57 by Carlos Raul Villanueva, integrates modern buildings with works by artists. Perhaps the most daring large-scale architectural project in Latin America was that for Brasília. The new capital of Brazil was planned by Lúcio Costa in 1957, and most of its buildings were designed after 1960 by Oscar Niemeyer. The city's spacious layout and graceful buildings were designed to bring the life of Brazil inland from the old coastal cities.

FLORENCIA BAZZANO NELSON
Rochester Institute of Technology

A warrior priest seizes a prisoner in this portion of an Aztec manuscript from about 1525–50. The Aztecs used such pictures to record information and events; the handwriting in this example was added by the Spanish.

LATIN AMERICA, LITERATURE OF

Latin American literature refers to works produced in countries of the New World originally settled by Portugal and Spain. It also includes writings in Spanish or Portuguese by exiles born in Latin America who reside in the United States, Western Europe, and other parts of the world. Finally, the term refers to writings in French in areas of the Americas, such as Haiti, that formerly belonged to France.

Latin American literature covers writings produced in the Latin American republics since their independence from Spain and Portugal in the early 1800's. It also includes literary works produced in the Spanish and Portuguese territories during the preceding colonial period, from the 1500's to the 1800's.

In addition, the writings of the native peoples before the Spanish conquest are considered part of Latin American literature. Examples of pre-colonial works by the Indians include the *Popol Vuh*, sacred books written in the Quiché language by the Mayas of Guatemala; manuscripts of the Aztec empire; and dramas by the Incas.

Furthermore, the culture of the native peoples had a great effect on Latin America's Spanish and Portuguese colonizers, and Latin American literature retains echoes of native culture to this day. Black slaves and various immigrant groups from around the world have also influenced Latin American literature.

Today, Latin American literature reflects the interest of its writers in U.S. and Western European writing. At the same time, however, Latin American literature is a distinct cultural tradition that has come to be respected throughout the world for its uniqueness and originality. Several Latin American writers have won the Nobel prize for literature.

▶ COLONIAL LITERATURE

Early examples of Latin American writing came from the centers of colonial rule. The grand courts of Mexico City and Lima had the most active cultural life, but Rio de Janeiro and Bogotá were also important.

Literature of Conquest. The first texts were chronicles of the conquest and descriptions of the original settlements. There was often a fascinating blend of objective fact and fantasy about the wealth and exotic natural wonders found in the New World. Christopher Columbus' diaries and Hernando Cortes' letters on the conquest of Mexico are some of the most famous of these texts.

Another early writer was Inca Garcilaso de la Vega, the son of a Spanish military man and an Inca noblewoman. His *Comentarios reales* (*Royal Commentaries*; 1609), written in Spanish, explain the history and legends of the Inca people. Bernal Díaz del Castillo wrote *Historia verdadera de la conquista de la Nueva-Espana* (*True History of the Conquest of New Spain*; 1632), the first eyewitness account of the conquest.

On the other hand, the missionary Bartolomé de las Casas wrote of the dark side of conquest in his *Historia de las Indias* (*History of the Indies*; 1552). It is one of the first documents concerning the treatment of the Indians by the Spaniards during the conquest and the early years of the colonies. It reflects a churchman's concern for the conquered native peoples and the need for the crown to protect them from abuse and exploitation. Las Casas' text opened a long debate over the legitimacy of the Spanish conquest, and it is today considered one of Latin America's first works of social consciousness.

In Brazil some one hundred years later another churchman, Antônio Vieira, also defended the rights of the Indians. Vieira's sermons and other works are among the greatest examples of prose writing in Portuguese.

Poetry. In other writing, especially poetry, Latin America developed during the 1500's and 1600's an artistic creativity as sophisticated as that of Spain and Portugal. Most notably, the Mexican nun Sor Juana Inés de la Cruz produced an extensive body of writings on a level with the best of European baroque literature. Sor Juana came to be known as the Tenth Muse and is considered Latin America's first great woman writer.

Satirical Writings. A third form of colonial literature criticized colonial society, often with dark humor and satire. Peru's Juan del Valle y Caviedes wrote more than one hundred scathing poems, few of which were ever published during his lifetime because of their harsh nature. Gregório de Matos in Brazil suffered less censorship with his equally critical views on colonial rule. In Colombia, Juan Rodríguez Freyle composed a biting history of Bogotá that was not published until two hundred years later, in 1859. The Brazilian Antônio Gonzaga, known for his love poems, anonymously published a satire of colonial government that led to his arrest in 1789.

▶ **INDEPENDENCE**

The independence movements in Latin America began in the late 1700's and arose from numerous problems between the crown and the colonists and from conflicts in the colonial administration. Independence, which was won by the 1820's in most of Latin America, had also been made possible by the invasion of Spain by the French under Napoleon.

Since independence meant a break from Spain, in the former Spanish colonies it also meant a break with Hispanic culture.

In the case of Brazil, however, the transition was more gradual. When the French invaded Portugal in 1807, the Portuguese emperor fled to Brazil, which became the center of the Portuguese Empire. When the emperor returned to Portugal in 1822, he left his son as the head of a new Brazilian Empire, which did not become a republic until 1889.

Nationalism and Romanticism. In most of the new countries there was an attempt to define a national literary identity—a distinct "Mexican" or "Argentine" or "Chilean" literature, for example. Although Spanish was retained, major influences from France and England occurred—in particular, a movement in romantic literature that stressed the importance of the individual and the importance of national culture.

One of the first great writers of the independence period was José Joaquín Fernández de Lizardi. His most important work is *El periquillo sarniento* (*The Itching Parrot*; 1816), often called the first Latin American novel.

Sor Juana Inés de la Cruz was a leading Latin American poet of the 1600's. Many of her works defend women's abilities and their right to pursue knowledge.

Argentina's gaucho, or cowboy, became a revered national symbol during the 1800's. Of the many literary works celebrating the life of the gaucho, the greatest was the epic poem *Martín Fierro* by José Hernández.

Three writers best represent the romantic poetry of the period. The Ecuadorian José Joaquín Olmedo wrote "Canto a Bolívar" ("Hymn to Bolívar"; 1825), one of the best-known examples of the nationalist writings following independence. The Cuban José María Heredia was the first romantic poet in the Spanish language to use the natural beauty of the Americas in poems such as "El Niagara" (1824). Andrés Bello, a Venezuelan poet and scholar, is known for his poems describing the tropics.

Many writings reflected the civil wars that followed the independence movement and the difficulties of establishing independent republics. Argentina's Esteban Echeverría composed one of the most famous texts of the period, a lengthy short story called "El matadero" ("The Slaughterhouse"; written in 1841 but not published until 1871). In it he portrayed the bloody effect of tyranny and social turmoil on the individual. Echeverría's story, composed in exile in Uruguay and not discovered until thirty years after his death, is considered the first truly Latin American short narrative and an example of the notable social content of so much of Latin American writing.

Argentina was a particularly fertile area for literature during the 1800's. Domingo Faustino Sarmiento, who later became president of Argentina, published *Facundo* (1845) during his exile in Chile. *Facundo* is the biography of a rural political leader who is portrayed as a symbol of the clash between "civilization and barbarism" in the young nation. This theme has become a permanent part of Latin American writing.

Argentina also produced a rich vein of folk literature based on the figure of the gaucho, the nomadic cowboy of the pampas (plains), who became a revered national symbol. The story of the gaucho was told in the long epic poem *Martín Fierro* (1872; second part, 1879) by José Hernández.

Urban Themes. Argentina's gaucho literature was essentially rural. In contrast, Peru's Ricardo Palma emphasized urban topics in his *Tradiciones peruanas* (*Peruvian Traditions*; 1872–1910), humorous and satiric sketches that reinterpret national history. The work represents the irreverent nature of much Latin American writing, as well as the need to reinterpret the past in ways that expose the hypocrisy of official versions.

Urban themes were especially important in Brazil, where such cities as Rio de Janeiro and São Paulo had developed into major metropolitan areas. Joaquim Maria Machado de Assis, one of Latin America's first prominent writers of black heritage, produced a significant number of realistic novels analyzing the values and conflicts of the Latin American urban middle class. Machado is probably the greatest Latin American writer of the 1800's.

▶THE MODERN ERA

In the late 1800's Latin America became a part of the international economy through the export of agricultural and other natural products. This brought enormous prosperity to such cities as Rio de Janeiro, Mexico City, Buenos Aires, and Montevideo. There emerged a sophisticated urban elite who demanded a Latin American literature of the same quality as that of France or England. The response to this was **modernism**, a movement that produced important works all over Latin America, particularly in urban centers. Modernism may perhaps be considered the first pan-American artistic movement.

The most important figure in modernism is Rubén Darío, a Nicaraguan who wrote poetry and prose reflecting the aesthetic refinement, as well as the internal contradictions, of the new wealthy class. Darío traveled extensively in Latin America, Spain, and Europe, and he came to symbolize the international interests and artistic accomplishments of a Latin American elite. His first book of poetry and prose, *Azul* (*Blue*; 1888), remains his most famous.

Mexican writer Octavio Paz, considered one of the major poets of the 1900's, won the Nobel prize for literature in 1990. His essays were also highly praised, especially *The Labyrinth of Solitude* (1950).

A Modern Latin American Poem

In "Alturas de Machu Picchu" ("The Heights of Machu Picchu"), modern Chilean poet Pablo Neruda seeks a connection with the people of Machu Picchu, an ancient Inca city. In this excerpt from the poem, he addresses the city's long-dead residents, describing the hardship and suffering they endured.

(Translated by Nathaniel Tarn)

Look at me from the depths of the earth,
tiller of fields, weaver, reticent shepherd,
groom of totemic guanacos,*
mason high on your treacherous scaffolding,
iceman of Andean tears,
jeweler with crushed fingers,
farmer anxious among his seedlings,
potter wasted among his clays—
bring to the cup of this new life
your ancient buried sorrows.
Show me your blood and your furrow;
say to me: here I was scourged
because a gem was dull or because the earth
failed to give up in time its tithe of corn or stone.
Point out to me the rock on which you stumbled,
the wood they used to crucify your body.
Strike the old flints
to kindle ancient lamps, light up the whips
glued to your wounds throughout the centuries
and light the axes gleaming with your blood.

I come to speak for your dead mouths.

* Wool-bearing animals of South America, related to the camel

---

Other important modernists were José Martí of Cuba and José Enrique Rodó of Uruguay. Martí, a playwright, poet, and essayist, died in the struggle for Cuban independence and is honored as a national hero. Rodó's essays, notably *Ariel* (1900), encouraged young people to forgo materialism in favor of idealism.

The 1900's. Following World War I (1914–18), Latin American culture profited from economic expansion, with growing numbers of writers and readers and increased opportunities for authors from very diverse backgrounds. Like most literature in the West, literature in Latin America became international in scope and style. At the same time, however, it continued to focus on regional and national problems, often in critical ways that brought harsh persecutions.

This was a period of important works of poetry, with Cuba's Nicolás Guillén, Peru's César Vallejo, Chile's Pablo Neruda, and Mexico's Octavio Paz emerging as the strongest voices. Guillén, who was black, denounced U.S. imperialism in the Caribbean, while Vallejo, who fought in the Spanish Civil War and died in Europe, wrote against social injustice, particularly European fascism.

Neruda and Paz incorporated native themes from their respective countries. Both authors won the Nobel prize for literature—Neruda in 1971 and Paz in 1990.

Neruda was not the first Chilean to win the Nobel prize. Gabriela Mistral, the "schoolteacher poet," received the prize in 1945. Her poetry, which looked forward to concerns

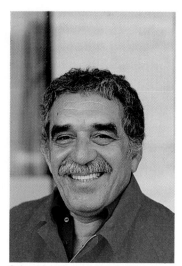

Colombia's Gabriel García Márquez led in Latin America's novel "boom."

Novels by Peru's Mario Vargas Llosa have political and cultural themes.

Argentina's Jorge Luis Borges is best known for his short stories.

identified by later feminists, is notable for its intense humanism.

It was prose that developed most fully during the mid-1900's. Paz authored one of the many essays of social and cultural analysis that have been an important ingredient of contemporary Latin American writing, *El laberinto de la soledad* (*The Labyrinth of Solitude*; 1950). In it, Paz analyzed the character of Mexico's people.

Perhaps the most exceptional writer of the 1900's is the Argentine Jorge Luis Borges who, over sixty years, wrote in every genre but the novel. His writings express a number of trends in contemporary Latin American writing. He is, however, best known for his abstract philosophical and psychological short stories, collected in *Ficciones* (1944) and other works. Borges came to reject the need for Latin American writers to concentrate on social reality. He was more concerned with the problems of understanding the universe and maintaining an individual identity.

The Novel "Boom." By contrast, the Colombian Gabriel García Márquez, who won the Nobel prize for literature in 1982, has striven to reaffirm the commitment to social reality. His internationally acclaimed *Cien anos de soledad* (*One Hundred Years of Solitude*; 1967) uses the story of one family dynasty as the image of all of Latin American social history. Márquez stresses the need for Latin Americans to understand their own history.

Márquez was one of the foremost authors of the novel "boom" of the 1960's that produced many important works. The boom novelists developed a style called **magical realism**, in which fantasy is combined with everyday reality in the quest for deeper meanings.

Contemporary novelists who have most attracted international attention have carried on Latin America's traditional literary commitment to social reality. Brazilian Jorge Amado's fame rests on his often humorous images of black society in Brazil's Bahia region, as in *Gabriela, cravo e canela* (*Gabriela, Clove and Cinnamon*; 1958). The novels of Mexico's Carlos Fuentes are pieces of a vast panorama of Mexican life. *La muerte de Artemio Cruz* (*The Death of Artemio Cruz*; 1962) describes the changes in Mexico after the 1910 revolution through the story of one man's rise to power. Peru's Mario Vargas Llosa has sought to record the contradictions in Peruvian society through novels like *La casa verde* (*The Green House*; 1966).

These novelists and others—including Paraguay's Augusto Roa Bastos; Puerto Rico's Luis Rafael Sánchez; Cuba's Alejo Carpentier; Mexico's Juan Rulfo; Argentina's Julio Cortázar and Manuel Puig; and Chile's Isabel Allende—present today's complex and problematic Latin American society.

DAVID W. FOSTER
Arizona State University
Editor, *Handbook of Latin American Literature*

LATIN AMERICA, MUSIC OF

Latin American music is rich in styles and performance traditions. It includes music produced in more than 25 countries over a large geographical area that extends from Mexico to the southern tip of Argentina.

Three worlds meet and mingle in Latin-American music. The first is quite old. It reaches back to the time before the discovery and conquest of America. This is the world of the native Indians. The second world came with the Spaniards and Portuguese, who brought the music of Europe to the New World. The third came with the Africans who were brought as slaves to work in the mines and on the plantations of the West Indies and South America.

Thus, many races make and enjoy Latin-American music. It can be heard at a market-place or a concert hall, at a family fiesta or a state ceremony. It is very old and very new; it is always colorful.

▶ MUSIC BEFORE THE CONQUEST

The Aztecs and Maya of Mexico and Central America and the Incas of Peru, Bolivia, and Ecuador were great painters, sculptors, and architects. They were also musicians. Stories of their gods and events of their history provided the subject of music. It was heard at great religious and civic festivals. It was played to accompany dances or epic poems that told the stories of the people. Music also served to accompany the more personal and private lyric poems.

Not much is known about this music. But ancient chants can still be heard in remote parts of Latin America. These show that the scale was pentatonic—that is, only five (in Greek, *penta*) tones were used. Pottery, paintings, and archeological excavations show that the ancient Aztecs, Maya, and Incas had wood and skin drums of various sizes; wood and bronze bells; bone scrapers and shakers. The most sophisticated instrument was the marimba, an instrument similar to the xylophone. The marimba is made of wooden bars of different sizes, with hollowed gourds or pumpkinlike fruits hung from each bar to produce greater vibration.

Wind instruments included reed pipes and panpipes—reeds of graduated lengths bound together that will reproduce the scale. There

Left: Wood-and-skin drums such as the Haitian *manman* are common Latin American percussion instruments.

Below: Stringed instruments were introduced to Latin America from Europe. Guitars and violins are played in the mariachi bands of Mexico.

Below right: The marimba is a percussion instrument played by striking wooden bars. Hollow gourds or boxes hung from the bars cause the sounds to resonate.

were also whistles, musical shells, and bird-shaped mouthpieces, now called ocarinas. There is no evidence of stringed instruments among the ancient Indians. The lute, the guitar, and the violin were brought to Latin America by the Europeans.

▶MUSIC SINCE THE CONQUEST

The Spaniards destroyed the Indian cities and suppressed the Indian arts. But they built cities, and they brought their own music and instruments. Soon the Indians adapted the new music and instruments to their own uses. After the 1500's African peoples added a new folk element to Latin-American music. Two traditions of music began to grow side by side in the New World. The first was a folk music combining Indian or African elements with European elements. The second was an art music that remained largely European in style until the close of the 1800's. But with the opening of the 1900's, Latin-American composers turned to the native folk music for new inspiration and forms.

Folk Music

In Latin America nearly every song can be danced and every dance has words. Since gaining independence in the 1800's each country has evolved its own national music.

Dance is an important form of musical expression in Latin America. Performances by the Ballet Folklórica of Mexico are based on traditional themes.

This evolution reflects the mixture of races of the particular country. The *zamacueca*, or *cueca*, of Chile, in 3/4 and 6/8 time, is very Spanish in feeling. So is the *pasillo*, a Spanish balladlike air sung in both Colombia and Venezuela. Mexico's *huapango*, a song and dance that uses the harp in addition to various guitars, and Mexico's *son* reflect the influence of Spain. The same is true of Argentina's dances, the *gato* and *cielito*.

But perhaps the best-known Latin-American folk music is the Mexican *corrido* and the Argentinian tango. The Mexican *corrido* is usually a narrative story set to a vigorous music. The words are about historical events and local, everyday happenings. The *corridos* are balladlike in form. The tango is very like Cuba's habanera; both are music in slow, syncopated 2/4 time. The tango, now a popular ballroom dance, grew up in the slums of Buenos Aires. In the best tangos not only the Spaniards but other Europeans—Italians, Frenchmen, and Jews, who immigrated to the country at the turn of the century—have found a means of self-expression.

The music of Brazil, Trinidad, Cuba, Haiti, the Dominican Republic, and Puerto Rico reflects the vitality and freshness of the African contribution to Latin-American music. The infectious Brazilian samba, a favorite all over the world, is in a highly syncopated 2/4 time. The *macumba*, also Brazilian, is a dance rich with religious folk themes and so varied in meter that it is hard to classify. The *macumba* has begun to influence modern dance-band music.

The rumba and conga are Cuban and began as chants in African rituals. They, too, have been adopted by the modern city dance bands. The merengue of the Dominican Republic, a merry dance with regional variations, and the witty, bubbling, and dramatic calypso of Trinidad are other examples of rhythmic and instrumental color in Latin-American music. In Haiti drums are used at voodoo ceremonies in a music that is deeply religious—a music to invoke the aid and spirit of ancestors and gods.

The latest influence on Latin-American folk music is jazz. European melodies, songs and dances in Afro-Caribbean and Afro-Brazilian traditions, and jazz are combined to create the mambo, bossa nova, cha-cha-cha, and other popular forms.

Art Music

Colonial. The first art music heard in the New World was that of the parent countries, Spain and Portugal. Choir music, religious songs of praise to the saints (*alabanzas*), and Christmas songs were among the first forms. But as a society began to develop in the colony, the music of the royal courts and the town mansions also began to be heard.

The Portuguese influence in Brazil and the Spanish influence in the rest of Latin America dominated the development of colonial music. With independence in the 1800's, conservatories, opera houses, and concert halls were founded in Mexico City, Mexico; Bogotá, Colombia; Lima, Peru; and Rio de Janeiro, Brazil. Through music teachers and conductors, the influence of Germany and Italy reached Latin America at the same time that it was reaching France, England, Spain, Portugal, and Russia.

The first important South American composer was the Brazilian Carlos Gomes (1836–96). He wrote *Il Guarany* (1870), an opera about Indian life in Brazil. But its text was in Italian, and he imitated Italian music. In Mexico, Melesio Morales (1838–1908) and Aniceto Ortega (1825–75), among others, wrote on native subjects with the colorfulness of the Italians. However, the Spanish *zarzuela* (operetta) and *sainete* (comic opera) were also popular.

Modern. Encouraged by the social revolutions of the 1900's, Latin-American composers turned to their own folk music to create a new and modern national music.

Manuel M. Ponce (1882–1948) is greatly respected in his native Mexico as a pioneer of modern Mexican music. He composed the famous song *Estrellita* (1912), as well as the *Concerto of the South* (1941) for orchestra and guitar. But Mexico's most famous composer is Carlos Chávez (1899–1978). Chávez was a conductor and a teacher and was considered a leader of the younger generation. In such works as *The Four Suns* (1925), the *Indian Symphony* (1936), and his Toccata for Percussion (1942), Chávez created a music that was purely Mexican. Other important Mexican composers are Silvestre Revueltas (1899–1940); Blas Galindo (1910–93), who used mainly folk themes; and Miguel Bernal Jiménez (1910–56), composer of religious works.

Another world figure in Latin-American music is the Brazilian composer Heitor Villa-Lobos (1887–1959). He created a music rooted in national life but with an appeal for the whole world. A composer of many songs, symphonies, and suites, such as *Discovery of Brazil* (1937) and *The Odyssey of a Race* (1945), he is most popularly known for *Bachianas Brasileiras* (1930–45), a series of Bach-like works on Brazil. Oscar Lorenzo Fernandez (1897–1948), Francisco Mignone (1897–1986), and particularly Camargo Guarnieri (1907–93) are also important figures in Brazilian musical culture.

A pioneer of music in Argentina was Alberto Williams (1862–1952), the grandson of an Englishman. He brought a fine European training to the composition of piano works based on Argentinian dances. Juan José Castro (1895–1968) and Juan Carlos Paz (1901–72) brought the leading styles of modern Europe to Argentina. This influence is best seen in the original and brilliant work of Alberto Ginastera (1916–83), who was Argentina's most gifted composer.

In Uruguay nationalism in music began with Carlos Pedrell (1878–1941). But it was Eduardo Fabini (1882–1950) who achieved originality.

Elsewhere in South America, noted composers are the Chileans Pedro Humberto Allende (1885–1959); Carlos Isamitt (1887–1974), who used Indian themes; and Carlos Lavin (1883–1962). In Peru the music of Raoul de Verneuil (1899–) is inspired by Indian life. The work of Juan Vicente Lecuna (1894–1954) is strongly Venezuelan in spirit. Guillermo Uribe Holguín (1880–1971) was a composer of distinction from Colombia.

The mixture of races and the drama and color of life in Central America and the West Indies have produced several noteworthy composers. Two of the best known are the Cubans Alejandro García Caturla (1906–40) and Amadeo Roldán (1900–39).

To the outside world the music of Latin America appears as a many-colored world of brilliant sounds and flashing and exotic rhythms. Behind this display there is an art of composition that has brought into unity the art and folk music of Latin America.

Reviewed by LEO PERACCHI
Composer, *Musica di Cena para a Plaça*

LATIN LANGUAGE AND LITERATURE

Latin is the language that was used by the ancient Romans and carried by them to much of Europe, the Near East, northern Africa, and even Britain. Millions of people have spoken or studied Latin over the past 2,500 years. Although Latin is no longer used for everyday speech in the world today, it is the official language of the Roman Catholic Church, and it is read and studied in schools in many parts of the world.

Anyone who speaks English speaks some Latin without realizing it, for more than half the words in the English language and many legal and scientific terms come directly from Latin. Some Latin words in common use are: *animal*, *area*, *capital*, *fact*, *genius*, *labor*, *minus*, *orator*, *resolve*, *senator*, and *senior*. Many Latin words have come into English with a slight change of meaning: "arena" (which in Latin meant "sand"), "campus" ("field"), "sinister" ("left").

Alphabet and Structure. The alphabet we use every day came to us from the Romans. It was developed from a Semitic alphabet through a western Greek form of writing used by the Etruscans, who dominated early Rome. It had only 21 letters until *Y* and *Z* were added in order to be able to spell words borrowed from Greek. *J* and *W* were not used. *I* was both a vowel and a consonant (with the sound of our *Y*). There was no sound like our *V*. The vowel sound *U*, as in "put," and the consonant sound *W*, as in "wine," were written with the letter *u*, which in capitals was *V*. Thus the Latin word for light, *lux*, looked like *LVX*. Vowels (*A*, *E*, *I*, *O*, *V*) were pronounced as long or short, but consonants had only one sound each, and that was much the same as in English.

Words in the Latin language change their endings to indicate different meanings. This process is called inflection. (Some English words inflect, too. For instance, the word "boy" adds *'s* to show the possessive, "boy's.") These endings on words make it possible to change the order of words around much more freely in Latin than in English.

Development. The Latin language was originally only one of many different languages spoken in Italy. It was the speech of the people who lived in the rich plain of Latium toward the mouth of the river Tiber in central Italy. These included the citizens of the city of Rome. The oldest complete books in Latin that have come down to us are the comedies of Plautus, written during the years around 200 B.C. They show that the early Latin language was lively, energetic, and full of variety.

The authors of Rome admired Greek literature and did their best to imitate it. Most of them wanted to make the Latin language as graceful and expressive as Greek. Terence the dramatist, Lucretius the philosophical poet, Cicero the orator, and many others worked to improve Latin.

Classical Latin is the Latin written and spoken by well-educated Romans from about 100 B.C. to about A.D. 150. During this time the best Latin books were written and the language was at its finest. In ordinary conversation and in friendly letters the Romans used short and simple phrases. But for books and speeches they usually chose dignified and imaginative words. They made their style very elaborate and filled their words with double and triple meanings. They built their sentences into beautifully proportioned paragraphs, taking great care with sounds and rhythms.

Classical Latin has never died out as a literary language. All through the Middle Ages and the Renaissance right down to the present time, people have gone on reading and writing it.

However, from about A.D. 200 onward, Latin began to change in several ways. Civil wars and barbarian invasions damaged the Roman Empire in the west. Libraries were destroyed and schools were closed. The level of education dropped. Fewer people were able to speak and write correct Latin or read the classical books. The Latin language finally broke up into rough dialects spoken by the farmers, the poor, and the invading barbarians. After many centuries these dialects grew into French, Italian, Portuguese, Romanian, Spanish, and other modern tongues. These are called the Romance languages, from a Latin word meaning "in the Roman fashion." Further changes were brought about by the Christians who spoke and wrote Latin.

The dialect spoken in central Italy grew into the language of nearly all Italy. Later it became the speech of all the western Roman Empire from Britain to North Africa. (Greek continued to be the language of most of the eastern provinces.) Finally it split up into classical Latin, a language read and written but not spoken; church Latin, the language of the western Christians; and the dialects that grew into the modern Romance languages.

Early Latin Literature. During the early period (before about 100 B.C.) Latin developed under the influence of Greek culture. Romans translated and adapted Greek works. They also wrote original patriotic histories and dramas in Latin. They invented poetic words and set up forms of drama, satire, and history.

The first real literature in Latin was a group of translations. Livius Andronicus (284?–204? B.C.) was a freed slave from the south of Italy, where Greek was spoken. He translated the Greek epic poem the *Odyssey* into Latin for use as a schoolbook. The epic form was used by Gnaeus Naevius (270?–201? B.C.) for a patriotic poem on the First Punic War, and by Quintus Ennius (239–169? B.C.) for his poem on the history of Rome, *Annales*. Both men wrote or adapted dramas on Greek and Roman themes. The greatest comic playwrights were Plautus (Titus Maccius Plautus, 254?–184 B.C.) and Terence (Publius Terentius Afer, 185–159 B.C.). Plautus, whose name means "Flatfoot," wrote many stories of mix-ups and tricks. Terence's stories and characters were deeper and more serious. Much sterner was Marcus Porcius Cato (234–149 B.C.), who wrote the first prose history, *Origines*, and a book on agriculture.

Literature of the Later Republic. Writers of the later republic (about 100–27 B.C.) showed continued Greek influence in their forms and philosophical thinking, but they were strictly Roman in their energy and political and moral consciousness.

Lucretius (Titus Lucretius Carus, 96?–55 B.C.) wrote the first great philosophical poem in Latin. His six-volume *De Rerum Natura* ("On the Nature of Things") preached the Epicurean philosophy of a well-balanced, peaceful life and gave a scientific theory of the universe that was based on the proposition that all matter is composed of atoms in motion. It was all done in beautiful poetry with rich vocabulary and skillful use of rhythm.

A very different poet was Gaius Valerius Catullus (84?–54 B.C.). Catullus wrote many short and a few long poems, most of them very artistic and highly polished in the style of the Greeks.

The greatest of all Latin prose writers, who set the style that is still considered the best classical Latin, was Marcus Tullius Cicero (106–43 B.C.). Cicero was most noted for his moving and powerful orations. These include his attacks on Verres and Catiline and his defense of his old teacher Archias. The speeches show precise sentence structure, long periods of carefully developed thought, very full vocabulary, and a stern dignity broken by occasional puns or jokes. As a professional orator Cicero wrote several books on the theory and practice of oratory. He also loved to read and discuss Greek philosophy. He reorganized and summarized the theories and ideas of the Greeks in many entertaining books of dialogues written in Latin.

Gaius Julius Caesar (102–44 B.C.) was most famous as a soldier and politician, but he deserves credit also as one of the best writers of Latin prose. His *Commentaries*, or *Notes*, on the Gallic and civil wars are written in clear, precise, straightforward, simple language and have been models for many later historians. Caesar was also an excellent orator, second only to Cicero.

The Augustan Golden Age. The period of the reign of the first emperor, Augustus (27 B.C.–A.D. 14), brought peace and prosperity to the Romans after a century of civil war. Great advances were made in art and culture. Romans had a new patriotism and a new zest for living that were reflected in their writings. Roman writers completed their mastery of Greek forms to produce the greatest Latin poetry of all time. Augustus himself encouraged literature, and it was natural for the poets of his day to idealize his reign as a new golden age.

Vergil (Publius Vergilius Maro, 70–19 B.C.) became the greatest poet to grace the Latin tongue. His first works were poems on rustic life, *Bucolics*, and on farming, *Georgics*. Augustus himself asked the young poet to write a great national epic, and Vergil spent the last eleven years of his life composing his masterpiece, the *Aeneid*. It is a long narrative poem in twelve books and tells the story of Aeneas, the legendary hero who came from Troy to found the Roman race in Italy.

Another poet who received support and encouragement from the Emperor was Horace (Quintus Horatius Flaccus, 65–8 B.C.). Horace wrote more than 100 odes, or songs, in meters copied from the Greeks. They deal with many themes—love, religion, the search for true happiness, and, occasionally, the decline of Roman morality.

Albius Tibullus (54?–18? B.C.) and Sextus Propertius (50?–15? B.C.) wrote elegies—poems of love and sadness and strange visions—in a polished, sophisticated style imitating the Greeks.

Ovid (Publius Ovidius Naso, 43 B.C.–A.D. 17?) wrote elegant little poems of love in elegiac meter, including his famous and rather scandalous *Ars Amatoria* ("Art of Love") and *Remedia Amoris* ("Remedy for Love"). Banished for some unstated offense against the emperor Augustus, Ovid wrote sad poems of his longing to be home. One of his more important books was the *Fasti*, an almanac in verse describing and explaining the religious celebrations of the Roman year. Ovid's most famous and enduring work is the 15-book *Metamorphoses*. It retells stories from mythology from the creation of the world to the deification of Julius Caesar. It is thanks to Ovid that we know as much of classical mythology as we do.

Livy (Titus Livius, 59 B.C.–A.D. 17) was a friend of Augustus' and the tutor of the later emperor Claudius. He wrote a history of Rome in 142 books, *Ab Urbe Condita*, covering more than 700 years from the founding of the city to the death of Augustus' best general, Drusus, in 9 B.C. Only about one fourth of this work survives. Livy is a strong moralist and a devoted Roman patriot. His style is wonderfully varied and yet always sounds vivid and natural. He is at his best in describing big crowd scenes, such as battles and stormy senatorial debates.

The Silver Age. From about A.D. 14 to about A.D. 130 Latin writers continued to flourish but did not achieve the greatness of those of the Augustan Age. Lucius Annaeus Seneca (4? B.C.–A.D. 65), the emperor Nero's tutor, wrote nine tragedies filled with horror and violence. Seneca also wrote several books on stoic moral philosophy and a satire about the emperor Claudius. Lucan (Marcus Annaeus Lucanus, 39–65), Seneca's nephew, composed a ten-book epic, *Pharsalia*, on the civil war between Caesar and Pompey. Petronius (Gaius Petronius Arbiter, ?–66?) wrote the *Satyrica*, a brilliant satirical novel about underworld life.

Aulus Persius Flaccus (34–62) wrote satires teaching stoic morals in private life. Martial (Marcus Valerius Martialis, 40?–104?), a clever Spanish poet who lived by his wits, produced twelve books of witty epigrams on the foibles and vices of Rome. The one surviving book of Quintilian (Marcus Fabius Quintilianus, 35?–95?) is a complete manual for the education of an orator. It is full of advice that is still valuable for speakers. Gaius Plinius Caecilius Secundus (62–113), Pliny the Younger, was also interested in oratory and wrote letters to be published, imitating Cicero. His uncle, Pliny the Elder (23–79), wrote an encyclopedic series of volumes on natural history.

Cornelius Tacitus (55?–117?), a friend of the younger Pliny and one of the great Latin historians, composed histories and annals covering most of the imperial period. Tacitus also wrote a biography of his father-in-law, Agricola, and a book on the Germans. Suetonius (Gaius Suetonius Tranquillus, 69?–140?) wrote biographies of famous men. One of the greatest writers of this period was Juvenal (Decimus Junius Juvenalis, 60?–140?). His satires in verse ridiculed such things as the noise and filth of the city of Rome and the vanity of human wishes.

Later Latin Writing. After the Silver Age, Latin literature fell into a decline. Marcus Cornelius Fronto (100?–175?) practiced oratory and urged a return to archaic style. He influenced two other writers of the 100's, Aulus Gellius, who produced a collection of essays called *Attic Nights*, and Apuleius, who wrote *The Golden Ass*, a fanciful story of a man turned into an animal.

Christian writers were trying more to persuade their readers than to produce lasting works of art. Tertullian (Quintus Septimus Florens Tertullianus, 160?–230?) wrote of Christian beliefs.

Perhaps the last of the literary Latin writers was Decimus Magnus Ausonius, a professor who lived in the 300's. He delighted in setting into Latin verse everything from the days of the week to a list of his ancestors. None of these writers can rank with the earlier ones for literary or artistic merit.

CAROL LAUER CHISDES
Wall Township (New Jersey) High School
Reviewed by GILBERT HIGHET
Columbia University

LATITUDE AND LONGITUDE

Anyone trying to find a place in a town or city can usually locate it by referring to a map that shows its different streets and avenues. But how do you locate yourself in a place such as an ocean or a river where there are no streets or avenues or even highways? You can use a system of imaginary east–west and north–south lines called latitude and longitude that crisscross the earth. With this system, in fact, it is possible to locate any point on the surface of the earth.

▶ LATITUDE

Latitude is a measurement of distance north or south of the **equator**, an imaginary east–west line that circles the earth halfway between the North and South poles. The equator divides the earth into a Northern Hemisphere and a Southern Hemisphere.

Other imaginary east–west lines circle the earth parallel to the equator and north and south of it. Because they are parallel to the equator, these lines are called **parallels**. Each parallel marks off a fixed distance north or south of the equator. This distance is called latitude. All points in the Northern Hemisphere have north latitude. All points in the Southern Hemisphere have south latitude.

Latitude Units

Latitude is expressed in degrees (°) based on the 360 degrees of a circle. It is measured from the equator, which is 0° latitude. The distance from the equator to the North Pole or to the South Pole is one fourth of a circle around the earth and is therefore equal to 90°. The North Pole has a latitude of 90° N, and the South Pole has a latitude of 90° S. These are the highest latitudes north or south of the equator. A point midway between the equator and the poles has a latitude of 45° N or 45° S, depending on the direction from the equator. A latitude of 30° is one third of the way from equator to pole, and so forth.

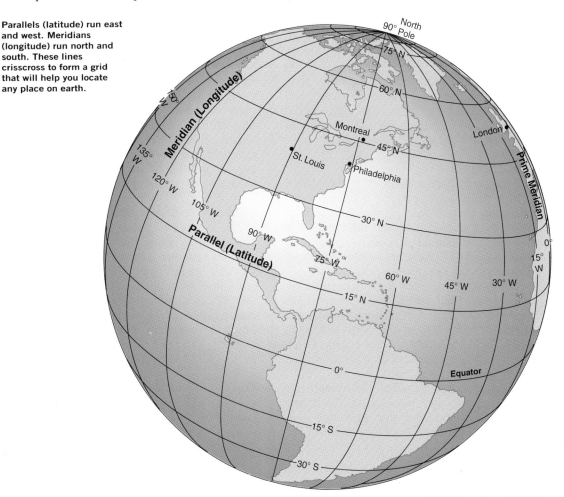

Parallels (latitude) run east and west. Meridians (longitude) run north and south. These lines crisscross to form a grid that will help you locate any place on earth.

Latitude and Miles

Even though latitude is always measured and expressed in degrees, it is easily converted into miles. The distance from the equator to either pole is 6,222 **statute miles**, or standard miles (10,013 kilometers). Divided by 90° from equator to pole, this equals about 69 statute miles (111 kilometers) for each degree of latitude. However, because the earth is not perfectly round, this figure varies slightly from the equator to the poles. The earth is flattest at the poles, and a degree of latitude is almost a mile longer there than at the equator.

If you know the latitude of a place, you can thus estimate its distance from the equator. For example, Montreal, Canada, is located at about 45° N latitude. By multiplying 45 by 69, you find that Montreal is about 3,105 statute miles north of the equator. Philadelphia, Pennsylvania, is located at about 40° N. Montreal is thus about 345 statute miles farther north than Philadelphia (5 degrees difference multiplied by 69 miles).

Degrees are too large for determining the precise locations of places. Therefore degrees are subdivided into minutes and seconds. Each degree has 60 minutes (60′), and each minute has 60 seconds (60″). One minute is equal to about 1 1/6 statute miles, or about 6,000 feet. One second is equal to about 100 feet. Latitude may thus be given more precisely in degrees, minutes, and seconds. The latitude of Montreal, for example, is 45° 31′ N.

▶LONGITUDE

Latitude by itself tells only how far a place is from the equator. It locates the place somewhere on an east–west parallel thousands of miles long extending around the earth. It is possible to pinpoint a place on any parallel by using a series of imaginary north–south lines that intersect the parallels at right angles.

The north–south lines that run perpendicular to the parallels are called **meridians**. Each meridian is a circle that runs north and south around the earth through the North and South poles. While parallels indicate distances in a north–south direction, meridians indicate distances in an east–west direction.

Unlike parallels, in which the equator is a natural midway line between the North and South poles, meridians have no natural midway line on the earth from east to west. The world's nations, however, have agreed on a starting line: the meridian that runs through Greenwich Observatory near London, England. This meridian is called the **prime meridian**, and its longitude is 0°. Every other meridian indicates a distance east or west of the prime meridian. This distance is called longitude.

Longitude Units

Longitude, like latitude, is measured in degrees. The half of the earth east of the prime meridian has longitude up to 180° E. The half west of the prime meridian has longitude up to 180° W. The 180th meridian, which lies directly opposite the prime meridian, is the same for both east and west longitude. It is therefore not referred to as 180° E or 180° W, but simply 180°. Midway between the prime meridian and the 180th meridian is 90° W or 90° E, depending on the direction from the prime meridian. One fourth of the distance is 45°, and so on.

Longitude and Miles

At the equator, 1° of longitude is about the same distance as 1° of latitude. Unlike parallels, however, meridians do not stay the same distance apart at all places on earth. As meridians move away from the equator they come closer and closer together until they finally meet at the poles. This means that the number of miles in 1° of longitude is different for each latitude. The poles have no longitude because all meridians meet there. Longitude degrees are also subdivided into minutes and seconds to locate places more precisely.

▶USING LATITUDE AND LONGITUDE

The location of places on the earth can be pinpointed by using both latitude and longitude. For example, St. Louis, Missouri, with a latitude of 39° N and a longitude of 90° W, is located where the 39° N parallel intersects the 90° W meridian. Places can be located even more precisely by expressing latitude and longitude in degrees, minutes, and seconds.

SAMUEL N. NAMOWITZ
Author, *Earth Science*

See also EQUATOR; INTERNATIONAL DATE LINE; TIME.

LATTER DAY SAINTS, CHURCH OF JESUS CHRIST OF. See MORMONS.

LATTER DAY SAINTS, REORGANIZED CHURCH OF JESUS CHRIST OF. See MORMONS.

LATVIA

Latvia is one of the Baltic States, a term often used in referring to three neighboring European countries situated on the eastern shore of the Baltic Sea in northeastern Europe. The other Baltic states are Lithuania, to Latvia's south, and Estonia, to its north. To the east, Latvia borders the Russian Federation and Belarus.

For much of their long history, the Latvians have been ruled by more powerful peoples—Germans, Poles, Swedes, Russians, and the Soviets. Latvia first proclaimed its independence in 1918, after the Russian Empire was overthrown, but in 1940 it was annexed by the Soviet Union. Latvians regained their independence as the Soviet Union was breaking apart in 1991.

The People. Of the once-widespread Baltic peoples, only the Latvians and Lithuanians have survived into modern times. The Latvian language is similar to Lithuanian. The Estonians, although geographically close, speak an unrelated language.

A Latvian farmhouse looks much as it did a century ago, when the population was mainly rural. Today, more than 70 percent of the people live in cities.

Latvians now make up about 52 percent of the country's population. Russians are the largest ethnic minority, with about 34 percent of the population. There are also smaller numbers of Belarusians, Ukrainians, and Lithuanians. Latvians formerly comprised more than 75 percent of the population. This decrease was due to the policy of the former Soviet government, which encouraged the immigration of Russians and other Slavs, threatening the very existence of the Latvian nation.

Most Latvians traditionally have belonged to the Lutheran Church. There are considerable numbers of Eastern Orthodox Christians, however, chiefly among the ethnic Russians, and nearly one third of the people are Roman Catholics. Almost all of Latvia's Jewish community was destroyed during the Nazi German occupation in World War II.

More than 70 percent of Latvians live in cities, the largest of which is Riga, the capital. Founded in 1201, Riga is a major port and center of industry and education. About half of Latvia's population lives in the city and its metropolitan area.

Way of Life. Religion was once a strong influence on Latvian life. It lost much of its

Riga is Latvia's capital and largest city, with about half the country's population residing in the city proper and its metropolitan area. Situated at the mouth of the Daugava River, which flows into the Baltic Sea, it has been an important Baltic port since the Middle Ages. Although the city was founded in 1201, a settlement existed on the site much earlier. Riga became the national capital in 1918.

vigor under the Soviet Communist regime, which discouraged religious observance, but is returning as Latvians rediscover their faith. Latvians, like the Lithuanians and Estonians, have a long tradition of choral singing, and national singing contests are organized regularly. Many of the songs are ancient, reaching back into pre-Christian times. The most popular festival is St. John's Eve, or Midsummer, celebrated in June, which combines pagan and Christian elements.

Industrious, hardworking, and competitive, the Latvians were strongly influenced by Germanic culture during the seven centuries of German rule.

The Land and Climate. Like the other Baltic states, Latvia has a flat landscape, which rarely rises above 600 feet (183 meters). The Ice Age that created the low-lying terrain also carved out thousands of lakes and rivers. Few of the rivers are of great extent, however, the longest being the Daugava (the Western Dvina in Russia). Latvia has four distinct provinces: Kurzeme (approximately historic Courland) in the west; the fertile central plain of Zemgale; Vidzeme (roughly ancient Livonia) in the northeast; and Latgale in the southeast. About 40 percent of the land is forested. There are few mineral resources, aside from some limestone, gypsum, and clays.

The climate is moderate, with generally mild winters and cool summers. January temperatures range from about 19°F (−3°C) in coastal areas to 27°F (−7°C) inland. In July temperatures vary from about 63°F (17°C) on the coast to 65°F (18°C) inland. Rainfall averages about 26 inches (660 millimeters) a year.

The Economy. Latvia was one of the most economically developed provinces of the Russian Empire, and its industrial growth continued under Soviet rule. It was a major supplier of such products as railway cars, buses, diesel engines and generators, telephone systems and equipment, textiles, chemicals, and processed foods. Independent Latvia is adjusting well to the new economic conditions. About 60 percent of its gross national product (the total value of its goods and services) comes from industry. With few natural resources of its own, however, Latvia must import much of its fuels and other raw materials.

FACTS and figures

REPUBLIC OF LATVIA is the official name of the country.

LOCATION: Northeastern Europe, on the Baltic Sea.

AREA: 24,600 sq mi (63,700 km²).

POPULATION: 2,700,000 (estimate).

CAPITAL AND LARGEST CITY: Riga.

MAJOR LANGUAGES: Latvian, Russian.

MAJOR RELIGIOUS GROUP: Christian (Lutheran, Eastern Orthodox, Roman Catholic).

GOVERNMENT: Republic, under an elected interim parliament, the Supreme Council, headed by a chairman (president). A new constitution is in preparation.

CHIEF PRODUCTS: Agricultural—meat and dairy products, rye, barley, oats, potatoes and other vegetables, fodder (livestock feed), sugar beets, corn. **Manufactured**—railway cars, buses, diesel engines and generators, telephone systems and equipment, textiles, chemicals. **Mineral**—limestone, gypsum, clays.

Latvia has an efficient agricultural sector, in which the production of meat, milk, and other dairy products was particularly important. The chief farm crops are rye, barley, oats, potatoes and other vegetables, fodder (livestock feed), sugar beets, and corn.

Early History. The Baltic ancestors of the Latvians first settled in the region in ancient times. In the A.D. 1200's, German missionary knights conquered the Latvian lands and converted the people to Christianity. Their successors, the Teutonic Knights, established the state of Livonia (including part of what is today Estonia), which dominated the region until the mid-1500's. Between 1561 and 1562, the Latvian lands were divided between Poland-Lithuania and the German-ruled duchy of Courland. In the 1600's, the area around Riga fell to the Swedes.

Russian and Soviet Rule. Sweden's defeat by Russia in the Great Northern War (1700–21) brought all of Latvia into the Russian Empire, although the provinces remained under the control of the German nobility. Latvian nationalist awareness emerged in the 1800's and reached its height in the early 1900's. Following the collapse of the Russian Empire in 1917, Latvians declared their independence, on November 18, 1918.

To maintain its freedom, Latvia had to repel both the Soviet Communist forces that had seized power in Russia and German troops. This it did, helped by the presence of the British navy, and in 1920 the Soviets recognized Latvian independence. It was to last for only 22 years. In 1939, just before the outbreak of World War II, a non-aggression pact between Nazi Germany and the Soviet Union gave the Soviets a free hand in Latvia. In June 1940, the Soviet Union occupied Latvia. A pro-Communist government was forced on the country, which was made a Soviet republic. The other Baltic states were similarly incorporated into the Soviet Union.

In spite of their treaty, Germany invaded the Soviet Union in 1941. Latvia remained under occupation until 1944, when the Germans were driven out by Soviet troops. The Soviet regime then completed the harsh transformation of Latvia into a Communist state. Industry and agriculture were brought under state control, religion and Latvian culture were suppressed, and Russians were brought in to administer much of the government and

Carrying the national flag, supporters of the Popular Front demonstrated in favor of Latvia's independence from the Soviet Union, which was achieved in 1991.

the economy. Thousands of Latvians had earlier escaped to the West. Many thousands more were now deported and imprisoned in Soviet labor camps.

Independence. The situation changed dramatically with the rise to power of the reformist Soviet leader Mikhail Gorbachev in 1985. In 1988 the non-Communist Latvian Popular Front was organized and won widespread support among the people. A new parliament was elected, which restored democratic practices and demanded gradual political self-determination. However, immediately after Communist hard-liners tried to overthrow the Soviet government in August 1991, Latvia's parliament declared full independence.

In 1999, Vaira Vike-Freiberga was elected president, succeeding Guntis Ulmanlis, who had served since 1993. In 2000, she appointed Andris Berzins, a former mayor of Riga, to the post of prime minister. Vike-Freiberga was easily re-elected in 2003.

In 2004, Latvia—along with several other former Soviet republics—joined both the North Atlantic Treaty Organization (NATO) and the European Union (EU).

V. STANLEY VARDYS
Coeditor, *The Baltic States in Peace and War*
See also ESTONIA; LITHUANIA.

LAUNDRY

Keeping clothes clean is always a problem. The most basic way to clean laundry is to scrub it in water with soap or detergent, rinse it, and then hang it up to dry. The invention of the washing machine in 1851 has made this process much easier.

Commercial Laundries. In some countries, businesses that wash clothes have operated for hundreds of years. Egypt had a laundry in 2000 B.C., and Greece and Rome also had launderers who washed and pressed clothes.

The first commercial laundry in the United States was set up in Troy, New York, to wash shirt collars made in factories. Today, there are many types of commercial laundries. They range from small, neighborhood shirt cleaners and coin-operated laundromats to large linen-supply laundries that launder and rent items such as sheets, pillowcases, tablecloths, and towels to hotels and restaurants.

Home Washing. To do your own wash, first read the care label found on your clothing. It will tell you what temperatures to use for the washing and drying. Sort the dirty clothes into separate piles. Most white cotton items can be washed in hot water. Other fabrics and colors are usually washed in warm water, except for those whose care labels call for cold water. Wash dark and light clothes separately. Instructions on the detergent container will list how much powder or liquid to use. Some fabrics, such as wool and silk, should be washed by hand in cool water or dry cleaned.

There are some special methods you can use to remove certain stains before washing: **Blood, fruit, ice cream, soft drinks**—soak or sponge with cold water as soon as possible. **Chewing gum**—harden with an ice cube, then rub until it crumbles away. **Chocolate**—scrape with a dull knife. **Grass**—sponge with alcohol, or wash in hot water and soap, rubbing the stain well. **Grease**—rub stain with detergent, then wash in hot water.

LEE JOHNSTON
American Institute of Laundering
See also DETERGENTS AND SOAP; DRY CLEANING.

LAUREL AND HARDY. See MOTION PICTURES (Profiles: Movie Stars).

LAURIER, SIR WILFRID (1841–1919)

Sir Wilfrid Laurier was Canada's first French-speaking prime minister. He was born on November 20, 1841, at St. Lin, Quebec, north of Montreal. He was elected to the Quebec legislature and in 1874 to the Canadian House of Commons. As the most promising young French Liberal, Laurier was made a cabinet member in the Liberal government of Alexander Mackenzie (1822–92) in 1877.

At that time Liberalism was unpopular in Quebec because some of the Roman Catholic clergy believed that all Liberals were against religion. In 1877 Laurier made an important speech showing that this was not true. His influence among Liberals grew until, in 1887, he was chosen leader of the party.

In the election of 1891, Laurier called for closer economic ties with the United States. This was an unpopular idea, and it helped defeat the Liberals. But in 1896 the Liberals won the election, and Wilfrid Laurier became prime minister. As prime minister, Laurier carried on many Conservative policies, such as favoring trade with Great Britain over trade with the United States. Canada was then growing very rapidly. Millions of immigrants settled in the Canadian Prairie Provinces. Two new trans-Canadian railways were built.

In 1910 Laurier started a Canadian navy. The next year he proposed reciprocity—a form of free trade—with the United States. These two policies were very unpopular and caused his defeat by Sir Robert Borden (1854–1937) in the election of 1911.

As leader of the Opposition, Laurier supported Canada's war effort during World War I. But in 1917 the Liberal Party was split over the plan to conscript men as soldiers. When he refused to join a coalition (joint) government with the Conservatives, many of the English-speaking Liberals joined the Conservative Party. Laurier was left with few followers except those from Quebec. Laurier, who had always worked for Canadian unity, was bitterly disappointed at this. He died on February 17, 1919, an unhappy and defeated man.

JOHN S. MOIR
University of Toronto

LA VÉRENDRYE, SIEUR DE. See NORTH DAKOTA (Famous People).

LAVOISIER, ANTOINE LAURENT
(1743–1794)

During Antoine Laurent Lavoisier's 51 years he was a chemist, a politician, and a lawyer. He was also a farmer and a banker. But it is as a chemist that he is remembered and honored today.

Lavoisier was born in Paris, France, on August 26, 1743. He was the son of a wealthy lawyer. Antoine studied law as his father wished, but he also attended many lectures on scientific subjects. Soon after graduating from law school he decided to follow a career of scientific research.

To carry on research, Lavoisier set up one of the finest laboratories in Europe. He insisted on exact measurements in all his experiments. He would accept no idea unless it could be proved. In this way he helped introduce methods of exactness in chemistry.

In 1771 Lavoisier married Marie Paulze, a brilliant, gifted girl 14 years younger than he. She acted as his secretary and later made many of the drawings for his books. They had no children.

▶ LAVOISIER'S WORK IN CHEMISTRY

In the 18th century chemists did not understand clearly what happened when a fuel burned. They thought a burning fuel gave up a weightless substance called phlogiston. Lavoisier found this hard to believe.

In 1772, he noticed that certain chemicals gained weight when they burned. This meant that something must have been added to these chemicals, instead of being lost. But he could not find out what this was.

In 1774, Lavoisier learned that the English chemist Joseph Priestley had discovered a gas that seemed to help things burn. Lavoisier repeated Priestley's experiments and added his own. These experiments convinced Lavoisier that this gas—which he called oxygen—is necessary for burning. When a fuel burns, he said, it combines with oxygen. There is no such thing as phlogiston.

In 1783 Lavoisier learned that another great English chemist, Henry Cavendish, had obtained water when he burned a gas then called "inflammable air." But Cavendish's explanation of why this happened did not satisfy Lavoisier.

Lavoisier added some careful measurements of his own to Cavendish's experiments. Then he announced that water was a combination of two gases, oxygen and "inflammable air." (He soon renamed this gas hydrogen.)

Lavoisier also carried out important investigations into respiration, or breathing. He showed that the body uses breathed-in oxygen to burn food, which gives the body its heat.

Up to that time there was no one way of naming chemicals. Lavoisier worked with several other chemists to set up a system of naming chemicals. It is in use today.

Lavoisier had long been a member of an organization that was much hated by the French people. The organization was called the Farm-General. Among its duties was the collection of taxes for the king. In 1789 a revolution broke out in France against the king. At the height of the French Revolution the members of the Farm-General were arrested, tried, and sentenced to death. Lavoisier was among them. On May 8, 1794, he was beheaded.

Antoine Lavoisier did not make many discoveries of his own. But he gave correct explanations of the discoveries of others. His explanation of combustion, or burning, changed the whole science of chemistry. Our modern science of chemistry is based on his work.

DAVID C. KNIGHT
Author, science books for children

See also CHEMISTRY, HISTORY OF.

LAW AND LAW ENFORCEMENT

Laws are rules that define our rights and responsibilities. Laws regulate the activities of citizens and of governments. They are made official through approval by a legislature, a court, or another governmental agency. Almost every aspect of our lives is affected by law. Criminal law helps keep people safe. Laws that apply to trade and business help our economy thrive. Laws limiting the power of government protect the freedom of citizens to speak openly, practice their chosen religion, and maintain their privacy.

▶ **HISTORICAL BACKGROUND**

Philosophers once believed that prehistoric people lived without laws, in a "state of nature." Back then, the philosophers thought, people obeyed only force. As a result, life became so dangerous that leaders had to create laws to protect people and property.

Scholars no longer believe this. Instead, it is thought, people probably worked out rules for getting along with one another as soon as they began living in groups. Group members came to accept and support the manners, customs, and beliefs that controlled the living habits and behavior of the group. These shared customs and habits of life (sometimes called "folkways") were most likely the real beginnings of laws and of moral codes.

Early Laws

Some of these customs were written down as the earliest recorded laws, or **codes** of law. In Egypt written laws date from about 3400 B.C. Those in Mesopotamia date from 3500 to 2360 B.C., the period of the Sumerians.

The Babylonians developed the Code of Hammurabi, one of the greatest of the ancient codes. Hammurabi was king of Babylonia from 1792 to 1750 B.C. His code was found on three fragments of a stone column at Susa, in what is now Iraq, in 1901. It included laws defining penalties for crime and laws governing the rights of those who were injured, owned property, or made loans. It also specified procedures for enforcing the law.

Among the Hittites, who were an ancient people of Asia Minor and Syria, written law was first recorded around 1300 B.C. Among the ancient Hebrews, written laws appeared around 1200 B.C. In European history, the most famous early written code was the Twelve Tables of Roman law. These rules governed crimes, property, debts, and injuries. They were recorded on bronze and wooden tablets ("tables") in 450 B.C. The complete body of Roman law was codified (written down) about a thousand years later, in A.D. 535, by order of the emperor Justinian. The Justinian Code had a great influence on the development of modern law in Europe and

The Roman emperor Justinian (483–565) and members of his court. Under Justinian, Roman law was codified, or written down. The Justinian Code had a great influence on modern law in Europe and America.

in countries around the world where Europeans exerted their influence.

Law in the Middle Ages

In medieval Europe, laws varied from place to place. Powerful landholders created and followed their own laws. Towns and small cities that were controlled by guilds also made their own laws. Special kinds of laws developed to govern social and economic relationships between localities. **Mercantile law**, for example, was a group of rules and regulations that governed the way merchants and traders across Europe conducted business. These rules were designed to prevent cheating in trade. The Roman Catholic Church had its own set of laws, called **canon law**. It incorporated some aspects of Roman law.

In the late Middle Ages (1300–1500), local laws and specialized laws began to give way to laws that governed entire nations.

Civil Law and Common Law

As new nations arose in continental Europe, many adopted national laws based on principles of ancient Roman law. The law of those countries that developed this way is called **civil law**. These laws were eventually codified in the 1800's. The most famous of the civil codes was the Napoleonic Code, or **Code Civil**, adopted in France in 1804.

A different system of law, called **common law**, evolved at the same time in England. In place of written laws, or **statutes**, common law relied on judicial decisions. That is, to decide a dispute, judges in common law courts would look to prior court decisions in similar cases. In contrast, judges in civil law courts would consult a code for guidance. Common law took form gradually, one case at a time, and established countless rules. Among them was the right of a person accused of a crime to have a jury trial and to be presumed innocent until proved guilty. A famous compilation of these rules is the treatise of Sir William Blackstone, written in the late 1700's.

The English jurist William Blackstone (1723–80). Blackstone's famous treatise codified English common law.

Because it served as the foundation for much of the law in the United States, English common law remains an important source of guidance for American courts today. Blackstone is still cited in decisions of the United States Supreme Court. The law of one state, Louisiana, grew out of the Napoleonic Code and from the civil-law tradition, not the common law, because Louisiana was settled by the French, not the English.

International Law

Just as small communities once banded together to develop national law, nations have developed international law to regulate relations with each other. As early as the 1500's in Europe, legal thinkers such as Hugo Grotius (1583–1645), a Dutch jurist and statesman, and Emerich de Vattel (1714–67), a Swiss jurist, worked out systems of international law. Then as now, the primary goals were to try to prevent war and promote good relations between countries.

International law today consists of treaties—formal agreements between countries—and long-standing customs. International law is enforced in international courts. The most important is the International Court of Justice at The Hague, in the Netherlands. (For additional information, see the article INTERNATIONAL LAW in Volume I.)

▶ THE LEGAL SYSTEM IN THE UNITED STATES

In the United States, laws exist at three levels. Federal laws apply to the entire country. State laws apply to activities within the borders of one state. Local laws apply within a city or township.

The supreme law in the United States—the law with which all other law must conform—is set out in the United States Constitution. States have adopted their own constitutions, governing the law in each state. These written documents determine the organization of government as well as the rights of the people. Like the United States Constitution, most

The Virginia state legislature in session. In the United States, federal, state, and local laws are adopted by legislatures— lawmaking bodies that are elected directly by the people.

state constitutions are quite short. They express rules in general terms, leaving courts and lawmakers to work out specific applications of the rules.

How Laws Are Made

At federal, state, and local levels, written laws are adopted by a legislature or, in the case of local laws, a council elected by the people. When a legislature approves a new law, it is said to enact legislation. In addition, government agencies are sometimes authorized by a legislature to develop rules in their area of expertise. These "administrative" rules and regulations have the force of law.

Federal laws are adopted by the U.S. Congress. A bill, which is a proposal for a new law, may be introduced in either house of Congress—the Senate or the House of Representatives. The bill is first reviewed by a committee of legislators who may hold hearings to get opinions from experts and others who may be interested in the issues addressed by the bill. The bill must be approved by the committee and then by both the House of Representatives and the Senate. Then, to become law, it must be signed by the president. (For more information, refer to the articles UNITED STATES, CONGRESS OF THE, and UNITED STATES, GOVERNMENT OF THE, in Volume U-V.) If the president vetoes, or rejects, a bill, the veto may be overridden by a vote of at least two-thirds of both the House

and Senate. Similarly, governors must sign state legislation, and state legislatures have the power to override a veto.

Statutes typically may be repealed (canceled) or amended (changed) by a majority of the legislature with the agreement of the executive. Constitutions are not as easy to change. Article V of the U.S. Constitution provides that any amendment must be proposed by two-thirds of both houses of Congress, or two-thirds of the states' legislatures. Then the amendment must be ratified (approved) by "the Legislatures of three-fourths of the several States, or by Conventions in three-fourths thereof."

Judges, as well as legislators, make law. Judges adopt rules of court that dictate procedures in the court system. Judges also interpret other sources of law, elaborating on the rules, expanding or narrowing their effects, or applying the rules to new situations. American courts, as the English courts before them, generally look to prior decisions on a legal issue for guidance on how to decide cases that raise a similar issue. By declaring legal rules and interpreting other sources of law such as the Constitution and statutes, courts provide guidance for those who seek to comply with the law and predict its requirements.

Did you know that...

the American Civil Liberties Union (ACLU) was founded in 1920 to protect the constitutional rights and liberties of people in the United States? The ACLU provides legal counsel in cases involving such civil liberties as freedom of speech, separation of church and state, due process of law, and the right to privacy. It also provides legal representation for people whose civil liberties have been violated.

Public Law and Private Law

U.S. law can be divided into two broad categories, **public law** and **private law**. Public law concerns the legal relationship between the government and citizens. It includes constitutional law, criminal law, regulations of administrative agencies such as the Internal Revenue Service and the Environmental Protection Agency, and the law governing court procedures. A violation of a person's civil rights, a theft or murder, and a case of illegal pollution are matters that involve public law.

Private law, often called civil law, regulates the relationships between private individuals and between individuals and nongovernmental entities, such as businesses and other organizations. Private law includes the law of contracts (agreements between people or between people and businesses), torts (wrongful acts that are not crimes but cause harm), and property. Matters such as the purchase of a home, a divorce, inheritance, and the formation of a corporation all involve private law.

▶ HOW LAWS ARE ENFORCED

Police, courts, and government agencies all play roles in enforcing the law. The role of the police is to investigate crimes and apprehend those suspected of committing crimes.

In the United States, each town, each county, and each state has its own police force. The federal government has several law enforcement agencies, including the Federal Bureau of Investigation and the Bureau of Alcohol, Tobacco, and Firearms. These various law enforcement agencies have to work together frequently. Sometimes they form task forces to coordinate their efforts to investigate particular types of crime.

The role of the courts is to provide a forum for weighing evidence of crimes and settling disputes fairly. The U.S. Constitution, as well as state and federal laws, sets out the minimum standards for fairness in court proceedings. These include the right of those accused of crimes or involved in disputes to be notified of the proceedings and to be heard by the court before a decision is made. The jury system is very important to the goal of fairness. Jurors are ordinary people who are chosen to hear and decide court cases. Their decisions are seen as fair because they are not associated with the government or with one side or the other in any case. Court pro-

ceedings are open to the public so that people can assess for themselves whether the processes are fair.

Government agencies may also help enforce the law. The Equal Employment Opportunity Commission (EEOC), for example, enforces the law prohibiting employment discrimination by seeking reinstatement or back pay for employees who can show that they have been denied a job or a promotion because of their race, sex, religion, veteran's status, age, or disability. Agencies may act through administrative sanctions or through lawsuits. Administrative sanctions are penalties imposed by an agency for violations of its rules. For example, the Internal Revenue Service may fine citizens who do not pay the taxes they owe.

A highway patrol officer tickets a truck driver for a traffic violation. To protect the community at large, the police must apprehend those who violate the law.

Enforcing Criminal Law

When a crime is committed, police and agents of law enforcement agencies such as the Federal Bureau of Investigation help uncover and collect the evidence. Then attorneys representing the government, called prosecutors or district attorneys, bring charges against the suspected lawbreaker in

A Glossary of Legal Terms

Act of God: A legal term for a natural event of overwhelming force, such as an earthquake or an accident that could not have been prevented by human action. Under the law of negligence, a person cannot be held responsible for damages or injuries caused by such an event.

Blue laws: Legislation that seeks to regulate matters of individual conscience or conduct, such as laws prohibiting drinking or working on Sunday. The term originated during colonial days in New Haven, Connecticut, where such laws were bound in blue paper.

Bylaws: Laws or rules by which a city, corporation, or other organization governs its affairs and members. In the case of a municipality, a bylaw has the force of law; in other private organizations, it is merely an agreement among members. The term also refers to a secondary rule subordinate to a constitution.

Capital punishment: The execution (killing) of a person found guilty of a serious crime. See the article CAPITAL PUNISHMENT in Volume C.

Class action: A type of lawsuit in which a few persons represent a large group of people with the same legal problem. Class actions are often brought in employment discrimination and consumer rights cases. The outcome of a class action affects all those in the group except those who opt out of the lawsuit.

Contempt of court: A term used in law courts to refer to an act that hinders or obstructs court proceedings or lessens the dignity or authority of the court. The term also refers to failure to comply with a court order. Persons charged with contempt may be imprisoned or fined.

Court martial: A military court responsible for trial of members of armed forces or those civilians who commit offenses against military or naval law in time of war or during military operations.

Double indemnity: Payment of twice the basic amount promised. Double indemnity clauses often appear in life insurance contracts, requiring that the beneficiary be paid double the amount of the policy if death of the insured is accidental.

Double jeopardy: Prosecution twice for the same criminal offense. "Jeopardy" begins when a jury is sworn in, or when evidence is first introduced. The United States Constitution prohibits double jeopardy. A second trial may be held, however, if the jury in the first trial could not reach a verdict or if the verdict is appealed on the grounds of procedural errors.

Due process: A term for legal proceedings that follow an established system of law. Due process is guaranteed by the U.S. Constitution. It ensures that a person accused of a crime will be treated fairly. Due process requires that an accused person understand the charges, be informed of his or her legal rights, and be given a fair trial. The concept of due process dates back to the English Magna Carta (1215), which stated that no person may be deprived of life, liberty, or property, except "by the lawful judgment of his peers and by the law of the land."

Estate: Property that a person owns, including personal possessions. For example, one may say, "He left an estate worth $500,000." An estate held by one person for another is called a trust.

Gentlemen's agreement: An agreement in which the parties involved are bound by honor and not by a legal contract. The term is applied to any such agreement between individuals, groups, or nations. It was used to describe an agreement between Japan and the United States in 1907. Japan agreed to restrict emigration of workers to the United States. In return President Theodore Roosevelt promised that no law would be passed to prevent Japanese from entering the United States.

A court officer swears in a witness. In trials, attorneys (foreground) question witnesses and present evidence. Jurors (at right) weigh evidence to determine guilt or innocence.

Habeas corpus: Latin for "you should have the body." A writ issued by a judge ordering an official to release a prisoner held in custody in violation of the law. It originated in early English law to prevent illegal imprisonment and is considered a cornerstone of civil liberty. According to the U.S. Constitution, the remedy of habeas corpus cannot be suspended unless, in cases of rebellion or invasion, public safety is at stake.

Injunction: A written court order either prohibiting a person or group from performing, or requiring them to perform, a certain act. Injunctions are often used in labor disputes and in instances of restraint of trade.

Inns of Court: The four legal societies that prepare students for the practice of law in England. Founded in London in the late 1200's and early 1300's, they are called Gray's Inn, the Inner Temple, Lincoln's Inn, and the Middle Temple.

Inquest: An inquiry made by a group of people appointed by a court. The term applies either to a jury that conducts a legal investigation of evidence or to the findings of such a jury. A coroner's inquest involves the investigation of the death of a person who may have died of unnatural causes.

Justice of the peace: An official of a town, county, or precinct, with limited judicial and administrative powers. The office may be elective or appointive. Powers and duties differ in different states. A justice of the peace may preside at the trials of small civil suits and crimes involving minor offenses. Among other duties, a justice of the peace may also perform marriage ceremonies. The office, which has existed in the United States since colonial times, began in the 1200's in England.

Kangaroo court: A court in which legal principles are ignored or perverted. The term usually refers to a prison court organized by the inmates to punish newcomers and those who do not conform to their rules or "code." The title is often applied to courts without legal standing set up in frontier territories. The phrase possibly originated in Australia, where kangaroos are found, when it was a British penal colony.

Limitations, Statute of: Law, originated (1623) under James I of England, limiting the period of time during which a person or group may bring claims to court, defend certain rights, or bring action against criminal offenders. It prevents prosecutors from delaying a trial until the evidence needed for defense has been destroyed or witnesses have died. In criminal cases, it supports the principle that the offender or suspect cannot be subject to prosecution forever.

Martial law: Rule by military forces. Martial law is usually declared by the head of a nation or state when danger, emergency, or panic creates a situation that cannot be handled by the local government. Martial law is usually temporary. But some nations have been ruled by martial law for long periods of time.

Miranda rights: Term from *Miranda* v. *Arizona* (1966), in which the U.S. Supreme Court ruled that statements made by suspects during questioning by police may not be used as evidence unless the suspects have been informed of their rights and warned that their statements may be used in court against them. These rights include the right to remain silent and to consult a lawyer.

Next of kin: The term for a person's nearest relative or relatives. It refers to those who may legally share in the estate of a person who died without making a will. The term usually applies only to people who are related by blood. But, in some areas, laws may also include a husband or wife.

Notary public: A public official authorized by a state government to certify official documents by signing them and stamping them with a notary public seal in order to give them credit and authenticity. Notary publics also administer oaths and take acknowledgements of documents.

Old Bailey: The common name for the Central Criminal Court in London, England. An older court that was the scene of many historic trials, it was described by Charles Dickens in *A Tale of Two Cities.* Newgate Prison, demolished in 1902–03, once stood opposite it. Old Bailey was so named because it was in a "bailey" (a space between the inner and outer walls) of early London.

Ombudsman: A public official appointed to receive, investigate, and channel complaints of citizens involving abuses of power by government officials. The ombudsman cannot order or reverse administrative action but can make recommendations for corrective measures. *Ombudsman* is a Swedish word meaning "representative."

Quorum: The number of members of an organization that must be present in order to conduct business legally. In England "quorum" originally referred to certain justices of the peace who were required to be present at court sessions.

Reprieve: From the French word *reprendre,* meaning "to take back." In criminal law, the postponement or suspension of the execution of a sentence. It is declared by a court or officials with pardoning power.

Search warrant: An order issued by a legal authority authorizing a particular officer to search a specific house or other premise for stolen property, unlawful goods, and occasionally persons. Usually the order requires that the goods or persons searched for and found be brought before the magistrate.

Sunset laws: Laws requiring periodic review of boards, commissions, and other agencies of government. These laws provide for automatic termination, or "sunset," of such agencies unless they are re-authorized. Many states of the United States have passed sunset laws in the hope of increasing efficiency in government.

Sunshine laws: Laws designed to keep government proceedings open to the public. These laws forbid or restrict closed sessions of many government boards and councils, except in specified situations.

court. The charges are reviewed by a judge or a grand jury to make sure they have some basis ("probable cause") for bringing the accused to trial. A judge decides whether the accused should be released pending trial or kept in jail. If the judge chooses to release the accused, an amount of money known as **bail** must be placed with the court as a guarantee that the accused will return at an appointed time to stand trial.

To help ensure fairness, defendants in criminal cases are protected by certain guarantees. For example, anyone accused of a serious crime, or felony (a crime carrying a penalty of over one year's imprisonment), has the right to a jury trial. Every person accused of a serious crime is also entitled to a lawyer to help present a defense against the charges. If the defendant (the accused person) cannot afford to pay a lawyer, the court will provide an attorney. People may represent themselves in court if they wish. But people without legal training are rarely skilled enough in the law to say and do the things that are needed to properly represent their own interests in court.

Only a small portion of criminal cases—10 percent or less—actually go to trial. Many criminal charges are dropped before trial or rejected by a judge or jury as unfounded. And most convictions are the result of guilty pleas before trial. Often the accused will plead guilty in exchange for a shorter sentence or the dismissal of another charge. This "plea bargaining" saves the government the cost of having to conduct a trial. It also allows prosecutors to handle more cases than they

could if each case went to trial before a judge or jury.

Criminal law is enforced through punishment, usually imprisonment and fines. Legislatures set limits on the penalties for each crime, and those limits are contained in the statutes defining the crime. While a jury may decide at trial whether or not a person committed the crime charged, it is usually the judge who decides what punishment to impose within the limits set by law.

Private Lawsuits

Laws other than criminal laws are enforced through private lawsuits. A person who claims that another has failed to obey the law may sue that person. The plaintiff (the person bringing the suit) asks the court for a judgment forcing the defendant (the person being sued) to comply or pay a sum of money. For example, a person who thinks another has failed to carry out a written agreement may sue for "breach of contract."

In lawsuits between private parties, the parties and their lawyers investigate the facts and present their sides of the story to the courts in written papers and at trial. The standard of proof required in private lawsuits is not as high as that required in criminal cases. Plaintiffs do not need to prove their claims "beyond a reasonable doubt," the standard in criminal trials. They only need to show that their claims are "probably true." However, most lawsuits are settled out of court. That is, the parties reach an agreement before the case goes to trial.

▶ CAREERS IN LAW

Lawyers help people understand the law and obtain the benefits and protections it provides. In the United States, lawyers (also called attorneys) are college-trained women and men who have completed law school and are licensed to practice law.

Legal Education

In law school, students learn how to analyze and present legal problems. They study the Constitution, treaties, statutes, and regulations of the United States, as well as state laws. Many students study the laws of other countries and international law. Law students also study court decisions and the ways that judges use them to decide new cases. As lawyers, they will be better able to predict how the courts will decide their cases, to advise their clients what actions to take, and to persuade judges why the law supports their clients' interests.

Basic courses cover criminal law, torts, contracts, and property law. Students also take courses in professional responsibility (the ethical standards required of lawyers), civil and criminal procedure (the rules that govern how laws are enforced), and special forms of law, such as tax law, copyright law, or family law. A huge variety of human activity is dis-

It takes hard work to succeed as a law student. Law school courses are demanding and call for excellent writing and research skills.

cussed in law school classes. Lawyers must learn how to study new subjects, spot problems, absorb information quickly, and present information clearly in writing and in speech.

After law school, a lawyer may decide to concentrate on a particular kind of law, such as criminal law, labor law, patent law, or tax law. Some of the special fields require additional training. Those who practice tax law, for example, usually have some training in mathematics and accounting.

Licensing

After students have completed formal law school training, they must secure a license to practice law. They must take and pass a difficult test, known as the bar examination. Usually lawyers must take a bar examination in each state in which they wish to practice, because each state has its own rules about training and licensing lawyers.

Applicants also must show that they are of good character. A committee appointed by the court or bar association investigates the background, training, employment, and past behavior of the applicant. Lawyers are bound by a code of ethics that requires them to maintain the highest standards of fidelity and honesty, and to devote themselves to the cause of their clients. The code requires that as well as being loyal to their clients, lawyers must be fair and honest with judges and other lawyers.

Ethical rules are enforced by the bar association and the courts of each state. Should a lawyer violate these ethical rules, the lawyer can be punished and may even lose his or her license to practice law.

Practicing Law

Much of a lawyer's work is carried on in an office, not in the courtroom. Lawyers advise clients about how to comply with the law, help clients resolve legal problems, and negotiate settlements in disputes. They help people set up and manage businesses and draw up wills and contracts.

When a dispute arises, lawyers may initiate a lawsuit, asking a court to decide whose position is right. For instance, a lawyer may help a person who has been injured by a product bring a lawsuit against the product's manufacturer. The process of preparing, developing, and resolving or trying these lawsuits is called **litigation**. It is usually much less costly to settle disputes out of court, before trial. The only disputes that end up in the courtroom are those that lawyers and clients cannot resolve in other ways.

In criminal cases, lawyers may be prosecutors or defense attorneys. Prosecutors present the evidence against the accused and argue for conviction. They work for the government. A defense attorney represents the defendant and tries to show why the defendant deserves to be released or acquitted, or to receive a less serious penalty. Public defenders are lawyers who are paid by the government to represent people who have been accused of crimes and cannot afford to hire a defense attorney.

Lawyers may work on their own or as members of a law firm. Law firms range in size from a few lawyers to hundreds. The largest firms have offices in several cities. Some lawyers work for only one business or client, as "house counsel," rather than for a

A lawyer explains the terms of a will to his client. The day-to-day work of many lawyers involves counseling individuals on legal issues pertaining to routine matters of life and death.

law firm representing many clients. Lawyers are involved in public interest litigation, too, working on cases involving welfare, education, the environment, or the rights of consumers. Some of these lawyers work for legal aid societies, unions, and other organizations that represent people who cannot afford to hire their own lawyers.

The broad and varied training lawyers receive helps many succeed in careers other than law. Lawyers often go into business or government. Some enter politics and run for public office. Of all the presidents of the United States, more than two-thirds were licensed to practice as lawyers. Lawyers also may become judges, either by election or political appointment.

▶ CAREERS IN LAW ENFORCEMENT

Police officers are government employees whose job is to protect their community from crime and enforce the

Alerted by a broken window, a police officer checks out the scene of a possible break-in. Police work is often dangerous.

law. Police officers investigate crimes, apprehend people suspected of crimes, collect evidence needed to prove crimes, and often testify in court about these activities. Police also work to prevent crime. They help control crowds and protect dignitaries, and they visit schools and other organizations to help teach others about safety and crime prevention. Police officers may specialize in a certain type of police work; for example, canine experts work with police dogs, and arson investigators become experts on fires. The term "police" usually refers to municipal law enforcement agencies. Agencies that perform similar duties include state highway patrols, public safety agencies, and county sheriffs' offices.

A variety of other careers are vital to fair and efficient law enforcement. Counselors and advocates help victims of crime and witnesses to crime. Scientists and other experts analyze evidence such as blood, fibers, drugs, and firearms. Government employees maintain arrest records, fingerprint records, even DNA profiles of offenders. Each court is staffed by administrators, secretaries, clerks, bailiffs, and security officers.

Probation officers prepare sentencing recommendations and monitor offenders who are released on probation—that is, on conditions such as maintaining employment or submitting to drug tests. Prisons employ guards, wardens, doctors, psychiatrists, and ministers. Parole boards in many states decide whether prisoners may be released from prison before the end of their sentences. Parole officers are similar to probation officers, keeping track of those who are released from prison and working with them to make sure they meet the conditions of release.

NANCY JEAN KING
Vanderbilt University
School of Law

See also CIVIL RIGHTS; COURTS; CRIME AND CRIMINOLOGY; FEDERAL BUREAU OF INVESTIGATION; JURY; JUVENILE CRIME; MUNICIPAL GOVERNMENT; ORGANIZED CRIME; POLICE; PRISONS; STATE GOVERNMENTS; VIOLENCE AND SOCIETY.

LAWRENCE, T. E. ("LAWRENCE OF ARABIA"). See WORLD WAR I (Profiles: Allied Powers).

LEAD

Lead is a soft, bluish gray metal. It is heavy, easily melted, and rustproof, and it forms many useful alloys and compounds.

People have used lead for several thousand years. The ancient Egyptians used it for making ornaments. Greeks, Romans, and Chinese used it in their coins. Women in ancient India used red lead as a cosmetic. The hanging gardens of Babylon were floored with sheets of lead to help hold moisture for the plants. Long before bullets were invented, lead was being used in warfare. Chunks of lead were hurled from slings at the enemy, and molten lead was poured down from forts onto attacking troops.

▶ USES OF LEAD

The most important use of lead today is in electric storage batteries that provide and store electricity needed to start automobiles, trucks, buses, and other vehicles. Much larger storage batteries are used for emergency power sources in hospitals, telephone exchanges, and industrial plants.

Because lead is easy to shape and resists corrosion (being eaten away), it is useful for such things as drainpipes and coverings for power and telephone cables. The Romans used large amounts of lead for water pipes. Some of this ancient pipe is in almost perfect condition. Our words "plumber" and "plumbing" come from the Latin name for lead, *plumbum.*

Lead melts at a lower temperature than most other metals. Solder, an easily melted mixture of lead and tin, is used to fasten metal parts together. Lead is also useful in making ammunition because it is dense and heavy. A lead bullet will fly straight and true through the air, while a bullet made of lighter metal might waver off course.

The heaviness of lead is useful in many ways. Lead weights are used to balance airplane propellers and automobile wheels and to help fishing tackle sink. In fact, lead is so dense that it can block dangerous rays from X-ray machines or from nuclear equipment. When standing behind a lead shield, a worker is safe from radiation. Lead-lined aprons are used to shield X-ray workers.

Combinations of lead and other materials are quite useful. Calcium has been alloyed with lead for use in maintenance-free batteries and in roofing. Lead alloys are used for making bearings and type for printing. Lead sheet can be attached to plywood, plasterboard, or plastic to make building materials that control noise and vibration. Lead and arsenic are combined to form an insect-killing material. Litharge, a compound of lead and oxygen, is used for making storage batteries, glass, and glaze on china. Tetraethyl lead—a compound of lead, carbon, and hydrogen—is well known as an antiknock ingredient of gasoline. When automobiles burn leaded gasoline, however, poisonous lead-containing particles are released into the air. The United States government now requires petroleum companies to make "lead-free" gasoline, and many auto-

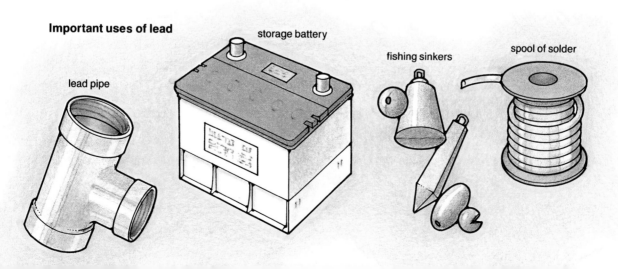

Important uses of lead

lead pipe

storage battery

fishing sinkers

spool of solder

mobiles are designed to use only this type of fuel.

The paint industry uses large quantities of lead compounds. Red lead, a compound of lead and oxygen, plays an important role in paint that is used to protect steel structures, such as bridges, from rusting.

▶ LEAD HAZARDS

It is now known that lead compounds are toxic to humans and other living things. In many homes built before 1980, the paint used on walls, ceilings, and trim is likely to contain lead. If children eat pieces of this paint or inhale lead-contaminated dust from peeling or cracking paint, they risk developing lead poisoning. Adults as well as children can also be exposed to lead in drinking water, soil, some types of ceramic dishes and cookware, and some canned foods. People who work in industries that use lead or that refine lead ores should also be concerned. In addition, the waste disposal from these plants can damage the environment.

The symptoms of lead poisoning include headaches, loss of appetite, stomachaches, and short-term loss of memory. Even if there are no physical symptoms, lead poisoning can interfere with the growth of a child's brain. For that reason, children from ages 1 to 6 should have their blood tested for lead every year.

In response to these health hazards, the law in many countries now requires that paints produced for use in homes contain no lead. In addition, most gasoline used today is unleaded. Also, there is a greater awareness of the risk of exposure to lead in homes and in the workplace. Older homes, apartments, and offices are often tested to determine the amount of lead in existing paint on walls, in drinking water, and in the plumbing, particularly the pipes used to carry drinking water. In industrial plants, waste disposal is monitored more closely.

▶ SOURCES OF LEAD

Lead is usually found in combination with other metals, especially with silver and zinc. The chief source of lead is the mineral called galena, a compound of lead and sulfur. Two other lead minerals, cerrusite and anglesite, are also found in nature.

Most of the world's lead is mined in China, Australia, the United States, Peru, Canada, Mexico, and Sweden. But lead ores are distributed around the world.

Because lead is almost indestructible, much of it can be used more than once. Old storage batteries, pipes, sheets, cable coverings, and solder are melted down, and the lead is reused in new products.

▶ PROCESSING THE ORE

Most ores are not rich enough in lead to be sent directly to a smelter. Usually waste rock and other materials must first be removed. Removing waste materials from lead ore is called concentrating the ore. The ore is crushed into small particles and mixed with water and oily chemicals. Blasts of air are blown through the mixture. The concentrate floats to the surface in a froth that is skimmed off. The waste materials sink to the bottom. With this flotation process, ores that contain even small amounts of lead can be mined economically.

After waste materials are removed, the concentrate is heated in air (roasted) to remove most of the sulfur. Then it is smelted in blast furnaces to produce lead metal and refined to obtain the desired purity. Commercial grades of lead are from 99.85 to 99.99 percent lead. Lead of even higher purity—99.9999 percent—is available for specialized uses.

ANDREW H. LARSON
Gould, Inc.

See also ALLOYS; METALS AND METALLURGY.

LEAGUE OF NATIONS

At the end of World War I (1914–18), most of the world's leaders saw the need for an international organization to promote peace. The idea for such an organization was conceived by U.S. president Woodrow Wilson, who outlined his plan in an address to Congress on January 8, 1918, in a famous speech known as the Fourteen Points. The last of these points put forth an idea of a League of Nations that would guarantee "political independence and territorial integrity to great and small countries alike."

The potential success of the League of Nations depended on a policy known as "collective security." Under this rule, if one nation were to attack another, it would be the duty of all other nations to come to the aid of the victim and stop the aggressor.

President Wilson went to Versailles, France, in 1918 to work toward establishing a League of Nations with America's wartime allies—Great Britain, France, Italy, and Japan. The leaders of these nations agreed with Wilson that the world had to be made, in Wilson's words, "safe for democracy" and that a League of Nations should be established to keep the peace.

President Wilson then returned to the United States only to face a bitter disappointment. The U.S. Senate refused to go along with his idea, since many Americans wanted to turn away from world affairs and not engage further in the disputes or wars between other countries. President Wilson warned the Senate, however, that any future war would hurt the United States and involve Americans whether they liked it or not. Therefore the United States should be prepared to help prevent such a war from occurring. Nevertheless, the Senate rejected Wilson's plan, and on January 10, 1920, the League of Nations was born, but without the crucial participation of the United States.

Organization. The League of Nations made the Palace of Nations in Geneva, Switzerland, its headquarters. The three main bodies of the League were the assembly, council, and secretariat. The League's organization also included the Permanent Court of International Justice, the Permanent Mandates Commission, the International Labor Organization, and sections concerned with health, communications, child welfare, and lowering barriers to international trade. In many ways, the organization of the League anticipated that adopted by the United Nations following World War II (1939–45).

The League in Action. The most successful years for the League of Nations were from 1920 to 1930, when it dealt successfully with disputes between Greece and Italy, Great Britain and Turkey, Greece and Bulgaria, and others. But the history of the League's later years was an unhappy one.

In 1931 the League was unable to stop the Japanese from attacking Chinese territory in Manchuria. Japan withdrew from the League in 1933, but no attempt was made to force Japan to return conquered territory. Then, in 1935, Benito Mussolini, the Fascist dictator of Italy, invaded Ethiopia. The member states of the League made a half-hearted attempt to help Ethiopia by stopping the shipment of oil and other vital war materials to Italy. But the effort failed, and Italy withdrew from the League in 1937.

In the following years, the League was also unable to stop the German leader Adolf Hitler from invading Austria and annexing portions of Czechoslovakia. Germany had gained membership to the League in 1926 but had withdrawn in 1933. Furthermore, in 1939, the League expelled the Soviet Union, a member since 1934, for attacking Finland. But by that time, World War II had already begun.

It is true that the League was not able to stop the aggressive actions of Japan, Italy, Germany, and the Soviet Union. But it must be remembered that the League was the first attempt by most of the nations of the world to join in an effort to preserve the peace. This first effort failed. But it served as an inspiration for a second try.

The League of Nations stayed in operation until 1946, when its functions were taken over by the United Nations, a much stronger and more vital organization that the United States joined from the very beginning. The United Nations has lasted and has steadily grown in strength and stature.

JOHN G. STOESSINGER
Author, *The Might of Nations:
World Politics in Our Time*

See also UNITED NATIONS; WILSON, WOODROW (Struggle for the League).

LEAKEY FAMILY

The Leakey family includes four distinguished anthropologists (scientists who study human beings and their culture). Over the years, Louis, Mary, Richard, and Meave Leakey made important contributions to the study of human evolution. Through their discoveries, the Leakeys were able to prove that humankind was far older than had previously been believed.

Louis Seymour Bazett Leakey (1903–72) was born in Kabete, Kenya. His parents were British missionaries to the Kikuyu tribe of Kenya. Growing up among the Kikuyu, Louis became interested in studying prehistoric cultures. He started by collecting prehistoric stone tools from fields near the mission. In England, he continued to follow his interests as he studied archaeology (the study of the remains of people and their culture) and anthropology at Cambridge University.

Louis and Mary Leakey compare the fossils of an early humanlike species they discovered with that of a modern human.

In 1926, Leakey led his first expedition to investigate Stone Age cultures in eastern Africa. In 1932, he began research at Olduvai Gorge in Tanzania, where he hoped to find evidence of prehistoric human life. Little did he know when he began his search that the Olduvai Gorge was to become the site of the family's most famous discoveries.

Mary Douglas Nicol (1913–96) married Louis Leakey in 1936. Born in London, England, she was a talented artist who studied archaeology at London University and made detailed drawings of archaeological finds.

Although the first finds at Olduvai Gorge were animal fossils and crude tools, the hard work paid off. Starting in the late 1940's, the Leakeys were credited with many significant discoveries. In 1948, Mary unearthed the skull of *Proconsul africanus*—a creature that lived in eastern Africa nearly 20 million years ago. Some scientists think that *Proconsul africanus* may be close to the common ancestor of human beings and apes.

In 1959, the skull of *Australopithecus boisei*, a humanlike species that lived more than 1.7 million years ago, was found. The next year, the Leakeys found fossils about 1.8 to 1.9 million years old. Louis considered them the remains of the earliest known human ancestor to use tools. He called his find *Homo habilis*, which means "handy man." In 1962, the Leakeys discovered a skull of *Homo erectus*, another early human ancestor that lived about 1.6 million years ago.

The Leakeys' findings shook the scientific world. Until the time of the Leakeys' research, most anthropologists searched for the fossil evidence of human origins in Java (now part of Indonesia) and China. However, the Leakeys' research clearly identified Africa as the center of human evolution.

Human culture was not the only interest of Louis Leakey. He was also a great lover of animals, both wild and domestic, and was a pioneer in the study of apes and monkeys. It was with his encouragement that such well-known scientists as Jane Goodall and Dian Fossey began studying chimpanzees and gorillas. Leakey also wrote several books, including *Olduvai Gorge, 1951–1961* (1961) and a two-volume autobiography, *White African* (1937) and *By the Evidence* (1974). After he died in 1972, the Louis Leakey Memorial Institute for African Prehistory was founded in Kenya in his honor.

Mary Leakey continued to do research. In 1978, she led the team that found footprints of a humanlike creature preserved in volcanic ash in Laetoli, Tanzania. Made 3.6 million years ago, they are among the oldest known fossils of a human ancestor. Mary Leakey's writings include *Africa's Vanishing Art: The Rock Paintings of Tanzania* (1983) and *Disclosing the Past* (1984), an autobiography.

Richard Erskine Frere Leakey (1944–   ) was born in Nairobi, Kenya. He was raised in Africa and often worked alongside his parents. At first reluctant to follow in their footsteps, Leakey instead led safaris and collected wild animals for study. However, in 1963, after finding the jawbone of an extinct near-human species while exploring in Tanzania, he decided to become an anthropologist after all.

Leakey became director of the National Museums of Kenya in 1968 and continued the search for evidence of early humans in Africa. In 1972, along the shore of Lake Turkana in Kenya, he discovered part of a skull of an early human who lived about 2.6 million years ago. Leakey believed this skull to be the oldest known fossil of *Homo habilis*. In 1984, Leakey and his British co-worker Alan Walker unearthed an almost complete skeleton of a *Homo erectus* teenager. Dubbed "Turkana Boy," its age matches that of the original *Homo erectus* skull found earlier by the Leakeys—about 1.6 million years old.

Noted fossil hunter Richard Leakey (*above*) has also actively supported wildlife conservation. Here, he oversees the burning of tusks seized from poachers who had hunted protected elephants in Kenya.

Meave Leakey (*left*) led a team in 1994 that discovered the first fossils of the oldest known human ancestor to walk upright. Here, she examines the skeleton foot of another primate species.

A noted lecturer and author, Leakey wrote many works, including *The Making of Mankind* (1981) and an autobiography, *One Life* (1983). Throughout his career, he actively supported wildlife conservation. From 1989 to 1994, Leakey headed the Kenya Wildlife Service.

In 1993, Leakey lost both legs below the knee after a near-fatal plane crash. Since then, he has learned to walk again using artificial legs. In 1995, Leakey entered politics, founding an opposition party to Kenya's ruling party in government.

Meave Gillian Epps (1942–   ) married Richard Leakey in 1970. Born in London, England, she studied zoology at the University of North Wales. In 1965, she took up a position at Louis Leakey's primate research center near Nairobi. Four years later, she was invited by Richard Leakey to join his field expedition at Lake Turkana, where she has continued the work of the Leakey family. From 1982 to 2001, she was head of paleontology at the National Museums of Kenya.

In 1994 near Lake Turkana, Meave Leakey and her co-workers discovered the first fossils of *Australopithecus anamensis*, the earliest known human ancestor able to walk upright. Tests on soil samples later confirmed that the fossils were about 4.1 million years old.

Louise N. Leakey (1972–   ) is the daughter of Meave and Richard Leakey. She was born in Kenya and spent much of her youth on field expeditions with her parents. This led her to pursue studies in paleontology at University College London. In 1999, she and her mother and co-workers discovered the skull of an early human that lived about 3.5 million years ago. Features of the skull suggest it belongs to a new branch of human ancestors, *Kenyanthropus platyops*.

KARYN L. BERTSCHI
Science Writer

See also EVOLUTION; FOSSILS; PREHISTORIC PEOPLE.

LEARNING

You begin to learn from the moment you are born. You cry and get a hug or some milk. You learn that crying brings attention and food. This is one of your first lessons.

Day by day, you learn more and more. You learn to crawl, walk, and run. Soon you learn to talk. By the time you are 3 years old, you know about 900 words.

By the end of third grade, you will probably know more than 14,000 words. You will be able to read books and add and subtract large numbers. Some of you will play the piano; some of you will play baseball. Some of you will begin to learn how to play chess; some of you will begin to study ballet.

How can you learn so much? Understanding how the human mind works and how young people learn is of special interest to many scientists and psychologists. These experts have explored many aspects of learning. There are scientists who study the best ways to motivate young students to learn. Other scientists concentrate on how we think about complicated ideas. Still others study how the brain learns new subjects. Some scientists and teachers explore ways to make learning easier. Because of the work of these people, we know a great deal about the human mind.

This article discusses the most important aspects of learning. While reading it you will also find suggestions that will help you become a better learner.

▶LEARNING BY REWARDS

Ivan Pavlov (1849–1936), a Russian physiologist (someone who studies how the systems in living things function), was one of the first modern scientists to study behavior and learning. During an experiment on the digestive system, Pavlov noticed that the mouths of the dogs used in the study would fill with saliva when they ate. This was their natural response to food.

Pavlov wondered if he could teach the dogs to salivate at other times. He started to ring a bell right before giving the dogs food. Soon they began to salivate whenever they heard the bell ring. After a while Pavlov stopped bringing food to the dogs. Even so, they salivated when they heard the bell. This was not an instinctive response to the bell ringing. This was a learned response. Pavlov had taught the dogs to salivate whenever they heard a bell ring. The dogs kept the behavior because they learned to associate food with a ringing bell.

After Pavlov, many scientists began to do learning experiments with animals. They discovered that you can teach rats to go through a maze; you can teach pigeons to turn lights on and off; and you can teach cats to escape from cages if you reward the animals with food or a pat on the head. Scientists call these rewards positive reinforcements. Scientists also discovered that you can teach animals not to do things by punishing them. Scientists call such punishments negative reinforcements.

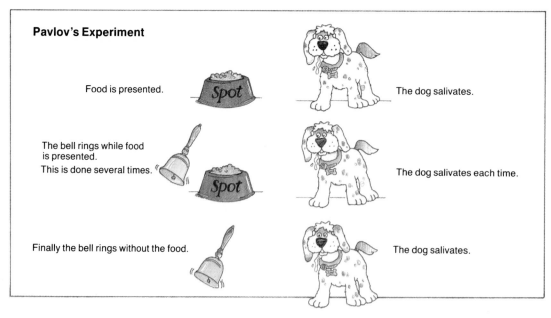

Pavlov's Experiment

Food is presented. — The dog salivates.

The bell rings while food is presented. This is done several times. — The dog salivates each time.

Finally the bell rings without the food. — The dog salivates.

B. F. Skinner (1904–90), an American psychologist (someone who studies human and animal behavior), believed that both positive and negative reinforcement can motivate learning, but that positive reinforcement works much better. He encouraged teachers to use praise or rewards and to avoid using criticism or punishment to achieve successful learning behaviors in students.

For example, when a teacher gives a student a list of ten addition problems to memorize, how can the teacher be sure that the student will learn the math facts? Using Skinner's ideas, the teacher promises a reward if the student answers correctly. If the student cannot answer correctly, the teacher does not get angry or punish the student, nor does the student receive the reward. The teacher sets a new goal and gives the student a second chance to succeed and get a reward.

▶ LEARNING IMPORTANT CONCEPTS

Imagine that you are attending a country carnival. Along comes a man who claims his horse can do math. He calls out a problem: 5 + 4. The horse pounds its hoof on the dirt nine times. Amazing! How did the horse do it? The man trained the horse to pound its hoof nine times whenever it heard the words "five plus four." He trained the horse with treats.

Does the horse understand what it is doing? Does it understand the idea of adding? Does it understand numbers? Of course not. Instead, the horse understands getting a treat. If you give the horse a new problem, a problem the owner did not train it to answer, the horse will not respond because it does not understand mathematical ideas. You do, however. Because you understand important number concepts, you can solve math problems you have never seen before.

Try this: 82,897 + 1. Most likely, you have never solved this problem before, but you can probably give the answer. How do you do this? You know what it means to add. By adding 1 to any number, you end up with the very next counting number. You may have never counted as high as 82,897. Still, because you understand how counting numbers works, you know the next number is going to be 82,898.

If you had to learn every math problem individually, you could never get very far in math. Instead you learn basic concepts and

these concepts allow you to solve any math problem—even if you have never seen it before. Learning concepts is different than memorizing the right answer, the way a carnival horse does.

Getting Ready to Learn

Jean Piaget (1896–1980), a Swiss psychologist, investigated the ways in which young people learn important concepts. As a result of his work, he determined that very young children cannot understand complex ideas until they are about 5 or 6 years old.

To investigate this idea, Piaget devised a series of tests to show whether or not a child is ready to learn complicated concepts. Here is one of the tests. An adult puts two even rows of five blocks each on a table. The adult asks a child if the rows have the same number of blocks. When the blocks are in even rows, the child sees that each row has the same number of blocks.

Then the adult spreads out the blocks in one of the rows.

A young child believes that the longer row has more blocks. An older child, however, knows that the two rows still have the same amount. The older child understands that moving the blocks does not change the amount of blocks on the table.

Why are young children confused about the number of blocks in this test? Piaget believed that they lacked the ability to think logically about them and that until they could think logically, they could not learn many mathematical concepts. Piaget also believed that children develop logical thinking on their own and that adults could not help children learn how to think in logical steps.

Discovery Learning

Jerome Bruner (1915–), an American psychologist, agreed with some of Piaget's ideas and not others. For example, unlike Piaget, he believed that adults can teach children conceptual ideas. He also proposed that young learners should not be asked to memorize important ideas. Instead, their lessons should be designed to help them discover important ideas on their own. Bruner's teaching technique is sometimes called the discovery approach to learning.

Exploring Ideas

According to both Piaget and Bruner, it is very important for young people to explore ideas in real-life situations. To learn about numbers, for instance, it is best to use beans, fingers, counters, and other real objects to make the mathematical ideas come alive. Imagine a youngster learning to count to five. The child says the words "one, two, three, four, five." The words do not explain much about the concept of five, however. To understand the concept, the child should count five cups, five beans, five fingers, or five blocks. After counting these objects, the child will understand more about five than the words alone could ever teach.

Patterns

The ability to discover patterns is another important tool. Look at these math problems:

$$1 \times 1 = 1$$
$$11 \times 11 = 121$$
$$111 \times 111 = 12321$$
$$1{,}111 \times 1{,}111 = 1234321$$

Now, look at this problem:

$$11{,}111 \times 11{,}111 = ?$$

If you study the pattern carefully, you can solve this problem without paper, pencil, or a calculator. The answer is: 123454321.

Logic

Logic is another tool. If you think logically, you can solve this problem:

There were three sisters. Betty is older than Susan and younger than Mary. Can you name the oldest sister?

Logic tells you that Betty is the middle child. She is younger than Mary. That means Mary is older. Since Betty is older than Susan, Mary must be the oldest child.

Logic helps you learn. Logic can help you understand patterns. Logic can help you organize information.

▶THE BRAIN

Remember the scarecrow in *The Wonderful Wizard of Oz*? Poor scarecrow, he did not have a brain. Without it he could not learn.

You do have a brain. Your brain is amazing. It controls your heartbeat. It controls your breathing. It controls your thinking and learning. It controls your memory so you can remember the things you learn.

When you learn, how does your brain work? Think of it as a machine with different connecting parts. Each part has a job.

Your brain's work begins when it gathers the information you want to learn. It does this through your five senses. Most often, you see or hear the information you want to learn. Scientists call this part of the brain the **sensory registers**.

The brain does not pay attention to all the information you see or hear. Instead, it focuses on the special information you want to learn. This information moves to the next part of the brain machine—the **working memory**. Working memory is the only place in the brain where you actually think about information. As long as you do think about the information, it stays in your working memory. When you stop thinking about the information, it leaves your working memory.

There are two things that can happen to information after it leaves your working memory. Either the information is forgotten altogether or it moves to your **long-term memory**. You do not think about the information in your long-term memory, but it can return to your working memory when you need it.

Imagine that you need to telephone a friend, but you do not know the phone number. Now your brain goes to work to help you learn the phone number.

First you open the phone book. Your brain's sensory registers see lots of numbers but only pay attention to your friend's number. Your brain moves this information into working memory. As long as you keep thinking about the phone number—repeating it over and over—it stays in working memory.

After dialing, you will probably forget the number. If you call your friend often, however, the number may then move into your long-term memory. When it is in long-term memory, you will not need to look it up again in the phone book. Instead, you simply pull the number from your long-term memory, move it into your working memory, and dial.

How the Brain Processes Information

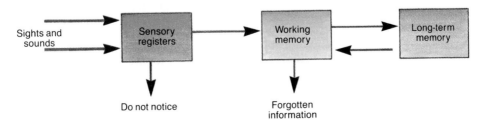

Working memory

You can only think about a fact, a word, or an idea when it is in working memory. But working memory can only hold about seven pieces of information at a time. In order for more information to enter working memory, some other information must leave.

Working memory holds information for about twenty seconds. This means that twenty seconds after you first see your friend's phone number in the phone book, the number leaves working memory. But if you want to keep the number in working memory, you can do it for as long as you want. You do this by continually thinking about the information. Of course, thinking about the number uses a portion of your working memory. Since working memory holds so little data, you will probably let that phone number leave working memory as soon as you dial.

Increasing Working Memory. You can increase the amount of information you can hold in your working memory. Let us say your friend's phone number is 845-3234. Like all phone numbers, it has seven digits. If you think of the number digit by digit—8 4 5 3 2 3 4—it takes up all of your working memory. If you group the numbers together like this, 845 32 34, you use only a portion of your working memory. You still have some working memory available.

Long-term Memory

Think about your last birthday. Did you have a party? Did you have a cake? Did you get presents? To think about this, you reach into your long-term memory and pull out thoughts of your birthday. Then you send these thoughts to your working memory. Twenty seconds after you stop thinking about the birthday, all thoughts about it will leave your working memory. You can always bring the birthday to mind, however. You pull the right thoughts out of long-term memory and your birthday will be on your mind again.

In addition to last year's birthday, long-term memory contains all your other memories, all the information you know, everything you have learned in school, everything you have learned out of school, all the words to all the songs you can sing, and more. You store everything you know in this part of your brain. There is no limit to the amount of information it can store.

USE WHAT YOU READ

Memory

Here is a game that can help increase the strength of your working memory. You will need at least two players for this game as well as seven small objects. You might use a paper clip, a penny, a pencil, a pair of scissors, a rubber band, a comb, and a piece of paper. Your opponent picks five of the objects and displays them on a table. You study them for as long as you want, then close your eyes. After you close your eyes, your partner removes one item from the table. You then open your eyes. Now, study the table. Can you name the missing object? If you can, you get a point.

Next, you and your opponent switch roles. You select five objects. Your opponent studies the table and then closes his or her eyes. You remove something from the table. Your opponent tries to name the missing item. Each remembered item is worth a point. The first player to get five points wins the game.

The next time you play the game, start with more objects on the table. See if you can work up to eight or nine different items.

Look at this table:

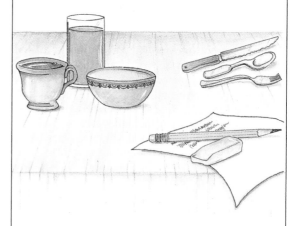

How can you remember so many objects? You can, if you combine the objects in meaningful groups like this:

cup	bowl	glass
paper	pencil	eraser
spoon	fork	knife

Now you have three groups to remember instead of nine objects.

Long-term Memory Problems. If all the information you have ever learned is waiting in long-term memory, why do you sometimes forget what 6×7 equals? Why is it so hard to remember certain spelling words?

All of these facts are in your long-term memory. You cannot, however, always get to the facts and bring them into working memory when you want them.

Imagine this school scene: Your teacher asks you a question. You know the answer, but you cannot remember it. You try hard. You want to answer, but you cannot. Later in the day, while walking home or riding your bike, the answer pops into your mind. How annoying! You could not think of the answer when you needed it. Now, hours later, you suddenly remember it.

There are other problems with long-term memory, too. Some scientists think that facts may decay in long-term memory. If the decay is too great, you cannot recall these facts easily or perhaps at all.

Occasionally information gets mixed up in long-term memory. Suppose your grandmother's phone number is 567-0987 and your friend's number is 576-0897. Because the two are so similar, you may confuse them.

Long-term Memory Storage. The way you store thoughts in long-term memory makes a difference in how easy the facts are to remember. If something is special, like a birthday, you are more likely to remember it.

Sometimes one memory leads to another. You may remember the pizza pies at your birthday party because one of them fell on the floor. What a mess! The pizza makes you think about the cake. The cake helps you remember the ice cream.

You may have a harder time remembering unconnected information. Who gave you that box of colored pencils? Was it Aunt Mary or Uncle Max?

Memories that have some order to them are easier to recall. Stray bits of information are harder to remember.

How Long-term Memory Works Best. If you think a lot about information while it is in working memory, you are more likely to have access to it in long-term memory. If you practice the multiplication facts often or study your social studies notes frequently, you are more likely to remember the information when you need it.

The more you know about a topic, the more likely you will be to remember new information about a subject. Let us say you are a baseball fan. You watch all the games you can. You follow the teams and the players. You go out to the stadium to see a game. The announcer gives the lineup of starting players. A while later, someone asks you who is playing today. This question is easy for you to answer. You can list all the names and even give the batting order.

Imagine that your cousin, who is not a baseball fan, goes to the game with you. Your cousin does not know much about the teams or the players and will not remember the lineup the way you do—even though you both heard the announcement of the starting lineup at the same time.

Do you have a better memory than your cousin? For baseball information you do. That is because you already know so much about the game. The more you know about a subject, the easier it is to learn and remember new information.

Relating the New and the Old. Your cousin may not know much about baseball but may be an expert on soccer. You begin to explain the rules of baseball and the importance of the different positions. Your cousin can remember all this new information more easily if it is

---

USE WHAT YOU READ

Use Your Brain!

Understanding how your brain works can help you be a better learner. Suppose your class is getting ready for a big social studies test. Everyone has a study sheet from the teacher and a chapter to read in a social studies textbook.

You might find it tempting to study the sheet without reading the chapter. You might think that this is a timesaving way to study. But if you remember how your brain works, you will change your mind. It is easier to remember new information when you already know a lot about the subject. Therefore, read the chapter first. Your study time will be more efficiently spent, and it will probably take you less time to learn the new material.

related to soccer—a game he or she already knows a lot about. When you link new facts to already known information—even if the subject matter is a little different—the new facts become easier to learn and to remember.

Helping Long-term Memory. Sometimes you study hard but still find it difficult to remember important facts. For example, you may know a lot about the American Revolution, but you forget what year the Declaration of Independence was signed. How can you help yourself remember 1776? You can use a memory aid.

Think of something that makes these numbers special so that they stick out in your mind. You might notice that there are double 7's in the middle of the date and the number 1 is at the beginning. Now note that $7 - 1 = 6$, and that gives you all the numbers. You may now find it much easier to remember the date 1776.

WONDER QUESTION

How does sleep affect learning?

The amount of sleep we get determines how much we are able to learn. Scientists think that sleep gives the brain a chance to form new connections among nerve cells. These connections help boost memory, concentration, creativity, and learning.

Therefore, not getting enough sleep makes it harder to learn. Some studies have shown that sleep-deprived students do not perform as well on tests that measure learning. Other studies have shown that students who do not sleep enough also get lower grades.

So how much sleep do you need? It depends on your age. Since the 1980's, researchers have found that adolescents need more sleep than was once thought—even more than younger children or adults. Beginning about age 10 or 11, most children need $9\frac{1}{2}$ hours per night. This requirement continues throughout puberty, until one reaches adulthood. Then the amount of sleep needed drops to $7\frac{1}{2}$ to 8 hours per night.

You can also tell how much sleep you need simply by how you feel during the day. Are you tired? Do you doze off in class or in front of the television? If so, consider an earlier bedtime. If you do this, you might also find it takes less time to get things done—including homework!

Some people find it easier to remember information when they turn it into a rhyme: "1776 and King George was in a fix."

Other people prefer visual aids. They will make a picture out of 1776 so they never forget the numbers.

Using Mnemonics. The use of memory aids such as pictures or rhymes is called **mnemonics.** Mnemonics are most helpful for remembering single facts that are important to learn but hard to keep in mind.

Suppose you have a long list of vocabulary words to study. There is one word on the list that you cannot remember. What can you do? Think of a way to make the word special. Let us say the troublesome word is "hover." The dictionary defines "hover" this way: to hang or suspend in air. You might notice that "hover" has the word "over" inside it. That helps. "Hover" means to "hang over."

As an alternative, you might draw a picture that shows the meaning of the word. Whichever method you choose, the word "hover" will be easier to remember.

Do you sometimes forget that $7 \times 8 = 56$? Use a memory trick to help yourself remember. Count: five, six, seven, eight. These counting numbers contain the math fact: Five, six—that is 56; seven, eight—that is 7×8. Now you have it. It is as easy as five, six, seven, eight.

You can make up memory aids such as these for almost any fact you must remember.

▶ ACTIVE LEARNERS

The most successful learners are active learners. Imagine that you are learning about colonial America. Your teacher tells you about the colonists. You learn how they lived. You learn how they spent their days. You find out a lot of information.

Active learners do more than just listen to all the facts. They think about the new information. First, they organize the information and look for patterns. They think about everyday life and divide the information into logical groups: houses, clothes, food, what children do, what adults do, and so forth. They do this without instructions from the teacher.

Active learners question information. They wonder why colonial children worked on farms instead of going to school. They wonder how the colonists got new clothes. They even question themselves. They wonder if they really understand how the farmers worked. They question themselves along with questioning the information.

Active learners compare the new information they learn by using information they already know. They compare the colonists' lives with their own lives. They compare the colonists' homes with their homes, and compare their work with the work people do today. They try to make the past real by comparing it to the present.

Active learners reflect. They think about information. They think before they answer questions. They may work more slowly, but they usually get good results.

The opposite of active learners are passive learners. Passive learners try to memorize the teacher's exact words. They do not organize facts or connect new information to facts they already know. Because of this, it is harder for passive learners to understand and remember information.

Metacognition

Active learners have many good strategies for learning. Many people develop and use

---

USE WHAT YOU READ

A Plan for Studying

There are many possible study plans. Here is one you may find useful whenever you have a lot of material to learn.

1. Pick a special time and quiet place for studying.
2. Scan the material first. Get a good idea of the job ahead. Read the headings; look at the pictures; look at the charts.
3. Ask yourself questions about the pages before you read. Let us say you are studying a chapter about farming in colonial America. You might wonder what crops the farmers planted. You might wonder how the farmers stored food after the harvest. You might wonder if the men, women, and children all worked together in the fields.
4. Read carefully. Study the learning aids in the text. Try to find patterns and to understand the ideas and concepts you are reading about. Try to connect new information to what you already know about the subject.
5. Think about the material. Reflect on the information and the ideas. Did you find answers to any of your questions?
6. Stop occasionally while reading to think about the ideas you are learning. Repeat some of the most important information to yourself in your own words.
7. Go back and review the pages. Review right away. Then review again before your next class or your next test.

You can call this the **SQ4R Method** because you **S**can, **Q**uestion, **R**ead, **R**eflect, **R**estate, **R**eview the Material.

---

these strategies without any help. Most people, however, need to learn how to learn. They need to learn how to study effectively. That is where **metacognition** comes in. Metacognition is a long word that describes a simple idea. It means thinking about learning. Metacognitive skills are the tools a good learner uses when he or she studies. You use these skills when you organize information, question facts, and reflect on ideas.

If you use a learning tool—like mnemonics—you are using a metacognitive skill. When you have a set plan for studying, you are using a metacognitive skill. If you leave your studying to chance or work without a plan, you are less likely to be successful.

▶ INTELLIGENCE AND EFFORT

Can we tell how smart a person is? One way people try to measure intelligence is to use mental ability tests, or intelligence tests. Today, however, experts believe that many factors contribute to a person's intelligence. Being a good learner is one of them. Does a high score on a mental ability test mean that a person is a good learner? Not always.

Imagine two students. One scores very high on mental ability tests. If this student tries hard in school and uses good learning strategies, he or she will probably be a good learner. If this student does not try or studies in a careless way, he or she will probably be a poor learner.

The other student's scores on mental ability tests are not as high as the first student's scores. But this student works hard, has good study habits, and puts in a lot of effort. This student is a good learner.

Unless you have special learning problems, effort is as important in learning as intelligence.

Special Learning Problems

Some people have special learning problems. These people may have trouble learning in school even though they are very smart and try very hard. Some of them have trouble taking in information. Others have a hard time organizing information, which makes it hard to learn. Some people have trouble holding information in working memory or transferring information from working memory to long-term memory and back again.

Special teaching techniques may help these people. Sometimes people with special learning problems in one subject area, such as reading, excel in another area, such as mathematics. Many famous people have had learning problems. Nelson Rockefeller, vice president of the United States from 1974 to 1977, had learning problems. He had troubling reading as a child and as an adult, but he was able to overcome this problem. People can overcome most learning problems with effort and hard work.

A Life of Learning

You started learning the moment you were born. You will continue to learn throughout your entire life. Human beings have the unique ability to learn, to understand, and to make use of ideas.

You can help yourself to be a successful student. You can motivate yourself with positive reinforcements. You can make a special effort to understand as you learn instead of simply memorizing information. When you must memorize information, you can use memory tricks. If you do all of these things, you will become an active, successful learner.

PEGGY KAYE
Author, *Games for Learning*

See also INTELLIGENCE; PSYCHOLOGY; TESTS AND TEST TAKING.

WONDER QUESTION

What is an IQ test?

An IQ test measures certain aspects of intelligence. Alfred Binet (1857–1911) and Theodore Simon (1873–1961) designed the first intelligence test in 1905. It had thirty questions that tested the general knowledge, vocabulary, and physical coordination of children. It was originally designed to identify mentally retarded children in the elementary schools of Paris.

Since 1905, scientists have designed many different intelligence tests. All of them consist of several sections. Some sections test vocabulary; others test general knowledge about the world; and others check memory, the ability to think logically, arithmetic knowledge, the ability to re-create pictures, and more.

The letters "IQ" stand for **intelligence quotient**. The quotient in an IQ test is the number you get when a person's test score is divided by that person's age and then multiplied by 100.

When a student takes an IQ test, the score is measured against the scores of other students who have taken the test. The average IQ is 100. If a score is over 100, it is above the average. If a score is under 100, it is below the average.

LEARNING DISORDERS

Learning disorders affect a person's ability to learn. People with learning disorders have normal or above normal intelligence, but their brains work differently from the brains of other people. There may be an interruption in the connection between what they see and hear and the message the brain receives. Or there may be difficulty bringing together information from various brain regions.

Students with learning disorders can find ways to get the correct message to or from the brain by replacing learning strategies that do not work with others that do. Sometimes this involves finding new ways to do homework assignments and other learning tasks.

Types of Learning Disorders

People with learning disorders have more than the usual trouble learning subjects that other people may find easy. Some have difficulty identifying written words or the words people use to explain things to them. Others have trouble with math skills. Some people cannot easily coordinate their body movements or understand the "body language" of those around them. Each of these problems can cause a student to do poorly in school.

Speech and Language Disorders. Some students have great trouble speaking or understanding words and language. Children with **expressive language disorders** have difficulty expressing themselves vocally. They may raise their hand to answer a question, but then are unable to find the words to respond. Other children have trouble understanding what people say. Their hearing is fine, but words and syllables jumble together or sound the same. This is known as a **receptive language disorder**. Often, expressive and receptive language disorders occur together because similar brain processes are involved in both skills.

Academic Skills Disorders. Academic skills disorders are learning problems that affect the core school subjects: reading, writing, and arithmetic. **Dyslexia** is a disorder that makes it difficult to read and understand printed words. People with dyslexia often substitute similar letters or words for the correct ones and may mix up the order of words in a sentence. Dyslexia can affect a person's ability to read individual words and to understand the meaning of sentences and paragraphs.

People with dyslexia may have difficulty with other subjects as well. For example, they may do poorly in math class because they mix up numbers or have trouble reading word problems. Similarly, it may be difficult for them to read textbook assignments for history or science. Children with dyslexia or language disorders often have trouble remembering a sequence of directions, telling time, and organizing their thoughts for written tasks.

Other people are good readers but have significant trouble doing math. The difficulty can be caused by several different problems. Some people have **visual-spatial disorders** that affect how they view the world around them. They have difficulty telling right from left and doing things in a particular order or sequence. In math class, these students have trouble reading charts and graphs and learning subjects such as geometry that deal with shapes. These individuals may also have trouble forming letters and numbers when they write and remembering how words are spelled. Other children seem unable to remember and process the numbers and symbols needed to solve math problems.

Some students have difficulty writing down their own words. People with **written-language disorders** have trouble writing sentences that make sense and are complete. In their heads the thoughts are correct, but they encounter trouble when they want to put the thoughts down on a page. This disorder tends to show up in the later grades and can cause problems in any subject in which a student has written assignments.

Motor Disorders. Some people have unusual difficulty getting the different parts of their bodies to work together smoothly for writing, drawing, and physical activities. They may feel and appear clumsy as they move about, and their handwriting is difficult for others to read. Such problems are referred to as motor disorders.

Twice Exceptional. "Twice exceptional" is a term used to describe children who have remarkably high ability in some areas of learning and severe impairments in other areas. For example, a student may be a math wizard but have great trouble reading. Some can tell wonderful stories but are unable to write down their own words. Because of high scores on intelligence tests these students may be called "gifted," yet certain subjects cause them extreme difficulty. These students need special attention from parents and teachers because their gifted abilities require that they be given challenges in their areas of strength, but they must also learn compensation strategies in their areas of weakness.

Other Learning Problems. Some disorders can negatively affect the learning process but are not learning disorders. For example, children with Attention-Deficit Hyperactivity Disorder, or ADHD, have difficulty concentrating and sitting still. Although ADHD is not considered a learning disorder by most experts, its symptoms make it difficult for a child to pay attention and learn. You can read more about ADHD in Volume A.

Other children have learning problems related to social cues. They are unable to understand the nonverbal messages others send them, such as facial expressions and "body language." Because of this, these children may behave in ways that are unacceptable without realizing they are doing so. They may have difficulty making friends.

Causes of Learning Disorders

Scientists believe that learning disorders have a biological basis—that is, the brains of people with learning disorders are physically different in some way from people who learn normally. Many learning disorders seem to be hereditary, which means a person's mother, father, or other relative has experienced a similar learning problem. Scientists have recently begun to identify the regions of DNA involved in specific learning disorders.

Learning disorders can also be caused by problems with brain development during pregnancy, injuries at birth, and accidents or illnesses during childhood. There may be other causes that have not been identified.

Identification and Education

Learning disorders can occur in young children, but they often are not recognized until a child begins school. Children develop and learn at different rates, so having difficulty with a subject does not necessarily mean one has a learning disorder. A learning disorder is formally diagnosed using tests that measure a person's skill level in a certain area and compare it to the expected level for a child of that age and intelligence. If there is a large difference between performance on the test and the expected score, it could indicate that the person has a learning disorder. Vision or hearing problems must be ruled out before a diagnosis can be made.

Public schools in the United States are required to provide specialized instruction for children with learning disorders. In some cases a child may spend the entire school day working on a specialized curriculum with a special education teacher. Other children may do well in the mainstream classroom and attend specialized classes a few days a week to explore new methods for learning. Most children with learning disorders can succeed in school using these approaches. Many go on to college and succeed there as well. Some colleges and universities have special support programs for people with learning disorders.

Overcoming Learning Disorders

People with learning disorders are not "dumb" or "lazy." Their brains work in ways that make it difficult for them to learn in the normal way. But they also have many strengths. Although there are no cures for learning disorders, people who have them can use their strengths to accomplish the tasks they find difficult. They should not pretend there is no problem. Telling a parent or teacher who can help find a way to deal with the problem is the best strategy.

Today people with learning disorders can take advantage of technologies that make it possible to compensate for certain difficulties. For example, students with receptive language disorders can tape record a lesson and play it back as many times as needed to understand the information. A student with a motor disorder that causes poor handwriting can type written assignments using a word-processing program. A student with dyslexia can use textbooks on tape to listen to lessons rather than reading them. Students with written-language disorders can use speech-recognition software so they can say what they want to write. And a person with a learning disorder in math can use a calculator. With hard work, creativity, and technology, learning disorders can be overcome.

SUSAN WINEBRENNER
Educational Consultant

See also LEARNING.

The unique qualities of leather—durability, suppleness, and beauty—make it an ideal material for a variety of products. Jackets, shoes and boots, and saddles and other riding gear are among the most popular leather items.

LEATHER

Leather is a durable and versatile material produced from specially treated animal skins. It has long been prized for its beauty and suppleness and for the protective covering it offers. It is used in a wide range of products, including shoes, clothing, handbags, belts, luggage, furniture, and sporting equipment.

▶ SOURCES OF LEATHER

The words "hide" and "skin" usually mean the same thing. But in the leather industry, these words refer to two different kinds of leather.

Hides. Hides come from large animals. Cattle—due to their large size and vast numbers—are the single most important source of hides. Cattle hides are the primary source of leather for shoes as well as furniture and car upholstery. Water buffalo hides are another source of upholstery. Horsehide is used to make cordovan leather, an extremely tough and durable material that is ideal for shoes.

Skins. Skins come from smaller animals such as calves, sheep, pigs, and goats. Pigskins are used for shoes, luggage, and gloves. Goat- and sheepskins are used for gloves, clothing, and handbags. The skin of any goat, old or young, is known commercially as kidskin.

Calfskin leather is finer grained and lighter in weight than cattle hide. It is extremely strong and handsome and is used for expensive shoes, handbags, and similar articles.

Skins of lizards and snakes provide leather of unusual textures and colors for shoes, handbags, and luggage.

▶ HOW LEATHER IS MADE

Turning hides and skins into high-quality leather products involves many steps.

Fleshing. Before the hide can be tanned, flesh and fat must be removed. This is done by a fleshing machine, which cuts away the unwanted material with a rapidly rotating spiral blade.

Curing. Curing preserves the raw hide or skin, preventing it from decaying.

There are two main ways of curing hides. The first method involves spreading salt over the flesh surface, or underside, of the hides. The second method, common in the United States, involves submerging the hides in large tanks containing a salt solution called brine.

A factory worker loads a piece of leather into a shaving machine. This machine adjusts the thickness of a piece of leather after a hide has been split into layers.

The salt partially dries the hides and prevents bacteria from damaging them.

The use of ice and refrigeration is a popular method of short-term preservation in Scandinavia (Denmark, Sweden, and Norway) and Australia. Preservation through drying is common in Africa, where the climate is extremely hot and dry.

Soaking. After curing, the hides are soaked in water, which removes the salt, dirt, grease, and dissolvable proteins that would inhibit the leather-making process. Soaking also replaces the moisture removed by curing, allowing the hides to easily absorb the tanning agents.

Unhairing. Next, the hair must be removed. Although furs and shearlings (the skins of sheared sheep or lambs) may be tanned with the hair left on the skin, most leathers have all the hair removed.

The hides are soaked in drums or vats equipped with paddles, which rotate the hides through a solution of lime and sodium sulfide. This solution also removes the epidermis (top layer) of the hides. Once the hair and epidermis have been removed, the lime and sulfide are neutralized and washed away. The hides may again be run through a fleshing machine to remove any remaining flesh.

Bating. The hides are then soaked in a solution of enzymes in a procedure known as bating. Bating removes any discoloration and much of the remaining hair. It also makes the hides soft.

Tanning. Tanning preserves and protects hides and skins, making them durable, flexible, and even softer. Most leather is made by either of two tanning methods—vegetable tanning or chrome tanning. Each process produces a very different type of leather.

Vegetable tanning uses extracts from the bark and wood of trees. These extracts are called tannins, from which the term "tanning" is derived. The process produces very firm leather for shoe soles and luggage.

In vegetable tanning, the hides are hung in a series of vats until the tannins have fully penetrated them. After tanning, the leather is bleached. This reduces the concentration of tannins on the surface of the leather, making it more flexible. Heavy leather for shoe soles and harnesses is "stuffed"—that is, clay, mineral salts, corn sugar, mineral oils, animal fats, and waxes are added. Lighter leather, for luggage, saddles, and belts, is treated (dressed) with oils and fats. Stuffing or treating adds weight to the leather and makes it last longer.

Chrome tanning is used to produce leather for shoe uppers, clothing, and a wide range of other leather articles. The leather is very soft, flexible, and durable, and it does not scratch or scuff easily.

During the chrome tanning process, which takes just a few hours, the hides are tumbled in wooden drums partly filled with chromium salt solutions that turn the skins a light blue-green color. After tanning has been completed, the leather is squeezed dry. Today, chrome tanning accounts for about 90 percent of the world's leather production.

Splitting. After tanning (or sometimes after unhairing), the hides are passed through a machine that splits them into layers of the desired thickness. The upper layer is called the grain split and has an even thickness. The lower layer is called the flesh split and contains variations in thickness that are characteristic of the original hide. One of these layers may be split a second time to give a middle split. A shaving machine is also used to adjust the thickness. The split layers are then ready for further processing.

Retanning, Dyeing, and Fatliquoring. Retanning involves the use of natural or synthetic tanning agents to improve the feel and durability of the leather. Dyeing produces the desired color, and fatliquoring uses oils to lubricate the leather fibers, making the leather more soft and flexible. Once the leather has been retanned, dyed, and fatliquored, it is known as crust leather.

Staking and Finishing. After the crust leather dries, it is passed through a staking machine. This machine pummels and stretches the leather, making it softer by separating the fibers and improving the fatliquor penetration. The final stage of leather production normally involves the application of a protective finish to the grain surface of the leather. Traditionally, natural substances such as milk and egg protein, waxes, shellac, and nitrocellulose were used to finish leather. Linseed oil was used to give patent leather its uniquely smooth and shiny appearance. Modern leather finishing uses polymers such as acrylic resins and polyurethanes to protect the leather and improve its appearance.

▶ **LEATHER ALTERNATIVES**

A number of fabrics, plastics, and composite materials have been created as substitutes for leather in many products. These synthetic materials do not possess the special combination of comfort, strength, beauty, and the ability to "breathe" (to allow air and water vapor to pass through) that is unique to leather. However, the synthetic substitutes can sometimes offer advantages. For example, shoe soles have traditionally been made of leather, but synthetic materials are now often favored because they are waterproof, softer, resistant to slipping, and easier and cheaper to make.

▶ **LEATHER THROUGH THE AGES**

The craft of leather making is ancient. In fact, tools for leather making have been discovered in Africa that date back 600,000 years. Early peoples used the skins of animals to make clothing, water containers, and tents.

The ancient Greeks placed their leather tanneries outside the city walls because of the bad odor. Greek, Roman, and Egyptian tanners all used limewater to help take the hair off hides, just as is done now. Oak and sumac bark extracts were used for tanning.

In the Middle Ages, England was a center for leather making and for the export of leather. Russia, France, Spain, Italy, and Germany also had important leather industries. However, only the wealthy could afford the products made of such leather, and since that time leather has been a symbol of luxury and wealth.

Some Native Americans were expert tanners. They used leather for clothing, tents, boats, and many other purposes. Their leather was very soft, pliable, and water-resistant.

In England, Sir Humphry Davy (1778–1829) discovered that oak and sumac barks were not the only barks that could be used for tanning. He also found tannin in the bark of the hemlock and mimosa and in the wood of the chestnut and the quebracho trees.

The invention of chrome tanning in 1884 by the American Augustus Schultz helped modernize the leather industry. Beginning in the 1900's, leather was commonly used in everyday items. More recently, the invention of new machinery, the growth of cattle herds, and the development of advanced retanning chemicals have all helped improve the value, availability, and desirability of this product.

WILLIAM RAPP
Director, Leather Industries of America
Reviewed by
Leather Research Laboratory
University of Cincinnati

See also SHOES.

In a method of drying called toggling, leather is stretched over a frame and held by toggles (clips) before being inserted into a drying oven.

LEAVES

Leaves are the "food factories" of plants, the sites where most of a plant's energy is produced. **Photosynthesis** is the process by which plants use light energy from the sun to produce food. Although photosynthesis may take place in any green part of a plant, it mainly occurs in the leaves. Earth's first land plants, which appeared more than 400 million years ago, had no leaves and carried out photosynthesis through their stems. The flowering plants that are familiar to us today first appeared on

Each kind of plant has its own characteristic leaves, such as (*clockwise from right*) the bright red leaves of a poinsettia, the giant round leaves of a water lily, the spiny leaves of a prickly pear cactus, and the furled leaves of lettuces and cabbages.

Earth more than 200 million years ago. Because these advanced plants have more numerous and larger leaves than did their primitive ancestors, they are more efficient at making their own food.

Leaves vary greatly in size, from a water plant leaf as small as the head of a pin to a tropical palm leaf that can grow more than 65 feet (20 meters) long. Along with size, there are also variations in how many leaves a specific species, or kind, of plant supports. For instance, a mature hardwood tree may produce several million leaves during its life span, while one plant specialized for life in the desert grows only two leaves throughout its entire life.

▶ PARTS OF A LEAF

If you look at the plants around you, you will see a wide variety of leaves. No other visible plant part can be found in as many different forms as leaves. Leaves may look like feathers, needles, or fans, and they may be smooth, sticky, or waxy, with edges that are smooth, toothed, or lobed. Still, most leaves share a common design and some basic features.

The External Structure of Leaves

The flattened, usually broad part of the leaf is the **blade**. The **petiole** is a stalk-like structure that supports the blade and attaches it to the twig or stem of the plant. The petiole holds the leaf at an angle that allows the leaf to receive the most sunlight possible. Some kinds of leaves also have **stipules**, tiny leaflike structures that grow at the base of the petioles.

Such characteristics as general structure, vein pattern, and arrangement on a plant help create each leaf's unique identity. Leaves have either simple or compound structures. **Simple leaves** have a single flat, undivided blade. **Compound leaves** have more than one blade, called **leaflets**, that are attached to a **midrib**, or central vein. On **pinnate compound leaves**, the leaflets look like feathers arranged along the midrib. Leaflets of

palmate compound leaves are arranged outward from a center point, like fingers from a palm.

Some leaves have a large midrib with a network of smaller veins branching from it. Other leaves have straight, parallel veins. Plant leaves can often be distinguished by this pattern of veins. The flowering plants known as **dicots** have leaves with a branching network of veins; those known as **monocots** have leaves with parallel veins. Dicots include most familiar trees, such as maples, oaks, and dogwoods, and most garden flowers. Common monocots are corn and grasses.

The site where a leaf attaches to a stem is called a **node**. The particular arrangement of leaves on a plant's stem allows for the most efficient exposure to the sun. Plants with **alternate** or **spiral** arrangements of leaves have one leaf attached at each node. Plants with **opposite** arrangements of leaves have pairs attached at each node. When plants have more than two leaves attached at each node, it is a **whorled** arrangement.

The Internal Structure of Leaves

The **epidermis**, a thin, tough layer of cells, covers the outside of each leaf. The epidermis secretes a thin waxy film, or **cuticle**, on the surface of the leaf. The cuticle protects the inside from injury and from losing moisture. Within the layer of epidermal cells are openings or pores called **stomata** (plural of **stoma**). Each stoma is surrounded by two balloonlike **guard cells**. Working as a pair, the guard cells change shape to open or close the stoma between them. Carbon dioxide enters through the stomata, and oxygen and water vapor exit.

Inside a Leaf

Cuticle
Mesophyll (palisade cells)
Chloroplasts
Xylem
Phloem
Upper epidermis
Lower epidermis
Stoma
Guard cells
Mesophyll (spongy cells)

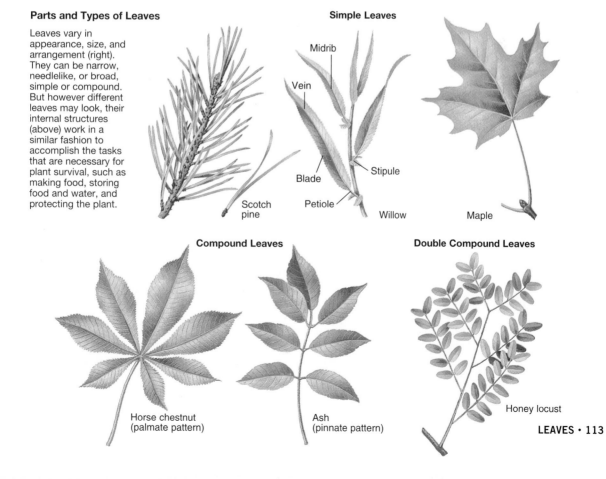

Parts and Types of Leaves

Leaves vary in appearance, size, and arrangement (right). They can be narrow, needlelike, or broad, simple or compound. But however different leaves may look, their internal structures (above) work in a similar fashion to accomplish the tasks that are necessary for plant survival, such as making food, storing food and water, and protecting the plant.

Scotch pine

Simple Leaves

Midrib
Vein
Blade
Stipule
Petiole
Willow
Maple

Compound Leaves

Horse chestnut (palmate pattern)

Ash (pinnate pattern)

Double Compound Leaves

Honey locust

The desert ocotillo (*left*) adapts to changes in the water supply, such as during dry spells (*bottom*), by limiting the number of leaves produced—fewer leaves means less water lost through evaporation.

Beneath the epidermis is the **mesophyll** tissue of the leaf. Mesophyll cells are designed to absorb light and exchange gases, processes that are necessary for the plant's production of energy and food. Within mesophyll cells are **chloroplasts**, the special structures that hold the green pigment **chlorophyll**. The number of chloroplasts in a plant cell varies, from as many as 300 to as few as 1. It is in the chloroplasts that photosynthesis occurs.

A network of channels made up of the tissues **xylem** and **phloem** forms a transport system that carries food, water, and other materials throughout the plant. Xylem tissues carry water and dissolved nutrients up from the roots to the rest of the plant. Phloem tissues transport food from the leaves, where it is made, to other parts of the plant.

▸ THE LIFE CYCLE OF A LEAF

Leaf activities are controlled by plant chemicals called **hormones**. The effects of any one plant hormone depend on the amount of hormone that is released and the amounts of other hormones present.

How a New Leaf Emerges

The leaves and stems of a plant make up the plant's shoot, or growth, system. The **apical bud**, found at the tip of each stem or branch, contains beginning leaves and the **apical meristem**. The apical meristem is a region of rapid cell division that leads to the development of several plant tissues, including leaves, flowers, and branches. As the cells of the apical meristem divide, the region moves forward on the lengthening stem. Some meristem cells remain behind on the stem's surface. These cells will become leaves. The tiny beginning leaves gradually emerge just below the apical bud and develop into mature leaves.

The arrangement of the leaves on the stem—alternate, opposite, or whorled—is determined as the leaves emerge. As the stem grows, the spaces between nodes grow larger. This growth allows the crowded young leaves to spread farther apart as they develop. New leaves continue to emerge in an orderly way as cells in the apical bud divide and develop.

Why Trees Shed Their Leaves

Mature leaves carry out their critical role for the plant, which is the production of the plant's food through photosynthesis. In the middle of summer, when trees appear their greenest, the rate of photosynthesis is at its peak. In winter, many wooded areas look very different, because trees have dropped their leaves. Trees that shed their leaves at the end of each growing season are called **deciduous**. The process of shedding is believed to help deciduous trees avoid water loss.

By the end of summer, the nutrients produced by leaves of deciduous trees have mostly been stored in the roots. Leaves then undergo **senescence**, a seasonal aging process that is triggered by such environmental cues as cooler temperatures and shorter days. Senescence is easy to spot in trees because it triggers the lovely colors of autumn. As leaves age, they stop carrying out photosynthesis. They no longer require the green chlorophyll pigments that are necessary for

How Leaves Develop

Inside a protective bud, immature leaves are folded tightly. A signal, such as warm weather, triggers the bud to become active. As the bud opens, the bud scales fall off and the young leaves unfold. Soon a twig develops and many more leaves appear.

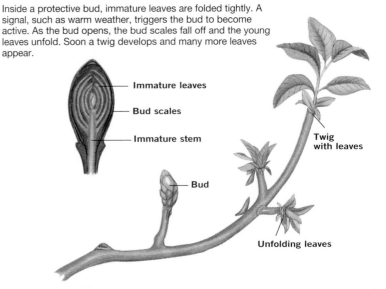

Immature leaves

Bud scales

Immature stem

Bud

Twig with leaves

Unfolding leaves

As the leaves of deciduous trees age, a riot of color emerges. This vibrant display occurs when a leaf's chlorophyll breaks down and pigments hidden throughout much of the year are revealed.

photosynthesis, and the plant breaks them down. Because chlorophyll is absent, the leaves no longer appear green. Instead, other pigments that were hidden by the chlorophyll-containing cells stand out as the weather grows colder. It is then that the pigments **carotenoid** and **anthocyanin** are revealed and the spectacular yellows, reds, oranges, and purples of fall leaves can be seen.

The actual shedding of leaves is called **abscission**. As a leaf grows older, a layer of tissue forms at the base of its petiole. Cued by the changing environmental conditions of autumn, cells of this abscission layer release an enzyme that breaks down their own cell walls. Because the leaf is attached only by threads of xylem and phloem, it is easily broken off by wind, rain, or any other disturbance. A scar forms on the branch where the leaf was attached. In regions where leaves fall before winter, plants generally become dormant, greatly limiting any processes requiring energy. It is not until spring that environmental conditions trigger the beginning of growth and the formation of new leaves.

▶ **LIFE PROCESSES**

All leaves must accomplish certain tasks during their life cycle to survive. A leaf must perform photosynthesis and respiration, obtain and transport food, and move water and other substances.

Photosynthesis

During photosynthesis, plants convert light energy from the sun into chemical energy. The chemical energy is then used to convert carbon dioxide, water, and minerals into food substances. These food substances are used to transport and store energy and to power other processes, such as respiration.

Leaves are specially designed for carrying out the process of photosynthesis. Their structures allow them to take in the substances that are necessary to make food. Chlorophyll traps the solar energy. Water and minerals are brought into the leaf from the roots

The philodendron's huge, dark green leaves allow it to absorb the maximum amount of light in dim environments.

PRESERVING LEAVES

Many people enjoy having a leaf collection. To keep the leaves you collect from curling up and cracking, they need to be pressed. Pressing requires a few simple materials: absorbent paper (such as newspaper), a piece of plywood, and a weight (such as a stack of books or bricks).

Arrange the leaves you have collected on top of several sheets of the absorbent paper. The leaves should not touch one another. Then cover the leaves with more of the paper. Put the plywood board and the weight on top.

The papers should be changed every day. Depending on the weather and the kind of plants, the leaves should be dry and flat after about a week. Each leaf can then be mounted on a separate sheet of stiff paper by placing a strip of tape across the tip and the petiole.

If Leaves Need Sunlight to Survive

During photosynthesis, light energy is captured by chlorophyll, the green substance in leaves, and turned into chemical energy. The chemical energy is then used to power chemical reactions within a plant's cells. The experiment below will let you see how important it is for leaves to have sunlight.

For this experiment, you will need a growing plant with large green leaves, black construction paper, scissors, and tape or paper clips. Use the scissors to cut a piece of the construction paper large enough to cover a leaf. Then cut three small circles, about the size of nickels, in the paper. Place the paper over the top of the leaf and gently clip or tape the paper in place. Only three small circles of the leaf should show through the black paper cover. Leave the plant, with the paper clipped to the leaf, in the sunlight for two days.

At the end of two days, remove the paper from the leaf. Observe the difference between those areas that were covered and those that remained exposed to the sunlight. In the absence of sunlight, the chlorophyll was used up and not replaced. Because chlorophyll gives leaves their green color, it is easy to

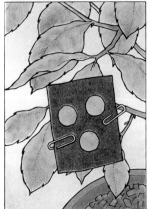 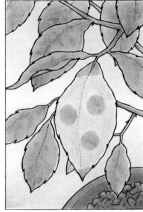

Leaf with paper blocking sunlight.   Leaf after paper is removed.

see that chlorophyll is missing from the areas that were covered by the paper. The leaf cells in the covered areas were not able to use sunlight to make food. If the leaf was kept covered, it would eventually die. Two or three days after removing the paper, look at the leaf again. Can you tell if the chlorophyll has been replaced?

by the xylem, and carbon dioxide enters from the air through the abundant stomata. The guard cells surrounding each stoma control the size of the stomatal opening, allowing for the exchange of water and gases. Generally, stomata respond to changes in light by opening during the day, when sunlight is available for photosynthesis, and closing at night. In dry weather, guard cells close the stomata to prevent water loss.

The spaces between mesophyll cells allow carbon dioxide to enter each cell. Within the chloroplasts, water molecules are split by light energy into their components—hydrogen and oxygen. The oxygen is released by the leaf through the stomata into the environment surrounding the plant, and the hydrogen combines with water to form the energy-rich sugar known as glucose. The glucose produced is a simple sugar that plants can convert into other food products, such as more complex sugars, starches, proteins, and fats. Some of the glucose, transported throughout the plant by the phloem, is used immediately to provide energy for growth and other functions. The remaining food is stored as starch, usually in the roots and stems but sometimes in leaves or other plant parts.

Cellular Respiration

As in all other living things, plant cells break down food to obtain energy. This process, called **cellular respiration**, takes place in all cells, unlike the process of photosynthesis, which takes place in a specialized few. During cellular respiration, glucose is broken down to release energy that can be used to power chemical reactions within the plant's cells. Along with freed energy, the process also yields carbon dioxide and water. In the presence of sunlight, these products can again be used to form food substances.

Photosynthesis and respiration are similar in that they both function to provide usable energy to the cell. However, unlike photosynthesis, which must take place during daylight hours, respiration occurs all the time, both night and day. In order to survive, then, a plant's photosynthesis effort must be as great as or greater than its respiration effort, so that it makes at least as much food as it uses.

Water and Mineral Transport

The veins that are often easy to see on leaves are the transport tissues—phloem and xylem. While food is carried through the phloem tissues, water and other materials are carried by the xylem tissues.

Water is transported in plants within the xylem in one direction, from root to shoot. It is pulled up the xylem by pressure changes that occur when water evaporates from leaves. The water evaporates through the stomata in a process known as **transpiration**.

As leaves transpire, water levels in mesophyll cells drop, causing the nearby water molecules to be drawn into the leaf tissue. Water molecules through-

Predators that try to dine on holly leaves (*below*) are discouraged by sharp edges that can tear their flesh. Painful skin inflammations are the result of an encounter with poison oak leaves (*left*).

out the xylem are so tightly bound to each other that they are pulled up the xylem together, creating a column of water. This in turn reduces water concentrations in the roots, causing more water to be pulled in from the soil. This force is so strong that water can be extracted from even very dry soils.

Transpiration allows water and minerals to be carried up to the leaves. It also helps with temperature regulation, as water evaporating from mesophyll cells removes heat and cools the leaf.

▶ SPECIAL FUNCTIONS OF LEAVES

Although a leaf's most important contribution to a plant is its role in photosynthesis and transpiration, many leaves provide other necessary functions. There are leaves that provide a protective service when a plant is under attack. Leaves may also serve as storage sites or help obtain food for a plant.

Defense

Leaves can protect plants from their enemies, such as animals, disease, and environmental extremes, through specific defense mechanisms. These defenses often involve spines or poisons to discourage predators. The spines of a cactus are modified leaves that protect the plant from predators while also reducing the amount of water lost through evaporation. Most leaves contain chemicals that make them more difficult to digest. Belladonna (deadly nightshade) and brittlewood shrubs both have highly poisonous leaves. If you often walk in the woods, you are probably familiar with the effective defenses of poison oak and poison ivy. These plants secrete oils that cause painful, itchy skin irritations.

Leaves can also provide protection by physically supporting the plant. **Bracts** are modified leaves that protect developing flowers. Because bracts can be colorful, such as the red bracts of poinsettias, they are sometimes mistaken for petals. Climbing plants such as peas often have vinelike leaves called **tendrils**. Tendrils cling to nearby objects to anchor the growing plant.

Food and Water Storage

Leaves may also serve as sites of food and water storage. Storage leaves are usually fleshy. The nutrient-rich bulbs of onions, daffodils, and tulips are the bases of storage leaves. Flowering plants have special leaves that store energy for the developing plant. Some plants adapted to dry environments, particularly deserts, have fleshy leaves for water storage. These plants are known as **succulents**. Leaves of succulent plants are usually covered with a thick cuticle to prevent water loss.

Some special leaves, such as the fleshy, overlapping bulb scales of an onion, are used to store a plant's extra food underground during the winter.

Obtaining Food

Probably the most unusual leaves are those that can actually catch food. One example is the butterwort plant, which is found in wet environments. It has flat, harmless-looking leaves, but they are actually covered with a sticky substance that traps those insects that land on them. The insects die while stuck to the leaves, and the leaves then curl inward to digest the insect.

Specialized Behaviors

Leaves are able to adapt to their environment. In response to signals given by particular hormones, they bend toward light—an important adaptation for performing photosynthesis in an efficient way. Like other kinds of organisms, plants compete with each other for resources. Among its neighbors, the plant that produces the most leaves is able to take in the most light, water, and nutrients and manufacture the most energy. It is also the one that is most likely to survive and create new plants.

Telltale signs of warm weather are rhododendron leaves that lie almost straight out (*above left*). When temperatures fall, leaves begin to droop and curl (*above right*).

In the swampy areas of the southeastern United States lives the meat-eating Venus's-flytrap. Each of its leaves has two halves that can close around an unfortunate insect victim.

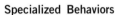

▶ THE IMPORTANCE OF LEAVES

Because leaves are the sites of food making in plants, they are important to a plant's survival. However, they are also important to other organisms for the same reason. We depend on the food made by leaves. When we eat lettuce, cabbage, and spinach, we are eating actual leaves. The food-making abilities of leaves produce the parts of plants that supply us with our other vegetables, fruits, nuts, and cereals. Some specific

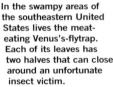

Signaled by hormones, sunflower leaves turn toward the sun—an important adaptation for performing photosynthesis efficiently.

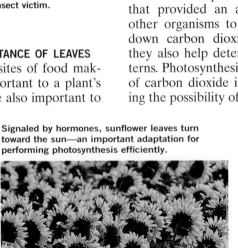

products are made directly from leaves, such as teas, herbs, and tobacco. Still other products, including milk, meats, and eggs, come to us as part of a plant-based food chain. For instance, plants make their own food, chickens eat the seeds or fruits of food plants, and we eat the eggs and meat chickens provide.

In addition to supporting lives, leaves are often responsible for saving them. Many medicines are extracted from leaves, such as the heart medicine digitalis, which is a product of dried foxglove leaves.

The most important contributions leaves make to our planet's ecosystems are through their processing of oxygen and carbon dioxide. Oxygen, though a waste product of photosynthesis, is essential to plant, animal, and human survival. It was the evolution of plants and the buildup of the oxygen they released that provided an atmosphere that allowed other organisms to evolve. As leaves break down carbon dioxide and release oxygen, they also help determine global climate patterns. Photosynthesis slows down the buildup of carbon dioxide in the atmosphere, reducing the possibility of global warming.

Leaves clearly play a large part in the daily existence of plants, animals, and humans. Without leaves, Earth would be an entirely different place.

MARY CATHERINE HAGER
Contributing Author,
Environment

See also FLOWERS; GRASSES; PHOTOSYNTHESIS; PLANTS; TREES.

LEBANON

Lebanon is a small nation located in Southwest Asia, in a part of the region known as the Middle East. It is situated on the eastern shore of the Mediterranean Sea and shares borders with Syria and Israel.

Lebanon first became a fully independent nation in 1943, but its history goes back thousands of years, to the Phoenicians, an ancient seafaring and trading people. Modern Lebanon, and especially its capital of Beirut, was the commercial center of the Middle East. Between 1975 and 1991, however, Lebanon was torn by a civil war that disrupted its economy, caused widespread loss of life, and made many of its people homeless.

▶ THE PEOPLE

Most of the people are Arabs. In addition to the Lebanese, the population also includes large numbers of Palestinians and Syrians. The Palestinians fled to Lebanon to escape the wars that followed the creation of the nation of Israel in a part of Palestine in 1948.

Language and Religion. Arabic is the official language of the country and is spoken by most of the people. Many educated Lebanese also speak French or English, or both.

About 60 percent of the Lebanese are Muslims, including both Shi'ites and Sunnis, who form the religion's two chief sects. Christians make up most of the rest of the population. Lebanon has the largest percentage of Christians of any nation in the Middle East. Many sects are represented. But the Maronites of the Eastern Catholic Church make up the largest group. Lebanon also has a considerable num-

The old and the new meet frequently in Lebanon. Here, two young Lebanese, wearing traditional Arab headdress but otherwise in Western-style clothing, view the remains of a Roman temple at Baalbek, in eastern Lebanon. The building dates from about 67 B.C. The Romans were one of many peoples who conquered, settled, or passed through Lebanon during its long history.

ber of Druzes, who broke away from the Muslim faith centuries ago and are usually considered a separate religion.

▶ THE LAND

Mountains, Plains, Rivers. Lebanon extends from north to south for a distance of about 130 miles (210 kilometers). A narrow plain, in some places just wide enough for the road, lies along the Mediterranean coastline. The Lebanon Mountains rise steeply from the coastal plain. Their highest point, Qurnat al-Sawda, is more than 10,000 feet (3,000 meters) above sea level. The Anti-Lebanon Mountains, on the Syrian border, are lower. Between these two ranges lies the fertile Bekaa plain.

The Litani and the Orontes are the major rivers. The Litani River rises in north central Lebanon. It cuts southwest across more than half the country before it finally breaks through the Lebanon Mountains. From there it flows into the Mediterranean Sea. The Orontes River begins in the Bekaa plain and runs north between the two mountain chains into western Syria.

Climate. Lebanon has a Mediterranean climate with cool, rainy winters and warm, dry summers. Temperatures on the coast average about 55°F (13°C) in January and 85°F (29°C) in August. It is cooler in the mountains, where the ground is snow-covered for much of the winter months. The mountains also receive more rainfall than other areas of Lebanon.

Natural Resources. Lebanon was once famous for its old and beautiful cedar trees, which became the symbol of the country and

The Bekaa plain lies between Lebanon's two mountain ranges. It is the country's most fertile area and the principal grain-growing region.

are shown on its national flag. Most of the trees were cut down in past centuries, and the few remaining groves are now found only in special areas, where they are protected from further destruction. In all, only about 8 percent of the land is forested, and Lebanon has to import nearly all its lumber.

Lebanon has few mineral resources, except for small deposits of iron ore, lignite (brown coal), and building stone.

▶ THE ECONOMY

Trade and Tourism. Trade traditionally has been the most important part of Lebanon's economy. As the center for much of the commerce of the Middle East, Lebanon had an extensive banking system. Tourism was also an important industry. The country's beautiful coastline and breathtaking mountains attracted tourists from all over the world. Lebanon was popular with vacationers for both winter and summer sports. Trade, banking, and tourism were all severely affected by the civil war.

Manufacturing and Agriculture. Lebanon has a small but important manufacturing sector, which employs about 10 percent of the work force. Chief products include processed foods,

---

FACTS AND FIGURES

REPUBLIC OF LEBANON is the official name of the country.

THE PEOPLE are known as Lebanese.

LOCATION: Southwest Asia.

AREA: 4,015 sq mi (10,400 km²).

POPULATION: 3,000,000 (estimate).

CAPITAL AND LARGEST CITY: Beirut.

MAJOR LANGUAGES: Arabic (official), French, English.

MAJOR RELIGIONS: Muslim, Christian.

GOVERNMENT: Republic. **HEAD OF STATE**—president. **HEAD OF GOVERNMENT**—prime minister. **LEGISLATURE**—National Assembly.

CHIEF PRODUCTS: Agricultural—citrus fruits, bananas, and other fruits, olives, wheat and other grains, vegetables. **Manufactured**—processed foods, refined petroleum and petroleum products, textiles, furniture. Other important economic activities include service industries, such as banking and tourism. **Mineral**—small amounts of iron ore, lignite (brown coal), and building stone.

MONETARY UNIT: Lebanese pound (1 pound = 100 piasters).

textiles, furniture, and a variety of consumer goods. Refineries process petroleum from other parts of the Middle East.

Agriculture is also important to the economy. Citrus fruits and bananas flourish in the coastal plain. Other fruits, olives, and vegetables are grown on the lower slopes of the Lebanon Mountains. Wheat and other grains are grown in the Bekaa plain.

Many Lebanese work abroad, and money they send home plays an important role in the economy.

▶CITIES

Beirut is Lebanon's capital, largest city, chief port, and the commercial heart of the country. Of all Lebanese cities, it suffered the most from the devastation caused by years of war. Founded by the Phoenicians in ancient times, Beirut first gained importance in about 15 B.C. as a Roman colony. The city later came under the rule of Arabs, European Crusaders, and the Ottoman Turks. It became the capital of Lebanon in 1920.

At the outbreak of the civil war in 1975, the city was divided into two zones—East Beirut, inhabited chiefly by Christians; and West Beirut, the home of most of the city's Muslims. Until 1991 the two parts of Beirut were separated by a deserted stretch of land called the Green Line, and the city was a battleground between armed militias of the warring factions. Israeli troops briefly occupied Beirut in 1982. Artillery battles between Lebanese Christian army troops and Syrian forces in 1989 caused further destruction.

Other major Lebanese cities include Tripoli, the second largest in population, in the north; as well as Juniye, Hamat, and the southern port cities of Sidon and Tyre. All suffered damage from the war.

▶HISTORY AND GOVERNMENT

Early History. The earliest known people in Lebanon were the Phoenicians. They arrived there around 3000 B.C. In the Bible they are referred to as the Canaanites. The Phoenicians founded a great empire using the city-states of ancient Lebanon as their base.

Among the most important of the city-states were Byblos, Sidon, and Tyre. At various times these states were conquered by Egyptians, Assyrians, Persians, and the Macedonians and Greeks under Alexander the Great. Later, Lebanon became a part of the Roman Empire.

Beirut is Lebanon's capital, largest city, and chief port. It was long a major commercial and banking center of the Middle East and a popular spot for tourists. Most of the commercial heart of the city was destroyed during a 15-year-long civil war. Many of its people were made homeless. Others, like this family (*in inset*), managed to live with a certain dignity amidst the ruins of war.

The Phoenicians, the earliest known inhabitants of Lebanon, built a great trading empire. Part of a bronze door from the 800's B.C. shows Phoenician ships unloading tribute for an Assyrian king.

During the Byzantine period, most of the people became Christians. In the A.D. 600's, when Lebanon was conquered by the Arabs, the Muslim religion was introduced into the region. Other religious groups, including Maronite Christians in the late 600's and Druzes in the 1000's, escaped persecution by setting up their own communities in the rugged Lebanon Mountains.

Lebanon was occupied by French Crusaders from the 1000's to about 1200, when the Muslims drove them out. Early in the 1500's, the Arabs, in turn, were conquered by the Ottoman Turks. British and French forces ended Turkish rule in the region in World War I (1914–18).

Modern Lebanon. After World War I ended, Lebanon was placed under French rule as a mandate of the League of Nations. In 1943 it achieved independence.

In 1958 the Lebanese government faced internal revolt from groups opposing its pro-Western policies. It asked the United States for help, and 10,000 marines were sent to the region. But no shots were fired, and peace was quickly restored. Lebanon did not take part in the 1956, 1967, or 1973 Arab-Israeli wars. It tried to maintain a noncombatant position in the conflict. This policy was opposed by Palestinian refugees and Lebanese radicals, mainly Muslims. From bases in Lebanon, Palestinian guerrillas attacked villages in Israel. Israeli forces counterattacked into Lebanon. In this way Lebanon was reluctantly drawn into the Arab-Israeli struggle. Tensions between the Palestinians and the Lebanese government increased.

Toward Civil War. Tensions between Muslims and Maronites had also been growing. The Christians, once a majority in Lebanon, had a greater proportion of representatives in the legislature. By an unwritten but strict tradition, the president of the country had to be a Maronite Christian. The president appointed the prime minister, who had to be a Sunni Muslim. Each Muslim and Christian sect was assured of representation. But the Muslims, who were now in the majority, demanded a greater voice in the government.

Outbreak of War. Full-scale civil war erupted in 1975. A number of cease-fires and truces were arranged, but none lasted long. At the request of the Lebanese government and the Arab League, Syria and some other Arab nations sent a peacekeeping force into Lebanon in 1976. The non-Syrian troops were later withdrawn.

Meanwhile, chaos continued. The central government had almost no power. More than forty armed groups controlled various parts of the country. Palestinian guerrillas set up military strongholds in refugee camps and attacked Israel from bases in southern Lebanon. The Syrians, who had originally backed the Maronites, began to support the Palestinians and other groups opposed to the Maronites. A Maronite-dominated government was reluctant to call on the nation's army to restore order for fear the army would split into rival groups.

In 1978, Israeli troops entered Lebanon in retaliation for attacks by the Palestine Liberation Organization (PLO). Under pressure from the United States and the United Nations, Israel withdrew its troops. A United Nations peacekeeping force took their place, but attacks by the PLO on Israel continued.

The War Expands. In an attempt to crush the PLO, Israeli troops invaded Lebanon in June 1982. Within a few days they had occupied all of south Lebanon, including parts of Beirut. After intervention by the United States, Israel lifted the siege of the capital, and PLO and Syrian forces in Beirut withdrew.

In August 1982, the Lebanese parliament elected Bashir Gemayel president. He was leader of the Phalangists, a Maronite Christian party with close ties to Israel. Many Muslim and leftist Lebanese opposed his election. In September, after Gemayel was assassinated,

Israeli forces and Phalangist militia occupied all of Beirut. Phalangists entered Palestinian refugee camps, where they killed hundreds of civilians. Gemayel was succeeded as president by his brother, Amin Gemayel.

Israeli forces left Beirut and were replaced by a multinational group of U.S., French, Italian, and British troops. In 1983, Shi'ite terrorists and leftist factions bombed U.S. Marine and French military headquarters, causing hundreds of casualties. The multinational force left Lebanon in 1984, and by the following year, Israeli troops remained only within a security zone in the south.

A Government Crisis. In 1988 a crisis over a successor to President Gemayel split the government into rival Maronite and Syrian-backed groups. Gemayel appointed General Michel Aoun, commander of the (mainly Christian) Lebanese Army, to head the government. But most Lebanese refused to accept Aoun's authority. A rival government, headed by a Sunni Muslim prime minister, was established in West Beirut under Syrian control.

The Compromise Agreement. In 1989, most Lebanese factions reached a compromise agreement. It divided representation in the national legislature equally between the various Christian and Muslim groups, and transferred some power from the Maronite president to the Sunni prime minister. The legislature elected a new president, René Moawad. But Aoun refused to recognize the new government. Just 17 days after taking office, Moawad was assassinated. He was succeeded by another Maronite, Elias Hrawi. In 1990, Syrian and Lebanese troops supported by militia units attacked Aoun, forcing him to abandon the presidential palace.

Recent Events. After Aoun's defeat, President Hrawi's government established control over all of Beirut, and a pro-Syrian national unity government was proclaimed. The constitution was revised in 1995, to allow Hrawi to serve a second term as president. He was succeeded by General Emile Lahoud in 1998.

The Israeli government withdrew its troops from southern Lebanon in 2000. But lasting peace hinged on a broader peace accord between Syria and Israel. In 2004, the Lebanese parliament again amended the constitution to extend the term of pro-Syrian president Lahoud for another three years.

Syrian troops patrol a devastated area of Beirut. Brought in as peacekeepers in 1976, the Syrians were caught up in the Lebanon conflict, which lasted until 1991.

In early 2005, Prime Minister Hariri, who had resigned his office to protest Syria's influence and the recent constitutional amendment, was assassinated. Lebanese opposition leaders blamed Syria. Riots broke out, and international pressure forced Syria to agree to remove its troops from Lebanon. But then hundreds of thousands of Lebanese organized by Hezbollah (an anti-Israeli, Shi'ite Muslim guerrilla group supported by Syria and Iran) rallied in support of Syria. A week later, as a countermeasure, even larger numbers turned out to oppose Syria and Lebanon's pro-Syrian government. This event became known as the Cedar Revolution (for the cedar tree emblem on the Lebanese flag). As a result, Syria withdrew all its last troops from Lebanon in late April, ending 29 years of military presence.

In June, an anti-Syrian alliance swept the parliamentary elections, and Fouad Siniora was named prime minister.

ALEXANDER MELAMID
New York University

Reviewed by DON PERETZ
Author, *The Middle East Today*

LE CARRÉ, JOHN. See MYSTERY AND DETECTIVE STORIES (Profiles).

LE CLAIR, JOHN. See VERMONT (Famous People).

Villa Savoye, built in 1929, shows Le Corbusier's use of simple concrete forms and large areas of glass.

LE CORBUSIER (1887–1965)

Le Corbusier was one of the most creative architects of the 1900's. He introduced many innovative architectural ideas in the buildings he designed throughout the world. His extensive writings also did much to stimulate acceptance of modern architectural styles. Most notable is his book, *Towards a New Architecture*, published in 1923.

Le Corbusier was born on October 6, 1887, in La Chaux-de-Fonds, Switzerland. He was named Charles Édouard Jeanneret but today is best known as Le Corbusier. He studied in Paris and Berlin. After World War I, he settled in Paris and later became a French citizen.

As an architect, Le Corbusier's prime objective was to improve the environment and to serve everyday human needs with greater efficiency. He gained a reputation for his pure white houses made of glass and stucco over reinforced concrete. These houses were supported on slender stilts, called **pilotis**, and contained freely flowing interior spaces. One of the finest examples is the Villa Savoye (Savoye House), built in Poissy-sur-Seine, near Paris, in 1929. Other important houses designed by Le Corbusier include the Villa La Roche, built in Paris in 1925, and the villa called Les Terraces, built two years later on the outskirts of Paris.

Sometimes Le Corbusier's works aroused great astonishment. For example, at the Paris Exhibition of 1925 he displayed a plan for a house with a living tree growing through it. Yet he was also instrumental in the mass production of housing and contributed many novel ideas for town planning in the 1930's and 1940's. In addition, he was a member of a committee of international architects who jointly designed the United Nations Headquarters building in New York City in 1949–51.

In the late 1940's, however, Le Corbusier's designs began to depart more and more from tradition. They started to take on the appearance of massive free-form sculpture molded in concrete. A significant example is the Unité d'Habitation, a large apartment building built in 1947–52 in Marseilles, France. The whole building (which included a kindergarten and shops as well as apartments) was supported on huge concrete pilotis. The exterior, or facade, of the building had a honeycombed design—a Le Corbusier creation that became a standard feature in apartment design.

Le Corbusier is also noted for his plan for the new city of Chandigarh, India. The city's government center, made of raw concrete, was built over a 13-year period, from 1951 to 1964. Perhaps his most striking and innovative work is the church of Notre Dame du Haut (1951–55), in Ronchamp in southern France. Its boldly curved roof is made of a thin shell of reinforced concrete held together by concrete struts, like the metal struts inside the wing of an airplane.

The only building in the United States designed entirely by Le Corbusier is the Visual Arts Center at Harvard University. It was finished in 1963, two years before Le Corbusier's death on August 27, 1965, in France.

HOWARD E. WOODEN
Director Emeritus
The Wichita Art Museum

LEE, HARPER. See ALABAMA (Famous People).
LEE, JASON. See OREGON (Famous People).

LEE, ROBERT E. (1807–1870)

Robert Edward Lee, the last commander in chief of the Confederate armies, was the most beloved general of the Civil War. He was born at Stratford, the Lee family home in Westmoreland County, Virginia, on January 19, 1807. His father was the famous "Light-Horse Harry" Lee, one of George Washington's generals and one-time governor of Virginia. His mother was Anne Hill Carter.

At 18, Robert entered the military academy at West Point. In 1829 he graduated second in his class and without a single fault on his record in four years. Two years later, Robert, newly commissioned a lieutenant in the U.S. Army Corps of Engineers, married Mary Randolph Custis, a great-granddaughter of First Lady Martha Washington. The years that followed were filled with routine engineering assignments. But during the Mexican War (1846–48), Lee, now a captain, greatly distinguished himself for his role in the capture of Veracruz and Mexico City. Later, as a lieutenant colonel of the cavalry, Lee served on the Texas frontier. Then in 1859 he led the raid on Harpers Ferry (West Virginia) that led to the arrest of the violent abolitionist John Brown.

▶ **A CONFLICT OF LOYALTY AND DUTY**

Lee was 54 years old and nearly ready to retire when the great crisis of his life occurred. In 1861 the states of the Deep South seceded from the Union and set up their own nation, the Confederate States of America. When Virginia seceded in April 1861, Lee was faced with the most difficult decision of his life: Should he stay with the Army of the United States or should he resign and go with his state? He did not believe in secession or in slavery. He was a soldier and the son of a soldier, and he had sworn allegiance to the United States. But he was first a Virginian, his roots deep in the soil of his state.

Yet to Lee the question was a simple one. "With all my devotion to the Union," he wrote, "I have not been able to make up my mind to raise my hand against my relatives, my children, my home." To General Winfield Scott, commander of the United States Army, he said: "Save in defense of my native State, I never desire again to draw my sword."

It was in defense of his state that Lee was now called upon to draw his sword. He had refused field command of the United States Army. Now Virginia put him in command of all its forces, and Confederate President Jefferson Davis appointed him as his military adviser.

Lee was in Richmond, Virginia, the Confederate capital, when a Union army of 100,000 troops, under General George McClellan, advanced to the outskirts of the city. On May 31, 1862, the Confederate and Union armies locked in combat at the Battle of Seven Pines. The Confederate commander, Joseph E. Johnston, was wounded, and President Davis appointed Lee to his place. Lee promptly gave the army the name that would become immortal—the Army of Northern Virginia.

Beyond any general in American history, Lee combined qualities that make for military greatness. First, he had an almost unfailing grasp both of grand strategy (the overall military policy) and of tactics (the direction of troops on the battlefield). Second, he showed himself always willing to take the offensive and to take risks. Third, he displayed an astonishing understanding of what the enemy was up to; thus he was able to outguess and outwit the other side. Fourth, and perhaps most important, Lee inspired limitless confidence and devotion in his men. "He is the only man whom I would follow blindfolded," said Stonewall Jackson. Lee had one other asset—a nobility of appearance and bearing. "He looked," said one Confederate general, "as though he ought to have been and was the monarch of the world."

Lee's immediate task was to save Richmond. His long-range task was to inflict such heavy losses on the Union forces that they would get fed up with the war and leave the South alone. In a series of battles called Seven Days, Lee and Stonewall Jackson hammered McClellan's army and sent it reeling back. Lee's losses were heavy, but Richmond was saved. The whole Union strategy was thrown off balance, and there was a new spirit of confidence in the Confederacy.

Swiftly, Lee marched north. He caught a second Union army, under General John Pope, by surprise, and at the Second Battle of Bull Run (Manassas) shattered the Union forces and sent them in full retreat to Washington, D.C. Now Lee decided to carry the war to the North. In September 1862, the Confederates splashed across the Potomac River. General McClellan advanced to meet Lee with some 70,000 men. Lee had sent Jackson to capture Harpers Ferry, so his forces were smaller than McClellan's. The two armies met at Sharpsburg, Maryland, on a little stream called Antietam. All day long the Union troops hurled themselves against the thin gray lines of the Confederate Army. As evening fell, Jackson's men came hurrying up from Harpers Ferry and saved the day for Lee. Yet it was not a clear Confederate victory, and Lee withdrew to Virginia.

Three months later a new Union commander, Ambrose Burnside, invaded Virginia. Lee moved swiftly to meet him near Fredericksburg and crushed Burnside's forces in a desperate battle. Next spring the Union tried again under a new commander, "Fighting Joe" Hooker. In one of the most brilliant actions of the war, Lee met Hooker in the tangled woods called the Wilderness and rolled him back with heavy losses. It was Lee's greatest victory but a costly one, for it was there that he lost his ablest general, Stonewall Jackson.

▶ THE TURNING POINT OF THE WAR

Once again Lee prepared to invade the North. He crossed into Pennsylvania and ran into Union troops at the little town of Gettysburg. The Battle of Gettysburg (July 1–3, 1863) was the worst fought of Lee's battles, partly because of mistakes by his generals. The result was a heavy defeat from which the Army of Northern Virginia never recovered.

On May 4, 1864, the new Union commander, Ulysses S. Grant, headed for Richmond with an army of well over 100,000 men. With only 60,000 men, Lee moved swiftly to stop him in the Wilderness. All month long the savage fighting went on, Lee outguessing Grant and stopping his advance. All together, Grant lost almost 60,000 men, and Lee half that number. Yet the Wilderness was a Union victory. Grant could replace his losses, but Lee could not. Grant finally swung his great army across the James River to Petersburg and began to move on Richmond from the south. Lee hurried to meet him and halted him. There, in front of Petersburg, the two armies dug in for the autumn and winter.

By now the fortunes of the Confederacy were at low ebb. In February 1865, Lee became commander in chief of all Confederate armies. But by then it was much too late for him to do anything effective. At the end of March, Lee decided that he must give up Richmond and retreat to the west. There he hoped to join up with remnants of other Confederate armies and make a last stand.

As Lee hurried west along the Appomattox River, Grant pursued him. At the same time, Union General Philip Sheridan's cavalry raced ahead of Lee, blocking his retreat. Lee was determined to avoid further bloodshed. On April 9, 1865, he met with General Grant at Appomattox Court House and surrendered what was left of his army. It was the end of the Confederacy.

▶ PEACE

"I believe it to be the duty of every one to unite in the restoration of the country and the re-establishment of peace and harmony," Lee wrote. He himself did his best for peace and harmony. In 1865 he accepted the presidency of Washington College (now Washington and Lee University) in Lexington, Virginia. He served as college president until his death on October 12, 1870.

Of all the military leaders in American history, very few can compare to Lee for qualities of spirit and of character. Honorable in all his actions, courageous and gallant in battle, patient in defeat, and generous in victory, Lee belongs not only to the South but to the whole nation.

HENRY STEELE COMMAGER
Author, *The Blue and the Gray*

See also JACKSON, THOMAS JONATHAN ("STONEWALL").

LEE, SPIKE. See MOTION PICTURES (Profiles: Directors).

LEE FAMILY

The Lees of Virginia were one of the most distinguished families in American history. From the settlement of Jamestown through the Revolution and the Civil War, the Lee family produced many exceptional statesmen, soldiers, and revolutionaries.

Richard Lee (1618–64), born in England,

Richard Henry Lee

was the first to come to America. He arrived in Jamestown, Virginia, about 1639. He rapidly acquired large amounts of land and became a prominent member of the Council of State, which governed the colony. His son, **Richard Lee** (1647–1715), and his grandson, **Thomas Lee** (1690–1750), also served on the Council of State.

Thomas' eldest son, **Philip Ludwell Lee** (1727–75), inherited Stratford Plantation, the family mansion his father built in Westmoreland County. He followed in his family's footsteps and was appointed to the Council of State. Two of his brothers, **Richard Henry Lee** (1732–94) and **Francis Lightfoot Lee** (1734–97), both born at Stratford, became rebels.

In 1758 Richard Henry was elected to Virginia's House of Burgesses. In his very first bill, he proposed to stop importing slaves into Virginia. Although this bill was defeated, he was among the first in the colonies to insist that Africans were "equally entitled to liberty and freedom by the great law of nature."

Later, he and his brother Francis Lightfoot were delegates to the Continental Congress (1775–79). On June 7, 1776, Richard Henry courageously proposed to Congress that the colonies should break free of their ties to England and become an independent nation. Richard Henry and Francis Lightfoot both signed the Declaration of Independence, the only brothers to do so.

Francis Lightfoot Lee

Richard Henry remained an active player in national politics. He served as president of Congress (1784–85) and later led the fight against the ratification of the U.S. Constitution, which he did not believe was forceful enough to protect individual liberties. After ratification, however, he served as a U.S. senator from Virginia (1789–92).

"Light Horse Harry" Lee

Matilda Lee (1764–90), the daughter of Philip Ludwell Lee, inherited Stratford. The Divine Matilda, as she was called, married a first cousin, **Henry Lee** (1756–1818).

Henry Lee was an outstanding cavalry leader in the Revolutionary War (1775–83). His lightning attacks on the British earned him the nickname Light Horse Harry. He fought the British for six years and was decorated for his leadership of the attack on Paulus Hook in New Jersey.

After the war, Henry became active in politics. He fought for the ratification of the Constitution and was elected to three 1-year terms as governor of Virginia. In 1794 during the Whiskey Rebellion, he was made commander of the federal army.

Henry Lee's wife Matilda died in childbirth in 1790. Three years later, Henry married **Ann Hill Carter** (1773–1829). In 1807, their fourth child, Robert E. Lee, who would later lead the Confederate Army during the Civil War, was born at Stratford. For more information, see the article LEE, ROBERT E. in this volume.

Light Horse Harry was not a good businessman. He was imprisoned for debt and only released after declaring bankruptcy. During the War of 1812, which he opposed, he was severely beaten by a mob in Baltimore. In 1813, anxious to avoid those to whom he owed money and to recover his health, he moved to the West Indies. His wife and children never saw him again.

JEANNE A. CALHOUN
Director of Research and Education
Stratford Hall Plantation

LEEUWENHOEK, ANTON VAN (1632–1723)

In 1673, the Royal Society of London began receiving letters filled with detailed drawings of strange creatures from a Dutch amateur biologist named Anton van Leeuwenhoek. Although few of the leading scientists of the day had heard of him, his letters immediately impressed the society's learned members. Many of the tiny creatures Leeuwenhoek described had never been seen before.

Over the next fifty years, Leeuwenhoek continued writing to the Royal Society about the unusual life-forms he was discovering using small but powerful microscopes he had made. Among his letters were the first recorded observations of **microbes**—organisms normally invisible to the naked eye.

Anton van Leeuwenhoek was born on October 24, 1632, in Delft, the Netherlands. By the time he was 22, Anton was married and owned his own fabric shop. A few years later he was appointed part-time caretaker of the Delft Town Hall. He ground lenses and made microscopes as a hobby. Later he gave up his fabric shop and devoted most of his time to grinding lenses.

Microscopes at that time were considered little more than scientific toys. Early compound microscopes—those that used more than one lens—could magnify objects, or make them appear larger, by 20 to 30 times their actual size. Leeuwenhoek's microscopes were much simpler, each having only one lens scarcely larger than the head of a pin. The lenses were ground so precisely, however, that they could clearly magnify objects 200 to 300 times.

Leeuwenhoek would spend hours peering through his tiny lenses. He looked at almost anything he could put under the lenses. He looked at the head of a fly, a piece of skin, a drop of rainwater, even the scrapings from his own teeth.

Leeuwenhoek discovered the one-celled animals we now call protozoa. He called them "animalcules" and "wretched beasties." He also discovered and made drawings of bacteria, but he could not explain what they were.

At that time people thought that certain forms of life came from air, mud, water, or decaying material. They thought life could even arise spontaneously—out of nothing.

But one day Leeuwenhoek examined some dirty rainwater under his microscope. In it he could see, as he wrote, "wretched beasties …swimming and playing, a thousand times smaller than one can see with the eye alone." He was puzzled. Did they come from the sky?

To find out, he collected some rainwater that had just fallen. There were no "beasties" in it. But after several days some did appear. He correctly concluded that they did not arise spontaneously at all but were carried by dust in the air. After hundreds of such experiments, he realized that even the lowest forms of life must have a parent.

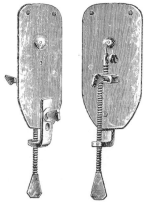

One time Leeuwenhoek looked at the tail of a tadpole through his microscope. He could see the flow of blood in tiny, thin-walled vessels—capillaries—connecting the veins and the arteries. William Harvey, who had discovered the circulation of the blood about 1616, had not been able to see the capillaries because there were no good microscopes in his time.

Leeuwenhoek lived to be 91 years old. He worked with lenses almost to his last day. He died in Delft on August 26, 1723.

DAVID C. KNIGHT
Author, science books for children

See also BIOLOGY; MICROBIOLOGY; MICROSCOPES.

Anton van Leeuwenhoek (**left**) discovered many tiny organisms, invisible to the naked eye, using his simple, handcrafted single-lens microscopes (**above**).

LEGENDS

Legends are a kind of folklore—the artistic and creative traditions of a society. They are stories about people or events that seem important and worth telling about, and they often reflect the values and beliefs of the people who tell them. In fact, one purpose of a legend is to maintain, reinforce, and validate the traditional beliefs and ideas of a particular culture. Legends can also teach about important historical figures or they can warn people against certain kinds of behavior. But the usual purpose of telling a legend is to entertain.

▶ CHARACTERISTICS OF LEGENDS

Legends are distinguished from other kinds of folklore by three essential characteristics. First, legends are believed to be true by the people who tell them (although people sometimes repeat legends they do not personally believe). Second, legends are realistic; they sound like they could have happened, and they are set in a specific time in history or even in the present. Third, legends always involve humans. They may also include supernatural beings, such as ghosts or vampires, but their focus is always on people and what happens to them in the real world.

The term "legend" comes from the Latin word *legenda*, meaning "things to be read."

But, although many legends were written down years ago, they began as oral stories that were passed on from person to person, often changing slightly in the process. The teller of a legend does not claim to be creating a story, like Mark Twain recounting the adventures of his fictional character Tom Sawyer. Even though a legend may find its way into print, it is not the original creation of a single author. A famous story, such as Washington Irving's "The Legend of Sleepy Hollow," may be based on a real legend—in this case, a story about a headless horseman—but Irving's story is literature, while the oral tales that must have circulated about the horseman were legends.

Many legends are quite old. We can prove their age by pointing to written versions of them in ancient texts, such as the Bible or the Sumerian poem the *Epic of Gilgamesh*. Some legends are **migratory**, meaning they are found throughout the world. Other legends are tied to a specific place, but even then the stories are known collectively by many of the people in that area.

▶ KINDS OF LEGENDS

Folklorists who study legends recognize four general categories of legend: historical, personal, supernatural, and modern or contemporary. Some legends have characteristics that would suggest they be placed in more

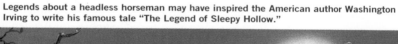
Legends about a headless horseman may have inspired the American author Washington Irving to write his famous tale "The Legend of Sleepy Hollow."

than one of these four categories, but usually it is relatively easy to determine where a legend belongs.

Historical Legends

Most place-name legends are considered historical legends since they account for a historical occurrence, such as how a place came to have the name it bears. However, even though a story is called a historical legend, and even though people may believe the story, the story may in fact be inaccurate. "Historical" in this case simply means that the story is tied to a historical event. There are many stories, for example, about how Indiana, a state in the American Midwest, came to be called the Hoosier State. One story includes reference to a construction boss whose last name was Hoosier; another relates the tradition of fighting on the early frontier and ends with the improbable question after the bloody fight—"Who's ear?"—which sounds like "Hoosier." There is no clear evidence for considering either story an accurate historical account, but both stories would be called historical legends.

Other historical legends include accounts of battles, natural disasters, famines, sinking ships, mining accidents, train wrecks, amazing rescues, famous contests, or bloody massacres. Some of these stories are of local events, but others, such as the story of American colonists dressed as Native Americans dumping British tea into Boston Harbor, are widely known and have national significance.

Personal Legends

Often closely related to historical legends are personal legends, stories that recount the acts of a specific individual. An example would be the well-known story of a young George Washington cutting down the cherry tree and saying, "I cannot tell a lie. I did it with my little hatchet." Important figures like Washington, Abraham Lincoln, or the Macedonian king Alexander the Great often have cycles of legends associated with them. A legend cycle is a series of tales revolving around one particular person or subject. An American hero from the early 1800's, Davy Crockett, was one of the first to use the newspaper to circulate his cycle of legends. More recently, popular entertainers and sports figures are often made "legendary" through the sto-

ries told about them through movies, television, and other media.

Folklorists often write book-length studies bringing together the many stories told and written about such well-known figures as Billy the Kid, Geronimo, Annie Oakley, Robin Hood, Lawrence of Arabia, Joan of Arc, King Arthur, Saint Patrick, or Marco Polo. Other personal legends are told about people who are known only in a specific region or country. For instance, the legend of the heroic outlaw Ned Kelly (who stole from the rich and gave to the poor, just like Robin Hood) is very familiar to people living in the southeastern part of Australia, but most people outside that area have never heard of it.

Historical and personal legends are more likely to have a basis in fact than are other kinds of legends. Public records and other documents can provide information about when or where legendary people actually lived and performed their famous deeds.

Supernatural Legends

Supernatural legends involve such phenomena as werewolves, ghosts, haunted houses, or people who return from the dead. They are often recounted piecemeal, with one person telling a part of the story and other persons adding more details. When such legends involve local people or places, often many people in the area will know the story and simply refer to it by a short phrase, such as the story of the House of Blue Lights (a ghost story told in Indianapolis, Indiana).

Supernatural legends are often far less easily tied to specific recorded facts, although they are often written down or published in the newspaper. A famous supernatural legend that is believed to have a historical basis is the vampire Dracula. Although the account in Bram Stoker's novel *Dracula* is fictional, the character is thought to be based on a brutal prince of Romania who lived in the 1400's and engaged in behavior that later became associated with vampires.

Modern, or Urban, Legends

Modern legends are also told as if true, or at least as if they could possibly have happened. But while supernatural legends may or may not be migratory, the same modern legends are found throughout the world. These contemporary legends are often spread through newspapers or television, and their setting is often the city rather than the countryside and small villages usually associated with supernatural legends. In fact, modern legends are often called urban legends even though not all of them are set in the city.

Modern legends tend to be short and often prefaced by a comment that lends credibility to the story by way of personal connection. That is, often the person telling the story claims that the mishap in the legend happened to a friend or relative of someone he or she knows—a "friend of a friend" or FOAF. This claim of authenticity, along with an ironic or dramatic twist to the plot at the very end of the story, is a hallmark of modern legends.

Urban legends that have become widely told include stories about alligators living in sewers, contaminated food, the deaths or strange behaviors of celebrities, and bizarre medical occurrences.

Modern legends continue the tradition begun long ago in the oral tales of our ancestors. Just as yesterday's legends did, the legends we create today and in the future will reveal our ever-changing beliefs, values, and perceptions of the world in which we live.

SANDRA K. DOLBY
Professor of Folklore, Indiana University

Three legends follow. The first is an urban legend found in many variations throughout the United States and elsewhere. Some versions of this tale are lent credibility with the "friend of a friend" element and even with reports in newspapers. The second legend originated in France and tells of Roland, nephew of the Emperor Charlemagne, and Oliver, nephew of Charlemagne's enemy, Count Girard. The third legend is one of many about England's Robin Hood. This version is based on a tale from *The Merry Adventures of Robin Hood* (1883), by the American author and illustrator Howard Pyle.

THE VANISHING HITCHHIKER

A traveling man who lived in Spartanburg was on his way home one night when he saw a woman walking along the side of the road. He stopped his car and asked the woman if he could take her where she was going. She stated that she was on her way to visit her brother who lived about three miles further on the same road. He asked her to get in the car and sit by him, but she said she would sit in the back of

the car. Conversation took place for a while as they rode along, but soon the woman grew quiet. The man drove on until he reached the home of the woman's brother, whom he knew; then stopped his car to let the woman alight. When he looked behind him, there was no one in the car. He thought that rather strange, so went into the house and informed the brother that a lady had gotten into his car to ride to see him, but when he arrived at the house the lady had disappeared. The brother was not alarmed at all and stated that the lady was his sister who had died two years before. He said that this traveling man was the seventh to pick up his sister on the road to visit him, but that she had never reached his house yet.

ROLAND AND OLIVER

In the days of the Emperor Charlemagne, Charles the Great of the Franks, who ruled France and Germany and fought so mightily against the enemies of Christendom, there lived a count named Girard. Count Girard held the city and the castle of Vienne and the land that lay about it, but he was no friend to his Emperor, and with his vassals and his knights he rebelled and made war on him. Charlemagne, much angered, called together his army and marched against Vienne, whilst Gi-

rard and his followers retreated into the city, defending the walls bravely. For many months the advantage fell to neither side, and time passed until the siege had lasted for two whole years, and many there were among the besiegers, as well as among the besieged, who longed for the war to be over. Yet the city could not be taken, so well was it defended, and Charlemagne, glad though he would have been to be at peace with all his subjects, could not bring himself to withdraw his army, lest it should seem as though he acknowledged himself defeated by a rebel.

With the Emperor's army were those who were considered the great champions of France: Duke Naimes, his most trusted counsellor, Ganelon, who later brought such sorrow on France, Ogier the Dane, Yve and Yvoire, Gerin, Engelier the Gascon, Turpin the Archbishop of Rheims, who could wield a sword in defence of his faith as well as any knight, Duke Samson and brave Count Anseïs: ten champions famed throughout France.

There, too, with Charlemagne was his young nephew Roland, son of the Emperor's sister Berthe. Roland had but lately been knighted and he was anxious to prove himself, yet so long as the siege lasted it seemed as though he would have little chance of showing his worth. The days went slowly for him, and with the other young knights and the squires he often left the camp and hunted in the woods near Vienne, or jousted with his companions; and among them there was no one more skilled at feats of arms than he.

Count Girard also had a nephew, Oliver, of an age with Roland; and one day, for an adventure, carrying plain arms, that he might be unknown, Oliver slipped unseen through the gates of Vienne and wandered into the Emperor's camp. Here in an open space he found Roland and his companions tilting together, and after watching for a while, he asked if he might join them. Though he was a stranger to them, they thought him one of the Emperor's men, and they lent him a horse and let him tilt with them. Soon it was apparent that Oliver surpassed them all. Not even Roland, who was accounted the best among them, was more skilled with lance and sword.

The youths were loud in admiration of the stranger and asked his name, but he only smiled and would not answer. Then someone whispered that he might be an enemy, since in two years no one of them had seen him before. And the murmur went round amongst them, so that their friendly smiles were changed to suspicious frowns, and they crowded about him, demanding his name. Rough hands were laid upon him, but he broke free, and leaping on a horse, rode for his life towards the walls of Vienne.

'After him!' cried Roland. 'He must not escape. He is too good a prize to lose.' And the young knights rode after him swiftly with Roland at their head. Steadily Roland gained on Oliver, until he was upon him, and close beneath the city walls, Oliver turned to face his pursuers, and Roland, in triumph, raised his sword to strike. But at that moment there came a cry of terror from the walls above, and Roland looked up and saw a maiden, the fairest he had ever seen, standing on the ramparts, her hands clasped in supplication and her face pale with fear. It was lovely Aude, the sister of Oliver. 'Spare my brother Oliver,' she pleaded. And Roland, staring at her, slowly lowered his sword and let Oliver ride on to the gates unharmed. 'I could not bring grief to so fair a maiden,' he said to himself.

During the days that followed, Roland thought much on Oliver and Aude, and wished that they had not been the Emperor's enemies. And for their part, they thought of Roland, and wished the war were at an end; and Oliver sought to persuade his uncle to peace.

After a time, his nephew's counsels prevailed, and Count Girard sent Oliver, well attended, to Charlemagne to ask that they might be accorded. 'If you will withdraw your army, sire, my uncle the Count will come forth from Vienne and swear allegiance, and he will serve you faithfully for all his life,' said Oliver.

But the Emperor, for all that he hated warring against his own vassals, could not find it in his heart to forgive Girard his rebellion so easily. 'Let Count Girard humble himself before me, and I will consider pardoning him,' he said.

'Sire,' replied Oliver, 'that would my uncle never do.'

'Then the war goes on,' said Charlemagne. But Duke Naimes spoke to him, counselling peace.

Oliver, standing before the Emperor, turned his head and looked at Roland and saw how he was watching him. He smiled and said impulsively, 'You and I are of an age and well matched. How say you, if our uncles are willing, shall we settle this war in single combat?'

'Gladly,' said Roland, and he begged the Emperor's permission. After thought, Charlemagne agreed. 'Go back and tell Count Girard,' he said to Oliver, 'that if you are victorious in this contest I will depart from his lands with all my army, and leave him in peace for ever. But if my nephew Roland is the victor, then must Count Girard lose Vienne and all his lands to me.'

'I shall tell him,' said Oliver; and he returned to the city.

And so it was decided that the outcome of the war should be determined by single combat between the two young knights, and a day was named upon which they should meet on a little isle in a river that ran between the camp and the city walls.

On the appointed day, Roland, armed and carrying his sword Durendal, which no blade could withstand, went to the islet to await Oliver. Soon Count Girard's nephew came out through the city gates, wearing the armour and bearing the sword which had been given to him by a good Jew of Vienne on the day he had been made a knight.

Eagerly all those from the Emperor's camp crowded about Charlemagne and the champions of France upon the bank of the river to watch the fight, whilst Count Girard and his family, and Aude with them, stood upon the walls of Vienne with the defenders of the city.

The two young men greeted each other courteously, and at once the battle began. They were indeed well matched, giving blow for blow; and at any one of their strokes a lesser knight would have fallen. Soon their shields were dented and their armour battered, links from their chain mail falling about them as they hacked with their good swords. But at last with a great stroke from Durendal, the strongest sword in all France, Oliver's blade was broken and he fell to his knees with the force of the blow. A cry of fear went up from the watchers on the walls of Vienne, but from the Emperor's knights a shout of triumph rose. Oliver thought, 'My last moment is come,' and he braced himself to meet the stroke which would end his life. But Roland flung Durendal aside. 'I cannot slay an unarmed man,' he said.

Oliver rose, and he and Roland tore up two saplings to serve them as clubs, and with these they continued their fight until the green wood was broken all to splinters. And then the young knights wrestled together, each striving unsuccessfully to throw the other, until, at midday, both locked in each other's grip, they fell to the ground at the same time, so that neither could be said to have thrown the other. They stood up, breathless and exhausted. 'The sun is high,' said Roland. 'It is too hot for fighting. Let us rest awhile.'

They took off their helmets and smiled at one another. 'I am happy,' said Oliver, 'that I am privileged to fight with so worthy an enemy.' And the two young men embraced and sat down upon the grass and talked together as though they had been old friends. Wine was brought to them from the city, and another sword for Oliver; and when an hour or two had passed and the sun was lower in the sky, they helped each other to arm again, and once more began their fight.

As before, neither proved the better, and for long the battle raged, until suddenly, stepping aside to avoid a blow from Oliver, Roland lowered his sword and said, 'Stay your hand awhile, for I feel a weakness come over me as though I had a fever, and I would rest.'

With courtesy Oliver set aside his sword. 'Rest for as long as you need, good Roland. I would not wish to be victor because you are unwell. Lie down and I will watch over you.'

Roland, who was merely feigning sickness in order to test Oliver, took off his helmet and lay down upon the grass. Oliver placed his shield beneath his head to serve him as a pillow and fetched water for him from the river in his own helmet.

Watching, Charlemagne thought, 'My nephew is

vanquished and I have lost the day.' While from the walls of Vienne fair Aude watched with pity; for though her brother's cause was hers, from her first sight of him she had felt a great admiration for Roland, an admiration which she knew could very easily turn to love.

But Roland sprang to his feet and laughed. 'I did but try you, Oliver. And so courteously have you treated me that I wish we were brothers or friends, and not enemies.'

'Brothers we could be,' replied Oliver. 'If we both live through this battle, I will give you my sister for your wife, since there is no other to whom I would rather see her wed. And as for friends, are we not friends already in our hearts?'

They fell once more to fighting, and again the advantage lay with neither, and still they fought as the sun went down the sky and sank from sight. Through the twilight they fought, while the watchers strained their eyes to see them and could not tell one from the other; and on into the darkness, so that only the sound of metal clashing upon metal told that the battle still went on.

And then at last from the darkness there was silence, as with one accord they ceased their strife. 'Heaven does not mean that to either of us shall be the victory,' they said. And they threw down their weapons and embraced, swearing friendship for ever. 'Never again shall we take arms against each other,' they vowed.

Each of them persuaded his uncle to be at peace, and for love of them Charlemagne and Count Girard were accorded, uniting against their common enemies, the Saracens, who held all Spain and were attacking France. And on a happy May morning Roland and Aude were betrothed, to their great joy and Oliver's.

From the day of their battle Roland and Oliver were comrades in arms, riding together against the Saracens and fighting side by side, winning such fame that they were accounted amongst the champions of France, the foremost of the twelve. Roland was ever brave, brave to the point of rashness, and very proud, and he hated the Saracens with all his heart and never trusted them. But Oliver, though no less brave, was gentle and cautious and never set his own glory before the good of France. Many adventures did the two young knights have in the years they were together, and until the day they died they were never parted.

THE LEGEND OF ROBIN HOOD

In merry England in the time of old, when good King Henry the Second ruled the land, there lived within the green glades of Sherwood Forest, near Nottingham Town, a famous outlaw whose name was Robin Hood. No archer ever lived that could speed a gray goose shaft with such skill and cunning as his, nor were there ever such yeomen as the sevenscore merry men that roamed with him through the greenwood shades. Right merrily they dwelt within the depths of Sherwood Forest, suffering neither care nor want, but passing the time in merry games of archery or bouts of cudgel play, living upon the King's venison, washed down with drafts of ale of October brewing.

Not only Robin himself but all the band were outlaws and dwelt apart from other men, yet they were beloved by the country people round about, for no one ever came to jolly Robin for help in time of need and went away again with an empty fist.

When Robin was a youth of eighteen, stout of sinew and bold of heart, the Sheriff of Nottingham proclaimed a shooting match and offered a prize of a cask of ale to whomsoever should shoot the best shaft in Nottinghamshire. "Now," said Robin, "will I go too, for gladly would I draw a string for the bright eyes of my lass, and a cask of good October brewing." So up he got and took his good stout yew bow and a score or more of broad clothyard arrows, and started off from Locksley Town through Sherwood Forest to Nottingham.

As he walked along with a brisk step and a merry whistle, he came suddenly upon some foresters seated beneath a great oak tree. Fifteen there were in all, making themselves merry with feasting and drinking as they sat around a huge pasty, to which each man helped himself, thrusting his hands into the pie, and washing down that which they ate with great horns of ale. Then one of them, with his mouth full, called out to Robin, "Hulloa, where are you going, little lad, with your one-penny bow and your farthing shafts?"

Then Robin grew angry, for no young man likes to be taunted with his green years.

"Now," said he, "my bow and my arrows are as good as yours; and moreover, I go to the shooting match at Nottingham Town, which has been proclaimed by our good Sheriff of Nottinghamshire. There I will shoot with other stout yeomen, for a prize has been offered of a fine cask of ale."

Then one who held a horn of ale in his hand said, "Ho! Listen to the lad! Why, boy, your mother's milk is scarcely dry upon your lips, and yet you speak of standing up with good stout men at Nottingham, you who are scarce able to draw one string of a two-stone bow."

"I'll hold the best of you twenty marks," said bold Robin, "that I hit the target at threescore rods, by the help of Our Lady fair."

At this all laughed aloud, and one said, "Well boasted, fair infant, well boasted! And well you know that no target is near to make good your wager."

And another cried, "He will be taking ale with his milk next."

At this Robin grew right mad. "Hark ye," said he; "yonder, at the glade's end, I see a herd of deer, even more than threescore rods distant. I'll hold you twenty marks that, by leave of Our Lady, I cause the best stag among them to die."

"Now done!" cried he who had spoken first. "And here are twenty marks. I wager that you shall cause no beast to die, with or without the aid of Our Lady."

Then Robin took his good yew bow in his hand, and placing the tip at his instep, he strung it deftly; then he nocked a broad clothyard arrow, and, raising the bow, drew the gray goose feather to his ear; the next moment the bowstring rang and the arrow sped down the glade as a sparrow-hawk skims in a northern wind. High leaped the noblest stag of all the herd, only to fall dead.

"Ha!" cried Robin, "how like you that shot, good fellow? I say the wager is mine, even if it were three hundred pounds."

Then all the foresters were filled with rage, and he who had spoken first and had lost the wager was more angry than all.

"Nay," cried he, "the wager is none of yours. Get you gone, straightway, or, by all the saints of heaven, I'll baste your sides until you will never be able to walk again."

"Know you not," said another, "that you have killed the King's deer, and, by the laws of our gracious lord and sovereign, King Harry, your ears should be shaven close to your head?"

"Catch him!" cried a third.

"Nay," said a fourth, "let him go because of his tender years."

Never a word said Robin Hood, but he looked at the foresters with a grim face; then, turning on his heel, strode away from them down the forest glade. But his heart was bitterly angry.

Now, well would it have been for him who had first spoken had he left Robin Hood alone; but his anger was hot, both because the youth had gotten the better of him and because of the ale that he had been drinking. So, of a sudden, he sprang to his feet, and seized upon his bow and fitted it to a shaft. "Ay," cried he, "and I'll hurry you anon." And he sent the arrow whistling after Robin.

It was well for Robin Hood that same forester's head was spinning with ale, or else he would have never taken another step; as it was, the arrow whistled within three inches of his head. Then he turned around and quickly drew his own bow, and sent an arrow back in return.

"You said I was no archer," cried he aloud, "but say so now again!"

The shaft flew straight; the archer fell forward with a cry, and lay on his face upon the ground. Then, before the others could gather their wits about them, Robin Hood was gone into the depths of the greenwood. Some started after him, but not with much heart, for each feared to suffer the death of his fellow; so presently they all came and lifted the dead man up and bore him away to Nottingham Town.

Meanwhile Robin Hood ran through the greenwood. Gone was all the joy and brightness from everything, for his heart was sick within him, and it was borne in upon his soul that he had slain a man.

"Alas!" cried he, "I wish that you had never said one word to me, or that I had never passed your way, or even that my right forefinger had been stricken off ere that this had happened! In haste I struck, but grieve I now at leisure!"

And so he came to dwell in the greenwood that was to be his home for many a year to come; for he was outlawed, not only because he had killed a man, but also because he had poached the King's deer. Two hundred pounds were set upon his head, as a reward for whoever would bring him to the court of the King.

Now the Sheriff of Nottingham swore that he himself would bring this knave, Robin Hood, to justice, and for two reasons: first, because he wanted the two hundred pounds, and next, because the forester that Robin Hood had killed was of kin to him.

But Robin Hood lay hidden in Sherwood Forest for one year, and in that time there gathered around him many others like himself. All, for one cause or another, had come to Sherwood to escape wrong and oppression.

So, in all that year, fivescore or more stout yeomen gathered about Robin Hood, and chose him to be their leader and chief. Then they vowed that even as they themselves had been robbed they would rob their oppressors, and that from each they would take that which had been wrung from the poor by unjust taxes, or land rents, or in wrongful fines. But to the poor folk they would give a helping hand in need and trouble, and would return to them that which had been unjustly taken from them. Besides this, they swore never to harm a child nor to wrong a woman; so that, after a while, when the people began to find that no harm was meant to them, but that money or food came in time of want to many a poor family, they came to praise Robin and his merry men, and to tell many tales of him and of his doings in Sherwood Forest.

LÉGER, FERNAND (1881–1955)

The French artist Fernand Léger is recognized as one of the 20th century's greatest painters. Léger painted pictures about modern times. In his paintings, he captured the excitement of everyday life in the new century—the energy of cities, of working people, and of the machine. His style ranged from fully abstract works made up of colored shapes to paintings of people, places, and objects.

Léger was born on February 4, 1881, in Argentan, France. He went to Paris to study painting in 1903 and was influenced by the painter Paul Cézanne and a new style of art known as cubism. During World War I (1914–18), Léger served in the army. After the war, he returned to Paris to paint again. The bright colors and shapes he saw in advertisements, shop windows, and traffic lights inspired him to create abstract pictures that suggested the liveliness of the city.

Léger also painted machines and machine-like forms invented from his imagination. He was fascinated by machine-made objects such as cups and bottles and painted them in unusual ways, using bold colors, geometric shapes, and new painting styles. *The City* (1919) and *Three Women* (1921) are two of his masterpieces. After 1932, Léger wanted his art to appeal to a wide audience, so he

The City (1919) by French artist Fernand Léger.

began painting huge murals such as *Composition with Two Parrots* (1935–39).

In 1940, to escape World War II (1939–45) in Europe, Léger moved to New York. He returned to France after the war and painted pictures of modern people at their jobs and at leisure. Léger also worked as a filmmaker, theatrical designer, and book illustrator and is known for his film *Ballet mécanique* (1924). Léger died at his farm in France on August 17, 1955. A museum, the Musée Fernand Léger, opened in Biot, France, in 1960.

JOYCE RAIMONDO
Department of Education
The Museum of Modern Art

LEGISLATURES

The word "legislature" comes from Latin and means "a body for proposing law." In other words, a legislature is a lawmaking body. A legislature may also approve the raising and spending of money by the government, and it may make amendments to the constitution. Sometimes it may approve or reject people who have been appointed to certain public offices.

More than half the national legislatures in the world today are **bicameral**. That is, they are divided into two houses, or chambers—an upper house and a lower house. The lower house may be elected directly by the people. Or it may be elected indirectly through an electoral college. Members of the upper house may be elected, as in the U.S. Senate, or appointed by the government, as in the Canadian Senate. They also may inherit the position, as do most members of the British House of Lords. In most bicameral legislatures, both houses must approve a bill before it becomes law. Some countries have **unicameral**, or one-house, legislatures.

Many countries also have regional legislatures representing states, provinces, or districts. Cities and other units of local government may have their own legislatures.

In democratic countries the national legislature represents and expresses the will of the majority of the people. Legislators are usually elected for two to five years. Historically, the legislature in democratic countries controlled the executive branch of government—the branch that carries out the laws. But in some governments, the executive is more powerful. Where there is only one political party, the legislature often does little more than approve party decisions automatically.

From the time of the ancient Greek city-states, countries have often had some form of legislature. The world's oldest existing legislature, the Althing, was founded in Iceland in A.D. 930. Governing bodies that represented all the people of England first met in the late 1200's, during the reign of Edward I.

The name of the national legislature is not the same in every country. For example, in Japan the legislature is the Diet, in Canada the Parliament, and in the United States the Congress. The legislature in most Latin-American countries is also called Congress.

JOHN S. MOIR
University of Toronto

See also GOVERNMENT, FORMS OF; PARLIAMENTS; articles on individual countries.

LE GUIN, URSULA K. See OREGON (Famous People); SCIENCE FICTION (Profiles).

EXAMPLES OF REPRESENTATIVE LEGISLATURES

Country	Legislative Body	Houses of the Legislature
Bangladesh	National Parliament	(unicameral)
Brazil	National Congress	Federal Senate, Chamber of Deputies
Canada	Parliament	Senate, House of Commons
China (People's Republic of)	National People's Congress	(unicameral)
Egypt	People's Assembly	People's Assembly, Advisory Council
France	Parliament	Senate, National Assembly
Germany	Federal Parliament	Bundesrat (Federal Council), Bundestag (Federal Assembly)
Greece	Chamber of Deputies	(unicameral)
India	Parliament	Council of States, People's Assembly
Indonesia	House of Representatives	(unicameral)
Israel	Knesset (Parliament)	(unicameral)
Italy	Parliament	Senate, Chamber of Deputies
Japan	Diet	House of Councillors, House of Representatives
Mexico	National Congress	Senate, Chamber of Deputies
Pakistan	Parliament	Senate, National Assembly
Philippines	Congress	Senate, House of Representatives
Russia	Federal Assembly	Federation Council, State Duma
South Africa	Parliament	National Assembly, National Council of Provinces
Switzerland	Federal Assembly	Council of States, National Council
Thailand	National Assembly	Senate, House of Representatives
Turkey	Grand National Assembly	(unicameral)
United Kingdom	Parliament	House of Lords, House of Commons
United States	Congress	Senate, House of Representatives

LEIBNIZ, GOTTFRIED WILHELM VON (1646–1716)

Gottfried Wilhelm von Leibniz was one of the greatest thinkers of his era and perhaps in all history. He traveled widely, and he mastered much of the available knowledge of his time. He made important contributions to mathematics, philosophy, law, politics, theology, physics, and history. Leibniz ranks with Descartes, Hobbes, Galileo, and Spinoza as an example of the rational and scientific spirit that marked the change from medieval to modern thought.

Leibniz was born on July 1, 1646, in Leipzig, Germany, where his father was a professor. His brilliance showed even when he was a child, and he received a doctorate in law at the age of 20. For most of his life he served as an adviser to a royal family, all the while carrying on study and research in various fields.

At almost the same time but independently of each other, Leibniz and Isaac Newton invented the system of mathematics known as the calculus. This was one of the most remarkable coincidences in the history of science. Both men claimed exclusive credit for the invention, but the verdict of history is that they deserve equal credit. Leibniz also attempted to merge mathematics and philosophy. He tried to devise a mathematical language in which all problems could be precisely defined and solved. He did not succeed, but he helped set the stage for developments in logic and in computer sciences three centuries later. Interestingly, Leibniz did succeed in building a calculating machine.

Leibniz proposed certain basic principles that have influenced science and philosophy ever since. Among these are the principle of indiscernibles—that no two things can be exactly alike; the principle of sufficient reason—that every fact must have a reason that fully explains it; and the principle of pre-established harmony—that God created this world to be the best of all possible worlds. Late in life, Leibniz developed the theory of monads, according to which everything is made up of infinitely tiny spiritual substances called monads.

Leibniz' most important philosophical writings are *Theodicy* (1710) and *Monadology* (1714). He died in Hanover, Germany, on November 14, 1716.

RAZIEL ABELSON
New York University

LEMON AND LIME

Lemons and limes have many uses. They flavor pies, puddings, frostings, candies, jams, and marmalades. They are served with fish and some kinds of meat. Lemon juice is used in salad dressings and in tea. Lemonade and limeade are popular hot-weather drinks.

Lemons and limes are also good for health. On long voyages, sailors once faced the danger of scurvy, a dreaded disease. What caused scurvy was a mystery, but by the 1750's, it was known that oranges and lemons could prevent the disease. The British explorer Captain James Cook provided his sailors with these fruits on a long voyage (1772–75), and none of them developed scurvy. By 1795 all British sailors were being given lemon or lime juice. ''Limey'' became a nickname for a British sailor. Now we know that a lack of vitamin C causes scurvy, and lemons and limes contain this vitamin.

Lemons, limes and citrons are citrus fruits, like oranges and grapefruit. Citrus fruits are native to southeastern Asia. Citrons (fruit with little pulp and a very thick peel) were brought to the Mediterranean area before Christian times. During the Middle Ages, Arabs brought lemons and limes to the area.

Columbus took lemon seeds to the New World on his second voyage, in 1493. The seeds were planted on the island of Hispaniola, where they took root quickly and the trees grew vigorously. In the 1500's, Spanish conquerers took the seeds to Mexico and Central America. The Spanish who settled in St. Augustine, Florida, in 1565 also planted lemon seeds. Portuguese settlers had planted lemons and limes in Brazil by 1540.

All citrus trees are evergreens with glossy green leaves and white or pink flowers. The skins of lemons, limes, and citrons are thick

Lemons (*left*) and limes (*right*) are citrus fruits.

rinds with many small glands full of fragrant oil. The flesh of the fruit is pulpy.

The trees grow well in hot, semi-dry climates. In a very good climate, lemon and lime trees bloom almost all the time. The fruit matures continuously and is self-fertile.

Lemon and lime trees are expensive to care for. They must be carefully sprayed to protect them from insects and disease. They must be irrigated when the weather is dry. They must be protected against frost. Heaters and wind machines are kept ready for use at any time. Heaters warm the air around the trees. Wind machines stir the air so that the cold air does not settle and freeze the trees.

▶LEMONS

The commercial growing of lemons began in Italy. Large quantities of lemons are also grown in Greece, Spain, and Turkey.

The first commercial lemon orchards in the United States were planted in Florida. These orchards were destroyed in the severe freeze of 1894–95. The industry did not start again for 60 years. The early growers did not realize that lemons are more sensitive to cold than oranges are. Lemons must be planted in very warm, but not too humid, citrus-growing areas. The trees develop many diseases in humid weather. Since 1955 there have been new plantings of lemon trees in southern Florida, but orchards are not widespread.

In Florida lemons cannot be shipped as fresh fruit. This is because they ripen there in September, when lemons are no longer in heavy demand. The greatest use of lemons is during the hot months. Therefore, the juice of Florida lemons is made into frozen concentrate and stored until the following summer.

The lemon industry was set up in California in 1880, near the warmer coastal areas. Since that time the state has become the largest producing area of fresh lemons in the United States. In California, lemons do not have to be picked all at the same time. The season extends over several months.

California lemons are picked while they are still green. They are then cured for a long period of time in cool, dry storage houses. During storage the green fruits slowly turn to a beautiful waxy yellow.

In one year the United States produces an average of about 1,000,000 metric tons of lemons. Most come from the California-Arizona area. The Mediterranean area produces even more, averaging about 1,400,000 metric tons a year. Lemons are also produced on a small scale in South America.

▶LIMES

The lime industry has never been very large. Mexico is the leading producer and exporter of limes. It produces more than 900,000 metric tons each year. The West Indies and Egypt have lime orchards, but the fruits are chiefly used locally. There is a small lime industry in southern Florida.

The lime is more likely to be injured by cold than is the lemon. Only the warmest and most humid areas can be used for lime growing.

There are two main varieties of acid limes. The most important is called the Mexican lime. It is a small, very sour fruit that grows on small, bushy trees. The other is called the

Tahiti lime. It has larger fruit, from taller and lovelier trees.

Not all limes are sour. Sweet limes are popular in Central and South America, India, and Egypt. Sweet limes have not been grown in Europe and the United States because there has been no demand for them.

▶ CITRONS

Citrons are used to make a candied peel. They are rarely used except in fruitcakes and some candies. Citrons are not commercially important. They grow wild in northern India, and a few are cultivated in southwest Asia, southern Europe, and the West Indies.

A citron called ethrog is used in the Jewish festival of Sukkoth. The real citrus-type citron should not be confused with a watermelonlike plant of the same name.

HARRY W. FORD
University of Florida

See also FRUITGROWING; ORANGE AND GRAPEFRUIT.

L'ENGLE, MADELEINE. See CHILDREN'S LITERATURE (Profiles).

LENIN, VLADIMIR ILICH (1870–1924)

On November 7, 1917, a group of revolutionaries seized control of the Russian government. Their success was due in large part to the efforts of one man—Lenin—who had long been working toward this goal.

Lenin was born Vladimir Ilich Ulyanov in Simbirsk (now Ulyanovsk) on April 22, 1870, one of six children of a middle-class family. His father was a school inspector with an honorary title as a hereditary nobleman.

In 1887, the year that Vladimir graduated from high school, his older brother was executed for taking part in a revolutionary plot. In the next few years Vladimir became interested in the theories of Karl Marx, a German philosopher. Marx saw history as a class war between poor workers and rich employers. In 1891, Vladimir received a law degree from the University of St. Petersburg. (The city was known as Leningrad from 1924 to 1991.) He never practiced seriously, for he spent most of his time spreading Marx's ideas.

V. I. Lenin.

In 1895, Vladimir was arrested for his activities. He was sentenced to jail and then exiled to Siberia. There he completed one of his best-known works, *The Development of Capitalism in Russia*. When he was released from exile, Lenin went to Germany and Switzerland. He published a newspaper, *Iskra (The Spark)*, calling for the overthrow of the czar. About this time he began to use the pen name Lenin. During the following years he traveled throughout Europe, strengthening his position in the Communist movement. His supporters were called Bolsheviks, which means "majority group" in Russian.

When World War I began, Lenin called on the working classes to turn the conflict into a struggle against the rich. In March 1917, the Russian people revolted, forcing the czar to abdicate. A provisional government took control. Lenin returned to Russia to unite the revolutionary forces. He issued his "April Theses," calling for the transfer of political power to soviets, or councils of workers. Finally his followers seized control and established what they called a dictatorship of the working class. Actually, it was a dictatorship of a single party—that of the Communists. Civil war broke out between Communists and anti-Communists. In 1921, the conflict ended in victory for the Communists.

Until his death on January 21, 1924, Lenin ruled the Soviet state. His body lies in a mausoleum in Red Square, Moscow.

Reviewed by BERTRAM D. WOLFE
Author, *Three Who Made a Revolution*

See also COMMUNISM; MARX, KARL; STALIN, JOSEPH.

LENSES

Thousands of years ago someone happened to look through a glass bead and noticed that it made things seem larger. The glass bead was really a crude lens because it had a rounded surface. Later, people found that they could shape glass into bigger lenses that would bring together the rays of the sun. Such "burning glasses" were used to start wood fires. And legends tell us that the ancient Greeks set fire to enemy ships with burning glasses.

Still later, people learned that lenses could reveal unknown wonders. One of the first persons to use lenses in this way was the self-taught Dutch scientist Anton van Leeuwenhoek, who was born in 1632. For a time Leeuwenhoek kept a shop and did other kinds of work. But his hobby was the grinding and polishing of lenses. He used his lenses to build some of the first true microscopes. With these instruments he was able to see details of plants and animals a thousand times smaller than anything the eye alone could see.

Leeuwenhoek's magnifying lenses opened up an unknown world. He found swarms of what he called "little animals" in drops of water from puddles. Actually, he was seeing the one-celled plants and animals that we

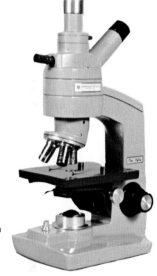

Cameras, binoculars, microscopes, telescopes, and television cameras are among the many instruments that make use of lenses.

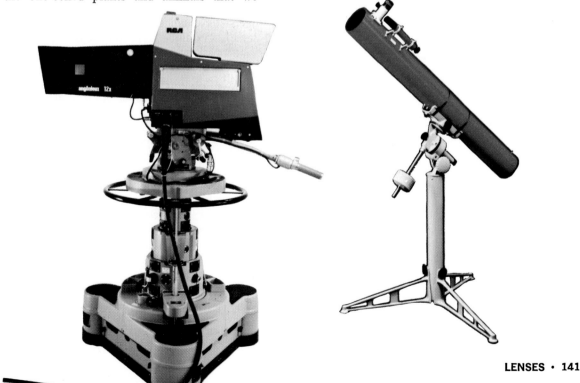

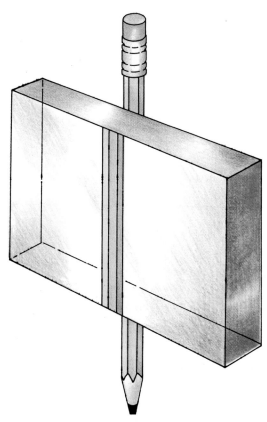

Figure 1. A pencil seems to be broken when seen through a thick plate of glass. This is because light rays are bent sharply when they pass from air to glass and from glass to air, as shown in the drawing below.

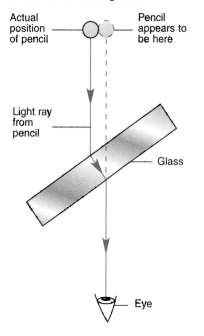

call bacteria and protozoa. In the tail of a tadpole, he also observed the threadlike blood vessels known as capillaries.

Even before this, the great Italian scientist Galileo had used lenses to make a telescope, with which he made several great discoveries. He was the first person to see the mountains and craters of the moon and the dark markings, now called sunspots, on the face of the sun. He also observed four moons circling the planet Jupiter. These and other unexpected discoveries by Galileo had a great influence on the beliefs of his time, as well as of later times.

Lenses are an important part of eyeglasses and of microscopes, cameras, movie projectors, and many other **optical instruments**. The word "optical" means "making use of light or sight." To understand how optical instruments work, we must learn something about lenses and about light itself.

▸ REFRACTION OF LIGHT

You know that a very hot object, such as a glowing coal or an electric lamp, gives off light. When some of this light enters your eye, you see the object. Objects that give off light are called light **sources**. Light from a small source streams away in all directions. It travels outward as lines of light called **light rays**. Light from a distant streetlight comes to you through the air. The light rays will be straight lines if all the air between you and the source is in about the same condition. But the rays will curve slightly if there are differences in temperature or in the amount of moisture in the air from place to place. In any case, you say that you see the source of light as long as some rays get to your eye.

Besides being able to go through air, light can pass through many other materials, such as water, glass, and some plastics. These materials are said to be **transparent**. Something special may happen to light rays when they go from one transparent material to another. For instance, suppose you look at a pencil through a fairly thick piece of glass held at a slant. The part of the pencil behind the glass seems to be broken off and moved to one side.

The pencil, like other objects in the room, reflects light coming from lamps or from

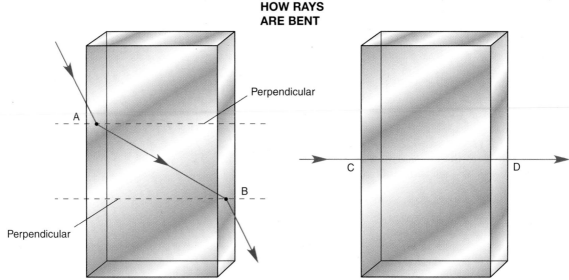

Figure 2. A ray of light is bent if it enters or leaves the glass at a slant. A ray entering or leaving perpendicular to the surfaces of the glass is not bent.

daylight. These reflected rays bend sharply when they enter the glass. And when they come out on the other side, they again bend sharply, in the opposite direction, as shown in Figure 1. This sudden change in direction of rays when they go from one transparent material into another is called refraction. Some materials are more refractive than others.

There is a rule for telling which way the rays will bend. In Figure 2, you see a ray coming at a slant toward a piece of glass. At A, where the ray enters the glass, a line is drawn perpendicular (at a right angle) to the surface of the glass. Another line perpendicular to the surface is drawn at B, where the ray leaves the glass. Here is the rule: Light bends *toward* the perpendicular when it passes into a more refractive material (such as glass) and *away from* the perpendicular when it passes into a less refractive material (such as air). But a ray is not bent at all if it enters or leaves at a right angle to the surfaces of the glass, as at C and D. This rule is important in understanding how a lens works.

▶ WHAT IS A LENS?

A lens is any piece of transparent material, such as glass, that has at least one evenly curved surface. Figure 3 shows cross sections of lenses. (A cross section is made by slicing, or cutting through, an object.) Some of the surfaces are curved outward. Some are curved inward. And two of the lenses have a flat side. All these lenses can be divided into two groups. The first three shapes are thicker at the center than at the edges. They are **converging lenses**. The second three are thinner at the center than at the edges. They are **diverging lenses**. The word "converge" means "to bring together." The word "diverge" means "to spread apart." And that is just what these lenses do to light rays.

Figure 3. Converging lenses are thicker in the center than at the outer edges. Diverging lenses are thicker at the outer edges than in the center.

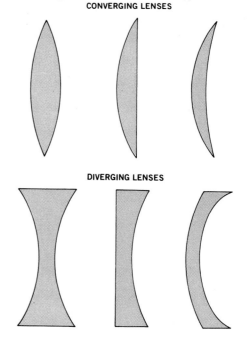

CONVERGING LENSES

DIVERGING LENSES

▶ CONVERGING LENSES

Figure 4 shows what happens to some parallel rays that are heading directly toward a converging lens. After passing through the lens, all the rays are moving in new directions except for the middle one. It keeps going straight ahead. All the other rays are refracted (bent aside) a little on going from the air into the glass. And they are refracted again in the same direction when they come out.

A converging lens is very useful because it can send the light rays toward a single point, called the **principal focus**. The distance between this point and the lens is the **focal distance**. The length of the focal distance depends on the material that the lens is made of and the way that the surfaces are curved. The focal distance tells a great deal about the way the lens will bend light rays.

Rays coming from a very distant source are nearly parallel, like those in Figure 4. A converging lens can bring them together at the principal focus to form a bright point of light. You can catch this spot of light on a card held at the principal focus. If the card is not there, the rays simply go on and fan out again after crossing at the principal focus.

The center of the lens is called the **axis**. The rays shown in Figure 4 are parallel to each other and to the axis. They pass through the lens and converge at the principal focus. What happens to parallel rays going in some other direction? They converge at a different place, a little off to one side.

Any object, such as a tree or a lamp, is really a collection of many points. Each of

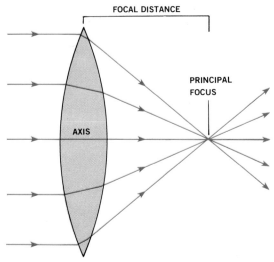

Figure 4. Converging lenses bring light rays together to a single point, or focus. When light rays travel in the same direction as the axis (the center line of the lens), the focus is on the axis.

these points reflects light or sends out light of its own. A set of light rays coming from any one of the points can be gathered together again by the lens and sent to a certain place on a card held at the proper distance from the lens. The whole set of these bright points forms a "light-picture" of the object from which the rays came. Such a picture, which you can see on the card in Figure 5, is called a **real image** of the object.

An ordinary magnifying glass is a converging lens. You can use it to form a real image of a lighted lamp on a card. Move the card slowly back and forth behind the lens until you see a sharp image of the lamp. Notice that the image is upside down. It is also reversed from side to side. Figure 5 shows how this happens. Rays from the top of the object

Figure 5. Rays from the top of the bulb are refracted, and they focus (come together) below the axis of the lens. Rays from the bottom of the bulb focus above the axis. The same thing happens in the sideways direction, with the focus to one side of the axis. As a result, the image is upside down, and its right and left sides are reversed.

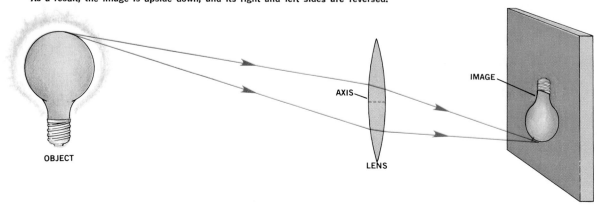

are brought to a focus below the axis. Rays from the bottom come to a focus above the axis. The same thing takes place in the sideways direction.

If the lamp is brought closer to the lens, the card must be moved a little farther away to get a sharp image. Scientists do not have to search for the location of the image. They have worked out formulas that show in advance where the image will fall for any lens setup. They can also figure out how to shape a lens to give it a desired focal distance.

▶ DIVERGING LENSES

If you try to do the lamp-lens-card experiment with a diverging lens, you find that you cannot get a real image anywhere on the card. That is because a diverging lens spreads light rays apart instead of bringing them together.

In Figure 6 you can see what happens to parallel rays moving toward a diverging lens parallel to its axis. After passing through the lens, the rays fan out in a way that makes all of them seem to be coming from a single point in front of the lens. This point is the principal focus of the diverging lens. Its distance from the lens is the focal distance.

Other bundles of parallel rays come in at a slant with the axis. They fan out in the same way after going through the lens. Each bundle seems to come from a different point off to one side or the other of the principal focus. A whole collection of such bundles, coming from various points of an object, forms a complete image. But this image is different in an important way from the real image formed by a converging lens—it cannot

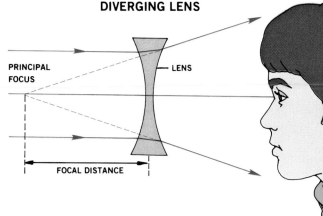

DIVERGING LENS

Figure 6. When light rays pass through a diverging lens, they fan out and seem to come from a focus in front of the lens.

be caught on a card. For this reason it is called a **virtual image**. This kind of image is only a collection of points from which the rays seem to come, as shown in Figure 7.

A virtual image formed by a diverging lens does not show up on a card. But it can be seen directly through the lens. That is because the eye furnishes an additional set of lenses to bring the rays together.

Look at any object through a diverging lens, such as the lens in a nearsighted person's eyeglasses. You will see a small, upright image. It seems to be located nearer to the lens than to the object itself. Diverging lenses always form virtual images that are right side up and smaller than the object. Figure 7 helps to show why this happens. Diverging lenses are almost always used in combination with other lenses.

Figure 7. If you look directly through a diverging lens, you see a small upright image. Your eyes provide an extra set of lenses to bring the light rays together.

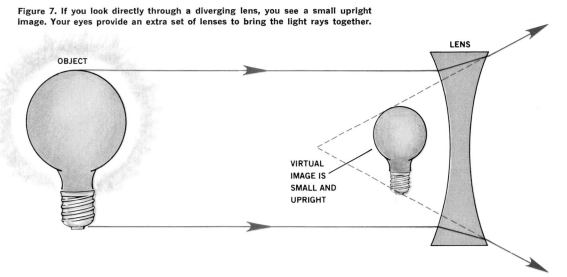

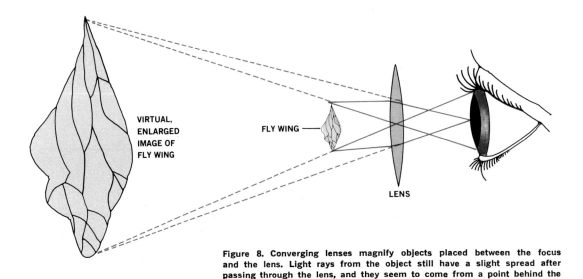

VIRTUAL, ENLARGED IMAGE OF FLY WING

FLY WING

LENS

Figure 8. Converging lenses magnify objects placed between the focus and the lens. Light rays from the object still have a slight spread after passing through the lens, and they seem to come from a point behind the actual object.

▶ MAGNIFIERS AND MICROSCOPES

If you bring an object closer to a converging lens than the focal distance, you find that there is no longer any place where you can get a real image on the card. The reason is that rays from any point on the object have such a great spread that the lens cannot bring them together again on the other side. But if you look directly into the lens, you see a much enlarged image of the object. This makes a converging lens useful as a simple magnifier.

Figure 8 shows what happens. Rays coming from any point on the object (here, the wing of a fly) are refracted by the lens. But they still have a slight spread after going through. These rays seem to have come from a point that is located by extending the final rays backward. For example, in Figure 8 the rays coming from the top of the wing can be traced back along the dotted lines to locate that part of the image. The same thing is true for the bottom of the wing and for all points in between. Your eye sees the complete image, which is virtual and enlarged. It is also right side up, which is convenient when the lens is used as a magnifier.

Leeuwenhoek's microscopes were one-lens magnifiers of this kind. They are called **simple microscopes**. To get better images and higher magnification, a combination of two converging lenses or sets of lenses must be used. A setup of this kind is called a **com-pound microscope**. That is the way all high-powered scientific microscopes are now made. Figure 9 shows how these instruments are constructed. A set of converging lenses, of very short focal distance, is mounted at

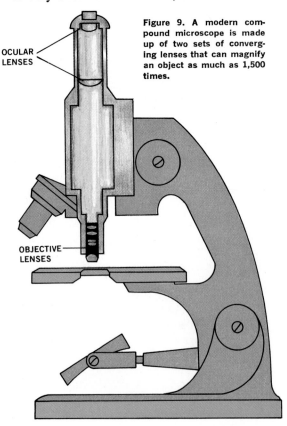

OCULAR LENSES

OBJECTIVE LENSES

Figure 9. A modern compound microscope is made up of two sets of converging lenses that can magnify an object as much as 1,500 times.

the bottom end of a tube. This set of lenses is near the object that is being magnified. It is called the **objective,** or set of objective lenses. A second set of converging lenses, of moderate focal distance, is mounted at the upper end of the tube. This set of lenses forms the **eyepiece,** or **ocular** (ocular lenses). The tube can be moved slowly up or down by turning a knob.

An object that is to be examined is placed right under the objective. Then the tube is moved carefully up and down until the image is sharp. This image is virtual, and it is very much enlarged. It is also upside down and reversed from side to side. It seems to be located some distance below the objective.

Modern compound microscopes used by biologists, geologists, and engineers can magnify things as much as 1,500 times. This would make a single hair look as broad as the trunk of a tree. At high magnification, only a small part of an object may be seen at one time.

▶ THE TELESCOPE

Telescopes are used to make distant objects appear nearer and larger. A **refracting telescope** has two sets of converging lenses, just as a microscope does. The important difference is that the objective system at the front end of the telescope has a very long focal distance, instead of a short one. As in the microscope, the final virtual image is upside down and reversed from side to side. This is troublesome for most uses of the telescope, and a third lens is sometimes put in to make things appear in their normal position. A better way of getting this result is to reflect the rays back and forth inside the instrument, using a pair of triangular pieces of glass, called **prisms.** At the same time this makes the instrument much shorter and more convenient to hold. A **prism binocular** is made up of a pair of such telescopes, one for each eye.

The biggest telescopes of all are the ones used in astronomy. These instruments must be able to take in enough light to make very faint or distant stars show up. In some cases, this means that the objective must be more than 1 meter in diameter. It is very difficult and expensive to grind and polish lenses of this size because the surfaces must be accurate to

within about 1/400,000 centimeter. For this reason most of the very largest telescopes use a hollowed-out mirror in place of a set of objective lenses. Such an instrument is called a **reflecting telescope**.

▶ THE CAMERA

The setup using the magnifying glass and card (Fig. 5) is like a camera. In place of the lamp, there can be a person or a house or whatever you wish to photograph. The camera lens takes the place of the magnifier, and the film takes the place of the card.

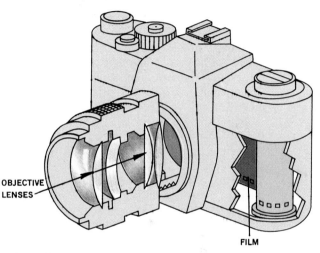

OBJECTIVE LENSES

FILM

Figure 10. In most cameras, a combination of lenses, called the objective, is used to give sharper images.

In a good camera a combination of several lenses is used instead of a single lens, to get a better image (Fig. 10). The whole set of lenses, firmly mounted in a metal tube, is the objective. To focus a camera on a subject, the objective is moved back and forth until the image is perfectly sharp on the film. You cannot do this by looking at the image directly because that would let light into the camera and expose the sensitive film. Instead, you use a distance scale marked on the objective or a viewer or range finder mounted on the camera.

Some movie cameras and television cameras are fitted with **varifocal objectives.** These make it possible to "zoom" in on a subject from far away, keeping it in focus all the while. This is done by moving some lenses of the combination back and forth, while the rest stay in place. The effect is the same as if the camera itself were moved toward or away from the subject.

In the objective of a camera, the reflection of light from the various lens surfaces can be troublesome. Light reflected back and forth between the lenses may cause extra images and haze. To prevent such reflections, the lens surfaces can be covered with a very thin chemical coating. This sends most of the reflected light back into the lens, where it helps strengthen the image. If your camera objective seems to have a purplish color, it is a **coated objective**.

There is more to a camera than the objective and the film. A **shutter** lets light come through the objective just long enough for the image to register properly on the film. There is also an opening that can be changed in size by a metal diaphragm. The size of the opening controls the brightness of the image.

▶ DEFECTS OF LENSES

Even the most carefully and exactly made single lens cannot give a perfect image. There are always shortcomings that are troublesome under certain conditions. These basic defects of lenses are called **aberrations**.

Rays going through the outer parts of a broad lens do not focus at exactly the same point as the rays nearer the axis. The result is that the image is not quite sharp. This effect is known as **spherical aberration** (Fig. 11). The remedy is to block off the outer parts of the lens by using a piece of metal that has a small, round hole in it. A better image is then formed because only the rays coming through the center of the lens are used.

That is what happens when you "stop down" the objective of your camera on a very bright day. This is done mainly to reduce the amount of light that comes in. But it also cuts down spherical aberration. As a result, the image is sharper than it would be with the objective "wide open." But if there is not much light, stopping down the objective would make the image too weak. Then the only practical remedy is to use lenses that have been ground to a special shape by hand. Such lenses are expensive. They are ordinarily used only in research instruments.

The images seen through a toy telescope or microscope often have annoying colored edges. This is another defect of lenses, called **chromatic aberration**. Ordinary daylight is really a mixture of all colors of the rainbow. When a ray of daylight enters a lens, the various colors in the light are refracted by slightly different amounts. Each color comes out again as a separate ray going in its own direction. The difference is quite small. But it is enough to make the focal length of a lens noticeably different for each color. This means that there is no one place where all

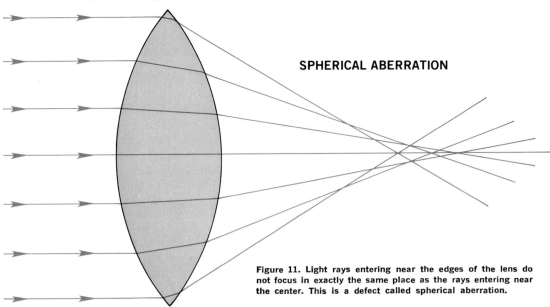

SPHERICAL ABERRATION

Figure 11. Light rays entering near the edges of the lens do not focus in exactly the same place as the rays entering near the center. This is a defect called spherical aberration.

the colors come together to form a sharp image.

Chromatic aberration is often corrected by using a special combination of two lenses in place of one. One of the pair must be a converging lens made of a lightweight kind of glass. The other must be a weakly diverging lens made of heavier glass. Each lens cancels out most of the color-spreading of the other, so that the image is sharp and fairly free of color. Pairs of lenses of this kind are found in optical instruments of high quality. Sometimes sets of three and four lenses are used for even better color correction.

There are several other lens defects that optical engineers must try to reduce or eliminate. In designing a new lens system, they may first make calculations to find which shapes and combinations will do what is needed. Then they trace some rays through the lenses on a large drawing of the setup. By such trials they find a design that makes the lens errors as small as possible. The final test is to grind the lenses, mount them carefully, and try the system under the conditions of actual use.

▶ THE EYE AND VISION

There is one optical instrument that nobody has ever been able to make. Yet it is by far the most important and useful of all. It is the eye. Your eye is like a color television camera because it can form images of things that are continually changing, and it can show them in their own colors.

Each eyeball is held in its socket by a set of muscles. The muscles can turn the eyeball, making the axis point in various directions. Figure 12 shows a cross section of the eye. Just behind the transparent front surface, or **cornea,** there is a salty liquid. Next comes the **crystalline lens,** built up of layers of transparent tissue. There is a chamber behind the lens. This chamber is filled with a thin, jellylike material. Together, the various parts act as a converging lens. They form images on the inner back surface of the eye, which is called the **retina.** From there, millions of nerves send sight messages to the brain.

Just in front of the crystalline lens is a small, round opening that controls the amount of light entering the eye. This opening is called the **pupil.** When you look at your pu-

CROSS SECTION OF THE HUMAN EYE

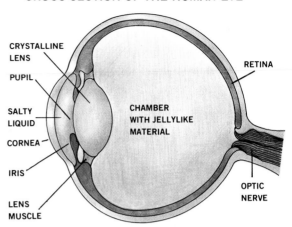

Figure 12. The human eye is made up of several parts that act together as a converging lens. These parts are the cornea, the salty liquid behind the cornea, the crystalline lens, and the jellylike material in the main chamber of the eye.

pils in a mirror, they appear to be black because you are looking into the dark, inside part of the eyeball. The pupil is surrounded by two sets of muscles, which form the colored part of the eye, or **iris**. These muscles automatically change the size of the opening to regulate the amount of light entering. In bright sunlight the pupil may close down to less than 3 millimeters (⅛ inch) in width. In a darkened room it may open up to more than twice that size. This action of the pupil is like the action of the automatic "stop" on some cameras.

You focus a camera for various distances by moving the objective in or out. The eye changes focus in a different way. When you look at something nearby, muscles around the edge of the crystalline lens squeeze it up. This shortens its focal distance until the image is sharp. When you focus on a distant object, the muscles relax, letting the lens flatten out.

There is a limit to how much the lens can be squeezed up. This **power of accommodation** allows a normal eye to focus on objects about 25 centimeters (10 inches) away without too much strain. With a magnifying glass you can bring things much closer and yet see them clearly. The power of accommodation lessens as a person grows older, making it more difficult to focus sharply on nearby objects.

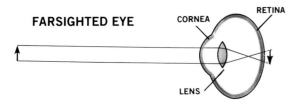

FARSIGHTED EYE

CORNEA · RETINA · LENS

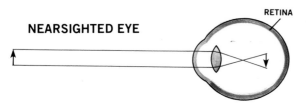

NEARSIGHTED EYE

RETINA

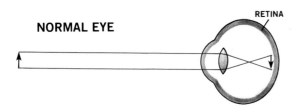

NORMAL EYE

RETINA

Figure 13. In a nearsighted eye the image is focused in front of the retina. In a farsighted eye, the image of the object would be focused behind the retina.

A **farsighted** eye (Fig. 13) can give clear images of distant things but not of those that are fairly near. The reason may be poor power of accommodation. Or it may be an eyeball that is too short, front to back, for a sharp image to form on the retina. In either case, the condition is helped by using eyeglasses with converging lenses, to help bring the rays together properly.

Some eyes are **nearsighted**. They cannot form sharp images of objects that are more than a few centimeters away. Usually this is because the eyeball is too long, front to back. This condition is helped by eyeglasses with diverging lenses. These lenses spread the rays slightly, so that a sharp image results.

Another common defect is called **astigmatism**. In this case the front surface of the eyeball is not of the same roundness in all directions. Examine the pattern of lines in Figure 14. If you have astigmatism, you will find that the various sets of lines will not appear equally sharp. One group will be clearer

than all the others. And the group that crosses it squarely will seem fuzzier than the rest. Astigmatism can be corrected by using eyeglass lenses that are curved more in one direction than in another.

An eye may need correction for nearsightedness or farsightedness and for astigmatism at the same time. The two lens shapes that are needed can be ground into the same piece of glass.

Small, thin lenses that rest on the eyeball itself have become very popular. These are called **contact lenses**. They float on the layer of moisture (tears) that covers the eyeball. Contact lenses are described in a separate article, on the next page.

▶ **WHAT YOU HAVE LEARNED ABOUT LENSES**

There are two special ways in which lenses can refract light rays coming from an object. A converging lens can bring the rays together to form a real image. A diverging lens bends the rays so that they all seem to come from a virtual image.

A real image formed by a converging lens can be caught on a card placed where the rays cross. It is always upside down and reversed from right to left. The image formed on the film by the objective of a camera is real.

Images formed by a diverging lens are always virtual. They are right side up and are not reversed from right to left.

Figure 14. These sets of lines will not appear equally clear to a person with astigmatism.

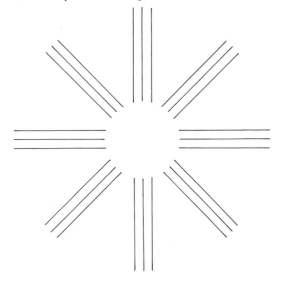

The principal focus of a lens is the place where it forms a point image of a far-off object. This point image is on the axis of the lens. The distance between the point image and the lens is called the focal distance.

Lenses can be combined to construct various optical instruments. The compound microscope uses a set of lenses of very short focus as an objective, plus an ocular. The refracting telescope uses an objective of very long focus, plus an ocular. A prism binocular is really a pair of refracting telescopes. All these lens systems are converging. Many other kinds of optical instruments are used for special purposes.

Single lenses have certain defects, such as spherical aberration and chromatic aberration. These can be corrected by using only the center part of the lens, by using certain combinations of different types of lenses, or by grinding the lens surfaces to special shapes.

The eye acts as a set of converging lenses, forming real images on the retina. If an eye cannot focus sharply on nearby objects, it is farsighted, and a converging eyeglass helps. If an eye cannot focus sharply on objects more than a few centimeters away, it is nearsighted, and a diverging lens helps. Astigmatism results when the front surface of the eyeball is not evenly rounded in all directions. The remedy is to use an eyeglass lens that is curved in a way that makes up for this defect.

IRA M. FREEMAN
Author, *Physics: Principles and Insights*

See also LIGHT; MICROSCOPES; OPTICAL INSTRUMENTS; TELESCOPES.

LEO III, POPE (?–816)

Leo III was pope from 795 until his death in 816. He is best known for crowning the Frankish ruler Charlemagne emperor of the Romans on Christmas Day, A.D. 800. This event is sometimes regarded as the founding of the Holy Roman Empire, which gave the Catholic Church greater power and authority in the West.

Leo was born in Rome in the 700's. Before becoming pope, he headed the pope's treasury and was a cardinal-priest of Santa Susanna, a church in Rome.

Although Leo had been unanimously elected by the other bishops, the Roman aristocracy opposed him. Pope Adrian, his predecessor, had been a Roman aristocrat, and Leo was not. Also, two of Adrian's nephews sought the papacy themselves.

Soon after becoming pope, Leo requested Charlemagne's protection by sending him the keys to the tomb of St. Peter and the standard (emblem or symbol) of the city. In return, Charlemagne sent Leo silver and gold.

Leo's opponents continued their efforts to unseat him and accused him of immorality and simony (the sale of sacred things). On April 24, 799, a group of important Romans—including relatives of Pope Adrian—brutally attacked him. It was hoped he would be so injured that he could no longer perform his papal duties. Leo escaped and was taken to Charlemagne in Saxony, where he reportedly recovered.

Leo then returned to Rome. In 800, shortly before he was crowned emperor, Charlemagne went to Rome to hear the accusations against the pope. Leo swore an oath of innocence before the king and was cleared. The pope's attackers were sentenced to death. However, Leo requested that they not be executed but exiled instead.

Upon Charlemagne's death in 814, Leo's enemies again began plotting against him. When Leo learned of this, he had them executed. Shortly thereafter, nobles from Campagna rose up against Leo but were defeated.

During his papacy, one of Leo's most notable actions was to uphold the original language of the Nicene Creed. This important church doctrine, a statement of belief in Jesus Christ's divinity, had been drawn up in 325.

Leo died on June 12, 816, in Rome. He was canonized in 1673.

KEVIN MADIGAN
Harvard Divinity School

LEO XIII, POPE (1810–1903)

Pope Leo XIII was born Gioacchino Pecci on March 2, 1810, in Carpineto, Italy, to a family of the minor nobility. He received his education at Jesuit schools, where he proved himself a bright student with a gift for languages. He studied law and received his doctorate in theology before entering the service of the Papal Government.

In 1838, after serving a successful term as governor of Benevento, Monsignor Pecci was transferred to Perugia. In 1843 he became an archbishop and Papal Nuncio to Belgium. After a few years in this post he returned to Perugia as archbishop. In 1853 Pope Pius IX made him a cardinal.

On February 20, 1878, Cardinal Pecci became Pope Leo XIII. At once he took steps to improve the poor relations that existed between the Holy See and almost every government in Europe and Latin America. Especially difficult were relations with the Kingdom of Italy, which had seized the Papal States in 1870.

The new Pope soon proved himself a skillful statesman. His expert diplomacy met with much success. He helped to bring about the end of religious conflict in Germany and tried to get French Catholics to accept the new Third Republic as their lawful government. He arranged the settlement of a dispute between Germany and Spain over the Caroline Islands. Only in Italy, where he would not accept the loss of the Papal States to the new Italian kingdom, did his efforts fail.

Pope Leo XIII took a deep interest in the social problems of his day. Among the greatest of his contributions are his brilliant encyclicals, or papal letters. The most famous of these, *Rerum Novarum,* discussed social progress and the conflict between workers and employers. Leo upheld the rights of the working man. He revealed his approval of trade unions and laws designed to improve the lot of the laborer. Above all, Leo showed great understanding of the new ideas spreading throughout the Western world.

Pope Leo XIII was a generous patron of scriptural and philosophical studies. He opened the archives of the Vatican to historians from all countries. He took an especially friendly interest in the English-speaking countries and was the first pope to write sympathetically of democracy. He is generally regarded as one of the ablest of all the popes. His 25-year reign was one of the longest in Catholic history.

Msgr. Florence D. Cohalan
Cathedral College

LEONARDO DA VINCI (1452–1519)

Perhaps no one in history achieved so much in so many different fields as did Leonardo da Vinci. An outstanding painter, sculptor, and architect, he also designed bridges, highways, weapons, costumes, and scientific instruments. He invented the diving bell and tank, and—though they could not be built with the materials of the time—flying machines. He made important discoveries about the structure of the human body.

From his notebooks we can tell that Leonardo approached science and art in the same methodical manner: after studying a problem, he made many sketches to help him find a solution. He saw no difference between planning a machine and a painting, and he became an expert in every field that interested him.

Leonardo da Vinci was born in the town of Vinci, Italy, in 1452. His father was a successful government official, and his mother was a peasant girl. Leonardo spent his early years on his family's farm. Free to explore in the fields and streams, he grew to love the outdoors. He had a keen interest in how things work. He bought caged birds in the marketplace and set them free. He did this because he could not stand to see birds in cages and also because he wanted to learn exactly how birds fly.

By 1469 Leonardo had moved with his father to Florence, where the young man was apprenticed to the painter and sculptor Andrea del Verrocchio (1435?–88). In the 7 or more years Leonardo spent in Verrocchio's studio he was especially inspired by his teach-

Self Portrait, drawn in red chalk by Leonardo da Vinci.

er's imaginative sculpture. By 1472, Leonardo became a master of the painters' guild. A few years later he painted such a beautiful angel that Verrocchio, his master, is said to have given up painting for good.

After this, Leonardo's skill as a painter must have been known, for he painted an altarpiece, *The Adoration of the Kings,* for the monks of Scopeto. The *Adoration* had a great influence on younger painters. The Virgin Mary is shown in a large landscape. She and the three kings stand out among the many figures because of Leonardo's use of **chiaroscuro** —contrasts of light and dark. He made many drawings for this work. What we see today is only the first stage, for Leonardo left the painting unfinished in 1481. Leonardo often abandoned works, regardless of their state of completion. After he had solved a particular problem, he went on to other projects that interested him.

About 1482, Leonardo left Florence to enter the house of Lodovico Sforza, Duke of Milan. While there, he painted court portraits, supervised pageants, designed costumes, built machines of war, and even installed central

heating in the palace. He also supposedly played the lyre and sang to entertain the Duke and his friends.

While in Milan, Leonardo worked on his magnificent painting, *The Last Supper.* Because he worked slowly, Leonardo painted in oil on a damp wall instead of using the **fresco** technique (painting with watercolors on wet plaster). This experiment was not successful, and the painting began to peel soon after Leonardo's death. Although it is now badly damaged, it is still an extraordinary picture. By cutting out all unnecessary details Leonardo emphasized the drama of the event. A photograph of *The Last Supper* may be found in the article on the Apostles in Volume A.

One of Leonardo's greatest interests was the study of the human body. At first, like other artists of the 15th century, he studied the outward appearance of the body. Then he became fascinated with its inner structure and dissected corpses to find out how the body was put together. His studies of the heart, especially, were quite advanced. Leonardo looked at plants as closely as he looked at people

Leonardo da Vinci's *Mona Lisa* is one of the most celebrated paintings in the world.

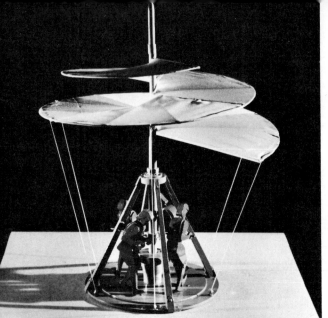

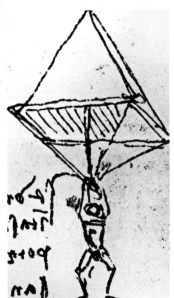

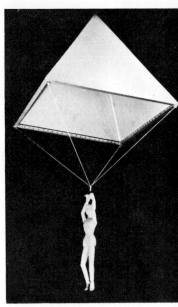

A modern model of a helicopter made from a drawing by Leonardo da Vinci.

Leonardo's design (*left*) and a modern model (*right*) of a parachute.

and animals, and he made many discoveries about plant growth.

Soon after he arrived in Milan, Leonardo began to write down things that interested him. His notebooks show the great variety and originality of his scientific observations. He illustrated his theories with very beautiful and exact drawings. By studying his drawings of machines, 20th-century engineers, with modern materials, have been able to build models that work perfectly. The notebooks are hard to read because he used mirror writing. He did not want his ideas to be stolen.

Leonardo's life in the court of Milan was suddenly interrupted in 1499 by the invasion of the French Army. Leonardo's patron, Lodovico, was taken prisoner, and Leonardo fled to Venice. The next year he went back to Florence, which was still an active center of art. He was given a commission to paint an altarpiece for the church of the Annunziata. When his full-scale drawing of the Virgin and Child with Saint Anne was placed on public view, people filed by for two days and admired it enthusiastically.

Leonardo briefly served Prince Cesare Borgia in Rome as a military engineer. In 1503 he returned to Florence, where he spent a few very productive years. The most outstanding and only completed painting of this period is his portrait of a Florentine lady, the *Mona Lisa*. This portrait is famous for the delicately painted features of the woman's face and for the rich **sfumato** ("smoky") effects of the mountainous landscape in the background. While in Florence, Leonardo was commissioned to paint a battle scene on a wall of the Great Hall of the Palazzo Vecchio. Again Leonardo experimented, this time with wax paint. The work began to melt even before he finished it. Leonardo was disappointed. But as a scientist, he knew that to achieve success, people must expect some experiments to fail.

In 1513 Leonardo was invited to Rome by Giuliano de' Medici, a brother of Pope Leo X. There he continued his experiments. Sometime in 1516 Leonardo left Italy to become chief painter and engineer to the king of France. King Francis I gave Leonardo a château near Amboise, where he was free to carry on his experiments.

While in France, Leonardo was stricken with partial paralysis. He had to stop painting, but his mind remained active. During his last years he received countless visitors, who listened with awe to the master's brilliant ideas about art and science.

People of the Renaissance set impossibly high goals for themselves. Leonardo da Vinci, the person who came closest to reaching all of those goals, died in his French château on May 2, 1519.

> Reviewed by AARON H. JACOBSEN
> Author, *The Renaissance Sketchbook*

LEONOV, ALEKSEI. See SPACE EXPLORATION AND TRAVEL (Profiles).

LEOPARDS

Leopards are often considered the most dangerous of all the big cats. They weigh about 100 to 175 pounds (45 to 80 kilograms), and some are more than 7 feet (2 meters) long. Although they are smaller than lions and tigers, they are fierce fighters.

Leopards usually have yellowish brown coats covered with large and small black spots. Some leopards, known as panthers, appear to be entirely black. But their spots are simply hard to see against the rest of their fur. A litter may include both normally spotted and dark leopards.

Leopards spend much of their time in trees. From the branches on which they lie hidden, leopards leap on the animals that pass underneath. They may eat the animal on the spot, or they may store part of the meat in a tree and eat it later. Leopards eat a variety of animals—among them cattle, sheep, monkeys, antelopes, dogs, and birds.

For the most part, leopards live and hunt alone. During the mating season, they will team up with a mate and hunt together. Two to four offspring, called cubs, are born about 90 days after mating. Shortly after the birth of the cubs, the male and female leopards separate. The cubs stay with the mother for about two years, until they are able to fend for themselves.

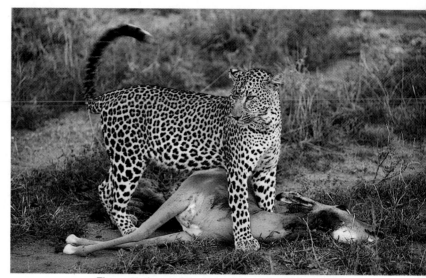

The spotted coat of the leopard keeps it well concealed from prey until it is too late for an unsuspecting victim to escape capture.

Leopards live to be some 20 years old. They are more common than lions or tigers and are found in a greater variety of places. They live in parts of Asia and in most of Africa. A few may still roam the Caucasus, east of the Black Sea in Europe.

Two other species of cats are also called leopards. They resemble common leopards, but they differ in skull structure and in other details.

The snow leopard is about the same size as the common leopard. It is found in cold, mountainous areas of central Asia. Its long, thick coat is grayish white, marked with large, broken black spots.

The smaller clouded leopard lives in southeastern Asia. It is grayish yellow, with darker spots, stripes, and other markings. For its size, it has very long fangs.

The practice of killing leopards for their beautiful fur has caused some varieties to become very rare. But today many areas where leopards range are protected by law, and reserves have been established. The governments of several nations have also placed restrictions on the importation of leopard skins.

Reviewed by ROBERT M. MCCLUNG
Science Writer

See also CATS, WILD.

LEPRECHAUNS. See FAIRIES.

While most leopards have yellowish brown coats with black spots, black leopards, or panthers, have coats that are so dark it is hard to distinguish the spots.

LESOTHO

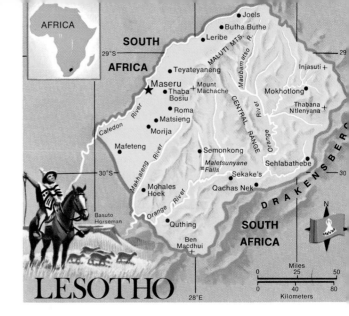

LESOTHO

Lesotho is a small kingdom in southern Africa. A rugged, mountainous country, it is entirely surrounded by the much larger territory of the Republic of South Africa. Lesotho was formerly known as Basutoland and was a British dependency before it gained independence in 1966.

▶THE PEOPLE

The people of Lesotho are the Basotho (or Basuto), who belong to the large and varied Bantu family. Most are Christian, though some Basotho maintain their old religious beliefs. Both English and Sesotho, the Basotho language, are official languages. Because many Basotho children attend at least primary school, Lesotho has one of the highest literacy rates in Africa. The majority of people can read and write either Sesotho or English.

The Basotho are traditionally farmers and herders of sheep, goats, cattle, and horses. But since only a small part of the land is suitable for agriculture, Lesotho has difficulty supporting its population. As a result, many of the Basotho men spend long periods away from home, working in the mines and industries of the Republic of South Africa.

Lesotho has no cities. Its largest town is Maseru, the capital. Most Basotho live in villages of varying size. Houses are usually round in shape, with stone walls and peaked thatched roofs. The most distinctive item of clothing worn by the people is the woven straw Basotho hat.

▶THE LAND AND THE ECONOMY

The western part of Lesotho is a high plateau that occupies about one-third of the country. Much of the population is concentrated here. The eastern two-thirds of the land consists of mountains that rise to a height of 11,425 feet (3,482 meters). The climate is generally dry and temperate. Rainfall is moderate except during the summer rainy season. Much of the usable land suffers from soil erosion.

The chief food crops are corn, wheat, sorghum, and beans. Lesotho can supply only

FACTS and figures

KINGDOM OF LESOTHO is the official name of the country.

LOCATION: Southern Africa.

AREA: 11,720 sq mi (30,355 km²).

POPULATION: 1,900,000 (estimate).

CAPITAL AND LARGEST TOWN: Maseru.

MAJOR LANGUAGES: English, Sesotho (both official).

MAJOR RELIGIOUS GROUP: Christian.

GOVERNMENT: Constitutional monarchy. **Head of state**—king. **Head of government**—prime minister. **Legislature**—National Assembly and Senate.

CHIEF PRODUCTS: Corn, wheat, sorghum, beans, livestock, diamonds.

MONETARY UNIT: Loti (1 loti = 100 lisente).

Lesotho has no cities and only a few towns. Most of its people live in villages of varying size. Traditional Lesotho houses are round with peaked thatched roofs.

about half its food needs. The rest must be imported. Wool from sheep and mohair from goats are exported. Lesotho has little manufacturing and few mineral resources, except for diamonds, which are exported. Lesotho's economy is dependent on South Africa, which handles much of Lesotho's trade.

▶ HISTORY AND GOVERNMENT

The ancestors of the Basotho migrated into the area between the 1500's and early 1800's. The various peoples were united between 1818 and 1830 by Moshoeshoe I, a chief of great ability. In the middle of the 1800's, the Basotho fought a series of wars with the Boers, descendants of Europeans who had settled in what is now South Africa. The Basotho lost much of their territory to the Boers. Fearing further domination, they appealed to Great Britain for help, and in 1868, Basutoland became a British protectorate.

Basutoland gradually progressed toward internal self-government, which it gained in 1965. The following year it became completely independent and was renamed Lesotho. A constitutional monarchy was established, with Moshoeshoe II (the great-grandson of Moshoeshoe I) as king and head of state, a prime minister as head of government, and an elected senate and assembly.

In 1970, Leabua Jonathan, Lesotho's first prime minister, suspended the constitution and dissolved the legislature. Jonathan held power until 1986, when he was overthrown by the military, led by General Justin Lekhanya. In 1990, Lekhanya deposed King Moshoeshoe II, replacing him with his son, Letsie III. Lekhanya himself was overthrown in 1991. A new constitution went into effect in 1993 that abolished the king's executive and legislative powers. In 1995, King Letsie III stepped down in favor of his father, but he returned following his father's death in 1996.

In 1998, charges of election fraud caused an army rebellion and anti-government riots, resulting in a wave of arson and looting that devastated the economy. Troops from South Africa, called in by Prime Minister Pakalitha Mosisile to help put down the rebellion, remained in Lesotho until May 1999.

HUGH C. BROOKS
St. John's University (New York)

LESSEPS, FERDINAND DE (1805–1894)

Ferdinand de Lesseps was the person responsible for the building of the Suez Canal. Construction of the Suez Canal, which connects the Mediterranean and Red seas, greatly shortened travel between Europe and Asia. De Lesseps also made the first—unsuccessful—attempt to build the Panama Canal.

Ferdinand Marie de Lesseps was born in Versailles, France, on November 19, 1805. His father was a diplomat, and young de Lesseps followed the same career. The turning point in his life came in 1849, when, after a dispute with his government, de Lesseps resigned from the French diplomatic service. He now turned to a project he had long thought of, construction of a canal across the Isthmus of Suez in Egypt. De Lesseps was not an engineer, but he raised the money needed to build the canal and guided it to completion. His stubborn determination overcame all obstacles. The work took ten years, and when the canal was opened in 1869, de Lesseps became the most famous man in France.

In 1879, de Lesseps formed a company to build a canal across the narrow Isthmus of Panama in Central America. The canal would link the Atlantic and Pacific oceans. Although now 74 years old, he began energetically. But the problems he encountered were greater than expected. The rocky soil of Panama was harder to dig than the sandy soil at Suez, and de Lesseps' attempts to build the same kind of canal in Panama as he had at Suez proved unworkable. Money ran out and in 1889 the company went bankrupt, with the loss of large sums of money to its investors. The scandal caused by the failure of the Panama canal project overshadowed de Lesseps' last years. He died on December 7, 1894, a poor man, having lost all his own money in Panama. He is remembered for the accomplishment of building the Suez Canal, still one of the world's most important waterways.

Reviewed by JEAN T. JOUGHIN
American University

See also PANAMA CANAL; SUEZ CANAL.

It is never too early to begin practicing and enjoying the art of letter writing. Whether it is a chatty note home from camp or a secret request to Santa, a letter is fun to write—and there is always that wonderful sense of anticipation as you await a reply.

LETTER WRITING

Letters help us to make friends and get along well in the world. A letter can jet you across the miles for a visit with a friend or faraway family member. It can say thank you, apply for a job, or issue an invitation.

Letters are written for both personal and business reasons. It is important to know the proper form to use for each type of letter. Good letter writing can be learned. Some people write so well that they make an art of letter writing.

▶FRIENDLY LETTERS

A friendly letter contains five parts: the heading; the salutation, or greeting; the body of the letter; the complimentary closing; and the signature of the writer. A friendly letter might look something like the ones on the opposite page.

Heading

The heading of a letter contains important information for the person to whom you are writing. It is placed in the upper right-hand corner of the page as in Letter #1. The heading has three parts: your street address or post office box number; your city, state, and ZIP code number; and the date. (If you are writing to a close friend or family member who knows where you live, you may omit your address.) The United States Postal Service has authorized two-letter state abbreviations for addresses. A listing appears in Volume P in the article POSTAL SERVICE.

Salutation

The salutation is the greeting. It tells to whom the letter is written. It begins at the left-hand margin and is followed by a comma. A letter to an adult might begin "Dear Grandmother" or "Dear Mr. Phillips." A close friend may be greeted with "Dear Ted" or "Dear Ann." A letter to an entire family may begin "Dear Folks."

Body

The body of the letter gives the news. It has as many paragraphs as there are topics. You show that you are changing topics by beginning a new paragraph.

The body of a letter is very important. It is you on paper. Reread your letter before you send it. Read it over first to be sure all your ideas are stated clearly and in a lively manner. It is a good idea to check for errors in spelling or punctuation. Be sure, too, that your handwriting can be read easily. If you know how to type, it is acceptable to type a friendly letter, especially if you have lots of news to deliver. It is all right to make small corrections in the margin. If you forget something you meant to say, you may add a P.S. (postscript) after your signature.

Complimentary Closing

The complimentary closing is your way of saying good-bye. It must be right for the person to whom you are writing.

"Lovingly," "With love," "Your friend," "Your loving son (or daughter)"—these are correct closings for letters to people close to you. "Sincerely" or "Sincerely yours" is used for people you do not know well. "Cordially" is "Sincerely" with an extra dash of warmth.

Notice that the complimentary closing does not begin where a new paragraph begins. It begins just far enough away from the left-hand margin to give a balanced look to the page. A comma always follows the complimentary closing.

Signature

The signature is your name in your own writing. Even in a typewritten letter you should write your name under the closing, not type it.

Planning the Letter

Planning a letter helps you to remember what you want to include. Keep the plan simple—just a few topics, such as "The Family," "Fun at School," "Camping Out Last Weekend." Each topic will require at least one paragraph. Start with whichever topic would most interest the person to whom you are writing. Grandmother wants news about the family and about you. Your best friend wants to know what you have been doing and thinking. The news may be the same in each letter you write, but the arrangement and emphasis will differ.

Before you start, be sure to read over the last letter you received from the person to whom you are writing. It is always annoying when a writer fails to answer questions.

Writing the Letter

A friendly letter should be as interesting as a lively conversation. Good letter writers describe everyday happenings much as they might relate the plot of a movie or a book. If you add descriptions and details and tell about your feelings, your readers will feel that they have shared your experience.

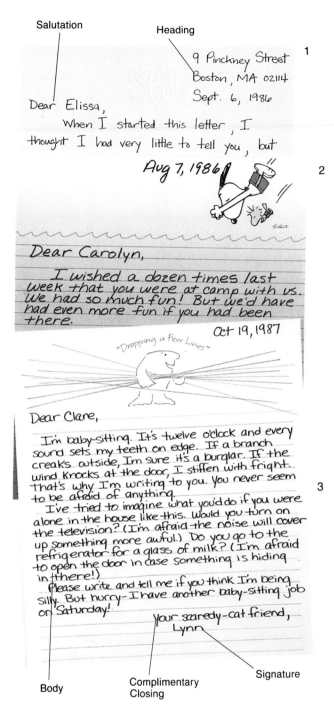

There are any number of ways to begin your letter. You can start right off with your first planned topic. Be sure to bring your reader into the first paragraph. Letter #2 above does this well.

Or you can begin by setting a mood as Letter #3 does.

From
Brad Wellington
12 Chestnut Rd.
Boulder, CO 03303

To

Alan J.

4

Peter Martin
9 Pinckney Street
Boston, MA 02114

Mr. John Pond
R.D. 2
Jaffrey, N.H. 03452

5

218 Waterford Street
Stratford, Ontario N5A 3C5
October 4, 1987

Dear Aunt Elsa,

How clever of you to send me blue beads! I was planning to wear a blue sweater and a plaid skirt to the harvest festival next Saturday, and the beads will match perfectly.

Our harvest festival is going to be bigger than ever this year. We're having exhibits of farm products, arts and crafts, books, and flower arrangements. In the evening there will be folk dancing and games. You should be there!

Thank you again for your thoughtful gift.

Your loving niece,
Joan

6

134 Sandburg Drive
Chicago, IL 60610
September 6, 1986

Dear Cousins (all five of you),

We've talked about nothing since we got home except the wonderful time we had visiting your farm. I get so lonesome for the pony I dream about him. Alan is counting the days until next summer. He misses the cows the most.

Do come to visit us as soon as you can, though it isn't so much fun in Chicago.

Thank you for a lovely visit. You can tell I enjoyed it because I gained two whole pounds!

Your cousin,
Nancy

Never start a letter with a weak excuse for not having written sooner. We can all find time to write if we really want to.

Try not to write a letter when you are angry about something. By the time the letter reaches its destination, your mood will very likely have changed. And the letter certainly will not make the reader glad to receive it. (If you must get something off your chest, writing a letter is a good way to do so—just do not mail it.)

Addressing the Envelope

After you have written the address on the envelope, check it carefully. Is it legible? Is it complete? Write the return address, too. Figure #4 shows an envelope with the address and return address in the correct position.

Thank-You Notes

A fifth grader once remarked that the reason it was better to give than to receive was that the receiver had to write the thank-you note.

Many people dislike writing thank-you notes. But sometimes it is easier to say thank you in writing than in person. Begin by thanking the giver. Mention something pleasing about the gift and explain, if you can, how you will use it as the writer of Letter #5 does. Then chat a little so that your ending will not seem too abrupt.

Bread-and-Butter Notes. A bread-and-butter note is a must after you have stayed in someone's home. Begin by saying thank you and then mention the highlights of your visit. You might also like to express a wish that your hosts may soon be your guests.

Nancy, her parents, and her brother, Alan, visited their cousins in the country. Afterward, Nancy wrote Letter #6 to thank them.

Notes of Appreciation. Some people write notes of appreciation at Christmas or Thanksgiving or on a birthday. If you are a newspaper carrier, you might write to your favorite customer. If you are a baby-sitter, maybe you have a favorite family. Perhaps a teacher has been especially kind to you. A doctor or nurse who took care of you or your camp counselor might appreciate a note, too. Even the president of the United States likes to get a note of appreciation.

Letter #7 on the opposite page is a note a Boy Scout sent to his Scoutmaster.

7

Fan letters. You may want to write a letter of appreciation to a well-known person you admire—a favorite musician, for example, or your senator. Most famous people enjoy hearing that their work is appreciated. Keep your letter short and to the point. You may even get an answer.

Letters to the editor. A letter to the editor of your local newspaper in praise of something or someone is a kind of fan letter. On the other hand, if you are angry about something or you want to let people know your opinion on a local or national event, a letter to the editor will serve this purpose, too.

Invitations

Most invitations—to a birthday party or to a dinner at home or to spend the weekend—are informal. They can be written simply, telling the time, date, and place, and expressing the hope that the person being invited will be able to come. Some invitations—to a ball or a diplomatic reception or a church wedding—are formal. They follow a set pattern and must be answered in a certain way. For instance, Figure #8 on this page is a formal invitation to a wedding.

An invitation to a church wedding does not have to be answered, but if you are also invited to the reception, you must send a reply. Usually a small card such as #9 on this page is enclosed with the invitation.

R.S.V.P. stands for the French words *Répondez s'il vous plaît,* meaning ''Please reply.'' Your reply should be written by hand on the first page of a folded sheet of note paper. Space the words just the way they are in the invitation. Letter #10 is an example of a formal acceptance.

If you cannot attend, the second line should say ''regrets that she is unable to accept.'' In most cases it is courteous to mention your reason for not being able to attend.

Get-Well Notes

A get-well note to someone who is sick should be designed to cheer up the patient. Letter #11 shows the way Richard began one to his friend Al.

Sympathy Notes

Sooner or later a friend of yours may lose a grandparent or some other loved one, and you will want to say how sorry you are. Like Let-

Box 19
Stamps, AK 71860
April 9, 1986

Dear Mr. Domoff,

I want to thank you for giving me the courage to own up to breaking Mrs. McKinney's window. I worked to pay off the damage, and now I have a regular job with her. You are a big help to all the scouts in our troop. We may not show it, but we really appreciate all you do for us.

Your friend,
Jerry

8

Mr. and Mrs. Albert Roy Marshall
request the honour of your presence
at the marriage of their daughter
Marilyn Marie
to
Mr. John Sherman Groves
on Friday, the twelfth of December
Nineteen hundred and eighty-seven
at two o'clock
Saint Mark's Lutheran Church
Madison, Wisconsin

9

Reception
following ceremony
in the Church Social Hall
1917 East Haven Avenue

10

Miss Lynn Hopkins
accepts with pleasure
Mr. & Mrs. Albert Roy Marshall's
kind invitation for
Friday, the twelfth of December

11

Dec. 8, 1986

CAUTION: POOR HANDWRITING

READ & PASS ON

Hi Pal!
Hurry up and get those bones knitted or crocheted or whatever. School is dead without you. We haven't had a laugh in a week. All the girls are looking sad.

READ AT YOUR OWN RISK
TOP SECRET

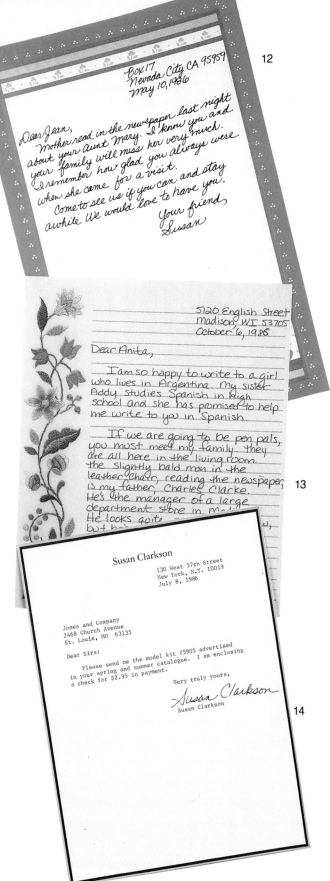

12

Box 17
Nevada City CA 95959
May 10, 1986

Dear Jean,
Mother read in the newspaper last night about your Aunt Mary. I know you and your family will miss her very much. I remember how glad you always were when she came for a visit.
Come to see us if you can and stay awhile. We would love to have you.
Your friend,
Susan

13

5120 English Street
Madison, WI 53705
October 6, 1986

Dear Anita,

I am so happy to write to a girl who lives in Argentina. My sister Addy studies Spanish in high school and she has promised to help me write to you in Spanish.

If we are going to be pen pals, you must meet my family. They are all here in the living room. The slightly bald man in the leather chair, reading the newspaper, is my father, Charles Clarke. He's the manager of a large department store in Ma...
He looks quite...

14

Susan Clarkson
130 West 57th Street
New York, N.Y. 10019
July 8, 1986

Jones and Company
2468 Church Avenue
St. Louis, MO 63135

Dear Sirs:

Please send me the model kit #5905 advertised in your spring and summer catalogue. I am enclosing a check for $2.95 in payment.

Very truly yours,

Susan Clarkson
Susan Clarkson

ter #12, your note should express sympathy without making your friend feel any worse.

Pen-Pal Letters

Many people have discovered that it is fun to write to someone in another part of the world. They call themselves pen pals. Their letters help them understand the way people in other countries live and think. Your school or your local newspaper can probably help you find a pen pal.

In your first pen-pal letter, you may want to introduce the members of your family to your new friend. Try to make a word portrait of each one. Letter #13 is a nice pen-pal letter.

As you get acquainted, you can share experiences and future plans. A pen-pal letter is a sharing between friends.

Do you own a home computer and a modem, which is a device that lets computers talk to each other over telephone lines? If you do, find out if any other computer users have set up a computer bulletin board in your town. By joining the group, you will be able to exchange electronic mail with your computer friends. Someday, most letters may be sent this way.

Some people also tape-record letters. This allows the person receiving the ''letter'' to hear not only your words, but also other sounds such as your pets, your piano lesson, and the voices of your family and friends. It is just as important to organize a tape-recorded letter as it is a written letter. Otherwise, you may be tempted to ramble on without saying anything important—or give your pen-pal a headache from all your scrambled sounds.

▶BUSINESS LETTERS

From time to time you will need to write a business letter. You may want to order something or apply for a job or request information.

Everybody has problems now and then. Some of them can be solved with a letter. A complaint letter should tell who the writer is, exactly what the problem is, and what you want the person or company to do for you. It should be as polite as possible but also to the point.

Other kinds of business letters include letters of appreciation to a person or organization for their help or their good business policies. And letters can get you in touch with the people who run your government.

A business letter has six parts. It has the same five parts as a friendly letter, with an inside address added. This is the same as the address put on the envelope. The salutation is followed by a colon instead of a comma, and the complimentary closing is more formal. Your name should be typed below your handwritten signature to be sure it can be read.

The letter should be typed or written carefully. Read it over to check the spelling, grammar, and punctuation. Keep the letter short, but give all the necessary information. Letters #14, #15, and #16 are samples of business letters.

▶PERFECTING THE ART OF LETTER WRITING

Writing letters easily is just a matter of getting into the habit. But there are a number of ways you can improve the quality of your writing by practicing with different kinds of letters and even make-believe letters. For example, try telling a familiar story in letter form. Number 17 is an exchange based on a familiar children's story.

You might also like to write a letter to yourself as you might be in the future. Write down how you feel about the important things now and keep the letter in a safe place to be "delivered" in a few years. Your future self will be very interested in hearing from you!

Other ways to practice letter-writing include sending picture postcards when you go on a vacation. A postcard is a kind of short letter. Taking telephone messages for other people and leaving notes for members of your family will give you practice in organization. Some families leave messages to one another on a special bulletin board or on the refrigerator. Try to make your message stand out.

Reading published letters, such as those on your newspaper's Letters to the Editor page or in the advice columns, will show you how other people write letters. You might try making up a letter of your own to a columnist or rewriting a published one.

Make letter writing a regular habit. It will get results for you, bring you closer to your friends and family, and lift your spirits when you receive letters in return.

MAUREE APPLEGATE
University of Wisconsin—La Crosse

Reviewed by MURRAY SUID
Co-author, *For the Love of Letter Writing*

See also ADDRESS, FORMS OF; AUTOGRAPHS.

15

362 Ash Avenue
Milford, CT 06460
June 3, 1986

Mr. Thomas Cook
Farm Machines, Inc.
28 Main Street
Milford, CT 06460

Dear Mr. Cook:

Your advertisement in this morning's Courier interests me very much. I am 15 years old and a sophomore at Winchester High School. Last summer I worked as a stock boy in the parts department of a large garage. The experience would help me in the stock job you have open.

If you wish to arrange an interview, I could come to your office any day after 3 o'clock. School closes on June 21.

Respectfully yours,

Jay Bennett

Jay Bennett

Diane Halliday

19 Cotswold Close
Singapore 10, Malaysia
April 19, 1986

United Nations Information Office
United Nations Secretariat Building
United Nations Plaza
New York, N.Y. 10017

Dear Sirs:

Our class in school is preparing a program on the activities of the United Nations. We plan to make a chart of the different member organizations and present dramatizations of the work they do. We should appreciate any information you can send us.

Thank you for your assistance.

Yours truly,

Diane Halliday

Diane Halliday

16

Dear Mrs. Wolf,   May 1, 1986
My piglets have written me that your son has threatened to blow their house down. Please talk to them about this!
Sincerely,
Mrs. Sow

17

Dear Mrs. Sow,   2, 1986
Your pigs are the trouble-makers. Tell them to stop calling my son names like "Big Bad Wolf."
I hate to cut this short but I'm making my son a sheep's costume for a Halloween party.
Sincerely,
Mrs. Wolf

LEUKEMIA. See DISEASES (Descriptions of Some Diseases).

LEWIS, CARL. See OLYMPIC GAMES (Profiles); TRACK AND FIELD (Profiles).

LEWIS, JOHN L. (1880–1969)

John Llewellyn Lewis, one of the most powerful labor leaders in the United States, was the son of an immigrant Welsh coal miner. He was born in Lucas, Iowa, on February 12, 1880. Lewis left school after the seventh grade to help support his family by working in the mines. At the age of 21, he traveled widely throughout the western states working at various jobs. Lewis married Myrta Edith Bell, a former schoolteacher credited with directing her husband's reading and helping him succeed as a labor organizer.

In 1906, Lewis was chosen a delegate to the national convention of the United Mine Workers of America (UMWA). During the years that followed, he held many posts in both the UMWA and the American Federation of Labor (AFL). In 1920 he became president of the mine union and served in that post for 40 years. In 1935, Lewis played a leading part in the creation of a new kind of labor organization called the Committee for Industrial Organization, which is known today as the Congress of Industrial Organizations (CIO). This group organized unskilled workers in the mass-production industries.

Lewis was sometimes criticized by other labor leaders and the public for what seemed to be his ruthless methods. During World War II, for example, Lewis called four major strikes in the coalfields. Charged with disrupting American industry when strikes were prohibited, he defended himself by pointing to the gains he had made for the miners.

Lewis was a tireless fighter for the rights of the worker. Under his direction, unions in the steel and automobile industries were organized. His persuasive powers as a bargainer won for the workers higher wages, better conditions, and many other benefits. With his great, booming voice, eloquent phrases, and shaggy hair, Lewis was often called "the roaring lion of labor." He died on June 11, 1969, at the age of 89.

Reviewed by GERALD KURLAND
Author, *John L. Lewis:
Labor's Strong-Willed Organizer*

See also LABOR MOVEMENT.

LEWIS, SINCLAIR (1885–1951)

The novels of Sinclair Lewis give a detailed picture of life in the American Middle West. Although Lewis often wrote about likable characters, his books were usually satires of the society he described. In 1930, Lewis became the first American to receive the Nobel Prize for literature.

Harry Sinclair Lewis was born in Sauk Centre, Minnesota, on February 7, 1885, the son of a doctor. He made few friends as he grew up in this small town or later when he attended Oberlin Academy, in Ohio. Lewis entered Yale University in 1903. By that time he knew that he wanted to be a writer, and he became editor of the *Yale Literary Magazine.* But he was often lonely and discontented. After graduation in 1908, he worked as a freelance journalist. In 1910 he moved to New York City to support himself by writing fiction and working in publishing.

Lewis' first successful novel was *Main Street,* published in 1920. It created a sensation with its portrayal of the narrow-mindedness of a typical small Midwestern town. It was followed by *Babbitt* (1922), the story of a small-town businessman; *Arrowsmith* (1925), an account of a young Midwesterner who wants to become a research scientist; *Elmer Gantry* (1927), a novel about a religious fanatic; and *Dodsworth* (1929), about an American's visit to Europe and its effect on him. In 1926, Lewis was offered the Pulitzer Prize for *Arrowsmith,* but he refused it.

Lewis was divorced from his first wife, Grace Hegger, in 1928. In the same year he married Dorothy Thompson, a well-known journalist. They were divorced in 1942. Lewis continued to write novels attacking those parts of American life that he thought were unfair or limited. But his later novels were less effective than those of the 1920's. Lewis died in Rome on January 10, 1951.

Reviewed by ERWIN HESTER
East Carolina University

LEWIS AND CLARK EXPEDITION

When Thomas Jefferson (1743–1826) became president of the United States in 1801, he set about planning an expedition to explore the little-known territory west of the Mississippi River. In January 1803, he asked Congress for $2,500 to fund an expedition of explorers to journey perhaps as far as the Pacific Ocean. However, the request and its approval were kept secret because much of the proposed region to be explored—a vast area between the Mississippi River and the Rocky Mountains called the Louisiana Territory—belonged to France. Beyond it lay the Oregon Territory, where Russian and British fur traders had already established a foothold.

Jefferson hoped that exploration of the West would open up additional territory to the American fur trade. He also wanted the members of the expedition to establish friendly relations with the Native Americans they might meet, so that they would be helpful contacts to fur traders.

In 1803, Jefferson bought the Louisiana Territory from France. Now that this unexplored territory belonged to the United States, Jefferson broadened his goals for the expedition and ordered the explorers to collect information about the plants, animals, climate, and geographical features. The party was also instructed to follow the Missouri River to its source—and seek an all-water route to the Pacific Ocean.

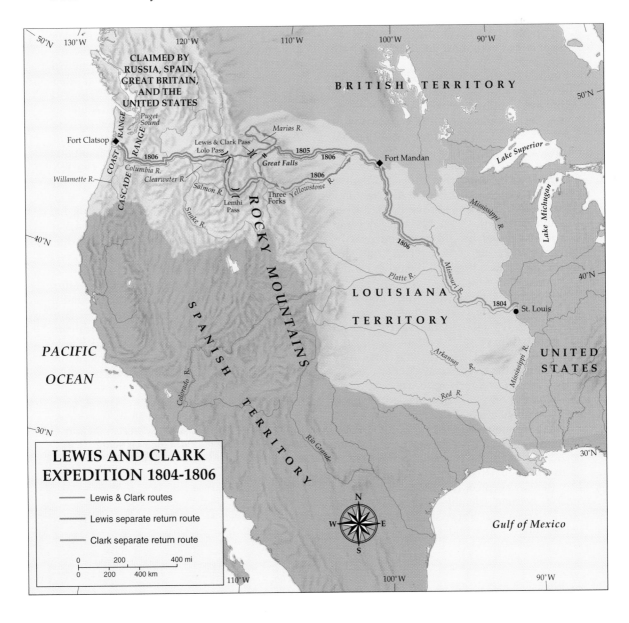

LEWIS AND CLARK EXPEDITION 1804-1806

—— Lewis & Clark routes

—— Lewis separate return route

—— Clark separate return route

0 200 400 mi
0 200 400 km

Jefferson appointed his private secretary, Meriwether Lewis (1774–1809), to head the expedition. As co-leader, Lewis chose William Clark (1770–1838), a younger brother of the Revolutionary War hero George Rogers Clark (1752–1818). Both Lewis and Clark were officers in the U.S. Army and experienced frontiersmen. They selected about 30 adventurous young men, some with military experience, to join the expedition.

The Expedition Gets Under Way

In December 1803, the party set up winter quarters in Illinois, across the Mississippi River from St. Louis. They held rifle practice and became skilled in ways of coping with hardships on the frontier. Aboard their canoes and keelboat the men stored nearly 100 barrels of food provisions and a supply of guns, ammunition, tools, drugs, medical instruments, and additional goods to trade with the Indians.

On May 14, 1804, the group started up the Missouri River—known as the Big Muddy. Some five months later they built a blockhouse, Fort Mandan, near the present site of Bismarck, North Dakota. They spent the winter there.

In the spring of 1805, 15 or 16 members of the party returned to St. Louis to analyze specimens of plant and animal life they had collected. The rest of the group headed west, accompanied by the French trader Toussaint Charbonneau and his Shoshoni Indian wife, Sacagawea. She agreed to act as translator for the party when it reached Shoshoni country in present-day Idaho.

During that summer the little band traveled through territory never before seen by non-natives. On June 13 the men gazed on the Great Falls of the Missouri River, near present-day Great Falls, Montana. Then they pushed on to the river's headwaters.

By this time the men were eager to reach the Shoshoni villages. They needed supplies, horses, and guides to lead them across the Rocky Mountains. Soon they would be unable to proceed farther by boat. At last the expedition found the Shoshoni on the banks of the Salmon River in present-day Idaho. The Indians seemed frightened at first but quickly became friendly when they recognized Sacagawea. They sold the travelers horses, supplies, and guides.

Reaching the Pacific

The expedition crossed the Rockies through the Lemhi and Lolo passes into the Clearwater River valley. Here they met the friendly Nez Percé Indians, who gave them food and shelter. They built dugout canoes and followed the Clearwater to the Snake River into present-day Washington State, where they picked up the Columbia River.

On November 7, 1805, they heard the roaring waters of the mouth of the Columbia River and thought they had reached the Pacific, but they were still 20 miles (32 kilometers) away. On November 15 they finally arrived at "this great Pacific Ocean," as Clark wrote in his journal, "which we have been so long anxious to see." Before winter set in, they built a shelter, Fort Clatsop, at the mouth of the river.

In March 1806, after enduring more than four months of rain, fog, and drizzle, the explorers began their journey back home. In the valley of the Bitterroot River, near what is now Missoula, Montana, the party split into two groups. Clark's group headed south to the three forks of the Missouri River, then on to the Yellowstone River. Lewis' group went north and crossed the Rocky Mountains through the Lewis and Clark Pass. The following August the two groups joined up again on the Missouri River. On September 23, the entire expedition arrived back in St. Louis, having traveled approximately 4,350 miles (7,000 kilometers). After 28 months, the historic journey had come to an end.

The Lewis and Clark expedition added to the geographical knowledge of the Missouri and Columbia valleys. It established friendly relations with a number of Indian tribes and opened up a new frontier for American fur trade activity. Finally, the Lewis and Clark Expedition began a new age of exploration and trailblazing, which later made possible the settlement of the western frontier.

OTIS K. RICE
West Virginia Institute of Technology
Reviewed by STEPHEN AMBROSE
Author, *Undaunted Courage: Meriwether Lewis, Thomas Jefferson, and the Opening of the American West*

See also FUR TRADE IN NORTH AMERICA (The American Trade); LOUISIANA PURCHASE.

LEWISTON. See MAINE (Cities).

LEXINGTON. See KENTUCKY (Cities).

LIBERIA

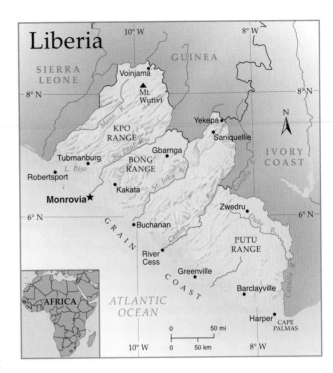

Liberia, whose name means "free land," is a nation on the west coast of Africa. It was established in 1822 by the American Colonization Society as a refuge for former slaves. When Liberia declared its independence in 1847, it became Africa's first republic.

The Americo-Liberian settlers dominated the indigenous (native) population, which led to hostilities that continue to this day. They remained in power until 1980, when an indigenous Liberian, Master Sergeant Samuel K. Doe, seized control in a military coup. The sudden change of government provoked a civil war that took more than 150,000 lives and severely damaged the economy. When the war ended in 1997, more than 1 million refugees returned home, and Liberia started the slow process of recovery.

▶ PEOPLE

About 95 percent of Liberia's population is indigenous to the area. They belong to some 16 different tribal groups, each with its own customs. The remaining 5 percent include Americo-Liberians, descended from the former American slaves, a few Westerners, and a growing number of immigrants from the Middle East.

Language. English is the official language of Liberia, but each tribal group has its own language or dialect. Among them are Kpelle, Bassa, Gio, Krahn, Mandingo, and Liberian pidgin English.

Religion. Most Liberians belong to one of three religious groups. About 70 percent are ancestral worshipers, who believe in a Supreme Being, the existence of spirits, and the ability of the dead (their ancestors) to in-

Left: Schoolboys enjoy a game of soccer.
Below: A girl in Monrovia sells vegetables at an outdoor market.

tervene with God on behalf of the living. The rest of Liberia's population is about 10 percent Christian and 20 percent Muslim.

Education. Prior to the establishment of western-style schools, many Liberians learned by observing older people and by attending traditional or informal schools. They were taught various survival skills and respect for community elders.

Today Liberia has many elementary and high schools run by Christian missionaries. There are three institutions of higher learning. The University of Liberia and William V. S. Tubman College of Technology were estab-

lished by the government. Cuttington University College is run by the Episcopal Church. However, because there is a lack of graduate and professional schools, many Liberians study abroad, particularly in the United States.

Rural Life. About 70 percent of Liberians live in small villages. A village is usually a group of round mud houses with palm-thatched roofs. Family ties are very strong. Each member plays a part in the livelihood of the village. The men clear timber from the fields and plant the rice. The women help harvest the crops and cook the food. The old men make fish traps. The young boys carry water, tend the goats, and drive the monkeys, baboons, and weaverbirds away from banana plants. All-night song and dance festivals are frequently held. Performances by local dancers are a great favorite of the people.

Polygyny (the practice of having multiple wives) is widespread, especially among Liberia's rural residents. Farmers want many children to help them till the land. And because of inadequate medical attention, many children die before the age of 5 or 6.

▶ LAND

Liberia lies about 300 miles (480 kilometers) north of the equator, on the western bulge of the African continent. It is bordered on the northwest by Sierra Leone, on the north by Guinea, on the east by the Ivory Coast, and on the south by the Atlantic Ocean. It covers an area of 43,000 square miles (111,370 square kilometers) and is slightly larger than the U.S. state of Virginia.

Land Regions. The country is divided into two land regions. One is a low-lying strip that stretches inland from the coast. The entire length of Liberia's Atlantic shore has long been known as the Grain Coast. Beyond this the land rises to a rough plateau about 800 feet (240 meters) above sea level. In many places the plateau is broken by small hills and mountain ranges, notably the Bong and Putu ranges. Liberia's high-

Loggers cut down trees in Liberia's dense forests. Timber is among the country's most valuable exports.

A young woman carries her baby on her back as she sows rice, the staple food. Most Liberians exist on the food they are able to grow themselves.

est peak, Mount Wutivi, rises 4,528 feet (1,380 meters).

Rivers and Lakes. Liberia's major rivers are the Mano, St. Paul, St. John, Cestos, and Cavalla. Its two largest inland bodies of water are Piso Lake and Shepherd's Lake.

Climate. Liberia has a tropical climate, with an annual rainfall of about 200 inches (5,000 millimeters). A rainy season lasts from May through October, and coastal areas receive about twice as much rain as the interior regions. A dry season lasts from November through April. Temperatures generally range between 70°F (21°C) and 82°F (28°C).

Natural Resources. Iron is Liberia's most important natural resource. Gold and diamonds are also mined.

A wide variety of wild animals are found in Liberia's dense forests. They include 16 species of monkeys, 15 species of snakes, 10 species of wild cats, and a rare species of pygmy hippopotamus. Elephants, buffalo, antelopes, hogs, lizards, crocodiles, and flamingos are also common.

▶ **ECONOMY**

Before the civil war began in 1980, Liberia was the world's fifth largest exporter of iron ore. Its economy also relied heavily on rubber, timber, gold, and diamonds. When the war ended in 1997, the economy was slow to improve, and the return of more than 1 million refugees raised unemployment rates as high as 70 percent.

Agriculture. Agriculture is the most important segment of Liberia's economy because it employs most of the workforce. Cash crops grown for export include rubber, cacao, coffee, and timber. The cultivation of rice, yams, cassava (a starchy root), and other crops by subsistence farmers has reduced the government's need to import food.

Transportation. The free port of Monrovia plays an important part in the commerce of western Africa. The harbor was built during World War II (1939–45) with assistance from the United States. Although the road systems have fallen into disrepair, two railroad lines connect the coast with important sources of iron ore in the interior.

▶ **MAJOR CITIES**

Monrovia, the capital and largest city of Liberia, has an estimated population of 500,000. The city was named for James Monroe, who was president of the United States when Americans established Liberia in 1822.

Much of the city of Monrovia, Liberia's capital and chief commercial center, was destroyed during a long civil war that raged in the late 1900's.

Monrovia is situated on the Atlantic coast. The city is the cultural and educational center of the country. And because of its fine harbor, it is also Liberia's chief port and commercial center. Large parts of Monrovia were destroyed during the long period of civil war.

▶ CULTURAL HERITAGE

The government attaches great importance to the native cultural arts, and efforts are being made to preserve them. A center for the display of native masks, handicrafts, and other visual and performing arts has been established outside Monrovia.

▶ HISTORY AND GOVERNMENT

Before the modern nation of Liberia was established, the region was inhabited by a variety of native groups. In 1364, France established the first colonial trading post there. Over the centuries the French were followed by the Portuguese, the British, and the Dutch, all of whom were engaged in the trans-Atlantic slave trade.

In 1822, Liberia became populated with West Indians and African Americans, including many former slaves, who moved to Africa under the sponsorship of the American Colonization Society. Anxious to maintain their links with the United States and remain separate from the native population, the settlers had their constitution drafted by American scholars. In 1847 the settlers declared Liberia independent and elected Joseph Jenkins Roberts as their first president.

Instead of setting up a liberal society, as might be expected from formerly oppressed peoples, the Americo-Liberians began acting like masters of the native population. The natives soon rebelled and battled with the Americo-Liberians over land issues, religious beliefs, forced labor, leadership of the country, and neglect of the rural areas.

In 1922, the American businessmen Charles Goodyear and Harvey Firestone found Liberia to be an ideal place for growing rubber. Encouraged by the U.S. State Department, the Liberian government signed an agreement with the Firestone company that leased them 1 million acres (400,000 hectares) for 99 years. But it soon led to an international scandal that caught the United States in an embarrassing situation. In 1929 a League of Nations investigation found the existence of forced labor and involuntary servitude in Liberia.

In 1944, William V. S. Tubman was elected president of Liberia. His reforms and concern for the indigenous peoples made him extremely popular. But when Tubman died in 1971, he was succeeded by his vice president, William R. Tolbert, Jr., who ordered his military and police forces to shoot at Liberians who were protesting against increases in the price of rice, the staple food. In 1980, Tolbert was removed from office in a bloody revolt led by Master Sergeant Samuel K. Doe, an indigenous soldier who sought to eliminate all political opponents. A failed attempt to unseat Doe led to an unstoppable cycle of ethnic violence, resulting in a civil war that led to the deaths of thousands of Liberians.

In September 1990, Doe was captured by soldiers of a rival rebel group and savagely beaten to death. After many failed attempts to reach a peace agreement among the combatants, the United Nations, the Organization of African Unity (OAU), and the Economic Community of West African States (ECOWAS) finally succeeded in negotiating a cease-fire. The war ended in 1997 with the election of Charles Taylor, the leader of the National Patriotic Front, as president.

Liberia made economic progress with the aid of the European Union, Japan, Libya, and the United States until 2001, when hostilities resumed between the government and rebel groups composed of Doe's loyalists. Furthermore, the international community imposed sanctions on Liberia because Taylor's government had been exporting arms to rebel forces in Sierra Leone.

By 2003, Liberian rebels had taken control of more than half the country, and Monrovia came under attack. After the United States and several West African nations sent troops, Taylor went into exile in Nigeria. He became the second incumbent leader in history to be indicted for war crimes by the United Nations. He was succeeded by Charles Gyude Bryant, who served as chairman of an interim government until new elections could be held.

In 2005, Ellen Johnson-Sirleaf was elected president. She was the first woman named head of state of a modern African nation.

HASSAN B. SISAY
California State University, Chico

LIBERTY, STATUE OF

On Liberty Island in New York Harbor stands a huge copper statue known as the Statue of Liberty. Its real name is *Liberty Enlightening the World*. The people of France gave it to the people of the United States as a memorial to American independence and a symbol of a friendship that began when France aided the colonies in the Revolutionary War. It was planned to commemorate the United States' centennial, or 100th anniversary of independence, in 1876.

The female figure, named Liberty, stands for freedom, or independence. The tablet in the left hand—with the date July 4, 1776—represents the Declaration of Independence. The right hand holds the Torch (or Light) of Freedom. The broken chain near the feet symbolizes the victory of Liberty over Tyranny.

In 1874 a committee of French citizens sent the sculptor Frédéric August Bartholdi to the United States to plan a memorial. When he sailed into New York Harbor, he realized that it would be a perfect setting for a monument —the figure of Liberty standing at the gateway to the New World. It was decided that the French would build the statue and the Americans would build the pedestal. The site chosen was old Fort Wood on Bedloe's Island (renamed Liberty Island in 1956).

Bartholdi first made a small model of the statue. The huge final form was built in 300 sections. Thin copper sheets were pressed and hammered into shape on wooden molds. The iron framework that supports the statue was designed by the engineer Alexandre Gustave Eiffel, who later built the Eiffel Tower in Paris. After a presentation ceremony in Paris on July 4, 1884, the statue was taken apart and packed into 214 cases for its journey to New York Harbor. Here it was erected on a pedestal designed by the architect Richard Morris Hunt. It was dedicated on October 28, 1886.

The statue became a national monument in 1924. Today the Statue of Liberty National Monument includes nearby Ellis Island—once an immigration center—and the American Museum of Immigration, in the statue's base. A three-year project to clean and repair the statue was completed in July, 1986, in time for a gala celebration of its 100th birthday.

Reviewed by PAUL O. WEINBAUM
Statue of Liberty National Monument

The Statue of Liberty stands 151 feet (46 meters) tall, from its sandals to the tip of its torch. It weighs 225 tons (204 metric tons). Its nose is 4.5 feet (1.37 meters) long, and each eye is 2.5 feet (.76 meter) wide. With pedestal and base, the statue rises to a height of 305 feet (93 meters). Inside, an elevator and stairway lead to the top of the pedestal. From there, spiral stairs take visitors to the crown.

A poem, "The New Colossus," by Emma Lazarus, is engraved on a bronze plaque inside the statue's pedestal. The poem ends:

". . . Give me your tired, your poor,
Your huddled masses yearning to breathe free,
The wretched refuse of your teeming shore.
Send these, the homeless, tempest-tost to me,
I lift my lamp beside the golden door!"

LIBERTY BELL

The Liberty Bell is one of the most prized symbols of the American past. It is a main attraction at Independence National Historical Park in Philadelphia. The bell once stood in a room on the ground floor of Independence Hall. In 2003, as part of a multimillion dollar renovation and expansion of Independence Mall, it was moved to a new home—Liberty Bell Center.

The Liberty Bell has had several names. It was first called the State House Bell. The Pennsylvania Assembly ordered it for the new State House (now Independence Hall). Thomas Lister of London, England, cast the bell for a price of about $300. It arrived in Philadelphia in 1752. The bell weighed more than 2,080 pounds (935 kilograms) and was more than 3 feet (1 meter) tall.

No one had ever rung the bell, so the new owners tested it. When the clapper struck the sides, the bell cracked. After local workers had recast it twice, it was hung in the State House belfry in 1753.

The bell rang on July 8, 1776, when Philadelphians celebrated the signing of the Declaration of Independence. The thought of a bell ringing out for freedom fired people's imaginations. The bell became a symbol of the Revolutionary War. When the British took Philadelphia in 1777, patriots rescued the bell. According to tradition, it was hidden in the basement of a church in Allentown, Pennsylvania, until the American colonial forces recaptured Philadelphia.

The Liberty Bell rang in 1783 to announce that the United States had won independence. From then on, the bell rang on all important patriotic occasions. It rang to mark the birthdays of famous people. And it tolled the public's grief when famous people died.

In 1835 the bell cracked while tolling the death of John Marshall, the fourth Chief Justice of the United States. After a period of neglect, the bell was repaired. Around this time the abolitionists (people who wanted to free the slaves) were becoming active in Philadelphia. The sentiment in Pennsylvania was so strongly against slavery that the bell was given its present name—the Liberty Bell. The bell had stood for independence from England, but it now began to symbolize a larger fight for freedom.

The bell cracked again as it rang for George Washington's birthday in 1846. This time no one was able to fix it. It was taken down from the belfry. After being placed in various parts of Independence Hall, the bell was finally set upon a framework on the ground floor of the tower in 1915. The wooden yoke that held the bell was weak with dry rot. Steel bars were added to give the yoke strength. Wheels were hidden under the framework so that the bell could be moved in case of fire.

Now people come from all over the world to visit the Liberty Bell in its new home. They remember its proud past and examine the zigzag crack running almost from top to bottom. And they can see that the words from the Bible around the top of the bell—"Proclaim Liberty throughout all the Land unto all the Inhabitants thereof"—mean as much for the future as for the past.

Reviewed by Hobart Cawood
Superintendent
Independence National Historical Park

See also INDEPENDENCE HALL.

LIBRARIES

The word "library" comes from the Latin word *liber,* meaning "book." The use of "library" to indicate a room, a set of rooms, or a building in which a collection of books and manuscripts is housed was first used in the 1400's. Libraries collect, preserve, and organize the knowledge that has accumulated throughout the ages—knowledge that educates us, entertains us, and opens doors to many new ideas and places.

▶ **EARLY LIBRARIES**

The library as we know it today, with shelves of books and other materials on every imaginable subject, had its origins in ancient libraries that go back at least 4,000 years to the 2000's B.C.

Babylonia and Assyria

In the 1840's, a British archaeologist and diplomat, Sir Austen Henry Layard (1817–94), conducted excavations in Babylonia and Assyria. At the site of the ancient city of Nineveh he discovered a library containing clay tablets. This library was founded during the 700's B.C. by Sargon II. His great-grandson Ashurbanipal (668–627 B.C.) organized and greatly enlarged the collection. It was probably housed in a temple or a palace, as were most libraries of that time. Librarians, called "men of the written tablets," were in charge of these collections. The heavy, durable tablets preserved information about affairs of daily life, especially trade and religion. Many of the tablets were used for record-keeping. Others told stories of heroic deeds.

Ancient Egypt

Libraries had existed in Egypt before the time of the temple libraries. The nobles of the feudal age may have gathered and maintained their own collections as early as 2000 B.C. Because perishable papyrus scrolls were used for recording information, however, we do not know very much about early Egyptian libraries.

We do know that a library existed in the temple of Horus at Edfu (now Idfu). This "House of Papyrus," dating from about 237 B.C., contained scrolls on astrology, astronomy, religion, and hunting. These scrolls were listed in a "catalog" that was cut into one of the library's stone walls.

Archaeologists working at the Karnak Temple at Thebes (now Luxor), in central Egypt, also discovered an inscription for a "House of Books." Other archaeologists unearthed the tombs of two librarians, a father and son, at Karnak. The job of librarian was probably inherited and, like many administrators, librarians were priests.

Above: In the earliest days of civilization, libraries were collections of inscribed clay tablets. *Below:* Later, in ancient Egypt, information was written on scrolls of papyrus, which were assembled to form libraries.

This article on libraries is divided into four main sections: (1) Early Libraries; (2) Modern Libraries; (3) Librarians and What They Do; and (4) How to Use Your Library.

Related articles in other volumes include BOOK REPORTS AND REVIEWS, BOOKS, CHILDREN'S LITERATURE, READING, REFERENCE MATERIALS, and RESEARCH.

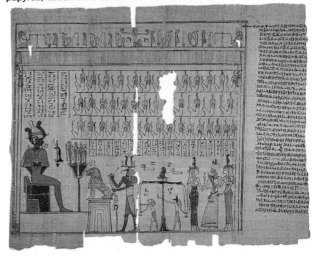

The greatest library of the ancient world was the library at Alexandria, in Egypt. It was founded by Ptolemy I (367?–283? B.C.). During his reign, Alexandria became the capital of Egypt, a place where scholars from all over the world gathered.

Ancient Greece

The first public library in the history of western civilization was probably founded in Athens in the 500's B.C. The first great private library of ancient Greece was established by Aristotle (384–322 B.C.). His collection grew from his need to gather materials to use in his research and teaching. After Aristotle died, the library was transferred to Asia Minor (then part of the Greek Empire), returned to Athens, and eventually taken to Rome by the Roman general and dictator Sulla (138–78 B.C.)

Rivaling the Egyptian library at Alexandria was the library of Pergamum, also in Asia Minor. It held 200,000 volumes.

Ancient Rome

The first libraries in Rome were filled with texts brought back from Greece by conquering generals. These texts spread the influence of Greek literature and thought among the Romans, who had no literature of their own.

Often the Roman libraries were located near and connected with temples. Manuscript rolls stored in these libraries were placed lengthwise on cupboard shelves or placed upright in boxes shaped like cylinders. The titles appeared on tags fastened to the rolls and boxes. Reading rooms often faced the east. This was partly for religious reasons. Also, the morning light made it easier for scholars to read, and the light helped ward off the dampness that is such an enemy of manuscripts and books.

The most celebrated Roman library was the Bibliotheca Ulpia, which was founded in Rome by Emperor Trajan (A.D. 53?–117). The library housed large separate collections of Latin and Greek manuscripts, and its walls were decorated with busts of writers.

The libraries of ancient Rome were not destined to survive. The Roman emperor Theodosius the Great (346?–395) closed the temples and with them the libraries. When the Goths and Vandals came down from the north and sacked Rome, some of the manuscripts were preserved, but the last of the Roman libraries vanished.

THE MIDDLE AGES

Between A.D. 100 and 400, scrolls were replaced by **codices**—the first bound books. A

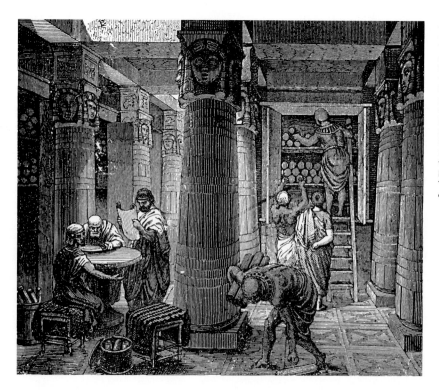

Left: The most famous library of the ancient world was the library at Alexandria, in Egypt. It contained more than 400,000 volumes, mainly Greek. The main part of the library was destroyed by fire in 47 B.C. *Opposite page:* The richly decorated Sistine Room in the Vatican Library in Rome is a treasure house of rare books and manuscripts. The Vatican Library dates from the 300's.

codex is a manuscript of sheets of parchment that are sewn together along one edge. The codex was easy to carry and easy to preserve. Because of this, the codex form was favored by the early Christians, who found it convenient for carrying the books of the Bible. As Christianity spread throughout the Roman Empire, the codex became established as the standard form for books.

The manuscripts that survived the demise of the Roman Empire had been hidden away or copied by monks in their **scriptoria**, special rooms used for writing. Cassiodorus (487?–583?), a Roman noble in the court of the Ostrogoth king Theodoric the Great (454?–526), was the most important force in establishing monastic libraries. He also developed rules for the care and preservation of books.

In the early Middle Ages, scribes made copies of books, such as Bibles and other religious and philosophical works, for the libraries of their monasteries.

Monastic libraries were not large. Indeed, they rarely contained more than several hundred volumes, which included encyclopedias, rules of the monastic orders, church law, the Old and the New Testaments of the Bible, the lives of saints, and classical works.

During the late Middle Ages the monastic libraries and scriptoria gradually lost their importance, due in part to the invention of the printing press around 1440 by Johann Gutenberg (1398?–1468). Since books could then be printed in quantity, they became more accessible. The rise of libraries in universities also contributed to the decline of the monastic libraries.

Renaissance and Reformation

Many of the great university libraries in Europe were founded during the 1300's. By the 1400's and 1500's, national libraries were established on the continent.

France. The first important national library was the Bibliothèque Nationale in France. It was developed from the libraries of such early French kings as Charles V, Charles VI, Charles VIII, and Louis XI. Francis I (1494–1547) first brought these royal libraries together at the palace of Fontainebleau. Then, during the reign of Louis XIV (1638–1715), the library was doubled in size by Jean-Baptiste Colbert (1619–83) and moved to its present site in Paris. The library became national property after the French Revolution. Today the library's collection includes books, photographs, prints, coins, and audiovisual materials.

England. The roots of the first great university library in England go back to the late Middle Ages. In 1444, Humphrey, Duke of

Gloucester (1391–1447), gave his collection of books to Oxford University. The library itself did not open until 1488. Then, during the stormy reign of Edward VI (1537–53), it was destroyed. Finally, through the efforts of Sir Thomas Bodley (1545–1613), the library was reopened in 1602 and it remains open to this day. The Bodleian Library of Oxford houses about 5 million books and 65,000 manuscripts. Its extensive Shakespearean and biblical collections are famous worldwide.

Italy. In 1440, about the time that Oxford University acquired the Duke of Gloucester's collection, Cosimo de' Medici (1389–1464) established Italy's first public library in Florence, in the cloisters of San Marco. De' Medici also started the collection that by the 1500's had grown into the state-supported Laurentian Library in Florence. The building housing the collection was designed by Michelangelo and contains such treasures as the manuscripts of Vergil, Cicero, and Dante.

The Vatican Library, the oldest public library in Europe, was formed in the 1400's, though its roots go back as far as the 300's and Pope Damasus I. Under Pope Pius XI (1857–1939) the collections were organized and cataloged for the first time. The library is known for the number of rare books and manuscripts in its collection.

The Western Hemisphere

The San Marcos University Library in Lima, Peru, founded by the Spanish in 1551, is the oldest library in the Western Hemisphere. The first library in North America was established in Canada in Quebec City, Quebec, in 1635. In the United States, libraries such as those at Harvard University in Cambridge, Massachusetts, the college of William and Mary in Williamsburg, Virginia, and Yale University in New Haven, Connecticut, had considerable collections by the middle of the 1700's.

Library of Congress. Founded by an act of Congress in 1800, the Library of Congress in Washington, D.C., is one of the world's largest libraries. Burned by British soldiers in 1814, it was re-established in 1815. Its main responsibility is to serve the Senate and the House of Representatives, but it is also considered to be the national library of the United States in much the same way as the British Library serves Great Britain and the Bibliothèque Nationale serves France.

Public Libraries. American public libraries had an early start when a Boston merchant, Robert Keayne, established a public library in 1653. The library continued to serve Bostonians for generations. Benjamin Franklin founded the first subscription library in the

Founded in 1895, the New York Public Library, in New York City, is the second largest library in the United States. The Library of Congress, in Washington, D.C., is the largest.

colonies in 1731. He and other Philadelphia citizens contributed books to a collection that they circulated among themselves, creating the Library Company of Philadelphia. The Redwood Library in Newport, Rhode Island, established in 1747, and the Charleston Library Society in South Carolina, established in 1748, were other important subscription libraries. All of these libraries are still in existence.

Farther west, in Amesville, Ohio, a "coonskin" library flourished in 1804, when settlers along the Ohio River offered Boston merchants raccoon skins for books.

In the middle of the 1800's free public libraries, supported by public taxation, were opened in New Hampshire, Maine, and Massachusetts. The first tax-supported library was established in Peterborough, New Hampshire, in 1833. By 1875 there were 2,000 free libraries owning more than 1,000 books each. By 1900 the free public libraries numbered 5,400.

The Boston Public Library, the largest in New England, opened in 1854. Its organization into both reference and circulating departments set the pattern for later public libraries. The New York Public Library, now the largest U.S. public library, was founded on May 23, 1895. The Astor and Lenox libraries formed the basis of its collection, and it was further aided by the Tilden Trust. It is financed primarily through public taxes but private funds from the Tilden Trust and from contributions of private citizens support the research collections and the work of the library.

Much of the growth of public libraries in the United States was due to Andrew Carnegie (1835–1919), the Scottish-born industrialist and steel tycoon. He made contributions totaling more than $5 million to the building of libraries on the condition that towns would set up and finance such libraries with taxes. The Carnegie fund still supports special library projects today.

Another factor in the development of early public libraries in the United States was the passage of state laws authorizing townships to create libraries. The first such law was passed in New Hampshire in 1893.

▶ MODERN LIBRARIES

When you think of a library, what comes to mind? Maybe you picture the school library students visit regularly during school hours.

Many libraries store materials on film, such as microfiche, because it allows them to maintain large collections in limited spaces.

Or you may picture the public library where you may have first experienced choosing a book for yourself. These are two types of libraries. There are also state libraries, provincial libraries (in Canada), and regional libraries, as well as university, research, and special libraries in government and business organizations, all of which house millions of volumes that are used for research in every imaginable field.

Public Libraries

Public libraries range in size from modest one-room facilities to large imposing buildings with many branches. In general, they are supported by taxes collected locally. The federal government may supply funds for special projects or materials. To meet the needs of library patrons of all ages and interests, the public library offers many different services.

Main Collection. In addition to keeping fiction shelves stocked with books from the great masterpieces of literature from the past to the latest bestsellers, the main collection in a library contains books and other materials on current events and a variety of other subjects. People look to the library to find out about all kinds of things. For example, the do-it-yourselfer fixing a faucet may need a book on plumbing. An aspiring cook may want to read the latest cookbooks. A traveler may look for information about sights to see and places to stay around the world.

With so many advances in medicine, science, and technology, information in these fields changes constantly, and it is very important to have up-to-date material available. Because it takes some time to publish books, libraries also have journals and magazines (periodicals), and newspapers in their collections to provide more immediate access to the most current information.

In addition to the books, periodicals, and newspapers in the main collection, computer programs, video and audio cassettes, recordings, prints, paintings, pamphlets, and maps may also be available. Books printed in large type for those with poor eyesight, as well as books in braille and on records and tapes, are a part of many collections.

Reference Collection. When library patrons look to the library as a source for answers to questions, it is important that the material containing the answers be on hand at all times. Therefore, this material is shelved in a separate section—the reference section. Reference librarians must be alert to the many kinds of published information that will meet the needs of patrons. They are trained to work with these resources and to help researchers find the information they need.

Encyclopedias, atlases, and dictionaries are the most frequently used books in the reference section, but there are thousands of other

books and materials covering most of the subject areas in the main collection.

Indexes to periodicals make it possible to find specific information from among thousands of publications. In large libraries, computers help to speed research by making it possible for users to scan all of the available sources of information on many particular topics quickly.

Most of the newspapers and periodicals, which would take up a great deal of space if they are stored, are photographed and stored on reels or cassettes of **microfilm** (a photographic record of printed material, in greatly reduced size) or on small sheets of film called **microfiche**. Many pages of a book or document fit on one microfiche card, which is

Most public libraries have special children's sections, where librarians offer story hours and programs to teach young readers how to find and use library materials.

Many school libraries offer a variety of nonbook materials as well as the equipment that may be needed to use them. These items are often kept in a special section of the library known as a media center.

about the size of a postcard. A microfilm or microfiche reader is used to scan the material, which is enlarged on a screen. Many of these readers are equipped to print copies of the pages.

Other materials found in the reference section include telephone books for large cities; consumer information guides that cover the purchase of everything from automobiles to toys; and books on law, science, literature, history, and career opportunities. The reference librarian also has access to materials in other libraries and will locate and borrow it for the patron. Much of this kind of searching for material is quickly done by computers.

Young Adult Collection. Some libraries have a separate collection for teenagers. The librarian specializes in working with young adults and searches for books that would appeal to them. Some of the books are written especially for teenagers, but many are selected from the general adult collection. Information on all aspects of the teenagers' world, including pamphlets, catalogs, and films on colleges, careers, and job opportunities, is usually available.

Children's Collection. Almost every library has an area or a separate room devoted to a collection of children's books—fairy tales, picture books, stories, and nonfiction books written especially for children. A popular activity in the children's room is the story hour. A specially trained librarian chooses stories to interest children of specific age groups. In addition to books, video cassettes, toys, and

games may be borrowed from libraries that have the funds to purchase them and the space to store them. Many libraries also make audio equipment and computers available to children.

School Libraries

In the United States, school libraries are often called media centers. Media centers are true centers of learning that use both print materials and nonprint materials such as computer programs, films, compact discs, and audio and video cassettes. Media centers have computer workstations, listening booths, media production and viewing areas, and individual desks for quiet study, as well as areas for discussions and conversations. They are important resources for modern teaching methods, which often require students to use different kinds of research materials instead of or in addition to textbooks in each subject. Some large high school libraries have resource centers that specialize in foreign languages, the sciences, and mathematics.

Media specialists are both teachers and librarians who instruct students in using the resources of the center. The materials in media centers also represent diverse political, religious, ethnic, and cultural viewpoints in order to help students develop into informed and responsible citizens.

State, Provincial, and Regional Libraries

The states of the United States and the provinces of Canada also maintain libraries. Originally set up to provide government officials and agencies with information required in their work, these libraries now have many other functions. They advise and help communities that want to establish a public library or to improve an existing one. State and provincial libraries lend material to local libraries on request, and they also encourage local libraries to cooperate in the collection and preservation of official papers.

A regional or county library is usually set up in a sparsely populated area to serve a single county or region. A regional library usually has headquarters in a central location and has numerous small book stations throughout the area.

The academic library at Merton College, Oxford University in England, was established in 1377. Note that the ancient volumes are chained to the shelves.

University and Research Libraries

There are more than 5,000 college and university libraries in the United States and Canada. The largest university library in the world is at Harvard University in Cambridge, Massachusetts, which has more than 14 million volumes.

University library collections may specialize in such subjects as physics, law, literature, architecture, or music. Specialists in science and technology, for example, often use the Linda Hall Library in Kansas City, Missouri. Researchers in the fields of literature, history, and fine arts might use the Newberry Library in Chicago, Illinois.

The libraries at Harvard, the University of California at Berkeley, the University of Illinois, and the University of Toronto are among North America's major research facilities. The libraries at Oxford and Cambridge universities in England are used by researchers from all over the world.

Unlike public libraries, which endeavor to provide the most up-to-date materials, college and university libraries offer researchers new as well as very old books that have become difficult to find. Some, such as the library at Yale University, are known for their rare book collections.

The New York Public Library is one of the greatest research libraries in the world, and the Center for Research Libraries in Chicago provides cataloging and storage space for books, magazines, and other materials that are rarely used in other research libraries in the United States.

The Library of Congress in Washington, D.C., is the world's largest library. Founded in 1800, it provides research material for the United States Congress as well as the general public. Its collections contain over 115 million items, including books, motion pictures, maps, audio recordings, and even telephone books.

The National Agricultural Library of the Department of Agriculture in Washington, D.C., houses many materials on agriculture, nutrition, water quality, and related topics. The National Library of Medicine, also in Washington, D.C., has a collection of materials on all kinds of medical subjects in almost every language.

Another national library with an extensive reference collection is the National Library of Canada, in Ottawa, established in 1953. It

The Library of Parliament in Ottawa, Ontario, Canada, is known as a special library. Its collection of more than half a million books was established to serve a specialized group of users—the nation's lawmakers.

publishes the national bibliography, which lists publications relating to Canada. It also maintains the Canadian Union Catalog, which is a key to the main library resources of that country.

The British Library was established after the British Library Act of 1972 separated the British Museum Library, which housed the United Kingdom's book and manuscript collection, from the British Museum. The library opened in 1973 and includes the National Sound Archive, the India Office Library and Records, the National Reference Library of Science and Invention, and a lending division.

The Russian State Library in Moscow and the Bibliothèque Nationale of France in Paris also have extensive research collections.

Special Libraries

Many business, industrial, research, and professional organizations maintain libraries that address their particular needs. Because these libraries have a single focus, they are called special libraries. The slogan of the Special Libraries Association, "Putting knowledge to work," gives a good description of what they do.

There are about 9,600 special libraries in the United States and about 1,300 in Canada. It is vital for these facilities to have up-to-date information found primarily in technical journals and reports, government documents, and newspapers.

▶ LIBRARIANS AND WHAT THEY DO

Librarians have always been classifiers, record keepers, information sharers, and promoters of books, reading, and research. Librarians must organize and be familiar with all material in a library system so that every library user may locate information quickly. When asked for help in locating material on a particular topic, a librarian must decide where to look for the best sources.

Librarians possess other valuable skills that relate to specific needs. Those who enjoy working directly with the public often work in local public libraries, both large and small, perhaps as reference or children's librarians. Public librarians also sometimes serve as coordinators of a variety of events and activities, such as short story and poetry readings, films, and seminars that take place at many libraries. School librarians work with young people of all ages and help teachers by providing information and supplementary materials that extend the work students are doing in their classrooms. They may also assist in organizing student exhibits and after-school activities, such as book clubs and study groups. In addition, there are librarians who are experts on various topics, who work in libraries that specialize in these areas.

How to Become a Librarian

To become a librarian in the United States and Canada, you first must obtain an under-

Librarians are the guardians of the materials in their libraries. But they also serve as guides to those materials, helping users find information ranging from basic facts to highly complex information.

graduate degree from a four-year college, and then a master's degree in library science (MLS) from a library school accredited by the American Library Association. The master's degree requires one to two years of full-time study that covers the theory of classification, information retrieval from a variety of sources, the development of library collections, laws and regulations affecting libraries, and administration.

Graduate schools look for an undergraduate emphasis in academic subjects, with courses in history, economics, government, literature, foreign languages, and the sciences. A school librarian would find education courses with a major in an academic subject useful. Since many libraries contain material in languages other than English, it is important to know at least one other language.

Because so many libraries and media centers are automated and connected to computerized on-line networks, computer skills are now in great demand.

Pioneers in Librarianship

Several American librarians of the 1800's made important contributions to the field that laid the groundwork for the library systems still used today.

William Frederick Poole (1821–94) developed the Newberry Library in Chicago into one of the great research libraries in America. His general index to periodicals, *Poole's Index to Periodical Literature*, is probably his most lasting contribution to the field.

Melvil Dewey (1851–1931) devised the Dewey Decimal Classification system that is used in many libraries. In 1887 he founded the New York State Library School, the world's first school for training librarians.

Minnie Earl Sears (1873–1933) was responsible for the *Sears List of Subject Headings for Small Libraries*, which has become a basic tool for librarians.

Isadore Gilbert Mudge (1875–1957) produced the classic *Guide to Reference Books* while teaching at the School of Library Sciences at Columbia University. She made reference service a respected and primary library function.

Professional Associations

Among the many professional associations for librarians is the American Library Association (ALA), which was founded in 1876. The ALA, with about 58,700 members, establishes standards for the education of its members and enforces the standards by accrediting schools of library and information science. The ALA cooperates with many other library associations in the United States, Canada, and other countries.

The Canadian Library Association, founded in 1947, develops standards and promotes public awareness of library and infor-

The American Library Association (ALA) is the largest professional organization for librarians in the United States. One of its functions is to encourage people to use their libraries by publicizing how useful and pleasurable a trip to the library can be.

use your library

mation services. The Special Libraries Association (SLA), established in 1909, represents libraries in business, industry, and the government, as well as organizations in the fields of medicine, science, technology, social sciences, and fine arts.

The American Society for Information Science (ASIS), which was founded in 1937, is the national organization for information scientists as well as for librarians who develop, manage, and use information systems and technology.

Other library associations include the Catholic Library Association, the Church and Synagogue Library Association, the American Association of Law Librarians, the Music Library Association, and the American Indian Library Association.

Professional Publications

The American Library Association, Special Libraries Association, and American Society for Information Science publish journals for the profession. Several publishing houses also publish materials to answer the needs of librarians. The H. W. Wilson Company publishes useful indexes, including the *Reader's Guide to Periodical Literature,* the *Education Index,* and the *Biography Index.* R. R. Bowker compiles current information about salary ranges, associations, awards, and book publishing statistics in its *Annual Library and*

Book Trade Almanac. Bowker's *Books in Print* is an invaluable reference in libraries, and its *Library Journal* publishes articles of interest and reviews of new books. Another source for reviews of books, films, videos, filmstrips, and software is the American Library Association's publication, *Booklist.*

▶ **HOW TO USE YOUR LIBRARY**

When you enter a library—no matter where it is or how large or small it is—there is one thing you immediately notice: It is quiet! The library is a place where people focus their attention on reading or research. Loud conversation, music, eating, drinking, and other distractions are not allowed because they make concentration difficult. Since the library is open to everyone, it is important that these rules be observed.

It is also important to know how to take care of the books and other materials provided by the library. If they are damaged or destroyed, they will no longer be available. Before you begin to look for a book, review these few rules for handling library materials: (1) always remove a book from the shelf by the middle of its spine; (2) open a book carefully so that the spine will not break; (3) turn

The ALA prints many colorful posters. This one reminds library users to return the materials they borrow so that others may use them as well.

I got carded at the library!

the pages by holding the upper right-hand corner; (4) use a flat bookmark—never turn down the corner of a page to mark your place; (5) do not write in—or highlight passages in—library materials; (6) do not tear out pages of books or magazines; (7) handle only the edges of filmstrips, compact discs, and computer discs, and never leave these materials in direct sunlight or on radiators; (8) always try to return the books you check out by their due dates.

How the Library Collection Is Organized

Now that you know how to care for the materials in the library, you are ready to start using them. Since libraries are all organized in much the same way, if you learn how to use even a small public or school library, you will find that the size of a library and the search for information need never be intimidating. There are two main standards of li-

brary organization in use in the United States: the Dewey Decimal Classification system and the Library of Congress Classification system.

Dewey Decimal Classification. The Dewey Decimal Classification system is a numerical scheme for the arrangement of subjects of nonfiction books. It is used in most public and school libraries. The system divides areas of knowledge into ten classes. Each of these classes is divided into ten divisions. For example, the 500's are divided as follows:

500 Pure Science
510 Mathematics
520 Astronomy
530 Physics
540 Chemistry
550 Geology
560 Paleontology
570 Biology
580 Botany
590 Zoology

Each division is divided into ten sections. By using decimals after the first three digits, each section can be divided indefinitely into subsections so that new subjects can be added anywhere.

According to the progression of the Dewey Decimal Classification, a book on radioactivity would be assigned the classification number 539.75.

500 Pure Science
530 Physics
539 Modern Physics
539.75 Nuclear Reactions

These classification numbers, called **class numbers**, are usually marked on a book's spine to make putting it in its correct place on the shelf easier and faster. Because there might be several books on the same subject

CLASSIFICATION SYSTEMS

Dewey Decimal Classification

000	General works
100	Philosophy
200	Religion
300	Social sciences
400	Language
500	Pure science
600	Technology (applied sciences)
700	Arts
800	Literature
900	History

Library of Congress Classification

A	General works	**L**	Education
B	Philosophy and religion	**M**	Music
C	History—auxiliary sciences	**N**	Fine arts
D	History and topography (except America)	**P**	Language and literature
E-F	American history	**Q**	Science
G	Geography and anthropology	**R**	Medicine
H	Social sciences	**S**	Agriculture
J	Political sciences	**T**	Technology
K	Law of the United States	**U**	Military science
		V	Naval science
		Z	Bibliography and library science

Books are arranged on shelves according to the classification system used by the library. The book *Radioactivity* has the Dewey Decimal system number 539.75. It is located next to others on similar subjects.

written by different authors, the library may add a letter (or letters) beneath the class number. This letter will be the first letter (or first three letters) of the author's last name. The combination of the class number plus the letter or letters is known as the **call number**. A book in the reference section usually has an "R" above the call number.

Nonfiction books are arranged on the shelf according to their class numbers, and then arranged in alphabetical order according to their call numbers.

For example, books of folk songs by Beatrice Landeck, Jean Ritchie, and Ruth Seeger would be shelved in this order:

784	784	784
L	R	S
(or **Lan**)	(or **Rit**)	(or **See**)

Biographies and autobiographies, books about the lives of real people, are usually grouped together in a special section. Generally, a book dealing with the life of one person will be given the classification B, with the name of the person about whom the book is written appearing beneath the B. It is shelved in alphabetical order according to the person's name. A book about the lives of several people is given the Dewey Decimal Classification number 920, with the first letter or letters of the author's last name appearing beneath the 920.

Fiction books, works written from the imagination, are generally shelved in alpha-

betical order according to the author's last name, and then alphabetically by title if there is more than one book by the same author.

Library of Congress Classification. The Library of Congress system is used by college and university libraries and by many large public library systems. Letters are assigned to each of twenty main divisions, and numbers are added for further divisions.

Using the Library of Congress system, the book *Radioactivity* by Tom McGowen would have the number QC 975. The Q stands for Science, the C for Physics, and the 975 for general works on that subject.

Nonfiction and fiction are organized in one group. General biography is assigned the Code "CT."

The Catalog

Many people enjoy browsing in a library; skimming through books on a topic of interest is satisfying because one can pick up each book and actually see if it contains something of special interest.

The majority of library users, however, are either looking for particular books, or for specific material on a subject. To help them find

Each book in the library appears in the card catalog. All books are cataloged alphabetically by author and by title. Nonfiction is also cataloged by subject.

what they are looking for, the catalog—the "guidebook" for the library—lists every book the library owns. Traditionally the library catalog has been in the form of index cards arranged alphabetically in file drawers. Each book has at least two cards, one for the author and one for the title. Nonfiction works will also have cards for the subject or subjects about which the book is written. The class number of the book, indicating in what section of shelves the book will be found, is usually located in the upper left-hand corner of the card. A book on astronomy, for example, with the class number 523, would be found in the section of shelves marked 500–599. A glance around the library will help you locate the section you want.

Using the Catalog

The number of subjects covered in a book usually determines the number of subject cards the librarian will use for the catalog. In the United States there are two standard lists for subject headings. School libraries and many public libraries use the *Sears List of Subject Headings*. Large public libraries and most college and university libraries, as well as those with computerized cataloging aids, use the Library of Congress subject headings.

Use of a standard list is important. For example, a book about the human body could have the following subject headings: Anatomy, Human Anatomy, or Human Body. Any of the three would be correct, but the librarian decides which subject headings will be used for such books, and always uses the same one. However, to help anyone searching for a book under either of the other two subject headings, a cross-reference card—a "see" reference—will be placed in the catalog for each of the headings not used. If two or more similar headings are used, a cross-reference card called a "see also" card directs the person to other headings that will be useful. Computerized catalogs often have the standard list of subject headings near the computer terminals so the user can find the correct heading before searching for a book on the computer.

Subject, Title, and Author Cards

The library card catalog contains subject, title, and author cards for each book. Each card gives the same information in different order, as shown here.

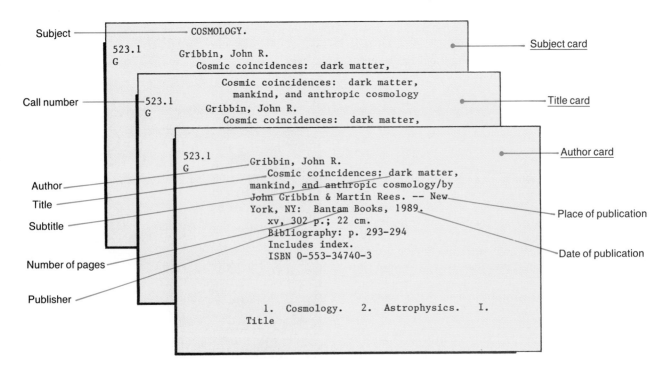

How to Use Your Library's Reference Collection

When you think of a reference collection, you probably think first of encyclopedias, dictionaries, and atlases. Most reference collections also have many other books and materials that contain information on a vast array of subjects. Do you know how to use these materials to research school projects or find answers to just about any question?

Below is a list of questions, followed by groups of reference books. Which books would you use to find the answers? (If you get stumped, you can refer to the boldfaced numbers following some of the titles.)

1. When were skateboards invented?
2. What makes an airplane fly?
3. What was Lewis Carroll's real name?
4. How old was Mozart when he wrote his first symphony?
5. What is circadian rhythm?
6. Who was the first to use the term "rock and roll"?
7. How many bones are in the human body?
8. What country has the most people?
9. When did John Steinbeck write *The Grapes of Wrath*?
10. What economic disaster occurred in the United States in October 1929?

Art and Music

History of Art for Young People (Abrams)
The New Grove Dictionary of Music and Musicians (Macmillan) **4**
The Oxford Junior Companion to Music (Oxford University Press) **4**
Rock Facts (Facts on File)
30 Years of Rock (Exeter) **6**

General Facts

Extraordinary Origins of Everyday Things (HarperCollins) **1**
Facts on File (Facts on File)
Current Biography (H. W. Wilson)
Guinness Book of World Records (Sterling)
Information Please Sports Almanac (Houghton Mifflin)
What's What (Hammond)
The World Almanac and Book of Facts

(Pharaos Books/Scripps Howard Company) **10**

History and Geography

America the Beautiful (Children's Press)
Chronicle of the Twentieth Century (Prentice Hall) **10**
Facts About the States (H. W. Wilson)
From Abenaki to Zuni: A Dictionary of Native American Tribes (Walker)
Geography on File (Facts on File)
National Geographic Picture Atlas of Our World (National Geographic) **8**
The Times Atlas of World History (Hammond) **8**
The World's Great Explorers (Children's Press)

Literature

Benet's Reader's Encyclopedia (HarperCollins)
Books in Print (R. R. Bowker)

Children of Promise: African-American Literature and Art for Young People (Abrams)
Sixth Book of Junior Authors and Illustrators (H. W. Wilson)
Something About the Author (Gale Research) **3, 9**

Science and Technology

The Book of Mammals (National Geographic)
Complete Guide to Computer Camps and Workshops (Bobbs Merrill)
Grzimek's Encyclopedia of Mammals (McGraw-Hill)
Human Body on File (Facts on File) **5, 7**
The New Illustrated Dinosaur Dictionary (Lothrup Lee & Shepard)
Science Experiments on File (Facts on File)
The Way Things Work (Houghton Mifflin) **2**

If you cannot get to a library, you can use this encyclopedia to find the answers to these questions. Each question number is listed below, followed by the appropriate encyclopedia article(s).

1. SKATEBOARDING
2. AERODYNAMICS; AIRPLANES
3. CARROLL, LEWIS
4. MOZART, WOLFGANG AMADEUS
5. BIOLOGICAL CLOCK; LIFE
6. ROCK MUSIC
7. BODY, HUMAN
8. CHINA
9. STEINBECK, JOHN
10. STOCKS AND BONDS

More and more libraries are using computerized catalogs instead of the traditional card files. This has influenced the organization of the "cards." If cards are filed manually, the librarian follows "as if" filing rules, which require filing "17" in the "S" drawer as if it were spelled out as "seventeen." "Dr." would be filed as "doctor," between "Dn" and "Dp." New filing rules have been adopted with computer capabilities in mind. The computer can only respond to what is typed, so the number 17 would be filed in the first drawer with other numbers, in numerical order, before any author, title, or subject. "Dr." would be filed between "Dq" and "Ds."

Some librarians may have made the decision to follow the new rules for filing the cards in the catalog. A quick look at the first few cards in the first drawer should enable you to determine if the cards are filed by the new or the old rules.

Using the Reference Collection

As the world around us becomes more complex, a dizzying array of materials covering a multitude of subjects has appeared. Since there are reference materials with the answers to almost any question, it is important to discover how easy and convenient this part of the library is to use. If you keep in mind that most questions fall into the familiar categories of who, what, when, where, and how, you can narrow your choice of sources and not waste time looking in the wrong place for the right answer. The current editions of most reference materials cannot be taken from the library, so you can almost certainly have access to them whenever you need to use them.

Computers have become an indispensable tool in today's libraries. They help people search the catalog of the library's holdings (*left*) and enable them to browse the Internet for information on just about any subject imaginable (*above*).

The Electronic Library

In addition to their growing use for cataloging books and searching for material at other libraries, computers today also provide access to vast amounts of information on the Internet. Newspapers, encyclopedias, almanacs, and many other sources of information are now available online.

By the end of the 1990's, approximately 70 percent of public libraries, 90 percent of public school (K-12) libraries, and 60 percent of academic (college and university) libraries in the United States were connected to the Internet. Internet access has made it easier for libraries and librarians to open the doors of knowledge to everyone.

ELSIE HORVAT
Media Specialist
Central High School, Bridgeport, CT
Reviewed by CAROLINE WARD
Chief, Youth Services
Nassau, New York Library System

LIBYA

Libya is an Arab nation of North Africa and the fourth largest country on the African continent. Situated along the coast of the Mediterranean Sea, it lies between Egypt, Tunisia, and Algeria. Although large in area, Libya is sparsely populated: About 90 percent of the land is covered by the Sahara desert. Libya has few natural resources. But its most important resource, oil, has transformed it from a poor nation into an economically important and relatively prosperous one.

▶ **PEOPLE**

Most Libyans are Arabs or have a mixed Arab and Berber heritage. The Berbers, who inhabited North Africa before the Arabs arrived in the area in the A.D. 600's, make up a minority of the population.

About 90 percent of Libya's people live in the fertile but narrow coastal region. Urban areas grew rapidly with the development of the oil industry, and more than half the population now lives in cities and towns.

Language and Religion. Arabic is spoken by nearly all the people and is the official language of the country. Almost all Libyans are Sunni Muslims, and religion plays an important role in the everyday life of the people. Muslim holidays and religious practices are strictly observed, and all laws must conform to sharia, or Muslim religious law.

Libya's population is made up mostly of Arabs (*far left*) and Berbers (*left*). About 90 percent of the landscape (*below*) is covered by desert or semi-arid regions.

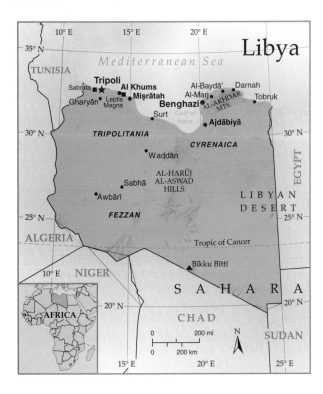

Libya

tional Libyan dish, couscous, is made of wheat and a sauce of meat, red pumpkin or squash, boiled eggs, and *filfil*, or red pepper. Other favorite dishes are whole roast lamb stuffed with rice, almonds, pine nuts, and spices and *bazin*, made of steamed wheat or barley with stewed vegetables and meat.

Festivals. One of the most colorful festivals in Libya is the *Mez*, which goes back to the time when Arab warriors first arrived in North Africa. At this festival the men dress in the style of clothes worn in ancient times, place beautiful silver rugs on the saddles of their horses, and perform trick riding.

▶ LAND

Geographically, Libya is divided into the historical provinces of Tripolitania in the northwest, Cyrenaica in the east, and Fezzan in the southwest. About 90 percent of Libya is desert or semi-arid land, with no lakes or permanent rivers. The only fertile areas are along the Mediterranean coast and on some patches in the desert called oases. South of the coast is a region of hardy grasses, shrubs,

Education. Increasing emphasis by the government on education has raised the literacy rate to about 70 percent. Literacy is highest among boys. Education is compulsory for all children between the ages of 6 and 12. Libya's universities include Al Fatah in Tripoli and Gar Yunis in Benghazi.

Family Life. As in other developing nations, many traditional ways of life in Libya are gradually changing. The traditional family was a large one, with many relations. The head of the family, a man, was obeyed by all its members. Marriages were arranged by the family. In the past, a woman was never seen by men unless they were members of her family. Women could only appear in public if covered by a long, loose robe called a *lahaf*, which revealed only their eyes.

Although family ties remain strong, the large, extended family is slowly becoming less commonplace. The role of women in particular has changed dramatically. While some women still wear the *lahaf*, in the cities and large towns most women wear modern dress. Women are also entering the workforce in increasing numbers.

Food and Drink. Tea drinking is a long-standing Libyan custom. It was once traditional to serve at least three cups of tea, each with a different taste and smell. The tradi-

---

FACTS and figures

GREAT SOCIALIST PEOPLE'S LIBYAN ARAB JAMAHIRIYA is the official name of the country. *Jamahiriya* means "state of the masses."

LOCATION: North Africa.

AREA: 679,359 sq mi (1,759,540 km²).

POPULATION: 5,500,000 (estimate).

CAPITAL AND LARGEST CITY: Tripoli.

MAJOR LANGUAGE: Arabic.

MAJOR RELIGIOUS GROUP: Sunni Muslim.

GOVERNMENT: Islamic socialist republic. **Head of state**—revolutionary leader (Muammar al-Qaddafi holds no official title but is de facto head of state). **Head of government**—secretary of the General People's Committee. **Legislature**—General People's Congress.

CHIEF PRODUCTS: Agricultural—wheat, barley, olives, dates, citrus fruits, vegetables, peanuts, soybeans, cattle. **Manufactured**—refined petroleum and petroleum products, processed foods, textiles, handicrafts, cement. **Mineral**—petroleum, natural gas.

MONETARY UNIT: Libyan dinar (1 dinar = 1,000 dirhams).

Oil is Libya's most important natural resource. It accounts for about 95 percent of the country's export earnings.

Libya's agriculture is limited by the small amount of land suitable for cultivation. Aside from wheat and barley, the chief agricultural products include olives, dates, oranges, lemons, and peanuts. The raising of livestock, including goats, sheep, camels, and cattle, is more suited to Libya's land and climate.

▶ MAJOR CITIES

Tripoli (Tarābulus al-Gharb in Arabic) is Libya's capital, largest city, chief port, and center of industry. Its population is about 1.2 million. Domed mosques (Muslim houses of worship) with minarets (towers) stand next to modern office buildings. Tree-lined boulevards add to the city's beauty.

Benghazi is Libya's second largest city. Until 1972 it was one of two Libyan capitals, along with Tripoli.

Ancient ruins are found near several cities. Roman temples, theaters, and marketplaces can be seen at **Sabrata** and **Leptis Magna** near Tripoli. Greek ruins thousands of years old are found in the region of Cyrenaica.

▶ GOVERNMENT

Libya's government is based on a constitution that was ratified in 1969. Since that time the country has been ruled by Muammar al-Qaddafi, an army colonel. Qaddafi holds no official post or title other than that of revolu-

and bushes where grains such as wheat and barley are grown. A series of high plateaus, where livestock graze, and rugged mountains form part of the landscape.

Climate. The Mediterranean Sea and the desert greatly influence Libya's climate. Coastal temperatures are warm in the summer and cool and rainy in the winter. Most of the interior has a hot, dry climate. A hot desert wind, called the *ghibli*, blows from the south and raises the temperature to as high as 136°F (58°C). The highlands are cooler, with occasional snow in the mountains.

Natural Resources. Libya has few but valuable natural resources. The most important are petroleum, natural gas, and gypsum.

▶ ECONOMY

Petroleum, discovered in Libya in 1959, is the mainstay of the economy. The country ranks among the world's leading oil producers, and about 95 percent of its export earnings are derived from this resource. A modern highway network connects the desert oases and petroleum fields with the coastal towns. Manufactured goods include petroleum products, processed foods, textiles, handicrafts, and cement.

Tripoli, situated on the Mediterranean Sea, is Libya's capital, largest city, principal seaport, and center of industry.

North African campaign. Italy lost the colony as a result of the war, and for a time Libya was governed by Britain and France. Libya gained its independence in 1951 and became a constitutional monarchy under King Idris I. But in 1969 the king was overthrown by Qaddafi in a military coup.

For many years Qaddafi was accused of promoting international terrorism. In 1986, U.S. warplanes bombed Libyan targets in retaliation for attacks against American military personnel. Libya's suspected involvement in the 1988 crash of a Pan Am jetliner over Lockerbie, Scot-

Roman ruins and other ancient artifacts can still be seen near Sabrata and elsewhere along Libya's Mediterranean coast.

Muammar al-Qaddafi sought to create a Libyan government that combined the principles of Islam and socialism.

tionary leader, but he is, in effect, the head of state. Qaddafi has sought to create a government based on Islamic principles combined with socialism.

In theory, power is exercised by the people through various levels of political bodies called people's committees. Members of the national legislature, the General People's Congress (GPC), are chosen by these local committees. The head of government is the secretary of the General People's Committee. The committee acts as a kind of cabinet and is responsible for foreign affairs and national security.

▶ HISTORY

Since ancient times Libya has been ruled by many different peoples, including the Phoenicians, Greeks, and Romans. Arabs conquered the region in the A.D. 600's. Libya was part of the Turkish Ottoman Empire from the 1500's until 1912, when it became a colony of Italy.

During World War II (1939–45), Libya was the scene of some of the great battles of the land, brought further international condemnation, and in 1992 the United Nations imposed sanctions on Libya. They were permanently lifted in 2003 when the Libyan government accepted responsibility for the crime. Later that year, to further improve relations with the West, Libya volunteered to dismantle its weapons of mass destruction.

JOHN WESLEY COULTER
University of Cincinnati

See also QADDAFI, MUAMMAR AL-.

LICHENS. See FUNGI.

LIDDY, G. GORDON. See WATERGATE (Profiles).

LIE, TRYGVE. See UNITED NATIONS (Profiles).

LIECHTENSTEIN

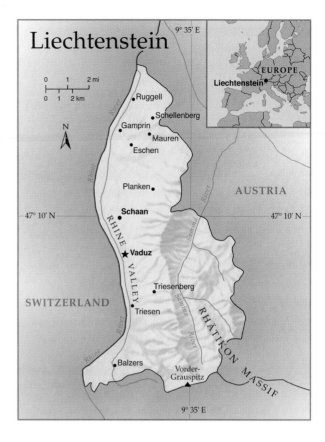

Liechtenstein

The Principality of Liechtenstein is a tiny nation in central Europe, located between Austria and Switzerland. The fourth smallest country in Europe, it is about the same size as Washington, D.C.

▶ PEOPLE

Most of the people of Liechtenstein are descended from the German Alemannic tribes that spread into the Alpine regions in the A.D. 500's. The official language is German, and Liechtensteiners speak the Alemannic dialect. Approximately three-fourths of the population is Roman Catholic. The literacy rate is high; 100 percent of the population age 10 and over can read and write.

▶ LAND

Liechtenstein lies along the east bank of the Rhine River, which separates it from Switzerland. Looking across the river from the Swiss side, one can see the Rhätikon Massif mountain range, part of the Central Alps; the highest point, Vorder-Grauspitz, rises to 8,527 feet (2,599 meters) in the south. A range of the Alps forms the eastern and northern border with Austria.

Because the mountain walls surround the country to the north and east, Liechtenstein has a surprisingly mild climate and is greatly affected by the warm southerly wind known

as the foehn. In winter the temperature rarely falls below 5°F (-15°C), while in summer the average daily maximum temperature varies from 68° to 82°F (20° to 28°C). These conditions allow for the cultivation of grapes and corn (maize), unusual in a mountainous area.

▶ ECONOMY

Liechtensteiners enjoy one of the highest standards of living in Europe. The principality's low business taxes and strict bank secrecy laws have encouraged many foreign businesses to register there; 30 percent of national revenues come from business services, banking, and company registration dues and fees.

Before World War II (1939–45), Liechtenstein was mainly an agricultural country.

A medieval castle overlooks Vaduz, Liechtenstein's capital city. Located in the Rhine Valley, the castle is the residence of the nation's ruling prince.

PRINCIPALITY OF LIECHTENSTEIN (Fuerstentum Liechtenstein) is the official name of the country.

LOCATION: Central Europe.

AREA: 62 sq mi (161 km²).

POPULATION: 33,400 (estimate).

CAPITAL: Vaduz.

LARGEST CITY: Schaan.

MAJOR LANGUAGE: German (official).

MAJOR RELIGIOUS GROUP: Christian (Roman Catholic, Protestant).

GOVERNMENT: Constitutional monarchy. **Head of state**—prince. **Head of government**—prime minister. **Legislature**—parliament (Landtag).

CHIEF PRODUCTS: Agricultural—wheat, barley, corn, potatoes, livestock, dairy products. **Manufactured**—electronics, metal products, dental products, ceramics, pharmaceuticals, processed foods, precision instruments, optical instruments.

MONETARY UNIT: Swiss franc (1 franc = 100 centimes).

Today more than half the working people hold jobs in industries in the Rhine Valley. Sleepy little villages have been transformed by the building of factories. Leading manufactures include electronics, metal products, dental products, ceramics, pharmaceuticals, and processed foods.

Tourism is also important to Liechtenstein's economy. Liechtenstein's roads are in excellent condition, and an international railroad linking Zurich, Switzerland, with Vienna, Austria, stops at the resort city of Schaan. Many tourists buy the nation's colorful postage stamps, which are much sought after by collectors, and view parts of the royal family's world-famous art collection at the art gallery in Vaduz.

Liechtenstein has been allied in a customs union with Switzerland since 1923. This means that Switzerland offers free access to its markets and allows Liechtenstein to use the Swiss franc and to export goods to Switzerland without customs duties. Switzerland also represents Liechtenstein abroad.

▶ **MAJOR CITIES**

There are no major cities in Liechtenstein. Most people live in one of 11 towns, or communes, in the Rhine Valley and the surrounding hills. There are also a few small resorts in the mountains. **Vaduz**, the nation's capital, has a population of about 5,000. A medieval castle is the home of the ruling prince. Vaduz is mentioned in documents dating from 1150 as the seat of the Count of Vaduz. **Schaan**, with a population of about 5,700, is the principality's largest town. Lying just north of Vaduz, it has been a settled site since Roman times. Both Vaduz and Schaan are popular tourist areas. Other important towns are Balzers, Triesen, and Eschen.

▶ **HISTORY AND GOVERNMENT**

The county of Vaduz and the barony of Schellenberg were ruled by several different families until 1699. In that year, the Austrian Prince John Adam of Liechtenstein took possession of the barony of Schellenberg. In 1712 he added the county of Vaduz to his realm. In 1719, Holy Roman Emperor Charles VI allowed Prince John Adam's successor, Prince Anton Florian, to unite these two regions in the Principality of Liechtenstein. Liechtenstein was a part of the Holy Roman Empire until 1806, when the ancient empire was dissolved. Liechtenstein was a member of the Confederation of the Rhine until it became independent in 1815.

Liechtenstein is a hereditary constitutional monarchy, ruled by the princes of the House of Liechtenstein. The present constitution dates from 1921. It provides for a legislature, the Landtag, whose 25 members are elected for four years. The government is headed by a prime minister, who is usually the leader of the majority political party in the Landtag and who is formally appointed by the reigning prince.

Prince Francis Joseph II came to the throne of Liechtenstein in 1938. He handed over executive power to his son and heir, Crown Prince Hans-Adam II, in 1984, but retained his official title until his death in 1989. Hans-Adam turned over many of the daily responsibilities to his son, Alois, in 2004.

A referendum in 1984 gave women the right to vote for the first time. Liechtenstein has no army, and public order is maintained by a small police force. The country became a member of the United Nations in 1990 and was accepted into the World Trade Organization (WTO) in 1995.

Reviewed by JONATHAN STEINBERG
Department of History, University of Pennsylvania

LIE DETECTION

People usually feel bad when they tell a lie. That bad feeling is called guilt. Feelings of guilt—and the fear of getting caught—often occur when someone is telling a lie. The fact that people usually have these feelings when they lie causes small changes in their bodies. If these small body changes can be accurately measured, they can sometimes help to determine if a person is lying.

When you tell a lie, you often get excited. Often your heart will begin to beat a little faster, the blood will move through your body with more force, and you will begin to breathe more quickly. These small body changes can be measured with a **polygraph**—the recording instrument sometimes called a lie detector.

Here is how a polygraph is used. Let us say Marilyn has been trained to operate a polygraph. She has taken special classes and has had hundreds of hours of practice using the polygraph under the guidance of a more experienced teacher. Marilyn is going to test Jack, who has been accused of robbing a store but who insists that he was elsewhere at the time.

Marilyn begins by placing some thin electrical wires on Jack's body. The wires do not hurt Jack because they have only a tiny amount of electricity running through them. They are connected to the polygraph, which measures and records on paper the changes in Jack's heart rate, blood pressure, and breathing as he is being tested. The polygraph may also record changes in the activity of the sweat pores in Jack's hand or changes in the movements of his muscles.

The first questions Marilyn asks are simple ones. (''What is your name?'' ''What day is this?'') These questions are called control questions. They give an indication of Jack's normal body activity when he is not lying. Then the important questions are asked. (''Where were you on the night of the robbery?'' ''Did you rob the store?'') If the polygraph records a big increase in Jack's excitement when he is answering the important questions, it may mean that he is lying.

We can only say that the person *may* be lying because polygraphs are not completely accurate. Polygraphs are so sensitive that they sometimes measure body changes a person might feel even when telling the truth. This is especially so when the operator has not been trained to ask the right kinds of questions in the right way. Another problem is that people can sometimes learn to make their bodies react in ways that fool the polygraph. Because polygraphs are not completely accurate, the results of a polygraph test usually cannot be used in court to definitely prove whether a person lied or committed a crime.

JERALD M. JELLISON
University of Southern California

During a polygraph test, the armband senses the subject's physical responses to the operator's questions. The polygraph machine records these responses on a moving graph.

LIES

"I never lie." Would you say that this statement about yourself is true or false? Most people are tempted to answer "true." But if they did, it would probably be a lie (an untrue statement). The truth is that very few of us can go through life without ever telling a lie or being dishonest.

▶BIG AND LITTLE LIES

People believe some lies are only "little white lies," while others are big lies. Whether a lie is big or small depends on many things. One way to judge a lie is by the harm it causes.

For example, imagine that Jenny and her mother are going shopping. Jenny is often late, and she is late again today. She is still in the house when her mother goes outside. When Jenny runs after her, her mother asks, "Did you check to make sure the front door was locked?" The truth is that Jenny was in such a rush she did not check the lock. If she tells the truth, her mother might get angry with her. So Jenny decides to answer "Yes."

Would you say that this was a big lie or a little one? What if the shopping trip took only 15 minutes, and no one entered the house while Jenny and her mother were gone? Some people (especially Jenny) might say that this was only a little lie because it did not cause any harm.

What if the shopping took several hours and a robber entered the house through the unlocked door? Jenny's lie would have caused a very serious problem, and almost everyone (even Jenny) would say it was a big lie.

Another way to judge lies is according to whether or not the person telling the lie knew it was a lie when he or she said it. For example, Jenny probably knew that she had not checked the lock on the door. Since she lied on purpose, that could be considered a big lie.

These are two of the ways that can help a person judge how serious (how big or small) a lie is.

▶WHY DO PEOPLE LIE?

Some people tell lies to avoid being punished for something. Often they lie because they want to cover up some mistake they have made. Jenny lied to avoid being scolded or punished by her mother for not checking the lock. The polite "social lies" people tell in order to avoid being. disliked often cause harm. Suppose you compliment a friend on her unflattering new outfit. She might then wear the outfit to a big party and get the reputation of having poor taste.

Another reason people lie is to make themselves seem better than they really are. For example, some boys at school are talking about a video game. Jeff is new at the school and he wants the boys to like him, so he lies and says that he has gotten a very high score on the game. By lying about how good he is, Jeff hopes to make the boys want him as a friend.

Some people lie in an effort to help solve their problems. But usually lying just causes more problems.

▶THE BAD EFFECTS OF LYING

People who tell lies can create trouble for themselves and other people. Suppose the other boys do not believe Jeff and ask him to play the game to prove he is really as good at it as he says he is? If he fails to live up to his big claims, it will be very embarrassing for him. Some of the boys might call him a liar and not want him as a friend.

Jenny's mother was counting on Jenny to tell the truth. Making certain the front door is locked is usually very important. When her mother discovers that Jenny lied, she might decide that Jenny cannot be trusted. Her mother might think she has to treat Jenny like a small child who cannot be trusted to take on grown-up responsibilities.

Being trusted by people and having good friends is very important. When people lie, especially if they do it repeatedly, they get the reputation of being untrustworthy. Once they have that reputation, it is very hard for them to win back other people's trust and friendship.

Even people who are basically honest sometimes tell a lie. Although telling the truth is much better than lying, the fact that a person occasionally tells a little lie does not mean that the person is completely bad. But people who intentionally tell big lies, and those who lie often, cause great harm to themselves and to others.

JERALD M. JELLISON
Author, *I'm Sorry I Didn't Mean to and Other Lies We Love to Tell*

Can you always recognize a living thing? Sometimes it is easy, as in this garden scene (*left*). The chipmunk and plants are alive; the large gray rock is not. Sometimes it is more difficult. In a magnified drop of seawater (*below*), diatoms may seem lifeless, but they are in fact tiny one-celled algae.

LIFE

All things in the world are either living or nonliving. Squirrels are living creatures, but stones are not. Trees are living things, but tennis balls are not. Birds are alive, but beds are not. Humans are living beings, but houses are not.

The line between the living and the nonliving is not always so clear, however. The differences are not always easy to see even though all living things have certain characteristics in common. From big to small, from giant whales to tiny bacteria, all living creatures are alike in the following basic ways. They can

- take in food and produce energy
- grow
- move
- respond to their environment
- adapt to their environment
- reproduce

These traits, taken all together, separate living things from nonliving things.

▶CHARACTERISTICS OF LIVING THINGS

All living things are called **organisms**. Many organisms, such as animals, grass, and trees, are familiar—we see them every day. But not all organisms are visible to the naked eye. Some can only be seen through a microscope. These tiny one-celled organisms are called **microbes**, or **micro-organisms**.

Taking in Food and Producing Energy

All organisms must either make their own food or take in food. Green plants make their

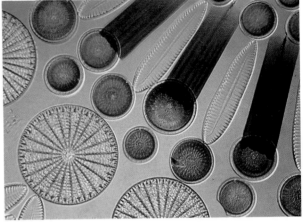

own food through the process of photosynthesis. Animals must take in their food. Once it is in the body, food is broken down into simpler substances. Some of these substances are used to make the organism larger or to repair cells. Some combine with oxygen to produce energy. The process in which food is broken down into simpler substances and combined with oxygen to provide energy and materials for growth is called **metabolism**.

When wood burns, it combines very quickly with oxygen and releases a great deal of heat energy. In cells, the oxygen combines slowly with substances such as fats and carbohydrates and releases a limited amount of heat energy. This is called **respiration**. Respiration is more than the simple act of breathing in and out. It refers to the entire process of taking in oxygen, using the oxygen in the body, and then breathing out the waste product, which is the gas carbon dioxide.

The monarch butterfly goes through several remarkable changes as it grows into an adult. An egg (*far left*) hatches into a striped caterpillar (*top center*). The caterpillar then becomes a pupa, resting inside a pupal case (*above*). At last the colorful adult monarch emerges (*left*), clinging to the pupal case until its wings dry and it can flutter away.

Growth

All living organisms grow and develop. Growth and development are the processes by which a fertilized egg becomes a tree, an elephant, or a newborn human baby. Nonliving objects such as tables, tissue paper, and tennis balls do not grow and change by themselves.

In a single-celled organism all of the activities needed to stay alive are carried out by the single cell. When the cell divides, the two new cells formed are smaller than the original parent cell. The new cells then grow until they are the same size as the parent.

Each many-celled organism starts as a single cell. The cell divides until it becomes many cells. These cells specialize. In animals, some become the skin, others become the bones, and still others become eyes, ears, and noses. In plants, different cells become stems, leaves, and flowers.

All organisms live for a certain period of time and then they die. The length of time from birth to death is known as the life span. During that time each organism passes through four stages in its life cycle—birth, growth, maturity, and death.

Movement

Some of the energy produced by the process of respiration is changed into motion or movement. For example, the material inside a cell is always moving. In addition to the movement within the cell, some one-celled organisms that live in water are able to move about by means of whiplike extensions called **flagella**. Others have many hairlike **cilia** that allow them to swim through the water. In many-celled animals, special cells called muscle cells are responsible for movement. These cells have the ability to contract, or become slightly shorter. When each one of the millions of muscle cells in an animal's legs contracts a tiny bit, the leg moves and the animal is able to walk or run.

Organisms such as plants and fungi cannot move about, but they can still become widely scattered. Their seeds and spores, which are tiny reproductive cells, can travel long distances. They may be light enough to be carried by the wind or to float on water. Some stick to passing animals, insects, or birds and travel far from the parent.

Responsiveness

Responsiveness, or the ability to react to conditions or events on the outside, is an important characteristic of living things. For example, simple organisms with only one cell can respond to light or food by moving closer to the food and avoiding the light. When certain fish swim near the tentacles that hang

Life span varies greatly among earth's many kinds of living things. The giant sequoia tree of California (*far left*) can live for more than 800 years. On its branches may sit a tiny mayfly (*near left*), a creature that lives at most for a day or two.

from the rim of a jellyfish's bell-shaped body, the jellyfish immediately responds. It injects a paralyzing substance into the fish's body. Then the jellyfish traps the helpless fish in its sticky tentacles and eats it.

Plants respond to light, to gravity, and to the presence of water. Some plants, such as those that trap insects in specialized leaves, respond to touch. The leaves of a houseplant placed on a windowsill will turn to face the sunlight; the growing tip of the stem always turns upward. At the same time, the roots of the plant turn downward and toward a source of moisture. The slow movements of plants in response to stimuli are called **tropisms**.

Adaptation

When organisms fit in very well with their environment, they are said to be well adapted. For example, the cactus is a plant that is well suited to live where there is little water. Over time the leaves of cactus plants modified, or changed, into needlelike spines. Much less water is lost from this type of leaf than from a broad, thin leaf. Because the leaves have been reduced to spines, the important process of photosynthesis is carried out in the thick green stems of the cactus. The stems are coated with a waxlike covering that also cuts down water loss. In fact, the plant stores water in its thick, fleshy stems. When the stems of a barrel cactus are mashed, they produce several quarts of watery liquid. All of these adaptations help the cactus survive in the extreme heat and dry conditions of a desert. Polar bears live in cold climates. They have a thick layer of fat under their white fur that keeps them warm.

Charles Darwin (1809–82) put forth a theory to explain how living things adapt to their environment. Darwin pointed out that there is variation within every group of plants or animals. Some are taller, some shorter. Some are stronger, some weaker. Some need high temperatures, others can live with less heat.

All living things respond to their environment in some way. The mimosa plant (*right*) is very sensitive. At the slightest touch the plant quickly folds its leaves tightly against the stem (*far right*).

Since there is never enough food and space to support every organism that is born, individuals have to compete in order to survive. Those that cannot compete successfully for food and spaces may die. If they die very young, they leave no offspring.

The organisms that have adapted to their environment do well. They are healthier and live longer. They leave more offspring, and their offspring resemble them. The traits that helped them survive are passed from generation to generation.

An example of this theory is the giraffe. Several theories have been proposed to explain why its long neck is a favorable characteristic. One theory states that long ago the ancestors of the giraffe had rather short necks. The giraffes with the shortest necks could reach only the lowest branches of the trees. Since there were many giraffes, those leaves were soon gone and many short-necked giraffes died of starvation.

However, among the giraffes that lived long ago were some with slightly longer necks. These giraffes were able to reach higher branches and get more food. They lived longer and had more offspring. Their offspring tended to be taller than the other giraffes. After many generations, giraffes came to have long necks. Long-necked giraffes are very well adapted to life on the African plains.

Reproduction

Living things reproduce themselves. The robin flying across the sky hatched from an egg laid by another robin. The oak tree growing in the forest came from a seed dropped by another oak tree. Each of us began with the joining of cells from two other human beings.

Reproduction is the ability of any organism to produce new organisms similar to the parents. Most plants and animals reproduce through the union of two specialized cells. This is known as **sexual reproduction**. The female parent produces an ovum, or egg cell. The male parent produces a sperm cell. The union of these two cells is called **fertilization**.

Some simple one-celled organisms reproduce in a different way. The amoeba and paramecium are two such organisms. In these organisms, the single cell simply divides in two and produces two new cells that are just like the parent. This process is called **asexual reproduction**.

▶ THE CHEMISTRY OF LIFE

Matter is made up of elements, either singly or in various combinations. An element is a substance that cannot be broken down into a simpler substance by ordinary means.

Every element is made up of units called **atoms**. The air you breathe is made up of atoms of oxygen and nitrogen, and the iron in your red blood cells is made up of atoms of iron.

Tasty leaves on high branches are out of reach for many animals—but not the giraffe. Its long neck and legs are adaptations that help it reach such food.

Even the smallest one-celled organisms can reproduce. This paramecium (*below*) is about to become two cells that are exactly alike—simply by splitting in two.

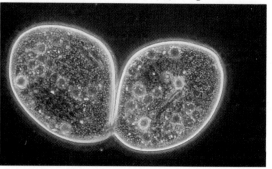

Atoms are almost always joined with other atoms to form **molecules**. A molecule is made up of two or more atoms. Some molecules are composed only of atoms of one element. For example, a molecule of oxygen (O_2) contains two atoms of oxygen. But an atom may also combine with one or more atoms of different elements. Substances formed from such molecules are called **compounds**. Water (H_2O), for instance, is a compound consisting of molecules that contain two atoms of hydrogen joined with one atom of oxygen.

Compounds that are part of organisms or that are produced by organisms are known as **organic compounds**. Today, many organic compounds are produced in laboratories or in large chemical plants. Organic compounds contain carbon in combination with other elements such as hydrogen, oxygen, nitrogen, and sulfur.

There are many kinds of organic compounds. Those that are necessary for life belong to one of four large groups—carbohydrates, lipids (or fats), proteins, or nucleic acids.

Carbohydrates

Carbohydrates contain atoms of only three elements—carbon, hydrogen, and oxygen. They are used in the cell as fuel, and they play an important role in the production of energy. Plants are made up largely of carbohydrates; smaller amounts are found in animals. Some common carbohydrates are sugars, starches, and cellulose.

Carbohydrates are formed from smaller molecules called sugars. **Glucose** is a simple sugar formed by plants as a result of photosynthesis. The sugar that you find in the sugar bowl at home is called table sugar, or **sucrose**. It is made up of two simple sugars—glucose and **fructose**—joined together. Sucrose comes either from sugarcane or from sugar beets. Starches such as cornstarch and potato starch are made up of long chains of glucose units linked together. Another carbohydrate made up of great numbers of glucose units is cellulose. Wood, cotton, hemp, and linen are a few well-known substances that are largely made up of cellulose. The cellulose molecule is even bigger than the starch molecule. While the starch molecule contains about 25 glucose units, the cellulose molecule may contain as many as 2,000 units.

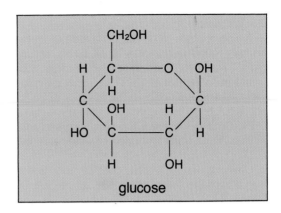

glucose

Lipids

Lipids, or fats, are made up of carbon, hydrogen, and oxygen atoms, just as carbohydrates are. But in lipids the proportions of each element are different. Usually, lipid molecules contain fewer oxygen atoms than are found in carbohydrate molecules. Lipids are used by cells as a source of energy. They do not dissolve in water, so they are useful in cell membranes for keeping different parts of the cell separate and for keeping the contents of the cell inside the cell.

Some familiar lipids are the solid white fat found on meat; butter, which is the fat from milk; and the oils that come from olives, cotton seeds, and peanuts.

Proteins

Proteins are vital to the structure and function of all organisms. They are also the most abundant of the organic compounds found in living things. Proteins contain carbon, hydrogen, oxygen, and nitrogen. In addition, they may also contain sulfur, phosphorous, and iron. Most protein molecules are very large. One molecule may be made up of thousands of separate atoms. As an example, hemoglobin, the oxygen-carrying part of the red blood cells, is a protein. Each molecule of hemoglobin contains more than 9,000 atoms.

Protein molecules are made up of smaller units called **amino acids**. There are 20 common amino acids. They are called the building blocks of proteins. Living things can construct a great number of different proteins by arranging two or more of these amino acids in various sequences. It is the particular proteins they produce that make one organism differ from another.

Nucleic Acids

Nucleic acids are long, threadlike compounds found in the cells of all living organisms. The two main types of nucleic acid found in living things are **DNA** (deoxyribonucleic acid), found only in the nucleus of cells, and **RNA** (ribonucleic acid), found throughout cells. Both DNA and RNA play a central role in passing all traits from one generation to the next.

Chromosomes, which contain the genes that determine traits, are made up largely of DNA. RNA directs the manufacture of the proteins that the cell needs.

▶ THE BASIC UNIT OF LIFE—THE CELL

Cells are the basic units of life in all living things. Every organism is made up of one or more cells. While cells show great variety in size, shape, structure, and function, all cells have certain things in common.

Most cells have a **nucleus**. The nucleus is usually spherical in shape and is found close to the center of the cell. Inside the nucleus are many fine threads or strands. These are the chromosomes. Also in the nucleus are the **nucleoli** (plural of nucleolus). They play a role in the growth of the cell. The nucleus is the control center for many of the cell's activities.

Surrounding the nucleus is the **nuclear membrane**. This membrane controls the movement of substances into and out of the nucleus. The material that fills the rest of the cell outside the nucleus is known as **cytoplasm**. The cytoplasm contains many vital structures, known as **organelles**. These structures are very small; they are barely visible with an ordinary microscope. They control many different functions of the cell, including energy production, elimination of wastes, and the manufacture of proteins.

The cell membrane surrounds the entire cell. This thin elastic covering controls the passage of substances into and out of the cell. In plants, the cell membrane is surrounded by a thick cell wall made of cellulose.

The cytoplasm in plant cells contains some structures not found in animal cells. These include bodies that contain chlorophyll, a pigment needed for photosynthesis. Also present are **vacuoles**, which are fluid-filled sacs within the cytoplasm that contain dissolved minerals.

Bacteria have cells that are not like those of other organisms. Bacteria do not have a nucleus enclosed in a membrane. Instead, they have a single molecule of DNA. They are missing many of the structures that are found in the cytoplasm of other cells. Although they have a cell wall in addition to the cell membrane, the wall is not made of cellulose as it is in plants. The bacterial cell may be one of the first kinds of cells to appear on earth.

In a single-celled organism, all of life's functions are carried out by the single cell. The cell takes in food, metabolizes the food, and gets rid of wastes. It reproduces by dividing in two. In a many-celled organism, different life functions are carried out by groups of cells that specialize in carrying out specific duties. A group of identical cells is called a **tissue**. For example, bone cells, which lay down hard layers of calcium minerals, form

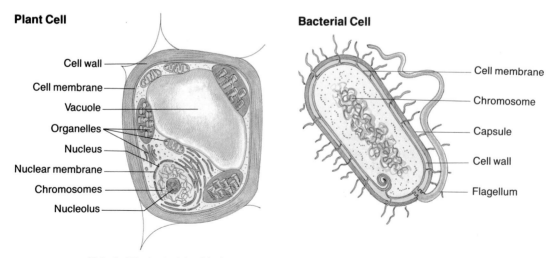

Plant Cell

Cell wall
Cell membrane
Vacuole
Organelles
Nucleus
Nuclear membrane
Chromosomes
Nucleolus

Bacterial Cell

Cell membrane
Chromosome
Capsule
Cell wall
Flagellum

Note that the bacterial cell lacks many of the internal structures that the plant cell has.

Some kinds of animals can control their body temperature, but reptiles cannot. This garter snake (*above*) lies in the sun to warm itself. A tiger salamander (*right*) cools off in the shade of a bush.

bone tissue. Muscle cells, which have the ability to contract, form muscle tissue.

An organ is made up of various tissues arranged to do special work for the body. Each organ, therefore, contains several different kinds of cells. The heart is an organ that pumps blood throughout the body; it is made up largely of muscle tissue. The eye is an organ for seeing; it contains tissue made up of cells that are able to sense light. The eye also contains muscle tissue to allow movement. The lungs contain tissue that is elastic and able to exchange gases easily. The stomach has muscle cells and cells that produce juices to digest food.

A set of organs in the body is grouped into a system. The framework of the body with all its bones forms the skeletal system. The muscles that move and support the skeleton and also move other parts of the body form the muscular system. The digestive system includes such organs as the stomach, liver, and intestines. All together, the systems of the body make up a living being, or an organism.

▶LIVING THINGS AND THEIR ENVIRONMENTS

The study of the relationship between living organisms and their environments is called **ecology**. Ecology is concerned with the **biosphere**—the part of the earth's air, land, and water that contains living things. It extends about six miles above sea level and as far into the soil as roots and micro-organisms are found. The biosphere includes the surface waters and the ocean depths. Compared to the size of the earth and the immensity of space, the biosphere is just a thin band.

Physical Environment

Conditions in the biosphere are controlled by many different physical factors. One of the most important factors is the movement of the earth around the sun, which causes the seasons. Another is the movement of air and water over the earth's surface. These factors cause a wide range in temperature and rainfall from place to place and at different times of the year. Surface features such as hills, mountains, and deserts also affect the kinds of plant and animal life found in different parts of the world.

Temperature. Living things can exist only within a very narrow temperature range, from about 32 to 120°F (0 to 49°C). There are few exceptions to this. Below these temperatures the water in cells freezes and many life processes stop, just as very high temperatures will affect the proteins in cells and stop life processes.

Some animals are able to control the temperature inside their bodies to a certain extent. These animals, known as warm-blooded animals, produce enough heat energy to keep their internal temperatures at a certain level even if the outside temperatures drop to a low level. They do lose heat, though, and must be protected by fur, feathers, or warm clothing if exposed to low temperatures for long periods. Birds and mammals, such as humans, horses, bears, and whales, are warm-blooded animals.

Plants and animals that need a warm, moist environment thrive in the Brazilian rain forest. Organisms adapted to other climates—such as the desert cactus or polar bear—could never survive here.

Other animals have body temperatures that change as the surrounding temperature changes. They are known as cold-blooded animals. Fish and reptiles, for example, are animals that are cold-blooded.

Temperature is affected by latitude, which is a measure of the distance north or south of the equator. The areas near the equator generally have the warmest temperatures, while the coldest temperatures are found in the areas around the North and South poles.

Temperature is also affected by the height above sea level, or altitude. The higher the altitude, the lower the temperature. Even near the equator the temperature on top of a mountain can be quite low.

Water. Water is essential for life. Many of the essential processes that take place in cells depend on water. For life to continue, therefore, there must be a plentiful supply of fresh water in the environment. Much of the water

on earth is in the world's oceans, lakes, and streams. The rest is either in soil or rock, in the atmosphere, in the bodies of living organisms, or frozen in polar ice and glaciers.

Water is a basic part of every cell in every living organism. About 70 percent of the human body is water. Water helps digestion by making it possible for the digestive chemicals to break the food down into molecules that can be used by the body's cells. Water in the blood helps to carry these molecules to all parts of the body. Water washes out wastes that accumulate in the body, and water helps to control body temperature, too, when it is released during the process of perspiration.

Some animals have become well adapted to living in an environment with little or no water. The kangaroo rat is a good example. This desert animal never drinks water. Its entire diet consists of dry seeds and other foods that contain little or no water, yet 65 percent of its body is water.

As the kangaroo rat burns food for energy in its body, a small amount of water is formed, and the animal is able to live on this water. Because it has sweat glands only on the pads of its toes and spends the hottest part of each day in cool burrows beneath the desert sands, it loses almost no water through perspiration.

Atmosphere. The atmosphere is the blanket of air that surrounds the earth. Air is a mixture of colorless, odorless, and tasteless gases. About four fifths of the air is nitrogen, and about one fifth oxygen. The rest is small amounts of gases such as carbon dioxide.

Most living things need oxygen in order to live. The oxygen is needed in chemical processes that change food into energy. Organisms that live on land take in oxygen from the atmosphere. Land animals have organs such as lungs to make this possible. Organisms that live in water take in oxygen that comes from air dissolved in the water. Fish, for example, have gills that allow them to take in oxygen.

The process of respiration in plants, whether on land or in the water, happens as they take in oxygen and give off carbon dioxide through small openings in their leaves. But unlike other living things, plants also carry on photosynthesis. In this process they take in carbon dioxide and give off oxygen.

There are certain organisms that can live without oxygen. In fact, they are not able to live in the presence of air. These organisms

are known as **anaerobic bacteria**. These tiny microbes usually live in soil, in water, or in places like the mud at the bottom of a pond or stream. A very dangerous kind of anaerobic bacteria can grow in airtight food containers if it is not killed by heat before the containers are sealed. These are the microbes that cause botulism, an often fatal food poisoning. A close relative of this bacterium is the one that causes a very serious infection called tetanus. This organism can grow in places such as deep puncture wounds, where there is no air.

Plants depend on soil for water and minerals, which are taken in through their roots. Soil is a mixture of particles of rock, water, air, tiny living organisms, and dead organic matter. It is formed by the weathering of rock, with the addition of material from organisms that are decaying.

Generally, plants prefer a certain kind of soil in which to grow. One type of plant may need a dry, sandy soil, while another may need a moist soil. For example, pine trees do best in sandy soil, while soil that includes clay, sand, and organic matter is best for forests of beech and maple trees. The wet, swampy soil of bogs is ideal for larch, white cedar, and cypress trees. The shallow, rocky soil on some mountain slopes favors forests of redwood and spruce.

Factors such as average temperature, amount of moisture available, and soil type affect the type of plant life that can grow in an area. A biome is a community of specific types of plants and animals that covers a large area of the earth's surface. Each biome is made up of many **habitats**—the place where a particular plant or animal normally lives and grows. The type of biome in a region is generally determined by the kind of climate in that region. For example, tropical rain forests can be found in areas of abundant rainfall and hot temperatures. In areas of hot temperatures where rainfall is severely limited, deserts can be found. The tundra is the area found around the Arctic and Antarctic circles and on some high mountaintops. The ground is permanently frozen just a few feet below the surface, and the plant life consists of mosses, lichens, grasses, and shrubs. (For a description of plant and animal communities around the world, see the article BIOMES in Volume B.)

Biorhythms. Living things are also affected by light in many ways. Because the rotation

The never-ending cycle of day and night affects many kinds of living things. The blossoms of the morning glory plant open in early morning sunlight (*top*) and close later in the day. This daily cycle is called a circadian rhythm.

of the earth on its axis causes night and day, organisms are exposed to alternating periods of light and dark. Organisms respond to this in various ways. Some flowers, for instance, open during the day and close at night. Many animals are active during the day and sleep at night, while others do just the reverse. In humans, there is a daily rise and fall in blood pressure, blood sugar level, body temperature, and other variables. These natural cycles are called **biological rhythms**. They can occur every few seconds, as in the beating of the heart, or within a single day, as in the opening and closing of flowers such as roses and morning glories. Changes that occur on a daily basis are known as **circadian rhythms**. There are also rhythms that occur on a monthly or yearly basis. Migrations of birds and other animals are examples of yearly cycles, which may be triggered by seasonal changes in the length of daylight and in temperature. All are examples of biorhythms.

It is important for plants and animals to produce offspring at a time of year when conditions are right for the survival of their young. It would be very difficult, for instance, if deer gave birth to fawns just as winter was beginning. A much more favorable time is in the early spring. It is believed that there is a **biological clock** in animals and plants that helps them respond to external clues such as changes in daylight and temperature. (See the article BIOLOGICAL CLOCK in Volume B).

Biological Environment

Living things are not only affected by the environment in which they live, they are also affected by other living things in their environment. One way to study the effects of living beings on one another is through the study of their groups. The two basic groups are populations and communities.

Populations and Communities. Most of us are familiar with the word "population." Knowing the population of a city, state, or nation means knowing how many human beings live there. But when biologists use this word, they have a different meaning in mind. They are talking about the number of any one kind of living thing with shared characteristics found in a particular place. As an example, a biologist might report a population of 200 snails of one species in a particular pond. Or, there might be a stand of 17 white birch trees in a particular forest.

A basic factor in determining the size of a population is the environment. In general, if there is plenty of water, good soil, and a suitable climate, the environment can sustain a large population. But if some elements are in short supply, only some individuals will survive. The others have to find another area or face the danger of dying.

A community includes populations of different species in a specific location interacting with each other. Usually a community is a complete system. It can sustain itself without taking in anything it needs from outside the community.

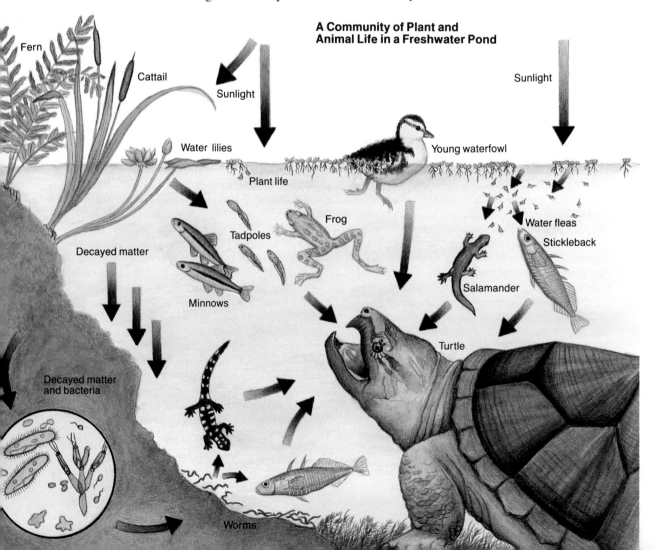

A Community of Plant and Animal Life in a Freshwater Pond

Fern

Cattail

Sunlight

Sunlight

Water lilies

Young waterfowl

Plant life

Decayed matter

Tadpoles

Frog

Water fleas

Stickleback

Minnows

Salamander

Decayed matter and bacteria

Turtle

Worms

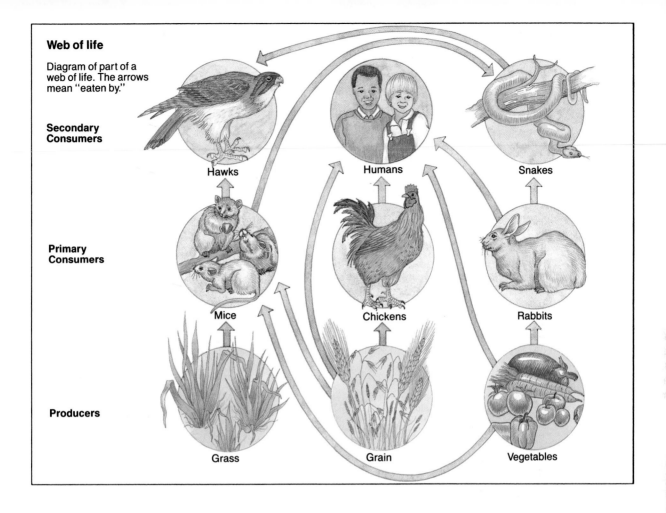

Web of life

Diagram of part of a web of life. The arrows mean "eaten by."

Secondary Consumers

Hawks

Humans

Snakes

Primary Consumers

Mice

Chickens

Rabbits

Producers

Grass

Grain

Vegetables

Webs of Life. Most communities contain one or more food chains. A food chain consists of a series of organisms, each one using the next one in the chain as part of its food supply. In the process, energy is transferred from one part of the chain to the next. Most biologists divide the members of a food chain into four separate groups.

1. Producers. Green plants are the primary producers of the food chain. They take minerals and water from the soil, carbon dioxide from the air, and energy from the sun to produce materials that make up their cells.

2. Primary consumers. These are the animals, called **herbivores**, that feed directly on plants. Cows and grasshoppers are both examples.

3. Secondary consumers. Organisms that feed on the primary consumers are known as secondary consumers. Wolves eat rabbits and other small animals. Some animals are pri-

mary and secondary consumers; bears, for example, eat plant berries and fish.

4. Decomposers. Decomposers feed on dead organisms. In this manner, the dead organisms are used to keep the food chain going. Bacteria, fungi, and some insects are among the decomposers. A simple food chain might look like the picture above.

The food chains within a community are often connected and related, one to the other. All together they form a food web, or web of life.

In some instances, there are special relationships between the members of a community. For example, some of the consumers are **predators**. Predators are animals that kill other animals, which are called prey, for food. Eagles, owls, wolves, and humans are a few well-known predators.

Predators are usually well suited for catching, killing, and eating their prey. They have keen senses of sight, smell, or vision, so they can detect other animals from far away. Many predators can move quickly to catch a fleeing creature. They have powerful claws and jaws to hold and kill their victims.

Some animals are **scavengers**. Scavengers eat the bodies of dead animals. By eating animals that have died or have been killed, scavengers return the materials of the dead animals to the food cycle. Vultures and jackals are scavengers.

Some organisms of different species in a community live together in special relationships. The general term for such relationships is **symbiosis**.

One form of symbiosis is **commensalism**. In commensalism one organism gains and the other seems to neither gain nor suffer. The remora is a small fish that uses a suction disk on top of its head to attach itself to a larger fish, such as a shark. The remora gains by being carried around its environment and by

Although the mistletoe plant can make its own food, it takes nourishment and water from various kinds of trees. For this reason it is called a parasite.

being able to eat scraps of the shark's food. The relationship does not seem to harm the shark in any way.

Another example of commensalism occurs when a woodpecker chisels out a hole in a tree and then abandons the hole. After the woodpecker is gone, a bluebird may make a nest in the hole. The bluebird has gained a home, and the woodpecker has lost nothing.

Mutualism is a type of symbiosis in which both organisms gain from each other. One kind of crocodile opens its mouth wide and allows a small bird, the Egyptian plover, to pick food particles from between its teeth. This helps both organisms. The crocodile gets its teeth cleaned while the plover gets a meal.

Mutualism is also found in the intestines of humans. Certain bacteria living there have a plentiful supply of food and water. In return, these bacteria produce vitamins that are helpful to humans.

Another kind of symbiosis, **parasitism**, occurs when one organism (the parasite) takes nourishment from another, usually larger, organism (the host) and harms the host in some way. A number of parasites cause human diseases. Some parasitic bacteria that live in or on human beings can cause such diseases as diphtheria and typhoid fever. Athlete's foot and ringworm come from another type of parasite, a **fungus**.

The opposite of symbiosis is **competition**. Competition can occur within one species, with individuals fighting each other for food, water, light, or living space. It can also occur between individuals of different species fighting over the same resources.

Deer living in communities near woodlands where humans are building houses must compete with other deer for the dwindling food supply. In many areas, there are too many deer for the amount of food that is available. As a result, large numbers of deer may die of starvation. In general, the ones who win the competition for food and space are those better equipped to find food and to fight off other hungry animals.

There are many examples of competition between species. Both hawks and owls eat mice. Every mouse that a hawk eats is one less for an owl, and, of course, the reverse is also true. Cattails and duckweed plants often grow next to each other and compete for space, light, and an adequate supply of water.

The domestic dog (*above*), the coyote (*far right*), and the wolf (*right*) share enough similarities to be grouped together in one genus, called *Canis*. However, because of differences in anatomy and behavior, each of these animals is a distinct and different species.

▶ THE KINGDOMS OF LIVING THINGS

The Greek philosopher Aristotle (384–322 B.C.) attempted to classify living things. He named two large groups: plants and animals. Plants were further divided into those with soft stems, those with one hard, woody stem (trees), and those with more than one woody stem (shrubs). The animal group was further divided into those that live in water, those that live on land, and those that live in the air. For many centuries Aristotle's system was accepted without question. It was not until the middle of the 1700's that a Swedish botanist and physician, Carolus Linnaeus (1707–78), introduced a new system that has become the basis for modern biological classification.

In the Linnaean system, the species is the basic unit of classification. Each organism is identified by two names. The first name is the **genus**, which is a group made up of similar **species**. The second name is the species, which is a more particular group of similar individuals. Members of one species can mate with other members of the same species but not with members of different species. The species name identifies the exact type of organism within the large group of the genus. For example, dogs, wolves, and coyotes all belong to the same genus, *Canis*. To make a distinction between these similar species, dogs are named *Canis familiaris;* wolves are named *Canis lupus;* and coyotes are named *Canis latrans.*

Using the genus and species name avoids much confusion. For example, the American mountain lion has close to 20 common names—among them are puma, cougar, panther, silver lion, king cat, and varmint. Using the scientific name, *Felis concolor,* is one way to make sure that people in different parts of the country are talking about the same animal.

The scientific name also helps to describe the organism and show its relationship to other organisms. For example, when they are given the scientific name of an organism with which they are not familiar, biologists will be able to tell you something about the organism's body structure, how it reproduces, what foods it eats, and other basic characteristics.

Species joined with similar or related species form the genus. The genus, too, can be joined with other similar genera (plural of genus) to form a larger group called a **family**. An example is the Apoidea, or bee, family. Among the genera in the family Apoidea are the honeybee (genus *Apis*), the bumblebee (genus *Bombus*), and the mason bee (genus *Chalicodoma*).

Families that have features in common can be grounded together to make an **order**. The Diptera order includes all the various families of flies and similar insects. There are families of fruit flies (Trypetidae), horseflies (Tabani-

The Kingdoms of Living Things

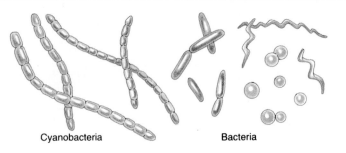

Kingdom Monera
One-celled, or form groups; cells lack organelles found in other kingdoms. Includes bacteria, such as cyanobacteria.

Cyanobacteria

Bacteria

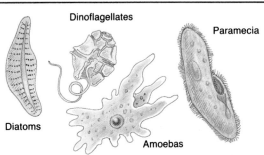

Dinoflagellates

Paramecia

Diatoms

Amoebas

Kingdom Protista
Usually one-celled, with organelles. Some carry on photosynthesis; some move by cilia, flagella, or a flowing movement. Includes amoebas, paramecia, diatoms, and dinoflagellates.

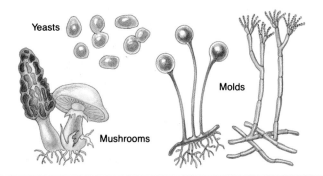

Yeasts

Molds

Mushrooms

Kingdom Fungi
Mostly many-celled; food obtained by absorbing material from dead organisms; cell walls made of chitin (carbohydrate found in insects). Includes mushrooms, molds, mildews, yeasts, water molds, and slime molds.

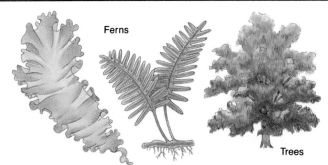

Ferns

Trees

Kingdom Plantae
Many-celled with organelles; tissues; organs; carry on photosynthesis; cell walls made of cellulose. Includes mosses, ferns, conifers, and flowering plants.

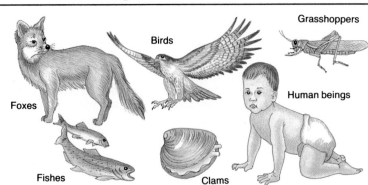

Grasshoppers

Birds

Foxes

Human beings

Fishes

Clams

Kingdom Animalia
Many-celled with organelles; tissues; organs; nervous system, in most; food obtained by ingestion. Includes sponges, corals, worms, mollusks, fishes, amphibians, reptiles, birds, and mammals.

dae), daddy longlegs (Tipulidae), and mosquitoes (Culicidae) within Diptera.

Groups of related orders make up a **class**, the next higher level of organization. The largest class of plants, Angiospermae, includes more than 280,000 species of flowering plants grouped into more than 50 different orders. Among the larger orders are Ranales (magnolias and buttercups), Rosales (roses), Geraniales (geraniums), and Umbellales (carrots).

Going one step further, related classes are combined to form either a **phylum** (for animals) or a **division** (for plants and plantlike organisms). As an example, the phylum Porifera contains all the sponges. There are more than 5,000 species. Most of them fall into three classes: Calcispongiae (shallow water), Hyalspongiae (deepwater), and Demospongiae (brightly colored).

In many classification systems, the highest level of organization is the **kingdom**. An early system defined just two kingdoms—Animalia (for animals) and Plantae (for plants). Later, as knowledge of life-forms grew, more kingdoms were added. The discovery of microscopic living things led scientists to add the kingdom Protista (for protists). These organisms did not fit into either the animal or plant kingdoms.

Classification also changed to show that life has two main branches, the prokaryotes and the eukaryotes. The prokaryotes lack a nucleus; the eukaryotes have a nucleus in their cells. The kingdom Monera was added to include prokaryotes such as bacteria. The other kingdoms were used for eukaryotes.

In 1959, the kingdom Fungi was first proposed. Unlike other organisms, fungi have cell walls made mostly of chitin. Also, fungi secrete enzymes that break down food before they ingest it. This is very different from animals, which ingest food before digesting it, and plants, which make their own food.

With the addition of the kingdom Fungi, scientists had devised a five-kingdom system. The chart on the opposite page shows the five kingdoms and gives characteristics and examples of the members of each kingdom. This system won broad support and remains popular, even though scientists continue to propose changes. For example, some scientists advocate a six-kingdom system. (For more information, see the article KINGDOMS OF LIVING THINGS in Volume JK.)

There are about 2 million known organisms. Scientists classify these organisms to show their relationships to each other and possibly their evolutionary paths. This is a difficult task and scientists do not always agree on the best method of classification. Comparing certain proteins of two different organisms has helped in some cases to determine how closely related the two organisms are.

▶ THE ORIGIN OF LIFE

No one knows exactly how or when life first appeared on earth. Most scientists guess that it was about 4 billion years ago. Scientists also do not know what the first living organisms looked like, although fossils of bacteria-like cells about 3.5 billion years old have been found. Over the billions of years since then, all other known life-forms evolved.

Theories of the Origin of Life

Religious Explanations. Some people reject the view that life on earth had such primitive beginnings. These people, called creationists, believe that the story of creation in the Bible is a literal explanation of the origin of life. In their view, God created all the living plants and animals as we now know them. Most scientists, however, feel that the Bible is not a literal or a scientific report.

Spontaneous Generation. For centuries, people believed that living things could arise from nonliving things. It was thought, for instance, that frogs were born from mud and that rotting meat gave rise to flies. This theory is known as spontaneous generation.

Italian physician and scientist Francesco Redi (1626–97) was one of the scientists of his time who did not accept the idea of spontaneous generation. In 1668, he performed an experiment that showed what actually happens. Redi placed pieces of meat in flasks with wide mouths. He left some of the flasks uncovered. The rest of the flasks were covered with cloth that had an open weave. Within a few days all of the meat began to decay. Flies, attracted by the smell, landed on the meat in the open flasks and laid eggs. Soon thereafter, the eggs hatched and small wormlike maggots hatched from the eggs and began crawling around the meat. Flies were also attracted by the smell from the other flasks. But, unable to reach the meat because of the cloth covering, they laid their eggs on the cloth. When these

Is cloning a way to create new life?

Cloning is a way to make genetically identical replicas of living organisms. It does not create life. However, it does allow scientists to select the cloned cells, thereby influencing reproduction of the cloned organism.

The science of cloning received international attention in 1997 when researchers in Scotland announced the birth of Dolly, a sheep that was cloned from cells taken from an adult sheep's udder. These udder cells contained the genetic material of the sheep from which they were taken. The researchers obtained egg cells from another sheep and removed the genetic material from them. The udder cells and the egg cells were then combined in a process that resulted in the creation of an embryo. The embryo was then implanted into a third sheep—a surrogate mother —where it matured and developed into Dolly, which would grow up to be an exact replica of the sheep from which the genetic material was taken. This was the first time that a mammal had been "produced" without the use of embryo cells.

Dolly's birth inspired widespread debate. Should cloning experiments be allowed? Could cloning be used in harmful ways? Could humans be cloned? If so, should they be?

These are not easy questions to answer. Cloning has some potential benefits such as helping to save endangered species by creating more of these animals.

But the possibility of cloning adult mammals —especially human beings—is troubling to many people. For example, it changes our ideas about parents and offspring. If a human could be cloned, who would its parents be? Would the cloned offspring have his or her own unique personality, character, and talents?

These types of difficult questions have led many nations to ban human cloning experiments. While recognizing the potential value of cloning for use on animals, these nations have determined that the moral, ethical, and legal issues related to human cloning do not justify such experimentation. Despite this, however, research into cloning—perhaps even human cloning—seemed certain to go forward.

eggs hatched, the cloth, not the meat, was covered with maggots.

Redi's work showed that the flies on rotting meat came only from other flies. It was more than 200 years later, though, that experiments by scientists such as Louis Pasteur (1822–95) finally convinced people that living things did not arise spontaneously from nonliving things.

Panspermia. Among other theories on the origin of life is the so-called germ theory, or panspermia. According to this theory, there are germs spread throughout the universe. These germs grow when they reach a place with favorable conditions such as the earth's. Panspermia maintains that the organisms we know of sprang from such germs. Few scientists today believe in this theory.

Modern Theories. In 1953, Stanley Miller, a young scientist, tried an experiment in which he re-created conditions thought to exist on earth before life was present. About 4 billion years ago the earth's atmosphere might have contained the gases methane, ammonia, hydrogen, and water vapor. The primitive seas would have been very hot; the atmosphere turbulent with violent lightning storms.

For his experiment, Miller placed hot water and the four gases found in the ancient atmosphere in a flask. Then he sent lightninglike sparks through the mixture of gases and water.

After a week, Miller found that the water had turned red and that two amino acids were present in it. As you know, amino acids are basic units of proteins, and proteins are the building blocks of all living things.

The steps between the formation of simple amino acids and the appearance of the first cell, however, are not at all clear. There are many theories but no real answers to the question of how life on earth began.

The theory demonstrated by Miller's experiment proposes that energy from bolts of lightning might have formed molecules of amino acids from the water and gases in the earth's atmosphere. In time, the seas were thick with amino acids. As the amino acids floated around, they kept bumping into one another. From time to time, some stuck together, forming large molecules. Eventually molecules that contained hundreds of these amino acids were formed. Then, by chance, different larger molecules formed. When these molecules bumped into certain smaller molecules, the smaller ones were added to the larger ones.

These big molecules were special in another way. They grew to a certain size and then divided. Instead of being one molecule, they became two identical molecules. Each new one went on taking in smaller molecules, growing, and then dividing again. In this way, complex molecules that eventually gave rise to DNA and RNA may have been formed.

▶ LIFE ON OTHER PLANETS

For many years humans have wondered whether life exists elsewhere in the universe. Many scientists today believe that there is a good chance of finding life on other planets.

Where Do Scientists Look for Life? For life as we know it to exist on another planet, the conditions would have to be suitable. The planet must be the right distance from its sun, so that the temperature is not too hot or too cold. There must be plenty of water and enough oxygen in the air to sustain life. In addition, the atmosphere must be thick enough to keep out ultraviolet rays and other dangerous radiation from space. Of course, there may be other kinds of living things in the universe that demand entirely different conditions.

How Do Scientists Look for Life? Over the years different scientists have suggested ways to make contact with creatures on other planets. In 1959, a research effort known as SETI, or *S*earch for *E*xtra*t*errestrial *I*ntelligence, was established. From its work came the abbreviation ET, for an *extrat*errestial—a creature living on another planet.

The tool used by SETI researchers is the radio telescope—a huge antenna, shaped like a metal dish up to 1,000 feet (300 meters) across.

Although they expect to hear signals from natural sources, SETI scientists are searching for special signals—ones with a form or pattern different from ordinary radio waves. Over the years, scientists have picked up some strange signals on their radio telescopes. Each time, though, they were able to explain them as resulting from natural causes.

Scientists also are trying to send messages to other life forms that might exist in the universe. In 1972, the Pioneer 10 space probe was launched from the Kennedy Space Center in Florida. It carried drawings of a nude man and woman, the Pioneer spacecraft and its path through the planets, the position of the sun in the galaxy, and a diagram of the hydro-

Huge radio telescopes aimed into space from planet earth may tell us whether or not intelligent life exists anywhere else in the universe.

gen atom are inscribed on the plaque. Perhaps some ET will spot Pioneer 10 during its long journey through space, will understand at least some of the drawings, and will find a way to contact us.

In 1974, scientists beamed a powerful signal into space as another way of making contact with ET's. Using the same binary system as computers, the message included the numbers from 1 to 10, the atomic numbers for several elements, the formula for DNA, a diagram of the structure of a DNA molecule, and the human population on earth.

Thus far, there is no direct evidence that ET's have sent us messages or received messages from us. But the scientists working for SETI are not discouraged. They think that we will be in touch with intelligent beings on other planets some day.

MELVIN BERGER
Author, *How Life Began*
Reviewed by BARBARA BRANCA
Author, *Animals and Plants*

See also ANIMALS; BACTERIA; BIOLOGICAL CLOCK; BIOMES; BODY, HUMAN; BODY CHEMISTRY; CELLS; EVOLUTION; FUNGI; GENETICS; PHOTOSYNTHESIS; PLANTS; VIRUSES.

LIGHT

Of all the forms of energy in nature, light is the most important to our lives. Without light there would be no life on Earth. Plants could not grow, and with no plants for food, animals could not exist. Light also enables humans and other animals to see. Because of light we can discover the world and the universe around us.

For as long as people have asked questions, they have wondered about light. Ancient peoples created myths to explain how the bright objects of the sky—the sun, moon, stars, and planets—made their light and how they moved. They knew how to make light from fire and invented torches, oil lamps, candles, and other ways to control it. Today we make light in many different ways, and we control and use it in many different devices.

A **source** of light is an object that creates its own light. The sun is the most important source of light for Earth. Other stars are also sources of light, but the sun appears much brighter because it is much closer to us.

Most objects are not sources of light. We see them only when light from a source strikes them and bounces off toward our eyes. This bouncing of light from matter is called **reflection**. The ancients thought the moon and planets were sources of light, but we now know they are not. We see them because sunlight reflects from their surfaces and travels to Earth.

The sun is our most important source of light, a form of energy essential to life on Earth. Light enables plants to grow and humans and other animals to see.

▶ **THE NATURE OF LIGHT**

As people developed science, they had more and more questions about light—how it is produced and how it behaves. One of the most important questions was posed in the 1600's by the English scientist and mathematician Isaac Newton. Newton wondered whether light spreads out from its source as a stream of tiny particles, or whether it travels through space as waves, like ripples in a pond.

A wave theory proposed earlier in the century by the Dutch physicist and astronomer Christiaan Huygens had already been widely accepted by many scientists. Huygens' ideas successfully explained the way light behaves as it reflects from matter or passes through it.

Newton did some experiments with shadows that showed that light travels in straight lines. If light behaved like water waves, it would not cast shadows. Instead, when light passed by an object, it would quickly fill in

Law of Reflection
The angle of incidence formed by an incoming ray of light is equal to the angle of reflection formed by the outgoing ray.

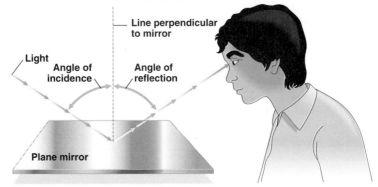

Line perpendicular to mirror

Light

Angle of incidence

Angle of reflection

Plane mirror

the space behind it, as water waves do when they pass a rock. Newton therefore concluded that light must not travel in waves. Rather, he theorized, it was made of tiny particles, which he called corpuscles. For many years, Newton's corpuscular, or particle, theory of light prevailed over wave theory. Which theory was correct?

Today scientists agree that light has both a wave nature and a particle nature. Light is an electromagnetic wave, made up of electrical and magnetic forces traveling together through space at a very high speed, and it is also a stream of particles of light energy called photons.

This understanding of the nature of light was achieved only after about 300 years of scientific experimentation and observation. Before we discuss these findings in detail, let us look at some of the basic behaviors of light.

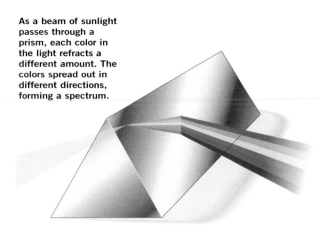

As a beam of sunlight passes through a prism, each color in the light refracts a different amount. The colors spread out in different directions, forming a spectrum.

▶ REFLECTION, REFRACTION, AND DISPERSION

When light strikes matter, it can bounce off, be absorbed by, or pass through the material. Lines can be drawn to show the direction in which light is moving. Such lines are called **rays** of light. When a ray of light shines on an ordinary surface such as a piece of cloth, it bounces off that surface in every direction. The one bright ray coming in becomes many not-so-bright rays going out. This is called **diffuse reflection**. ("Diffuse" means going in all directions). It is the way we see most objects.

Some surfaces, especially metals, are smooth and shiny. When a bright ray of light strikes a shiny surface, it bounces off in only one direction. If the ray strikes the surface perpendicularly (head-on), it bounces straight back in the opposite direction. In the illustration on the opposite page, you can see that if the ray strikes the surface at an

Light rays change direction, or refract, when they pass from one transparent material (air) to another (water). This bending of light makes the straw appear to be broken.

angle, the outgoing ray makes the same angle with the surface as the incoming ray. The law of reflection says that these two angles are always equal. This type of reflection is called **specular reflection**, and the reflecting surface is called a mirror. ("Specular" is derived from the Latin word for "mirror.")

Newton's Prism Experiment and Refraction

As Newton studied light and color, one of his first findings was that sunlight contains all the colors. Newton observed sunlight as it came through a hole in the window shade of a darkened room. When this light passed through a prism (a solid, three-sided piece of glass), a band of colors appeared on the opposite wall. The colors changed gradually from red at one end to violet on the other, with regions of orange, yellow, green, blue, and indigo in between. Newton called this spread of colors a **spectrum** (plural: spectra).

Newton experimented with the spectrum until he was convinced that sunlight was a mixture of all the colors and that the prism separated the colors.

How does a prism produce a spectrum? A material that lets light pass through is said to be **transparent**. When light crosses a boundary from one transparent material, such as air, to another, such as glass, it changes direction, unless it is traveling exactly perpendicular to the boundary. This change of direction is called **refraction**.

MIRRORS AND REFLECTION

Plane Mirrors

When a ray of light from an object strikes a mirror and reflects toward your eye, it is traveling exactly as if it had come from a similar object located the same distance behind the mirror. Looking into the mirror, you see an image of the object. Because the image appears to be in a place where there is no actual light from the object, it is called a **virtual image**.

If you stand directly in front of a plane, or flat, mirror, you see a virtual image of yourself. This image is right side up and the same size as you, but the left and right sides of your body are reversed. If you raise your right arm, the image in the mirror seems to be raising its left arm.

A virtual image of an object as seen in a flat mirror appears to be standing as far behind the mirror as the object is in front of it.

Concave Mirrors

If a mirror is curved like the inside of a bowl, it is called concave. All the rays coming straight into a concave mirror reflect to a single point called the **focus**. The distance from the mirror to the focus is called the **focal length**.

People often use concave mirrors to magnify their faces when applying makeup or shaving. If a face or any object is closer to a concave mirror than its focal length, an upright, magnified virtual image of it appears to be behind the mirror.

If an object in front of a concave mirror is farther away than the focus, you cannot see its image by looking into the mirror. If you aim the reflected light toward a wall or screen and carefully adjust the distance, you can cast a clear, upside-down image on the screen. This is called a **real image** because the light is actually where it appears to be.

When an object is less than twice the focal length away from a concave mirror, its image is magnified and farther from the mirror than the object. When an object is farther than two focal lengths from a concave mirror, its image is reduced in size and closer to the mirror.

Images seen in the convex mirror on the passenger side of a car appear to be smaller and farther away than they really are.

When you look into a flat mirror, your image seems to be as far behind the mirror as you are in front of it. It is a virtual image because light appears to be coming from a place where it is not.

Convex Mirrors

Convex mirrors are shaped like the outside of a bowl. They cannot be used to project or magnify an image, but they enable you to see a wider view.

Passenger-side mirrors on cars are usually convex. They help the driver see a wider area, to change lanes more safely. The images in such mirrors appear smaller and farther away than they really are.

How to Produce a Real Image

You and a partner can produce a real image using a small concave mirror, a large flashlight, an 8-inch (20-centimeter) square of white cardboard, and a yardstick or meterstick.

Turn on the flashlight. Look inside the bulb and note the size and shape of the glowing filament. Place the flashlight about 1 1/2 focal lengths from the mirror. Aim it toward the mirror at a slight angle.

Place the mirror on a table or on the wall. Find the focal length of the mirror by moving away from it until it no longer produces an image of your face. Have your partner measure the distance from the mirror to your face at that place.

Have your partner hold the white cardboard at the opposite angle to that of the flashlight, at a distance about 3 focal lengths from the mirror. Move the cardboard in and out until you get a sharp image reflected on it. Because this real image is magnified by the mirror, you should be able to see details of the flashlight filament clearly.

Did you know that...

you see scattered light every time you look at the sky? If the Earth had no atmosphere, we would only see sunlight if we looked directly at the sun. The rest of the sky would be black except for the faint light of the distant stars, the moon, and the planets. Because of the gas and dust in our atmosphere, light scatters away from the main beam of the sun. A light beam can scatter many times before it reaches our eyes.

Because light at the violet end of the spectrum scatters more than light at the red end, the light that reaches our eyes from parts of the sky away from the sun has a bluish color.

At sunrise and sunset, the sun is low in the sky and the sunlight has to travel through more of the atmosphere to reach our eyes. That means more light is scattered away from the direct sunlight than at other times of the day. Since the light scattered most is at the violet end, the remaining light is red. We then see a beautiful sunrise or sunset.

Newton's prism experiment is illustrated on page 213. A narrow beam of light strikes the left side of the prism. It changes direction, shifting closer to the perpendicular. Each color in the light refracts a different amount, red changing direction the least and violet the most.

When the separated colors pass through the opposite side of the prism, they again refract, this time shifting away from the perpendicular. Again the red changes direction less than the violet. As a result, each color is now going in a different direction. When the light strikes and reflects off the wall, the spectrum is clearly visible. This spreading of colors due to refraction is called **dispersion**. Dispersion of light in raindrops is responsible for producing rainbows. (For more information about how rainbows are formed, see the article RAINBOWS in Volume R.)

Scattering

When light passes through a gas or liquid, each time it strikes a dust particle or a molecule it changes direction. Thus the beam of light is made to spread out in every direction.

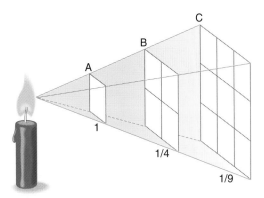

The intensity of light weakens as the light spreads from the source. The candle illuminates the surface at A with a certain intensity. The surface at B is twice as far from the candle as A, but the intensity is only $\frac{1}{4}$ as great. At C, three times as far away as A, the intensity is only $\frac{1}{9}$ as great.

This process is called scattering. Colors near the violet end of the spectrum scatter more than those at the red end. Scattering causes dispersion of colors just as refraction does, but it does not create a spectrum.

Color

The color of an object depends on the way it reflects and absorbs light. The object absorbs certain colors and reflects others. The color we see is a combination of all the colors that the object reflects. An apple looks red because the surface of the apple reflects colors from the red end of the spectrum and absorbs the rest. Black objects absorb all colors. White objects reflect all colors.

▶ INTENSITY OF LIGHT

The brightness of a light source is measured in **candles**, a name that goes back to the old days of wax candles. The amount of light received by an object, or its illumination, depends on how far away the light source is. Suppose a single candle shines directly on a flat surface 1 foot away. Then it lights this surface with an intensity,

or brightness, of 1 **footcandle**. The average 60-watt lightbulb emits about 1 footcandle for each watt, or about 60 footcandles.

Using metric units, the flat surface is placed 1 meter from the candle. The intensity of the light is then called 1 **meter-candle**, or 1 **lux**. One footcandle is the equivalent of 10.76 meter-candles.

As the distance between a light source and an object increases, the intensity of illumination decreases. Also, if the surface is slanted, instead of being perpendicular to the incoming rays, the intensity at each spot on the surface is less.

▶ DIFFRACTION, INTERFERENCE, AND WAVE THEORY

A different behavior of light was incorporated into an experiment by the English physicist Thomas Young in 1801. The results made a convincing case for the wave theory of light.

Scientists had noticed that objects with sharp edges cast shadows that are not as sharp. Light seems to bend a little bit around the edge of the object, producing a fuzzy boundary between light and darkness. This bending of light as it passes the edge of an object is called **diffraction**. Young wondered if diffraction could be used to prove that light is made of waves.

Young's Interference Experiment

Screen 1: A single pinhole allows light to pass through and spread, or diffract.
Screen 2: Each of the two pinholes allows light to pass and spread. Light waves are in perfect step with each other.
Screen 3: Alternating areas of brightness and darkness on the screen are the result of interference. Brightness occurs where waves are in step, making the combined wave brighter. Darkness occurs where waves are out of step, canceling each other out.

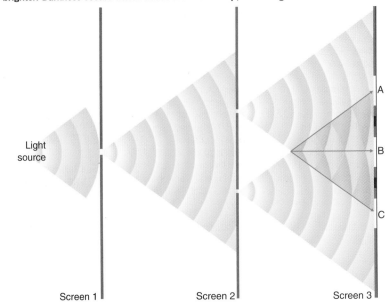

How Light Travels in Straight Lines

Make a Shadow

You will need a small table and a table lamp without its shade. Place the lamp on the table so that it is facing a blank, light-colored wall. Turn the lamp on. Stand between the lamp and the wall, facing the wall. You should see a fairly sharp shadow of your body on the wall.

This shadow is the result of light moving in straight lines from the lamp to the wall. The shadow is the dark space where your body blocks the light from the lamp. The edge of the shadow can be traced by imagining straight lines drawn out from the lamp and just touching the edge of your body all around.

Use a Pinhole Camera

You will need a cylindrical box, wax paper, a rubber band, and a candle in a holder.

Make a pinhole camera, or *camera obscura*, following the directions in the article Experiments and Other Science Activities in Volume E. Because it requires the use of a lit candle, have an adult supervise this demonstration.

Light the candle and place it in front of the pinhole you made in the camera. You should see an image of the candle flame on the wax-paper screen, but the image will be upside down. Why?

The only light that can reach the screen from the candle is light that falls directly on the pinhole. Light coming from the top of the flame goes straight through the hole and falls on the lower end of the screen. Light from the bottom of the flame goes through the

hole and falls on the upper end of the screen. Light from other parts of the flame falls at other parts of the screen, forming a complete upside-down image of the flame.

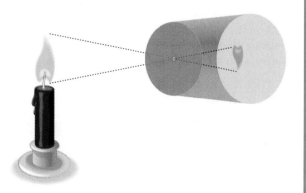

It was known that diffraction also occurs when light passes through a very small opening, causing the light to spread out on the other side of the opening. As shown in the illustration opposite, Young created a point source of light by passing sunlight through a pinhole in a light-absorbing screen. He allowed that light to spread out a bit before it struck a second screen with two pinholes close together. It then continued to a third screen, where any patterns might be observed.

If the particle theory was right, the third screen would be brightest in the middle with the intensity dropping off toward the edges. If the wave theory was right, the brightness pattern would be very different.

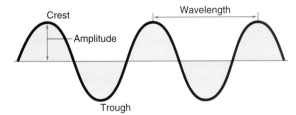

Waves have crests and troughs. The distance from crest to crest or trough to trough is the wavelength. The amplitude, or height of the wave, is half the distance from a crest to a trough.

Since the original light came from a tiny hole, Young reasoned that the crest, or high point, of each wave would reach the two pinholes at the same time. You can see that happening on Screen 2 of the illustration. The two pinholes would then act like two sources, putting out crests and troughs (low points of waves) in perfect step with each other. The waves would not simply add together when they reached the third screen. Instead, they would interfere with each other, as you can see on Screen 3.

Young realized that this **interference** would distinguish wave behavior from particle behavior. At the center of the screen, Point B in the illustration, the waves would meet crest-to-crest and trough-to-trough, making the combined wave much brighter. A short distance to the left or right of Point B, one of the two pinhole waves would have traveled a half-wavelength farther than the other. (A wavelength is the distance between crests or troughs.) There the two waves would meet crest-to-trough, canceling each other and leaving a dark spot. A little farther left or right and the waves would have traveled distances that differ by a whole wavelength. Again these waves would meet crest-to-crest and trough-to-trough, producing bright spots at Points A and C.

The net result would be a series of bright and dark bands on the third screen, and that is exactly what Young saw. From that point on, the wave theory of light was favored over the particle theory.

The effects of interference can be seen in many natural objects and in products of technology. Interference is responsible for the variations of color you see in an opal, a film of oil, and the surface of a compact disc. One of the most fascinating uses of interference is in the creation of three-dimensional images called holograms. (To find out how holograms are made, see PHOTOGRAPHY in Volume P.) Interference also played an important role in the development of Albert Einstein's famous theory of relativity. (Refer to RELATIVITY in Volume R for more information.)

▶ ELECTROMAGNETIC WAVES

In 1865 the wave theory of light became even stronger when the Scottish physicist James Clerk Maxwell published a set of mathematical formulas to describe the relationships between electricity and magnetism. His formulas led him to predict the existence of electromagnetic waves. Maxwell was able to arrive at his formulas and predictions because of several basic discoveries about electricity and magnetism that had been made previously by the French physicists Charles-Augustin de Coulomb and André-Marie Ampère and the English scientist Michael Faraday.

Coulomb's discoveries were expressed in what we now call Coulomb's Law. It contains a mathematical value called a constant that relates the force between two electrical charges to the amount of each charge and the distance from one to the other. Ampère discovered that two wires carrying an electric current had a magnetic force between them. Ampère's Law contains a constant that relates electric currents, the distance between

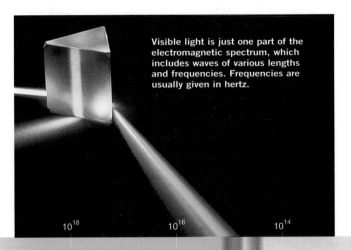

Visible light is just one part of the electromagnetic spectrum, which includes waves of various lengths and frequencies. Frequencies are usually given in hertz.

| 10^{24} | 10^{22} | 10^{20} | 10^{18} | 10^{16} | 10^{14} | 10^{12} |

| Gamma rays | | X rays | Ultraviolet | Visible light | Infrared |

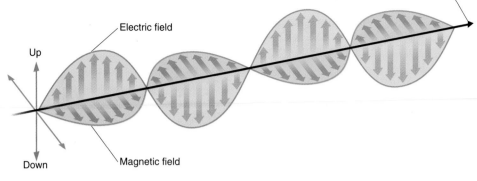

An electromagnetic wave is made up of two different fields, an electric field and a magnetic field, that change at the same rate and move at right angles to one another.

Electric field

Up

Direction of travel

Down

Magnetic field

the wires, and the magnetic force between them. Faraday learned that moving a magnet through a wire can create an electric current. Faraday's Law related the rate of change of a magnetic field to the amount of electrical current it produced. Maxwell's formulas were mathematical restatements of all three of these laws.

Measuring the Speed of Light

Maxwell was also able to use the constants of Coulomb and Ampère to compute mathematically the speed of electromagnetic waves. He found that it nearly matched the best experimental measurement of the speed of light at that time. He concluded that light itself was an electromagnetic wave.

The measurement Maxwell used for the speed of light had been made in 1849 by the French physicist Hippolyte Louis Fizeau. Fizeau set up a bright light source on one hill and a mirror on another hill several miles away. Using a rapidly spinning toothed wheel that created short flashes of light, Fizeau was able to determine how long it took the light to travel from the first hill to the second and back again. Knowing this time and the distance between the hills, he was able to compute the speed of light.

Improved measurements using other techniques were made by the French scientist Léon Foucault in 1850 and by the American physicist Albert Michelson in the 1920's. Today the speed of light and all other electromagnetic waves traveling through empty space is usually given as approximately 186,000 miles (300,000 kilometers) per second. When light travels through substances such as water or glass, its speed is not as great. The speed of light in water, for example, is about 124,000 miles (200,000 kilometers) per second. Scientists have even managed to stop a beam of light in the laboratory by passing it through a specially prepared container of gas. The light was stopped, stored, and then released.

What Are Electromagnetic Waves Like?

Electromagnetic waves have many similarities to ocean waves—and some important differences. As ocean waves pass through water, the water level rises and falls at a steady rate, which is called the **frequency**. The wave crests are evenly spaced, separated by a distance called the **wavelength**. The speed of the wave can be calculated by multiplying the frequency by the wavelength. The wave crests and troughs are above and below the normal ocean level by an amount that is called the **amplitude**.

Electromagnetic waves have wavelength, frequency, and amplitude as well. But one of the important differences between water waves and electromagnetic waves is that water waves need matter to exist, while electromagnetic waves can travel in empty space.

If an electromagnetic wave is traveling in empty space, how can you measure its amplitude? Scientists measure the electrical and magnetic environment of a region of space by quantities called the electric field and the magnetic field. The strengths of those fields tell us how large a force an electric charge and a magnetic pole would experience if they were placed there and in which direction that force would be.

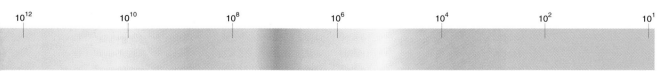

| 10^{12} | 10^{10} | 10^{8} | 10^{6} | 10^{4} | 10^{2} | 10^{1} |

Infrared Microwave Radar Short radio wave Long radio wave Induction heating AC power

The electromagnetic wave is made up of two amplitudes, one related to the other. It is as if one ocean wave (think of it as the electric field) were moving up and down, while the other wave (think of it as the magnetic field) were moving left and right along the surface of the water. One of Maxwell's equations describes how a changing electric field induces, or creates, a magnetic field, which changes at the same frequency as the electric field. The direction of the magnetic field is at right angles to the direction of the electric field.

Another of the equations describes how a changing magnetic field induces an electric field, which changes at the same frequency as the magnetic field. Again, the two fields are at right angles. The wave of changing electromagnetism constantly induces itself to move forward through space at the speed of light.

The Electromagnetic Spectrum

Maxwell's equations also predicted that an electromagnetic wave can have any frequency. Visible light has very short wavelengths and very high frequencies. Each color on the visible light band has a different frequency. Frequencies for visible light range from about 425 trillion cycles (or waves) per second for red to about 750 trillion cycles per second for violet.

Visible light is just one part of the electromagnetic spectrum. Most of the spectrum is not visible. Lower frequencies include radio waves, microwaves, and infrared light. Higher frequencies correspond to ultraviolet light, X rays, and gamma rays.

A yellow flower (*left*) looks quite different in ultraviolet light (*below left*). Many flowers have markings that are visible only to bees and other insects, which can see ultraviolet light.

Radio Waves

Radio waves have the longest wavelengths in the electromagnetic spectrum. People have produced and detected waves that stretch out as much as several miles from crest to crest. Radio waves were discovered by the German physicist Heinrich Hertz in 1888 and were at first called Hertzian waves. In 1901 the Italian scientist Guglielmo Marconi succeeded in sending the first radio signals across the Atlantic Ocean, using a transmitter he made himself. Today radio waves carry both radio and television signals, as well as signals to pagers, cellular telephones, and other communications devices.

In the 1930's, scientists detected radio waves coming to Earth from various directions in space. Large curved antennas called radio telescopes were built to gather the waves. With these instruments, astronomers have been able to identify many stars and galaxies as sources of radio signals.

When ultraviolet light strikes fluorescent materials, the materials absorb it and produce light visible to the human eye. Such materials glow when seen under ultraviolet "black light."

Microwaves

Radio waves that are shorter than approximately 12 inches (30 centimeters) are called microwaves. Like other radio waves, microwaves are used to carry telephone and other communications signals. They are also used in radar to detect aircraft and other objects. Their ability to heat certain materials has led to many other uses, including microwave cooking.

Infrared Light

About the year 1800, the English astronomer William Herschel set up an experiment to show the relationship between light and heat. He held a thermometer at various places in the spectrum of light formed by a prism. The temperature was highest at the red end and lowest at the violet end. Then he held the thermometer just outside the red limit. To his surprise, the temperature was higher there than anywhere in the spectrum itself. This meant that sunlight must contain a strong, invisible radiation with a wavelength that is greater than that of visible light. Radiation of this kind is called infrared. Compared with radio waves, infrared light has a much higher frequency, and it also has much shorter wavelengths.

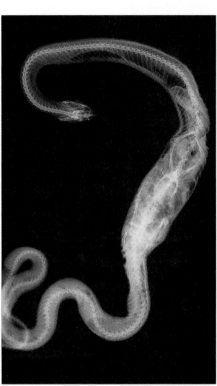

An X-ray photograph of a snake clearly reveals that it has recently made a meal of a frog. X rays, which can pass through soft body tissue and many other materials, are widely used in science and medicine.

Strong infrared light is emitted by glowing, hot objects such as the sun, electric lights, and flames. Even things that are not hot enough to glow—such as electric irons and hot pavements—send out strong infrared radiation.

Infrared radiation can be detected with special cameras and other types of instruments. With these devices the United States Coast Guard can locate an unlit ship at night, and astronomers can measure the temperature of a single star.

Ultraviolet Light

Just outside the violet end of the visible part of the spectrum is radiation with a shorter wavelength than violet light, called ultraviolet. It can have frequencies of more than one thousand trillion cycles per second.

When ultraviolet light strikes certain materials, the materials absorb it and produce visible light. Many minerals, oils, plant juices, and other materials can do this. Such materials are **fluorescent**.

The inside of a fluorescent lamp tube is coated with a chemical that fluoresces. When an electric current passes through the gas in the tube, ultraviolet radiation is given off. When that radiation hits the coating, the fluorescent material puts out a strong, visible glow.

In small amounts, ultraviolet light from the sun has a good effect on our bodies because it forms vitamin D in the skin. Too much exposure, however, can damage the cells of the skin, which may lead to the development of skin cancers.

Since ultraviolet radiation can kill bacteria, it is sometimes used to sterilize foods and water. Police scientists may use ultraviolet light to detect bloodstains, forged documents, and faked oil paintings.

X Rays

In 1895 a German physicist, Wilhelm Roentgen, discovered a range of radiations with wavelengths much shorter than those of ultraviolet waves. Roentgen had begun to experiment with a special kind of lamp called a cathode-ray tube. He noticed that when the tube was turned on, a glow came from a chemically treated piece of paper some distance away from the tube. This happened even when he wrapped the tube in cardboard to hold back any visible light. Apparently

How do polarized sunglasses work?

When sunlight scatters to create a blue sky, the scattering also produces partially polarized light. Some materials allow light with one direction of polarization to pass through them but block light polarized at right angles to that direction. Polarized sunglasses are made of such materials.

Because we know the primary direction of polarized sunlight, sunglasses are made to block that direction of polarization and permit light polarized at a right angle to that direction to pass through. On a bright day, polarized sunglasses can protect the eyes from glare quite effectively.

If you have a pair of polarized sunglasses, hold them in front of one eye as you look at a bright area of the sky in a direction away from the sun. Then slowly rotate the glasses. You will notice the sky getting lighter and darker as you change the alignment of the polarized lenses. When the sky looks darkest, the lenses are blocking the major direction of polarization of sunlight. In the direction at right angles to that, the greatest amount of light passes through and the sky looks brightest.

some unknown radiation from the tube was causing the glow.

Roentgen named the new radiation X rays. He found that these rays could pass through many materials, such as wood and cloth. They could even go through the soft parts of the body and cast shadows of the bones on a fluorescent screen. Soon doctors were using the rays when setting broken bones. Today you may have a chest X ray when you get a physical examination, and your dentist probably takes X rays of your teeth at regular intervals. X rays are also used as a security measure in airports to examine the contents of suitcases and other packages.

Gamma Rays

Not long after Roentgen's discovery, it was found that certain minerals continually emit radiation that is even more penetrating than X rays. The work of the French scientists Marie and Pierre Curie led to the discovery of radium and other chemical elements that send out these rays. This is called natural radioactivity. Most of the other elements are not naturally radioactive. But when they are placed in a nuclear reactor, they change to radioisotopes, which continue to give off strong radiations for some time.

Part of the radiation is in the form of gamma rays, which, on the average, are more than a thousand times shorter than X rays—shorter than the width of an atom. Gamma rays have frequencies of about one hundred million trillion cycles per second and can easily pierce through materials like concrete and steel. Nuclear explosions release gamma rays that can destroy living cells and cause radiation sickness. However, they are also used by physicians to kill cancerous or diseased cells in the body.

▶ POLARIZED LIGHT

Maxwell's equations also allow for a kind of light called polarized light. For example, the electric field of a particular light ray may be moving up and down while the magnetic field moves from left to right. We can describe that ray as having up-down polarization. Another light ray may have the electric field moving from left to right while the magnetic field moves up and down.

We can say that ray has left-right polarization. Or we may imagine the polarization direction of a ray at any angle between up and down or left and right.

If a light source puts out all its rays in the same direction of polarization, the light is called polarized. If the rays have random polarizations, it is unpolarized.

▶ THE PARTICLE THEORY RETURNS

Because of Maxwell's work, scientists were now convinced that light was an electromagnetic wave. It appeared to be the end of the particle-or-wave debate, but it was not. Toward the end of the 1800's, the German physicist Max Planck discovered a new way to explain some peculiar results in the study of radiation from hot bodies.

The Quantum Theory

Every object, no matter how hot or cold, produces some electromagnetic radiation. If an object is hot enough, it radiates visible light. In the late 1800's scientists were measuring the spectra of radiating bodies, examining how much energy is radiated at each wavelength. They found that although the theory they were using was in very good agreement with the measured spectrum in the visible light range, it matched very poorly in the ultraviolet. The theory predicted a rapid increase of intensity in the ultraviolet part of the spectrum. However, the experiment showed that the intensity was actually decreasing instead.

Planck devised a theory that explained this spectrum mathematically. However, it required light energy to be radiated in packets, which he called quanta (singular: quantum, from the Latin word for "bundle"). The energy of each quantum was mathematically equal to the frequency of the light wave times a value that came to be known as Planck's constant.

Planck's ideas started a whole new line of scientific thinking in what came to be called quantum theory, or **quantum mechanics**.

Planck's quantum theory was first presented in December 1900. It surprised scientists by bringing back the old particle theory of light in a different form. Planck's constant was regarded primarily as a clever mathematical device to explain the spectrum of light radiation from hot bodies, but scientists did not view quanta as real. Five years later they were forced to take quanta more seriously.

The Photoelectric Effect

In 1905 the German scientist Albert Einstein applied Planck's theory to a recently discovered phenomenon called the photoelectric effect.

When light shines on certain metals, it releases electrons from the metal and creates an electric current. This is called photoelectricity. When the American physicist Robert Millikan studied this phenomenon, he discovered that applying a high enough electrical voltage, called the stopping potential, to the metal would completely halt the photoelectricity. Even the most intense light would fail to free electrons from the metal. The current could be started again, however, by changing to a source of higher-frequency light (more toward the violet and ultraviolet portion of the spectrum), no matter how dim.

Einstein realized that if light really came in quantized packages, Millikan's discovery would make sense. When a light quantum struck the metal, an electron would absorb its energy and would fly off, carrying that energy as kinetic energy (energy of motion). The stopping potential would be like an electrical hill. If the quantum had enough energy, the freed electron would be able to clear the hill, and a current would flow. Otherwise, no matter how many electrons absorbed quanta, the result would be nothing but a lot of electrons that do not quite escape from the metal—and thus no current would be produced.

Using Planck's theory, Einstein calculated the energy of the light quanta. Then he computed the energy necessary to clear the stopping potential. The results were the same. The photoelectric effect demonstrated that Planck's quanta were far more than just a mathematical invention. They were real. Light came in packets of energy—particles called photons—just as surely as it came in electromagnetic waves.

Today, as noted earlier in this article, scientists agree that light has both a wave nature and a particle nature.

Biographical information on Planck, Einstein, and Millikan can be found by consulting the Index.

▶ LIGHT AND MATTER

The quantum theory describes not only the behavior of light, but also the properties of atoms and subatomic particles, the building blocks of all matter. Since it was no longer possible to avoid the conclusion that light has both wave and particle properties, scientists posed a new question: Do electrons and other particles have wave-like properties?

One of the first scientists to show how quantum theory could be used to understand the behavior and structure of atoms was the Danish physicist Niels Bohr. Bohr's research in the early 1900's involved working with a particular kind of spectrum. (A biography of Bohr can be found in Volume B.)

Line Spectra

Sunlight or radiation from a hot body, such as a lamp filament, can be dispersed by passing it through a prism or a raindrop. The colors spread out and blend into one another with no breaks between colors. This spread is called a **continuous spectrum**.

Although light with a continuous spectrum is most familiar to us in everyday life, you have also seen light with a different kind of

A popular kind of display lighting uses neon and other gases that emit colored light when an electric current is sent through them.

a line spectrum whose frequencies follow a simple mathematical relationship. For these reasons, Bohr set out to see if he could discover a way to understand the spectrum of hydrogen using the newly discovered quantum. Bohr's idea was to describe an atom as a miniature solar system, with electrons carrying a negative charge in orbit around a positively charged nucleus. This is called the Bohr Model of the atom.

The Bohr Model had one serious problem, which Bohr himself recognized. According to the laws of electromagnetism, when a charged particle moves in a curved path (such as the curved orbit of an electron), it radiates electromagnetic waves and loses energy. This energy loss would cause the elec-

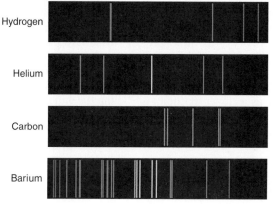

Hydrogen

Helium

Carbon

Barium

A line spectrum appears as a pattern of bright lines of color separated by dark areas. Each element produces its own unique pattern; thus line spectra can be used to identify substances in laboratory analyses.

spectrum. A number of stores and other businesses use signs with colored lighting. The colors are created by passing electricity through a gas-filled tube. A tube filled with neon gas produces a bright red light. Other colors are produced by other gases and metallic vapors, such as mercury and sodium.

Only certain frequencies are present in the light emitted by each different kind of material, and only certain colors will show up in its spectrum. When the light from one of these gas-filled tubes is dispersed, the resulting spectrum is a series of bright narrow lines of different colors separated by dark spaces. This is called a **line spectrum**, or an emission spectrum. Because each element or material produces its own pattern of spectrum lines, line spectra can be used to identify which materials are present in a given sample.

The Bohr Model

Hydrogen is the simplest of all atoms— with only one electron and one proton. It has

tron to spiral inward into the nucleus, and that would be the end of the atom.

So Bohr invented a rule. Electrons in certain special orbits, he proposed, do not radiate. What makes such orbits special? If you multiply the mass of the electron by its speed, and then multiply that by the circumference of the orbit, you get Planck's constant, or twice Planck's constant, or three times Planck's constant, and so forth.

From that model Bohr developed a formula for the energy level of each special, or "allowed," orbit. To go from one orbit to another, the electron must either absorb or emit a photon. The energy of that photon must be equal to the gain or loss of energy between the orbits. Knowing the photon's energy and Planck's constant, Bohr computed the frequency of the light that would be produced.

Considering all the allowed orbits, Bohr computed the line spectrum of hydrogen. The computed spectrum matched the actual measured spectrum. With Bohr's successful theory, quantum mechanics was established as the basis of understanding all matter and energy in the universe. After Bohr's work, other scientists continued to work on quantum theory, developing it more completely. A fuller understanding of atomic spectra now requires us to think of an electron as having both particle-like and wave-like properties—an idea that first emerged from the study of light.

▶ USING OUR KNOWLEDGE OF LIGHT

Using devices called spectroscopes, often attached to other instruments, scientists study light to learn about many different fields, especially chemistry and astronomy. They have also used their knowledge of light to create lasers, which produce a special kind of light that has certain advantages over ordinary light.

Absorption Spectra and Astronomy

Most of our knowledge about the makeup of stars comes from an examination of the

Bohr Model of the Atom

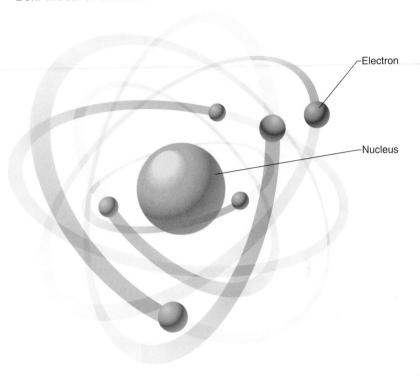

How an Atom Emits Light

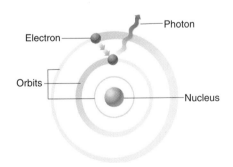

When an electron falls from an outer orbit to an inner orbit, it loses energy. This energy is emitted as a quantum of light, or photon.

dark lines that appear within their continuous spectra. These lines come about because the outside of a star is much cooler than its interior. Light created in the interior is absorbed by the atoms in the outer part of a star. The absorbed light has exactly the same spectrum that would be produced by those atoms if they were hot. This is called an **absorption spectrum**.

An absorption spectrum, like a line spectrum, can be used to identify elements. Thus the absorption spectrum of the sun, which is made up mostly of hydrogen and helium, has dark lines that match the spectra of those two elements, as well as several others. Because helium does not react chemically with any other atom, it was unknown until it was discovered in the absorption spectrum of the sun. Its name comes from *helios*, the Greek word for "sun." (You will find an image of the sun's absorption spectrum in the article SUN in Volume S.)

When a source of light moves toward us or away from us at very high speed, we can detect its motion by changes in the frequency of its light waves. The frequency change is simi-

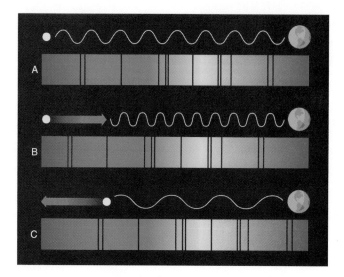

Compared with the spectrum of a star at rest in relation to Earth (A), the absorption spectrum of a star moving toward Earth (B) shows a shift to the blue end of the spectrum. The spectrum of a star moving away from Earth (C) shows a red shift. The shift can be seen by comparing the spectrum lines.

lar to what happens when you listen to the whistle of a passing train. The frequency, or pitch, of the whistle is higher when the train approaches and lower when it is going away. This is called the Doppler effect, after the Austrian physicist Christian Doppler, who explained it in 1842.

The absorption spectrum of a star shifts toward a higher frequency when the star is moving toward Earth. This is called a blue shift. When a star is moving away from Earth, the spectrum shifts toward a lower frequency. This is a red shift.

After years of observing the spectra of stars and galaxies, the American astronomer Edwin Hubble announced in 1929 that all stars outside our own galaxy and the neighboring galaxies have red shifts. The farther from us a galaxy is, the greater is its red shift, and the faster it is moving away from Earth. Hubble concluded that the whole universe is expanding at a measurable rate.

Lasers

The name "laser" is a shortened form of the term "light amplification through stimulated emission of radiation." What is meant by this term?

Lasers work because of the energy levels of atoms in matter. A laser device contains an active material that produces light. That material absorbs energy, causing huge numbers of electrons to go into a higher than usual energy level, called an excited state. An atom with these high-energy electrons is called an excited atom.

When an electron in an excited atom falls back to a lower level of energy, called the ground state, it produces a photon. This photon passes by another excited atom and stimulates the electron there to fall back to its ground state. That releases another photon in perfect step with the first photon. This process repeats until a highly focused, high-energy beam of light emerges from the device. This is laser light, that is, light that has been amplified because of the stimulation of atoms within the device.

Lasers have many practical applications in a wide range of professions, including medicine, science, business, and industry. (For more information about lasers, refer to the article LASERS in Volume L.)

ALFRED B. (FRED) BORTZ
Author, science books for children

See also COLOR; LASERS; LENSES; MICROSCOPES; MIRAGE; OPTICAL INSTRUMENTS; PHOTOELECTRICITY; RADIATION; RELATIVITY; TELESCOPES; X RAYS.

At a supermarket checkout, a laser beam scans the Universal Products Code, a pattern of lines and bars by which a product and its price are identified.

LIGHTHOUSES

Thousands of years ago, the Egyptians kindled fires on high hilltops to guide their ships at night. As water traffic increased on the Nile River, the Egyptians built stone towers to serve as lighthouses. Priests tended the flames that burned all night in the towers. The priests and the guiding fires were both considered holy by the ancient Egyptian mariners.

About 280 B.C. the Egyptians began to construct the tallest lighthouse ever built in ancient—or modern—times. This was the Pharos of Alexandria, one of the seven wonders of the ancient world. The lighthouse, built on the island of Pharos near Alexandria, was over 120 meters (400 feet) high. At the top of the tower, open fires were kept burning. They served as a beacon for Mediterranean voyagers for about 1,500 years.

Today most nations operate some form of lighthouse, to help mariners at night determine the positions of their ships. Lighthouses are located in fixed positions at known locations. Each lighthouse has its own identifying flashing signal. Lighthouse engineers know the amount of pressure that winds and waves cause on any surface area. They erect buildings and beacons that can outlast the pounding of seas and the battering of storms.

▶ LIGHTHOUSE CONSTRUCTION

John Smeaton, a British engineer, constructed the first modern lighthouse in 1759. This was built on a submerged (underwater) foundation—the famous Eddystone Rock outside Plymouth, England. The lighthouse was made of huge blocks of interlocking stones held together with bars of iron. Smeaton's basic design for building a lighthouse on an underwater foundation has been copied by every country throughout the world.

Lighthouses are built on mud, on soft sand, on lonely sections of rockbound land jutting out to sea, and on rocks that are seldom above water. Lighthouses are built where there is a good view of the ocean, so that the light is visible over great areas. Lighthouses built on shoals, coral reefs, and sandbanks are usually made of masonry and concrete. Cylinder, or hollow-caisson, construction is used for underwater foundations that support the lighthouse towers. Huge steel cylinders are riveted or welded together on shore, towed out to sea

Portland Head Light, commissioned by George Washington, is Maine's oldest lighthouse. Completed in 1791, it towers 31 meters (101 feet) above the pounding surf.

on a barge, and then slipped into the water. One end stands on the sea bottom, and the other is above the surface of the water.

▶ LIGHTS

Lighthouse beacons have ranged from primitive signal fires to candles, oil lamps, and electric incandescent bulbs many times more powerful than household bulbs.

Augustin Fresnel, a French physicist, designed the first modern lighthouse lens in 1822. The Fresnel lens concentrates the light beam and makes it visible for many miles. This type of lens is still used today.

The lens is made of glass held together by bronze fittings, with from 1 to 24 inner circles called bull's-eyes. Triangular prisms of glass are placed around the bull's-eyes. The lens, driven by a suspended weight, a clockwork motor, or a small electric motor, rotates smoothly. As the lens rotates, each bull's-eye sends out a shaft of light. Unlimited combinations are obtained by using different numbers of bull's-eyes and different speeds of rotation. Some lights burn steadily. Others go on and off. With a flashing light, the period of light is shorter than the period of darkness.

With an occulting light, the period of light is longer than the period of darkness. In an equal-interval light, the periods of light and darkness are the same.

Navigation lights are white, red, green, or a combination of these colors. A ship's captain, after sighting and timing a light with a stopwatch, consults a light list. The captain identifies the light, takes an accurate bearing, and figures out the ship's exact position.

Electric incandescent lamps use bulbs of up to 1,500 watts each. The bulbs are placed inside the lens. Lighthouses using electric lamps were once also equipped with kerosene lamps, in case of electricity failures during storms. Today generators and storage batteries provide emergency electric power.

In isolated, wave-swept places and treacherous shoals where it is impossible for lighthouse keepers to live, automatic acetylene gas burners were formerly used. These brilliant lights were able to flash 100 times a minute. The burners had valves that automatically turned them on every evening and off every morning. Today batteries and electric eyes have replaced acetylene burners. Lights go on automatically at night and off at daybreak.

Ambrose Light, off New York Harbor, has a beacon that can be seen for about 30 kilometers (18 miles).

SOUND GUIDEPOSTS

When fog engulfs the sea, a light, no matter how bright, is of little help to the mariner. Sound must then be used to guide ships.

During the 1700's, lighthouse keepers fired cannons once every hour to warn ships of danger during a fog. Some lighthouse keepers rang bells. Today fog signals have been perfected so that warning sounds can be heard far out at sea.

Fog signals have different sounds and their own identifying numbers of blasts. Foghorns with deep, steady tones and sirens that sound like fire engine signals give fog warnings. The diaphone, one of the most effective fog signals, has two tones—a high screech and a low grunt. The high note can be heard for 11 kilometers (7 miles). The low note can be heard even farther. Lighthouse stations also use radio beacons that transmit warning signals through the densest fog.

LIGHTSHIPS

Lightships are positioned where lighthouses are impossible to erect. Lightships carry the same warning equipment as light stations. Lights, radio beacons, and radar are used for guidance. Lightships go nowhere. They are anchored in place with chains and heavy anchors except when they are moving to or from stations.

Lightships are expensive to maintain, so they are not used much today. The last United States lightship was anchored off the island of Nantucket, Massachusetts. It was removed from service in 1984. Some lightships were replaced by platforms called light towers or by large buoys.

LIGHTHOUSE AUTHORITY

In the United States, lighthouses, lightships, and light towers are under the jurisdiction of the Coast Guard, which patrols the seacoast and the Great Lakes. The Coast Guard also operates electronic aids to navigation in some other countries, including Spain, Iceland, Turkey, Japan, and several African nations.

Lights that are staffed by trained civilian personnel or Coast Guard members are officially called light stations. Lights that have no staff or only part-time help are usually referred to as lighthouses. A civilian employed part-time by the Coast Guard to attend a light station is called a lamplighter. A civilian employed full-time is called a keeper.

Because of its historical significance, Boston Lighthouse, in the harbor of Boston, Massachusetts, is the only remaining United States lighthouse with a staff. All other lighthouses in the United States now operate automatically and thus require no crew.

In the past, a lighthouse crew had many responsibilities. They reported weather conditions, checked equipment, and observed the surrounding sea. If fog rolled in and decreased visibility enough to endanger ships and mariners, the fog signal was started.

On calm, clear days, the staff was assigned duties outside the light station. Care was taken to keep a light station clean both inside and outside. Machinery, floors, and equipment shone. Often it would take a whole day just to clean and polish the lens. This and the lantern room windows had to be spotless so the light would be as bright as possible. The whitewashed look of a light station was kept up by frequent painting and scrubbing. Some light stations had quarters for the families of station personnel.

Reviewed by AIDS TO NAVIGATION BRANCH
United States Coast Guard

Lighting is essential to the life of a big city, or even a small town. People depend on it in homes, offices, factories, stores, restaurants, hospitals, streets—everywhere.

LIGHTING

The earliest humans had no control over their light. In order to see, they had to rely on the sun, the moon, and the stars. Once humans learned to use fire, they struggled to break the blanket of night with a flickering torch or the small, fluttering flame of an oil lamp. These were the first forms of artificial lighting.

Today most artificial lighting is electric. It makes it possible for people to perform all sorts of tasks at any time under easy seeing conditions. If a room is dark, a person can flip a switch and sit down to read a book or sew. Outdoor lighting lets us watch a baseball game or attend an outdoor concert at night.

Controlled artificial lighting also provides safety and allows emergency tasks to be performed at any time of day or night. Streetlights, automobile headlights, airport signal lights, and ship beacons help us travel in safety. In modern hospitals good lighting makes it possible for surgeons to perform operations at any hour. In factories good lighting reduces the number of accidents.

In addition to practical uses, artificial lighting has decorative and creative applications. At home, strings of colored lights are used to decorate a Christmas tree. A small spotlight can draw attention to a valued painting. On storefronts and street corners, neon lights bent into the shapes of letters are familiar nighttime advertising signs. Flash equipment makes photography possible in the dark. Floor lights and spotlights illuminate the theater stage and can be used for dramatic effect. Elaborate, colorful light shows entertain audiences at rock concerts, and special lighting effects are an attraction in dance clubs and other night spots.

▶ PRE-ELECTRIC LIGHTING

The earliest lighting of all came from wood fires. If a person wanted to have light away from the fire, one of the burning sticks could be picked up and used as a torch. People learned that torches dipped into animal fat lasted longer and threw a stronger light. Torches were used for many, many years.

About the year A.D. 450, tarred torches were used to light the streets of Antioch. This Greek city in the Near East was the first in the world to light its streets. Torches like these continued to be used into the Middle Ages.

Another natural torch material was the candlefish, which was used in Alaska. The candlefish was dried and held in a split stick. It was so oily that it held a good flame. The stormy petrel, a seabird found in the Shetland Islands, was used in the same way.

Some American Indians used pine knots for light. The first Europeans to settle in North America followed that practice. Pine-knot torches were made of thin slices of wood from pine trees. They were so full of pitch and turpentine that they burned with an especially bright flame.

Other kinds of lighting before electricity were oil lamps, rushlights, candles, lanterns, kerosene lamps, and gas lighting.

Oil Lamps

The first oil lamps were open stone dishes with wicks of reeds or plant fibers. These lamps supplied the light used by Stone Age people when they painted pictures on cave walls.

Lamps have been found from as long ago as 3000 B.C. Some of these early lamps were made from shells or from the skulls of small animals. Conch shells were especially useful for lamps. They have a perfect shape for holding a good amount of oil and for supporting a wick. Hardened clay dishes were used next. When metalworking was developed, lamp makers made metal lamps.

The first oil used in these early lamps came from animals. In northern regions of the world, the fat of birds, whales, and fishes was important. In warm regions, vegetable oils from olives, linseed, grape seeds, and coconuts were used. Butter made from water-buffalo milk is still used for oil lamps in India. Fish oils are still used in South America and other parts of the world.

In early America, oil lamps were filled with whale oil. The demand for whale oil helped make whaling an important industry in the United States in the first half of the 19th century. As the demand for whale oil grew, better lamps were invented for burning it. A lamp with two wicks, which gave a better light than one-wick lamps, was made by Benjamin Franklin.

Rushlights

A waxed reed, something like a candle, was called a rushlight. Traces of rushlights have been found in Europe from before the Middle Ages. A rush is a grasslike plant that thrives in marshland. It has a long branchless stem and flattened leaves or a thick, tufted tip. Rushes grow in many parts of the world, including New England, where they often were used for lighting in the early colonial period.

STONE AGE LIGHTING

STONE LAMP

SHELL LAMP

BURNING BRAND

TWISTED BIRCH-BARK TORCH

CANDLEFISH TORCH

LIGHTING FROM THE GREEKS THROUGH THE MIDDLE AGES

EGYPTIAN LAMP

MEDIEVAL LANTERN

ROMAN LAMP

GREEK TORCH

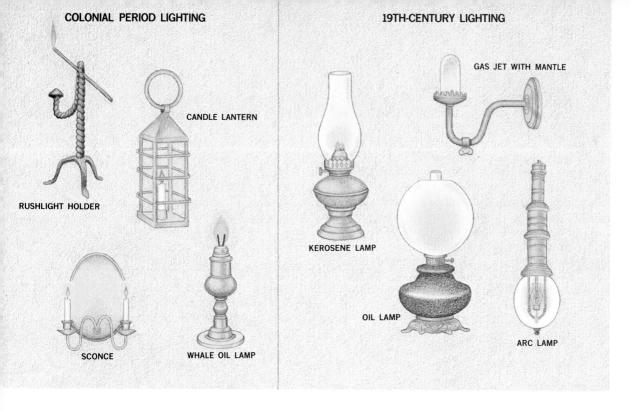

RUSHLIGHT HOLDER

CANDLE LANTERN

SCONCE

WHALE OIL LAMP

GAS JET WITH MANTLE

KEROSENE LAMP

OIL LAMP

ARC LAMP

To make a rushlight, part of the rush stem was peeled away, leaving a narrow section that held together the pith or center stem. This round stem was dipped several times in melted fat or tallow (fat from cattle or sheep) and served as a wick.

The flame of the rushlight was about twice as large as the flame of a kitchen match. The rush wick ordinarily burned to ashes without being messy, but sometimes charred chunks would fall from it. Rushlights were very cheap and easy to make but were replaced by candles whenever possible.

Candles

The first candles apparently were reeds or stalks filled with tallow or beeswax from hives. They were much like rushlights. The ancient Egyptians had wickless candles made of lumps of tallow wrapped with rags to keep them from melting apart as they burned. The Romans used candles made with sticks.

Candles were made in decorative styles and colors. Some, in glass containers, were used for religious purposes. Some candles were 3 meters (10 feet) tall and lasted for years.

One trade secret among candlemakers was discovered about 1874. Several strands of a woven wick were treated with a chemical, nitrate of bismuth. This made the end of the burnt wick bend over and burn up completely. Before this, candles had to be trimmed every few minutes or they smoked badly. Trimming was done with a scissorlike tool with a box on one side. The box caught the bits of wick that the scissor blades snipped off.

The material used for candles in the early days of America was tallow, or if the family was wealthy, beeswax or spermaceti. Spermaceti was a wax from the sperm whale. Most candles today are made of wax combined with stearin, a product made from paraffin. Stearin increases the burning rate because it makes the wax melt faster.

Lanterns

Lanterns, protective cases for lights, were common from at least the 5th century B.C. They were lighted with candles or oil lamps. Lanterns were designed in many different shapes. Cylindrical lanterns and square types with conical tops were popular. They were made of many materials—metal, wood, pottery, and even leather.

With their feeble flames and dark frames, lanterns could have given but little light. Sometimes the sides of the lantern were fitted with thin plates of mica or horn, through which the light could shine. Later on, glass was used.

Candle lanterns held three, sometimes four, candles, but most often only one. Before glass-sided lanterns were perfected, tin lanterns were typically used. These had holes punched in their sides. The light shining from hundreds of tiny holes made a beautiful, lacy pattern on the ground, but the light was almost too feeble to allow a person to walk safely or ride horseback. Later lanterns had "bull's-eyes" of glass with thick centers. They gave a spotlight effect.

Ships' lanterns were made of heavy glass and metal. Sometimes the lantern was attached to the compass on a stand called a binnacle. Other lanterns aboard ship were (and still are) red- and green-sided. This tells sailors which way a ship is headed.

In wealthier homes in the 17th and 18th centuries, elaborate lanterns were used in halls and entryways. Large dining rooms might have three lanterns hanging from the ceiling. Each time one had to be lighted or put out, a servant had to climb a stepladder.

Today electric lanterns are very important in railroading. Railroad lanterns are carried by brakers who ride in the caboose at the end of a long train of freight cars. The braker swings a lantern a certain number of times to signal the engineer in the locomotive to go ahead, to back up, or to stop.

Kerosene Lamps

Before 1859 the best lamp oil that money could buy was whale oil. Unrefined petroleum had been used in lamps for many years, but it gave a feeble and dirty flame. In 1859 petroleum oil was discovered in Pennsylvania. Shortly before this it had been learned that kerosene could be separated out of petroleum.

Kerosene gave a better light than had ever been known before. People could more easily read by it in the evening. Oil refining became an active business, supplying kerosene around the world.

At first, kerosene was burned in open lamps. The open flame flickered and was dangerous to use. Then glass chimneys were made for kerosene lamps. The flame became steady and gave more light. With a glass chimney to protect it from the wind and a little roof to protect it from the rain, kerosene lamps could be used outdoors for streetlights. A lamplighter had the job of lighting them every evening and turning them out in the morning.

Kerosene lamps had flat wicks. By the turn of a small knob, the wick could be raised and lowered and the lamp's light could be adjusted. This was a great advantage over other lighting. A circular wick, which allowed air to circulate inside as well as outside of it, made a lamp that burned much brighter. This was the Argand oil lamp, invented in Geneva by Aimé Argand in 1784. It was used in lighthouses and in great oil chandeliers, as well as in homes and offices.

In homes of the early 1800's, candles and oil lamps were rival light sources. In the average home there was a large oil lamp on a table in the center of the living room. There father read his paper, mother sewed or knitted, and the children read or played games. But when the children went upstairs to bed, they carried a candlestick to light their way. Candles were safer than oil lamps to carry about. If an oil lamp was dropped, the burning oil might set the house on fire.

In areas of the world where there is no electricity, kerosene lamps are still used. And in many homes with electricity, especially homes in country areas, kerosene lamps are kept on hand. When the electricity goes out in heavy storms, the kerosene lamps are used. Kerosene lanterns are sometimes used on highways to show detours or repairs in the roadway. Even now there are farmers who carry a lantern to the barn when they are milking the cows or doing other chores.

Gas Lighting

Late in the 1700's, people learned how to make gas from coal. With this new discovery, people began to think how they might use gas for lighting. Many experiments were made. By 1813, Westminster Bridge in London was lighted with gas. The bright, unusual lights astonished the people. But not many people used this new lighting in their homes until about 50 years later. The main problem was that the pipes in which gas traveled were leaky. Leaking gas was very dangerous and frightened people. Gas in large quantities makes people suffocate and also explodes very easily. But gaslight was so much brighter than kerosene light that it was soon used for lighting streets.

Manufactured gas was made by heating coal or by distilling petroleum. Many natural-gas wells were found as well. Both manufactured

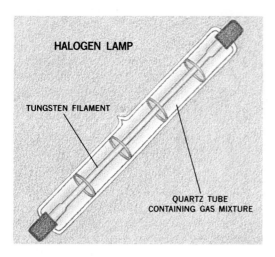

HALOGEN LAMP

TUNGSTEN FILAMENT

QUARTZ TUBE CONTAINING GAS MIXTURE

gas and natural gas were growing competitors of oil in the United States up to 1910. Fishtail-shaped gas jets on the ends of pipe brackets that swung out from the wall were the pride of many householders. But the bare flames were dangerous, and they flickered. They made sooty spots on the ceiling. Later, white-glass and clear-glass globes that enclosed the flames made cleaner gas lamps.

In 1885, Carl Auer von Welsbach of Austria invented the gas mantle. This was a loosely woven cotton cover for gas jets. The threads were filled with chemicals. They glowed so brightly that the light was increased about five times. This mantle is the one used in gasoline lanterns today, and also in the post lanterns in some front yards.

Gas was seldom used outside cities. It was difficult and expensive to lay the gas piping for long distances. Even now, when gas is a common fuel for heating and cooling, it is not often used in rural communities except where bottled gas can be supplied. Electricity is used instead.

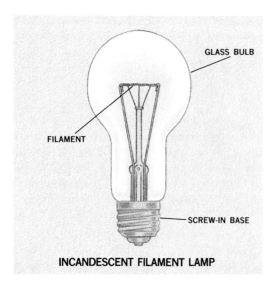

GLASS BULB

FILAMENT

SCREW-IN BASE

INCANDESCENT FILAMENT LAMP

▶ELECTRIC LIGHTING

The electrical lighting industry began with Thomas Alva Edison's first practical incandescent lamp in 1879. Many scientists knew how electricity worked. They had been trying to make electric lamps for a number of years. But no one had been able to make one that worked well. Work done by a British physicist and chemist, Sir Joseph Wilson Swan, helped Edison in his invention.

Edison tried again and again before he found how to make a lamp filament last more than a few hours. He used hundreds of materials. One day he even tried a whisker from the beard of one of his assistants. Finally he tried sewing thread from Mrs. Edison's sewing basket. He carbonized the thread. It worked! That first lamp lasted for 40 hours. Edison and his assistants watched it all day and half the night.

For more information on Edison, see the article EDISON, THOMAS ALVA in Volume E of this encyclopedia.

Filament Lamps

The type of electric lamp made by Edison is called a filament lamp. A filament lamp lights when a thread inside it heats up to incandescence—that is, when it gets so hot that it glows with light.

There have been big improvements in filament lamps since the time of Edison. Later filament threads were made of carbonized wood from selected Japanese bamboo, and then from carbonized cellulose. (Cellulose is found in cotton or wood fiber.) But carbon filaments could not operate at a high enough temperature to be very efficient. Tungsten filaments, introduced about 1904, were more efficient, but they broke easily. In 1910 a way was found to draw tungsten wire through a die (mold). This made a strong tungsten filament. As a result, tungsten replaced carbon as filament in incandescent bulbs.

Edison's lamps were evacuated. That is, the air was pumped out of the bulbs, creating a vacuum. Then the bulbs were sealed. This was done to keep the filament from burning up by combining with oxygen in the air. But the filaments still evaporated. When the filament became hot, particles escaped from its surface and settled on the glass of the lamp. After a time the inside of the lamp became blackened by these particles. Finally the filament broke in two, so that no current could pass through. The lamp was "burned out."

Then in 1913 an American scientist and engineer named Irving Langmuir filled a lamp with a chemically inactive, or inert, gas. The pressure of the gas tended to keep tungsten particles from escaping from the filament, so the lamp lasted much longer than a vacuum lamp.

Edison himself had experimented with lamps filled with the gas nitrogen, another gas that does not readily combine with other elements. But his experiments had not been successful. To get a good light from a nitrogen-filled lamp, the filament had to be thick. Yet a thick filament used up too much current. Langmuir solved this problem, too. Taking a thin tungsten wire, he coiled it into a spiral, like a coil spring. The spiral, which had as much surface area as a thick filament, glowed brightly. Yet the thin wire of which it was made drew little current.

Today all filament lamps are filled with chemically inactive gases, usually a mixture of nitrogen and argon. Lamps larger than 25 watts have coiled filaments.

Halogen Lamps

A special type of tungsten-filament lamp—called a quartz-iodine, or halogen, lamp—takes the form of a short, narrow tube or a small bulb. The lamp contains a gas mixture that includes a small amount of one of the halogen gases—usually iodine. The iodine, when hot, combines with tiny tungsten atoms that have evaporated from the filament. The result is a colorless gas called tungsten iodide. This gas, in turn, is broken down by the heat inside the bulb. The tungsten atoms then are replated on the filament, and the whole cycle starts over again.

Because of the extremely high temperature needed in the halogen lamp, glass cannot be used for the bulb. Only quartz can withstand the extreme heat. However, because the tungsten filament stays undamaged, the halogen lamp lives longer than an ordinary incandescent bulb. It also burns brighter while using the same amount of electricity. A 500-watt quartz-iodine tube is only as large as a lead pencil.

Halogen lamps are extremely useful because they produce a brilliant light from a small bulb. The first ones were used on the wing tips of airplanes. Halogen lamps are also used for floodlighting and to illuminate athletic stadiums at night. Most new automobiles today have halogen-gas headlights.

Carbon Arc Lamps

Edison's filament bulb was not the first electric lamp. The electric arc lamp was developed several decades earlier, but it had a number of disadvantages.

A simple arc lamp was made of two carbon rods about 15 millimeters (½ inch) thick. The rods were placed vertically so that the ends touched each other when the current was off. When the switch was closed, the rods were mechanically drawn apart. This drew an arc of light between them. The arc light was a continuous spark that was as bright as a tiny sun. To keep the arc stream steady, the rods had to be the same distance apart. Because the carbon rods burned away rather rapidly, a feeding device was necessary to maintain that distance between them. The first arc lights burned in the open air, but later ones had glass globes.

Except in some factories and other large workplaces, arc lighting was not practical to use indoors. It made smoke and fumes. But the lights were much bigger than Edison's light. This made arc lighting a favorite for lighting streets in the 1890's and early 1900's. Today high-intensity arc lamps are used for motion-picture projection, searchlights, and large theater spotlights.

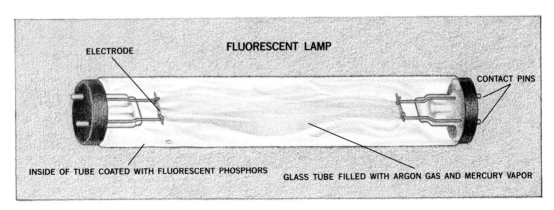

FLUORESCENT LAMP

ELECTRODE

CONTACT PINS

INSIDE OF TUBE COATED WITH FLUORESCENT PHOSPHORS

GLASS TUBE FILLED WITH ARGON GAS AND MERCURY VAPOR

Fluorescent Lamps

A fluorescent lamp is a long glass tube with a filament at each end. The tube is filled with mercury vapor. Coating the inside surface of the glass are powders called phosphors.

When the lamp is switched on, the electric current passes from one end of the lamp to the other through the mercury vapor. The vapor conducts electricity as if it were an invisible wire. When the current passes through the mercury vapor, it produces ultraviolet radiation, which is invisible. When this radiation hits the phosphors that line the tube, the phosphors change it to visible light.

The fluorescent lamp was developed in the 1930's. It proved to be highly practical for indoor illumination. Fluorescent lighting is common in schools, stores, and other large buildings. In homes it is used most often in kitchens, bathrooms, and laundry areas. The quality of light emitted by the fluorescent tube makes it well suited for desk lamps and draftsman's lamps.

Because fluorescent light comes from a long tube, it is spread out, or diffused, as compared with light from an incandescent filament, which is small and localized. Well-diffused light produces almost no shadows or bright spots, and is often called **soft light**.

Fluorescent light is more efficient than incandescent light. That is, more visible light is produced for each watt of electric energy consumed. This means that for a given amount of light, fluorescent lamps cost less to operate, produce less heat, and help conserve energy. Thus, less cooling (usually air conditioning) is needed in interiors illuminated with fluorescent light.

Neon, Mercury, and Sodium Lamps

Before the introduction of fluorescent lighting in the 1930's, several other gas- or vapor-filled lamps had been developed. These were simpler than fluorescent lamps because they did not involve the use of phosphors. Electricity simply passed through the gas or vapor, producing colored light.

One of the earliest of these lamps was a tube that was filled with neon gas. When high-voltage electricity was applied, the neon gave off a deep red light. Neon tube lamps were not practical for indoor illumination, but they found widespread outdoor use in glowing, lettered signs.

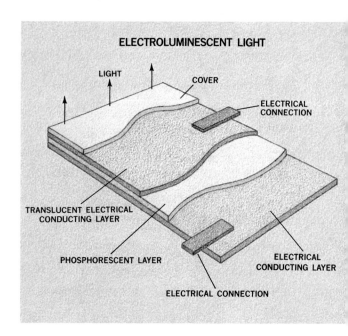

ELECTROLUMINESCENT LIGHT

LIGHT

COVER

ELECTRICAL CONNECTION

TRANSLUCENT ELECTRICAL CONDUCTING LAYER

PHOSPHORESCENT LAYER

ELECTRICAL CONDUCTING LAYER

ELECTRICAL CONNECTION

Meanwhile, experiments were being conducted with bulbs containing mercury vapor or sodium vapor. In these lamps, electricity is released in a short arc between two electrodes. The vapors produce colored light. Mercury lamps give off a bluish green light. Under this light, red looks nearly black, and people look like ghosts. Sodium lamps give off a yellowish light.

Sodium and mercury lamps found application in streets, tunnels, parking lots, and factories. Over the years, engineers have made major improvements. The color of vapor-discharge lamps was improved by the use of phosphors inside the bulb and by increasing the vapor pressure.

Electroluminescent Lamps

The electroluminescent lamp is unique. It is the first electrical device to change electricity into light without first heating a filament or creating an arc. Electroluminescent lamps look like thick pieces of plastic or plastic-coated plates. They are made in three layers, like a sandwich. The two outer layers conduct electricity; one of them is transparent. The middle layer is a coating of phosphor powder. When the current is turned on, the phosphor glows with a dim light. The color and brightness of the light depend on the frequency and voltage of the electrical current.

Lamp Research and Development

The major forms of electric lighting—incandescent, fluorescent, and vapor-discharge—continue to undergo improvement and change. Researchers are finding new ways to make light sources more energy-efficient, longer-lasting, and more compact. One example is a small fluorescent bulb that screws into an ordinary home light fixture. Scientists continue to search for a more efficient material to replace the tungsten filament, and experiment with new gases for the vapor-discharge lamp. The xenon lamp, for example, produces an intense white light.

As technology has advanced, new lighting systems have found valuable applications in many fields. One important area of development is called **fiber optics**. In fiber-optic technology, light is conducted by extremely thin, flexible glass fibers. The light enters one end of the fiber and emerges at the other end with practically no loss of energy. A number of fiber-optic instruments have been developed for use in medicine, electronic communication, astronomy, photography, and other fields. The "endoscope," for example, allows doctors to view the interior of human organs.

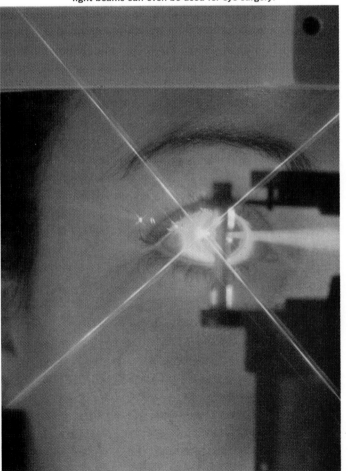

Lasers are a special form of light with uses in medicine, communications, and other fields. These narrow, intense light beams can even be used for eye surgery.

▶RULES OF GOOD LIGHTING

Most of our impressions about the world around us come by way of our eyes. In our use of artificial light from day to day, it is important that we make things easy on our eyes. Whether reading, doing homework, watching television, or playing a quiet game, it is important to control the lighting in two ways: (1) make sure there is enough light, and (2) reduce glare.

Rules of good lighting are best understood when we can measure lighting and have some idea of how much light we need. We think of a moonlit night as being very bright compared with a pitch-black night. But if you measured moonlight with a sensitive light meter, it would be only about 0.04 Dekalux (about 1/25 footcandle). Moonlight is only as strong as the light from a candle 1.5 meters (5 feet) away. After about 10 minutes in moonlight, your eyes get used to the low level. Some people try to read by moonlight. Try it some night. Your eyes will soon tire, and you will learn one principle of good lighting: It is necessary to have plenty of light to avoid eye fatigue.

In contrast to moonlight, bright summer sunshine is between 7,500 and 9,000 Dekalux (about 8,000 to 10,000 footcandles). If the air is particularly clear, sunshine can measure up to 11,000 Dekalux (12,000 footcandles). Indoors, near a window on a bright day, it may be 375 to 450 Dekalux (400 to 500 footcandles). On dull days the light in a classroom may be only a few Dekalux. Turning on the lights should bring it up to 75 Dekalux (80 footcandles) or more.

How Light Is Measured

Quantities of light are measured with a light meter similar to that used by photographers. The markings on the meter's scale are either in "footcandles" or in "lux."

One **footcandle** is the amount of illumination that falls on a flat surface 1 foot away from a light source equivalent to a standard candle.

Lux and **Dekalux** are measures of light in the metric system. One lux is the amount of light that falls on a flat surface 1 meter away from a standard candle. One Dekalux equals 10 lux, or 1.076 footcandles.

Different amounts of light are recommended for different tasks. For reading a book, about 30 Dekalux (32 footcandles) are needed. For shaving or for sewing on light-colored fabrics, 50 Dekalux (54 footcandles) are recommended; for sewing on dark fabrics, 100 Dekalux (110 footcandles) are suggested.

Glare should be avoided. It is uncomfortable for the eyes and makes seeing difficult. Glare is present when you look at a bright bulb, for example. Avoid glare reflected from your work, too. Do not place a lamp in front of you so that the rays reflect off the page and glare into your eyes. If you work near a window, place your chair so that you do not directly face the window or shadow your work.

Remember this: The proper amount of glare-free light can make your "eye work" easier and less tiring. You can work longer and with greater accuracy and comprehension.

▶ ILLUMINATING ENGINEERING

The study and practice of electric lighting has become a profession in itself. It is called illuminating engineering and is a branch of electrical engineering.

Illuminating engineers are concerned with both natural and artificial light. They develop lighting and set lighting standards for almost every kind of environment—streets, homes, offices, factories, theaters, stadiums, television and movie studios, airports, and so on. They work with architects, doctors, bulb manufacturers, and many other people to provide the best lighting for each situation. For example, the colors and materials in a room can affect the seeing comfort of the people in it. Therefore, illuminating engineers work with paint manufacturers to determine how light is reflected from walls and ceilings.

▶ THE FUTURE OF LIGHTING

In the future, lighting will be more efficient, more comfortable, and more useful. Scientists will continue to invent new light sources and lighting equipment—many of which we cannot even imagine yet.

Meanwhile, illuminating engineers will help make the most of the new technology. Increasingly, offices, factories, and schools will be designed with lighting, heating, and air-conditioning systems that are part of a single energy-efficient package. In homes of the future, attempts will be made to create lighting with the best quality, quantity, and seeing comfort. Streets, highways, parks, shopping centers, and vehicles all will be better illuminated and more colorful places in which to travel, play, work, and shop.

KARL A. STALEY
Illuminating Engineering Society
Reviewed by EDWARD A. CAMPBELL
Better Light Better Sight Bureau

See also CANDLES; EDISON, THOMAS ALVA; ELECTRIC LIGHTS; FIBER OPTICS; LANGMUIR, IRVING; LIGHT; NEON AND OTHER NOBLE GASES.

LIGHTNING.   See THUNDER AND LIGHTNING.

LILIUOKALANI.   See HAWAII (Famous People).

Outdoor sound and light shows—or *son et lumière*—are held at many historic sites. In these spectacles, stories are told with projected light images and recorded narration.

LIMA

Lima is the capital of Peru and the nation's economic, financial, and cultural center. It is one of Latin America's largest cities: Since 1940 the population of Greater Lima has increased from several hundred thousand to nearly 8 million. Nearly one-third of all Peruvians now live there.

Located in the Rímac River valley on Peru's central coast, Lima is surrounded by deserts and mountains. Rain rarely falls in Lima, but during the winter a heavy mist called the *garúa* dampens the city. Lima has had many earthquakes. It had to be almost completely rebuilt after the most serious of these earthquakes, in 1746.

Modern Lima bears little resemblance to the original Spanish colonial city, founded in 1535 by Francisco Pizarro, the Spanish conqueror of the Inca Empire. For the first 250 years of its history, Lima was the seat of the Spanish viceroyalty of Peru. The city was surrounded by a great stone wall to protect it against pirate raids. In colonial times, Lima was the center of political, economic, and religious power in Spanish South America. It was considered so important to be in Lima that criminals were often punished by being sent away to other cities.

A half century after Peru declared its independence in 1821, the great city wall was torn down. During the 1920's it was replaced by broad avenues lined with elegant buildings.

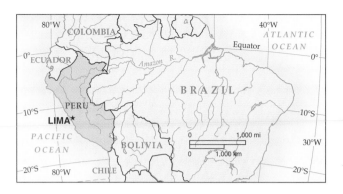

Almost 30 percent of Peru's population lives in Lima, the nation's capital. Located on Peru's central coast, it is one of Latin America's largest cities.

Since that time, Lima has again changed. Today freeways extend to suburbs such as Miraflores and San Isidro, with their modern office and apartment buildings.

During the 1960's and 1970's, Lima was one of the world's fastest-growing cities. Two-thirds of its adult residents were born elsewhere. Today the migrants, and Lima's poor in general, have founded hundreds of squatter settlements on the fringes of the city. Over time most families in these settlements have converted their bamboo homes into brick and concrete dwellings. Their determination to find a better life has changed both Lima and the country.

The Contemporary City. Contemporary Lima is a mixture of wealth and poverty. Many fine museums, theaters, and universities have made the city the cultural and educational center of Peru. Thousands of pleasure-seekers enjoy its beaches, restaurants, soccer stadiums, and race track, as well as one of the world's oldest bullrings. Most Peruvian industry is located in Greater Lima, including the adjoining port of Callao. From the city's factories come furniture, automobiles, processed foods, and cotton and woolen textiles. But many of Lima's poor are unable to find regular work. They struggle to support themselves as street vendors or hold only part-time jobs.

The presidential palace and the national parliament and ministries are all located in Lima. Peru's leaders—and the elected local officials who govern Lima—face growing demands to create more jobs and to improve the services provided to city residents.

Reviewed by HENRY DIETZ
University of Texas

LIME. See LEMON AND LIME.
LIMERICKS. See NONSENSE RHYMES.
LIMESTONE. See ROCKS (Sedimentary Rock).
LINCOLN. See NEBRASKA (Cities).

ABRAHAM LINCOLN (1809-1865)

16th President of the United States

FACTS ABOUT LINCOLN

Birthplace: Near Hodgenville, Kentucky

Religion: Christian (no specific denomination)

College Attended: None

Occupation: Lawyer

Married: Mary Todd

Children: Robert, Edward, William, Thomas (Tad)

Political Party: Whig; Republican

Office Held Before Becoming President: Congressman

President Who Preceded Him: James Buchanan

Age on Becoming President: 52

Years in the Presidency: 1861–1865 (assassinated in office; died April 15)

Vice President: Hannibal Hamlin (first term); Andrew Johnson (second term)

President Who Succeeded Him: Andrew Johnson

Age at Death: 56

Burial Place: Springfield, Illinois

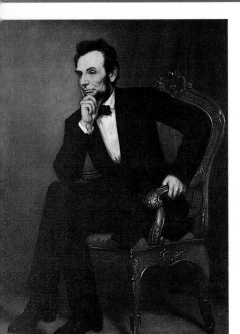

Abraham Lincoln

DURING LINCOLN'S PRESIDENCY

Above: The Confederate attack on Fort Sumter in Charleston Harbor, South Carolina (1861) marked the first hostilities of the Civil War. The Department of Agriculture was created by Congress (1862). The Homestead Act (1862) helped open up the West by offering free land to settlers. The Morrill Act (1862) provided for the establishment of land-grant colleges. The Emancipation Proclamation (1863) was the first great step toward the abolition of slavery. West Virginia (1863) and Nevada (1864) became states. *Below:* General Robert E. Lee surrendered to General Ulysses S. Grant at Appomattox Court House, Virginia (1865), effectively ending the Civil War.

LINCOLN, ABRAHAM. The election of a Republican president in 1860 provoked the Southern states of the United States to secede from the Union and led to four tragic years of civil war. In this time of grave crisis it at first seemed unfortunate that the American people had not chosen a more experienced leader. Yet the tall, awkward man from Illinois who took the presidential oath proved equal to his enormous responsibilities. Gradually, as the war progressed, Abraham Lincoln placed the mark of his greatness upon American history. He guided the nation through the perils of war to peace and reunion. He struck the fatal blow at slavery, and he reaffirmed the dignity of free people in language of simple beauty. Death came to him with dramatic violence before his work was done. But death only hastened his elevation to a place beside George Washington in the memory and gratitude of his country.

▶ EARLY YEARS

Abraham Lincoln was born on February 12, 1809, in a rude log cabin near present-day Hodgenville, Kentucky. His parents, who already had a little daughter named Sarah, were hardworking, uneducated pioneers. They probably saw nothing unusual about their son, except that he grew unusually fast. Thomas Lincoln, Abraham's father, was a man of ordinary abilities whose ambition apparently did not extend beyond owning a good farm. Like many western settlers, he tended to believe that there were better opportunities somewhere over the horizon. Of Abraham's mother, Nancy Hanks Lincoln, little is known. She and her two small children experienced the usual hardships and few pleasures of pioneer life. She must have left a mark upon Abraham's character, but the nature of her influence is lost to history.

In December 1816, the Lincolns packed their belongings and moved about 100 miles (160 kilometers) to southwestern Indiana.

They spent that winter in a rough shelter with an open side. A forest full of wild game surrounded their lonely new home. Lincoln later remembered shooting a turkey, watching for bears, and listening at night to the "panther's scream." In the spring, Abraham, now 8 years old, began to help his father in the hard daily labor of pioneering. They had to clear the land of trees, plant crops, build a permanent cabin, and split rails for fences. Lincoln became skillful in the use of the ax but never cared much for hunting and fishing. He acquired no love for the life of a farmer. It seemed to be all heavy toil with small reward.

Lincoln had little formal schooling, but he read widely as a boy and educated himself. Splitting rails for fences was one of his tasks on his father's farm.

The saddest days of Lincoln's childhood came in 1818, when his mother died and was buried in the nearby forest. A year later Thomas Lincoln married Sarah Bush Johnston, a widow with three children of her own. Between the boy and his stepmother there grew a bond of deep affection, and she lived to see him become president.

Much of Lincoln's learning was the practical kind that boys picked up from their work and play in a backwoods community. Lincoln attended school, in his own words, "by littles"—that is, only occasionally and for just a few weeks at a time. But he soon knew more than either of his parents about reading, writing, and arithmetic. School was probably what was known as a "blab school." Pupils studied their lessons aloud, and the noise could be heard some distance away. Lincoln later said that his total schooling did not amount to more than one year. But he read whatever he could lay his hands on. At home there was the Bible, and he walked long distances to borrow books like *Robinson Crusoe, Aesop's Fables*, and Weems's *Life of Washington*. In the process, Lincoln not only educated himself but became a master of the English language.

▶ YOUNG MAN IN ILLINOIS

In 1830 the Lincolns moved again, this time to Illinois. They traveled in ox-drawn wagons, with Abraham as one of the drivers, and built a cabin near Decatur. Dissatisfied there, Thomas Lincoln moved a year later to Coles County. But this time his son did not go along. Abraham Lincoln was now 22 years old. He stood 6 feet 4 inches (163 centimeters) tall and was thin but physically strong. Although he still had no definite ambition, he was ready to start life on his own.

A few years earlier, Lincoln had made a trip to New Orleans as a hired hand on a Mississippi River flatboat. Now, in the spring of 1831, he undertook a similar journey down the Mississippi. On his return he became a storekeeper in New Salem, Illinois. His friendliness, honesty, and talent for storytelling soon made him a popular local figure. He decided to enter politics, and in March 1832, he announced his candidacy for the state legislature.

At this point the Black Hawk War, an Indian war, began in northern Illinois. Lincoln volunteered and served for three months, first as the elected captain of his own company, then as a private under other commanders. But he engaged in no actual fighting. Back home by July, he had only a few weeks for his political campaign. Election day brought defeat, but Lincoln was encouraged by the fact that he had run eighth in a field of 13 candidates. Next, he and a partner opened a store in New Salem. Lincoln also became the village postmaster. The store was a failure, however, and he took up surveying to earn a living and pay his debts.

IMPORTANT DATES IN THE LIFE OF ABRAHAM LINCOLN

1809 Born near present-day Hodgenville, Kentucky, February 12.

1816 Moved to Indiana.

1831 Settled in New Salem, Illinois.

1834–42 Served in the Illinois legislature.

1837 Moved to Springfield; began law practice.

1842 Married Mary Todd.

1847–49 Served in the U.S. House of Representatives.

1858 Ran unsuccessfully for the U.S. Senate against Stephen A. Douglas; Lincoln-Douglas debates held.

1861 Inaugurated 16th president of the United States; Civil War began.

1863 Issued the final Emancipation Proclamation; delivered the Gettysburg Address.

1864 Appointed General Ulysses S. Grant commander of Union armies; was re-elected president.

1865 Inaugurated for a second term; Civil War ended; Lincoln shot by John Wilkes Booth, April 14; died in Washington, D.C., April 15.

▶ STATE LEGISLATOR AND LAWYER

In 1834 the 24-year-old Lincoln ran once more for the state legislature. This time he was successful, and Illinois voters would re-elect him for three more terms. It was also in 1834 that Lincoln began to study law. Here again he educated himself, reading borrowed law books in his spare time, and he passed the bar examination two years later. Soon after, he moved to Springfield, the new state capital, where he began his law practice.

For the next 24 years, with one brief interruption, Lincoln practiced law in Springfield. He did not grow wealthy but always earned a comfortable living. Fair and conscientious, he gave clients a feeling of confidence. Although never very learned in the law, he nevertheless knew the fundamentals well. His greatest asset in court was the ability to go directly to the heart of a matter. Long before the presidential election of 1860 he had become one of the most distinguished lawyers in Illinois.

In 1844, Lincoln began his lasting partnership with William H. Herndon. Although ten years younger than Lincoln, Herndon proved to be an excellent choice, and the two of them worked well together in both law and politics. Herndon's biography of his famous partner, known as *Herndon's Lincoln*, written many years later, is one of the classics of Lincoln literature.

▶ HUSBAND AND FATHER

Lincoln's famous romance with Ann Rutledge is apparently just a legend. He knew Ann in New Salem and was undoubtedly saddened by her death in 1835. But there is no reliable evidence that they were ever in love with each other. He did court a young woman named Mary Owens. There was a lack of enthusiasm on both sides, however, and she refused to marry him. In Springfield, Lincoln met Mary Todd, daughter of a prominent Kentucky family. She was a popular girl in local society—attractive, high-spirited, and intelligent, but somewhat temperamental. Her short and rather plump figure contrasted sharply with Lincoln's lank frame when he acted as her escort. They became engaged in 1840, then broke apart when Lincoln went through a long period of doubt and melancholy. Reconciled after a time, they were married at last on November 4, 1842.

Mary Lincoln, although not always easy to live with, was a good and loyal wife who probably spurred her husband's ambition. Their marriage had its troubled moments, but on the whole they were happy together. In 1844, Lincoln bought a house, which still stands at Eighth and Jackson streets in Springfield. There the Lincolns lived until their departure for Washington in 1861. Four children, all boys, were born to them. Robert, the oldest, later became a corporation executive and secretary of war under two presidents. Edward died in his 4th year. William died in the White House when he was 11. Thomas, nicknamed Tad, survived his father but died in 1871 at the age of 18. Lincoln was a loving and indulgent parent, but his frequent absences from home on his law practice placed the upbringing of the boys largely in Mary's hands.

▶ CONGRESSMAN

In the Illinois legislature, Lincoln became a member of the Whig Party, whose most prominent national leaders were Senator Henry Clay of Kentucky and Senator Daniel Webster of Massachusetts. Lincoln's major interest at this time was the promotion of better transportation facilities for his state. He soon advanced to the front rank of Illinois Whigs and by 1842 had emerged as a candidate for the U.S. House of Representatives. Two other men claimed the party's nomination, however, and Lincoln had to wait his turn. Finally, in 1846, he was elected to a seat in Congress.

Lincoln's congressional term began in December 1847, when the Mexican War was nearing its conclusion. Soon after taking his seat, he joined the Whig attack upon the war policy of President James K. Polk, a Democrat. Lincoln also introduced a bill for the gradual emancipation, or freeing, of slaves in the District of Columbia, but it got nowhere. He was careful and hardworking, but on the whole, his two years as a congressman were undistinguished.

Lincoln's criticism of the Mexican War was unpopular in Illinois, and he was not renominated for Congress. He then campaigned for Zachary Taylor, a fellow Whig, in his race for the presidency, helping Taylor win election in 1848. Offered the governorship of the Oregon Territory as a reward, Lincoln declined the appointment and resumed the practice of law. His political career had apparently reached a dead end.

See the article MEXICAN WAR in Volume M.

▶ **THE REPUBLICAN PARTY**

Several years went by, and then in 1854 came a decisive turn of events. Senator Stephen A. Douglas of Illinois, one of the leaders of the Democratic Party, secured passage of the Kansas-Nebraska Act. The measure created the two new federal territories of Kansas and Nebraska and left it up to the people there to decide whether to permit or exclude slavery, a doctrine known as popular sovereignty. The measure set aside the Missouri Compromise, which had limited the expansion of slavery.

Throughout the North there were angry protests against the Kansas-Nebraska Act from many Democrats and from most Whigs, including Lincoln. He had long considered slavery morally wrong, yet he respected the constitutional rights of slaveholders. If slavery could just be prevented from expanding, Lincoln reasoned, it might eventually die away in the Southern states. To such hopes the Kansas-Nebraska Act was a serious blow.

Those opposed to slavery's expansion began to form a political alliance. Lincoln became a leader of this "anti-Nebraska" movement in Illinois. In 1856, with the Whig Party breaking up, he helped organize the various anti-Nebraska groups into the Republican Party of Illinois. At the Republican National Convention in June 1856, Lincoln received strong support for the vice presidency. Although he did not win the nomination, he campaigned vigorously for the new party's presidential candidate, John C. Frémont, who was defeated by Democrat James Buchanan.

▶ **THE LINCOLN-DOUGLAS DEBATES**

In 1858, Illinois Republicans nominated Lincoln to run for the U.S. Senate seat then held by Stephen Douglas. In accepting the nomination, Lincoln made his famous House Divided speech. "A house divided against itself cannot stand," he said. "I believe this government cannot endure permanently half slave and half free."

The high points of the campaign were a series of debates between the candidates, held in seven Illinois cities and towns. Of the two men, Douglas was far better known at the time. He was a national figure, while Lincoln was little known outside his own state.

Lincoln debated Stephen Douglas in his 1858 campaign for the U.S. Senate. Although Lincoln lost the election, the debates made him known nationally.

Underlying the debates was the momentous issue of slavery. Both men emphasized their basic principles. Lincoln's was that slavery was wrong because it denied to the slaves the rights stated in the Declaration of Independence. He stressed the point, however, that he did not intend to interfere with slavery in the states where it legally existed but that he opposed its expansion. Douglas' position was that democratic self-government, as expressed in his policy of popular sovereignty, was more important than slavery itself.

Large crowds attended the debates, and newspapers all over the country reported on the campaign. The election itself was very close, but Douglas emerged as the winner. Lincoln's reaction was that, politically, he would now be forgotten. In this he was to be proved wrong.

See the article on Stephen A. Douglas in Volume D. A separate article on the Kansas-Nebraska Act can be found in Volume J-K and one on the Missouri Compromise in Volume M.

▶ THE PRESIDENTIAL CAMPAIGN OF 1860

In spite of his own feeling, the defeat did not hurt Lincoln politically. The debates with Douglas had brought him national attention, and before long he was being mentioned as a presidential prospect. During the next two years he gained further recognition by making speeches in many states. The climax of his efforts was an address delivered in February 1860, at Cooper Union in New York City. When the Republican National Convention met in Chicago in May 1860, Lincoln had more support than any other candidate except the favorite, William H. Seward of New York. Seward took the lead in the first round of balloting, but then Lincoln pulled almost even, and on the third ballot he was nominated for the presidency. (Lincoln would later appoint Seward to his cabinet as secretary of state.)

Meanwhile, the Democrats were split over the slavery issue. The Northern Democrats nominated Douglas. The Southerners chose John C. Breckinridge. Still another candidate, John Bell, was put forward by a remnant of the Whigs called the Constitutional Union Party. Thus Lincoln had three opponents in the race. Following the custom of the time, he did no active campaigning himself but directed strategy quietly from Springfield. Out of the South came ominous warnings that his election would mean the end of the Union. At the polls on November 6, only about 40 percent of the ballots were cast for Lincoln. But since most of them were concentrated in the heavily populated free states, he won a clear majority of the electoral votes.

The Republican Party had elected its first president.

▶ SECESSION AND CIVIL WAR

South Carolina promptly seceded from the Union, in December 1860. When efforts at compromise failed, six other Southern states followed its example. Together they formed the Confederate States of America. All this

Left: The Lincoln home in Springfield, Illinois. Lincoln and his son Tad can be seen in the inset. *Top:* Lincoln as he looked early in the 1860 presidential campaign. He grew the familiar beard soon after.

Lincoln visited the Union camp at Antietam, Maryland, in 1862, after the decisive but costly Battle of Antietam during the Civil War.

happened before Lincoln became president on March 4, 1861. In his inaugural address he pleaded for harmony and insisted that the Union could not be dissolved. He hoped for a peaceful solution but was prepared to risk war rather than see the nation permanently divided.

The critical spot was Fort Sumter in Charleston Harbor, South Carolina. This was one of the few places within the Confederacy still held by Federal troops. Lincoln, proceeding cautiously, planned to send supplies but not reinforcements to the garrison there. Early in the morning of April 12, however, Southerners opened fire on the fort and soon forced its surrender. Lincoln immediately proclaimed a blockade of the Confederacy and issued a call for volunteers to suppress the rebellion. This provoked the secession of four more Southern states. As spring gave way to summer, both sides were preparing hastily for war.

▶ WAR PRESIDENT

From the beginning, Lincoln understood the essential nature of the Civil War better than most of his generals. The Confederacy could gain independence merely by defending itself successfully. However, the Union forces had to conquer the enemy in order to win. Most of the material advantages were with the North. It had greater manpower, wealth, and industrial strength. Lincoln's task was to mobilize Northern superiority and make it effective on the battlefield. He favored pressing forward on several fronts to prevent the Confederates from concentrating their defenses. He also believed that the primary aim of Union strategy should be the destruction of Southern armies rather than the capture of Southern cities like Richmond, Virginia, the Confederate capital. In the early part of the war, however, Lincoln was unable to find a general capable of maintaining an offensive against the great Confederate general Robert E. Lee.

The Battle of Bull Run in July 1861 was only the first of many Union defeats and disappointments on the Virginia front. More successful in the West, Union forces captured New Orleans and were gaining control of the lower Mississippi. At the end of 1862, however, the war was obviously still far from over.

Although military affairs occupied much of his attention, Lincoln had many other presidential duties to perform. On the whole he was content to allow his cabinet members a free hand in the administration of their departments. He rarely sought to influence Congress and seldom used his veto power. Among the important pieces of legislation that he signed were the Homestead Act, which provided free land in the West to settlers; the Pacific Railway Act; and the National Banking Act.

▶ EMANCIPATION

Despite his own strong antislavery feelings, Lincoln insisted at first that the purpose of the war was to save the Union, not to destroy slavery. But pressure from abolitionists, who demanded an immediate end to slavery, steadily increased, and the president decided that emancipation could be justified as a military measure to weaken the enemy. It would also make the Northern cause more noble in the eyes of the world. After announcing his intention in September 1862, Lincoln issued the final Emancipation Proclamation on January 1, 1863.

Since it applied only to the areas still under Confederate control, the proclamation did not actually free very many blacks from bondage. Yet it was a symbol and a commitment that changed the nature of the war. From then on, everyone knew that a Northern victory would mean the end of slavery. Emancipation became complete and final with the 13th Amendment to the Constitution. Approved by Congress at Lincoln's urging, it was not ratified by a sufficient number of states until after his death. See the article on the Emancipation Proclamation in Volume E.

▶ TOWARD VICTORY

The responsibilities of his office and the mounting toll of battle casualties weighed heavily on Lincoln's spirit. For relaxation he swapped jokes, read books of humor, and visited the theater. In his more serious moments, however, he turned to Shakespeare and the Bible. Pondering the causes of the war, Lincoln came to believe that it was a divine punishment of all Americans for the sin of slavery.

The turning point of the war came in early July 1863. Lee's army, attempting a second invasion of the North, was defeated at the battle of Gettysburg in Pennsylvania. At the same time, General Ulysses S. Grant captured Vicksburg, the last important Confederate stronghold on the Mississippi River. Later that same year Lincoln helped dedicate the military cemetery at Gettysburg. His memorable address of only a few hundred words

The Lincolns in the White House, with sons Tad (in the president's lap), Robert, and William. Mary Lincoln is at right.

summoned the nation to complete the great task in which so many men had given "the last full measure of devotion. ..."

Early in 1864, Lincoln promoted Grant to the command of all Union armies. Grant then began the hard, bloody work of driving Lee back toward Richmond. At the same time, General William T. Sherman launched an invasion of Georgia. When his troops occupied Atlanta in September 1864, the war entered its final phase.

Meanwhile, the time for another presidential election had arrived. Lincoln, although opposed by some dissatisfied Republicans, won renomination without much trouble. The Democrats chose General George B. McClellan as their candidate, with a platform demanding immediate peace. For a time Lincoln despaired of victory, but Sherman's progress in Georgia helped his cause. Union soldiers voted overwhelmingly for Lincoln, and he was re-elected.

▶ THE LAST FULL MEASURE

As the Union armies pressed forward, Lincoln gave increasing attention to the problem of restoring peace when victory was achieved. It must be done, he said in his second inaugural address, "With malice toward none; with charity for all. ..." Desiring the speedy "reconstruction" of a united republic, he set forth a simple plan. Ten percent of the voters in a Confederate state, if they took an oath of allegiance to the United States, could organize a government and resume their old place in the federal union. By 1865 several states were putting the plan into operation. But strong opposition had developed in Congress. Many Republicans believed that such generosity was unrealistic. They felt that there should be more punishment for Southern traitors and more protection for freed slaves. The whole question of Reconstruction remained unsettled at the time of Lincoln's death.

On April 9, 1865, Lee surrendered to Grant at Appomattox Court House in Virginia. Throughout the North there were joyful celebrations. Five nights later, Lincoln and Mary attended a play at Ford's Theater in

Excerpts from Lincoln's speeches, letters, and other writings

... [as] soon as I discover my opinions to be erroneous, I shall be ready to renounce them.

Lincoln's first political address, as candidate for the Illinois legislature, March 9, 1832

The legitimate object of government, is to do for a community of people, whatever they need to have done, but can not do, *at all*, or can not, so *well do,* for themselves. ...

In all that the people can individually do as well for themselves, government ought not to interfere.

Fragment, probably 1850's

As a nation we began by declaring that *"all men are created equal."* We now practically read it "all men are created equal, *except negroes."* When the Know-Nothings get control, it will read "all men are created equal, except negroes, *and foreigners, and catholics."* When it comes to this I should prefer emigrating to some country where they make no pretence of loving liberty. ...

Letter to Joshua Speed, August 24, 1855

I will say here ... that I have no purpose directly or indirectly to interfere with the institution of slavery in the States where it exists. I believe I have no lawful right to do so. ...

Lincoln-Douglas Debates, Ottawa, Illinois, August 21, 1858

... he who would *be* no slave, must consent to *have* no slave. Those who deny freedom to others, deserve it not for themselves. ...

Letter to Henry L. Pierce and others, April 6, 1859

In *your* hands, my dissatisfied fellow countrymen, and not in *mine*, is the momentous issue of civil war. ... We are not enemies, but friends. We must not be enemies.

First Inaugural Address, March 4, 1861

With malice toward none; with charity for all; with firmness in the right, let us strive on to finish the work we are in; to bind up the nation's wounds; to care for him who shall have borne the battle, and for his widow, and his orphan—to do all which may achieve and cherish a just, and a lasting peace, among ourselves, and with all nations.

Second Inaugural Address, March 4, 1865

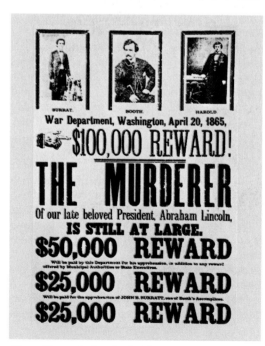

Above: The wanted poster for Lincoln's assassin, John Wilkes Booth, and his accomplices. *Top:* Lincoln's statue in the Lincoln Memorial in Washington, D.C.

Washington. There he was shot by John Wilkes Booth, an actor devoted to the Confederate cause. Lincoln never regained consciousness and died the next morning, April 15. Booth escaped to Virginia but was later trapped by Union soldiers and killed. An article on John Wilkes Booth appears in Volume B.

While the news of the assassination sped across the country, Vice President Andrew Johnson hastily took the oath of office as president. The war had ended, but the war leader had fallen. A crowd of mourners gathered at each railway station as the funeral train rolled westward toward the Illinois prairie, to Springfield, where Abraham Lincoln was buried. It was a tragic ending but also a triumphant one, for he left behind a nation reunited and a people set free.

DON E. FEHRENBACHER
Stanford University
Author, *Prelude to Greatness: Lincoln in the 1850's*

See also CIVIL WAR, UNITED STATES; CONFEDERATE STATES OF AMERICA; RECONSTRUCTION PERIOD.

LINCOLN CENTER FOR THE PERFORMING ARTS

Lincoln Center for the Performing Arts is located in New York City. It includes Avery Fisher Hall, the New York State Theater, the Metropolitan Opera House, the Vivian Beaumont Theater, the Library and Museum of the Performing Arts, and The Juilliard School and Alice Tully Hall. The center began functioning in 1962 and was completed in 1969 at a total cost of $185,000,000. This money was raised from many sources—government funds, foundations, industry, foreign donations, national organizations, and private individuals.

The Lincoln Center Council co-ordinates program schedules for the various resident companies, organizes festivals, and commissions new works in all the arts. There are also co-operative programs involving energy conservation, maintenance and security, and fund raising. The council also organizes the *Live from Lincoln Center* television series. This series broadcasts presentations of the performing arts live over public television.

Avery Fisher Hall, formerly Philharmonic Hall, opened in 1962 with a week of concerts by some of the country's leading orchestras. It was originally designed by the architect Max Abramovitz. In 1976, Avery Fisher Hall emerged with a new interior designed by Cyril M. Harris, a noted specialist in acoustics, and architect Philip Johnson. The new concert hall pleased both musicians and audiences.

The New York State Theater is the home of the New York City Ballet and the New York City Opera. It was opened in the spring of 1964. This theater, seating 2,729, was also designed by Philip Johnson.

The Vivian Beaumont Theater opened in 1965. The designers were Eero Saarinen Associates, with stage designer Jo Mielziner (1901–76) collaborating. The main theater seats over 1,000, and the Mitzi E. Newhouse Theater, a small amphitheater, seats 299.

The Library and Museum of the Performing Arts was designed by Skidmore, Owings & Merrill. It contains the Bruno Walter Auditorium, which seats over 200, and the Heckscher Children's Oval, which seats 100. The library houses the New York Public Library's performing arts research and reference materials. Its programs include films, concerts, dramatic readings, dance performances, lectures, and exhibitions.

The Metropolitan Opera House was designed by Wallace K. Harrison. It seats over 3,700. South of the opera house are Damrosch Park and the Guggenheim Band Shell.

The designers of the Juilliard School were Pietro Belluschi and Catalano & Westermann. It contains the Juilliard Theater, Paul Recital Studio, and the Juilliard Drama Workshop. It also houses Alice Tully Hall, home of the Lincoln Center Chamber Music Society.

Several cities in the United States have built vibrant arts centers. Lincoln Center is among the largest and most ambitious.

Reviewed by JOHN W. MAZZOLA
President
Lincoln Center for the Performing Arts

LINDBERGH, CHARLES (1902–1974)

Charles Lindbergh was one of the world's great aviators. His dramatic solo nonstop flight across the Atlantic—the first in history—made him a world hero.

Lindbergh was born on February 4, 1902, in Detroit, Michigan. He grew up in Little Falls, Minnesota, and in Washington, D.C., where his father spent ten years as a congressman from Minnesota, from 1907 to 1917.

In 1920, Lindbergh went to the University of Wisconsin to study mechanical engineering. Two years later, however, he left the university to go to flying school. He then worked as a barnstormer, or stunt flier, and later as an airmail pilot.

In the 1920's, airplanes were seen primarily as novelties with limited uses. Few people could imagine them as a reliable means of transportation for large numbers of passengers. Yet engineers and pilots were continually improving planes and expanding their capabilities. In 1926, Lindbergh heard about a $25,000 prize that was being offered for the first successful nonstop flight from New York to Paris. Lindbergh helped design and build a single-engine plane that he believed could make this flight. His plane, *Spirit of St. Louis*, was named for the group of St. Louis business people who had paid for the venture in hopes of getting publicity for their city.

On the morning of May 20, 1927, Lindbergh took off from Roosevelt Field in Long Island, New York. Some 33½ hours and 3,600 miles (5,800 km) later, he landed near Paris, France. The first transatlantic solo flight had been successfully completed, and it changed the way many people thought about the airplane. Lindbergh's flight made him an international hero, and he became known as "Lucky Lindy" and "The Lone Eagle" to millions of people around the world.

In 1929, Lindbergh married Anne Morrow. He taught her to fly, and she was his co-pilot and radio operator on flights to many parts of the world. She wrote about these trips in her books *North to the Orient* and *Listen! the Wind*.

During the 1930's, Lindbergh served as technical advisor to two airlines, Transcontinental Air Transport and Pan American Airways, and he developed many of the routes used by these companies. Lindbergh contin-

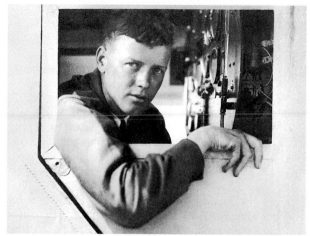

Charles Lindbergh at Curtiss Field just a few days before his 1927 flight across the Atlantic in the *Spirit of St. Louis*.

ued to be an aircraft consultant throughout his life, and he supported early rocket research essential to the future of space exploration.

In 1932, tragedy struck the Lindberghs. Their 20-month-old son, Charles, was kidnapped and murdered. Because Lindbergh was so famous, this tragedy became known worldwide. In the United States it influenced members of Congress who passed the "Lindbergh Law," which made kidnapping a federal crime punishable by death if the victim was brought across state lines. (This law was changed in 1956 to allow the Federal Bureau of Investigation to enter any kidnapping case after 24 hours. If no deaths result, the maximum penalty is life imprisonment.)

Airplanes had been important in World War I, but they were vital to both sides in World War II. Although Lindbergh first opposed United States entry into the war, after it entered, he served as an aircraft consultant and test pilot and he flew several missions as a civilian.

Lindbergh wrote five books about his life and his flying experiences: *We*, *Of Flight and Life*, *The Spirit of St. Louis*, *Autobiography of Values*, and *Wartime Journals*. He also became a leading conservationist, championing causes to preserve the atmosphere and to protect endangered species. Lindbergh died in Hawaii on August 26, 1974.

RACHEL KRANZ
Editor, Biographies
The Young Adult Reader's Adviser

See also AVIATION.

LINEN. See FIBERS.

LINNAEUS, CAROLUS (1707–1778)

Carolus Linnaeus was a Swedish naturalist, known particularly for his work in botany—the study of plants. "Carolus Linnaeus" is the Latin form of his Swedish name, Carl von Linné. At the time he lived, most scientific books were written in Latin. Because he, too, wrote in that language, he used his Latin name in his scientific work. He is generally known by this name.

Linnaeus was born in southern Sweden on May 23, 1707, the oldest of five children. His father was a country clergyman. From the time Carl was a little child, he showed an unusual interest in flowers. His father, very fond of flowers himself, taught his son about them. Carl enjoyed growing unusual plants in his garden.

When Carl was 7 years old, his parents hired a teacher to educate him at home. But this did not turn out to be successful. After two years, Carl was sent to school in the town of Växjö, about 25 miles away. His father hoped his son would become a clergyman like himself. But because Carl did poorly in school, this did not seem likely. His science teacher, however, thought Carl was the most promising of all his students. He urged the boy's parents to let Carl attend a university to study to become a doctor.

Linnaeus went first to Lund University in southern Sweden. After a year he moved to Uppsala University, near Stockholm. Here, while a student, he began scientific research. He spent a summer in Lapland, in the far northern part of Sweden, studying the plants and animals there. In 1735, after several years of study at Uppsala University, Linnaeus went to the Netherlands. He received the degree of doctor of medicine at Hardewijk University that same year.

Also in that year, 1735, Linnaeus published a book called *Systema Naturae* ("The System of Nature"). This book explained a system he had invented for classifying plants and animals. According to this system, each plant and animal had two Latin names, one telling its group (genus) and the other its kind (species). This made it simple for scientists to recognize the name of a plant or animal, no matter what its common name was. Linnaeus' system of classification was quickly accepted throughout Europe.

Carolus Linnaeus, the Swedish naturalist, created the system for classifying plants and animals that has been used for more than 260 years.

Whenever Linnaeus saw a collection of things, he had a burning desire to arrange them in an orderly way. He became famous for his system of arranging animals, minerals, and most of all, plants. The *Systema Naturae* was only the beginning of his work in classifying living things.

Linnaeus returned to Sweden in 1738. During his three years abroad, he had become very well known among European scientists. He was appointed professor of medicine and of natural history at Uppsala University and physician to the king of Sweden.

People from all over the world sent Linnaeus specimens of shells, insects, minerals, and plants. His collection of dried plants was the largest in the world. It was sold after Linnaeus' death and is now in England.

Linnaeus died in Uppsala on January 10, 1778, having become known as the "prince of botanists."

DUANE H. D. ROLLER
University of Oklahoma

See also TAXONOMY.

LINOLEUM-BLOCK PRINTING

Linoleum-block printing is a method of relief printing; that is, the image to be printed is raised above the rest of the printing plate. Relief printing is one of the oldest forms of printing. The Chinese and the Japanese were the first to use it, printing images from woodblocks. The earliest block prints were made in Japan about A.D. 770.

Today, linoleum, a common floor covering, is a popular material for relief printing. Linoleum prints, called linocuts, make attractive greeting cards, illustrations, and pictures. One carved linoleum block can print 50 to 100 copies clearly.

How to Make Your Own Linocut. At an art supply store, you can buy a linoleum block, a tube of water-based printing ink, a small cutting tool called a gouge, rice paper, a tablet of newsprint paper, and a rubber roller about 4 inches (10 centimeters) wide. You will also need a large wooden spoon and a tray, such as an old cookie sheet, on which to roll out your ink.

First, draw a picture on your mounted linoleum block. Remember that everything you draw will appear in reverse when you print your linocut. If you decide to print words or letters, draw them in reverse. Your print will be made from the parts of the block that you do not cut away. Following the lines of your drawing, gently cut into the linoleum with the gouge. Cut only the general shape of your design at first, leaving the details for later.

Linoleum is very easy to cut, but there is one safety rule to keep in mind: Always cut away from your body. If you must change the direction of your cut, do it by turning the linoleum, not your hand. Keep the hand holding the block behind the hand holding the gouge.

After you have cut the general shape of your design, you are ready to "pull" a proof (sample print). Squeeze a little ink onto your tray. Spread the ink with the roller until the roller is evenly coated. Roll the ink over the linoleum in thin layers, so that it builds up evenly. Place a piece of newsprint over the block, smooth it with your hand, and rub the surface with the back of your wooden spoon.

Now lift off the paper and study your proof. If you want to make changes or add details, clean the ink off the block and go back to cutting. Pull a proof whenever you want to see how the linocut looks. When you are satisfied, decide how many copies you want to make, and use the rice paper for finished prints.

After you become more experienced, you can use more complicated techniques. You can buy a linoleum cutting set, which includes a handle and a variety of gouges. Each gouge cuts a different kind of line. You can also experiment with printing a picture in more than one color, cutting a different block for each color. Making a good linocut in several colors takes a great deal of experimentation, but the results are worth the effort.

CLARE ROMANO
Coauthor, *The Complete Printmaker*

See also GRAPHIC ARTS.

STEPS IN MAKING A LINOCUT

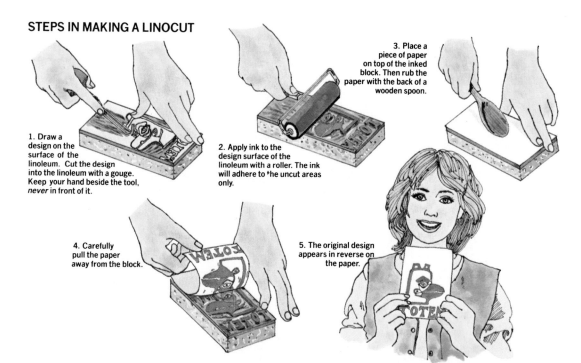

1. Draw a design on the surface of the linoleum. Cut the design into the linoleum with a gouge. Keep your hand beside the tool, *never* in front of it.

2. Apply ink to the design surface of the linoleum with a roller. The ink will adhere to the uncut areas only.

3. Place a piece of paper on top of the inked block. Then rub the paper with the back of a wooden spoon.

4. Carefully pull the paper away from the block.

5. The original design appears in reverse on the paper.

251

LIONS

Lions are very large, strong cats. The male lion may weigh 400 pounds (180 kilograms) or more. The female weighs less—usually no more than 300 pounds (135 kilograms).

Male lions are the only members of the cat family that have manes. The mane is usually the same color as the coat, but it can be black. Both male and female lions have a tuft of dark hair at the end of their tails. Inside this hair is the so-called claw—a tough patch of skin at the tip of the tail. No one knows what function this serves, if any, but no other cat has it.

Lions are meat eaters, and they are well suited to a life of hunting. They can run fast for short distances—up to 40 miles (65 kilometers) an hour when charging prey. They have powerful muscles for leaping. Their sharp, hooked claws are dangerous weapons. Like other cats, a lion can retract its claws and walk very quietly on the soft pads of its feet.

Like the rest of the cat family, lions hunt mostly at night. But unlike most other cats, lions hunt in groups. Zebras and antelopes are their favorite prey. Males and females often work together. The females may lie hidden, waiting quietly while the males round up the prey. The males drive the antelopes or other animals toward the females. When the antelopes are nearby, the females spring out and attack. When a kill is made, the lions usually feed from it for several days. When they have used up their food, they make a new kill. Lions kill only for food or when defending themselves or their young.

Young lions, or cubs, are born about three and a half months after the parents have mated. From two to six cubs are born at one time. They are about the size of small house cats and are spotted and striped. When half grown, lions are good climbers. But as they grow older and heavier, they rarely climb.

Young lions grow quickly. At the end of a year, their spots have faded or disappeared completely. Now they begin to make their own kills. In two years they mate and start to raise families. Their manes begin to grow when they are about 3.

Lions once lived in parts of Europe, Africa, and Asia. Today they are found only on open plains and grasslands in protected areas of Africa south of the Sahara and in a wildlife sanctuary in northwest India. The Indian lions are an endangered species.

Reviewed by ROBERT M. McCLUNG
Author, science books for children

See also CATS, WILD.

LIPINSKI, TARA. See OLYMPIC GAMES (Profiles).
LIPPMANN, WALTER. See JOURNALISM (Profiles).
LIPREADING. See DEAFNESS.

Lions are social animals and live in groups called prides. A pride consists of one to four males and many females and cubs. Only the females stay with the pride for life.

LIQUID OXYGEN AND OTHER LIQUID GASES

Almost any gas can be turned into a liquid if it is made cold enough. This is an important fact because liquid gases have many uses in science and industry.

The most common liquid gases are oxygen, nitrogen, hydrogen, helium, and neon. All of them are extremely cold in their liquid forms. They are sometimes called cryogenic gases. **Cryogenics** is the science that deals with phenomena that take place at very low temperatures. The name comes from the Greek word *kryos*, which means "icy cold." Nothing you usually see is even close to being so cold—as cold as the unlighted side of the moon.

The temperatures at which these substances **boil** (change to vapor) give some idea of just how cold liquid gases are. Methane boils at −263°F (−164°C), oxygen at −297°F (−183°C), nitrogen at −320°F (−196°C), hydrogen at −423°F (−253°C), and helium at −452°F (−269°C).

One of the most important fields for the use of liquid gases is missile and rocket aviation. Liquid gases are used to test the operation of spaceships and their electronic equipment in the very low temperatures they will meet in outer space. Liquid nitrogen, hydrogen, and helium are used to chill the test chambers. Liquid hydrogen is the most powerful rocket fuel known. Liquid oxygen is used to release the energy in the hydrogen fuel. Liquid nitrogen helps cool the tanks and compartments of a missile during countdown.

The extreme cold of liquid gases makes them ideal for use in refrigeration. Refrigerated trucks and railway cars use liquid nitrogen to cool fruits and vegetables. Medical laboratories store serum and blood plasma in containers refrigerated by liquid gases. Before some surgical operations, the area to be operated on is frozen with liquid gas. The very low temperature makes all normal biological activity stop.

Cooling electrical conductors is another important job of liquid gases. At extremely low temperatures, some metals and ceramic materials have no resistance to the flow of an electric current. This unusual characteristic is called **superconductivity**. Superconductors are cooled with liquid nitrogen, liquid hydrogen, or liquid helium. Scientists are experimenting with ways to achieve superconductivity at less extreme temperatures.

Familiar substances take on strange new properties at cryogenic temperatures. Mercury freezes so solid that it can be used as a hammer. Rubber becomes stiff and brittle. Soft, flexible plastics become rigid and can be shattered to pieces by a hammer blow.

Liquid gases are used in many scientific research laboratories. They are also used by many big industrial companies in testing and developing new materials.

Making Liquid Gases

Liquid gases are made in devices called **cold boxes**. The technical name of the cold box is **liquefaction fractional distiller**. Some are as large as a house; others can fit into a small laboratory. All of them work in much the same way.

Air is compressed and cooled. It then passes through a valve into a tank where it can expand. As the air goes through the valve and expands, its temperature drops. The slightly cooled, expanded air in the tank is used to precool new compressed air flowing toward the valve. This makes the temperature drop still farther. The temperature of the air slowly gets lower and lower until the air begins to condense. When all of the gases in the air have condensed, they can be evaporated (boiled) to separate each gas. The separated gases are then recondensed into liquid form.

There is a problem in keeping the gases liquefied. A certain amount of liquid gas is always boiling off at room temperature. Fortunately it takes a great deal of heat to boil off even small amounts of liquid gas, so the loss from evaporation is low.

Storing liquid gas in outer space is easier, because temperatures there are at the cryogenic level. The main problem is shielding the liquid gas from the radiant heat of the sun or from heated space capsules. To solve this problem, thin sheets of aluminum-coated plastic, which reflect radiation, can be wrapped around the liquid-gas tanks so liquid hydrogen can be kept in outer space for long periods of time.

FRANKLIN D. YEAPLE
President, TEF Engineering

Reviewed and updated by ROBERT GARDNER
Author, *Science Projects about Chemistry*

See also FUELS; GASES; ROCKETS.

The cohesive forces of mercury are stronger than the adhesive forces between mercury and glass, so mercury forms a convex surface. Water (dyed red here), whose cohesive forces are weaker than the adhesive forces between water and glass, is pulled up the side of a container and forms a concave meniscus.

LIQUIDS

Liquids are one of the three states of matter. The other two are gases and solids. The most common and familiar liquid is water.

▶ PARTICLES IN A LIQUID

Like all matter, liquids are made up of tiny particles called atoms and molecules. In some ways, the particles in liquids act like those in solids. In other ways, they act like particles in gases. Particles in a liquid remain close together, just like those in a solid. Therefore, a particular quantity of liquid takes up a fixed amount of space and has a definite **volume** just as a solid does.

However, the particles in a liquid, unlike those in a solid, are not fixed firmly in place. Like particles in a gas, they can move around one another. This means that a liquid, unlike a solid, has no definite shape. It takes the shape of the container in which it is placed. Because the shape of a liquid and the shape of a gas can change, they are able to flow, so liquids and gases are called fluids.

▶ PROPERTIES OF A LIQUID

If a liquid is heated to a sufficiently high temperature, its particles move apart and separate. At that point, the liquid boils; it changes from a liquid to a gas. The temperature at which a liquid boils is called its **boiling point**. For example, the boiling point of water is 212°F (100°C). At this temperature, water changes to steam.

If a liquid is cooled sufficiently, its particles lose the ability to move about freely. They become fixed in position; that is, the liquid becomes a solid. Water changes to ice at 32°F (0°C). This temperature is the **freezing point** of water. Every liquid has its own characteristic boiling point and freezing point.

Liquids exist over a range of temperatures. It is possible to have blazing-hot liquid iron as well as super-cold liquid helium. The range over which any substance remains a liquid depends on its boiling and freezing points. For water, the range is 180°F—from 32° to 212°F (100°C—from 0° to 100°C).

Many liquids and solids can be mixed together to form solutions. In a solution, the molecules of the solid spread evenly throughout the liquid. We say the solid **dissolves** in the liquid. Salt and sugar are solids that dissolve in water; sand and starch do not.

Liquids have other properties that make them unique. The molecules of a liquid tend to stick together. This sticking together is called **cohesion**. But liquids are also attracted to other substances. For example, a liquid may be attracted to the sides of the container in which it is placed. This attraction is called **adhesion**. Water particles are attracted to glass. We say water wets glass. To see this for yourself, pour some water into a tall, narrow tube such as a test tube or an olive jar. You can see that the water is pulled up the side of the container, giving the surface of the water a rounded concave (curving inward) surface called a **meniscus**. The narrower the tube, the higher the water will rise. The movement of water up narrow tubes is called **capillarity**.

To see how capillarity works, tape glass tubes, open at each end and with different diameters, to the inside and just above the bottom of a rectangular container that contains some colored water. Then watch the water rise to a different height in each tube (Figure 1).

Capillarity is related to the size of the tube. The narrower the tube, the higher the water rises in it.

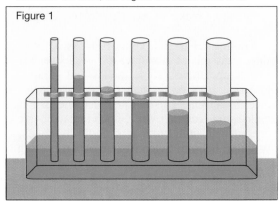

Figure 1

Within a liquid, cohesion causes the molecules to be attracted equally in all directions. As a result, the molecules can move freely about one another. But molecules on the surface of a liquid are all pulled inward by the molecules below them and along their sides. There are no molecules above them and, therefore, no balancing pull outward from above. This inward pull on the surface of a liquid creates what is called **surface tension**.

The inward pull on the surface molecules makes water act as if it had a skin. To see the skinlike effect caused by surface tension, fill a clean glass with water. Then use a dinner fork to place a paper clip gently on the surface of the water (Figure 2). Amazingly, the water surface supports the steel wire. If you look closely, you can even see the indentations of the paper clip in the water's "skin."

Surface tension always acts to reduce the amount of surface present. For that reason, small drops of liquid are always spherical in a weightless environment. The reason is that a sphere has the smallest surface for its volume. By forming a sphere, the liquid has pulled together as much as it possibly can.

On Earth, the force of gravity tends to flatten a drop of liquid. To demonstrate this, use an eyedropper to place single drops of water on a sheet of waxed paper (Figure 3). Notice how the water pulls together into a slightly deformed sphere rather than spreading out over the waxed surface. If you make the drop grow by adding more drops, the water becomes flatter because of the added weight.

When dissolved in a liquid, some substances will reduce the attraction among the molecules of the liquid. The reduced cohesion and surface tension make it easier for the liquid to be attracted to other substances. Soap

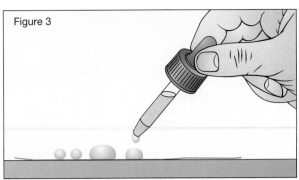

Figure 3

Drops of water on waxed paper are almost spherical.

affects the surface tension of water. When soap dissolves in water, the water will then wet oily or greasy surfaces, making it easier to wash the oil and grease off these surfaces. This is why you need to wash your hands with water and soap instead of only water.

To demonstrate how soap affects the surface tension of water, fill a vial with water. Then use an eyedropper to add water a drop at a time (Figure 4). You will be amazed to see how much more water can be added to the vial. Surface tension allows the water to be "heaped" well above the rim of the vial.

Next, prepare a small amount of soapy water. Using the eyedropper, carefully add a single drop of soapy water to the water you heaped above the rim of the vial. As the soapy water is added, the "heaped" water will run down the side of the vial and the water level will drop because the soap has reduced the water's surface tension, weakening its "skin." To see a similar effect, add a drop of soapy water to the glass with the floating paper clip. The soap reduces the water's surface tension and the paper clip sinks.

Figure 4

The cohesive forces in water allow it to hold together well above the rim of its container.

ISAAC ASIMOV
Author, *Asimov's New Guide to Science*

Reviewed and Updated by ROBERT GARDNER
Author, *Science Projects About Chemistry*

See also GASES; MATTER; SOLIDS; WATER.

LISA, MANUEL. See NORTH DAKOTA (Famous People).

The "skin" on the surface of water is strong enough to support a paper clip.

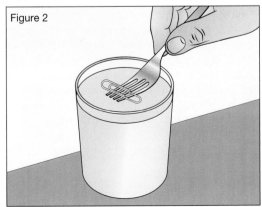

Figure 2

LISBON

Lisbon (Lisboa in Portuguese) is the capital and largest city of Portugal as well as its chief port and commercial center. The population of the city proper is over 800,000, while more than 2 million people live in its metropolitan area. The city is situated on the northern bank of the Tagus River, about 8 miles (13 kilometers) from where the Tagus flows into the Atlantic Ocean. Nearby is Cape Roca, the most westerly point on the mainland of Europe.

The City. Lisbon is built on a series of hills, which rise steeply from the Tagus. The oldest part of the city is the Alfama, an area of narrow, winding streets dominated by the castle of São Jorge (St. George). The Lisbon cathedral is also located here. West of the Alfama is the Cidade Baixa (Lower City), the center of the city. Rebuilt, along with much of the rest of Lisbon, after a devastating earthquake in 1755, it consists of handsome buildings and numerous squares, including the Praça do Commercio (Commerce Square) and the Rossio. The main thoroughfare is the Avenida da Liberdade (Avenue of Liberty). The Bairro Alto (Upper District), to the northwest, is the newest part of the city.

The suburb of Belém has several landmarks of particular interest. Among these are the Tower of Belém, built in the 1500's to guard the port of Lisbon, and the San Jerónimos monastery, dating from the same period.

The Praça de Dom Pedro IV, or the Rossio, is one of Lisbon's numerous squares. A statue of Dom Pedro IV, who became emperor of Brazil, stands in the center.

Economic Activity. Lisbon owes much of its economic importance to its harbor, one of the finest in Europe, which handles some two-thirds of Portugal's trade. The city has a petroleum refinery and produces a variety of manufactured goods, including construction materials, steel, processed foods, and textiles.

History. An ancient city, Lisbon may have been settled by the Phoenicians as early as 1200 B.C. It was ruled, in turn, by the Carthaginians, Romans, and Visigoths, before falling to the Moors, Muslim invaders from North Africa, in the A.D. 700's. The Moors, whose influence can still be seen in some of the city's oldest structures, were displaced, in 1147, by King Alfonso I of Portugal, who made the city his capital in 1256.

Lisbon reached its greatest heights in the 1400's and 1500's, during the great age of exploration and discovery, when the Portuguese created a vast maritime empire. It declined when Portugal was under Spanish rule (1580–1640) but regained its importance in the 1700's. During the Peninsular War, Lisbon was vital to the British as a base of operations (1808–14) against the French, who had occupied Spain and part of Portugal. The royal family, which had fled after the French invasion, returned to the city in 1822. In 1910, Lisbon became the capital of the newly proclaimed Portuguese republic.

Portugal was neutral during World War II (1939–45) and Lisbon became a haven for refugees. A suspension bridge across the Tagus was completed in 1966, aiding in the economic development of the city. In 1988 a fire destroyed part of the commercial area of the Bairro Alto. It was the most severe natural disaster since the 1755 earthquake.

ARTHUR CAMPBELL TURNER
University of California, Riverside

LISTER, JOSEPH (1827–1912)

Joseph Lister, born in Upton, England, on April 5, 1827, was a British doctor who developed the idea of germ-free, or antiseptic, surgery. This idea became one of the most important advances of modern medicine.

Lister decided to become a surgeon while still at University College, London. He graduated from medical school in 1853 and began his work in Edinburgh, Scotland, as an assistant to James Syme, a famous surgeon. He then went to Glasgow, Scotland, where he was appointed professor of surgery at Glasgow University in 1860.

A year later, Lister was elected to take charge of the surgical wards at the Glasgow Infirmary, the largest hospital in that city. While working in the surgical wards, he treated many people who had developed wound infections. Without a way to stop infections from spreading, death was always a possibility once a wound became infected.

Lister became interested in preventing such infections. It was after learning of Louis Pasteur's work, which showed that bacteria in the air could cause the spoiling of milk and the rotting of food, that Lister thought that infections in wounds could also be caused by tiny airborne germs.

Using a chemical called carbolic acid on the wounds, Lister was very successful in killing harmful germs and in reducing the number of infections. In 1867, he wrote an article about his method of wound treatment for an important medical journal. At first, Lister's theory was not readily accepted. But within 25 years most surgeons were using antiseptics (germ killers) to treat wounds and to prevent infections during surgery.

Lister returned to London in 1877 and devoted much of his time to developing better methods for antiseptic surgery. He was one of the founders of a medical research institute now known as the Lister Institute of Preventive Medicine. In 1897, he was given the title of baron by Queen Victoria, a former patient. He died on February 10, 1912.

DUANE H. D. ROLLER
University of Oklahoma

LISZT, FRANZ (1811–1886)

Franz Liszt, one of the greatest pianists of all time, was also a famous conductor and composer. He was born on October 22, 1811, in Raiding, Hungary. When he was 6 years old, his father started teaching him to play the piano. At 9, Franz gave his first public performance. A year later he went to Vienna, where his genius was recognized by the aging Beethoven. In Vienna he studied piano with Carl Czerny and composition with Antonio Salieri. At the age of 12, Franz set out on his first concert tour.

In 1827, Liszt settled in Paris, where he met Frédéric Chopin, Hector Berlioz, and Niccolò Paganini. Paganini's exceptional mastery of the violin inspired Liszt to a like mastery of the piano. Liszt composed and performed some of the most technically difficult pieces ever written for the piano. In 1839, Liszt started on a concert tour of Europe that lasted nine years and established his fame.

Liszt accepted the position of court music director in Weimar, Germany, in 1848. Here he wrote his greatest compositions—the *Hungarian Rhapsodies,* the *Faust* symphony, and his first piano concerto. He also developed a new orchestral form, the symphonic poem—a one-movement work that tells a story or describes a picture in music. *Les Préludes* is a famous symphonic poem by Liszt.

Always interested in helping young composers, Liszt used his position at Weimar to perform their compositions. He taught many pupils and invented the master class in which a celebrated teacher could work with several students at once. He conducted the first performance of the opera *Lohengrin* by Richard Wagner (who later married Liszt's daughter Cosima), and was one of the first to recognize Wagner's genius.

In 1859, Liszt resigned his position in Weimar, and two years later, he settled in Rome. He continued teaching, performing, and composing. During this period he wrote many songs and choral works, as well as piano and orchestral compositions.

Liszt died on July 31, 1886, in Bayreuth, Germany, while visiting his daughter Cosima.

Reviewed by ROBERT C. MARSH
Music Critic, *Chicago Sun-Times*

Literature forms a written record of people's thoughts and ideas throughout time. The vast body of world literature is an almost infinite source of knowledge and enjoyment.

LITERATURE

Literature may be described as the record in words of what people have thought and felt from the ancient past to the present day. More exactly, literature is good writing that helps us understand that human beings in all times and places have much in common.

Some literature belongs to what scholars call the oral tradition. This includes folktales, ballads, and nursery rhymes, which were passed by word of mouth from one generation to the next. But most literature comes to us in written form—manuscripts, scrolls, and the printed page.

▶ FORMS OF LITERATURE

Literature is divided into two broad classes, **fiction** and **nonfiction**. The word "fiction" comes from the Latin *fingere*, which means "to form." Fiction is something that the writer invents or imagines. It aims to stir our feelings and imaginations by describing moods of joy or sadness, by telling us exciting stories, and by introducing us to characters whose emotions we may all understand and share. Fiction can be in verse or prose—in the form of a play or a poem, a novel or a short story.

Nonfiction is the kind of writing we turn to when we want to learn the facts about a certain subject, such as science or history. This kind of writing may enter the realm of litera-ture when the ideas are beautifully expressed in language that gives added pleasure. Great works of religion and philosophy often become nonfiction literature.

Biographies, autobiographies, diaries, and essays are also nonfiction. An autobiography is the author's own life story. A biography is the life of someone other than the author. An informal essay—a short piece of prose—discusses a subject from a personal point of view.

Nonfiction can also teach us how to do things—how to play games, run a machine, or even conduct a business. But books of this kind are not often considered literature.

The two kinds of literature are not entirely separate, for nonfiction may move us strongly by its well-presented arguments, and fiction may reveal, in the course of a story, new facts

This article provides a brief overview of litera-ture. The various forms of literature are discussed in greater detail in such articles as FICTION, NOVELS, POETRY, and SHORT STORIES. Related articles in *The New Book of Knowledge* include CHILDREN'S LITER-ATURE, FAIRY TALES, and FOLKLORE.

The literature of individual countries is surveyed in numerous articles, including AFRICA, LITERATURE OF; AMERICAN LITERATURE; GERMANY, LITERATURE OF; LATIN AMERICA, LITERATURE OF; and RUSSIA, LANGUAGE AND LITERATURE OF.

Consult the Index to find the many biographies of authors contained in this encyclopedia.

and ideas. Nevertheless, fiction is most often what we study as "literature."

Epics

Imaginative literature belongs to all ages, but different forms emerged at different periods of history. The ancient Greeks were outstanding writers of epics—long story-poems about heroic events. Homer's *Iliad* describes the ten-year-long siege of Troy; the *Odyssey* recounts the heroic adventures of Ulysses on his voyage home from Troy. Later examples of the epic are Vergil's *Aeneid* and Milton's *Paradise Lost*. Although we still read the great epics of the past, the epic is no longer a popular literary form.

Drama

A drama is a story meant to be acted out on the stage. The Greeks invented drama as we know it today. But for most of us, the great age of dramatic writing was the reign of England's Queen Elizabeth I (1558–1603). And the greatest of the Elizabethan dramatists was William Shakespeare, the master of both comedy, as in *Twelfth Night*, and tragedy, as in *Hamlet*. Shakespeare's rivals included Christopher Marlowe and Ben Jonson, who were also very gifted dramatists.

Like the Greek playwrights, the Elizabethans wrote their dramas in poetic form. In more recent times most playwrights have written in prose.

Poetry

Poetry differs from prose in having a regular rhythm, sometimes using rhyme, and employing a more careful and beautiful selection of words. Lyric poetry is short, very personal, and songlike. The ode, a form of lyric poetry, is dignified in style. Narrative poetry tells a story.

Nearly every age has left some memorable poems. But in the early 1800's, the period known as Romantic, poetry was the chief literary form. William Wordsworth, Percy Bysshe Shelley, and John Keats are known for their splendid lyrics and odes. Wordsworth's "Intimations of Immortality" is among the greatest odes. Samuel Taylor Coleridge's "The Rime of the Ancient Mariner" is a ghostly tale of magic and mystery.

These four poets brought new subjects into verse and found a new richness of language.

The Romantics influenced the poets of later generations, including Alfred Tennyson, Robert Browning, Matthew Arnold, and Walt Whitman. These in turn prepared the way for the modern poets, such as T. S. Eliot, Robert Frost, and Ted Hughes.

Novels and Short Stories

A novel is a long story, often with many characters and an involved plot. It is the youngest of the literary forms. *Don Quixote* by Cervantes, perhaps the first great novel, was completed in 1615. But the great age of the novel was the Victorian period.

By the middle of the 1800's, fiction in prose form had replaced poetry as the most popular literary form both in England and America. A few titles will be enough to suggest the range and quality of the great age of the novel: Charles Dickens' *David Copperfield*, Charlotte Brontë's *Jane Eyre*, Herman Melville's *Moby Dick*, and Mark Twain's *Huckleberry Finn*.

The popularity of the novel continued into the 1900's. Theodore Dreiser, Stephen Crane, and others wrote realistic novels. Later, James Joyce, Ernest Hemingway, William Faulkner, and many Latin American writers expanded the scope of the novel.

Short stories are much shorter than novels, but they differ in more than length. A short story usually has only a few characters and focuses on a single incident. While novels were gaining popularity in the 1800's, Nathaniel Hawthorne, Edgar Allan Poe, and other writers were developing the short story as a distinctively American literary form.

▶ JUDGING LITERATURE

The basic tests for high literary quality remain much the same for all periods. Good literature from any age is judged on the power and beauty of its language.

Every true poet and storyteller achieves his or her own style, or original way of presenting impressions and ideas. Each tries to find just the right word to express an exact meaning, or just the right figure of speech (such as a metaphor or simile) to compare newly imagined characters and objects with persons and things already known. Each has some special skill in giving his or her writing excitement—perhaps by colorful phrasing or humorous detail, or by lively, realistic dialogue.

GLOSSARY OF LITERARY TERMS

Allegory: An extended metaphor; a tale in which characters or actions symbolize or suggest certain ideas, morals, qualities, or beliefs.

Alliteration: The use of the same first letter or sound in a group of words. An example is found in the first line of *The Fall of the House of Usher*, a short story by Edgar Allan Poe: "During the whole of a dull, dark, and soundless day. . ."

Analogy: A comparison between two basically different things possessing a similar characteristic, such as a mechanical clock and a heart (both produce a regular beat).

Assonance: The repetition of a sound within several words, such as in this line by the British poet Thomas Gray: "The lowing herd wind slowly o'er the lea. . ."

Elegy: A mournful poem written in praise of someone who has died.

Epilogue: The conclusion of a literary work; a speech concluding a play.

Eponym: The name of someone so often associated with a particular characteristic that the name comes to stand for that characteristic. For instance, the character's name Scrooge from Charles Dickens' *A Christmas Carol* has come to mean a miserly person.

Euphemism: A vague or indirect expression used in place of a more exact word or statement that is thought to be too direct or offensive; for example, saying "passed away" instead of "died."

Fable: A short and simple tale designed to teach a truth; usually features animals as the main characters.

Figure of speech: An expression that uses an imaginative rather than a literal meaning of words. Similes, metaphors, and irony are all figures of speech.

Hyperbole: The use of excessive exaggeration to make a point.

Irony: A figure of speech in which the literal meaning of what is said is the opposite of what is meant.

Metaphor: A direct, imaginative comparison made between two dissimilar things. When the English poet William Blake wrote "Tyger Tyger, burning bright/In the forests of the night. . ." he was speaking metaphorically; obviously the tiger was not on fire, but rather its colors had the vivid brightness of flames.

Onomatopoeia: Words that sound like what they describe, such as "slap," "hiss," or "buzz."

Oxymoron: The combination of two contradictory words or phrases to produce a new, unique meaning, such as "loud silence."

Palindrome: A word or group of words that read the same backward and forward, like the name "Anna."

Parable: A story meant to teach a lesson or moral by comparison to actual events.

Paradox: A statement that appears to contradict itself but actually makes sense as a figure of speech, such as Shakespeare's statement "Cowards die many times before their deaths."

Parody: A mocking imitation of a type of literature or a specific work.

Personification: When a writer gives human qualities (such as emotions, behaviors, or physical appearances) to animals, objects, or ideas.

Poetic license: The freedom a writer takes when he or she ignores established facts, conventions, or the proper use of language to achieve a desired literary effect.

Pseudonym: The name an author uses instead of his or her own. Also called a pen name. Famous pseudonyms in literature include Mark Twain (Samuel Langhorne Clemens), Lewis Carroll (Charles Lutwig Dodgson), George Eliot (Mary Ann Evans), and George Orwell (Eric Blair).

Satire: A literary work that uses humor and wit to ridicule its subject. Two famous works of satire are Jonathan Swift's novel *Gulliver's Travels* and Lord Byron's comic poem *Don Juan*.

Simile: A comparison of two things that are not alike, using words such as "like," "as," or "as if." The poet Lord Byron used a simile when he wrote "She walks in beauty like the night/Of cloudless climes and starry skies. . ."

Soliloquy: A speech made by a character in a play who is thinking out loud.

Symbol: An object, or sometimes a character, that represents an idea.

Theme: The overall meaning of a literary work, or the various subjects that recur within the work.

How are we to judge the success of imaginative literature? We may know at once what we like most in our reading. Yet we should try to consider the reasons for our choices. Experienced readers have discovered that the good poem or story is the one that is read over and over again with pleasure. It has a fresh style and a pattern that fits its separate parts—character, plot, and theme—into a well-shaped, pleasing whole.

We may ask ourselves a few helpful questions when we try to explain our literary likes and dislikes. For example, does the language used by the writer seem perfectly suited to the poem or story? Do the characters seem lifelike? Do their actions strike us as probable? Do the descriptions succeed in bringing the setting clearly before us? Above all, does the writer really stir our feelings and stimulate our imaginations?

When we can answer some of these questions, we can begin to understand something of the lasting power of good literature.

JEROME H. BUCKLEY
Harvard University

LITHOGRAPHY. See GRAPHIC ARTS.

LITHUANIA

Lithuania is the largest and most populous of the three European nations known as the Baltic States, a name derived from their location on the eastern shore of the Baltic Sea. Latvia lies just to its north. Estonia, the third Baltic state, is situated north of Latvia. In addition to Latvia, the countries bordering Lithuania are Belarus on the east, Poland on the south, and Russia on the southwest.

An important power during the late Middle Ages, Lithuania became a part of the Russian Empire in the 1700's. It declared its independence in 1918 but was forcibly annexed by the Soviet Union in 1940. After more than half a century of Soviet rule, Lithuania gained its independence for a second time in 1991, amid the breakup of the Soviet Union.

The People. The Lithuanians are a Baltic people—not Slavic, as is often thought—whose ancestors inhabited the region as early as 3000 B.C. Of the numerous Baltic peoples who once lived here, however, only the Lithuanians and the Latvians have survived.

Lithuanians constitute about 80 percent of the country's population. The largest minorities are Russians (with about 9 percent of the population), Poles (about 7 percent), Belarusians (nearly 2 percent), and Ukrainians (about 1 percent). Jews, Latvians, Germans, and Gypsies make up most of the rest of Lithuania's varied peoples. The percentage of Russians, many of whom were government administrators, more than tripled during the years of

Crosses decorate a shrine in the Lithuanian countryside. It is an ancient custom in Lithuania to erect crosses at wayside shrines in order to commemorate important family or national events.

Soviet rule. Most of Lithuania's Jews, who were once more than 7 percent of its population, were massacred by the Nazis during World War II.

Language and Religion. The official language is Lithuanian, an ancient tongue related to Latvian. The various ethnic groups usually speak their own languages. The government also supports schools in which instruction is given in Russian and Polish.

The great majority of Lithuanians are Roman Catholics. The major religious holidays, such as Christmas, Easter, and All Souls' Day, are state holidays. Despite severe persecution of the church under the Soviet Communists, the majority of Lithuanians have remained deeply religious. In addition to Roman Catholics, the other significant religious denom-

Sheep graze peacefully on a Lithuanian meadow. The country's landscape consists mostly of open plain or gently rolling hills. The Ice Age glaciers that created Lithuania's flat terrain also carved out thousands of small lakes and numerous short rivers.

inations are the Lutherans, Calvinists, and Eastern Orthodox Christians.

Way of Life. Lithuania today is an industrialized nation, with about two thirds of its population city dwellers. But until fairly recent times, it was still a largely rural country in which most of the people were peasant farmers. Rural traditions included elaborate weddings lasting several days. Such celebrations are now usually reserved for special occasions, as is the wearing of traditional folk dress.

The Lithuanian tradition of choral, or group, singing, however, has remained very much alive, and huge song festivals are organized regularly. Although forbidden by the Communists, the custom of erecting crosses at wayside shrines to commemorate family or national events has also survived, so much so that frequently the countryside seems covered with crosses. Lithuanian families remain closely knit. Family size has diminished, but Lithuania's birth and population growth rates are still among the highest in Europe.

Recreation. Lithuanians are avid movie, theater, opera, and ballet fans. The most popular sport is basketball. Lithuania won the European basketball championship in 1938 and 1939, and today Lithuanians play as professionals on U.S. and European teams. Most city dwellers spend as much time as they can out of doors, often tending the small garden plots found by the thousands around cities and towns. Camping, fishing, and hunting are also popular activities.

The Land. Lithuania's terrain was shaped by glaciers during the Ice Age. It is mostly an open plain, with the highest elevation, about 960 feet (300 meters), in the southeast. Some

3,000 lakes and about 750 rivers dot the landscape. The chief river is the Nemunas. The Baltic Sea shore is a favorite resort area. The country's most fertile areas are in the southwestern and central regions.

Climate and Natural Resources. Lithuania has a moderate climate. Temperatures vary from an average low of 27°F (−3°C) in winter to an average high of 64°F (18°C) in summer. Rainfall averages from 22 to 34 inches (559 to 864 millimeters) a year.

Lithuania is not rich in natural resources. It has modest amounts of oil and as yet untapped sources of thermal energy and deposits of iron ore. Dolomite, quartz, sand, clay, and gravel provide raw materials for fine quality cement, glass, ceramics, and building stone.

FACTS and figures

REPUBLIC OF LITHUANIA is the official name of the country.

LOCATION: Northeastern Europe, on the Baltic Sea.

AREA: 25,174 sq mi (65,200 km²).

POPULATION: 3,740,000 (estimate).

CAPITAL AND LARGEST CITY: Vilnius.

MAJOR LANGUAGES: Lithuanian (official), Russian, Polish.

MAJOR RELIGIOUS GROUP: Christian (Roman Catholic).

GOVERNMENT: Republic. **Head of state**—president. **Head of government**—prime minister. **Legislature**—parliament.

CHIEF PRODUCTS: Agricultural—meat and dairy products, wheat and other grains, flax, sugar beets, potatoes. **Manufactured**—metal products, motors, consumer goods, processed foods, furniture, fertilizers, textiles, fishing vessels. **Mineral**—dolomite, quartz, clays.

Major Cities. The capital and largest city is Vilnius, situated in the eastern part of the country. Founded in 1323, it is now a center of industry, with a population of about 580,000. Other major cities include Kaunas, second largest in population, and the port city of Klaipéda.

The Economy. Industry accounts for about 55 percent of Lithuania's gross national product. Its chief manufactures include a variety of metal products, motors, television sets, washing machines, tape recorders, bicycles, processed foods, furniture, fertilizers, plastics, and textiles. Shipbuilding (particularly large fishing vessels), oil refining, the production of nuclear-powered electricity, and the fishing industry are also of importance.

Lithuania's agriculture emphasizes meat and dairy production. Wheat and other grains, flax (used to make linen), sugar beets, potatoes, and other vegetables are the chief crops.

Early History. The Lithuanian tribes were first united as a nation in about 1230 under Duke Mindaugas. In 1251, Mindaugas was converted to Christianity and crowned king. However, his nobles revolted and killed him, and Lithuania returned to the pagan worship of nature. In 1387, Grand Duke Jogaila (Jagiello) accepted the Polish crown and in return established a personal union with Poland. He became a Christian and, with his cousin, Grand Duke Vytautas, converted the Lithuanians to Christianity. Under Vytautas, Lithuania expanded from the Baltic to the Black Sea. In 1569, Lithuania and Poland were united into a single state.

Russian and Soviet Rule. In 1795, in the final partition (division) of Poland, Lithuania was absorbed by the Russian Empire. A Lithuanian nationalist movement began in the 1800's, and after the Russian Empire was overthrown in 1917, Lithuania proclaimed its independence, on February 16, 1918.

When World War II broke out in 1939, Lithuania declared itself neutral. In 1940, however, as a result of a secret pact between Nazi German and Soviet leaders, Lithuania was annexed by the Soviet Union. Aside from the interval of German occupation from 1941 to 1944, Lithuania remained a Soviet republic until 1991. Lithuanian armed resistance to the Soviets caused tens of thousands of casualties. The Soviets deported an estimated 300,000 people, suppressed liberties,

Lithuanians celebrate Independence Day. Lithuania was the first of the Baltic nations to proclaim its independence from the Soviet Union, in 1990.

and made the country economically dependent on the Soviet Union.

Independence. In 1988, Lithuanians organized a massive reform movement, called Sajudis, which forced a break with the Soviet Communists in 1989. Multiparty elections for a new parliament in 1990 were won by Sajudis. Lithuanian independence was proclaimed and Vytautas Landsbergis was elected president. The Soviet Union responded with an economic blockade and a show of military force. Both failed, and in 1991, it recognized Lithuania's independence.

Presidential elections in 1993 resulted in a victory for the Democratic Labor Party's leader, Algirdas Brazauskas. In 1998, independent candidate Valdas Adamkus, a World War II refugee who lived for more than forty years in the United States, was elected president. He was succeeded in 2003 by Rolandas Paksas, who was later charged with corruption and removed from office. In 2004, Adamkus was re-elected president. That same year, Lithuania joined the North Atlantic Treaty Organization (NATO) and the European Union (EU).

V. STANLEY VARDYS
University of Oklahoma
Author, *Lithuania Under the Soviets*

Baseball fans throng the grandstands to watch the Little League World Series, which is played each summer at Little League headquarters in Williamsport, Pennsylvania.

LITTLE LEAGUE BASEBALL

Little League Baseball is a nonprofit organization providing organized baseball and softball for young people between the ages of 9 and 18. It is the only organization of its kind to have the official support of the United States government in the form of a federal charter. Both the baseball and softball programs have a Little League division for youngsters 9 to 12 years old, a Junior League division for 13- to 14-year-olds, a Senior League division for 14- to 16-year-olds, and a Big League division for players 16 to 18. In addition, players between the ages of 5 and 10 may participate in a special Tee Ball instructional program.

Today approximately 2.4 million players in some 100 countries participate in Little League, Junior League, Senior League, and Big League baseball and softball. There are more than 18,000 leagues.

▶ DEVELOPMENT OF LITTLE LEAGUE

The organization began in Williamsport, Pennsylvania, with one league of three teams. Growth was slow at first, because of World War II. But in 1947, Little League began to expand rapidly. In 1948 there were 94 leagues. Within a year these numbers had more than tripled, to 307 leagues. By 1955 every state in the United States had Little League teams.

Also in the 1950's, Little League became international, with teams formed in Britain, Germany, Venezuela, Mexico, and Canada.

In 1961 the Senior League Baseball division was begun, and in 1968 the Big League Baseball division was organized.

An important change occurred in Little League Baseball in 1974. President Gerald R. Ford signed legislation permitting girls to play on the formerly all-boy teams. Since then, girls have been avid players.

In 1974–75, Little League and Senior League softball programs were organized. Big League Softball and Junior League Baseball divisions were created in 1980, and a Junior League Softball division was established in 1999.

▶ PLAYING FIELD AND EQUIPMENT

Little League Baseball is played on a scaled-down version of a major league baseball diamond. The distance between bases is 60 feet (18.3 meters). The pitching distance is 46 feet (14 meters). The outfield fence is 200 feet (61 meters) from home plate. In Junior League, Senior League, and Big League baseball, the baselines are 90 feet (27.4 meters), the pitching distance is 60 feet, 6 inches (18.4 meters), and the outfield fence is 300 feet (91.4 meters) from home plate. All four softball divisions play on regulation Little League fields. The only exception is that the pitching distance in softball is 40 feet (12.2 meters).

Little Leaguers use bats (wood and metal) and balls that are lighter in weight than regular baseball equipment. The players wear regular uniforms and shoes with rubber or molded cleats.

Safety is extremely important. All batters, base runners, base coaches, and on-deck batters must wear protective batting helmets. The catcher must wear the long-model chest protector and foam throat protector, shin guards, catcher's helmet with attached face mask, and a protective groin cup supporter.

▶ LITTLE LEAGUE SPONSORS

There are no owners of Little League teams, but there are sponsors. The sponsors, who have no voice in the administration of the leagues, are usually civic groups, such as the Chamber of Commerce, the Young Men's Christian Association, B'nai B'rith, veterans' organizations, or police and fire departments, as well as various business organizations in the community. Usually a local league is started by a small group of parents and other interested adults in a neighborhood, who then enlist the support of sponsoring agencies.

Sponsors give money for the players' uniforms and equipment. But they do not run the team they sponsor. They cannot appoint managers or coaches or dictate rules or policy. Team managers and coaches are chosen by a committee of volunteer adults.

Girls have played in Little League since 1974, when President Gerald R. Ford signed legislation allowing girls to play on formerly all-boy teams.

Each team in the league has a sponsor. It costs hundreds of dollars to supply a league with enough uniforms and equipment for all its players. The sponsors of the teams split the expenses among themselves. At the end of each season, all the playing gear is turned in to the League officials, except for the baseball caps. These the players are allowed to keep.

Before it can be officially considered a member of Little League Baseball, a new league must apply for a certificate of charter (right to play). The national headquarters will send all necessary information to any group wishing to form a new league. The full address is Little League Headquarters, P.O. Box 3485, Williamsport, Pennsylvania 17701. Little League Baseball also has regional offices in St. Petersburg, Florida; Bristol, Connecticut; Indianapolis, Indiana; San Bernardino, California; and Waco, Texas.

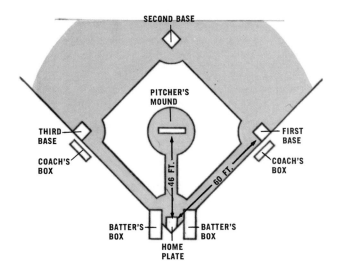

LITTLE LEAGUE WORLD SERIES CHAMPIONS

1947	Williamsport, Pennsylvania	1967	West Tokyo, Japan	1987	Hua-lien, Taiwan
1948	Lock Haven, Pennsylvania	1968	Wakayama, Japan	1988	T'ai-chung, Taiwan
1949	Hammonton, New Jersey	1969	Taiwan Red Leafs	1989	Trumbull, Connecticut
1950	Houston, Texas	1970	Wayne, New Jersey	1990	T'ai-nan, Taiwan
1951	Stamford, Connecticut	1971	Taiwan all-star team	1991	Taipei, Taiwan
1952	Norwalk, Connecticut	1972	Taiwan all-star team	1992	Long Beach, California (by forfeit)
1953	Birmingham, Alabama	1973	T'ai-nan, Taiwan	1993	Long Beach, California
1954	Schenectady, New York	1974	Kaohsiung, Taiwan	1994	Maracaibo, Venezuela
1955	Morrisville, Pennsylvania	1975	Lakewood Township, New Jersey	1995	T'ai-nan, Taiwan
1956	Roswell, New Mexico	1976	Tokyo, Japan	1996	Taipei, Taiwan
1957	Monterrey, Mexico	1977	Taipei, Taiwan	1997	Guadalupe, Mexico
1958	Monterrey, Mexico	1978	P'ing-tung, Taiwan	1998	Toms River, New Jersey
1959	Hamtramck, Michigan	1979	Pu-tzu, Taiwan	1999	Osaka, Japan
1960	Levittown, Pennsylvania	1980	Taiwan all-star team	2000	Maracaibo, Venezuela
1961	El Cajon, California	1981	T'ai-chung, Taiwan	2001	Tokyo, Japan
1962	San Jose, California	1982	Kirkland, Washington	2002	Louisville, Kentucky
1963	Granada Hills, California	1983	Marietta, Georgia	2003	Tokyo, Japan
1964	Staten Island, New York	1984	Seoul, South Korea	2004	Willemstad, Curaçao
1965	Windsor Locks, Connecticut	1985	Seoul, South Korea	2005	Ewa Beach, Hawaii
1966	Houston, Texas	1986	T'ai-nan, Taiwan		

▶ **CANDIDATES FOR LITTLE LEAGUE**

Every year, tryouts are held in the spring for all the teams of a league. In a community, boys and girls between the ages of 5 and 18 are eligible to become candidates if they have their parents' written permission and a physician's approval. During spring training, players can bat and field in the positions of their choice, competing with players their own age. The managers judge the players' abilities and then bid for the players at an auction. Instead of money, credits are used. Each league team has the same number of credits to spend.

A Little League Baseball team may have from 12 to 15 players. The teams must be balanced so that all the best players are not on

LITTLE LEAGUE TEE BALL

Little League Tee Ball is an instructional program for players aged 5 to 8. The game uses an adjustable batting stand, or "tee," rather than a pitched ball. The batter tries to hit the ball from the nonmoving tee. A baseball or a softball may be used. Each inning each player is allowed a turn at bat, regardless of how many outs are made. This and other rule changes from conventional baseball or softball are designed to aid instruction.

Generally, most of the rules of Tee Ball are identical to those of Little League Baseball. But the local league may change Tee Ball rules to serve the best interests of the young players. As a result, Tee Ball rules may vary slightly from league to league.

Tee Ball developed as a way of allowing younger players to practice running, fielding, and throwing before they mastered the more difficult skills of pitching and of hitting a pitched ball. It is also good batting practice to attempt to hit a ball off a tee. As young players become better at all the baseball skills, they may move on to play conventional baseball or softball.

One of the interesting aspects of Tee Ball is that a team manager or coach may request a "time out" from the umpire during the game in order to demonstrate a technique or explain a play. Because Tee Ball is instructional, players are encouraged to learn in addition to having fun. Competition—winning and losing—is considered less important.

the same team. For example, teams in the major division may have no more than eight 12-year-old players.

A Little League Baseball game consists of six innings, and every league must play at least 36 games in a season. The winning team becomes the champion of its league. An all-star team composed of the best players from all teams in the league goes on through various levels of play to compete for the regional championship.

In addition to the eight Little League divisions in the United States, the others are Canada, the Trans-Atlantic, the European, the Caribbean, Latin America, Mexico, Asia, and the Pacific. The champions from each league play in the Little League World Series, held annually in Williamsport, Pennsylvania.

The first Little League World Series took place in 1947. The champions were from Williamsport, Pennsylvania. Ten years later, a team from Monterrey, Mexico, became the first champion from outside the United States. Between 1969 and 1996, teams from Taiwan dominated the series, winning 17 championships, including five in a row (1977–81). Teams from the United States, however, have won the World Series 26 times, more than teams from any other country.

▶ LITTLE LEAGUE GRADUATES

Most young people who play Little League dream of becoming professional baseball players. However, because of the skill and athleticism required, only a small percentage actually make it. Little Leaguers who did make it to the major leagues and become stars of the game include Rod Carew, Nolan Ryan, Tom Seaver, Steve Carlton, Carl Yastrzemski, Cal Ripken, Jr., and Derek Jeter.

Reviewed by STEVE KEENER
Little League Baseball, Inc.

LITTLE ROCK. See ARKANSAS (Cities).

LITTLE TURTLE. See INDIANS, AMERICAN (Profiles).

LIVER

The liver is the largest organ in the body, weighing more than 3 pounds (1.4 kilograms). A wedge-shaped, reddish structure, it lies at the top of the abdominal cavity, fitting snugly under the diaphragm (the sheet of muscle that forms the floor of the chest cavity) on the right side of the body.

Performing more than 500 known functions, the liver is also the body's most versatile organ. It receives the food-laden blood flowing from the digestive organs, processing about a quart of blood each minute. The liver helps regulate the composition of the blood, storing some nutrients and subjecting others to various chemical reactions. It produces important blood proteins, recycles worn-out red blood cells and antibodies, and changes poisons and other harmful substances to less damaging forms. It also produces a substance called **bile** that helps in the digestion of fats. The liver helps regulate the volume of blood flowing through the body, as well. Normally the liver contains about a pint of blood—about 10 percent of the body's total blood volume—but it can expand to hold two or three times that much.

▶ PARTS OF THE LIVER

A tough ligament divides the liver into two main parts, or **lobes**. The **right lobe**, about six times larger than the left lobe, lies above the right kidney and a loop of the large intestine. The **left lobe** lies above the stomach. On the underside, the right lobe is further divided into two smaller lobes, the **quadrate lobe** (which covers the gallbladder) and the **caudate lobe**.

Most organs receive blood carried by arteries and are drained by veins. The liver, however, is supplied with blood from two separate sources. The **hepatic artery** brings oxygen-rich blood to the liver. After providing for the needs of the liver cells, this blood is carried away by the **hepatic vein** and eventually is returned to the heart. The liver also receives blood—about 80 percent of its total supply—from the **hepatic portal vein**, which carries blood gathered from the digestive system. After it is processed by the liver, this blood also drains out into the hepatic vein.

The lobes of the liver contain about 100,000 small structures called **lobules**. These are the working units of the liver. Inside each

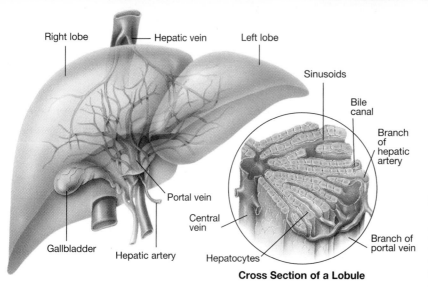

Right lobe — Hepatic vein   Left lobe

Sinusoids

Bile canal

Branch of hepatic artery

Portal vein

Central vein

Branch of portal vein

Gallbladder   Hepatic artery

Hepatocytes

Cross Section of a Lobule

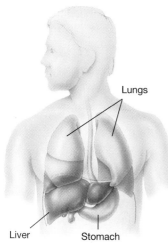

Lungs

Liver   Stomach

Serving as the body's master chemical laboratory, the liver performs more than 500 essential functions. Located in the upper right portion of the abdomen, the liver is the largest internal organ. The right and left lobes make up most of the liver. Each lobe is made up of many smaller six-sided units called lobules. The work of the liver takes place in the lobules, which interconnect with elements of the circulatory system, the bile-collecting system, and the lymphatic system.

proteins to pass freely into the narrow spaces around the liver cell plates. The excess fluid drains into the **lymphatic vessels** and is eventually mingled with the blood returned to the heart.

▶ HOW THE LIVER WORKS

The liver is like a vast chemical factory in which hundreds of chemical reactions take place constantly, affecting nearly every part of the body. Working on the food-filled blood delivered by the hepatic portal vein, hepatocytes process all the major types of nutrients—carbohydrates, fats, and proteins.

Starches and sugars in foods are digested into **glucose** and other simple sugars, which can be used in body cells to release energy. Liver cells convert some of the glucose in the blood to an animal starch, **glycogen**, and store it until the body needs more energy fuel. If the body's glucose supplies are very low, the versatile hepatocytes can also produce glucose from amino acids and glycerol, the building blocks usually used to form proteins and fats. (This formation of "new" glucose is called **gluconeogenesis**.)

Fats are also important energy fuels for the body, and the liver plays an important role in processing and storing fats. In the liver, fatty acids are oxidized to release energy, and carbohydrates and proteins are converted to fat. Liver cells also produce phospholipids, which help to form cell membranes, and cholesterol. About 80 percent of the cholesterol produced in the liver is used to form bile, which emulsifies fats (breaks them down into smaller particles) so that the digestive enzymes can reach them more effectively. Bile also helps in the excretion of body wastes, such as the breakdown products of old red blood cells. About a pint of bile is formed each day.

The amino acids that make up proteins contain nitrogen, which must be removed for proteins to be used for energy or converted to carbohydrates and fats. Hepatocytes remove the nitrogen-containing amino groups from amino acids in the form of ammonia,

lobule, liver cells called **hepatocytes** form one-cell-thick plates arranged like the spokes of a wheel around a **central vein**. The spaces between the liver cell plates, called **sinusoids**, receive blood from the portal vein. After the blood has been processed by the hepatocytes, it empties into the central vein and eventually drains into the hepatic vein. Running between the liver cells in each plate are small channels, or **bile canals**, which empty into the tubular **bile ducts** that carry bile to the gallbladder. (The gallbladder is a small, pearshaped sac that temporarily stores bile.)

The lining of the sinusoids in the liver lobules also contains special cells called **Kupffer cells**. Like the white blood cells that patrol the blood and tissues, Kupffer cells can gobble down bacteria, damaged blood cells, and bits of debris. Many openings or pores in the lining of the sinusoids allow fluid and even

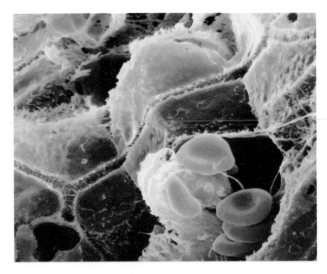

In this color-enhanced view of a liver, a few disk-shaped red blood cells surround a yellow Kupffer cell, which patrols the liver for foreign materials and debris. Green bile ducts branch through a one-cell-thick section of red-brown hepatocytes.

which is then converted to **urea**, a waste product that is carried out of the body in urine. Liver cells can also form amino acids and convert them to other amino acids. In addition, the liver produces about 90 percent of the proteins in blood plasma, including **albumin**, as well as the proteins involved in blood clotting and proteins that transport chemicals in the blood.

The liver stores reserves of many important compounds needed by the body. The fat-soluble vitamins (A, D, E, and K), as well as vitamin B_{12}, are stored in the liver. This organ also stores iron recycled from the hemoglobin contained in worn-out red blood cells that the Kupffer cells have captured. (A colored substance called **bilirubin** is formed in the breakdown of hemoglobin; it gives bile its typical greenish-orange color.) Lipid (fat) deposits in the liver store various fat-soluble poisons such as DDT, which the liver cells have taken out of the blood. Other poisons are converted to less harmful substances by the liver cells, or they may be bound to the bile salts and sent out of the body through the digestive tract.

The Kupffer cells lining the liver sinusoids are very efficient in cleaning the blood that flows in from the hepatic portal vein. By the time the blood leaves the liver, about 99 percent of the bacteria it contained have been removed.

▶ DISORDERS OF THE LIVER

As the body's main organ for coping with poisons, the liver is equipped to take a lot of punishment and still go on working. However, some poisons—including drugs and environmental pollutants—as well as viruses, bacteria, and certain parasites can damage the liver and hinder its functioning.

The most familiar sign of liver disorder is **jaundice**, a yellowness of the body tissues, especially noticeable in the skin and eyes. This color results from abnormally large amounts of the bile pigment bilirubin in the blood. Jaundice may be caused by an unusually high level of destruction of red blood cells; this form is called **hemolytic jaundice**. (In this case the liver is working properly but so much bilirubin is formed that it cannot be excreted fast enough, and some remains in the blood that leaves the liver.) An inability of the liver cells to take up or transport bilirubin results in **hepatocellular jaundice**, which may be due to hepatitis, cirrhosis, poisoning, or tumors. Blockage of the bile ducts, preventing bile from flowing out into the digestive tract, results in **obstructive jaundice**. Tests for particular forms of bilirubin in the blood and urine can help to determine the cause of jaundice. Tests of liver function can also help to diagnose liver disease, assess the damage, and evaluate how well a treatment is working.

Hepatitis is the general term for inflammation of the liver. Viral infections are the most common cause of hepatitis. At least five viruses have been found to infect the liver. Some, such as hepatitis A,

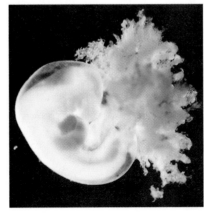

As seen in this 5-week-old fetus, the liver and heart begin to take shape in the earliest stages of development.

A healthy liver (*right*) contrasts with a liver badly damaged by cirrhosis (*below right*), a disease in which scar tissue impairs the liver's ability to function.

are transmitted by drinking polluted water or eating foods that have come in contact with it—for example, berries picked from plants watered from a contaminated source. Other hepatitis viruses, including hepatitis B and C, are transmitted from person to person through infected body fluids. For example, these viruses may be transferred through the sharing of contaminated needles among abusers of intravenous drugs. Blood transfusions used to be a common cause of viral hepatitis, but now blood tests screen for hepatitis contamination. A vaccine to prevent hepatitis B is available. Usually a person with hepatitis recovers fully. Sometimes, however, the virus remains in the body, producing a chronic infection that may be transmitted to others even if there are no apparent symptoms. This condition may result in more serious liver damage—a progressive scarring called **cirrhosis**.

Although cirrhosis of the liver can result from viral infections, obstruction of the bile ducts, and certain hereditary diseases, one of the most common causes is chronic alcohol abuse. Alcohol is a poison, and the continual intake of large amounts of alcohol damages the liver cells. Hepatocytes die and are gradually replaced by bands and lumps of scar tissue. In the early stages there are no symptoms. As the damage progresses, the liver becomes less able to perform its functions, and the pressure in the hepatic portal vein rises. Fluid may accumulate in the abdominal cavity and cause the ankles to swell, as a result of the high portal blood pressure and the failure of the liver cells to produce enough albumin for the blood plasma. With fewer working liver cells, poisonous nitrogen compounds formed in the digestion of proteins build up in the blood and are carried to the brain. There they may destroy nerve cells, and the person may develop memory problems, thinking difficulties, and muscle tremors. Although the parts of the liver damaged by cirrhosis can never completely return to normal, eliminating the cause—for example, abstaining from alcohol—can stop the progressive damage.

Cancer of the liver is very common in some areas of the world (such as certain African countries) but is rare in others (including the United States and western Europe). Substances found in certain local diets can cause liver cancer. These include plant chemicals used to brew native teas, as well as aflatoxin, a substance produced by mold that grows on damp peanuts. Viral hepatitis and cirrhosis due to chronic alcohol abuse can also make a person more likely to develop liver cancer. If the cancer has not spread too widely, the tumor can be removed by surgery.

A liver can still function when as much as 75 percent of it has been lost as a result of disease or surgery. However, severe liver damage can result in death. Very severe liver disease may be treated by removing the damaged liver and replacing it with a healthy liver from someone who has died in an accident. Such **liver transplants** are most successful in young patients. An artificial liver called ELAD (Extracorporeal Liver Assist Device) is being developed to help people with chronic liver disease.

ALVIN SILVERSTEIN
VIRGINIA SILVERSTEIN
Coauthors, *Hepatitis; The Digestive System*

See also BODY, HUMAN.

Did you know that...

the liver is one of the few parts of the body that can regenerate? If part of the liver is damaged or removed, the lost part can grow back! Doctors use this amazing ability in liver transplants for young children. A section of healthy liver from an adult can take the place of the child's diseased liver; meanwhile the donor's liver soon grows back to its full size.

LIVESTOCK

The term "livestock" refers to various domestic animals that are used for essential human needs, such as food, clothing, shelter, fuel, and draft (or work). Livestock have been important to people for thousands of years. Goats were one of the first animals to be domesticated, or tamed, about 10,000 years ago. Later, pigs, sheep, cattle, and horses were domesticated.

The various ways of breeding, raising, and caring for livestock are called **animal husbandry**. Animal husbandry practices are influenced by such factors as the environment, available natural resources (food and water, for example), and the needs of the people raising the animals. In developing countries, livestock are often raised by individual families using local resources. In developed nations, livestock production has become "industrialized," meaning that animals are raised in vast enclosures with specialized feed, modern medicines, proven managment practices, and efficient processing systems.

Livestock production methods range from simple to complex. A rancher on horseback (*above*) drives a herd of sheep. Beef cattle (*left*) eat nutrient-packed grain from an automated feeding system.

▶ LIVESTOCK AND THEIR USES

No matter what type of production is used, livestock are raised to provide products ranging from milk and meat to pharmaceutical drugs, glue, and fertilizer. The types of livestock most widely used around the world include cattle, sheep, swine (pigs), poultry, goats, horses, buffalo, and camels.

Cattle

Cattle are found in almost every part of the world. The largest population is in India, where cattle are considered sacred and are not killed or eaten. Brazil ranks second in cattle numbers, followed by the United States, China, Russia, and Argentina.

In developing countries, cattle are used for work, milk, and meat. Cattle dung is used as fuel and fertilizer in some developing countries. In industrialized nations, cattle are se-lected for special traits, such as high-quality meat or large-volume milk production. In many countries, cattle graze on grasses and other plants, usually on land that is unsuitable for growing crops. In the United States and other nations, beef cattle are often fed high-energy grain diets, which speed the time needed for the cattle to be ready for market.

Texas, Kansas, Nebraska, and Oklahoma are the leading cattle-producing states.

Sheep

Sheep are found in most parts of the world. Domestic sheep are noted for their wool and meat, but in many cultures they also provide milk and cheese.

The leading sheep-producing countries are Australia, China, New Zealand, Iran, India, and Turkey. Colorado and Texas are the leading states for lamb production.

Pigs

Pigs are members of the swine family and are usually called hogs when raised as livestock. They were domesticated more than 5,000 years ago to provide meat, known in its various forms as pork, ham, bacon, sausage, and lard. Swine production farms, where up to 50,000 animals are fed special grain diets, are typical in industrialized nations such as the United States.

China produces almost half of the world's swine, followed by the United States, Russia, Poland, and Germany.

Poultry

The term "poultry" covers domesticated birds that are raised to provide meat and eggs. The most important poultry are chickens, turkeys, ducks, and geese.

Selective breeding, special diets, and automated facilities enable farmers to produce large quantities of meat and eggs. Arkansas, Georgia, Alabama, North Carolina, Mississippi, Texas, Maryland, and Delaware are the leading egg-producing states.

People throughout the world depend on livestock for basic work. A Peruvian farmer (*right*) uses oxen to plow a field. A camel caravan in Africa (*below*) carries firewood to market.

Goats

Native to the mountains of southwestern Asia, goats are important livestock throughout the world because of their small size, efficient milk production, and fertility. Goats are able to eat scarce and poor-quality plants that most other animals cannot use. They can share land with grazing cattle because they do not compete for the same food.

Large numbers of goats are found in central and north Africa, the Middle East, southern Asia, and China. Goats are becoming more important in the United States for their milk, meat, and their hair, which is spun into yarn. California is the leading goat-producing state.

Horses

Domesticated between 5,000 and 6,000 years ago, horses have been raised primarily for riding and draft purposes. Ponies and donkeys, relatives of the horse, are also raised as draft animals.

Horses are classified by body type, size, and use. The "light horse" group includes breeds used for riding and racing. Draft horses have more muscular bodies and bigger bones, making them useful for pulling carriages and plows and performing similar work. On most modern farms, draft horses have been replaced by tractors and other mechanical equipment.

China, Brazil, and Mexico are the three leading countries in horse production, followed by the United States, Ethiopia, Argentina, and Russia. Recreation with horses is an important industry in the United States. Texas is the leading horse-producing state.

Buffalo

Buffalo are widely used in Africa and Asia for meat, milk, and work. They are distantly related to the American bison, which is often called buffalo incorrectly. True buffalo originated in Asia, where they are called water buffalo.

Camels

Camels were domesticated in Asia and the Middle East. They still are important there as a source of meat, milk, cheese, leather goods, cloth, and transportation.

Other Livestock

Other domestic animals are also used for food, shelter, and transportation. Llamas and alpacas, natives of the Andes mountains of South America, provide wool and are used as pack animals. In cold climates, reindeer and caribou provide work, food, and clothing to people in Russia, Siberia, Finland, Norway, and Sweden. Deer farming is widely practiced in Europe, New Zealand, Canada, and the United States.

Smaller animals are also raised as livestock. Rabbits, guinea pigs, and the capybara, a large rodent, are used in some communities for food. Wild animals such as alligators, ostriches, and emus are also raised for food and other products, such as leather.

▶ MODERN LIVESTOCK PRODUCTION

An important goal of livestock production is to produce healthy animals that yield high-quality, abundant products. Modern animal husbandry practices have achieved just that. For example, in the past fifty years, milk production in the United States has increased even though the number of dairy cows has dropped by one-half.

Scientific developments such as artificial insemination, embryo transfer, gene manipulation, and animal cloning have greatly improved livestock production. They have also contributed to human medicine. Products such as hormones, vaccines, and even vital organs are being developed in livestock animals for use in people.

Intensive animal production is not without problems. Livestock can become stressed from crowded conditions; the environment can be damaged by enormous herds of animals; and human health can be put at risk from drugs, or additives, that are used to speed the rate of an animal's growth.

Some animal activists, environmentalists, vegetarians, and medical professionals work diligently to put an end to modern animal food production. With continued population growth on an increasingly crowded planet, society must decide how best to use and protect its animal resources.

LARRY BOLEMAN
Texas A & M University

See also BUFFALO AND BISON; CAMELS; CATTLE; FISHING INDUSTRY; GOATS; HORSES; PIGS; POULTRY; RABBITS AND HARES; SHEEP.

LIVINGSTONE, DAVID. See STANLEY, HENRY MORTON, AND DAVID LIVINGSTONE.

LIVINGSTON FAMILY

The Livingstons were an important family of merchants, landowners, and political leaders in early America, especially in New York and New Jersey, where several family members played key roles in the American Revolution. In addition to holding appointed and elected offices, the Livingstons were leaders in the Dutch Reformed and Presbyterian churches. They also led the movement to establish a college in the colony (now Columbia University) and were charter members of the New York Society Library. Several Livingstons also served on the committees that organized colonial resistance to British policies before the Revolutionary War.

Robert R. Livingston (1746–1813)

Robert Livingston (1654–1728), the founder of the family in America, was born in Scotland. In 1663, Livingston's parents, who were Presbyterians, moved their family to the Protestant Netherlands to escape religious persecution. But in 1673, Robert moved on to America, where he settled in the prosperous town of Albany, New York. In 1679 he married **Alida Schuyler Van Rensselaer** (1656–1726), a member of two of New York's most prominent families.

Robert succeeded in the fur trade and performed important duties for New York's colonial governors. In 1686, in return for his services, he was granted 160,000 acres (64,000 hectares) in the Hudson River valley, which became known as Livingston Manor. While Robert was engaged in politics and business in New York City, Alida oversaw milling, baking, and trading operations at the manor. Tenant farmers produced wheat for local sale and export.

Robert and Alida's eldest surviving son, **Philip Livingston** (1686–1749), inherited Livingston Manor when his father died in 1728. He diversified his family's business interests by producing iron at the manor. Philip's eldest son, **Robert Livingston** (1708–90), the third lord of the manor, expanded the ironworks, making it one of the most profitable and productive in colonial America.

Robert's younger brother, **Philip Livingston** (1716–78), became a member of the Continental Congress (1774–78) and signed the Declaration of Independence (1776). Robert and Philip's younger brother, **William Livingston** (1723–90), commanded the New Jersey militia (1776) and served as that state's first governor (1776–90). William's daughter, **Susannah Livingston Symmes** (1748–?), became a heroine of the Revolution when she prevented her father's public papers from falling into British hands during a raid on their home. William later represented New Jersey at the Constitutional Convention (1787).

Robert R. Livingston (1746–1813), a cousin, was a member of the Continental Congress (1775–77; 1779–81); sat on the congressional committee that drafted the Declaration of Independence (1776); and served as the U.S. minister of foreign affairs (1781–83). As chancellor of the state of New York (1777–1801), he gave the oath of office to George Washington when he became president in 1789. Later, as U.S. minister to France (1801–04), Robert helped negotiate the Louisiana Purchase (1803). His younger brother, **Edward Livingston** (1764–1836), served as mayor of New York City (1801–03), then moved to Louisiana, which he represented as a U.S. congressman (1823–29) and senator (1829–31). In 1831 President Andrew Jackson appointed him secretary of state. He later served as U.S. minister to France (1833–35).

In recent times, **Robert (Bob) Livingston** (1943–   ) also served as a U.S. representative (1977–99) from Louisiana.

Cynthia A. Kierner
Author, *Traders and Gentlefolk:
The Livingstons of New York, 1675–1790*

LIVING THINGS. See Kingdoms of Living Things.

LIVY (59 B.C.–A.D. 17)

Titus Livius, or Livy, as he is called in English, was one of the greatest Roman historians. He was born in Padua, Italy, in 59 B.C., but spent most of his life in Rome. He was a friend of the emperor Augustus, and he encouraged Claudius, who later became emperor, to study history.

Livy wrote several books on philosophy and literary criticism, but his masterpiece was his history of Rome. He worked on it for 40 years. In 142 volumes he covered more than 1,000 years, from the founding of Rome down to his own time. He undertook this enormous work because he believed that the Romans had become rulers of much of the Western world through their strength of character and that the people of his own time had lost much of this strength. By describing how the early Roman heroes had built up their homeland into a great empire, he hoped to inspire his fellow Romans to imitate the behavior of their ancestors.

Livy was saddened also by the collapse of the Roman republic. Although he thought Augustus was a skillful statesman, he felt that something noble had been lost forever when the republic was changed into a monarchy. In writing Rome's history, he consoled himself by looking back at its past greatness.

His history was called *Ab urbe condita* ("From the Foundation of the City"). It came out in installments and brought him great fame. Only 35 of the 142 volumes still exist, but extracts from the other books and summaries of their contents have been preserved.

Livy gathered his material from many earlier Greek and Roman writers and molded it into a single story. He was sometimes careless about checking facts, but he wrote with energy and color. His history can be put next to Vergil's *Aeneid* as an epic in prose.

Livy died in Padua in A.D. 17.

Gilbert Highet
Author, *The Classical Tradition*

LIZARDS

Lizards are reptiles that are closely related to snakes. Like all reptiles, lizards have scaly skin and are **ectotherms**—cold-blooded animals whose body temperature varies with the temperature of their surrounding environment. More than 3,000 lizard species have been identified. Most lizards are native to the tropics, but a number of species are found in temperate regions. Lizards cannot survive long periods of cold weather, so they do not live in polar regions. Some types of lizards are kept as pets, either confined in terrariums or allowed to run free to aid in keeping down populations of insect or rodent pests.

The rough skin of the prehistoric-looking iguana, like that of all lizards, is covered with dry scales.

▶ CHARACTERISTICS OF LIZARDS

Chameleons, iguanas, skinks, monitors, anoles, and geckos are some of the many different types of lizards. Most lizards walk on four legs, dragging a long tail behind them. However, some run on two legs, like a small two-footed dinosaur. In others, the legs are tiny or missing altogether. These lizards slither along on their bellies like snakes.

Most lizards are less than 16 inches (40 centimeters) long. The world's largest lizard is the Komodo dragon, which can grow as long as 10 feet (3 meters) and weigh up to 300 pounds (135 kilograms). The smallest lizard species is a type of gecko. Measuring less than ¾ inch (2 centimeters), this lizard is also the world's smallest reptile.

The features that distinguish lizards from their closest relatives, the snakes, are subtle. Lizards, even limbless ones, all have shoulder bones, which snakes lack. Lizards have a more complex skull structure than do snakes. Other characteristics of lizards are quite variable. Lizards show a variety of adaptations to particular environments.

▶ THE LIFE OF LIZARDS

Many lizards are **diurnal**, which means they are active during the day. Early in the morning, these lizards usually find a sunny, protected spot where they can warm up for a few hours. The lizard usually spends the rest of the day hunting for food. Most diurnal lizards have excellent eyesight; many also use their sense of smell to help them hunt. Like snakes, lizards "smell" by flicking their tongue to catch molecules floating in the air. They deposit these molecules on the **Jacobson's organ**—a set of sensitive pits on the roof of the mouth where scents are analyzed.

Some lizards are **nocturnal**, which means they are active at night. The ability to close down the pupil to a narrow slit helps nocturnal geckos protect their sensitive eyes from strong light and reduce glare. Geckos are also the only type of lizard to make barking, squeaking, clicking, or chuckling sounds.

WONDER QUESTION

Why do chameleons change color?

Many lizards change the color of their skin from light to dark to help them warm up in the sun or to help them hide in shadows. Green anoles, sometimes misnamed chameleons, can shift from green to brown to yellow or to a multicolored pattern. However, the true chameleons, found mainly in Africa and Madagascar, are among the greatest color-change artists of all animals. They show an amazing variety of changing colors and patterns.

Chameleons change color not for camouflage but for display. When an intruder threatens a chameleon's territory, the chameleon takes on a bright, threatening color. Male chameleons ready to mate also become very colorful. Besides changing their skin color, they may also change their eye color to a bright, fiery yellow or orange. Females recognize the male's signals and change colors in response. These color changes help chameleons identify members of their own species and recognize chameleons of the opposite sex.

A chameleon snatches an insect with its sticky-tipped tongue, which is longer than its body (*left*). A frilled lizard assumes a threatening stance—mouth open and large neck frill unfolded—to frighten off adversaries (*lower left*).

These signals help geckos communicate at night, warning of potential predators or advertising for mating partners.

Mating. Before mating, male lizards often bob the head as a display to the female. After mating, many male and female lizards remain together for the rest of the breeding season or longer.

Most lizards lay eggs, which they bury in the soil or hide in decaying logs. Some lizards lay a single egg each season; others lay as many as fifty eggs in a **clutch**, or nest. Many lizards lay eggs with leathery shells, which protect the eggs and prevent them from drying out.

A number of lizard species do not lay eggs at all, but give birth to live young. Some lizards are **ovoviviparous**—they carry thin-skinned eggs inside the body, and the baby lizards hatch from these internal eggs. A few lizard species are **viviparous**—that is, they form a **placenta** in much the same way as mammals do. A placenta is an organ that helps nourish the young as they develop inside the mother's body.

Growth. Once baby lizards hatch, they are totally independent of their parents. Most are fully grown after a few months, but larger species may take a few years to mature. Adult lizards, however, differ from many other animals in that they continue to grow slowly throughout their lives.

The lizard's outer skin, with its stiff, sometimes bony scales, does not expand as the lizard grows. Lizards shed their skin, or **molt**, as they grow. Some lizards rub up against trees or rocks to scrape off patches of their molting skin. With other lizards, the skin slips off in one piece, leaving a thin, papery cast of the lizard's body.

Protective Behavior. Lizards are prey to many animals, such as birds, mammals, and reptiles, including other lizards. So they have developed a wide range of defenses. Most lizards have coloration that allows them to blend in with the background. Diurnal lizards are often very fast runners. If they are threatened, they scurry away to hide.

Some lizards, when caught, fool predators by breaking off part of their tail. The detached tail temporarily twitches and writhes on its own. This draws the predator's attention away from the lizard, which then quickly runs away. The lizard grows a new tail in a short time. A few lizards defend themselves by squirting blood from broken vessels in their eyelids.

Two lizard species, the Gila monster of the southwestern United States and its close relative, the beaded lizard of Mexico, are poisonous. Their bite can stun or kill other animals, though it is rarely fatal to people.

▶ LIZARDS AND THEIR ENVIRONMENT

Lizards adapt in a variety of ways to particular environments, including forests, deserts, and water environments.

In the Forest. Many lizards live in trees. They may be green to blend in with the leaves or brown to blend in with the trunk or branches. Some lizards have a flat green tail that looks like a leaf. This provides additional camouflage protection in the forest.

Many tree-dwelling lizards are excellent climbers. Some have sharp claws that help them grip tree bark. Others have special pads on their toes that act like tiny suction cups, allowing the lizard to cling to small branches and even to leaves. Many lizards that live in trees have a **prehensile tail**—a tail that can be used to grip branches. A few tree-dwelling species get around not by walking, but by gliding. These lizards have a flap of skin on either side of the body, which extends out like a wing when the lizard spreads its legs. With a leap from a branch, the lizard can sail through the air.

Chameleons are slow-moving lizards that spend most of their lives sitting quietly in trees. Several adaptations allow them to hunt successfully for insects without leaving their protected perch. Their eyes move independently in all directions, so the chameleon does not even need to move its head to locate its prey. Once the chameleon spots an insect, it takes careful aim and shoots out its long, muscular tongue to make the capture.

In the Desert. A number of lizard species have adapted to life in the desert. Some desert lizards have toes fringed with spiny scales to help them run across the sand without sinking. Others burrow into the sand to escape the desert's intense heat, to hide from predators, or to search for small animals that they prey upon. Some burrowing lizards even have clear scales on their eyelids that protect their eyes but still allow them to see while they move under the sand.

In the Water. Some lizard species spend time in the water, where they may fish for food or hide from land-dwelling predators. These species have webs of skin between their toes to help them swim. Marine iguanas, native to the Galápagos Islands in the Pacific Ocean, dive deep under the sea for the seaweed on which they live.

▶ **ENVIRONMENTAL THREATS TO LIZARDS**

Although it is less common today, lizards were once killed for their skins and for their meat. Some species of lizards, especially larger lizards or those that are native to isolated islands (such as the Galápagos Islands, or Mauritius in the Indian Ocean), are endangered. New predators or diseases introduced to these islands could quickly wipe out vulnerable populations.

The dozens of chameleon species native to the island of Madagascar, off the east coast of Africa, are similarly threatened. Many of

Lizards protect themselves in various ways. A green anole blends into its surroundings (*below left*). A five-lined skink breaks off its tail (*below right*); the wriggling tail distracts an enemy while the skink escapes. The basilisk lizard rises up on its hind legs and races away from danger (*bottom*).

these chameleon species have adapted to living on specific plants of the Madagascan rain forest. The rain forest is being cut down at a rapid rate. If the chameleons of Madagascar cannot adapt to new habitats, they may die out. With irrigation of the desert and rapid growth of cities in the southwestern United States, the Gila monster of that area is similarly threatened by destruction of its habitat.

ELIZABETH KAPLAN
Author, *Biology Bulletin Monthly*

See also REPTILES; SNAKES.

LLAMAS

With their calm manner and quick intelligence, llamas make an ideal beast of burden. Sure-footed and strong, they can cover 20 miles (32 kilometers) a day carrying more than 100 pounds (45 kilograms).

Llamas are native to the Andes mountains of South America. They were domesticated by the Inca peoples at least 4,000 years ago and no longer live in the wild. Llamas belong to the camelid family, a group that also includes alpacas, guanacos, vicuñas, and camels. While camels live in Asia and northern Africa, all other camelids live in South America.

Used for thousands of years in mountainous regions of South America, llamas are highly social domestic animals.

▶ CHARACTERISTICS OF LLAMAS

Llamas are well suited to life high in the mountains. Adults stand about 4 feet (1.2 meters) tall at the shoulder and weigh 250 to 300 pounds (113 to 135 kilograms). Their feet have two toes, each with a long nail curving over the top. Soft pads provide traction on rough terrain. The llama's long silky hair insulates the animal against cold, wind, and moisture. Coat color may be brown, black, gray, white, or red, often with spots or other patterns.

Although llamas eat mainly hay, they also browse on a variety of shrubs and other plants. After eating, they slowly chew the **cud**, a wad of partly digested food. They swallow the cud again, and digestion is completed in the animal's three-chambered stomach. With this thorough digestive system, llamas can handle a poor-quality diet that other animals cannot.

Llamas communicate with sound and body language. When curious or disturbed, they hum, a sound something like human humming. If danger approaches, they will sound a high-pitched alarm call. Llamas also signal their mood through head and ear position. Ears forward mean the llama is relaxed, while ears pinned back and nose tilted up mean the llama is worried.

Spitting is the llama's way of saying "Stop it!" Females spit more often than males, usually to establish dominance in the herd or to fend off an unwanted suitor. A common belief is that llamas spit on people. In truth, only a llama that has been mistreated or raised improperly will spit on a person.

▶ THE LIFE OF LLAMAS

Female llamas are usually ready to breed at 2 years of age. They give birth to one youngster at a time, and pregnancy lasts 335 to 355 days. Baby llamas, often called **crias**, weigh 15 to 20 pounds (7 to 9 kilograms) at birth. Within half an hour they are up and walking. Young llamas spend much of their time playing with each other and prancing about. After 4 to 6 months they are weaned, and by age 4 they are fully grown. Most llamas live from 20 to 25 years of age.

The Incas first raised llamas for their meat, wool, and dung, which they used for fertilizer and fuel. Later, llamas became important pack animals, carrying silver ore, farm crops, and other goods over rough mountain trails. Known as ships of the Andes, they remained the main form of land transport until roads were built in the early 1900's.

Llamas were first brought to the United States in the late 1800's by zoos and private collectors. In recent years, llama breeding has become a growing industry.

Hikers and hunters may rent llamas to carry their gear. Llamas are also featured in parades and even as golf caddies. Craftspeople sell clothing, blankets, and rugs made of llama wool. Because they are so easy to care for, and because they get along well with people, llamas are likely to remain popular.

CARRIE DIERKS
Science Writer

See also CAMELS.

LLOYD GEORGE, DAVID (1863–1945)

British statesman and social reformer David Lloyd George served as prime minister (1916–22) of Great Britain during the last half of World War I (1914–18).

He was born on January 17, 1863, in Manchester, England. After his father's early death, young David was taken by his mother to live in Wales, where her brother, a village shoemaker and Baptist minister, became David's guardian and nurtured his genius.

As a young man, Lloyd George worked locally as a lawyer, defending poor farmers and quarrymen. An impressive and inspiring public speaker, he soon made a name for himself as an agitator for Welsh causes. From the first, his ambition was unlimited. In 1890, he was elected to Parliament as a Liberal for the region of Caernarvon Boroughs.

In 1908, Lloyd George became chancellor of the exchequer, the nation's chief minister of finance. In that capacity, he promoted far-reaching social reforms, including old-age pensions and national health insurance. His "People's Budget" of 1909, which increased taxation of the rich, angered the Conservatives in the House of Lords. The conflict led to a constitutional crisis in 1911, after which the Lords no longer had the power to reject finance legislation.

In 1915, a year after World War I broke out, Lloyd George founded a munitions ministry to hasten the flow of guns and ammunition to the battlefronts. The following year he was chosen to succeed Lord Kitchener as minister of war. Soon after, with the support of a coalition of the Conservatives, Labour, and some Liberals, Lloyd George became prime minister.

In 1918, after the war was won, Lloyd George and his coalition government won a huge election victory. The following year he attended the Paris Peace Conference to negotiate the Versailles Treaty with representatives of the other victorious nations. In 1921, he negotiated a treaty to create the Irish Free State, but this helped to lose him the support of the Conservatives, and he fell from power in 1922.

Lloyd George remained in Parliament for the rest of his life, serving as Liberal Party leader from 1926 to 1931. Shortly before his death on March 26, 1945, he was granted a title of nobility and became the 1st Earl Lloyd-George of Dwyfor.

JOHN GRIGG
Author, *Lloyd George: The People's Champion*

LOBEL, ARNOLD. See CHILDREN'S LITERATURE (Profiles).

LOBSTERS

Lobsters are marine animals that live in all the world's oceans except for the cold polar waters of the Arctic and Antarctic. They are most closely related to crabs, shrimp, and crayfish. Along with their close relatives, lobsters belong to a group of animals called **crustaceans**—aquatic (water) animals that live inside hard external shells.

The approximately 160 species, or kinds, of lobsters are divided into three main groups: true lobsters, spiny lobsters, and slipper lobsters. True lobsters, the most well known group, have front legs that have been modified into large, powerful claws used in defense and in capturing and crushing prey. The familiar American lobster is a true lobster. Spiny lobsters lack the imposing claws of true lobsters. Instead, they have a shell covered with prickly spines that serves as protection. Slipper lobsters lack both claws and spines. They have wide, flat bodies with dull shells that help them blend in with their surroundings.

Characteristics of Lobsters. The lobster is an invertebrate—that is, an animal without a backbone. Covering its body is a hard, segmented shell called an **exoskeleton**. The lobster's exoskeleton serves the same purposes as the bony skeleton of the human body. The lobster's muscles are attached to the shell, and its internal organs are protected by this tough covering. Like many other marine animals, lobsters breathe through gills.

Various appendages are attached to the segmented body of the lobster. On its head are two pairs of antennae and a pair of compound eyes. Lobsters wave their slender, sensitive antennae in the water to detect food, predators, and possible mating partners. Each eye contains hundreds of lenses joined together and is mounted on a retractable stalk.

The large and powerfully clawed American lobster lives along the Atlantic coast. It is prized as a seafood delicacy.

When hidden in cracks between rocks or buried in sand or mud, a lobster can extend its eyestalks to search for food.

Lobsters are **decapods**, meaning they have ten legs. The five pairs of jointed legs are attached to the middle part of the lobster's body. True lobsters have large claws at the ends of their front legs. The larger of the two claws has toothlike bumps and is used for crushing clams and other shelled animals. The smaller is used for ripping up meat or plants for food. Lobsters also use their claws for fighting and for self-defense. The remaining four pairs of legs are used mainly for walking.

The lobster has a strong, flexible tail that it uses to escape predators. By flexing its powerful tail, the lobster is able to propel itself backward through the water. A lobster's color also offers protection from enemies. Most lobsters are a mottled brown or greenish color, which helps camouflage the lobster on the ocean floor.

The Life of Lobsters. Most lobsters live in shallow waters—about 100 to 130 feet (30 to 40 meters) deep. A few species live at depths of more than 3,000 feet (900 meters). While most lobsters live alone, spiny lobsters live in groups that can have from two to a hundred members.

Lobsters are nocturnal animals, which means they are active at night. During the day, they stay in caves, beneath rocks, or in burrows along the seafloor. Under cover of darkness, they crawl along the ocean floor, hunting for food. Fish, shrimp, clams, sea urchins, worms, algae, and plants are all part of their diet.

A female lobster usually produces offspring once every two years. Lobsters form in tiny eggs that the female carries on the underside of her body for weeks or months, depending on the species. When the eggs are ready to hatch, the female gently fans them with her **swimmerets**, which are small appendages attached underneath the tail. This shakes the lobsters out of their shells. Just hatched, a lobster looks like a tiny shrimp or insect larva.

Within its shell, the lobster grows quickly. But its hard shell cannot expand as the lobster grows. So, in order to increase its size, a lobster casts off the old shell and hardens a new one around itself. This process is called **molting**. At first the shell is soft. During the several days it takes for the shell to harden, the lobster is left vulnerable to its enemies. After several molts, the lobster sinks to the ocean floor where it spends the rest of its life.

Lobsters and Their Environment. Small lobsters are prey to large, predatory fish. However, large lobsters usually can defend themselves against any fish. They are prey only to humans, who prize them as a delicacy.

Millions of lobsters are caught each year, and per pound they are worth more than almost any other seafood. However, lobsters used to be much more abundant. Colonial New Englanders could go to the shore and pick up lobsters with pitchforks. Today strict laws control the trapping of lobsters. Lobsters under a certain size must be released. Any female lobster carrying eggs must also be returned to the sea. Trappers and scientists mark large females so that they will be released to continue breeding. These measures may help keep lobster populations stable and prevent overfishing.

ELIZABETH KAPLAN
Series coauthor, *Ask Isaac Asimov*

Did you know that...

an American lobster was recorded as the heaviest crustacean ever caught? In 1977, this lobster was caught off the northeast coast of the United States. It weighed more than 44 pounds (20 kilograms) and measured 3 1/2 feet (1 meter) from the end of its tail to the tip of its largest claw. Some species of spiny lobster may grow to 20 pounds (9 kilograms), but most other lobster species grow to no more than 2 to 3 pounds (1 to 1.4 kilograms).

LOCH NESS MONSTER

The Loch Ness monster is a legendary animal that is said to live in the waters of Loch Ness, a large lake in northern Scotland. The creature supposedly resembles a giant sea serpent, but no one has been able to prove that it really exists.

Legends about the monster have been told for many centuries. The first known written account dates from the year A.D. 565. Saint Columba, an Irish missionary working in Scotland, was said to have seen a large animal in Loch Ness.

Sightings of a monster in Loch Ness increased greatly in 1933, when a new road provided easy access to the rugged and isolated region surrounding the lake. Newspaper reports spread accounts of people who thought they saw Nessie, as the monster is sometimes called. Since the 1930's, many photographs of "sightings" have been taken, although most are not clear enough to distinguish an actual animal. Others have proved to be hoaxes.

During the past several decades, scientists have used modern equipment, such as sonar,

This famous 1934 photo is now thought to be a hoax.

to search for evidence of Nessie's existence. Unfortunately for those who hope to find a real monster, Loch Ness is vast and difficult to explore. The water is murky, and underwater caves may exist far below the surface.

Despite the lack of evidence, many people still think that a large serpent-like creature lives in Loch Ness. Could it be a dinosaur-like reptile that never became extinct? Could it be a new kind of animal, previously unknown to science? Or perhaps Nessie exists only in the imaginations of people who like a good mystery. For now, no one can say for sure.

BARBARA ROSS
Science Writer

LOCKE, JOHN (1632–1704)

John Locke was one of the greatest and most influential of English philosophers. He is considered the founder of British **empiricism**, the doctrine that all knowledge is acquired from experience.

Locke was born on August 29, 1632, in Wrington, Somerset, the son of a lawyer. After attending Westminster School and Oxford University, Locke had a brief taste of diplomatic service in Europe. He returned to England in 1666 to study medicine. He did not graduate as a doctor, but he became medical adviser to his friend and patron, Anthony Ashley Cooper. Lord Ashley, an enemy of the Stuart kings, fell into disfavor and fled to Holland. Locke followed him in 1683. He did not return to England until after the revolution in 1688, when William and Mary came to the throne.

Locke published his famous *Essay Concerning Human Understanding* in 1690. In it he expressed the belief that a person's mind

at birth is a *tabula rasa*, or blank slate, on which experience writes.

Locke's most important political work is his *Two Treatises of Government* (1690). In this work he argued that there is no divine right of kings to rule. He proposed that by nature all people are equal and independent and that government is formed by a social contract with the governed. He also held that a government must protect its citizens' natural rights to life, liberty, and property. When governments fail to do so, citizens have the right—and even the duty—to rebel.

Locke's political ideas influenced the leaders of the American Revolution. Thomas Jefferson used many of Locke's ideas in writing the Declaration of Independence.

In his later years, Locke's health was poor, but he kept up a busy schedule until his death in Oates, Essex, on October 28, 1704.

Reviewed by WILLIAM RADTKE
Seton Hall University

LOCKS AND KEYS

Once only the wealthy could afford the human guards needed to protect their property. But today every home, automobile, bicycle, and school locker can be made reasonably secure with an inexpensive key or combination lock. Even banks or businesses with large quantities of cash and other valuable items can reduce the need for human protection by installing very strong and complex mechanical or electronic locks.

▶ TYPES OF LOCKS

A lock is a device that prevents such things as opening the bolt or latch on a door or turning the ignition switch to allow the flow of electricity needed to start a car's engine. Some locks, called padlocks, are portable.

Most common locks are opened by a key— a piece of metal that is grooved, notched, or otherwise shaped to fit the locking mechanism exactly. Some are opened by turning a dial to the correct series of numbers called the combination. Computer-controlled locks are opened with an electronically coded plastic card or by the voice or handprint of an authorized person.

Warded Locks. One of the simplest locks is the warded lock. A ward is a guard put on the inside of the lock. Only a key with notches or slots cut in it to match the wards can move around them and slide the bolt. A warded lock is easy to open without its key because a straight piece of wire can slide around the guard. (Opening a lock without a proper key is called "picking the lock.") Ward locks are used for closets, cupboards, and doors to rooms and in some inexpensive padlocks.

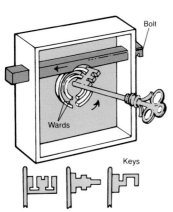

Warded Lock

Inside a warded lock there is a maze-like series of obstacles called wards. In order to work the lock, a key must be notched so as to be able to pass through the wards and reach the bolt.

Lever Tumbler Locks. Lever tumblers are thin strips of metal of different heights that swivel on a post. A key is notched to raise each tumbler to the correct height. When all the tumblers are in the proper position, a bar

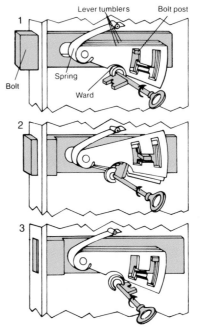

Lever Tumbler Lock

Each lever tumbler has an opening through which the bolt post must slide as the bolt moves. In the **locked** position (1) these openings are not lined up. A spring holds the tumblers in place. This lock also has a ward that fits the notch on the front of the key. Each of the other notches on the key is positioned to raise one of the tumblers. To unlock the tumbler, all of the openings are lined up (2) and the bolt post is free to move as the turning key pushes the bolt. In the **unlocked** position (3) the tumblers drop and hold the bolt post in place again.

on the bolt is freed and the bolt is moved by turning the key. Some lever tumbler locks have a separate bar for each tumbler, making it harder to pick the lock. Lever tumbler locks are frequently used for mailbox locks and as inexpensive padlocks.

Dual Control Locks. This type of lever tumbler lock is used for safe-deposit boxes in banks. The lock has two separate keyholes, and it must be opened with two separate keys. One is kept by the person who rents the safe-deposit box, and the other by the bank itself. The guard on duty in the safe-deposit vault first puts in and turns the bank's key. This raises the lever tumblers to a certain height. The tumblers are not high enough to throw the bolt, but they are high enough to clear the way for the renter's key. When the renter's key is turned in the second keyhole, the levers are raised, and the bolt is thrown.

The Pin Tumbler Cylinder Lock. The most familiar key-operated lock is found on the doors of the majority of homes in North America. It is based on a tumbler lock made in Egypt

Pin Tumbler Cylinder Lock

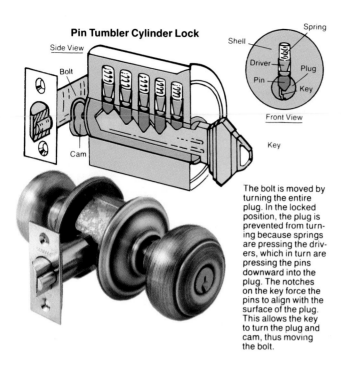

Side View

Bolt

Cam

Shell

Spring

Driver

Pin

Plug

Key

Front View

Key

The bolt is moved by turning the entire plug. In the locked position, the plug is prevented from turning because springs are pressing the drivers, which in turn are pressing the pins downward into the plug. The notches on the key force the pins to align with the surface of the plug. This allows the key to turn the plug and cam, thus moving the bolt.

nearly 4,000 years ago. Both locks raise a series of tumblers with a key. The pin tumblers in the modern lock are set in holes in a rotating cylinder, or **plug**. The plug is enclosed in a case, or **shell**. In the locked position, the pin tumblers lie partly in the plug and partly in the shell. Springs press the tumblers down and the plug cannot turn. But each pin tumbler is divided into two parts, the lower pin and the upper **driver**. When the correct key is put in the keyhole, the point of the key passes under the pins. It raises them until they rest in the notches, or **bits**, of the key. This pushes them exactly the right amount so that the top of each one lines up with the top of the plug. The key can then turn the plug. The most common cylinder lock has five pin chambers.

A system of pin tumbler cylinder locks can be designed to be opened by one special key called a **master key**. Some of the pins in each lock are cut into two parts. The lock's own key raises all the pins so one cut in each pin is flush (even) with the plug, allowing it to turn. A master key raises the divided pins so the second cut is flush and it also raises the undivided pins to their flush position. If some of the pins are cut into three parts, the locks can be opened by yet another key, called the **grand master**. Thus the owner of a building can open every door with the grand master.

Disc or Wafer Tumbler Locks. Many automobile locks, small padlocks, and cabinet locks use disc or wafer tumblers. The operation of this type of lock is similar to that of a pin tumbler lock, and the keys look almost identical; but instead of pins, the plug contains flat tumblers called discs or wafers. The tumblers have a rectangular hole in them; the key passes through the hole and lifts the tumbler. If the correct key is used, all of the tumblers will be pulled inside the plug and the lock will open. When an incorrect key is used, some of the tumblers will be too high or too low, which will prevent the plug from turning.

Combination Locks. The familiar combination lock works without any key at all. It can be opened only by turning a dial to the right numbers or letters. These locks are often used on school lockers and bicycle padlocks as well as on vaults and safes.

Combination locks used in schools usually have three disc-shaped tumblers inside. Each tumbler has a notch cut in it. Turning the dial rotates the tumblers. If you stop turning the dial at the correct number, the notch will be lined up with a lever. Turning the dial in the opposite direction leaves the first tumbler aligned with the lever and turns the second tumbler. When all three tumblers are lined up with the lever, the lever can fall into the notches and the lock will open.

Time Locks. Time locks are used on bank vaults. They have no levers or tumblers. Instead, the operation depends on the mechanical works of at least two clocks. (This is required in case one clock should break down.) These special clocks are set to show the time when the vault or safe is to open for

Simple Combination Lock
(parts separated for easy viewing)

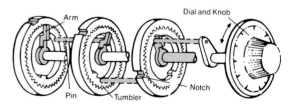

Arm

Dial and Knob

Pin

Tumbler

Notch

A combination lock has a movable dial marked with numbers. To release the lock, the dial must be turned to a certain sequence of numbers known as the combination. Each turn of the dial moves a different pin — one at a time. Each pin pushes an arm, which in turn moves a notched tumbler. The object is to line up the notches in all of the tumblers, at which point the lock will open.

business. The clocks are in a large case that has a hole in one side. When the vault is locked, a cover slides automatically over the hole. As soon as the clocks reach the time set for opening, the cover slides back. A steel bar connected to the lock mechanism enters the hole and fastens onto the handle on the outside of the vault door. The handle can then be turned to move back the bolt so the vault can be opened.

Time locks are wound and set by a special key for different periods. They can be set so they will not open between the close of business on Friday and the time when the bank reopens on Monday morning.

Electronic Locks. Electronic locks are really small computers. Instead of releasing with a mechanical key, an electronic lock may be opened with a small card, similar to a credit card, that holds coded information. Some electronic locks may require a combination to be typed on a keypad. Other electronic locks are programmed to recognize the voice or handprint of authorized users.

The main advantage of electronic locks is that they can be reprogrammed quickly. This makes them useful in industrial and commercial buildings such as hotels. For example, the hotel clerk enters a code into a terminal when a guest checks in. The guest's card matches the newly coded lock to the room. Cards used by the former guests in that room will not operate the lock. If the card is lost or stolen, the code to the lock of the room can be changed immediately and a new card issued to the guest. Electronic locks usually have a backup battery or a mechanical override in case of power failure.

▶ **HISTORY OF LOCKS AND KEYS**

The first known lock was a wooden Egyptian tumbler lock invented about 2000 B.C. It required the bolt to be on the outside of the door. Later, the Greeks designed a lock to operate a bolt on the inside of a door. They inserted a key through a hole from the outside. The Greek key was a curved bar about 40 inches (1 meter) long. It slid through the keyhole above the bolt until its tip caught a notch in the bolt to slide it back.

The Romans made a tumbler lock with a keyhole and inside bolt. In the Roman lock the ends of the tumblers and the pegs on the keys were cut in a variety of shapes that had to

Ancient Egyptian Pin Tumbler Lock

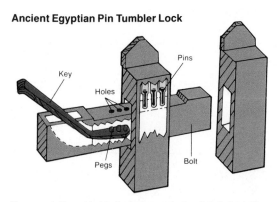

Pins are positioned inside the lock so as to drop into holes in the bolt, thus holding the bolt in place. A series of pegs stick up from the key in positions corresponding to those of the pins. When the key is slid into the lock, the pegs raise all of the pins at once, thus allowing the bolt to slide free.

match. The Romans also invented the first portable lock, or padlock, with the small keys often made to be worn as rings. The Romans may also have invented warded locks.

A thousand years later, during the Renaissance, the next major improvement was made in lock design. This was the lever tumbler lock, with wards. It was harder to pick than the simple warded lock, but it could be opened with a **skeleton key**, a long straight key with one tooth on the end. It could be slipped around the wards to raise the tumbler.

In the late 1700's an Englishman, Robert Barron, invented a lever tumbler lock with double action. If the lever was raised too high by an improper key, it hit a bar on the bolt that kept the bolt from moving. Lever locks based on Barron's design are still in use.

In 1818 another English inventor, Jeremiah Chubb, used the lever tumbler principle to invent an almost pick-proof lock. Six tumblers had to be raised to exactly the right height. There was a detector tumbler that was sprung if any tumbler was raised too high by the use of an improper key. This detector tumbler jammed the lock until the owner inserted the correct key and turned it in the opposite direction than was usual.

In 1861, Linus Yale, Jr., invented the pin tumbler cylinder lock, which could be mass produced. This meant that an inexpensive, secure lock was available to nearly everyone. With modern improvements, it is still the most secure key-operated lock.

Reviewed and updated by SAM ALLEN
Author, *Locks and Alarms*

LOCOMOTIVES

An important development in the history of transportation, the locomotive has fascinated people for almost 200 years. The impact of the locomotive cannot be underestimated, especially on life in the 1800's. Locomotives not only made travel faster and more convenient, but they also made it possible to ship heavy loads of freight overland. Lands that were previously inaccessible and unsettled became just a train ride away.

A locomotive is a self-propelled vehicle system that uses energy created from fuel or electricity to move railroad cars along rails. An engine is simply part of the system, though locomotives are often called engines.

Since its invention in the late 1700's and early 1800's, the locomotive has undergone many changes and technical improvements. By the 1940's, the largest locomotives measured more than 130 feet (40 meters) long, weighed more than 1 million pounds (450,000 kilograms), and could produce more than 6,000 horsepower. By comparison, today's diesel locomotives produce the same horsepower in a vehicle that measures 90 feet (27 meters) long and weighs half as much as the 1940's locomotive.

▶ TYPES OF LOCOMOTIVES

There are three chief types of locomotives: steam, diesel, and electric. Except for electric locomotives, all locomotives produce their own power.

Steam Locomotives

The first locomotives were steam powered, and for more than 100 years steam was the chief source of rail power all over the world. Today the diesel locomotive has taken the place of the steam locomotive in many countries, and only a few steam locomotives remain in service. Some of those are used on railroads that have been preserved for recreational purposes and as attractions for tourists and railroad enthusiasts. In Europe, South Africa, and Russia, several historically important steam locomotives are kept operational for special occasions. China still uses steam locomotives to transport freight in the northern regions of the country.

Diesel locomotives commonly move the biggest loads and longest trains. A huge diesel engine works with powerful electric motors to drive the wheels.

Steam locomotives burn fuel (usually coal or wood) to heat and boil water, which produces steam. Contained in a boiler, the steam passes into a cylinder near the driving wheels. In the cylinder, the steam expands against and moves a piston. The back-and-forth motion of the piston turns the driving wheels—the wheels that move the locomotive—through a system of rods and cranks. Steam locomotives commonly have two cylinders powering four, six, eight, or ten driving wheels.

The steam boiler is essentially a large steel cylinder with chambers at each end. At the rear is a firebox, where the combustion occurs. The smoke and heat flow through a network of narrow tubes, called **flues**, that run the length of the boiler and then out the smokestack. The firebox and the flues are surrounded by water. The heat from the fire causes the water to boil and creates the steam.

Steam exhausts from the cylinders and passes out the smokestack, creating the familiar "chuff, chuff, chuff" sound. The force of the exhaust creates a vacuum that draws air from the opposite end of the boiler and through the burning fuel. This causes the fuel to burn efficiently.

Fuel and water are carried in a special car called a **tender**, which is coupled, or joined, right behind the locomotive. For more than 100 years, locomotives were fueled by hand. This process is called **stoking**. During the 1920's, a mechanical stoker—powered by the

Steam locomotives, the first type of locomotive invented, dominated the railroad industry for more than 100 years.

steam locomotives are often classified according to their wheel arrangement? This classification system, known as the Whyte system, was developed in 1901 by mechanical engineer F. M. Whyte of the New York Central Railroad. According to this system, the number of leading, driving, and trailing wheels are listed in order. For example, the *Pacific* locomotive is a 4-6-2, having 4 leading wheels, 6 driving wheels, and 2 trailing wheels. The *Mogul* locomotive (2-6-0) has 2 leading wheels, 6 driving wheels, and no trailing wheels.

Certain wheel arrangements were so popular that several railroads gave different names to one type. For example, the 4-8-4 was a *Pocono*, a *Greenbrier*, a *Niagara*, and a *Dixie*, to name some examples.

2 - 6 - 0   4 - 6 - 2   4 - 8 - 4

same steam that propels the locomotive—was successfully developed.

Early steam locomotives burned coal or wood, depending on which type of fuel was most plentiful and least expensive. American-built steam locomotives were primarily wood-fired until the 1870's. In the 1920's, oil became more common as a locomotive fuel, primarily in western areas of the United States, where coal was scarce.

Steam locomotives are classified according to the number and arrangement of their wheels. They usually have smaller wheels in front of and behind their big driving wheels. These small wheels help carry the weight of the locomotive and guide it around curves, but they have no power. The small wheels are set in frames called **trucks**, which are pivoted underneath the engine frame so that they can swing right or left.

Diesel Locomotives

The first experimental diesel locomotives were developed around 1910 in Germany. The diesel locomotive was first tried in the United States in 1923, and the first commercial diesel locomotive in the United States was put into use by the Central Railroad of New Jersey in 1925.

By the 1930's, Electro-Motive Corporation (EMC) was offering streamlined diesel locomotives for passenger service. In 1939, EMC produced a bulldog-nosed model FT, which toured North America and proved it could outperform steam.

After World War II (1939–45), a major conversion from steam locomotives to diesel locomotives began. Production of new steam locomotives by commercial builders ended in 1949, and by 1960 steam locomotives were rarely used in the United States.

There were many reasons for such a quick turn to diesel power. In general, though, diesel locomotives proved to be much simpler, more reliable, and cheaper to operate than steam locomotives.

An oil-burning internal-combustion engine is the heart of the diesel locomotive, also called the diesel-electric locomotive. Oil is sprayed into the cylinders of the engine, where it burns with almost explosive force. The rapidly expanding gases from the burning oil force the pistons downward. The diesel engine, in turn, drives an electric generator that supplies power to **electric traction motors** located near the driving wheels. These electric traction motors, mounted in truck assemblies, turn the wheels.

At one time all electric traction motors ran on direct current (DC). Today, however, alternating current (AC) traction is revolutionizing diesel locomotive design. These locomotives generate alternating current—electric current that constantly reverses the direction in which it flows. They then convert it to direct current, which flows in just one direction. Sophisticated electrical equipment and computers convert the direct current back into specific forms and quantities of alternating current needed by the electric traction motors.

AC traction motors controlled by high-speed computers provide modern diesel locomotives with more precise control over speed, fuel economy, and wheel slippage than was possible on older DC-driven locomotives.

One widespread type of speed control in diesel locomotives—dynamic braking—was introduced in the late 1930's. When running downhill, the traction motors act as generators. Electric current from the traction motors is directed toward electrical grids (networks of electrical conductors), which absorb high amounts of current to slow the motors and the train.

Electric Locomotives

The first electric locomotives can be traced back to 1842 in Scotland, where battery-powered mine locomotives, known as lokies, were tried out. But a truly useful electric locomotive was not possible until a simple method of producing electricity was developed. Once the electric generator was perfected in 1873, practical electric locomotion became possible.

Overhead wires feed electric power to this 7,000-horsepower electric locomotive. The electric power is then transferred to strong electric motors that drive the wheels.

Best Friend of Charleston

LOCOMOTIVE FIRSTS

England was the birthplace of the steam locomotive. Richard Trevithick, a successful English mining engineer, built the first steam locomotive in 1804. Even though it was too heavy for the tracks, it inspired others to build steam locomotives. The *Stourbridge Lion*, imported from England in 1829, was the first locomotive to run on a regular railroad in North America. In 1830, the *Best Friend of Charleston* became the first locomotive built in the United States to perform regular service.

Trevithick's Locomotive

Stourbridge Lion

During the 1880's electric traction motors were used to power streetcars, also known as trolley cars. In 1890 the world's first electric subway opened in London. In 1895 the Baltimore & Ohio used an electric locomotive to pull trains through a tunnel in the city of Baltimore—the first use of an electric locomotive on a main-line railroad. This success

encouraged other railroads in the United States and Europe to begin electrifying parts of their main lines, especially around cities, where the smoke of steam locomotives was a problem. But the high cost of electrification limited its use.

Electric locomotives get energy from power plants that supply electricity either to an overhead wire, called a **catenary**, or to a third rail alongside the track.

Powerful electric motors connected to the wheels drive electric locomotives. Contacts on the locomotive pick up the electric power delivered through a third rail or a catenary. Big transformers and rectifiers inside the locomotive change the current as received from the power plant to a form best suited to the motors, which drive the wheels through gears.

Many innovations helped electric railroads expand from single-city people movers to systems that connected several cities. These railroads were referred to as **interurbans**.

The sleek, electrically powered Eurostar train carries almost 800 passengers at up to 186 miles (300 kilometers) per hour between European cities.

Today electric locomotives primarily provide passenger service in cities and built-up areas. Amtrak and the commuter railroads serving New York, Philadelphia, Baltimore, Boston, and Washington, D.C., all use 6,000- or 7,000-horsepower electric locomotives. These locomotives are fast, powerful, and dependable. They are also good for these areas—now and in the future—because they make no smoke or fumes.

Cog, or rack, railways are used to climb steep grades. The Mount Washington Cog Railway conquers the highest peak in the northeastern United States.

The fastest trains in the world, including the French TGV and the Japanese bullet trains, all use electric locomotives.

▶ **SPECIAL-PURPOSE LOCOMOTIVES**

Mountain railroads, with their sharp curves and steep grades, need special locomotives. These locomotives must have great power, yet be able to swing around curves easily. To meet these needs, articulated (jointed) locomotives were invented.

One type was invented by Anatole Mallet, a Swiss, in 1887. Mallet's locomotives had two engines under one big boiler. One of the two engines pivoted so the locomotive could make sharp bends. The Union Pacific Railroad's 4-8-8-4 Mallets, known as "Big Boys," were the largest steam locomotives ever built, measuring 133 feet (40.5 meters) long.

Geared locomotives were used primarily in logging and mill areas on grades of up to 10 percent—rails that climb as much as 1 foot (0.3 meter) for every 10 feet (3 meters) of track. Cog, or rack, railroads were developed to climb grades of 30 percent or more. To climb such steep grades, most cog railroads use a toothed cog wheel on the locomotive that meshes into a ladderlike rack rail. The rack rail is mounted between the two typical outer rails. The steepest cog railway in the world, the Mt. Pilatus Railway in Lucerne, Switzerland, climbs grades of 38 percent.

MICHAEL J. DEL VECCHIO
Railway Historian and Transportation Consultant

See also DIESEL ENGINES; ELECTRIC MOTORS; RAILROADS; STEAM ENGINES.

LODGE, HENRY CABOT. See UNITED STATES, CONGRESS OF THE (Profiles: Senators).

LOGIC

Logic is the study of the correctness or incorrectness of arguments. An argument consists of one or more statements called **premises** and a final statement called the **conclusion**. In logic, arguments are determined to be correct or incorrect, depending on whether or not the premises give sufficient evidence to support the truth of the conclusion.

Logicians (people who study logic) classify arguments as **inductive** or **deductive**, based on whether or not the premises are intended to give complete evidence for the truth of the conclusion.

In a correct inductive argument, the premises are meant to provide some evidence for the truth of the conclusion, always allowing for the possibility that the conclusion may be false even though the premises are all true. Here is an example:

All observed swans are white.
Therefore, probably all swans are white.

Here the premise refers only to observed swans, but the conclusion speaks of all swans. The conclusion that all swans are white is probably true, but not necessarily true.

In a correct deductive argument, the conclusion must be true if the premises are true. Look at the following argument:

All birds have backbones.
All penguins are birds.
Therefore all penguins have backbones.

Here the conclusion that all penguins have backbones follows necessarily from the two premises. Can you tell why? Because in a correct deductive argument it is never possible for the premises to be true and the conclusion false.

▶ SYLLOGISMS

The Greek philosopher Aristotle (384–322 B.C.), in a collection of works titled *Organon*, or "Tool," gave us the first systematic treatment of deductive logic. Aristotle developed the idea of the **syllogism**, a three-part deductive argument containing two premises and a conclusion. The deductive argument examined above is an example of a syllogism.

The Greek philosopher Aristotle, a founder of logic, developed the type of argument known as a syllogism.

Logic and Validity. If the conclusion in a deductive argument follows necessarily from the premises, logicians say the argument is **valid**. Deductive logic is the study of how to determine whether a deductive argument is valid or not.

How can we tell whether an argument is valid or invalid (not valid)? Let us look at the following situation. If we get into our car in the morning and it will not start, we may conclude that the car is out of gas. This may be set up in the form of an argument:

The car will not start.
Therefore the car is out of gas.

In this example, the conclusion may follow from the premise, but not necessarily. There may be other reasons why the car will not start. The starter may be broken, for instance. For this particular argument to be valid, therefore, it must be stated in a different form. We can start with the premise "The car will not start only if it is out of gas" and then develop the rest of the syllogism:

The car will not start only if it is out of gas.
The car will not start.
Therefore it is out of gas.

This argument is logically valid. Remember, this means that the premises cannot be true without the conclusion being true also. We can question the truth of the conclusion only by questioning the truth of at least one premise. If the premise "The car will not start" is an undeniable fact, then we can reject the conclusion only by rejecting the other premise, "The car will not start only if it is out of gas." This would involve actually examining other cases in which the failure of the car to start is not due to its being out of gas. This, however, is beyond the scope of deductive logic. In this example the logic is valid even though common sense may cast doubt on one of the premises.

Categorical Syllogisms. A categorical syllogism, sometimes called an Aristotelian syllogism, is a particular kind of syllogism. In it, the components of the premises and the conclusion are generally common nouns or noun phrases, called **terms**, which stand for categories, or groups of objects having certain common traits. The terms are related by means of the words "all," "no," "some," or "not," and "are" or "are not." Using these words, each statement in a categorical syllogism may take one of the following four forms:

All x are y.
No x are y.
Some x are y.
Some x are not y.

The following argument is an example of a valid categorical syllogism:

All mammals are things that have lungs.
All whales are mammals.
Therefore all whales are things that have lungs.

In this syllogism the terms are "mammals," "whales," and "things that have lungs." Each term is used twice. In the premises, two terms are related to a common third term so as to reveal their relation to each other in the conclusion. In our example, the terms "whales" and "things that have lungs" are related to the term "mammals" in such a way that we conclude that whales have lungs.

USING RULES TO DETERMINE VALIDITY

Logicians have developed a number of rules to tell whether syllogisms are valid or not. One such rule is "From two negatives nothing follows." Applying this rule, is the following a valid argument?

No crickets are worms.
No worms are insects.
Therefore no crickets are insects.

Both premises are negative, so this argument violates the rule. The argument is invalid because the premises are true and the conclusion is false.

Representing Terms with Symbols. To make it easier to tell valid from invalid forms, logicians use letters to represent the terms. The letters S and P are commonly used to represent the subject and predicate terms of the conclusion, and the letter M for the middle term (the term found in both premises). Using symbols, a logician can quickly determine, without knowing what the terms are,

whether a syllogism is valid or invalid. Look at this syllogism:

No heroes are cowards.
Some people are cowards.
Therefore some people are not heroes.

Can you tell which are the subject, predicate, and middle terms? Here is how the syllogism looks when symbols are used to stand for the terms:

No P are M.
Some S are M.
Therefore some S are not P.

S (the subject term) stands for people, P (the predicate term) stands for heroes, and M (the middle term) stands for cowards. This is a valid syllogism.

OTHER FORMS OF DEDUCTIVE ARGUMENTS

Some deductive arguments have statements instead of terms as components. These statements are related by the words "If …then …," "…or …," and "not." In the argument below, for example, the statements in the major premise are related by the word "or."

Either the butler stole the money or the chauffeur did.
The chauffeur did not.
Therefore the butler stole the money.

MODERN LOGIC

In 1847 George Boole, a British mathematician, developed what he called an "algebra of classes," also called an algebra of logic. In Boole's system, algebraic symbols are used to represent terms and relations in arguments. Modern logic, based on Boole's system, is therefore often referred to as symbolic or mathematical logic. In the 1900's it was shown that Boole's symbolic logic could be used to program the operations of electronic computers.

Today inductive, deductive, and symbolic logic have many applications in mathematics and the sciences, as well as in engineering, law, philosophy, and other areas.

WILLIAM RADTKE
Seton Hall University

See also ARISTOTLE; MATHEMATICS.

LOGUEN, JERMAIN. See UNDERGROUND RAILROAD (Profiles).

LONDON

London, or Greater London, as it has been officially known since 1965, is the capital and largest city of the United Kingdom of Great Britain and Northern Ireland. It is also the nation's predominant banking, business, and cultural center. Thus, in American terms, London combines the roles of New York City and Washington, D.C.

London attracts millions of tourists every year, and they encounter a fascinating mix of sights and sounds—historic buildings and places, museums and art galleries, beautiful gardens and parks, fine restaurants and elegant shops, and outstanding theatrical, musical, and dance performances. Londoners are as diverse as their city. While most are of British ancestry, immigrants from many parts of the world have settled in London, making it a truly multicultural metropolis.

More than two hundred years ago, the great English writer Samuel Johnson wrote, "When a man is tired of London, he is tired of life; for there is in London all that life can afford." This is still true today. Founded by the Romans nearly 2,000 years ago, London, with its blend of the past and the present, is one of the most exciting cities in the world.

▶ LAND

London, which covers 610 square miles (1,580 square kilometers), is located in southeastern England on the banks of the Thames, England's principal river. The Thames flows

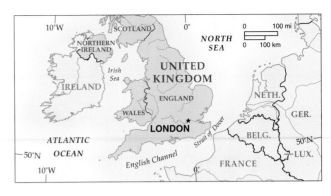

into the North Sea some 40 miles (65 kilometers) east of London.

A few tributary streams enter the Thames in the Greater London area. They are the Colne, Crane, Lea, and Roding rivers in the northern part of the city and the Ravensbourne, Wandle, Hogsmill, and Mole rivers in the south. Some tributaries originate in the hills of northern London. A few of these hills rise to 450 feet (137 meters) and are the city's highest points. The lowest point in the city, the floodplain of the Thames, is just a few feet above high-tide level.

Climate

London has temperate summers and mild winters. Temperatures average about 63°F (17°C) in July and 39°F (4°C) in January. Because temperatures rarely fall below the freezing point, the Thames is navigable throughout the winter. Precipitation averages 23 inches (584 millimeters) a year.

London was once known for its thick winter fog. Londoners called it a pea-soup fog because the fog and coal smoke from factories mixed, making the air a yellowish-green.

Tower Bridge crosses the Thames River, connecting London's north and south banks. London is the capital of Britain and one of the world's great cities.

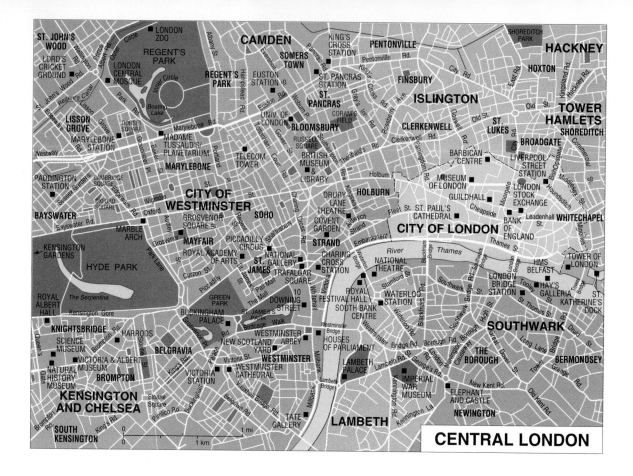

CENTRAL LONDON

Since the passage of the Clean Air Act in 1956, these fogs have ended, and today London has more sunshine than ever before.

▶ **GREATER LONDON**

London is made up of 13 inner boroughs, 19 outer boroughs, and the City of London, which is commonly called the City. It and two other inner-borough areas, the West End and the South Bank, make up Central London. Central London is much like the borough of Manhattan in New York City, for it is the area that attracts most of the tourists.

The City, London's financial district, is the original and most historic part of London. It is only 1 square mile (2.6 square kilometers) in size, and is often called the Square Mile. After William the Conqueror invaded England in 1066, he built a castle there to guard London Bridge. This fortress, the White Tower, was the beginning of the Tower of London. The Tower, at first the home of the kings, later became a prison. Today it is a museum where the Crown Jewels are kept. Colorfully dressed Yeomen Warders of the

Tower, called Beefeaters, guide people around. West of the Tower is St. Paul's Cathedral, which was designed by Sir Christopher Wren and completed in 1710.

In addition to St. Paul's, the City has many other places of architectural interest. The Royal Exchange is topped by large golden grasshoppers. The Bank of England building was completed in 1734, but it was enlarged in the 1920's and 1930's, while keeping the original Palladian facade. The Guildhall, completed in 1430, is the seat of the City's government; it is the next-to-largest timber hall in England. (The largest is Westminster Hall, in Westminster Palace.) Lloyd's of London, the London Stock Exchange, and the Natwest Tower are striking new buildings. The Barbican Centre is a large commercial, cultural, and residential development.

The West End, to the west of the City, is the center of Britain's government. It grew up around Westminster, the most important of all the villages that became part of London. Westminster had its start when King Edward the Confessor (1002?–66) built his palace

London is a city of time-honored traditions and historic landmarks. *Top to bottom:* The changing of the guard at Buckingham Palace is a daily occurrence. The clock tower of Big Ben stands next to the Houses of Parliament, seat of the British government. Young visitors enjoy the pigeons in Trafalgar Square.

there. Nearby is Westminster Abbey, where monarchs of Britain have been crowned ever since the time of William the Conqueror. Westminster Palace, seat of the Houses of Parliament, stands where King Edward's palace once stood. Victoria Tower is at one end of the huge building, and the clock tower of Big Ben is at the other end. Big Ben strikes the hour in distinctive tones.

Most government offices are just north of the Houses of Parliament, on Whitehall. And on a small street running off from Whitehall is one of England's most famous addresses: Number 10 Downing Street, official residence of the prime minister.

A little farther west, Henry VIII converted an old hospital into St. James's Palace. The British court is still known as the Court of St. James, although the royal family now makes its London home in Buckingham Palace. This palace, just south of St. James's, became the royal residence in the 1800's. Guards in red coats and tall hats parade up and down in front of the palace. People throng to watch the colorful changing-of-the-guard ceremony each morning.

Northwest of Buckingham Palace, at the corner of Hyde Park and Oxford Street, is Marble Arch. Originally built as a gateway for the palace, it was moved to its present site in 1851. Marble Arch is a well-known stop on the Underground (subway). People get off there to shop at Selfridge's, a big department store, and other shops on Oxford Street.

South of Oxford Street, and running more or less parallel to it, is a broad av-

Theaters, stores, and giant advertising billboards are features of Piccadilly Circus, one of London's busiest traffic circles.

enue called Piccadilly. At its eastern end is Piccadilly Circus, one of London's main traffic centers. Regent Street, Shaftesbury Avenue, and the Haymarket (which once really was a hay market) all lead into Piccadilly Circus. All around are theaters and movie houses. People, cars, buses, and taxis jam the traffic circle. They swing around a traffic island where there is a fountain. On top of the fountain is a statue called Eros, a popular landmark.

West of Regent Street, toward Hyde Park, are the hotels, restaurants, and foreign embassies of the Mayfair district. East of Regent Street lies the district known as Soho. Although this historic area is being rebuilt, parts of it are still a maze of little courts and dark, narrow streets crowded with busy coffeehouses and restaurants.

East of Piccadilly Circus is Leicester Square, the heart of the movie and theater district. Still farther east is Covent Garden, where the Royal Opera House stands. A famous produce market stood nearby for almost 150 years. It was moved to a location south of the Thames in 1974, and a shopping complex now occupies the site.

Two Londoners chat in front of one of the many small neighborhood shops that dot the city.

South of Leicester Square, on Charing Cross Road, is another London landmark, Trafalgar Square. This square is named in honor of Admiral Horatio Nelson's victory over the French at the Battle of Trafalgar in 1805. In the center is a tall column topped by a statue of Admiral Nelson.

The South Bank, or Bankside, has in recent years developed into one of London's most interesting areas. In addition to the Imperial War Museum, the South Bank is home to the Museum of Garden History, the Florence Nightingale Museum, and the Museum of the Moving Image. The latter museum is part of the South Bank Centre, an important arts complex at the southern entrance of Waterloo Bridge.

▶ **PEOPLE**

London, like New York and other major cities, began to lose population to its suburbs in the years following World War II. From a population of 8.6 million in the late 1930's, the city has shrunk to 6.6 million. At the same time, London's ethnic composition was also undergoing change.

Until the late 1800's, most immigrants to London came from other parts of England and from Scotland, Wales, and Ireland. Then small numbers of immigrants began arriving from other European countries, primarily France, Italy, Germany, Poland, and Russia. Jewish immigration increased during and after World War II. Other immigrant groups during this pe-

Left: The early Greek sculptures known as the Elgin Marbles are a highlight of the British Museum's outstanding collection of ancient art. *Below:* Passersby outside Harrod's, a famous London department store, reflect the city's ethnic variety.

riod included Chinese and Greek and Turkish Cypriots.

Beginning in the 1950's, as immigrants from Britain's former Caribbean and African colonies made their way to England, London's black population increased. So too did the number of people from India, Pakistan, and Bangladesh. Somalis, Iranians, Arabs, and Latin Americans were among the other ethnic groups that settled in London. Today London is a multicultural community: One-quarter of its people are immigrants or the children and grandchildren of immigrants.

Perhaps the most distinctive Londoners are the Cockneys. Traditionally, Cockneys are said to be people born within the sound of Bow Bells—the bells of St. Mary-le-Bow, a historic church in the City. Cockneys have a special costume for festival days, and their speech has a number of unique features. For example, they tend to ignore *h* as a first letter but add it to the beginning of words that begin with a vowel. Thus, they say "'appy" instead of "happy" and "Hoxford Street" instead of "Oxford Street."

Education and Libraries

More than a million students attend London's elementary and secondary schools. Among the city's famous private schools are Harrow, Westminster, and St. Paul's. London's major center of higher education, and the largest university in Britain, is the University of London. A federation of colleges and faculties, it includes the London School of Economics and Political Science, King's College, Imperial College, and University College.

London's more than 500 public libraries are administered by the public library authorities of the boroughs. Among the city's major libraries is the British Library, now housed in the British Museum but scheduled for relocation. Other major libraries include the London Library and the University of London Central Library. Museums such as the Science Museum and the Victoria and Albert Museum maintain specialized library collections, as do such institutions as the Royal Geographic Society.

Museums and Art Galleries

London has more than 250 museums. Among the most notable are the Victoria and Albert Museum, with its collections of fine and applied arts; the National Maritime Museum at Greenwich; and the Natural History Museum. The Science Museum has a special children's gallery where visitors push buttons to make different exhibits work.

The National Gallery, National Portrait Gallery, Tate Gallery, and British Museum house outstanding art collections.

Theater, Music, and Dance

London is one of the world's leading centers for the performing arts. Among its best-known theaters are the Royal Opera House at Covent Garden, home to both the Royal Opera and the Royal Ballet; the Sadler's Wells Theatre, which hosts visiting troupes; and the Drury Lane Theatre, which is London's oldest theater. The Royal Albert Hall is known for its summer-evening Henry Wood Promenade Concerts.

The Barbican Centre, an arts complex in the City, hosts the Royal Shakespeare Company and the London Symphony Orchestra. Another center for the arts is located on the South Bank of the Thames. The Royal National Theatre is there, as is a recently completed replica of William Shakespeare's Globe Theatre. The Royal Philharmonic and the London Philharmonic both perform at the South Bank's Royal Festival Hall.

Workers outside the Stock Exchange, in London's financial district. Financial services are the most important component of the city's economy.

Parks

London has many beautiful parks. Regent's Park, a 465-acre (186-hectare) oasis of greenery with beds of roses and other flowers, is in northwestern London. The London Zoo is in the northern part of the park, and the beautiful Y-shaped Boating Lake is in the southern end. A canal, built in the early 1800's, circles the northern perimeter of the park. Boat cruises on the canal are popular with visitors.

Kensington Gardens and Hyde Park, in Westminster, form a single 615-acre (246-

hectare) expanse of trees, greenery, and flowers. The Serpentine, a giant artificial lake, runs through both parks. Kensington Palace is a popular attraction in Kensington Gardens. Speaker's Corner, near the northeastern entrance to Hyde Park, is where people gather to listen to soapbox orators make speeches on many different subjects.

To the east of Hyde Park are the smaller Green Park and St. James's Park. St. James's, with its view of Buckingham Palace, is especially beautiful.

Sports

London's best-known sporting event is the annual tennis tournament at Wimbledon. Held in southern London, it is one of the Grand Slam tennis tournaments that also include the U.S. Open, French Open, and Australian Open. Another annual event is the London Marathon, which attracts some 25,000 runners every April.

Soccer, called football in Britain, is London's top spectator and participant sport. There is no single London soccer team, but 13 professional clubs represent different parts of the city. The annual championship is held at Wembley Stadium. Cricket is London's other important spectator and participant sport. During the summer months, almost 1,000 cricket clubs vie for dominance. Important matches are played at Lord's Cricket Ground in northern London.

▶ ECONOMY

London is the United Kingdom's most important center of economic activity. Its businesses and industries account for about 15 percent of the nation's gross domestic product (GDP; the total value of goods and services produced in a year) and employ 20 percent of the nation's workforce. In the last half century, with the decline of manufacturing, service industries have become the major contributors to the city's economy.

Services

London is one of the world's great centers of international finance, and financial services are the most important sector of London's economy, producing nearly 40 percent of the city's GDP. The London Stock Exchange, the

Bank of England, Lloyd's and other insurance companies, and many more financial institutions are located in the City, London's financial district. Tourism is another major contributor to the city's economy. Other service industries include health services, business services, and wholesale trade.

Manufacturing

London was once a major manufacturing city. But like other large cities worldwide, it has witnessed the relocation of factories and plants to the suburbs and other areas. As a result, the percentage of London's labor force that engaged in manufacturing declined from about 50 percent in the early 1960's to 10 percent in the late 1990's.

Today London's manufacturing sector, though diminished, is quite diverse. Among the major products are clothing, leather products, furniture, household appliances, food products, pharmaceuticals, and other consumer goods. Precision instruments, computers, and printing and publishing products are also important.

Transportation

Numerous bridges connect London's north and south banks. London Bridge, the oldest, has been rebuilt many times, most recently in 1972. Two other bridges, Westminster and Blackfriars, were built in the mid-1700's. During the 1800's many more were built, including Tower Bridge.

London has six great railway stations, and some 1.25 million commuters travel in and out of London by train every day. Trains from the Waterloo International Terminal, completed in 1994, take passengers to Paris in three hours by way of the English Channel Tunnel (or Chunnel), or to Brussels in three and a quarter hours.

Probably no other city in the world is better served by public transportation than London. Its bus and subway systems carry 5 million passengers a day. The red double-decker bus is the best known of all London forms of transportation. London also has one of the most extensive underground, or metro, systems in the world. Londoners call their subway system the "tube." The first subway line, the Metropolitan Line, was built in the 1860's. The most recent addition, the Jubilee Line, is to be extended east to the Docklands, a new commercial, housing, and recreational development east of the City.

London has five airports: Heathrow, Gatwick, Stansted, Luton, and London City. The last, constructed as part of the Docklands redevelopment, is only 20 minutes from London by road. Heathrow, about 15 miles (24 kilometers) west of London, is the busiest international airport in the world.

London was once one of the busiest ports in the United Kingdom. Its docks were located downriver from the Tower of London. But they were unable to handle the huge container ships that shippers started to use in the late 1950's. As a result, modern facilities were built east of London at Tilbury, and the old docks became the site of the new Docklands development.

Communication

London is the center for the United Kingdom's communications media. Fleet Street, in the City, was once the heart of the newspaper publishing industry. But most publishers have moved to other parts of London. London's daily newspapers include the influential *Times*. Book and periodical publishers also have their headquarters in London, as does the British Broadcasting Corporation (BBC), the national radio and television network.

▶ GOVERNMENT

Greater London is governed by the Greater London Authority (GLA), which consists of an elected mayor and a 25-seat assembly. The GLA is responsible for citywide services as well as planning and development.

Each of London's 32 boroughs elects its own government council, which is responsible for local matters. The City of London also retains authority over local matters. It is governed by the Corporation of London, an organization that acts through an elected Court of Common Council.

For much of its history London had no elected central government. Beginning in 1889, the London County Council and later the Greater London Council (GLC) supervised some common services. The GLC was abolished in 1986. In 1998, Londoners voted to establish a new citywide government. And in May 2000 the city's first popularly elected mayor and an assembly were chosen to form the GLA.

A concerned citizen airs his views at Speaker's Corner in Hyde Park, where crowds gather to hear speeches.

▶ HISTORY

After the Romans invaded Britain in A.D. 43, they built a walled town they called Londinium on the banks of the Thames. By the 200's about 15,000 people lived there.

The Romans left Britain in the 400's, and London was deserted. But King Alfred the Great rebuilt it in the 800's. By the time William the Conqueror, Duke of Normandy, invaded England in 1066, London was inhabited by people used to running their own affairs. William made the city his capital, and Londoners accepted him as their king because he granted them self-government.

During the Middle Ages (500–1500), London became the richest city in England. It prospered even more during the reign of Queen Elizabeth I (1558–1603), becoming a great cultural center and an international port. But as trade increased, the walled City became terribly overcrowded, and two tragedies struck. In 1665–66, the Great Plague killed almost 100,000 people, and in 1666 the Great London Fire burned down most of the old City. Thereafter, new houses were built of brick or stone instead of wood, and streets were widened. England's great architect, Sir Christopher Wren, built about 50 churches in the City, including the magnificent St. Paul's Cathedral, and other important structures.

In the late 1600's and early 1700's, London expanded westward into Westminster—the other historic center of modern London—and eastward into the area known as the East End. By 1800, Lon-

The damage inflicted by the German Blitz during World War II was captured on the cover of a London newspaper.

don had a population of about 1 million and was the world's largest city.

During the mid-1800's, as more and more people moved farther from the center of London, many railroad stations were built to accommodate them. London also became the first city to build an underground railroad.

London continued to expand during the early 1900's. During World War I (1914–18), it suffered only minor damage from German bombs, but the damage during World War II (1939–45) was extensive. The German Blitz—bombing and rocket attacks—killed more than 30,000 people and seriously damaged or destroyed 250,000 homes. Much of the old City of London was destroyed.

An energetic program of rebuilding has been going on since the mid-1950's. A Green Belt, or band of open country, was set up to control further growth. New suburbs were established. The M25 ring road, which encircles London, was built. Many high-rise buildings were constructed, including One Canada Square, one of Europe's tallest buildings. It is not far from remnants of the Roman wall built around the city of London almost 2,000 years ago. Notable landmarks of the new millennium include the enormous Millennium Dome and the London Eye, the largest observation wheel ever built.

On the morning of July 7, 2005, four bombs exploded in London, killing 52 people riding on public transportation. The attacks, carried out by British Islamic terrorists to protest Britain's military involvement in Iraq and Afghanistan, were condemned worldwide.

ARTHUR CAMPBELL TURNER
University of California, Riverside

See also ENGLAND; UNITED KINGDOM.

LONDON, JACK (1876–1916)

Jack London's life was as rugged and adventurous as the tales he told. Born in San Francisco on January 12, 1876, he grew up in and around the docks of San Francisco and Oakland, California. At 13 he left school to help support his family. But normal occupations did not appeal to him, and he joined a gang of men who illegally caught oysters at night and sold them the next morning. At only 15 years of age, Jack London was one of the most successful oyster pirates working San Francisco Bay.

London maintained a strong love for books while he practiced his pirate trade. In fact, his continuous reading was often compared to his hard drinking—he did both with equal zest. London moved from place to place and from job to job. He hunted seals in the Pacific, worked in a jute mill, and went prospecting for gold in Alaska.

London was an active socialist and joined a march to Washington, D.C., in 1894 to voice demands for social and economic justice. But his own words sum up his attitude: "I became a tramp . . . because of the life that was in me, of a wanderlust in my blood which would not let me rest."

London began writing down his adventures, and in 1893 he won a newspaper short-story contest. This success encouraged him to write more. His early works were rejected by publishers, but a series of stories based on his experiences in the Far North met with greater success. Between 1900 and 1916, he became the most widely read author of his time.

Most of London's stories are about the struggle for survival that he knew well. His short stories of the Klondike, such as "To Build A Fire," drew on his own experiences there. The autobiographical novel *Martin Eden* (1909) tells of the time he first began to write. And anyone who reads his novels *The Sea Wolf* (1901), *The Call of the Wild* (1903), and *White Fang* (1906) will come to know the life and personality of Jack London.

Unfortunately, London's life came to a tragic end. Ill and burdened by debts, unable to help people to whom he had often given money and shelter, he took an overdose of drugs. He died on November 22, 1916.

JAMES K. BOWEN
Southern Oregon State College

▶THE CALL OF THE WILD

Jack London's best-known novel tells the story of Buck, a dog stolen from his California home and brought to the Klondike to work as a sled dog during the 1890's gold rush. This excerpt shows how Buck, used to the pampered life of a family pet, learns to survive in his new, harsh environment.

That night Buck faced the great problem of sleeping. The tent, illumined by a candle, glowed warmly in the midst of the white plain; and when he, as a matter of course, entered it, both Perrault and François bombarded him with curses and cooking utensils, till he recovered from his consternation and fled ignominiously into the outer cold. A chill wind was blowing that nipped him sharply and bit with especial venom into his wounded shoulder. He lay down on the snow and attempted to sleep, but the frost soon drove him shivering to his feet. Miserable and disconsolate, he wandered about among the many tents, only to find that one place was as cold as another. Here and there savage dogs rushed upon him, but he bristled his neck-hair and snarled (for he was learning fast), and they let him go his way unmolested.

Finally an idea came to him. He would return and see how his own team-mates were making out. To his astonishment, they had disappeared. Again he wandered about through the great camp, looking for them, and again he returned. Were they in the tent? No, that could not be, else he would not have been driven out. Then where could they possibly be? With drooping tail and shivering body, very forlorn indeed, he aimlessly circled the tent. Suddenly the snow gave way beneath his fore legs and he sank down. Something wriggled under his feet. He sprang back, bristling and snarling, fearful of the unseen and unknown. But a friendly little yelp reassured him, and he went back to investigate. A whiff of warm air ascended to his nostrils, and there, curled up under the snow in a snug ball, lay Billee. He whined placatingly, squirmed and wriggled to show his good will and inten-

tions, and even ventured, as a bribe for peace, to lick Buck's face with his warm wet tongue.

Another lesson. So that was the way they did it, eh? Buck confidently selected a spot, and with much fuss and waste effort proceeded to dig a hole for himself. In a trice the heat from his body filled the confined space and he was asleep. The day had been long and arduous, and he slept soundly and comfortably, though he growled and barked and wrestled with bad dreams.

Nor did he open his eyes till roused by the noises of the waking camp. At first he did not know where he was. It had snowed during the night and he was completely buried. The snow walls pressed him on every side, and a great surge of fear swept through him—the fear of the wild thing for the trap. It was a token that he was harking back through his own life to the lives of his forbears; for he was a civilized dog, an unduly civilized dog, and of his own experience knew no trap and so could not of himself fear it. The muscles of his whole body contracted spasmodically and instinctively, the hair on his neck and shoulders stood on end, and with a ferocious snarl he bounded straight up into the blinding day, the snow flying about him in a flashing cloud.

LONG FAMILY

The Longs, Louisiana's most significant and colorful political family, influenced Democratic politics for nearly sixty years.

Huey Pierce Long (1893–1935), known as the Kingfish, was born near Winnfield. He became a lawyer in 1915 and won his first public office in 1918 as a railroad commissioner. In 1924 he ran for governor, finishing third behind better-known candidates. But he easily won the job four years later, after his strongest opponents had died.

As governor (1928–31), Long passed many social and public works programs to help the poor, which made him enormously popular.

But much of his power came through his ruthless use of bribes and threats. He also appointed friends to high offices. In 1929, the state legislature tried but failed to impeach him on charges of misusing state funds.

In 1930, Long ran for the U.S. Senate and won. But even while he was serving as senator (1931–35), he continued to rule Louisiana state politics unofficially through his successors in the governor's office. Meanwhile, in Washington, D.C., Long devoted much of his energy promoting his social programs, notably his Share Our Wealth plan. It proposed guaranteeing each family a minimum income and land allowance, to be financed by raising the taxes of millionaires. Long's proposals were particularly attractive to the millions suffering the effects of the Great Depression. It was widely believed that Long would successfully challenge Franklin D. Roosevelt for the presidency. His autobiography, *Every Man a King*, was published in 1933.

On September 8, 1935, Huey Long was shot at the Louisiana state capitol in Baton Rouge. He died two days later. Many believe he was assassinated by Carl A. Weiss, a physician whose family members were Long's political enemies. But Long's bodyguards killed Weiss at the scene before a trial could establish his guilt or innocence.

Earl Kemp Long (1895–1960), Huey's brother, was also born in Winnfield. Elected lieutenant governor of Louisiana in 1936, he

Despite charges of corruption and fraud, Huey Long was one of the most popular politicians ever to serve the state of Louisiana.

succeeded Richard Leche as governor in 1939 and was the first to serve more than two terms (1939–40, 1948–52, and 1956–60). Like his brother, Earl was accused of corruption and overspending.

Although Earl Long was no champion of the rights of African Americans, he was the first white candidate for governor to court the black vote and was a moderate on racial issues at a time when some other Louisiana politicians were trying to prevent blacks from voting at all.

Russell Billiu Long (1918–2003), Huey's son, was born in Shreveport. In 1948, at the age of 29, Russell was elected to the U.S. Senate. (He turned 30, the minimum age for senators, before taking his seat.) Although he, too, was a champion of social welfare, Russell was more conservative than his father. He served in a number of leadership positions, including chairman of the powerful Senate Finance Committee (1966–81) and assistant majority leader (1965–69). In 1980 a national news magazine ranked him the eleventh most influential person in the country.

GLEN JEANSONNE
Author, *Messiah of the Masses: Huey P. Long and the Great Depression*

LONGFELLOW, HENRY WADSWORTH (1807–1882)

The American poet Henry Wadsworth Longfellow was born in Portland, Maine, on February 27, 1807. He was the second child in a family of eight. His father was a lawyer, and his mother was fond of music and poetry.

Henry was an excellent student. At age 14 he went to Bowdoin College in Brunswick, Maine. His father wanted him to study law, but he was proud when poems and essays Henry wrote were published.

Longfellow was offered a chance to teach modern languages at Bowdoin if he would study abroad at his own expense. After graduating, Longfellow went abroad for the first time. He came home after three years knowing four languages.

Longfellow taught at Bowdoin from 1829 to 1834. Up to that time, Latin and Greek had been the only languages taught extensively, and there were no really good French or Spanish textbooks. So Longfellow wrote textbooks for his students.

In 1831, Longfellow married Mary Storer Potter. Three years later he was offered a position as professor of modern languages at Harvard. First Longfellow asked for time to study abroad again. He and Mary visited London, Hamburg, Denmark, and Sweden. Longfellow studied Scandinavian poetry and translated some of it into English verse.

In 1835, Mary died in Holland. Hard work seemed to help Longfellow overcome his grief. He continued his European journey, studying at the famous university in Heidelberg, Germany.

In December 1836, Longfellow began teaching at Harvard. He had a way of making foreign languages interesting and exciting to his students. For the next 18 years he was one of Harvard's best-loved professors.

Longfellow rented rooms at Craigie House, a mansion built before the American Revolution. His windows overlooked the gardens and open fields that stretched down to the Charles River. He was happy but very lonely. In 1843 he married Frances Appleton of Boston. His father-in-law bought Craigie House for the Longfellows. Longfellow loved people, and there were many parties in the big house on Brattle Street.

Longfellow's six children were all born at Craigie House. He wrote "The Children's Hour" for them. In "The Song of Hiawatha," he wrote of Indians like those he had seen during his own boyhood in Portland, when Indians used to come to trade their furs. "Paul Revere's Ride" came from stories his Grandfather Wadsworth used to tell him.

In 1861, Frances died when her dress caught fire from some sealing wax she was using. Longfellow was badly burned trying to save his wife. Later he wrote about her in the touching sonnet, "The Cross of Snow."

Again Longfellow turned to work for comfort. He spent years translating some of Dante's work into English poetry. He finished writing *Tales of a Wayside Inn*. He went to England again, and Queen Victoria invited him to call on her at the royal palace. Oxford and Cambridge gave him honorary degrees.

Longfellow died in Cambridge, Massachusetts, on March 24, 1882. A monument to him stands in the Poets' Corner in Westminster Abbey, London.

LOUISE HALL THARP
Author, *Tory Hole, The Peabody Sisters of Salem*

LONGITUDE. See LATITUDE AND LONGITUDE.

LONGSTREET, JAMES. See CIVIL WAR, UNITED STATES (Profiles: Confederate).

LOPEZ, NANCY. See GOLF (Great Players).

LORENZ, KONRAD (1903–1989)

Konrad Zacharias Lorenz, an Austrian naturalist, was one of the founders of an entirely new branch of science. His studies of animals in their natural environments led to the establishment of **ethology**, the study of animal behavior. For his work, Lorenz was a co-winner of the Nobel Prize in physiology or medicine in 1973.

Lorenz was born on November 7, 1903, in Vienna, Austria, and grew up in the small village of Altenberg. Young Konrad loved animals and cared for many pets. As a student at the University of Vienna, Lorenz kept a pet bird, a jackdaw he named Jock. The notes he kept on Jock became his first published account of animal behavior.

After completing his medical degree (1928) and earning a Ph.D. in zoology (1933), Lorenz joined the University of Vienna faculty. There he began to study and develop his theory of imprinting, which involves a type of instinctive behavior. Lorenz discovered that certain species of animals receive fixed impressions shortly after birth. Lorenz found that baby geese think the first moving object they see is their mother—even if the moving object is not a goose. He became known for the greylag geese that became imprinted on him, following along behind him during walks near his home.

Geese that became imprinted on Lorenz as babies followed the naturalist as if he were their mother.

Lorenz later compared his studies of animals with human behavior. His book *On Aggression* (1963), which discusses the similarities of aggression in animals and in humans, sparked controversy and brought Lorenz wide public attention.

From 1961 to 1973, Lorenz directed the Max Planck Institute for the Physiology of Behavior in Germany. He wrote hundreds of scientific papers and also a number of books, including *King Solomon's Ring* (1949), *Man Meets Dog* (1950), and *The Year of the Greylag Goose* (1978). *The Foundation of Ethology* (1982) describes much of his life's work.

Lorenz died on February 17, 1989, at his childhood home in Altenberg.

BARBARA ROSS
Science Writer

LORENZO THE MAGNIFICENT. See MEDICI.

LOS ANGELES

Los Angeles, the second largest city in the United States, is located on the Pacific coast of southern California. The city, the seat of Los Angeles County, covers an area of 466 square miles (1,207 square kilometers) and is home to approximately 3.7 million people.

More than 16 million people, or about half of California's total population, live in the sprawling metropolitan area known as Greater Los Angeles. It encompasses dozens of other well-known cities, such as Long Beach, Burbank, Santa Monica, Glendale, Anaheim, Santa Ana, Pasadena, Pomona, Beverly Hills, Malibu, Riverside, and San Bernardino.

Known as the City of Angels, Los Angeles is the largest center of manufacturing and the second largest center for finance and banking in the United States. It is renowned for its pleasant climate, decorative palm trees, and sandy beaches stretching from Malibu to San Juan Capistrano. But Los Angeles is probably best known as the heart of the nation's television and motion picture industries.

▶ LAND

Los Angeles was founded along the banks of the Los Angeles River, 15 miles (24 kilometers) inland from the shores of Santa Monica Bay. Much of the city is situated on a plain that gently rises up from the Pacific Ocean to low mountains or hills. North of the Santa Monica Mountains lies the enormous San Fernando Valley. Additional mountain systems in the northeast, east, and southeast enclose more valleys and basins in a sort of great bowl. The San Andreas Fault—one of the largest fractures in the Earth's crust and a primary source of earthquakes—runs just east of the city.

Approximately 90 percent of the city's water is piped in through aqueducts from northern California and from the Colorado River far to the east. The city gets much of its electrical power from Hoover Dam, also on the Colorado River.

Climate

Los Angeles has a sunny, pleasant climate, although summers can sometimes be quite warm. Winter temperatures rarely fall below freezing. Rainfall occurs mostly in the winter when storms arrive from the Pacific Ocean. Dry conditions in the summer and fall can lead to dangerous wildfires. Smog, caused by automobile exhaust and industrial gas fumes, is also a source of ongoing concern.

▶ PEOPLE

The people of Greater Los Angeles represent a wide variety of world cultures, making the city an interesting place to live and visit.

Los Angeles is the second largest city in the United States. Its sprawling metropolis lies between several mountain ranges and the Pacific Ocean.

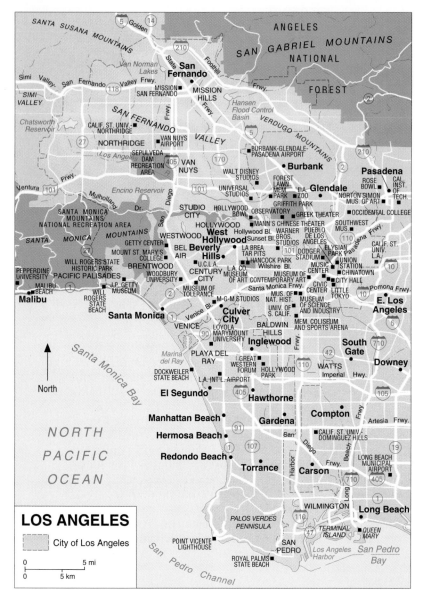

LOS ANGELES

City of Los Angeles

| 0 | 5 mi |
| 0 | 5 km |

located just north of the downtown area and the other in Monterey Park, an eastern suburb of the city. Monterey Park is the only city in the United States where people of Chinese ancestry form the majority. Approximately 250,000 Japanese Americans live in Los Angeles. Little Tokyo, a business center and limited residential district that borders Los Angeles' Civic Center, serves as a cultural center for the community and contains the Japanese American National Museum. Koreatown, home to some 200,000 Korean Americans, has emerged to the west and southwest of the downtown area. Little Saigon, located in the suburban city of Garden Grove in neighboring Orange County, is the business and cultural center for approximately 200,000 Vietnamese Americans.

Notable concentrations of more recent immigrant groups include roughly 300,000 Armenians, many living in Glendale, and growing numbers of Russian communities south of Hollywood.

African Americans make up approximately 12 percent of the population of Greater Los Angeles. Major communities are located in the south central part of the city and in Pasadena, Pomona, Long Beach, and suburban communities in neighboring Riverside and San Bernardino counties.

In addition to large national ethnic groups, Greater Los Angeles contains the second largest Jewish community in the United States, with approximately 550,000 people.

Education and Libraries

Los Angeles has many public universities. The University of California at Los Angeles (UCLA) has the largest enrollment. Additional University of California campuses are located in Irvine and Riverside. California

People of Latino (Latin American) origins, including Mexicans, Guatemalans, and Salvadorans, account for more than 40 percent of the population of Greater Los Angeles. Latinos are concentrated particularly in the downtown areas and in the many suburban towns that stretch eastward through the San Gabriel and Pomona valleys.

People of Asian ancestry, particularly Chinese, Japanese, Koreans, Filipinos, and Vietnamese, make up about 11 percent of the population. Greater Los Angeles is home to more than 300,000 Chinese Americans. Many live in one of two Chinatowns, the oldest one

State University (CSU) has six campuses, including Long Beach (the largest), Los Angeles, Northridge, Dominguez Hills, Fullerton, and San Bernardino. Among the local private institutions of higher learning are the University of Southern California (USC), Occidental College, Pepperdine University, California Institute of Technology (Caltech), Loyola Marymount University, California Institute of the Arts (Cal Arts), Art Center College of Design, Otis College of Art and Design, Fashion Institute of Design and Merchandising, and five campuses of the Pomona-Claremont colleges.

Museums

Many fine museums are found in Greater Los Angeles. The Los Angeles County Museum of Art has an outstanding collection of paintings and sculptures, as do the J. P. Getty Museum, in Malibu, and the Getty Center, housed in a massive building complex atop the Santa Monica Mountains. The Getty museums have the richest endowment of any museums in the world.

The California Museum of Science and Industry features industrial, agricultural, and recreational exhibits. The Southwest Museum has fascinating displays about the Indians of the Southwest. The Los Angeles County Museum of Natural History offers lectures, films, and historical and scientific exhibits. It also administers the George C. Page Museum, which displays a fine collection of Ice Age fossils, and Hancock Park, the site of the La Brea Tar Pits, where the remains of saber-toothed tigers, mastodons, giant bison, bears, and other animals were uncovered. Other museums include the Museum of Contemporary Art (MOCA) and the Museum of Tolerance, which focuses on the Holocaust.

Theater, Music, and Dance

The city has four major musical and theatrical performance centers. The largest among them, the Music Center for the Performing Arts, features theater, ballet, symphonic music, and opera in three different buildings—the Dorothy Chandler Pavilion, the Mark Taper Forum, and the Ahmanson Theatre. Additional concert facilities include

Above: Korean Americans are among the fastest-growing ethnic groups in Los Angeles. *Left:* The mechanical shark from the movie *Jaws* remains one of the most popular attractions at Universal Studios.

the indoor Universal Amphitheater and two outdoor forums, the Greek Theater and the Hollywood Bowl.

Parks

Amusement parks are numerous throughout the Los Angeles area. Disneyland, located in nearby Anaheim, was dubbed "the happiest place on Earth" by its creator, Walt Disney. Universal Studios in Universal City, north of Hollywood, contains the world's largest movie and television studios and is one of the nation's most visited theme parks. Other major amusement parks include Knott's Berry Farm in Buena Park, Six Flags Magic Mountain in Valencia, and the Raging Waters water park in the Pomona Valley.

From Malibu to San Juan Capistrano, visitors as well as native Angelenos enjoy the beautiful beaches along the Pacific coast.

One of Los Angeles' most popular public parks is Griffith Park, which contains the Los Angeles Zoo. Covering 4,200 acres (1,680 hectares), it is one of the largest city parks in the world.

Sports

Professional and collegiate sports are popular, and people turn out in large numbers to cheer their teams. The Rose Bowl, in Pasadena, and the Memorial Coliseum and Sports Arena, in central Los Angeles, host football, soccer, and other outdoor events. Dodger and Anaheim stadiums are home to the Los Angeles Dodgers of baseball's National League and the Anaheim Angels of baseball's American League. Other professional teams include the Los Angeles Lakers and the Los Angeles Clippers of the National Basketball Association and the Los Angeles Sparks of the Women's National Basketball Association. Ice hockey teams include the Los Angeles Kings and Anaheim Mighty Ducks. Hollywood Park and Santa Anita racetracks provide Thoroughbred horse racing. Fontana Speedway offers regular auto racing, and the Long Beach Grand Prix road race is a popular annual event.

▶ECONOMY

The making of motion pictures is Los Angeles' best-known industry, and it has spawned many other businesses that have become vital to the local economy. These range from companies that create television programs, musical recordings, and advertising campaigns to those that manufacture cosmetics and clothing, particularly women's apparel and accessories.

The manufacture of aircraft and aerospace products—very important until the 1990's, when defense-related spending went into decline—stimulated the development of related industries, such as the design and production of electronics goods. Electronics brought in the computer industry, and today the creation of software programs and computer equipment is a major industry in Greater Los Angeles. Other important manufactures include jewelry, chemicals, metals, home and office furnishings and supplies, food products, medical equipment and supplies, and refined oil and oil-based products, such as plastics, medicines, and fuels.

Tourism is also a major contributor to the city's economy. Only Las Vegas, Orlando, and Greater New York City have more hotel and motel rooms than Greater Los Angeles. The region's many beaches are a major attraction in the summer months.

Transportation

The combined ports of Los Angeles and Long Beach are the busiest in the country. Four major airports serve the region. Among them is Los Angeles International Airport, which ranks third in the United States and fourth in the world in number of passenger arrivals and departures.

The major communities of Greater Los Angeles are linked by an extensive freeway network for automobiles, containing more miles of roads than any other city in the world. The first step in the development of a rapid transit rail system was introduced in 1990. In addition, Metrolink, a lightweight commuter-railway connecting downtown Los Angeles with outlying communities, has been developed on former railroad routes.

Communication

More than 20 English-language daily newspapers are printed in Greater Los Angeles. The *Los Angeles Times*, with a daily distribution of more than 1 million copies, has the widest audience, followed by the *Orange County Register* and the *Long Beach Press-Telegram*. The Spanish-language daily *La Opinion* is also widely read. Weekly newspapers are published in Chinese, Thai, Korean, Japanese, Farsi, Vietnamese, Armenian, Hebrew, and Russian, as well as in English.

Greater Los Angeles supports 24 television stations, including 1 Spanish station. There are more than 130 radio stations, broadcasting primarily in English and Spanish.

▶ GOVERNMENT

Los Angeles has a complex system of government. The City of Los Angeles is run by a mayor, elected to a 4-year term, and a city council made up of 15 council members, also elected to 4-year terms. Other elected officials include a city attorney, a city controller, and seven members of a board of education that governs the nation's second largest public school district. The Los Angeles Department of Water and Power, a utility company owned by the city, provides water and electricity to all city residents. City appointed commissions manage the Los Angeles International Airport and Los Angeles Harbor.

Because Greater Los Angeles sprawls across portions of five counties, approximately 160 independent cities within it are self-governing. There are 88 cities in Los Angeles County alone. In addition, each of the five counties is governed by a board of supervisors, which is responsible for offering services not provided by the cities.

▶ HISTORY

Los Angeles was founded in 1781 by the Spanish governor of California, Don Felipe de Neve. He called the town El Pueblo de Nuestra Señora la Reina de Los Ángeles de Porciúncula, which means "the town of Our Lady the Queen of the Angels of Porciúncula." Olvera Street, along with the neighboring plaza and the city's first church, is now part of El Pueblo de Los Ángeles State Historic Park.

The town grew slowly until California became a part of the United States in 1848, after the Mexican War. Its population then was about 1,500. Soon farms sprang up around the town, producing oranges, grapefruit, lemons, walnuts, avocados, and grapes.

The Southern Pacific Railroad reached Los Angeles in 1876, followed nine years later by the Santa Fe. For a time a ticket from Chicago cost only one dollar—far less expensive than to go east. This bargain rate was intended to attract new settlers to the area.

Los Angeles began to grow after oil was discovered after 1890, but for a time the city was very short of water. In 1913 engineers built facilities to bring water in from Owens Valley, below the Sierra Nevada mountain range.

In the early 1900's, motion picture producers discovered that the combination of open space and a sunny climate made Los Angeles a perfect location for the young film industry. In a very few years Hollywood became one of the film capitals of the world. It was not until after World War II (1939–45) that Los Angeles greatly expanded and diversified its industry and commerce.

The Beverly Hills Hotel is a familiar landmark in one of Los Angeles' most celebrated neighborhoods.

Famous People

For information on individual movie stars and directors associated with Los Angeles, see the profiles in the article MOTION PICTURES in Volume M.

Thomas (Tom) Bradley (1917–98), born in Calvert, Texas, was the first African American mayor of Los Angeles (1973–93) and the first person elected to that office five times. A former member of the Los Angeles Police Department (1940–61), Bradley established a law practice and served on the Los Angeles city council from 1963 until he became mayor in 1973. He ran unsuccessfully for governor of California in 1982 and 1986.

Norman Chandler (1899–1973), born in Los Angeles, was the publisher of the *Los Angeles Times* (1944–60) and one of the city's greatest benefactors. He and

Louis B. Mayer

William Mulholland

his wife, **Dorothy Buffum Chandler** (1901–97), who was born in Lafayette, Illinois, were great patrons of the arts. They raised funds to rescue the deteriorating Hollywood Bowl and to build the Los Angeles Music Center, which includes the Dorothy Chandler Pavilion. The Chandlers also served as trustees of the University of Southern California and the California Institute of Technology. Their son, **Otis Chandler** (1927–), born in Los Angeles, became publisher of the *Los Angeles Times* on the retirement of his father. Under Otis' leadership, the paper's parent corporation, the Times-Mirror Company, became a major publisher of newspapers, magazines, and books. In 1980, Otis was named chairman of the board and editor in chief of Times-Mirror. He also helped found the Los Angeles Times–Washington Post News Service.

(Delorez) Florence Griffith Joyner (1959–98), born in Los Angeles, was a sprint champion who earned three gold medals and one silver medal at the 1988 Olympic Games in Seoul, South Korea. Popularly known as Flo-Jo, she set the world records in the 100 m (10.49 sec) and 200 m (21.34 sec). Her sister-in-law, **Jackie Joyner-Kersee**, also an Olympic champion, is profiled in the article TRACK AND FIELD in Volume T.

Louis B(urt) Mayer (1885?–1957), born in Minsk, Russia, was among the most powerful film studio heads in what

Florence Griffith Joyner

was known as the Golden Age of Hollywood. As first vice president in charge of production of the Metro-Goldwyn-Mayer Corporation (1924–51), Mayer was a master of the "studio system," in a time when major stars performed under contract to one film company. Mayer built the careers of such actors as Greta Garbo, Clark Gable, and Joan Crawford. His motto for M-G-M was "More stars than there are in heaven." Mayer's son-in-law, **David O(liver) Selznick** (1902–65), born in Pittsburgh, Pennsylvania, formed his own company, Selznick International Pictures. He produced several of Hollywood's most popular films, including *Gone With the Wind* (1939) and *Rebecca* (1940).

William Mulholland (1855–1935), born in Belfast, Ireland, engineered systems to bring water to the residents of Los Angeles, making possible the growth of the city. As superintendent and chief engineer of the Los Angeles City Water Company, Mulholland built a system of aqueducts across mountains, valleys, and desert regions to carry water from Owens Valley in the Sierra Nevada into the city. He also formulated the plans that brought additional water resources from the Colorado River.

Earl Warren (1891–1974), born in Los Angeles, served as governor of California for three terms (1943–53) and as chief justice of the U.S. Supreme Court (1953–69). During Warren's tenure as chief justice, the Court passed down many historic decisions involving civil rights, notably *Brown* v. *Board of Education of Topeka*, which declared it unconstitutional to separate black and white students in the public school system. He headed the Warren Commission (1963–64), which investigated the assassination of President John F. Kennedy.

Like many cities, Los Angeles has had problems, and it is trying to cure its urban ills. In 1971 and 1994, the city had to endure the destruction caused by two large earthquakes. In 1975 and 1992, discontent among lower-income segments of the population led to widespread riots, looting, and arson. In 1993, fires and mudslides caused local devastation. The early 1990's was also a time of economic

slowdown and decreasing property values. By the new millennium, however, the city's economic growth had bounced back as industries boomed, employment levels rose, and tourism reached new highs.

JOEL SPLANSKY
California State University, Long Beach

LOUGANIS, GREG. See OLYMPIC GAMES (Profiles).

LOUIS

Louis (pronounced LOO-ee) was the name of many kings of France who reigned (r.) between 814 and 1848. The original Germanic name was Chlodowech, which meant "famous in battle." In France the name evolved from Clovis to Louis. In Germany the name became Ludwig.

▶ THE CAROLINGIANS

The first five kings named Louis belonged to the Carolingian family of rulers, who were descendants of the emperor Charlemagne, also known as Charles the Great.

Louis I (778–840) (r. 814–40), Charlemagne's only surviving son, became Holy Roman emperor in 814. Known as Louis the Pious, his first acts were to reform the imperial court, which had become notorious for its immorality, and to reform the monasteries, which had ceased to enforce the strict rules of religious life.

Louis's reign was undermined by his sons, who battled each other for the inheritance of the empire. After Louis's death, his empire was divided into three parts. The western part, which became the kingdom of France, was left to his youngest son, Charles II (Charles the Bald).

Louis II (846–79) (r. 877–79), son of Charles the Bald, was known as Louis the Stammerer. He had a short and inglorious reign.

Louis III (863?–82) (r. 879–82), son of Louis II, ruled France jointly with his brother Carloman. Louis ruled over the north and west and his brother over the south and east. In 881, Louis III won renown for a great victory over the invading Vikings, although their devastating raids lasted another generation.

Louis IV (921?–54) (r. 936–54), half-nephew of Louis III, was reared in exile in England until 936, when he was called back to France to be crowned king. Nicknamed *d'Outremer* ("from beyond the seas"), Louis IV proved to be the strongest of the Carolingian kings. At first he fought with Holy Roman Emperor Otto I over possession of Lorraine, but they were reconciled in 942. Otto then gave Louis help in his struggle against the most powerful of his subjects, Hugh the Great, duke of Francia, whom they subdued in 950.

Louis V (966?–87) (r. 986–87), grandson of Louis IV and the last Carolingian king of France, died in a hunting accident one year after his coronation. He was succeeded by Hugh Capet, son of Hugh the Great.

▶ THE CAPETIANS

Five descendants of Hugh Capet bore the name Louis.

Louis VI (1081–1137) (r. 1108–37), son of Philip I, was known as Louis the Fat. He was widely regarded as a protector of the poor, the church, the peasants, and the towns. An ardent warrior, he spent much of his time putting down the rebellions of the barons in his royal domains. By the end of his reign he had largely succeeded in establishing law and order in northwestern France.

Louis VII (1121?–80) (r. 1137–80), son of Louis VI, was known as Louis the Young. Never as strong a figure as his father, Louis VII was exceedingly religious and led an expedition to the Holy Land during the Second Crusade (1146–48). His marriage to Eleanor of Aquitaine gave him control over her lands in southwestern France until they divorced in 1152.

Louis VIII (1187–1226) (r. 1223–26), grandson of Louis VII, was known as Louis the Lion. He attacked Aquitaine and annexed the provinces of Poitou and Saintonge. He then revived the religious crusade against the Albigenses, a group in southern France who refused to follow the teachings of the Roman Catholic Church. Louis conquered Albigensian lands in Avignon and Languedoc. He died while returning from the expedition.

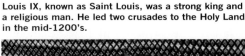

Louis IX, known as Saint Louis, was a strong king and a religious man. He led two crusades to the Holy Land in the mid-1200's.

Louis IX (1214–70) (r. 1226–70), son of Louis VIII, was known as Saint Louis. Combining religious piety with political authority, Louis crushed feudal uprisings and gave his kingdom strong government. He issued ordinances forbidding private warfare, tournaments, and the carrying of arms in times of peace; he ended trial by battle in the royal courts; and he extended the use of royal coinage throughout his realm. He also made peace with the kings of Aragon and England, who had long been at war with France. Louis is best remembered for leading two crusades (1248–54; 1270) to regain the Holy Land for the Christians, but he died of disease in Tunis. Louis was made a saint of the Roman Catholic Church in 1297.

Louis XI ruled during the early Renaissance period, when France regained strength in the aftermath of the Hundred Years' War.

Louis X (1289–1316) (r. 1314–16), great-grandson of Saint Louis, was known as Louis the Quarrelsome. He inherited the kingdom of Navarre from his mother in 1305 and the kingdom of France on his father's death in 1314. His brief reign is chiefly noted for the charters of liberties he granted to leagues of nobles in the provinces.

▶ THE VALOIS

Two French kings of the Valois family, a branch of the Capetian dynasty, were named Louis.

Louis XI (1423–83) (r. 1461–83), son of Charles VII, inherited a kingdom that was weakened by the waging of the Hundred Years' War (1337–1453) and the aftermath of the Black Death, which had killed approximately one-quarter of the population. Louis's achievements lay in his ability to win the loyalty of the great nobles of his kingdom, who had once attempted to overthrow him; to increase the territorial size of France, specifically by taking over the regions of Burgundy, Picardy, and Artois; and to forge a series of foreign alliances with other European states. His cunning skills at diplomacy and politics gained him the nickname the Spider King.

Louis XII (1462–1515) (r. 1498–1515), a cousin of his predecessor Charles VIII, is largely noted for a reign of peace and prosperity. He was the first French monarch to put his own likeness on silver coins of the realm. He had no male heir of his own, and at his death the crown passed to a distant cousin, who became Francis I.

▶ THE BOURBONS

The Bourbons, another branch of the Capetian dynasty, were the last royal family to rule France. Six of the Bourbon kings were named Louis.

Louis XIII (1601–43) (r. 1610–43), son of Henry IV and Marie de Médicis, inherited the French crown as a young boy upon his father's assassination. His early reign was dominated by his mother, but once Louis came of age, he quickly established his own authority. In 1624 he appointed Cardinal Richelieu to the royal council. Richelieu quickly put down the Huguenot (French Protestant) rebellions that broke out in the 1620's, ending with a siege at La Rochelle in 1628. In the 1630's, also at Richelieu's urging, Louis entered the Thirty Years' War against the Habsburg rulers of Spain and the Holy Roman Empire. Louis's victories over the

In the mid-1600's, Louis XIII fought the Thirty Years' War with Spain and the Holy Roman Empire, setting the stage for France's supremacy among European powers.

Habsburgs set the stage for France to replace Spain as Europe's most powerful state, which it did when the Thirty Years' War ended in 1648, five years after Louis's death. (For more information, see the article on Richelieu in Volume Q-R.)

Louis XIV (1638–1715) (r. 1643–1715), son of Louis XIII, was the longest-reigning monarch in European history. A separate article on Louis XIV follows this article.

Louis XV (1710–74) (r. 1715–74), great-grandson of Louis XIV, inherited a weakened throne at the age of 5. His kingdom, continuously drained by years of unsuccessful warfare—particularly the War of the Austrian Succession (1740–48) and the Seven Years' War (1756–63)—was nearing bankruptcy, making it necessary for the king to raise new taxes. These efforts resulted in mounting public opposition, especially in the law courts known as *parlements*.

Louis XVI was the last absolute monarch to rule France. He was put to death in 1793 during the French Revolution.

Many of the judges in these courts eventually denounced the king for overstepping his royal authority. In 1770, encouraged by his chancellor René Maupeou, Louis issued a number of edicts that took away many of the judges' privileges. When they rebelled, Maupeou replaced them with judges more willing to accept the absolute power of the king.

Although Louis's actions against the *parlements* were successful in the short term, they caused a lasting distrust of the monarchy that eventually led to the French Revolution. Louis was also faulted for the power he bestowed on his mistresses, notably the Marquise de Pompadour (1721–64) and Madame Du Barry (1746–93), who was later executed during the Revolution.

Louis XVI (1754–93) (r. 1774–92), grandson of Louis XV, dismissed the unpopular minister Maupeou and restored to the *parlement* the judges his grandfather had fired. But another military involvement, this time supporting the Americans in their war for independence from England, resulted in an-

other serious financial crisis in the 1780's. By 1786 the French kingdom was again close to bankruptcy, and all the royal efforts to raise additional revenues were once again being denounced by the *parlements*.

In order to pay his bills, Louis was forced to call an emergency meeting of the Estates-General, an advisory body, in May 1789. He found himself at the mercy of a large group of deputies who demanded a new constitution and an end to privilege. A republican spirit overtook the country, and the French Revolution began. In June 1791, Louis, his wife Marie Antoinette, and their children fled the court at Versailles and escaped to Varennes, where they were recognized and captured. A newly elected group of deputies ultimately voted to abolish the monarchy in September 1792. After a very heated trial, Louis XVI was found guilty of treason and sentenced to death on January 21, 1793. (For more information, see the article FRENCH REVOLUTION in Volume F.)

Louis XVII (1785–95), the young son of Louis XVI and Marie Antoinette, died in captivity during the French Revolution. He was never crowned and did not rule as king.

Louis XVIII (1755–1824) (r. 1814–15; 1815–24) was the younger brother of Louis XVI. In 1814, after the collapse of Napoleon I's empire, the Bourbon monarchy was restored to power, although Louis ruled only as a constitutional monarch, willing to compromise with the new republicans. However, the Chamber of Deputies, where elected officials gathered, proved to be a battleground between supporters of the Revolution and its royalist opponents. Louis sought to steer a middle path between these two groups, ultimately preserving the peace of the nation.

▶ **THE BOURBON-ORLÉANS**

Louis Philippe (1773–1850) (r. 1830–48), the last king of France, came to power after his cousin, King Charles X, was overthrown in the July Revolution of 1830. Known as the Citizen King, Louis Philippe reigned until 1848, when he himself was overthrown by another revolution.

Louis Philippe, duke of Orléans, was born on October 6, 1773. During the French Revolution (1789–99), his father, Philippe, supported the republicans and voted for the execution of his cousin, King Louis XVI. The young Louis Philippe renounced his royal titles and fought with the republican army. Nevertheless, the family was suspected of conspiring to restore the monarchy, and Louis Philippe was forced to flee the country after his father was executed in 1793.

In 1814, as the era of Napoleon I was coming to an end, the monarchy was restored in France, first under Louis XVIII and then under Charles X, both brothers of the executed Louis XVI. But in 1830 the conservative Charles X refused to accept the results of an election that favored the liberal party. When Charles attempted to censor the press, street riots erupted in Paris, and Charles was forced to abdicate (give up the throne). Without much support or enthusiasm, Louis Philippe was chosen to replace him. Some people thought that other royal family members had a greater claim to the throne. Many others did not want a king at all.

Government corruption, followed by an economic depression in 1846, weakened Louis Philippe's already fragile position. In 1848, after his government rejected a proposal to extend the vote to the poorer classes, Louis Philippe called in his troops to put down public demonstrations. But he had little support, even from his own military, and was forced to abdicate and take refuge in England, where he died two years later.

FRED A. CAZEL, JR.
The University of Connecticut
MACK P. HOLT
George Mason University
JEREMY BLACK
University of Exeter

See also FRANCE (History).

LOUIS XIV (1638–1715)

Louis XIV, known as the Sun King, ruled France for 72 years (1643–1715), the longest reign of any European monarch. Born on September 5, 1638, the son of Louis XIII and Anne of Austria, he was only 4 years old when he inherited his father's throne.

▶ THE REGENCY PERIOD (1643–52)

Louis's reign began with a regency government, required whenever a new king was still a minor. Until he came of age at the beginning of his 14th year, according to the unwritten French constitution, his kingdom would be ruled by his mother and her chief minister, Jules Mazarin (1602–61), a cardinal of the Roman Catholic Church.

In 1648 a brief period of political crisis and unrest broke out in France. The judges in the Parlement of Paris (the highest law court in

Louis XIV brought France to the height of its power. An absolute monarch, he once declared "*L'état c'est moi*" ("I am the state").

France) and several provincial *parlements* revolted against Mazarin and the regency government. The uprising, known as the *Fronde*, was joined by several powerful nobles at court. Anne, Mazarin, and young Louis were forced to flee for their safety.

These events made a big impression on the 10-year-old king. When he came of age in 1652, ending the regency period, Louis made every effort to restore the authority of the crown that had been undermined in his early years.

▶ ABSOLUTE POWER

When Cardinal Mazarin died in 1661, the 23-year-old Louis announced that he would govern the state by himself. He would still appoint ministers to his council to advise him, but decisions of politics, finance, peace, and war would be his alone. He also made it clear to the judges in the Parlement of Paris that he was the sole dispenser of justice in his realm. Louis was determined to rule without interference.

There were three components to Louis's success as an absolute monarch. First, because he needed a state bureaucracy that could carry out his will in the provinces, Louis hired hundreds of officials who were loyal to him. The most significant of these were the *intendants*, whose important duties included assessing and collecting taxes in the provinces. Second, he organized a standing army of 70,000 men—unequaled in Europe—to enforce his will. And third, Louis recognized the need to come to an agreement with the aristocracy in the provinces. The nobles had held power since the Middle Ages, and Louis realized he could never succeed without their support.

Louis XIV used his power to make France the greatest and most powerful state in Europe. At Versailles, just outside Paris, he constructed the largest and costliest royal palace in Europe to boast his grandeur. France also produced many great artists during Louis's reign, including the playwrights Jean Baptiste Molière and Jean Racine, the architect Louis Le Vau, and the artist Charles Le Brun, who not only decorated the palace at Versailles but influenced the entire Louis XIV period of art and design.

In 1660, Louis XIV married Marie-Thérèse (1638–83), the daughter of Philip IV of Spain. The marriage temporarily concluded a long period of warfare with Spain. But in 1668, Louis began a series of wars to further expand his territory. Thereafter, his great French army was fighting almost continuously against the kingdom of Spain, the Dutch Republic, and eventually England and many lesser states.

▶ LOUIS'S ADVISERS

In 1661, Louis appointed Jean Baptiste Colbert (1619–83) as his superintendent of finances. Colbert introduced a series of economic reforms to help pay for Louis's costly wars. Another gifted minister, François Michel Le Tellier, Marquis of Louvois

(1639?–91), organized and supervised the king's army. Louis also relied on the advice of his favorite mistress, the Marquise de Maintenon (1635–1719), whom he secretly married after the death of Marie-Thérèse.

▶ EUROPE UNITES AGAINST FRANCE

Louis's aggression led to a coalition against him of virtually every major state in Europe. He was particularly despised in Protestant kingdoms for revoking the Edict of Nantes in 1685, which since 1598 had guaranteed the Huguenots (French Protestants) the right to worship in France.

When Louis attempted to seize the Spanish throne during the War of the Spanish Succession (1701–14), his army suffered a humiliating defeat. Although Louis had succeeded in making France the most powerful single state in Europe, he could not defeat all the European powers when they united against him.

Death came to the Sun King in 1715. Louis, who outlived his son and grandson, left his crown to his great-grandson, the 5-year-old Louis XV.

MACK P. HOLT
George Mason University

LOUISIANA

In February 1682, the French explorer Robert Cavelier, Sieur de La Salle, canoed down the Mississippi River with a party of some fifty Frenchmen and Indians. When they reached the mouth of the Mississippi on the Gulf of Mexico on April 9, La Salle claimed the entire Mississippi Valley for France. He named the vast area Louisiana in honor of France's king, Louis XIV.

Louisiana's traditional nickname is the Pelican State. The eastern brown pelican is a native bird that nests in the salt marshes of the Gulf Coast and the Mississippi Delta. Recently, Louisiana has been called the Sportsman's Paradise, because it affords almost limitless outdoor activities year-round.

State flag

Louisiana, a southern state, is bordered on the north by Arkansas, on the east by Mississippi, and on the west by Texas. To the south lies the Gulf of Mexico. The state's location at the mouth of the Mississippi River has shaped its development in many ways. Louisiana is a land of bayous—the word "bayou" comes from an Indian word meaning "river" or "creek." Bountiful coastal marshes, teeming cypress swamps, expansive prairies, and rolling hill country also contribute to the state's geographical diversity. In addition to its scenic beauty, Louisiana enjoys an abundance of mineral wealth that has been important to its economic development.

Because Louisiana was originally founded as a colony of France, the French cultural heritage is visible everywhere. Louisiana's legal system, for example, is based partly on a system of laws created by French emperor Napoleon I. The celebration of Mardi Gras, which means "fat Tuesday" in French, is a custom brought to Louisiana from France in colonial times. But many other ethnic groups have added to Louisiana's diverse culture.

Louisiana's history is as rich as its cultural background. Its strategic location prompted European monarchs to contend for control of Louisiana until the United States purchased the Louisiana Territory from France in 1803. From this area came the state of Louisiana and all or the greater parts of twelve other states. Ever since, Louisiana has played an important role in American history, especially during the War of 1812 and the Civil War.

For most of its history, Louisiana was rural and agricultural. But during the 1900's it became industrialized and urbanized. These changes brought increased prosperity, but they also gave rise to problems—such as pollution and economic readjustment—that the state is trying to address.

Louisianans have traditionally been known as a fun-loving people, and *Laissez les bon temps rouler* ("Let the good times roll") is the unofficial state motto. Indeed, music and festivals are mainstays of Louisiana life. But Louisianans also consider themselves a hardworking and devout people.

▶ LAND

Louisiana is shaped like a short boot with the toe pointing east. It lies within a large natural region of the United States called the Coastal Plain.

Land Regions

Geographers divide the state into three major land regions—the East Gulf Coastal Plain, the Mississippi Alluvial Plain, and the West Gulf Coastal Plain. Each of these regions consists of upland areas and lowlands. Marshlands, which are part of the lowlands, extend the length of Louisiana's coastline.

The East Gulf Coastal Plain extends from the Mississippi River eastward to the Pearl River

Opposite page, clockwise from top left: Cypress trees draped with Spanish moss grow in one of Louisiana's many bayous. A costumed reveler celebrates Mardi Gras in New Orleans. Crawfish boiled with corn and potatoes is a staple of Louisiana's famous cuisine.

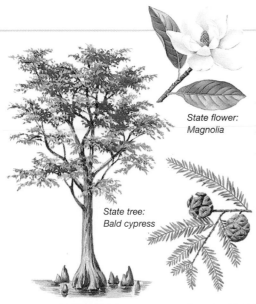

State flower: Magnolia

State tree: Bald cypress

FACTS AND FIGURES

Location: South central United States, bordered on the north by Arkansas, on the east by Mississippi, on the south by the Gulf of Mexico, and on the west by Texas.

Area: 49,651 sq mi (128,595 km²); rank, 31st.

Population: 4,468,976 (2000 census); rank, 22nd.

Elevation: *Highest*—Driskill Mountain, 535 ft (163 m); *lowest*—at New Orleans, 5 ft (1.5 m) below sea level.

Capital: Baton Rouge.

Statehood: April 30, 1812; 18th state.

State Motto: *Union, justice, confidence.*

State Song: "Give Me Louisiana."

Nicknames: Pelican State; Bayou State; Sugar State; Creole State; Sportsman's Paradise.

Abbreviations: LA; La.

State bird: Eastern brown pelican

and from Lake Pontchartrain north to the Mississippi border. The southern third of this area is marshy, but in the north there are areas of gently rolling hills covered with pine trees.

The Mississippi Alluvial Plain generally follows the course of the Mississippi River from the Arkansas border to the Mississippi Delta. The Mississippi and other rivers have deposited so much sand, silt, and other material that they now flow on land that is higher than the surrounding floodplains. The banks of the rivers make natural levees, or dikes. The higher lands sloping away from the rivers are known locally as frontlands. These lands are suitable for crops. The adjoining lands are known as backlands. The land in the delta, formed by silt over millions of years, is very fertile.

The West Gulf Coastal Plain lies to the west of the Mississippi Alluvial Plain. The northern part of the plain contains the largest hills in Louisiana, including Driskill Mountain, the state's highest point. South of this upland area are the coastal prairies, which slope gently south and merge with the coastal marshes.

Coastal Marshlands cover the southernmost parts of the three major land regions. These flat, swampy plains are covered with grass and rushes and dotted by hundreds of lagoons and shallow lakes. They are separated from the Gulf of Mexico by long, low ridges of sand and shells called barrier beaches. Throughout the marshes are ridges, called cheniers, that once were barrier beaches. Hills known as land islands, or salt domes, rise high above the surrounding marsh. They are the tops of huge domes of rock salt; some also contain sulfur and petroleum.

Rivers, Lakes, and Coastal Waters

Louisiana's most important river is the Mississippi. It zigzags through the state and forms part of its eastern boundary. Levees have been built along the river to keep it from overflowing. The Atchafalaya Basin Floodway and the Bonnet Carré Spillway also help to prevent flooding. The Red River, which drains the northern part of the state, is the Mississippi's major tributary in Louisiana. The Sabine River forms much of the Louisiana-Texas border, and the Pearl River in the southeast forms part of Louisiana's boundary with Mississippi.

Louisiana has three kinds of natural lakes—coastal, oxbow, and flood lakes. The largest coastal lakes are Pontchartrain, Maurepas, and Borgne. Oxbow lakes were created when the Mississippi River cut across its own huge bends, forming lakes in the shape of oxbows. An example of an oxbow lake is False River near Baton Rouge. Many of the lakes in northern and central Louisiana were caused by the flooding of the Red River.

Because Louisiana's coastline is very irregular and constantly changing, determining the exact coastline is difficult. The general coastline of the state is 397 miles (639 kilometers) long. Counting all the inlets, bays, and islands, the total shoreline measures 7,721 miles (12,423 kilometers).

Climate

Louisiana has a humid subtropical climate. Winters are mild and wet, and summers are long and hot. In the south, winters are slightly warmer than in the north, whereas summers are about the same or even cooler. Average January temperatures range from 48°F (9°C) in the north to 54°F (12°C) along the coast. The average July temperature is 82°F (28°C).

Louisiana is one of the wettest states. Annual precipitation averages about 58 inches (1,473 millimeters). Thunderstorms are frequent during the summer, and hurricanes and tornadoes are a constant threat. The growing season can range from 230 to 250 days in the north and from 270 to over 300 days in parts of the south.

Plant and Animal Life

Just over half of Louisiana's total land area is forested. Pine forests, hardwood forests, and cypress swamps can be found in different parts of the state. Louisiana is noted for its beautiful live oaks, which keep their leaves year-round and grow to a huge size. Trees are often draped with Spanish moss, which is not really a moss but a plant that belongs to the pineapple family. Shrubs and flowers, including honeysuckle, camellia, azalea, and jasmine, grow throughout the year. Lilies, irises, and other bulbed flowers are found in many varieties.

Louisiana has large numbers of muskrat, otter, and other fur-bearing animals, as well as many deer. It even has some black bears, timber wolves, and cougars. Many North American birds and waterfowl make their winter homes in the coastal areas. Native seabirds include the brown pelican, the laughing gull, and the royal tern.

The coastal waters, swamps, and many lakes and streams are filled with aquatic life.

A tanker makes its way along the Mississippi River, Louisiana's major avenue of commerce. Oceangoing vessels can travel as far north as Baton Rouge.

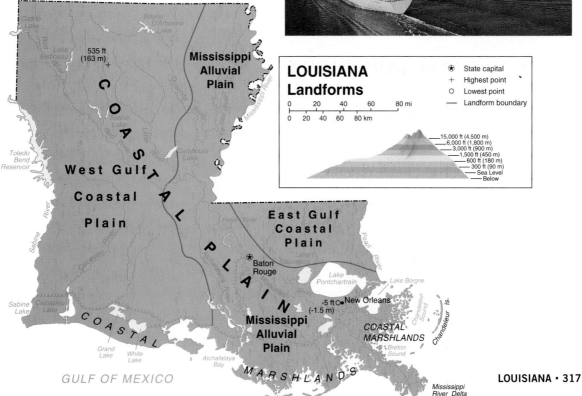

LOUISIANA
Landforms

✷	State capital
+	Highest point
O	Lowest point
—	Landform boundary

0   20   40   60   80 mi
0 20 40 60 80 km

15,000 ft (4,500 m)
6,000 ft (1,800 m)
3,000 ft (900 m)
1,500 ft (450 m)
600 ft (180 m)
300 ft (90 m)
Sea Level
Below

Caddo Lake
Bayou D'Arbonne Lake
Lake Bistineau
Red River
535 ft (163 m) +
Ouachita River
Mississippi River

Mississippi Alluvial Plain

C O A S T A L

Toledo Bend Reservoir

Little River
Catahoula Lake

West Gulf Coastal Plain

Sabine River

P L A I N

Calcasieu River

East Gulf Coastal Plain

Pearl River

✷ Baton Rouge

Lake Maurepas
Lake Pontchartrain
Lake Borgne

-5 ft O New Orleans
(-1.5 m)

Chandeleur Is.

Sabine Lake
Calcasieu Lake

C O A S T A L

Mississippi Alluvial Plain

COASTAL MARSHLANDS

Chandeleur Sound

Breton Sound

Grand Lake   White Lake

Atchafalaya Bay

M A R S H L A N D S

GULF OF MEXICO

Mississippi River Delta

The Preservation Hall Jazz Band performs in New Orleans. The city is world renowned as a center of jazz; many people believe it was the music's birthplace.

Dozens of varieties of saltwater fish and shellfish live in the offshore waters and in the bays and bayous, while freshwater fish are abundant throughout the state.

Natural Resources

Among Louisiana's most important natural resources are rich soils and large supplies of petroleum and natural gas.

The alluvial soils along the rivers are among the best in the United States. Many crops, including cotton and sugarcane, are produced in these fertile soils. The sandy soils of the uplands are good for vegetable and strawberry crops, and the hill soils support pine forests and peach orchards.

Louisiana's principal mineral resources are petroleum and natural gas. Most petroleum comes from the northwest and the Gulf Coast, but fields are scattered throughout the state. The greatest natural gas fields are in the northeast. Sulfur is found in the coastal regions, especially near the mouth of the Mississippi River. The state also has stores of salt, sand and gravel, clay, and stone.

State agencies monitor air and water pollution. Flood control, soil conservation, and forest and wildlife preservation have been accomplished through the efforts of governmental agencies and private business.

▶ PEOPLE

In the past, Louisiana was a rural state. Most of the people lived on farms or plantations. It is now considered an urban state, with more than two-thirds of the people living in the larger cities and towns.

Louisianans have a rich mix of customs, languages, and ancestries. Descendants of the original French and Spanish settlers live mainly in southern Louisiana and are called Creoles. Also in that area are the Cajuns, descendants of French Canadians from Acadia, or Nova Scotia.

The central and northern parts of the state were settled in the late 1700's and early 1800's by pioneers from nearby states, mostly of British ancestry. African Americans, the largest single ethnic group, make up almost 33 percent of the population. Louisiana is also home to people of German, Swiss, Irish, Italian, Hungarian, and Chinese descent. Since the 1980's, many Vietnamese immigrants have settled in Louisiana.

Education

The first schools in the Louisiana area were established in New Orleans during the 1720's by Catholic priests and nuns. Even after statehood in 1812, there was little

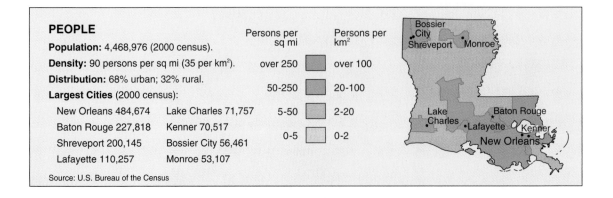

PEOPLE

Population: 4,468,976 (2000 census).

Density: 90 persons per sq mi (35 per km²).

Distribution: 68% urban; 32% rural.

Largest Cities (2000 census):

New Orleans 484,674	Lake Charles 71,757
Baton Rouge 227,818	Kenner 70,517
Shreveport 200,145	Bossier City 56,461
Lafayette 110,257	Monroe 53,107

Source: U.S. Bureau of the Census

Persons per sq mi		Persons per km²
over 250		over 100
50-250		20-100
5-50		2-20
0-5		0-2

progress in establishing public schools. The constitution of 1845 provided for a statewide educational system. Today each parish (unit of local government) in the state has a public school system.

Louisiana has more than twenty colleges and universities. The largest of them is the state-supported Louisiana State University, with campuses in Baton Rouge, Alexandria, Eunice, New Orleans, and Shreveport. The next largest state-supported school is the University of Southwestern Louisiana in Lafayette. Southern University is the nation's largest predominantly African American university. The main campus is in Baton Rouge, with branches in New Orleans and Shreveport. Other state-controlled colleges are in Grambling, Hammond, Lake Charles, Monroe, Natchitoches, Ruston, and Thibodaux.

The largest private institutions of higher education are Tulane University, Loyola University, and Xavier University of Louisiana. All are in New Orleans. Other private institutions include Louisiana College, in Pineville, and Centenary College, in Shreveport.

Libraries, Museums, and the Arts

The Louisiana State Library in Baton Rouge provides library services throughout the state. It also lends books and films from its large collections. Most of the parishes have their own libraries, as do some cities. The library at Louisiana State University in Baton Rouge has a notable collection of books and documents pertaining to the history of the state, as does the Louisiana State Archives, also in Baton Rouge. Other important histor-

Students chat on the main campus of Louisiana State University, in Baton Rouge. LSU is Louisiana's largest state-supported institute of higher education.

ical collections are maintained by the New Orleans Public Library and by the Howard-Tilton Memorial Library of Tulane University. Also at Tulane is the Latin American Library, which has many books on Mexico, Central America, and the West Indies.

The New Orleans Museum of Art includes a collection of Renaissance paintings and sculpture. It also exhibits paintings and sculpture by Louisiana artists. Louisiana State Exhibit Museum in Shreveport has displays of Louisiana's natural resources and their products. Louisiana State Museum in New Orleans consists of two historic buildings. The Cabildo, built in 1795, was once the headquarters of the Spanish governors. Among the displays in this building are Mardi Gras costumes and mementos of the pirate Jean Laffite. Another building, the Presbytère, dates from 1793 and houses natural history exhibits.

A gambling casino in Lake Charles. Legalized in 1991, gambling has brought much-needed employment and revenue to many Louisiana parishes.

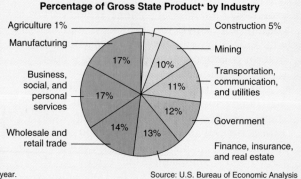
New Orleans is the birthplace of jazz. New Orleans-style jazz can be heard throughout the city, and the annual Jazz and Heritage Festival attracts performers and fans from around the world each spring. Cajun and zydeco music (blues-influenced Cajun music) is played at fairs, festivals, and celebrations throughout the year. New Orleans hosts a symphony orchestra and ballet, as well as operatic and theatrical productions. Symphony orchestras also perform in Baton Rouge, Shreveport, and Lake Charles.

▶ ECONOMY

A favorable climate and rich soils have long made Louisiana an important farming state. But industry, commerce, and services have also become important.

Services

Louisiana's service occupations employ about 80 percent of the state's workforce and produce more than 65 percent of the gross state product (GSP)—the total value of goods and services produced in a year.

Wholesale and retail trade together employ over 20 percent of the workforce. Wholesale trade includes the distribution of products entering the state through the deepwater ports at New Orleans, Baton Rouge, and Lake Charles. Retailers, including supermarket chains and the fast-food industry, rank among the state's largest nongovernmental employers. Shopping malls and other retail outlets have sprung up all over the state, providing thousands of jobs.

With some 350,000 employees, the state, local, and federal governments employ about 20 percent of the workforce. The tourist industry is also a major employer, and legalized gambling has brought much-needed employment and revenue to many parishes.

Other leading service industries include business, social, and personal services; trans-

Louisiana is a leading shrimp-catching state. *Left:* A shrimp boat fishes the waters of a bayou in the Mississippi delta. *Right:* Workers prepare the shrimp for market.

portation; communications; research; and public utilities. Health care is one of the fastest-growing industries in the state.

Manufacturing

Chemicals and petrochemicals—chemicals made from petroleum and natural gas—are Louisiana's most important manufactured products. They are used to make numerous other items, such as plastics, detergents, and fuels for rocket engines. Processing petroleum and coal products is another important industry, as is the production of ships, aircraft, and other transportation equipment. Paper products are made by pulp and paper mills located throughout the state.

The food processing industry is vital to Louisiana's economy. The leading processed foods are coffee, soft drinks, and sugar. Refineries in Louisiana produce much of the nation's sugar.

Agriculture and Fishing

Louisiana produces a wide variety of field crops, fruits, and vegetables. Soybeans are the leading field crop. Rice and cotton are important as well. Louisiana is also well known for sugarcane. Some corn is grown everywhere in the state except in the rice area. Louisiana ranks high among the nation's growers of sweet potatoes. Other important cash crops are strawberries and honey.

Livestock farming is also important. Cash receipts from beef cattle and calves are higher than receipts from any one of Louisiana's crops, except soybeans. Dairying also brings a large income, as does the raising of poultry.

Louisiana's most valuable fishing grounds are in the Gulf of Mexico. Shrimp and oysters are sold throughout the United States. Among the commercial fish from the Gulf are speckled trout, redfish, red snapper, flounder, Spanish mackerel, menhaden, and tuna. Freshwater fisheries have large catches of spoonbill catfish and gaspergou (a local name for freshwater drumfish).

An oil rig lies in the marshlands of southern Louisiana. With both offshore and onshore oil fields, the state is an important producer of petroleum and petroleum products, including petrochemicals.

Mining and Construction

Louisiana's chief minerals are petroleum and natural gas. Other important minerals include salt, sand, and gravel. Sulfur is mined by the Frasch process, which was developed in Louisiana. Very hot water is used to melt the underground sulfur deposits. Then the liquid sulfur is forced to the surface.

The 1960's and 1970's witnessed a boom in the state's construction industry. New homes and housing subdivisions sprang up, while suburban shopping malls serviced the needs of these new communities and created a demand for construction workers. In New Orleans, the construction of office buildings, hotels, and the Louisiana Superdome, completed in 1974, provided thousands of jobs. Construction declined in the mid-1980's, but there has been a modest recovery since.

Transportation

The first roads in Louisiana were its rivers and bayous, and water transportation remains important. Barge lines operate on the Intracoastal Waterway and the Mississippi, Ouachita, and other rivers. The largest ports in the state are New Orleans, Baton Rouge, and Lake Charles. Oceangoing vessels dock at these ports daily. A direct route between New Orleans and the Gulf of Mexico is provided by the Mississippi River–Gulf Outlet, a 76-mile (122-kilometer) canal opened in 1963.

Places of Interest

Oak Alley Plantation, on the River Road near Vacherie

Café in New Orleans' French Quarter

Acadiana, encompassing the parishes of south central and southwestern Louisiana, has been home to Louisiana's Cajuns since the 1760's. It is known for its teeming swamps, open prairies, and picturesque villages and towns, including New Iberia and St. Martinville, on Bayou Teche, and Lafayette, Opelousas, and Lake Charles. Charming churches, courthouses, and other buildings, some dating from the 1700's, are characteristic of the region.

Aquarium of the Americas, on the banks of the Mississippi River in New Orleans, features aquatic life from the Amazon rain forest and the Caribbean, as well as from the Gulf of Mexico and the Mississippi River. Over 4,000 specimens, including a rare white alligator, are housed in more than a million gallons of water.

Avery Island, near New Iberia, is one of the state's major land islands, or salt domes. In the area are the Jungle Gardens, a large salt mine, and a small factory that makes a famous pepper sauce—Tabasco sauce. The Jungle Gardens consist of more than 200 acres (80 hectares) of wooded areas, tropical gardens, and a special sanctuary for egrets.

French Quarter, a historic section of New Orleans and the oldest part of the city, is also known as the Vieux Carré (Old Square). Laid out in a grid pattern in 1721, the quarter is home to one of the nation's great clusters of colonial and antebellum architecture. It is known for its antique shops, art galleries, restaurants, jazz clubs, and nightclubs. Important sites within the French Quarter include Jackson Square, St. Louis Cathedral, the Cabildo, the Presbytère, and the French Market.

Jungle Gardens, Avery Island

Grand Isle, located on the Gulf Coast just west of Barataria Bay, is a favorite summer resort. A popular spot for fishing, camping, and other outdoor activities, it offers large beaches, pleasant lodgings, and fine seafood restaurants.

Hodges Gardens, situated in forestlands south of Many, has nearly 5,000 acres (2,000 hectares) of beautiful gardens, an arboretum, and a refuge for deer, elk, and other animals. The site also contains a lake that shelters migratory waterfowl.

Jean Lafitte National Historical Park and Preserve, near New Orleans, preserves natural and historical resources of the Mississippi Delta. The Chalmette Unit, formerly Chalmette National Historical Park, was the site of the Battle of New Orleans, the last major battle of the War of 1812.

Kisatchie National Forest is Louisiana's only national forest. It is spread out over central and northern Louisiana in six divisions.

The River Road, actually two roads—one on each side of the Mississippi River between Baton Rouge and New Orleans—hosts some of the finest surviving antebellum mansions anywhere in the South. One of these, Oak Alley Plantation, near Vacherie, was built in the 1830's and is a good example of Greek Revival architecture. An avenue bordered by 300-year-old live oaks extends from the mansion all the way to the river.

The Shadows, on the banks of the Bayou Teche in New Iberia, is a Greek Revival–style mansion built about 1830. Carefully restored, it is considered one of the best examples of plantation-house architecture in the United States.

State Recreation Areas. Louisiana maintains numerous state parks, state preservation areas, and state commemorative areas (including museums). For more information, write to the Office of State Parks, P.O. Box 94291, Baton Rouge, Louisiana 70804.

Railroad operations began in 1831. At present there is a well-developed system of railroads. New Orleans, Alexandria, and Shreveport are the major rail centers. Each major urban area has a good airways network, served by a well-planned airport.

A network of local, state, and national highways connects all sections of the state. Interstate highways speed traffic through or around the densely settled areas.

Communication

Most of the early newspapers were French. The first was *Le Moniteur de la Louisiane* ("The Louisiana Monitor"), begun in New Orleans in 1794. The oldest and largest of present-day newspapers is the New Orleans *Times-Picayune*, founded in 1837. Each parish has at least one weekly paper. The total number of dailies is about 25.

All cities and many smaller towns have at least one radio station each. There are about 30 television stations in the state.

▶ CITIES

All sections of Louisiana have large cities. These include New Orleans and Lake Charles in the south, Shreveport and Monroe in the north, and Alexandria in the center of the state.

Baton Rouge, the state's capital and second largest city, was established about 1720. Since that time, many flags have flown over the city, including those of France, Spain, Great Britain, and the United States. The name "Baton Rouge" is the French form of an Indian term meaning "red post." It is said that Native Americans had placed a reddened post at the site to mark the dividing line between two of their nations.

Baton Rouge is a deepwater port and a busy industrial city. One of the largest oil refineries in the world is located there. Baton Rouge is also the home of Louisiana State University. Points of special interest include the Old State Capitol, which resembles a medieval castle, and the present capitol.

New Orleans, the largest city in Louisiana, is an important seaport on the Gulf of Mexico. An article on New Orleans is included in Volume N.

Shreveport, the third largest city, is situated on the banks of the Red River in the northwestern part of the state. It was named for Henry Miller Shreve, a steamboat captain and builder of steamboats. Shreve designed the first snag boats. These boats were used to remove snags—sunken trees, stumps, and logs—from riverbeds. In the 1830's, Shreve directed a project to clear the Great Raft—a huge mass of snags—from the Red River. The opening of the river was a major factor in the development of Shreveport and northern Louisiana.

Today Shreveport is a leading cotton market and the center of one of the most important oil and gas areas in the United States. Bossier City, twin city to Shreveport, has grown rapidly in recent years.

Lafayette is the largest city in Acadiana and one of the fastest-growing cities in the state. The seat of Lafayette Parish, Lafayette was first known as Vermilionville when the city was founded in 1824, but the name was later changed. Lafayette is located in a highly productive agricultural area, but in recent years it has also become an important center for the petrochemical industry.

Lake Charles is located on a wide part of the Calcasieu River not far from the Texas border. It has been called a Louisiana town with

A paddleboat churns along the Red River at Shreveport, Louisiana's third largest city and a center of oil and natural gas production.

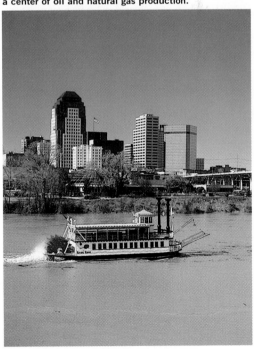

a Texas flair. Early settlers had a more informal name for the town—Charlie's Lake. It is one of Louisiana's three deepwater ports. Oil refining is a major industry.

▶ **GOVERNMENT**

Since statehood in 1812, Louisiana has had eleven state constitutions. The present constitution was adopted in 1974.

The state capitol building in Baton Rouge. The city has been the state capital since 1882; prior to that it was the capital from 1849 to 1862.

GOVERNMENT

State Government
Governor: 4-year term
State senators: 39;
  4-year terms
State representatives: 105;
  4-year terms
Number of parishes: 64

Federal Government
U.S. senators: 2
U.S. representatives: 7
Number of electoral votes: 9

For the name of the current governor, see STATE GOVERNMENTS in Volume S. For the names of current U.S. senators and representatives, see UNITED STATES, CONGRESS OF THE in Volume U-V.

INDEX TO LOUISIANA MAP

Place	County	Grid
Abbeville ●	(Vermilion)	C4
Alexandria ●	(Rapides)	C2
Amite ●	(Tangipahoa)	E3
Arabi ●	(St. Bernard)	G1
Arcadia ●	(Bienville)	C1
Atchafalaya National Wildlife Refuge		D3
Avondale ●	(Jefferson)	F1
Baker ●	(E. Baton Rouge)	D3
Bastrop ●	(Morehouse)	D1
Baton Rouge ★	(E. Baton Rouge)	D3
Bayou Cane ●	(Terrebonne)	E4
Bayou Sauvage National Wildlife Refuge		F3
Belle Chasse ●	(Plaquemines)	G2
Benton ●	(Bossier)	B1
Bogalusa ●	(Washington)	F3
Bossier City ●	(Bossier)	B1
Breaux Bridge ●	(St. Martin)	D3
Breton National Wildlife Refuge		F4,G4
Bridge City ●	(Jefferson)	F1
Bunkie ●	(Avoyelles)	C3
Cameron ●	(Cameron)	B4
Carencro ●	(Lafayette)	C3
Catahoula National Wildlife Refuge		D2
Chalmette ●	(St. Bernard)	F4
Chitimacha Indian Reservation		D4
Clinton ●	(East Feliciana)	D3
Colfax ●	(Grant)	C2
Columbia ●	(Caldwell)	C1
Convent ●	(St. James)	E3
Coushatta ●	(Red River)	B1
Coushatta Indian Reservation		C3
Covington ●	(St. Tammany)	E3
Crowley ●	(Acadia)	C3
Delta National Wildlife Refuge		F4
Denham Springs ●	(Livingston)	E3
De Ridder ●	(Beauregard)	B3
Des Allemands ●	(St. Charles)	E2
Destrehan ●	(St. Charles)	F1
Donaldsonville ●	(Ascension)	E3
Edgard ●	(St. John the Baptist)	E3
Estelle ●	(Jefferson)	G2
Eunice ●	(St. Landry)	C3
Farmerville ●	(Union)	C1
Franklin ●	(St. Mary)	D4
Franklinton ●	(Washington)	E3
Grambling ●	(Lincoln)	C1
Greensburg ●	(St. Helena)	E3
Gretna ●	(Jefferson)	E4
Hahnville ●	(St. Charles)	E1
Hammond ●	(Tangipahoa)	E3
Harahan ●	(Jefferson)	F1
Harrisonburg ●	(Catahoula)	D2
Harvey ●	(Jefferson)	G2
Homer ●	(Claiborne)	B1
Houma ●	(Terrebonne)	E4
Jena ●	(La Salle)	C2
Jeanerette ●	(Iberia)	D4
Jean Lafitte National Historic Park and Preservation (Barataria Unit)		G2
Jefferson	(Jefferson)	F1
Jennings ●	(Jefferson Davis)	C3
Jonesboro ●	(Jackson)	C1
Kenner	(Jefferson)	E4
Kisatchie National Forest		B1,B2,B3,C1,C2
Lacassine National Wildlife Refuge		C4
Lafayette ●	(Lafayette)	C3
Lake Charles ●	(Calcasieu)	B3
Lake Ophelia Nat'l. Wildlife Refuge		D2
Lake Providence ●	(East Carroll)	D1
Laplace ●	(St. John the Baptist)	E1
Leesville ●	(Vernon)	B2
Livingston ●	(Livingston)	E3
Luling ●	(St. Charles)	F1
Mansfield ●	(De Soto)	B1
Many ●	(Sabine)	B2
Marksville ●	(Avoyelles)	C2
Marrero ●	(Jefferson)	E4
Meraux ●	(St. Bernard)	G1
Metairie ●	(Jefferson)	E4
Mimosa Park ●	(St. Charles)	F1
Minden ●	(Webster)	B1
Monroe ●	(Ouachita)	C1
Morgan City ●	(St. Mary)	D4
Moss Bluff ●	(Calcasieu)	B3
Napoleonville ●	(Assumption)	D4
Natchitoches ●	(Natchitoches)	B2
New Iberia ●	(Iberia)	D3
New Orleans ●	(Orleans)	E4
New Roads ●	(Pointe Coupee)	D3
New Sarpy ●	(St. Charles)	F1
Norco ●	(St. Charles)	E1
Oakdale ●	(Allen)	C3
Oak Grove ●	(West Carroll)	D1
Oberlin ●	(Allen)	C3
Opelousas ●	(St. Landry)	C3
Pineville ●	(Rapides)	C2
Plaquemine ●	(Iberville)	D3
Pointe a la Hache ●	(Plaquemines)	F4
Ponchatoula ●	(Tangipahoa)	E3
Port Allen ●	(W. Baton Rouge)	D3
Poydras ●	(St. Bernard)	H2
Rayville ●	(Richland)	D1
River Ridge ●	(Jefferson)	F1
Ruston ●	(Lincoln)	C1
Sabine National Wildlife Refuge		B4
St. Francisville ●	(West Feliciana)	D3
St. Joseph ●	(Tensas)	D2
St. Martinville ●	(St. Martin)	D3
St. Rose ●	(St. Charles)	F1
Salvador Wildlife Management Area		F2
Shreveport ●	(Caddo)	B1
Springhill ●	(Webster)	B1
Sulphur ●	(Calcasieu)	B3
Tallulah ●	(Madison)	D1
Tensas River Nat'l. Wildlife Refuge		D1
Terrytown ●	(Jefferson)	G2
Thibodaux ●	(Lafourche)	E4
Tunica-Biloxi Indian Reservation		C2
Upper Ouachita National Wildlife Refuge		C1
Vidalia ●	(Concordia)	D2
Ville Platte ●	(Evangeline)	C3
Violet ●	(St. Bernard)	H2
Waggaman ●	(Jefferson)	F1
Westlake ●	(Calcasieu)	B3
West Monroe ●	(Ouachita)	C1
Westwego ●	(Jefferson)	G2
Winnfield ●	(Winn)	C2
Winnsboro ●	(Franklin)	D1
Zachary ●	(E. Baton Rouge)	D3

● County Seat   Counties in parentheses   ★ State Capital

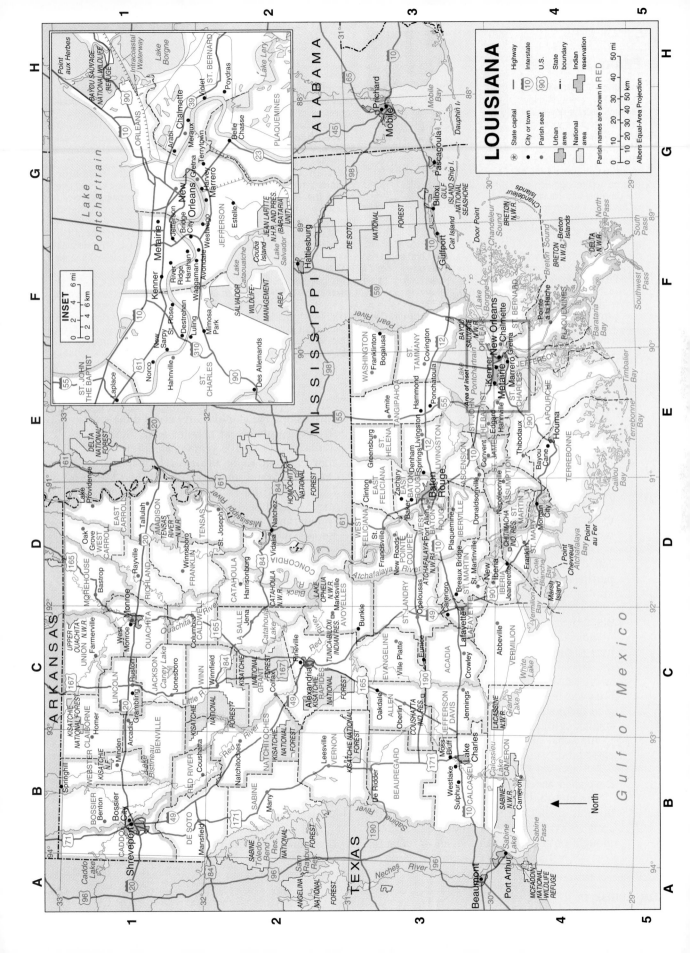

Famous People

Louis Armstrong (1900–71), born in New Orleans, was a legendary jazz musician and singer and popular entertainer. After playing the cornet in his teens, he switched to the trumpet in the 1920's and gained recognition as the greatest jazz musician of his day. Known for his distinctive gravelly voice, he invented scat singing, in which nonsense syllables are substituted for words. By the 1950's, Armstrong was one of the world's best-known entertainers.

Judah Philip Benjamin

Judah Philip Benjamin (1811–84), lawyer and Confederate political leader, was born on the Caribbean island of St. Thomas. He came to Louisiana as a young man. From 1853 to 1861, he was a U.S. senator. During the Civil War, he was attorney general, secretary of war, and secretary of state of the Confederacy.

Jean-Baptiste Le Moyne, Sieur de Bienville (1680–1768), a French Canadian explorer, has been called the Father of Louisiana. With his brother Pierre Le Moyne, Sieur d'Iberville, he helped establish the first settlements in the Louisiana area. Bienville founded New Orleans in 1718 and served four times as the governor of the French colony of Louisiana, the last from 1733 to 1743.

Truman Capote (1924–84), a writer born in New Orleans, achieved fame for his first novel, *Other Voices, Other Rooms* (1948). His best-known book was *In Cold Blood* (1965), a carefully researched account of an actual murder case, which he called a nonfiction novel. Capote's other works include the novella *Breakfast at Tiffany's* (1958) and a short story collection, *Music for Chameleons* (1980).

William Charles Coles Claiborne (1775–1817), a native of Virginia, was one of the two commissioners who received possession of Louisiana for the United States after the Louisiana Purchase. In 1804 he was appointed governor of the Territory of Orleans, and in 1812 he was elected the first governor of the new state of Louisiana.

Lillian Hellman (1905–84), born in New Orleans, was a noted playwright and screenwriter. The American South figured prominently in her work. She first gained fame with her Broadway plays *The Children's Hour* (1934), *The Little Foxes* (1939), and *Watch on the Rhine* (1941).

The chief executive officer is the governor, who serves a 4-year term and is limited to two consecutive terms. The legislative branch has two houses, a senate and a house of representatives. In both houses, members are elected for 4-year terms. The judicial branch is headed by a supreme court. Lower courts include courts of appeal, district courts, municipal courts, and family courts.

Units of local government in Louisiana are called parishes instead of counties. Most parishes are governed by elected bodies known as police juries.

▶ HISTORY

Indian cultures had been thriving in what is now Louisiana for about 10,000 years before the arrival of the first Europeans. One of the strongest and most important groups in the area was the Caddo confederacy, which occupied the northwestern part of the state. Other smaller groups, such as the Natchez, the Chitimacha, and the Choctaw, lived in the east and the south.

Exploration and Settlement

The mouth of the Mississippi River probably was sighted by Spanish explorers in the early 1500's. But Hernando de Soto is thought of as the first European to reach the Mississippi. He and his party crossed the river in 1541, probably at a point near Memphis, Tennessee. Over 100 years passed before further exploration of the river took place. In April 1682, the French explorer Robert Cavelier, Sieur de La Salle, reached the mouth of the Mississippi. He claimed the Mississippi Valley and named the area Louisiana in honor of King Louis XIV of France. Two years later, La Salle made an unsuccessful attempt to establish a colony on the delta.

The next attempt at settlement in the Louisiana area was made by two French Canadians—Pierre Le Moyne, Sieur d'Iberville, and his younger brother, Jean-Baptiste Le Moyne, Sieur de Bienville. In early 1699, they sailed up the Mississippi River, probably as far as the Red River. They chose a place near present-day Biloxi, Mississippi, for the first settlement. Early in 1702 the colonists were moved to a better location—a site near present-day Mobile, Alabama, which was named Fort Louis de la Mobile. Bienville was named governor of Louisiana, and Fort Louis became the headquarters for the colony.

Colonial Period

In 1712, King Louis XIV gave control of Louisiana to Antoine Crozat, a merchant.

Her memoirs—*An Unfinished Woman* (1969), *Pentimento: A Book of Portraits* (1974), and *Scoundrel Time* (1976)—were also immensely popular works.

Jean Laffite, or **Lafitte** (1780?–1826?), born in Bayonne, France, became famous as the Pirate of the Gulf and as a hero of the War of 1812. A biography of Laffite appears in this volume.

Mary Landrieu (1955–   ), a U.S. senator, was born in New Orleans. The daughter of former New Orleans mayor Maurice "Moon" Landrieu, she served as a state legislator and state treasurer before making an unsuccessful bid for governor in 1995. The following year, she was elected the first female U.S. senator in Louisiana's history.

Louis Armstrong

Mary Landrieu

Huey Pierce Long (1893–1935) born near Winnfield, was governor of Louisiana (1928–31) and U.S. senator (1932–35). A biography of Long appears in this volume.

Henry Hobson Richardson (1838–86), born in St. James Parish, was a renowned architect whose "Richardsonian architecture" influenced a generation of younger architects. His first major work was Trinity Church in Boston.

Alexander Pierre Tureaud (1899–1972), born in New Orleans, was an attorney and civil rights leader. He was the only practicing African American attorney in Louisiana between 1937 and 1947 and the lawyer of record in virtually every civil rights and desegregation case in the state.

Edward Douglass White (1845–1921) born in Lafourche Parish, was a justice of the U.S. Supreme Court from 1894 to 1921. After serving as an associate justice, he was appointed chief justice in 1910. Earlier he had been a U.S. senator (1891–94). His father, also named Edward Douglass White (1795–1847), was a governor of Louisiana (1835–39).

About two years later, Fort St. Jean Baptiste was established at present-day Natchitoches. This was the first permanent settlement in the area now known as Louisiana. But Crozat failed to develop the colony. In 1717 it was turned over to another businessman, John Law.

Many settlers came to Louisiana, attracted by stories of quick riches. Most of the French settlers were not interested in farming. To encourage agriculture, leaders of the colony brought slaves from the West Indies and Africa to work in the fields. They also brought farmers from Germany, Switzerland, and other European countries. Many Germans settled along the Mississippi above New Orleans, which became the new capital in 1722. But the colony did not develop, and it was returned to the French king in 1732.

By the Treaty of Fontainebleau in 1762, France ceded Louisiana west of the Mississippi River and New Orleans to Spain. Louisiana east of the river was ceded to Britain. The French were glad to get rid of Louisiana, because it had been a heavy drain on the French treasury. But in 1768 the French people of New Orleans rebelled against the Spanish governor and declared their allegiance to France. Spanish authority was restored in 1769.

Between 1764 and 1790, more than 4,000 Acadians settled in Louisiana. The Acadians were French Canadians whose ancestors had settled in Acadia, or Nova Scotia, Canada, in the early 1600's. They were expelled from Nova Scotia, beginning in 1755, for refusing to adopt British customs and obey British laws. The Acadians settled mainly in the Bayou Teche country, west of New Orleans. They eventually became known as Cajuns.

During the Revolutionary War, Louisiana aided the American colonies, and after the war, American settlers thronged to the upper Mississippi Valley. The Mississippi River became their main artery of commerce, with New Orleans as the most important seaport.

To solve shipping problems, the United States wanted to buy the Isle of Orleans—an area including New Orleans and the mouth of the Mississippi. But Louisiana was now back in French hands, Spain having returned it in 1800. In early 1803, President Thomas Jefferson sent his special agent, James Monroe, to Paris with instructions to pay not more than $10 million for the Isle of Orleans. Monroe found that Napoleon I, ruler of France, was willing to sell the entire Louisiana area, some 800,000 square miles (2 million square kilometers). The United States purchased Louisiana for about $15 million.

The Battle of New Orleans was the final encounter between the Americans and British in the War of 1812. It was actually fought two weeks after the war ended.

Territorial Period and Statehood

In 1804, the part of the Louisiana Purchase south of 33 degrees latitude—the present state of Louisiana—was organized as the Territory of Orleans. In 1811, Congress authorized the territory's residents to draw up a constitution. On April 30, 1812, Louisiana was admitted to the Union as the 18th state.

Almost immediately after becoming a state, Louisiana got involved in the War of 1812. In 1815, General Andrew Jackson defeated the British in the Battle of New Orleans. After the war, Louisiana grew rapidly. Cotton and sugar plantations thrived. Railroads were built, and steamboats came to the Mississippi. By 1840, New Orleans was second only to New York City as a port.

Civil War and Reconstruction

From 1861 to 1865, Louisiana was involved in the Civil War. It withdrew from the Union in January 1861 and joined the Confederacy. In 1862, Admiral David G. Farragut captured New Orleans and Baton Rouge for the federal government. During the rest of the war, these cities and other areas were administered by a federal governor. The Confederate state capital was moved to Opelousas and then to Shreveport.

The period after the Civil War, known as Reconstruction, was one of the most controversial periods in Louisiana's history. African Americans gained political rights, but there was much violence. Reconstruction ended in 1877 after federal troops were withdrawn from the state. Economic recovery after the war was slow.

Modern Times

About 1900, Louisiana began large-scale production of petroleum, natural gas, sulfur, and other minerals. The traditional crops—cotton, sugarcane, and rice—continued to be important. But many farmers turned unproductive land into pasture for beef cattle. Dairying, poultry raising, and truck farming added to the variety of agriculture.

Still, by the early 1900's Louisiana continued to lag behind the country in many areas of life. Then in 1928, Huey Long was elected governor. Long promised to provide paved roads, build new schools and hospitals, and provide free textbooks to school children. He was later elected a U.S. senator but continued to run Louisiana.

Under Long, Louisiana made great progress. But he also ruled Louisiana like a dictator, and many people began to oppose him. He was assassinated in 1935. After Long's death, his supporters continued his public works and social welfare programs. Earl Long, Huey's younger brother, became leader of the "Longites" and served three separate terms as governor from the 1930's to the 1950's. (See LONG FAMILY in this volume.)

After World War II ended in 1945, industry expanded greatly. The petrochemical industry experienced tremendous growth, and thousands of people, attracted by jobs and good wages, moved to the state. But the collapse of the oil industry in the mid-1980's brought economic hardship. Gambling was legalized in 1991 to help replace lost revenue. Meanwhile, increased urbanization brought more crime, pollution, and traffic congestion to Louisiana. The issue of race relations remained a major concern.

Hurricane Katrina

Louisiana made important gains in attracting industry and jobs to the state. But on August 29, 2005, catastrophe struck when Hurricane Katrina hit the Gulf Coast and Mississippi Delta. Hundreds of thousands of people were evacuated from the region, and nearly 1,000 Louisianans were killed. New Orleans, the city most vulnerable to flooding, was devastated and left completely uninhabitable. For more information, see the article NEW ORLEANS in Volume N.

JOHN C. RODRIGUE
Louisiana State University

LOUISIANA PURCHASE

The Louisiana Purchase was one of the largest land purchases in history. In 1803, the United States bought from France a vast area of some 828,000 square miles (2,144,520 square kilometers), a territory covering the central third of what are today the "Lower 48" states. The area stretched from the Mississippi River in the east to the Rocky Mountains in the west and from the Gulf of Mexico in the south to the Canadian border in the north. Before territorial boundary adjustments were made, the territory included all or parts of what became 15 states. These are (with the dates of their admission to the Union): Louisiana (1812), Missouri (1821), Arkansas (1836), Texas (1845), Iowa (1846), Minnesota (1858), Kansas (1861), Nebraska (1867), Colorado (1876), North Dakota (1889), South Dakota (1889), Montana (1889), Wyoming (1890), Oklahoma (1907), and New Mexico (1912).

▶ **BACKGROUND**

In the 1500's, this vast region was explored by the Spanish conquistadores Francisco Vásquez de Coronado (1510?–54) and Hernando de Soto (1500?–42). In 1682 a Frenchman, Robert Cavelier, Sieur de La Salle (1643–87), named it Louisiana in honor of his king, Louis XIV. Early in the 1700's the French founded settlements along the Mississippi River. The most important one, New Orleans, was founded in 1718 on the east bank of the river, 90 miles (145 kilometers) from its mouth.

At the end of the French and Indian War (1754–63) in North America, France lost its lands east of the Mississippi to Great Britain. In a separate treaty, France gave up Louisiana—New Orleans and the French lands west of the Mississippi—to Spain.

In the late 1700's, Napoleon Bonaparte (1769–1821) became the first emperor of France. One of his many ambitions was to build a colonial empire in North America. In

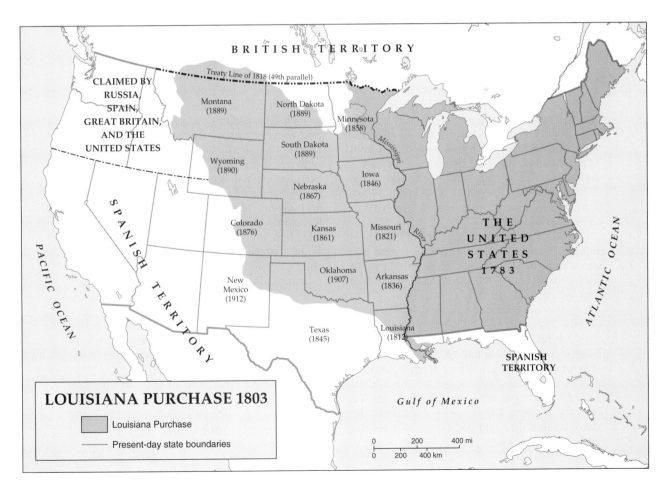

1800, Napoleon persuaded the Spanish to sign the secret Treaty of San Ildefonso and transfer Louisiana back to France.

CRISIS OVER LOUISIANA

When President Thomas Jefferson (1743–1826) learned of the secret agreement, he was very worried. He did not welcome the idea of gaining as a neighbor in the west a strong France in place of a weak Spain. Jefferson was also afraid that when the French controlled New Orleans they would close the Mississippi River to American trade. This happened sooner than he expected.

On October 15, 1802, the king of Spain finally gave the order transferring Louisiana to France. But the Spanish governor in New Orleans did not know of this order. The following day he suddenly withdrew the **right of deposit**, the right that allowed American shippers to leave their goods at New Orleans while awaiting transfer onto oceangoing vessels. Seeing their means of making a living threatened, western fur trappers and traders demanded that the United States seize Louisiana by force. As it turned out, this was not necessary.

Jefferson ordered Robert R. Livingston (1746–1813), the American minister to France, to explore the possibility of purchasing New Orleans and West Florida. Jefferson used psychology to force Napoleon's hand. He permitted certain letters to fall into the hands of French agents that hinted at a joint U.S.-British attack on Louisiana. One of the letters to Livingston said, "The day that France takes possession of New Orleans …we must marry ourselves to the British fleet and nation."

In March 1803, James Monroe (1758–1831) left for Paris as a special envoy. Congress had given him the power to offer Napoleon up to $10 million for New Orleans and a tract of land on the Gulf of Mexico.

By the time Monroe arrived in Paris on April 12, Napoleon had already decided to give up his plans for a New World empire. Napoleon needed money to finance a war he was planning against Great Britain, and he feared that once that war began, the United States would take advantage of the situation and try to seize Louisiana. Furthermore, he doubted that he could defend both Louisiana and Haiti, France's most valuable sugar colony, which was at that time undergoing a violent slave rebellion. Thus, Napoleon decided to sell Louisiana rather than fight for it.

THE SALE AND TRANSFER

Livingston and Monroe were startled at being offered so much more than they had hoped to buy. And because Napoleon was in a hurry to finish the business, they finalized the deal without referring the matter back to President Jefferson.

A treaty dated April 30, 1803, and signed May 2 sold Louisiana to the United States for about 80 million francs, or $15 million. Of this amount, $11.25 million was for the territory itself. The rest covered debts owed by France and Spain to American citizens, mostly for property damages, which the United States agreed to pay.

At first Jefferson did not know exactly how to take the surprising news. The Constitution said nothing about acquiring foreign territory. But popular enthusiasm for the purchase swept his doubts aside. The treaty was ratified by the Senate in October. On December 20 a colorful ceremony was held at New Orleans. French, Spanish, and American onlookers watched as the French flag came down and the Stars and Stripes fluttered to the top of the flagpole. The following year, Louisiana was divided into the Territory of Orleans (which later became the state of Louisiana) and the District of Louisiana (later divided among 14 states).

In time, disputes arose because the U.S. boundaries had not been exactly defined in the purchase treaty. In 1818 the United States and Great Britain established the United States' northern boundary at the 49th parallel. Then in 1819, Spain gave Florida to the United States to settle $5 million worth of claims against Spain by U.S. citizens. With the Louisiana Purchase, the United States took a giant step in expanding its national territory "from sea to shining sea."

Reviewed by CARL J. RICHARD
Author, *The Louisiana Purchase*

See also TERRITORIAL EXPANSION OF THE UNITED STATES.

LOUIS NAPOLEON. See NAPOLEON III.

LOUIS PHILIPPE. See LOUIS (The Bourbon-Orléans).

LOUISVILLE. See KENTUCKY (Cities).

L'OUVERTURE, TOUSSAINT. See TOUSSAINT L'OUVERTURE.

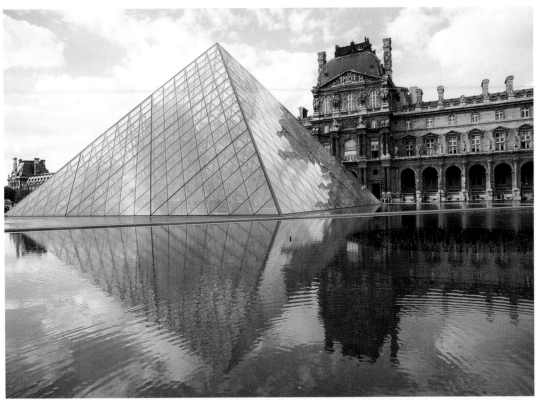

The Louvre, once a royal residence, is now the national art museum of France. Visitors enter the museum through a glass pyramid designed by modern U.S. architect I. M. Pei.

LOUVRE

The Louvre is the national art museum of France. Its buildings form a vast rectangular complex on the right bank of the Seine River in Paris. Once a residence of the kings of France, today the Louvre houses one of the world's greatest collections of art.

▶COLLECTIONS

The famous collections of the Louvre grew from the works of art bought by the kings of France. Ruler after ruler added more treasures. Occasionally a king sold something to pay for the expenses of war, but most of the original works remain. The royal collections have been enlarged by gifts and purchases.

Each year more than 3 million visitors come to see the great works of art gathered in the Louvre. The museum's extensive collections are divided among seven departments: Oriental antiquities, Egyptian antiquities, Greek and Roman antiquities, sculpture, paintings, drawings, and decorative objects.

The collections of antiquities (art of ancient times) are outstanding. The Egyptian section was founded in 1825 by Jean François Champollion, who was the first person to decipher (decode) ancient Egyptian hieroglyphics (picture-writing). One of the Near Eastern works is a carving inscribed with the code of Hammurabi, the oldest known collection of laws. This carving dates from the 1700's B.C. Among the important pieces of sculpture from ancient Greece are the *Winged Victory of Samothrace* and the *Venus de Milo*.

The museum's collection of more than 5,500 paintings includes the most extensive collections of French paintings in the world. The work of every period from medieval to the middle of the 1800's is represented. Next to the collection of French paintings, the Italian collection is the largest. There are also fine collections of Spanish, Dutch, and Flemish paintings. One room contains 24 paintings from the 1600's by the Flemish painter Peter Paul Rubens and his pupils. All these paintings show scenes from the life of Marie de

Médicis, Queen of France (1573–1642). Also on display at the Louvre is one of the most famous paintings in the world, the *Mona Lisa*, by the Italian Renaissance artist Leonardo da Vinci.

Sculptures include examples of French works from the Middle Ages to the mid-1800's, as well as Italian Renaissance and other European sculptures. The collection of decorative arts includes enamels, ceramics, gold and silver work, ivory carvings, furniture, tapestries and carpets, and the crown jewels of France.

▶HISTORY OF THE BUILDINGS

The buildings of the Louvre are important in the history of French architecture and culture. Many of the country's most talented and famous architects, sculptors, and painters helped to create and decorate them.

The original building was a royal fortress built for King Philip Augustus about 1200. This stronghold was made into a royal palace in the 1300's. When Francis I (1494–1547) came to the throne, the palace was in a state

of decay. In 1546 the King hired the architect Pierre Lescot to design a new palace. Only the west wing and part of the south wing of Lescot's design were completed.

Francis I was France's first great art patron. He bought important paintings by Raphael and Leonardo da Vinci—including the *Mona Lisa*—that are owned by the Louvre today. By the time Francis I died, the royal collections had been enriched by many valuable works of art. As the royal collections grew, so did the Louvre complex. Work on the Louvre was continued by Charles IX (1550–74) and by Henry III (1551–89).

During the reign of Henry IV (1553–1610), a long wing called the Grand Gallery was added to the palace. Today some of the most famous French paintings of the 1600's and 1700's hang there.

Below: An artist copies one of the many great paintings in the Louvre galleries. *Right:* Among the best-known works in the Louvre is Leonardo da Vinci's *Mona Lisa*.

Above: One of the many outstanding sculptures that can be seen at the Louvre is the *Venus de Milo*, a Greek statue probably carved about 100 B.C.

Right: Another of the Louvre's treasures from ancient Greece is the *Winged Victory of Samothrace*, a marble statue that dates from about 200 B.C.

Construction was resumed in 1624 by Louis XIII (1601–43), who employed the architect Jacques Lemercier to add to the buildings. The next ruler, Louis XIV (1638–1715), also made additions. The most important was the Louvre colonnade (a series of columns supporting a roof). Designed by Claude Perrault, it was begun in 1667 and completed in 1670. It is considered one of the finest examples of French classical architecture.

After Francis I, Louis XIV was the most outstanding royal collector. However, he was more interested in his palace at Versailles, which he decorated with many of the treasures from the Louvre. When the King deserted the Louvre to live in Versailles, the people of Paris moved in, setting up ramshackle houses and shops in the big courtyards.

By 1710, nearly 2,400 paintings were in the royal collection, and plans were made to restore the royal palace. In 1793 the palace was officially opened as a museum.

After Napoleon I (1769–1821) became emperor, he had the huts and booths cleared away from the courtyards. He sent away the artists who had been living in the Louvre. Napoleon had his architects, Charles Percier and Pierre Fontaine, build a large triumphal arch in the courtyard, and one of the halls was made into a riding ring.

The buildings of the Louvre were completed by Emperor Napoleon III between 1852 and 1857. The palace of the Tuileries, which adjoined the Louvre, was destroyed by fire in 1871. But the Louvre remained much the same for more than 100 years.

A new entrance to the Louvre, a giant glass and steel pyramid 65 feet (20 meters) high, was completed in 1989. The pyramid, designed by American architect I. M. Pei, is situated in an inner courtyard. It leads to a large underground hall linking the various sections of the museum and providing space for exhibits, shops, restaurants, and other facilities.

Reviewed by CATHERINE BELANGER
Musée du Louvre

LOVELL, JAMES. See SPACE EXPLORATION AND TRAVEL (Profiles).

LOWELL, ROBERT (1917–1977)

The American poet Robert Lowell was born in Boston, Massachusetts, on March 1, 1917. He was a member of one of Boston's most prominent families. He received his college education at Harvard University and Kenyon College. Lowell spent several months in jail during World War II after refusing to serve in the armed forces.

Lowell's early poetry, published in *Land of Unlikeness* (1944) and *Lord Weary's Castle* (1946), was dense and complex. His subjects were frequently taken from the history of New England and of his own family. At this time, Lowell was a Catholic convert; he was especially interested in religious questions such as the existence of God and the problems of evil. His early poems often record the struggle between obedience and rebellion, a theme that would persist in his later work.

Lowell remained sternly critical of American politics throughout his career. He called the postwar years the "tranquilized fifties." In the 1960's he was a leading opponent of the war in Vietnam. He also spoke out vigorously for civil rights. "For the Union Dead" (1963), written on the 100th anniversary of the Emancipation Proclamation, combines a tribute to the black and white soldiers killed in the Civil War with a demand for racial justice.

Lowell was acclaimed as the leading poet of his generation, but his private life was shaken by turmoil. He was married three times and was hospitalized for mental illness. He called his poetry an "autobiography in verse." Beginning in the mid-1950's, his poems became more personal, and he was regarded as a central figure among the writers known as confessional poets. He abandoned the traditional forms of the early poems, adopting a looser, more conversational style. *Life Studies* (1959), a major achievement of modern poetry, provided glimpses into his most private and painful experiences.

Lowell continued to reveal himself in many of his later volumes, including *Notebook 1967–68* (1969) and his last book, *Day by Day* (1977). He died in New York City on September 12, 1977.

Peter Conn
University of Pennsylvania

LOWRY, LOIS. See Children's Literature (Profiles).

LOYOLA, SAINT IGNATIUS (1491–1556)

Saint Ignatius Loyola founded a religious order of Catholic priests and brothers known as the Society of Jesus. Its members are known as Jesuits. Ignatius was born in 1491 in the castle of Loyola in northeastern Spain, the youngest son of a wealthy family. In 1521 he fought against the French when they besieged the Spanish city of Pamplona.

During the battle, Ignatius was severely wounded in the legs. While he was recovering, he began to read the life of Christ and the lives of saints. Deeply moved by these stories, Ignatius resolved to change his former way of life and dedicate himself to God. When his wounds had healed, he went to Montserrat, a famous monastery in northeastern Spain. After three days of prayer, he vowed to become a soldier of God.

Ignatius then began a life of prayer and penance. He supported himself by begging. In 1523 he made a trip to Jerusalem. He returned to Spain the following year and began to study for the priesthood. In 1528 he went to Paris to continue his studies. There he and six other young men, all eager to serve God, took vows to lead a religious life, to teach Christianity to unbelievers, and to make a pilgrimage to Jerusalem.

In 1537, Ignatius and his companions tried to make this pilgrimage. But war had broken out in Jerusalem, and they got no farther than Italy. In Venice, Ignatius and some of his companions were ordained priests in June of 1537. Two years later they formally organized the Society of Jesus, a teaching order. Pope Paul III approved the society in 1540, and Ignatius was elected its first leader.

Ignatius died in Rome on July 31, 1556. By then, Jesuits were working in Portugal, Spain, Italy, France, and Germany, as well as in South America and Asia. He was canonized in 1622, and his feast day is July 31.

Kathleen McGowan
Catholic Youth Encyclopedia

LUBRICATION AND LUBRICANTS

Lubricants reduce friction and wear between the surfaces of machines and keep them running smoothly. Lubricants are important for the proper operation of automobile and aircraft engines, construction machinery, bicycle chains, and nearly every other machine with moving parts.

Any surface, no matter how smooth it may appear, looks very uneven and bumpy under a microscope. Whenever two surfaces move against each other, there is a force that works against that movement. That force is friction.

Sometimes friction is very useful and, in fact, necessary. There must be friction between an automobile's tires and the road. Otherwise, the tires would just spin and the automobile would not move, as often happens on icy or other slippery surfaces.

There are many places, however, where friction is a nuisance. If there is too much friction in a machine, extra power is needed to make it run. This makes running the machine very expensive. In some machines friction can produce enough heat to cause the parts to be welded together.

When an oil is used as a lubricant, friction is reduced by separating the two surfaces with a thin oil film so that they do not touch. When the two surfaces are moved, the fluid between them acts like a deck of cards, moving in layers. The resistance of the fluid layers to movement is called fluid friction, or **viscosity**. Liquids of high viscosity are thick and do not flow as easily as low-viscosity liquids.

There are four kinds of lubricants: gases, liquids, semisolids, and solids.

Gaseous Lubricants. A gas such as air or nitrogen can be pumped between the surfaces of bearings to separate them, thus reducing friction and wear. The principle is much the same as on an air hockey table, where a puck slides over a layer of air jets. One high-technology application of gaseous lubricants is in the disk drive of a desktop computer, where bytes of information are stored on a rotating disk. As the disk rotates, the bytes sweep past a recording head, which transmits the information to the computer. To prevent friction and wear in the disk drive, these surfaces must be lubricated, but because of the degree of cleanliness required, oils cannot be used. Instead, air acts as the lubricant, separating the disk and recording head by only 15 to 50 nanometers. (A nanometer is one-billionth of a meter.)

Liquid Lubricants. Petroleum oils, by far the most common liquid lubricants, are made in many different viscosities. Oils are often graded according to their viscosity using a scale established by the Society of Automotive Engineers (SAE). To reduce friction as much as possible, it is necessary to use oil of the lowest viscosity possible. But where pressure between the parts of a machine is great, a thin (low-viscosity) oil would be squeezed out, leaving the parts without lubrication. Here it is necessary to use thicker (higher viscosity) oil. Sometimes synthetic materials such as silicons and chemical groups called esters and synthetic hydrocarbons are used for special lubricating purposes.

Lubricating oils tend to thin when they are heated and thicken when they are cold. However, additives can help keep oils at the same viscosity when temperatures change.

Semisolid Lubricants. Lubricating greases are liquids that have been thickened by the addition of special substances. Metallic soaps (similar to the soap you use to wash your hands) are the most common thickening agents. Uses of semisolid lubricants include lubricating ball bearings and the joints of the steering and suspension in automobiles.

Solid Lubricants. Most solid lubricants reduce friction because their molecules form very thin plates or sheets that slide over one another very easily. The main advantage of solid lubricants is that they remain in place longer than oils or greases. One example of a solid lubricant is graphite powder, a form of carbon, which is commonly used to lubricate the inner workings of door locks.

Reviewed by JONATHAN WICKERT
Carnegie Mellon University

See also PETROLEUM AND PETROLEUM REFINING; WORK, POWER, AND MACHINES.

LUCAS, GEORGE. See CALIFORNIA (Famous People).

LUCE, CLARE BOOTHE. See NEW YORK CITY (Famous People).

LUCE, HENRY R. See JOURNALISM (Profiles); NEW YORK CITY (Famous People).

LUCID, SHANNON. See OKLAHOMA (Famous People).

LUDENDORFF, ERICH. See WORLD WAR I (Profiles: Central Powers).

Lullabies are meant to send a child off to sleep. Some do so with soothing words and bright promises, while others coax or even threaten the fretful child.

LULLABIES

Lullabies are usually the first melodies babies hear sung to quiet them and make them ready for sleep. Almost every language has its own word for lullaby: The Germans call it *Wiegenlied*, the French *berceuse*, the Swedish *vaggvisa*, the Spanish *nana*, the Italian *ninnananna*.

Lullabies developed from wordless crooning or humming that was meant to soothe a fretful infant. In fact, we still use some of those nonsense syllables such as "loo-loo" and "la-la," from which the English word "lullay" or "lullabye" comes, though it is more directly associated with the verb "to lull."

Most lullabies carry the intent to soothe into the lyrics. They charm, coax, and promise the wakeful child. A Yiddish lullaby says "Mama is standing near," and a German song wishes "May your slumber be deep."

Other lullabies speak of warm, homey virtues. "Hush little baby, don't say a word/Mama's gonna buy you a mocking bird" sings an Appalachian lullaby from the southern United States. And the Czechoslovakian cradle song "Hej Pada Pada" talks about raindrops falling

Rock-A-Bye Baby

With a rocking manner

Rock-a-bye ba - by, on the tree-top,

When the wind blows, the cra-dle will rock.

When the bough breaks,the cra-dle will fall, And

down will come ba - by, cra-dle and all.

Brahms's Lullaby

Sweetly

Lull-a - by, and good night, With ro - ses be-dight,— With lil - ies be- decked Is— ba - by's wee bed. Lay thee down now and rest, may your slum-ber be blest.— Lay thee down now and rest, may your slum - ber be blest.

▲ The melody of this famous lullaby was written by the world-famous composer Johannes Brahms. The lyrics were written in German by his friend and publisher Fritz Simrock. This translation is one of several that have become popular since 1868, the year the song was introduced in America.

◄ A printed version of this song was found as far back as the 18th century. Tradition has it that the song was actually written by a young man on the *Mayflower* after he watched Indian women rock their children in birch-bark cradleboards that they hung on tree branches. Cradleboards were used by most of the Indian tribes because they made handling a baby easier. The board could be strapped on the mother or father's back, laid on the ground, or hung by a rope from a tree. A string attached to the cradleboard was pulled back and forth to keep the cradle rocking gently in the tree.

from the skies. A Kwakiutl baby might hear "When I am a man, then I shall be a hunter, harpooner, canoe-builder." A Hopi sleep song talks about beetles riding on each other's backs. A Tsimshian Indian girl from the Northwest coast of America would hear "The little girl was born to gather wild roses" just before she fell asleep.

But a number of lullabies are of a more threatening nature, as if warning the child to go to sleep—or else. A South African tune, "Siembamba," states: "Twist his neck and hit him in the head//Roll him in the ditch and he'll be dead/Siembamba." An English melody promises that the giant Bonaparte will carry off any naughty baby who will not go to sleep right away. A Japanese lullaby threatens with the figure of Hotei, who has eyes in the back of his head and who will not bring gifts to wide-awake children. Occasionally an animal acts as the punishing figure, as in the German lullaby in which two sheep, one black and one white, will "give your little toe a bite." And even the American lullaby "Rock-a-bye Baby," which has been called the world's most famous song, has verses that can hardly be considered soothing as they detail how the baby's cradle will fall down from the treetops when a bough breaks off in a windstorm.

It is interesting to note as well that the age-old caution "Hush-a-by," which can be found in many English-language lullabies, is thought to be a corruption of the French phrase *"He bas, la le loup"* ("Hush, here comes the wolf"), an expression used by nurses in France to quiet unruly children.

Many of the songs we sing today as lullabies contain popular nursery rhymes written by anonymous writers. But well-known poets have also composed lines for cradle songs. Alfred Lord Tennyson's "Sweet and Low" is a famous lullaby. The English clergyman Isaac Watts wrote "Hush my dear, lie still and slumber." A number of famous composers have included lullabies in their musical plays and operas. Even such a rousing thunderous opera as Wagner's *Siegfried* contains a lullaby in it. And one of the world's most famous lullabies, "Now I lay me down to sleep," comes from Humperdinck's opera *Hansel and Gretel*.

JANE YOLEN
Editor, *The Lullaby Songbook*

LUMBER AND LUMBERING

The forest has served the needs of people for centuries. Wood is used to make homes and other buildings. It is used to make furniture. Wood is used to make pulp and paper. It is still used by many people as fuel. But no matter how we use wood, people must first go into the forest and log the trees.

There are forests all around the world. But nowhere have forests been more important in meeting the needs of people than in North America. The story of logging and lumbering

The lumber-making process begins with the harvesting of timber from forests and its transportation, usually by truck or rail, to sawmills.

is largely the story of logging and lumbering in North America.

The United States is the world's largest user of lumber. It is also the largest producer of lumber. It produces about one-quarter of the world's total. It also produces more than one-third of the wood pulp in the world. Together, the United States and Canada produce nearly half the world's supply of newsprint.

North American forests are rich in trees that are strong, beautiful, and useful. In the northeastern states there are white pine, hard maple, oak, basswood, and beech. In eastern Canada there are spruce and balsam fir, and white, red, and jack pine. On the Pacific slope

there are Douglas fir, hemlock, western red cedar, and spruce. California is known for its redwood and the South for its pine **stands** (a stand is an area in which only one type of tree grows). There are almost 1,000 different kinds of trees growing in the United States. About 100 of these kinds of trees are used for lumber.

▶ EARLY LOGGING AND LUMBERING

Logging and lumbering played a major role in the development of North America. The forests provided shelter, fuel, game, and furs, but they also occupied great areas of fertile land needed for crops. The work of clearing the land was difficult and wearying.

But from the earliest days there were many settlers for whom logging and lumbering provided a livelihood. Sawmills were built to cut lumber for building construction. Railroads and canals were built so that new stands of timber could be tapped. Lumber was produced for export to England.

The value of this lumber from the colonies was well appreciated in England. The great white pines made excellent masts for ships. Trees that were as tall and straight as these pines could not be found in Europe. Therefore men were sent out by the British Navy to mark the tallest trees of the colonial forests with the sign of a broad arrow. This meant that they were for the king. Any settler who cut down or damaged a marked tree received the death sentence.

For nearly 300 years after Jamestown was settled in 1607, the white pine remained the most useful tree in the United States. The white pine stands of Maine were easily reached. So it was in this area, in York, Maine, in 1623, that the first sawmill in the United States is believed to have been built.

The forests of Canada were developed for war purposes after 1534, when Jacques Cartier claimed the land for France. The lumber was used by France to build ships of war. After the British conquered Canada in 1763, timbers from its forests were used to build the ships of the Royal Navy. Today Canada remains a major lumber-producing country.

LOGGERS

Many years ago a lumberjack who went into the woods to earn a little money might walk from 25 to 50 miles (40 to 81 kilometers) along bad roads, carrying the 30 pounds (14 kilograms) or so of luggage needed to winter in the **bush**, or wilderness. Now planes, buses, or snowmobiles are used. Many lumberjacks in eastern operations are farmers who turn to logging to earn some money in the winter. Others are professional loggers, for the use of specialized machines calls for skilled people.

Some loggers live in comfortable, well-equipped camps, although the construction of roads into the bush has turned most loggers into commuters who live in their own homes and go to the woods each day.

Right: A highly skilled logger cuts a wedge into a 500-year-old tree to control the direction of its fall. *Below:* In high-lead logging, a winch-driven cable attaches at one end to a spar, or steel tower. The other end of the cable attaches to, lifts, and drags the log over the ground.

METHODS OF LOGGING

Methods of logging vary according to the type of tree, its location, and the way in which the wood is to be used. There are four basic steps, however, that are common throughout the world. First, the tree must be cut down, or **felled**. Second, the tree must be cut, or **bucked**, into suitable lengths. It may be bucked into 16-foot (4.9-meter) lengths if the logs are going to the sawmill to be made into lumber. It may be cut into 4-foot (1.2-meter) lengths if the logs are going to a newsprint or pulp mill. Third, the bucked logs must be dragged, or **skidded**, out of the woods to a central assembly point, called a landing. A landing may be located on a road, a railway,

or a riverbank. The fourth major step is the **hauling**, or transportation, of the logs to the mill. Transportation may be by truck, railroad, or barge. Sometimes logs are still floated down waterways to mills.

From the time of the first settlers until the end of the 1800's, men, animals, and the natural force of streams and rivers were of great importance in North American logging. Lumberjacks felled the trees with powerful strokes of the ax. Horses or oxen skidded the logs out of the woods to the landing. The spring river drive swept the logs to the mill in a rush of water and melting ice. Where there were no waterways, wagons or sleds drawn by mules or horses hauled the logs to the mill.

Today good roads, special tractors, long cables, powerful winches (machines that haul or hoist items by coiling ropes, cables, or chains

Most sawmill operations today employ highly automated, accurate equipment and computers. *Right:* Rotating grinders remove bark from logs. *Far right:* Stripped logs are conveyed to processing areas. *Below:* Electronic scanning equipment determines a log's shape. Then a computer calculates how the log should be sawed to produce the most lumber. *Bottom:* Large saws precisely cut the logs into boards of a specified thickness.

onto a turning drum), and other logging equipment have replaced animals in skidding and hauling logs. A grapple-loader (a machine with a large claw-like clasping tool at the end of a long boom) lifts the logs onto trucks waiting at the landing.

Before logging begins, the logging manager works with a forester. The forester determines which trees should be cut and how to protect the area for future use through reforestation. Roads must be engineered. Forest fire hazards must be avoided, and fire drills organized. People using the forest for camping, sports, and other recreation must be encouraged to help prevent forest fires. The manager of a large operation often plans a logging program years in advance.

Sometimes **selective cutting**, or prelogging, is carried out to remove timber ready for harvesting without damaging the young, growing crop. Sometimes **salvage logging** is planned to follow the major logging operations, so that all remaining usable wood is removed from the site. The logging plan may call for all timber in an area to be logged. This is called **clear-cutting**. Other timber may be **patch logged**. In this method, cleared areas, or patches, are separated by stands of trees that serve as firebreaks or seed trees, trees used for reseeding part of a forest.

Some logging is done throughout the year. But in eastern Canada and the United States, most logging takes place in the winter. Since a large part of the forest is swampy, loggers cannot transport wood in hot weather. In winter, snow forms white highways through the forest, and the frozen lakes can withstand the weight of a load of logs.

The loggers go into the eastern forests in the later summer or early autumn. First they must open up trails and build roads. Trees are felled to open up trails. Stumps are pulled out or blasted. Hollows are filled and streams bridged. In winter the snow is rolled until it is packed hard. Then it is sprinkled with water to give it an icy surface so that larger loads can be pulled more easily.

The fallers and buckers go into the woods alone or in pairs. Fallers must have great skill. A skilled faller can drop a tree exactly as planned. After being felled, the trees are bucked and skidded to the landing.

far up a mountain as the cables could reach from the railcars.

The rugged landscape and the giant trees of the western timber stands make it very difficult to skid and haul logs. Because of this, machines and steel cables are used to swing the logs over narrow canyons or up steep mountain slopes. Two types of cable-logging systems are used: high-lead logging and skyline logging.

How a Log Is Used

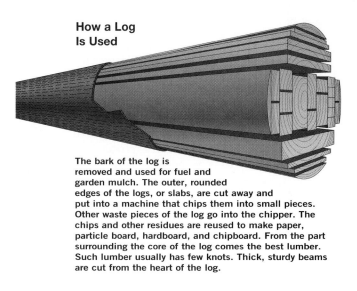

The bark of the log is removed and used for fuel and garden mulch. The outer, rounded edges of the logs, or slabs, are cut away and put into a machine that chips them into small pieces. Other waste pieces of the log go into the chipper. The chips and other residues are reused to make paper, particle board, hardboard, and chipboard. From the part surrounding the core of the log comes the best lumber. Such lumber usually has few knots. Thick, sturdy beams are cut from the heart of the log.

Cutting Methods

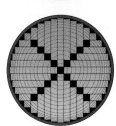

Top: Plain sawing makes the best use of the log. The boards are cut through the tree rings. Such lumber is inexpensive but will warp easily. *Bottom:* In quarter sawing, the log is first cut into quarters. Then cuts are made from the outer edge across the rings toward the center of the log. Quarter-sawed lumber is very strong and seldom warps.

Time is important in winter operations, for the wood must be ready to move with the spring freshets, great rises in the streams and rivers due to melting snow. Sometimes the logs are piled at the riverbank. Sometimes they are dumped onto the frozen surface of a lake. Then, when the ice melts in the spring, the logs are left in the water and can be rafted and towed to the river outlet. When the freshet comes, nimble lumberjacks drive the logs down the river, jumping from one to another of the big, slippery logs as they swirl through the waters.

On the Pacific slope, logging is done in the summer or in all but the snowiest months of the year. Railroad logging was developed in the period from 1890 to 1930 to tap the remote stands of timber in the western United States. Here the trees were too big and the mountain streams too fast and furious to permit stream driving. The railroads usually ran along the mountain valleys or along the lower mountain slopes. Trees were logged as

In **high-lead logging**, one end of a cable is attached to the log to be skidded. The other end of the cable is fastened to a transportable steel tower, called a **spar**. By means of a powerful engine-driven winch, the log is lifted at one end and is dragged over the ground to the landing.

A similar process is used in **skyline logging**, except the whole log is picked up and swung through the sky to the landing. Because the logs are not dragged, skyline logging causes less damage to the forest floor than high-lead logging.

Logs arriving at the landing are stacked in piles until they can be transported—by truck, railroad, or barge—to a sawmill.

▶ **SAWMILLING**

The sawmiller takes over from the logger when the logs reach the yard or millpond. The basic steps in sawmilling are essentially the same throughout the world. The logs are carried into the mill by means of a moving

Most of the lumber produced in the United States goes into the construction of homes and other buildings.

jack ladder (a conveyor-like chain with hooks along it) and put through the head saw. The **band saw** and the **circular saw** are two common types of saws. These either cut the logs into planks roughly 3 inches (8 centimeters) thick or **slab** the logs on two sides (remove the thick outside slices). The slabbed log moves along a series of rollers and chains. It goes through the **gang saws**, which cut it into several boards. **Resaws** are used in some mills to slice the thick planks or boards into thinner sizes. Because the blades of the resaws are thin, less of the log is turned into sawdust.

Then the boards go through the **edgers** and **trimmers**, which trim off the bark and reduce the boards to standard widths. To be planed, they go to the planer mill, which may be either next to the sawmill or some distance away. When the boards leave the planer mill they are smooth and lustrous. In the mill yard the lumber is stacked in neat rows.

Sawmills typically use special machines called **chippers** and **barkers**. These salvage the chips, bark, and other parts of the log wasted in the sawing process and prepare them for use in pulp mills. Workers in some mills use closed-circuit television to watch the progress of the boards along the rollers and chains. Automation is an important part of the lumber industry.

Lumber must be sorted and graded, for boards sawed from average logs vary widely in quality. A perfect board is free of knots and has a straight grain. A poor board may be scarred, stained, or knotty.

In the raw state of the wood, the water content of a board may equal the weight of the wood itself. This moisture must be removed or reduced before lumber is used. Also, moisture encourages rot and stain and increases the cost of shipping lumber.

Sometimes lumber may be dried in the open air. But if the lumber is to be used in flooring or furniture or for general interior use, air drying alone is not enough. Lumber for these uses is stacked in an airtight structure called a **dry kiln**. Here it is dried to the correct moisture content in hours or days—much faster than air drying, which can take weeks or months. After the drying process, the lumber is ready to be shipped to market.

▶ TRENDS

New pulp-making and papermaking processes have led to the use of some varieties of trees previously left in the woods. Some countries are planting new varieties of trees to suit special needs. For instance, Australia and other countries in the Southern Hemisphere have started planting softwoods that are easier to convert into lumber and pulp than their native hardwoods are.

New roads, railroads, and reservoirs created behind hydroelectric dams have opened up stands of timber that were unreachable before. More efficient machines have made it possible to log timber that once was too difficult and costly to log. Modern loggers work the mountainsides in places where their grandfathers logged only the valleys. Even helicopters have been used in the logging of extremely hard-to-reach locations.

In recent years, however, there has been a growing movement to restrict logging in places where **deforestation** (the loss of forests) could endanger species and cause other environmental problems. Also, many countries now require logging companies to replant trees in areas they have harvested.

PAT CARNEY
Former business columnist, Vancouver *Sun*

See also BUILDING CONSTRUCTION; FORESTS AND FORESTRY; WOOD AND WOOD PRODUCTS.

LUNGS

Nestled inside the curving cage formed by the ribs and a muscle called the diaphragm, the lungs are shaped like upside-down cones. With each breath that is drawn in, air travels down a series of branching tubes to these vital organs. There, in millions of tiny compartments, an exchange of gases takes place. Oxygen from the air passes from the lungs into the bloodstream and is carried to the body's cells. In the cells, oxygen is used to produce the energy necessary to power the processes that sustain life. Meanwhile, carbon dioxide, a waste product formed when energy is produced, passes from the blood into the lungs. The carbon dioxide leaves the lungs when we breathe out. If this exchange were to stop, even for a few minutes, we would die.

▶ THE PARTS OF THE LUNG

The two lungs take up most of the space inside the chest cavity. The right lung is divided into three parts, called **lobes**; the smaller left lung is divided into only two lobes. The lungs are pink and spongy and look a bit like balloons. Each lung is surrounded by a thin, airtight membrane called a **pleura**.

Together with the lungs, the **pharynx**, the cavity located behind the nose and mouth; the **larynx**, or voice box; and the **trachea**, or windpipe, make up the respiratory system. From the nose, air passes through the pharynx to the larynx and then into the strong, flexible trachea. The trachea, which extends into the chest, is 4 to 5 inches (10 to 13 centimeters) long and up to 1 inch (2.5 centimeters) in diameter. Within the chest cavity, the trachea branches into two narrower tubes. Each tube, called a **bronchus**, enters a lung and branches again and again, into still narrower tubes. The smallest of these, the **bronchioles**, are only about $1/25$ inch (1 millimeter) in diameter.

Each bronchiole ends in a grapelike cluster of tiny sacs, called **alveoli**. Each alveolus is only $1/125$ inch (0.2 millimeter) in diameter. The inner walls of the alveoli are coated with a **surfactant**, a chemical that keeps the alveoli from sticking together and makes it easier for them to inflate. The 300 to 400 million alveoli in each lung provide an enormous surface area—about 80 to 100 square yards (67 to 84 square meters), or about 40 to 50 times the total skin area! This large surface allows the rapid exchange of gases to take place.

Each alveolus is surrounded by a network of tiny capillaries, which receive waste-carrying blood that is pumped from the heart. The walls of the alveoli and the walls of the capillaries surrounding them are moist and very thin, so gases can pass easily between the tiny air sacs and the blood flowing through the capillaries around them. It is here that the transfer of gases takes place: Oxygen

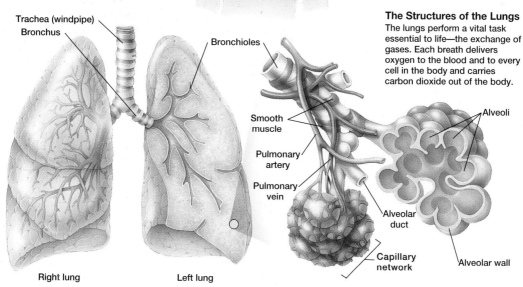

Trachea (windpipe)
Bronchus
Bronchioles
Smooth muscle
Pulmonary artery
Pulmonary vein
Alveoli
Alveolar duct
Capillary network
Alveolar wall
Right lung
Left lung

The Structures of the Lungs
The lungs perform a vital task essential to life—the exchange of gases. Each breath delivers oxygen to the blood and to every cell in the body and carries carbon dioxide out of the body.

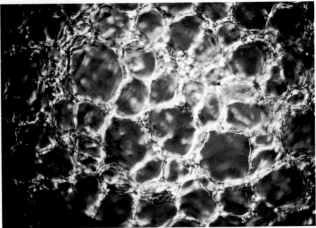

Within the lungs, air travels through the bronchial tree (*left*), a system of tubes that branch again and again into ever smaller tubes, to the alveoli. The large surface area provided by the millions of alveoli lining each lung (*above*) guarantees that a rapid exchange of gases will take place.

breathed in moves out of the air sacs into the blood, and carbon dioxide moves out of the blood into the air sacs. The blood, now free of waste products and rich in oxygen, is carried back to the heart and then pumped throughout the body.

▶ HOW THE LUNGS WORK

Normally breathing is automatic, even when sleeping. All the work of breathing is coordinated in the brain without our having to think about it. With each breath, an adult takes in about 1 pint (0.5 liter) of air, or about 12 pints (6 liters) per minute. With a deep breath, nearly 4 quarts (about 3.5 liters) can be taken in. During exercise, when the muscles are working hard, the body needs more oxygen. So the breathing rate speeds up, and more air is taken in with each breath. During hard exercise, a person may take in 15 to 20 times as much air as usual—more than 200 pints (100 liters) of air per minute.

The lungs do not have any muscles of their own, so they are not able to move by themselves. Breathing depends on movements of the diaphragm and the **intercostals**, the muscles between the ribs. When we **inhale**, or

breathe in, the diaphragm contracts, moving downward, while the chest muscles contract, moving the ribs upward and outward. With these movements, the chest cavity expands, lowering air pressure in the lungs. Because air always moves from a high-pressure area to a low-pressure area, air moves from the higher-pressure area outside into the lungs. When we **exhale**, or breathe out, the muscles relax and the chest cavity becomes smaller. This increases the air pressure inside the lungs, so that the air, moving to what is now the lower-pressure area outside, rushes out of the lungs.

When air is inhaled, the alveoli expand like little balloons. Oxygen passes out, or diffuses, through their thin walls and into the surrounding capillaries, where it is picked up by the red blood cells. Meanwhile, the red cells have released their loads of carbon dioxide, gathered from the body cells on their last trip through the body. This carbon dioxide diffuses through the capillary walls, enters the alveoli, and then is exhaled. Not all of the air in the alveoli leaves the lungs during exhalation. Nearly 3 pints (at least 1.2 liters) remains in the lungs, even if a forceful effort is made to blow the air out. This remaining air is called the **residual volume**.

There are several safeguards that help keep the lungs in working order. Bristly hairs in the nose trap large particles, and the sticky substance called **mucus** picks up smaller ones. The lining of the respiratory tubes provides two kinds of protection to keep dust and other solid particles from reaching the alveoli. Some cells in the lining secrete mucus, which traps particles that have gotten through the first line of defense. Other cells are studded with tiny hairlike structures called **cilia**. The cilia wave back and forth, creating currents in the mucus that carry trapped particles upward, away from the lungs. Sometimes the trapped particles are carried out of the respiratory passages during a sneeze or cough. Typically the particles trapped in mucus are swept into the throat. The mucus, which is swallowed, reaches the stomach where any germs are killed by stomach acid and pass harmlessly out of the body.

In addition to their important work as respiratory organs, the lungs perform some other functions. They help excrete waste products and other substances. They also help in forming the sounds of speech. When the exhaled air is forced through the folds of tissue in the larynx called the **vocal cords**, the tissue vibrates, producing sounds.

▶ DISORDERS OF THE LUNGS

Most people know that smoking can lead to lung cancer. As lung tissue is invaded by cancer, the number of alveoli able to carry on the normal breathing functions decreases. Cancer cells may also break away and travel through the blood and lymph, settling down in other organs and forming tumors there as

well. Air pollution can also contribute to the formation of cancers.

Smoking and air pollution can cause another kind of serious lung disease: **emphysema**. Smoking irritates the bronchioles and paralyzes the action of the cilia. In this way it interferes with the normal cleaning action of the cilia, so that the tars and other solid particles introduced into the airways by smoking cannot be cleared away. The results of smoking can be seen on a smoker's lungs. A long-time smoker has lungs that are gray rather than pink, from all the soot and tar deposits. Both smoking and air pollution can lead to chronic infections. The excess mucus and inflammation that result may obstruct bronchioles, making it difficult to exhale. Air stays trapped in the alveoli and stretches them, leading to destruction of their walls. As alveoli are destroyed, breathing becomes more and more difficult.

Pneumonia is a term for lung infections in which the lung tissue is inflamed and the alveoli are filled with fluid and blood cells. It may be caused by bacteria or viruses. **Tuberculosis** is a lung infection caused by a type of bacteria called tubercle bacilli. The lung tissue fights the infection by walling off the bacteria in pockets called tubercles. This helps to keep the infection from spreading, but sometimes the bacteria break free and spread through the lungs, damaging tissues and decreasing the number of alveoli.

Obstruction of the airways by mucus or by a cancerous tumor may lead to **atelectasis**, a collapse of the alveoli. It may affect a small area, a whole lobe of a lung, or an entire lung. In babies born prematurely, the alveoli may collapse for a different reason: a lack of the surfactant that helps to keep their walls from sticking together. This condition is called **respiratory distress syndrome**.

Asthma is a disorder in which spasms of the bronchioles occur, making it difficult to breathe. In young people, it is generally the result of allergic reactions to plant pollens or other substances in the air. Air pollution can also bring on asthma attacks, especially in older people. Drugs to open the bronchioles can help to ease the breathing distress.

ALVIN SILVERSTEIN
VIRGINIA SILVERSTEIN
Coauthors, *The Respiratory System*

See also BODY, HUMAN.

LUTHER, MARTIN (1483–1546)

Martin Luther was the first and most important leader of the reform movement in European Christianity known as the Protestant Reformation. One of the major branches of the Protestant church, Lutheranism, is named for him. Except for a brief trip to Rome, Luther spent his busy life—studying, teaching, preaching, and writing—within a small circle of towns in central Germany. From there his name and influence spread throughout Europe.

Luther was born in Eisleben, Germany, on November 10, 1483. He was given a better than average education by his father, who wanted his son to study law. At the age of 18,

Martin Luther, leader of the Protestant Reformation, in a portrait by Lucas Cranach the Elder.

Luther entered the University of Erfurt. He received his master of arts degree in 1505 but gave up his law studies and entered a monastery in Erfurt. In 1507 he was ordained a Catholic priest. In 1512 he received a doctorate in theology from the University of Wittenberg, where he became a professor.

As he struggled to find the meaning of faith and salvation, Luther became dissatisfied with the traditional ways of thinking. Gradually he turned to the teachings of the Bible, especially the letters of Saint Paul, and to the writings of Saint Augustine. Luther came to believe that God freely offers forgiveness, faith, and new life to anyone who puts his trust in Jesus Christ as the mediator between man as sinner and God as savior. This view became known as the doctrine of justification by faith.

Luther was not, at first, in rebellion against the church. But he was unhappy with the religious ignorance and immorality of the time. A pilgrimage to Rome about 1510 left him disappointed with the church's lack of spiritual truth in contrast to its material wealth and power.

A basic issue that roused him to action was the church's sale of indulgences. These were documents sold for cash by representatives of the Pope, promising forgiveness for sins. Luther argued that forgiveness is not something one can buy or deserve but is the gift of God. He prepared a list of 95 theses, or statements, on the subject of indulgences and nailed them as a public notice on the church door in Wittenberg. The date—October 31, 1517—is often considered to mark the birth of the Reformation.

Luther, against his original intentions, was now thrust into a debate with the church on fundamental issues of church authority and religious truth. He came to be regarded as a dangerous heretic. He was excommunicated (expelled from the church) in January 1521.

In a series of public hearings, Pope Leo X tried to persuade Luther to change his mind and withdraw his objections against the church. The most famous of these was a diet (meeting) held in the city of Worms, Germany, in April 1521. There Luther defended his position, claiming the authority of the Bible as higher than the authority of the Pope. He refused to alter his views, saying: "My conscience is bound by the Word of God; I cannot and will not recant anything. …Here I stand; I cannot do otherwise."

Luther became the leader of the growing protest, or Protestant, movement throughout Germany. One of his most important acts was to translate the Bible into German. For the first time people could read the Bible in their own language, rather than hearing it read in church in Latin. He also wrote many books and essays and a number of hymns, notably "A Mighty Fortress Is Our God."

The last years of Luther's life were marked with difficulties. These arose not only with Rome but within Protestantism and even within the emerging Lutheran Church itself. Stubborn and unyielding, he often clashed with other reform leaders. Though he won the political protection of the German rulers, Luther lost some popular support.

However, Luther found personal happiness through his marriage in 1525 to Katherine von Bora, with whom he had six children. He died in Eisleben on February 18, 1546.

HUGH T. KERR
Princeton Theological Seminary

See also REFORMATION.

LUXEMBOURG

Luxembourg is a small landlocked nation in western Europe, bordered by Germany, France, and Belgium. Its official name is Grand Duchy of Luxembourg, and its head of state is a grand duke or grand duchess. It is the only grand duchy in the world.

▶ PEOPLE

Luxembourgers originally descended from the Belgae, an ancient Celtic people. But since the region was located at an important crossroads in Europe, many Germanic and Frankish tribes also settled there. By the 1800's, three-quarters of Luxembourg's original land area had been lost to Germany, France, and Belgium; the remaining people, struggling for complete independence, expressed their desires in the national motto, "We wish to remain what we are."

The official language of the country is Luxembourgisch (Lëtzebuergesch), a dialect of German with some French words. French is the administrative language of government, and German is widely used in commerce. Most Luxembourgers are Roman Catholics.

Education is free and compulsory for all children between the ages of 6 and 15. German is the first language of instruction in primary school. French is added soon after and becomes the main language in secondary school. The literacy rate is 100 percent.

▶ LAND

Luxembourg has two distinct geographic regions. The northern third of the country, known as the Oesling, is part of the Ardennes plateau which extends into Belgium. This rugged, forested region rises to 1,834 feet (559 meters) at Buurgplaatz, the country's highest point. The southern two-thirds of the country is known as the Gutland, or Bon Pays ("Good Earth"). With its fertile, rolling land, the Gutland is Luxembourg's agricultural and industrial region; it is also home to the nation's two largest cites, Esch-sur-Alzette and the capital city of Luxembourg. The Our, Sûre, and Moselle rivers form most of the country's eastern border with Germany.

The city of Luxembourg is the capital of the Grand Duchy of Luxembourg. The site was a Roman fort in ancient times.

▶ ECONOMY

For its size, Luxembourg is one of the world's most highly industrialized nations. The production of iron and steel has long been its most important industry. Other leading manufactured products are chemicals, plastics, rubber goods, and mechanical and electrical equipment. Luxembourg is also one of Europe's most important banking and financial centers. About 23 percent of the land is suitable for farming. The chief agricultural products are barley, oats, potatoes, and wheat.

▶ MAJOR CITIES

Luxembourg, the capital and largest city, has a population of more than 77,000. The city's site is an ancient one, dating from Roman times. The European Court of Justice, the secretariat of the European Parliament, and other European Union and international offices are located in the city.

Esch-sur-Alzette is the chief industrial city and the second largest in population, with nearly 28,000 people. The city's iron and steel industry, which began in the mid-1800's, made Luxembourg one of the leading iron and steel producers in Europe.

▶ HISTORY AND GOVERNMENT

Luxembourg's history as an independent state dates from the year 963, when Siegfried, Count of Ardennes, acquired an old Roman fortress on the site of the present city of Luxembourg. The fortress was called Lucilinburhuc ("small fortress"), from which the name Luxembourg is derived.

Under Siegfried's successors, the fortress of Luxembourg became one of the strongest in Europe. Several of the counts of Luxembourg became rulers of other lands as well. Four of them were emperors of the Holy Roman Empire, the group of states from which modern Germany developed. Luxembourg's national hero is John (Jean l'Aveugle), the blind king of Bohemia. In spite of his blindness, he led an army at the Battle of Crécy, where he met his death in 1346.

As it grew larger, Luxembourg was less able to defend its territory. In 1443 it was conquered by Philip the Good, Duke of Burgundy (now part of France). For the next four centuries, Luxembourg was a prize fought over by various European nations. Luxembourg was made a grand duchy in 1815 by the Congress of Vienna and placed under the rulership of William I, prince of Orange-Nassau and first king of the Netherlands. The duchy dates its modern independence from 1839; although the Treaty of London granted half of Luxembourg's territory to Belgium, the duchy's current boundaries were set and it gained more autonomy. The Conference of London granted the grand duchy neutrality and full independence in 1867.

Although Luxembourg's neutrality had been guaranteed by the European powers, the country was invaded by Germany during World War I (1914–18) and World War II (1939–45). After recovering from the devastation of World War II, Luxembourg took a leading role in the creation of the European Economic Community (now the European Union, or EU). In 1999, the nation adopted the euro, the EU's common currency.

Luxembourg is a hereditary constitutional monarchy. The ruling family is the house of Nassau-Weilburg; the present head of state, Grand Duke Henri, came to the throne in 2000. The legislature, the Chamber of Deputies, is elected for five years. The government is headed by a president of government (prime minister), who leads the Council of Ministers. An advisory body, the Council of State, is appointed by the grand duke.

Reviewed by JOHN B. RONEY
Sacred Heart University

LYME DISEASE. See TICKS.

FACTS and figures

GRAND DUCHY OF LUXEMBOURG is the official name of the country.

LOCATION: Western Europe.

AREA: 998 sq mi (2,586 km²).

POPULATION: 463,000 (estimate).

CAPITAL AND LARGEST CITY: Luxembourg.

MAJOR LANGUAGES: Luxembourgisch (Lëtzebuergesch; official), German, French.

MAJOR RELIGIOUS GROUP: Roman Catholic.

GOVERNMENT: Constitutional monarchy. **Head of state**—grand duke. **Head of government**—prime minister. **Legislature**—Chamber of Deputies.

CHIEF PRODUCTS: Agricultural—barley, oats, potatoes, wheat, fruits, wine grapes, livestock. **Manufactured**—iron and steel, processed foods, chemicals, metal and engineering products, tires, glass, aluminum. **Mineral**—iron ore.

MONETARY UNIT: Euro (1 euro = 100 cents).

LYMPHATIC SYSTEM

The lymphatic system is a network of tiny tubes, similar to blood vessels, that branch throughout the body. These lymphatic vessels collect fluid from the body tissues and return it to the blood. In fact, the lymphatic system is so closely associated with the blood and blood vessels that it is sometimes considered a part of the circulatory system. The lymphatic system also helps in digestion, by absorbing and transporting fat nutrients, and it links the organs of the immune system, which works to defend the body against infection.

▶ STRUCTURES OF THE LYMPHATIC SYSTEM

The tiniest vessels of the lymphatic system, the **lymphatic capillaries**, branch through nearly all the tissues of the body. Unlike blood capillaries, which are all linked together into a network, lymphatic capillaries begin as a series of tiny closed tubes. The walls of lymphatic capillaries are just one cell thick, but the edges of the covering cells overlap, forming tiny flaps. Fluid from the tissues can flow into the capillaries through the gaps between cells, but the flaps close to prevent it from flowing out again.

The tiny lymphatic capillaries join to form larger vessels, called **lymphatics**. Lymphatic vessels are similar to the veins of the circulatory system. Like veins, the lymphatics have valves that allow fluid to flow in only one direction.

All of the fluid carried by the lymphatics flows into two large vessels that empty into the large veins that return blood to the heart. The **thoracic duct**, which lies along the front of the spine, collects fluid from the entire lower part of the body, as well as from the left arm and the left halves of the upper body and head. Fluid from the right arm and the right halves of the upper body and head flows into another large collecting vessel, the **right lymphatic duct**.

The clear, straw-colored liquid carried by the lymphatic system is called **lymph**. It con-

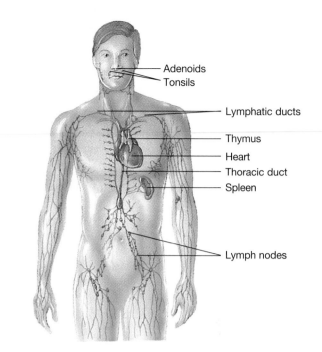

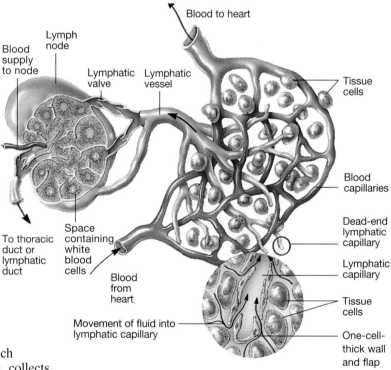

The lymphatic system, a body-wide network of interconnecting vessels, collects and drains excess fluid (interstitial fluid) from the body tissues. The lymphatic system also plays important roles in defending the body against disease and in absorbing and transporting fats to all parts of the body. Interstitial fluid enters the lymphatic system through tiny gaps in the one-cell-thick lymphatic capillary walls. One-way valves direct the fluid through the lymphatics to lymph nodes, where concentrations of white blood cells help filter harmful substances from the lymph fluid before it returns to the blood.

sists of the fluid gathered from the spaces between body cells and is somewhat similar to blood plasma (the liquid part of the blood).

Lymph nodes are oval masses of tissue from $1/25$ to 1 inch (1 millimeter to 25 millimeters) in diameter, scattered along the lymphatic vessels. Large numbers of lymph nodes are bunched together in the neck, armpits, and groin and also near organs and large blood vessels in the chest and abdomen. Tough covering tissue surrounds the lymph nodes and divides each one into compartments, through which lymph flows. The lymph nodes contain numerous white blood cells. One type, called **macrophages**, can swallow up germs or bits of debris. Another kind, the **lymphocytes**, defend the body against germs and cancerous cells.

Other organs of the lymphatic system include the tonsils and adenoids, the spleen, and the thymus. They all contain **lymphoid tissue** and are part of the body's immune defenses. The two masses of lymphoid tissue at the back of the throat are one of three pairs of **tonsils**. Another pair, called the **adenoids**, are found in the nasal passages. The third pair of tonsils lie at the base of the tongue. The **spleen** is a deep red bean-shaped organ about 5 inches (13 centimeters) long. Its structure is similar to that of the lymph nodes, but it contains blood. The **thymus** is a butterfly-shaped lymphoid organ behind the breastbone.

▶ **HOW THE LYMPHATIC SYSTEM WORKS**

The capillaries of the circulatory system are rather leaky. Fluid, consisting of water, nutrients, dissolved salts, and some protein, continually passes out through their thin walls and accumulates in the spaces between cells. This liquid, called **interstitial fluid**, bathes and nourishes the body tissues. An important function of the lymphatic system is to return the excess interstitial fluid to the circulatory system. Fluid passes into the lymphatic capillaries through the gaps between the cells that form their walls. As nearby muscles contract, the tissues surrounding the lymphatic capillaries squeeze them, sending the fluid toward the larger vessels. The muscular walls of

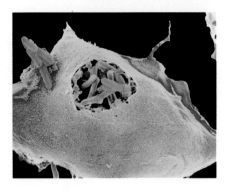

In this color-enhanced photomicrograph, a macrophage (yellow) engulfs and will digest disease-causing bacteria (green).

the lymphatics contract automatically when these larger vessels fill with fluid, pumping the lymph along.

Specialized lymphatic capillaries in the intestines, called **lacteals**, absorb fat nutrients from the digested food and transport them to the blood to be distributed through the body.

The lymph nodes filter the lymph that flows through them. Macrophages sweep up dead cells and other debris and eat up microbes. If foreign particles are too large for these white cells to swallow, they may work together to surround them and wall them off, preventing them from spreading through the body. The macrophages also help to stimulate other white cells, the lymphocytes, to attack invading microbes. In the spleen, blood is filtered and "policed" in a similar way. T cells, one type of lymphocyte, mature in the thymus before traveling to the lymph nodes.

▶ **DISORDERS OF THE LYMPHATIC SYSTEM**

Inflammation of the lymphatic vessels, injury, or parasites may block the flow of lymph and prevent the return of fluid to the circulatory system. Then the amount of interstitial fluid continues to increase, causing the tissues to swell—a condition called **edema**.

When the body is fighting an infection, lymph nodes or tonsils may become enlarged and painful. Swollen glands (enlarged lymph nodes) in the neck are a common symptom of mumps, a viral disease. An early symptom of AIDS (*a*cquired *i*mmune *d*eficiency *sy*ndrome) is **lymphadenopathy**, a swelling and inflammation of lymph nodes.

Cancer sometimes develops in lymph tissue and may lead to the production of large numbers of abnormal white blood cells. One type of **lymphoma** (cancer of lymphoid tissue), **Hodgkin's disease**, occurs mainly in young adults and in people over 50.

ALVIN SILVERSTEIN
VIRGINIA SILVERSTEIN
Coauthors, *The Circulatory System*

See also AIDS; BODY, HUMAN; CIRCULATORY SYSTEM; IMMUNE SYSTEM.

Index

HOW TO USE THE DICTIONARY INDEX

See the beginning of the blue pages in Volume 1.

L (twelfth letter of the English alphabet) **L:**1 *see also* Alphabet
Labatt Brier (curling tournament) **C:**615
Label (in heraldry) **H:**118
Labels (on food packaging) **F:**345–46, 348
  bottles labeled by machine **B:**347
  consumer involvement **F:**338
  genetically modified organisms **B:**214
  health foods **H:**79
  herbal medicines **H:**119
  milk **D:**9
  nutrition **N:**428–29, 430
  percents, uses of **P:**146
  picture(s)
    example of U.S. food label **F:**346
Labels (on household products) **P:**356
Labe River (Europe) *see* Elbe River
Labia (female anatomy) **B:**287
Labor
  African Americans in organized labor **A:**79k
  automation **A:**529–33
  capitalism **C:**103
  child labor **C:**227
  clocks record employees' work time **C:**369
  contract and wage agreements **L:**5
  disabilities, employment of people with **D:**180
  economics **E:**57
  ethnic groups **E:**335
  farm labor **A:**100
  government regulation **L:**5–7
  guilds **G:**403–5
  Hispanic Americans **H:**148, 149
  how to be an entrepreneur **B:**472
  immigration, problems of **I:**91
  Industrial Revolution **I:**221–22, 224
  industry's needs **I:**225–26
  International Labor Organization (ILO) **U:**69
  Labor, United States Department of **L:**2–3
  Marx, Karl **M:**117
  Massachusetts, labor troubles in **M:**150
  May Day and Labor Day **H:**169
  New Deal **N:**138h
  occupational health and safety **O:**13
  older people **O:**100
  Oriental Exclusion Acts **O:**228
  poverty and the decline of traditional occupations **P:**419
  segregation **S:**113
  serfs under feudalism **F:**102
  slave labor **S:**192–97
  sweatshops in early clothing industry **C:**380
  trade, productive factor in **T:**264
  unemployment and unemployment insurance **U:**28–29
  vocations **V:**375–76
  women's rights movement **W:**212b, 213
  workers' compensation **W:**253
Labor, United States Department of **L:**2–3; **O:**13; **P:**447
Laboratories
  archaeological work **A:**355–57
  forensic science **F:**372–73
  medical laboratory tests **D:**207–8
  space stations **S:**349–50
  underwater laboratories **O:**40; **U:**24–25
Labor camps (for criminals) **P:**481

Labor Day **H:**169 *see also* May Day (International Labor Day)
Labor-management relations **L:**3–10
Labor-Management Relations Act (Taft-Hartley Act) (United States, 1947) **L:**7, 8, 16; **T:**326
Labor-Management Reporting and Disclosure Act (Landrum-Griffin Act) (United States, 1959) **L:**7
Labor movement **L:**11–18
Labors of Heracles (in mythology) **G:**365–67
Labor Statistics, Bureau of **C:**533; **L:**3
Labor unions **L:**11–18 *see also* National Labor Relations Act
  capitalism modified by **C:**103
  Debs, Eugene V. **D:**53
  Gompers, Samuel **G:**261
  guilds **G:**403–5
  Industrial Revolution **I:**224
  labor-management relations **L:**7–10
  Lewis, John L. **L:**162
  organized crime **O:**225
  Pennsylvania, history of **P:**140
  railroad workers **R:**86
Labour Party (Great Britain) **B:**254; **E:**253; **P:**373; **S:**224; **U:**62
Labrador (Canada) *see* Newfoundland and Labrador
Labrador City (Newfoundland and Labrador) **N:**141
Labrador Current (Arctic Current) (of Atlantic Ocean) **A:**479; **C:**58; **G:**413; **I:**18; **N:**140, 291
Labrador Inuit Association **I:**276
Labradorite (gemstone) **G:**73
Labrador retrievers (dogs) **D:**246, 257
La Brea Tar Pits (Los Angeles, California) **L:**305
La Bruyère, Jean de (French social critic) **F:**439
Labyrinth (in Greek mythology) **G:**366, 368
Labyrinth (of the ear) *see* Inner ear
Lac (resin) **R:**184
Lacalle, Luis Alberto (Uruguayan president) **U:**241
Lacandon Mayas (Indians of South America) **I:**195
Lace (fabric) **L:**19; **T:**145
Lacewood (tree)
  picture(s) **W:**223
Lachaise, Gaston (French-born American sculptor) **S:**103; **U:**133
Lackland Air Force Base (San Antonio, Texas) **U:**108
Laclède, Pierre (French fur trader) **F:**522; **S:**16
Laclos, Pierre Choderlos de (French writer) **F:**440
Lacombe, Albert (Canadian missionary) **A:**172
Lacombe, Patrice (Canadian writer) **C:**87
La Condamine, Charles de (French scientist) **R:**347–48
Lacquers **D:**72; **F:**508; **J:**50–51
  picture(s) **D:**71
Lacrimal glands **G:**226
Lacrosse (game) **L:**20–21
Lactase (digestive enzyme) **D:**164
Lacteals (in the intestines) **D:**165; **L:**350
Lactic acid (in sour milk) **M:**307
Lacto-ovo vegetarians **V:**293
Lactose (milk sugar) **M:**307; **S:**482
Lactose intolerance (digestive disorder) **M:**307
Lacto vegetarians **V:**293
Ladakh (Kashmir) **K:**197, 198
Ladd, William (American worker for peace) **P:**105
Ladder bucket dredge **D:**322
  picture(s) **D:**321

Ladders
  superstitions about **S:**504
  picture(s)
    on fire engines **F:**150
Ladies' Home Journal, The (magazine) **M:**19
  picture(s)
    1909 cover **M:**20
Ladies Professional Golf Association (LPGA) **G:**258, 260–61
La Digue (island, Seychelles) **S:**131
Ladino (language spoken by Jews in Spain) **S:**370
Ladinos (a people of Guatemala) **G:**394
Ladoga, Lake (Russia) **E:**346; **L:**25, 31; **R:**362
Lady (British title) **K:**277
Lady Amherst's pheasant
  picture(s) **B:**235
Lady, Be Good! (musical by Gershwin) **M:**554
Ladybird beetles (Ladybugs) **B:**127; **F:**482; **I:**236; **P:**290
  picture(s) **B:**126; **I:**244, 245, 250
"Lady of Shalott, The" (poem by Alfred, Lord Tennyson)
  excerpt from **T:**101
Lady's slipper (flower) **P:**317
  picture(s) **M:**327; **P:**319, 461
Lady Suffolk (race horse) **H:**235
La Farge, John (American glassmaker) **S:**418
Lafayette (Louisiana) **L:**323
La Fayette, Marie, Comtesse de (French novelist) **F:**439
Lafayette, Marquis de (French statesman and soldier) **L:22**
  honorary citizen of the United States **C:**324
  National Guard so named to honor Lafayette **N:**42
  Revolutionary War **R:**203
  wife saved from guillotine by Elizabeth Monroe **F:**166
Laffite (Lafitte), Jean (French-born American pirate) **L:23,**
  322, 327 *profile;* **P:**263 *profile*
Lafleur, Guy (Canadian ice hockey player) **I:**30 *profile*
La Follette, Philip F. (American statesman) **W:**206
La Follette, Robert Marion (American political leader) **U:**138
  profile; **W:**206
  picture(s) **W:**206
La Fontaine, Jean de (French writer of fables) **F:**3, 438
Lafontaine, Louis (Canadian statesman) **C:**83
Lafontaine, Mademoiselle (French ballerina) **B:**26
Laforet, Carmen (Spanish writer) **S:**392
LAFTA *see* Latin American Free Trade Association
Lagan (items thrown overboard from a ship that are attached to
  a buoy indicating the owner) **S:**158
Lagash (Sumerian city) **S:**487
Lager beer **B:**115
Lagerkvist, Pär (Swedish author) **S:**58i, 527
Lagerlöf, Selma (Swedish author) **S:**58i, 527–28
Lagomorpha (order of mammals) **R:**24
  picture(s)
    rabbit as example **M:**75
Lagoon **P:**3
Lagos (Nigeria) **N:**256
  picture(s) **N:**254, 256
Lagos Escobar, Ricardo (Chilean president) **C:**255
La Grande River (Quebec) **C:**62
Lagrange, Joseph Louis de (French mathematician) **M:**168
Lag screws **N:**3
La Guardia, Fiorello (American congressman and mayor) **L:23**
  picture(s) **N:**233
La Guardia International Airport (New York City) **N:**232
Laguna (Indians of North America) **I:**183
Lahaf (robe worn by Libyan women) **L:**188
Lahaina (Maui, Hawaii) **H:**52
Lahontan, Lake (Nevada)
  picture(s)
    Pyramid Lake a remnant of **N:**127
Lahore (Pakistan) **P:**39
Lahoud, Émile (president of Lebanon) **L:**123
Laidlaw Foundation **F:**391
Laika (dog sent into space) **S:**350
Laín Entralgo, Pedro (Spanish philosopher) **S:**392
Lais (short poems) **F:**436
Laissez-faire **E:**60, 298

La Jolla (California) **S:**30
Lake (chemical compound used in dyeing) **D:**377
Lake Champlain, Battle of (1814) **W:**11
Lake Champlain Maritime Museum (Vergennes, Vermont)
  V:314
Lake Charles (Louisiana) **L:**320, 321, 323–24
  picture(s)
    gambling casino **L:**319
Lake District (in northwestern England) **E:**233; **U:**52–53, 54
"Lake Isle of Innisfree, The" (poem by Yeats) **Y:**354
Lake Mead National Recreation Area (Arizona–Nevada)
  picture(s) **N:**123
Lake of the Clouds (Michigan)
  picture(s) **M:**260
Lake of the Woods (Minnesota–Ontario) **L:**34; **T:**104
Lake Placid (New York) **B:**271; **L:**33
Lakes **L:**24–34 *see also* the land section of country, province,
  and state articles; the names of lakes, as Erie, Lake
  acid rain **A:**9, 10
  Antarctic lake hidden beneath ice sheet **A:**293
  Asia **A:**438g
  Europe **E:**346, 348
  eutrophication **W:**63
  freezing of water **I:**3–4
  national lakeshores **N:**55
  North America has largest number **N:**287
  precipitation, effects on **R:**97
  salt lakes **O:**17
  South America **S:**281
  tides · **T:**196
  What seas are actually lakes? **L:**26
  table(s)
    world's largest lakes **L:**30
Lake Shore area (of Chicago, Illinois) **C:**218
Lake Shore Drive Apartments (Chicago, Illinois)
  picture(s) **M:**306
Lake Washington Ship Canal (Washington) **W:**21
Laki (volcano, in Iceland) **I:**37
Lakota (Indians of North America) **F:**43; **I:**180, 182
Lakshmi (Hindu goddess) **H:**141; **R:**155
  picture(s) **H:**139
"L'Allegro" (poem by John Milton)
  excerpt from **M:**312
Lalo, Edouard (French composer) **F:**446
Lam, Wilfredo (Cuban painter) **C:**609; **L:**64
Lamaism (Tibetan Buddhism) (religion) **B:**155, 425, 427;
  M:416; **T:**189, 191
  Dalai Lama **D:**12
Lamar, Mirabeau Buonaparte (American statesman and soldier)
  T:139 *profile*
Lamartine, Alphonse de (French poet) **R:**303
Lamb (meat of young sheep) **F:**331; **M:**196, 198
  picture(s)
    cuts of lamb **M:**197
Lamb, Charles (English essayist and critic) **E:**283–84, 321;
  L:34
Lamb, Mary (English writer) **L:**34
Lambaréné (Gabon) **G:**3; **S:**63
Lambert, Johann (Swiss-German mathematician) **G:**128
Lambert, Louis (pen name of Patrick S. Gilmore) **B:**40
Lambs (young sheep) **E:**44; **F:**502; **S:**147
Lambton, John George (English statesman) **C:**83; **O:**135
Lame duck amendment *see* Twentieth Amendment
Lamellae (parts of fish's gills) **F:**191
Lamentation, The (fresco by Giotto di Bondone)
  picture(s) **G:**211
Lamentations (book of the Old Testament) **B:**163
La Mettrie, Julien Offroy de (French physician and philosopher)
  E:297 *profile*
  picture(s) **E:**297
Laminae (thin plates or scales) **T:**355
Laminar airflow **A:**40
Laminated wood **F:**514; **W:**227
Lamizana, Sangoulé (president of Upper Volta) **B:**454
Lamm, Heinrich (German scientist) **F:**106

Lammergeiers (vultures)   V:394
Lamont, Johann von (Scottish-German astronomer)   A:471
L'Amour, Louis (American writer)   N:334 profile
Lamplighters (for lighthouses)   L:229
Lampman, Archibald (Canadian poet)   C:86
Lampreys (eel-like fish)   F:184
   picture(s)   F:185
Lamps   L:230–38
   electric lights   E:150–51
   kerosene lamps   K:235
   picture(s)
      Tiffany lamps   A:316
Lamy, John Baptist (French missionary)   N:192–93 profile
LAN (Local-area network) (of computers) see Local-area network
Lanai (one of the Hawaiian Islands)   H:51, 60
Lancashire (England)   E:233
   picture(s)   E:234
Lancaster, House of (English royal family)   E:241, 244; H:110
Lance-headed vipers   S:216
Lancelot (knight of King Arthur's court)   A:438
   picture(s)   M:289
Lances (weapons)   K:273
Lan Chang (Lan Xang) (former kingdom, Laos)   L:43
Land see also Agriculture; Soils; the agriculture section of
      country and state articles
   agricultural management   A:95–96
   alien land laws   A:460
   clearing of land by pioneers   P:251–52
   climatic control   C:361
   conservation   C:523–27
   environment and overcrowding   E:301
   feudal system of serfs working the land   F:102
   food supply   F:351
   forest land conversion to non-forest use   F:376
   irrigation   I:339–41
   land laws for pioneers   P:260–61
   Mexican land reform   M:250, 251
   Namibian redistribution of farmland   N:9
   Oklahoma land rush   P:261
   public lands   P:516–17
   real estate   R:112d–113
   surveying   S:519–20
   picture(s)
      Oklahoma land rush   P:260
Land, Edwin Herbert (American scientist and inventor)   P:215
Land Between the Lakes (TVA recreation area,
      Kentucky–Tennessee)   K:220
Land Between Two Rivers (nickname for Iowa)   I:291
Land breezes   W:82, 187
Land bridges (linking continents)   M:298
Land claims
   Aborigines, Australian   A:512, 517
   Hispanics and Indians in New Mexico   N:194
   Inuit   I:276; N:413
   Maine   M:50
   Yukon   Y:371
Landers
   lunar see Lunar module
   Viking space probes   S:362
Landfills (for burying of solid waste)   H:73; P:326; S:33
Land flowing with milk and honey (name for Canaan)   M:469
Landforms (of Earth's surface)   G:99 see also the land and
      landform sections of continent, country, province, and
      state articles
   continents   C:537–38
   physical relief maps   M:96
Land grants
   colleges   A:96; P:517; U:220
   railroads, history of   R:89
Landi, Stefano (Italian composer)   O:139–40
Land iguana
   picture(s)   A:275
Landing gear (of an airplane)   A:114–15
Landini, Francesco (Italian composer)   I:410; M:296–97

Landis, Kenesaw Mountain (American baseball commissioner)
      B:91
Landlords (owners of rental housing)   H:190
Landlord's Game   G:14
Land Management, Bureau of (United States)   I:256
Lando (pope)   R:292
Land of Enchantment (nickname for New Mexico)   N:180
Land of Lincoln (official nickname for Illinois)   I:62, 63
Land of Opportunity (nickname for Arkansas)   A:406, 407
Land of Pagodas (nickname for Myanmar)   M:557
Land of Sky-Blue Waters (nickname for Minnesota)   M:327
Land of Steady Habits (nickname for Connecticut)   C:508, 509
Land of 10,000 Lakes (nickname for Minnesota)   M:326,
      327
Land of the Dakotas (nickname for North Dakota)   N:322, 323
Land of the Midnight Sun (nickname for Alaska)   A:144, 145
Land of the Midnight Sun (nickname for Norway)   N:346
Land of the Shining Mountains (Indian name for Montana)
      M:428
Landon, Alfred Mossman (American statesman)   K:189 profile
   political anagram   W:236
Land reclamation see Reclamation, land
Landrieu, Mary (American political figure)   L:327 profile
   picture(s)   L:327
Landrum-Griffin Act see Labor-Management Reporting and
      Disclosure Act
Landry, Bernard (Canadian political leader)   Q:17
Landry, Tom (American football coach)   F:359
Landsat (United States satellite)   S:54
   picture(s)   S:53
Landsbergis, Vytautas (Lithuanian political leader)   L:263
Landscape gardening   G:26, 29
Landscapes (in art)
   American art   U:129
   Australian painting   A:501
   China, art of   C:274–75
   Cole, Thomas   N:224
   Dutch and Flemish art   D:318, 365
   English   E:261–62
   Hokusai   H:159d
   Japanese woodblock prints   J:50
   romanticism   R:303
   Turner, Joseph Mallord William   T:354
Land's End (England)   E:234
Landslides (movements of rock and soil down hillsides)
      A:557–58; P:161
   picture(s)   A:558; E:199
Landsteiner, Karl (Austrian physician)   B:261; T:273
Lane, Dick (American football player)   F:363 profile
   picture(s)   F:363
Lane, Ralph (English colonist)   T:165
Lang, Andrew (Scottish writer)   S:464
Lang, Fritz (German filmmaker)   S:83
Lange, David (New Zealand political leader)   N:242
Lange, Dorothea (American photographer)
   picture(s)
      Migrant Mother, Nipomo, California (photograph)
         D:120; W:273
Langévin, Paul (French physicist)   R:41
Langhorne, Nancy (British political figure) see Astor, Lady
Langi (a people of Africa)   U:4
Langland, William (English poet)   E:269
Langley (aircraft carrier)   U:118
Langley, Samuel Pierpont (American aeronautical pioneer)
      A:561
Langmuir, Irving (American scientist and engineer)   L:35, 235
Langston, John Mercer (American educator and diplomat)
      A:79h; V:359 profile
Langton, Stephen (English theologian)   E:239; M:26
Language arts   L:36 see also Compositions; Grammar; Letter
      writing; Reading; Reports; Spelling
   handwriting   H:22–25
   learning disorders   L:107
   punctuation   P:541–44

Language arts (cont.)
    reading   **R:**108–11
    speech   **S:**395–96
    spelling   **S:**398–400
    vocabulary   **V:**373–74
Languages   **L:**37–40 *see also* Alphabet; Dialects; Grammar;
    Linguistics; Semantics; Speech; Universal languages;
    Writing systems; individual country articles; the
    names of principal languages and language groups
    Africa   **A:**56–57
    African tone languages   **A:**79
    alphabet   **A:**194–94c
    Anglo-Saxon (Old English) in *Beowulf*   **B:**144a–144b
    animal signals   **A:**284
    anthropological studies   **A:**302–3
    Asia   **A:**445
    baby's talk   **B:**4
    Bible translations   **B:**157–58
    child development   **C:**225–26
    Chinese   **C:**258
    Christmas greetings in ten languages   **C:**301
    communication by speech and writing   **C:**463
    computer programming languages   **C:**483
    days of the week in five languages   **D:**46
    dictionaries   **D:**156–57
    Europe   **E:**352–53
    folk speech   **F:**307
    French is official language of many countries   **F:**433
    grammar: the way a language works   **G:**288–90
    Grimm, Jacob, made the first scientific study of German
      grammar   **G:**382
    Hawaiian   **H:**55
    India's regional languages   **I:**117
    Inuit-Inupiaq language family   **I:**273, 276
    Japanese   **J:**30
    judging literature   **L:**259–60
    lack of a common language is a problem in many countries'
      schools   **E:**75
    Latin once a world language   **L:**74
    North America   **N:**298
    phonics   **P:**194
    pronunciation   **P:**486
    Romany (gypsy)   **G:**434
    semantics   **S:**116
    slang   **S:**191
    South America   **S:**285, 288
    speech   **S:**395–96
    spelling   **S:**398–400
    taxonomy: a kind of universal language   **T:**29
    tongue twisters   **T:**225–26
    treaties   **T:**298
    universal *see* Universal languages
    word origins   **W:**238–41
    writing   **W:**329–32
    map(s)
      North America   **G:**102
Languedoc Canal *see* Canal du Midi
Langurs (monkeys)   **M:**422
    picture(s)   **M:**422
La Niña (Pacific Ocean current)   **W:**83
Lanolin (fat from wool)   **C:**560; **F:**109; **S:**147; **W:**78, 235
L'Anse aux Meadows (Newfoundland and Labrador)   **C:**79;
    E:312; **N:**145, 147; **V:**343
    picture(s)   **N:**147
Lansing (capital of Michigan)   **M:**265, 267–68
    picture(s)   **M:**269
Lansky, Meyer (Polish-born American mobster)   **O:**225 *profile*
Lanston, Tolbert (American inventor)   **T:**371
Lantern Festival (in China)   **H:**161
Lanterns (protective casings for lights)   **L:**232–33
    picture(s)   **F:**296
Lanterns, Feast of the (Japan)   **J:**32
Lanthanide series (of elements)   **E:**168, 170
Lanthanum (element)   **E:**170, 174

Lanting, Frans (Dutch photographer)   **P:**218 *profile*
    picture(s)
      photograph of albatross   **P:**218
Lao (Asian people)   **L:**41, 43
Laocoön (in Greek mythology)   **T:**316
Lao Lishi (Chinese diver)   **O:**119
Laos   **L:**41–43
    Buddhism   **B:**424, 427
    economy   **S:**332
    Geneva Accords   **G:**93
    Vientiane   **S:**334
    World War II   **W:**298
    picture(s)
      farmers' market   **S:**332
      flag   **F:**234
      Mekong River   **L:**41
      monks   **L:**42
      women planting rice   **L:**43
Lao She (Chinese writer)   **C:**279
Lao Theung *see* Kha
Laotian Americans
    picture(s)   **A:**458
Lao-tzu (Lao-tse; Lao-tsze) (Chinese philosopher)   **C:**278;
    R:151
La Palma (El Salvador)   **E:**197–98
Laparoscopy (surgery through very small incisions)   **S:**515
La Pasión River (Guatemala)   **G:**396
La Paz (capital of Bolivia)   **B:**308, 309
    picture(s)   **B:**309
Lap dogs *see* Toy dogs
Lapilli (rock fragments)   **V:**383
Lapis lazuli (Lazurite) (gemstone)   **D:**70; **G:**73
Laplace, Pierre Simon, Marquis de (French mathematician and
    astronomer)   **A:**476 *profile;* **M:**168
Lapland   **L:**44–45; **S:**58f
    Arctic region   **A:**380
    Finland   **F:**134
    Norway   **N:**344
    map(s)   **L:**45
    picture(s)
      reindeer   **E:**351; **F:**134; **R:**138
      Sami couple guiding tourists   **L:**44
La Plata (Spanish viceroyalty)   **S:**293
La Plata, Río de *see* Plata, Río de la
Lappeenranta (Finland)   **F:**135, 137
Lapps (European people) *see* Lapland; Sami
Laps (rolls of raw cotton)   **C:**569
Lapta (Russian bat-and-ball game)   **R:**360; **U:**36
Laptev Sea   **O:**46
Laptop computers   **C:**480; **O:**55
    picture(s)   **C:**481
Laramie (Wyoming)   **W:**338, 341
Larboard (port or left side of a ship)   **S:**154
Larceny (crime)   **J:**167
Lard (fat obtained from hogs)   **O:**79, 80
Lardner, Ring (American writer)   **M:**273 *profile*
Lardner, Ring, Jr. (American film writer)   **U:**13
Large Glass, The (artwork by Duchamp)   **D:**344
Large intestine (of the body)   **B:**282; **D:**163, 165
Large numbers, law of (in mathematics)   **I:**251
Large-print books   **B:**257
Largo (musical term)   **M:**536
Lariat (rope)   **C:**577; **K:**286; **R:**336
Larible, David (Italian-born American clown)   **C:**310
Larionov, Igor (Russian hockey player)   **I:**31
Larionov, Mikhail (Russian artist)   **R:**378
Lark bunting (bird)
    picture(s)   **C:**431
Larkin, Philip (English poet)   **E:**290
Lark's head knot (in macramé)   **M:**7b
    picture(s)   **M:**7a
Larkspur (Delphinium) (flowering plant)
    picture(s)   **G:**27
Larnaca (Cyprus)   **C:**617
La Rochefoucauld, François, Duc de (French writer)   **F:**439

Larra, Mariano José de (Spanish writer) S:389
Larsen, Don (American baseball pitcher) B:93
Larsen, Henry A. (Canadian sailor) N:339
Larvae (early forms of animals that must undergo
        metamorphosis) M:237–38
    amphibians A:223
    ants A:321, 322
    bees B:119
    beetles B:125, 127
    butterflies and moths B:475–76; H:261
    crabs C:581
    crustaceans C:602
    eels E:94
    eggs and embryos E:96
    frogs and toads see Tadpoles
    insects I:232
    mollusks M:407
    shrimps S:168
    ticks T:192
    zooplankton P:283, 284
    picture(s)
        bees B:118
        insects I:244
Laryngitis (inflammation of the larynx) D:191
Larynx (voice box) D:191; L:343; V:377
    respiratory system B:282–83
    speech S:395, 396
La Salle, Robert Cavelier, Sieur de (French explorer) L:46
    Canada C:80
    exploration of the New World E:408
    Louisiana, history of L:314, 326
    Mississippi River I:74; M:360, 364
    Missouri M:379
    Ohio River O:78
    Saint Lawrence River S:14
    Tennessee, history of T:84
    Texas, history of T:137
La Scala (opera house, Milan)
    picture(s) I:411
Las Casas, Bartolomé de (Spanish missionary and writer) L:67
Lascaux Cave (France)
    picture(s) P:436
Las Cruces (New Mexico) N:187, 189
Laser diodes T:276
Laserdisc players T:66
Laser guide stars (used to align telescopes) L:46d
    picture(s) L:46d
Lasers (devices for amplifying light waves) L:46a–46d
    bar codes read by A:532
    cane for the blind B:257
    communication, advances in C:467, 468
    compact discs S:267a
    dermatology D:124
    digital recording of music H:133
    DVD players and recorders V:332f, 332g
    electronics E:160
    experimental aircraft powered by A:572
    fiber optics F:107; T:48, 54
    gravure printing P:477
    gyroscope G:438
    holography P:208
    laser mirror on moon S:340h
    light L:226
    planetarium laser systems P:272
    plastics manufacturing P:329
    science, milestones in S:74
    semiconductors M:153
    Townes, Charles I:283
    welding W:118
    diagram(s) L:46a
    picture(s) L:46d, 237
        air pollution research E:217
        construction uses T:337
        dermatology D:123
    glaucoma diagnosis L:46c
    metal cutting L:46b
    projection system L:46a
Laser scanning confocal microscopes M:284–85
Las Minas, Cerro (mountain, Honduras) H:206
Lassen Peak (California) C:18
Lassoing (catch-roping) K:286; R:335
Lassus, Roland de (Belgian composer) C:283; D:373;
        R:173–74
Last (foot-shaped form used in shoemaking) S:160
Last Frontier (nickname for Alaska) A:144, 145
Last Judgment (fresco by Michelangelo) M:257; V:281
    picture(s) M:256
Lastman, Pieter (Dutch artist) R:156
Last of the Mohicans, The (novel by James Fenimore Cooper)
        C:549
    excerpt from C:549–50
Last Supper (of Jesus Christ) J:87–88 see also Eucharist
    Holy Thursday E:43
Last Supper, The (painting by Dierik Bouts)
    picture(s) D:362
Last Supper, The (painting by Leonardo da Vinci) L:153
    picture(s) A:328
"Last Word of a Bluebird, The" (poem by Robert Frost) F:480
Las Vegas (Nevada) N:122, 125, 126, 129, 131
    picture(s) N:123
Latakia (Syria) S:549
Lateen sails T:283
Late fetal death see Stillbirth
La Tène (Iron Age culture) C:164
Latent period (time between exposure to occupational danger
        and appearance of symptoms) O:13
Latent viruses V:367, 369
Lateral buds (of plants) P:304
Lateral line system (of fish) F:192
Lateral pass (in football) F:358
Lateral undulation (movement of snakes) S:209–10
Lateran Treaty (1929) I:380, 390; R:294; V:282
Latexes
    carpet backing R:355
    paints for exterior use P:32
    rubber R:344–45, 348a
    synthetic latexes R:346
Latgale (province, Latvia) L:80
Lathes (machine tools) F:507; T:231, 232, 235; W:231
Latimer, Lewis Howard (American inventor) E:150; I:283
        profile
    picture(s) I:283
Latin America L:47–59; S:274–75 see also Central America;
        South America
    baseball B:85
    Bolívar, Simón B:305
    bullfighting B:450–51
    Christianity, history of C:295
    education E:75
    good neighbor policy M:427
    guerrilla warfare G:400
    holidays H:165, 167
    immigration H:144, 149; I:93
    Monroe Doctrine M:427
    Organization of American States O:221
    poverty P:418, 419
    segregation S:115
    theater T:162
    universities U:226
    map(s) L:54
Latin America, art and architecture of A:367; D:72–73;
        L:60–65
Latin America, literature of L:66–70; N:363
Latin America, music of C:406–7; D:340; L:71–73; P:163
Latin-American dancing D:27–28, 30–31
Latin American Free Trade Association (LAFTA) S:292
Latin American Integration Association (LAIA) S:292, 295
Latin Fathers see Fathers of the Church
Latin grammar schools E:81, 82, 83

Latin language   L:74–76; R:309
   abbreviations of Latin phrases   **A:**4
   ancient Roman civilization   **A:**239
   Bible, early Latin translation of   **B:**157
   days of the week   **D:**46
   education, history of   **E:**79, 81
   English language influenced by   **E:**265
   German language influenced by   **G:**174
   given names derived from   **N:**7
   humanism   **H:**284
   international language of scientific names   **K:**254
   Italian developed from Latin   **I:**404
   Old French   **F:**433, 434
   taxonomy   **T:**29
   word origins   **W:**238–39
Latin literature   L:74–76
   Aeneid   **A:**36; **V:**304–5
   Caesar   **C:**6
   Cicero   **C:**303
   Horace   **H:**227
   Livy's history of Rome   **L:**274
   novel, beginnings of the   **N:**358
   Ovid   **O:**283
   Renaissance interest in   **R:**159
   Roman drama   **D:**299
   Vergil   **V:**304–5
Latinos *see* Hispanic Americans
Latin Quarter (of Paris)   **P:**69
Latitude   L:77–78
   climate control   **C:**361, 362
   equator   **E:**308
   horse latitudes   **W:**189
   maps and globes   **M:**92, 94
   navigation   **N:**74
   temperature of environment affected by   **L:**202
   trade winds   **T:**268
Latium (plain on which Rome is located)   **R:**310
Latona (Roman goddess) *see* Leto
Latortue, Gérard (prime minister of Haiti)   **H:**12
Latosolic soils   **S:**237
La Tour, Charles (French fur trader)   **N:**138g
Latrines (for campsites)   **C:**47
Latrobe, Benjamin (American architect)   **C:**104; **U:**128
Latter-day Saints *see* Mormons
Lattices (grids)   **N:**381
Latticinio (glass design)   **G:**231
   picture(s)   **G:**230
Latvia   L:79–81
   disintegration of Soviet Union   **C:**460
   independence   **U:**44
   non-Slavic peoples in former Soviet Union   **U:**34
   World War I   **W:**290
   World War II   **W:**296, 312
   picture(s)
      flag   **F:**234
      girl wearing traditional bow   **E:**340
      Popular Front demonstration   **L:**81
      Riga   **L:**80
      woman in front of farmhouse   **L:**79
Lauan (Philippine mahogany) (tree)
   picture(s)   **W:**223
Laud, William (English prelate)   **E:**245; **P:**550
Laughing Cavalier, The (painting by Hals)
   picture(s)   **H:**15
Laughing gas *see* Nitrous oxide
Laughing hyenas   **A:**277; **H:**317–18
   picture(s)   **H:**317
Laughing philosopher *see* Democritus
Laughter *see* Humor
Launch vehicles (to send satellites into orbit)   **R:**257, 261; **S:**54
Laundromats   **L:**82
Laundry   **L:**82 *see also* Dry cleaning
   picture(s)
      pioneer life   **P:**255

Laura (heroine of Petrarch's poetry)   **I:**406
Laura Ingalls Wilder Award (book award)   **C:**240; **W:**170
Laurasia (primitive land mass)   **O:**16
Laurel (tree) *see* California laurel; Mountain laurel
Laurel and Hardy (American film comedy team)   **M:**489 *profile*
Laurel wreath (ancient decoration of merit)   **D:**69
Laurence, Margaret (Canadian writer)   **C:**87
Laurent, François *see* Arlandes, Marquis d'
Laurentian Library (Florence, Italy)   **L:**174
Laurentian Plateau *see* Canadian Shield
Laurentide Ice Sheet   **G:**224
Laurentius (antipope) *see* Lawrence
Laurier, Sir Wilfrid (Canadian statesman)   **C:**84; **L:**82; **Q:**16
   picture(s)   **C:**76; **P:**459
Lausanne (Switzerland)   **O:**116; **S:**544
Lava (volcanic molten rock)   **R:**266–67; **V:**380, 382–83
   caves   **C:**157
   ever-changing earth   **E:**15
   moon   **M:**452, 453, 455
   Venus   **V:**303b
   picture(s)
      caves   **C:**156
Laval, Carl Gustav de (Swedish engineer)   **M:**307; **T:**342
Laval, François (French bishop)   **Q:**19
Laval, Pierre (French political leader)   **W:**298
La Valette, Jean de (French knight of Malta)   **M:**64
Lavallée, Calixa (Canadian composer)   **N:**20
Lavalleja, Juan Antonio (Uruguayan patriot)   **U:**241
Laval University (Quebec City)   **C:**53; **Q:**19
Lavender (plant used for medicinal purposes)   **H:**119
Laver, Rod (Australian tennis player)   **T:**97 *profile*
   picture(s)   **T:**97
La Vérendrye, Pierre Gaultier de Varennes, Sieur de (French explorer)   **E:**408; **N:**335 *profile;* **S:**51
Lavin, Carlos (Chilean composer)   **L:**73
Lavoisier, Antoine Laurent (French chemist)   **C:**208–9; **L:**83
   named hydrogen   **H:**316
   nitrogen   **N:**262
   oxygen   **O:**288
   science, milestones in   **S:**72
   picture(s)   **B:**202; **S:**72
Law, John (American businessman)   **L:**327
Law and law enforcement   L:84–92 *see also* Civil rights; Lawyers
   abortion   **A:**8
   adoption laws   **A:**28
   air pollution, control of   **A:**125
   Anglo-Saxon basis of English law   **E:**237, 238
   animal rights   **A:**261
   arbitration, enforcement of   **A:**349
   automobiles   **A:**540, 547, 552
   Bill of Rights   **B:**181–84
   business organization, types of   **B:**470–71
   Canada   **C:**78
   capital punishment   **C:**104
   child labor laws   **C:**227
   citizenship, legal requirements for   **C:**322–24
   civil rights, protection of   **C:**325–26
   codes *see* Codes (of law)
   consumer protection   **C:**533–35
   copyright   **C:**555
   courts   **C:**574–76
   crime and criminology   **C:**584–86
   dairying   **D:**7, 9
   disabilities, discrimination in employment of people with   **D:**180
   divorce   **D:**230–31
   draft laws   **D:**293
   drugs, control of   **D:**330, 333
   endangered species, protection of   **E:**209, 210–11
   ethics   **E:**328
   Federal Bureau of Investigation   **F:**76–77
   flotsam, jetsam, and lagan   **S:**158
   food regulations and laws   **F:**345–47

French civil law in Quebec (Canada)   **C:**82
French law based on Napoleonic Code   **F:**473
Good Samaritan laws   **F:**157
government, forms of   **G:**272–73
government regulation of businesses   **B:**473
gun control   **G:**426
Hammurabi, Code of   **B:**5
Hittites   **H:**155
homosexuality   **H:**204
hunting laws   **H:**301
immigration, legislation on   **I:**91–93
international law   **I:**267–68
Islamic law   **I:**347–48
Jim Crow laws   **J:**109
jury   **J:**163–64
Justice, United States Department of   **J:**164–66
juvenile crime   **J:**167–70
legislation   **U:**163, 168–69
legislatures   **L:**137
Magna Carta   **E:**239; **M:**26
marriage laws   **W:**101
Marshall, John   **M:**111
narcotics, legal measures to control use of   **N:**15
naturalization laws   **N:**61
occupational health and safety   **O:**13
oceans, control of   **O:**29
patents   **P:**99
pioneer life   **P:**258–59
Plymouth Colony   **P:**347
police   **P:**363–68
postal inspectors   **P:**400
president's executive orders   **P:**450
prisons   **P:**480–82
refugees, protection of   **R:**137
Roman law   **A:**239; **R:**313
Russia   **I:**413d; **R:**370
sanitation standards   **S:**33
seat belt laws   **A:**552
Supreme Court of Canada   **S:**505–6
Supreme Court of the United States   **S:**507–10
trademarks are protected   **T:**266
traffic regulations   **T:**269–70
Treasury, United States Department of the   **T:**294–95
United States Constitution   **U:**145–60
What does it mean to be "admitted to the bar"?   **L:**90
wills   **W:**177
Lawman (English priest) see Layamon
Lawn bowling see Bowls
Lawn games
badminton   **B:**13–14
bowls or lawn bowling   **B:**350a
croquet   **C:**595–96
horseshoe pitching   **H:**246
tennis   **T:**88–99
Lawn sprinklers   **J:**90
Lawn tennis see Tennis
Law of see the inverted form as Moses, Law of
Lawrence (antipope)   **R:**292
Lawrence (Massachusetts)   **M:**145
textile strike (1912)   **M:**150
Lawrence, D. H. (English novelist)   **E:**289; **F:**116; **N:**361
Lawrence, Jacob (American painter)
picture(s)
illustrations in The Great Migration (book)   **C:**247
Lawrence, James (American naval captain)   **W:**10
Lawrence of Arabia (Thomas Edward Lawrence) (British archaeologist, soldier, writer, and diplomat)   **G:**399; **W:**283 profile
picture(s)   **W:**283
Lawrencium (element)   **E:**174
Laws see Law and law enforcement
Lawson, Henry (Australian writer)   **A:**500, 501
Lawton (Oklahoma)   **O:**89, 91

Lawyers   **L:**87 see also the names of lawyers
courts   **C:**574, 575, 576
divorce   **D:**230
jury trials   **J:**163, 164
Middle Ages   **M:**294
nurse attorneys   **N:**419
What does it mean to be "admitted to the bar"?   **L:**90
Lawyers' Committee for Civil Rights under Law   **C:**326
Laxness, Halldór (Icelandic writer)   **I:**36
Layamon (English priest)   **A:**438c; **E:**269
Layard, Sir Austen Henry (British archaeologist and diplomat)   **L:**171
Laye, Camara (Guinean novelist)   **A:**76d
Lay investiture (in Roman Catholic Church)   **R:**288
Laylat al-Qadr (Muslim holiday)   **I:**349; **R:**155
Layout (diving position)   **D:**225
picture(s)   **D:**224
Layouts (in bookmaking)   **B:**329; **C:**457; **M:**17; **P:**470
Layout tools (in woodworking)   **W:**231
Lazarus (in the New Testament)   **B:**160
Lazarus, Emma (American poet and essayist)
The New Colossus, excerpt from   **L:**169
Lazurite see Lapis lazuli
Lazy daisy stitch (in embroidery)   **N:**98
picture(s)   **N:**99
LCD see Least common denominator
L.C.D. see Liquid crystal display
LDL's (Low-density lipids)   **O:**80
Leaching (in soapmaking)
picture(s)   **D:**139
Leaching (of ores)   **M:**233; **O:**217
Leaching (of soils)   **I:**339
Leaching fields (for wastewater disposal)   **S:**33
Leacock, Stephen (Canadian economist and humorist)   **O:**135
Lead   **E:**174; **L:**93–94
automobile batteries   **B:**103b
galena, ore, cleavage of   **M:**315
glass, used in making   **G:**229
Missouri deposits   **M:**366, 371, 374–75
particulate pollutant   **A:**123
pencils   **P:**143
poisons in the home   **P:**356
pottery glazes   **P:**411
radioactive elements break down to form lead   **R:**65, 74–75
retardation, mental, can be caused by ingestion of   **R:**190–91
Roman plumbing systems of lead pipes   **P:**340
white lead a pigment in paints   **P:**32
white lead formerly used in cosmetics   **C:**560, 561
X-rays stopped by   **X:**351
table(s)   **M:**235
Lead (South Dakota)   **S:**321, 325
Lead crystal (glass)   **G:**233
Leaded brass (alloy)   **B:**410
Leading (adjusting line spacing in printing)   **T:**370
Leading tone (in music)   **M:**536
Lead pencils   **P:**143–44
What is the "lead" in a lead pencil?   **L:**94
Leaf (of a plant) see Leaves
Leaf-cutter ants   **A:**267, 322
picture(s)   **A:**323
Leaf-cutter bees   **B:**121
picture(s)   **B:**121
Leaf-legged bug
picture(s)   **I:**248
Leaflets (parts of compound leaves)   **L:**112
Leaf rollers (insects)   **I:**247
Leaf springs (of suspension systems)   **A:**551
Leafy sea dragon (fish)
picture(s)   **F:**187
League Championship Series (in baseball)   **B:**93
League of Nations   **L:**95; **W:**291, 294
approved British mandate over Palestine   **J:**84; **Z:**386

League of Nations (cont.)
    Canada **C**:84
    Coolidge opposed **C**:548
    Ethiopia **E**:333
    Geneva (Switzerland) **S**:544
    international relations **I**:270
    peace movements **P**:106
    slavery in recent times **S**:197
    United Nations charter has similar principles **U**:64
    United States, history of the **U**:192
    Wilson, Woodrow **W**:182–83
League of Women Voters **W**:212b
Leah (Biblical character) **B**:160
Leakey, Louise N. (Kenyan anthropologist) **L**:97
Leakey, Louis Seymour Bazett (British-Kenyan anthropologist)
    F:380; **L**:96; **S**:74
    picture(s) **L**:96
Leakey, Mary Douglas Nicol (British anthropologist) **L**:96;
    S:74
    picture(s) **L**:96; **S**:75
Leakey, Meave Gillian Epps (British anthropologist) **L**:97
    picture(s) **L**:97
Leakey, Richard Erskine Frere (Kenyan anthropologist) **L**:97
    picture(s) **L**:97
Leakey family (anthropologists) **L**:96–97
Leander (in Greek mythology) *see* Hero and Leander
Lean dough **B**:387
Leaning Tower of Pisa (Italy)
    picture(s) **I**:391
Lean-to (pioneer shelter) **P**:251
Leaphorn, Joe (fictional character) **M**:565
Leap year **C**:14, 15; **F**:74; **S**:111
Lear, Edward (English writer and artist) **C**:232–33;
    N:274–75, 276; **P**:353
    picture(s)
        illustration by Eckert for *Scroobious Pip* **C**:237
Learning **L**:98–106
    brain function **B**:367
    child development **C**:223–26
    Dewey's "learning by doing" **D**:144
    dreaming may strengthen **D**:320
    How does sleep affect learning? **L**:104
    learning disorders **L**:107–8
    Pavlov's discovery of the conditioned reflex **P**:103
    play **K**:246–50; **P**:333–34
    programmed instruction **P**:483
    sleep, importance of **S**:198
    study, methods of **S**:470–72
    tests and test taking **T**:118–23
Learning disorders **D**:178; **L**:106, 107–8; **M**:223–24
Learning from Las Vegas (book by Venturi, Brown, and Izenour)
    A:376
Learning resources centers *see* Media centers
Leary, J. Scott (American swimmer) **S**:536
Lease (real estate contract) **R**:112d, 113
Least bitterns (wading birds) **H**:124
Least common denominator (LCD) **F**:399
Leather **L**:109–11 *see also* Fur
    animal rights supporters avoid using **A**:261
    armor **A**:423
    books on parchment and vellum **B**:319–20
    dolls made of **D**:268
    rope **R**:334
    shoes **S**:160
Leatherbacks (turtles) **T**:355
Leathercraft **I**:358; **N**:257
Leathernecks (nickname for Marines) **U**:122
Leatherstocking Tales (novels by James Fenimore Cooper)
    A:208; **C**:549
Leavened breads **B**:385–87, 388a; **F**:89
Leavenworth (Kansas) **P**:480
Leavers machine (for lace making) **L**:19
Leaves (of plants) **L**:112–18; **P**:305–6
    collections, how to make and keep **L**:115
    foliar (leaf) feeding of plants **F**:482
    food from plants **F**:329–30; **P**:297
    photosynthesis **P**:219
    rain-forest plants **R**:99
    trees and their leaves **T**:301–4, 307–8
    Why do leaves change color in the autumn? **P**:306
    picture(s)
        balanced design, example of **D**:132
Leaves of Grass (book of poetry by Walt Whitman) **W**:167
Leavitt, Henrietta Swan (American astronomer) **A**:476 *profile*
    picture(s) **A**:476
Lebanon **A**:347; **L**:119–23
    Arabic literature **A**:342
    civil war **M**:305
    Israeli invasion **I**:376
    Syria, relations with **S**:552
    picture(s)
        flag **F**:234
        Syrian troops patrolling **L**:123
Lebanon Mountains (Middle East) **L**:120
LeBel, Louis (Canadian Supreme Court justice)
    picture(s) **S**:505
Lebombo Plateau (Swaziland) **S**:521
Le Brun, Charles (French baroque artist) **F**:427, 510; **P**:72;
    T:22
Le Carré, John (English writer) **M**:565 *profile*
Lechfeld, Battle of (955) **O**:258
LeClair, John (American hockey player) **V**:318 *profile*
Le Corbusier (French architect) **L**:124
    India, art and architecture of **I**:139
    modern architecture **A**:374, 375; **F**:432
    picture(s)
        Notre Dame du Haut (Ronchamp, France) **A**:375
Lecuna, Juan Vicente (Venezuelan composer) **L**:73
Lecuona, Ernesto (Cuban musician) **C**:609
Leda (in Greek mythology) **G**:366, 368
Lederer, John (American explorer) **W**:136
Ledger lines (in musical notation) **M**:534, 536
Ledgers (in bookkeeping) **B**:312
LED's *see* Light-emitting diodes
Lee, Ann Hill Carter (mother of Robert E. Lee) **L**:127
Lee, Charles (American soldier) **R**:204
Lee, Francis Lightfoot (American political figure) **L**:127
    picture(s) **L**:127
Lee, Harper (American novelist) **A**:143 *profile*
Lee, Henry "Light Horse Harry" (American officer) **L**:127;
    R:208; **W**:37
    picture(s) **L**:127
Lee, Jason (Canadian-born American pioneer) **O**:211, 214
    profile, 216, 276
Lee, Manfred B. (American author) *see* Queen, Ellery
Lee, Matilda (first wife of Henry "Light Horse Harry" Lee)
    L:127
Lee, Peggy (American singer) **N**:334 *profile*
Lee, Philip Ludwell (American statesman) **L**:127
Lee, Richard (American statesman; 1647–1715) **L**:127
Lee, Richard (English-born American statesman; 1618–1664)
    L:127
Lee, Richard Henry (American political leader; 1732–1794)
    D:60; **L**:127
    picture(s) **L**:127
Lee, Robert E. (American military leader) **L**:125–26, 127
    Arlington House memorial **N**:27; **V**:354
    Brown, John **V**:360
    Civil War **C**:336, 339, 340–41, 343, 347, 497
    Grant and Lee **G**:295
    holiday on his birthday **H**:165
    lost United States citizenship **C**:324
    Mexican War **M**:239b
    picture(s) **C**:341, 495; **L**:125
        Civil War **C**:346
Lee, Sammy (American diver) **A**:459; **D**:229
Lee, Spike (American film director) **M**:495 *profile*, 497
    picture(s) **M**:495
Lee, Thomas (American statesman) **L**:127

Lee, Tsung Dao (Chinese American physicist)   A:459
Leeches (worms)   W:319, 321
Leeds (England)   U:59
Lee family (in American history)   L:127
Leek (plant)   O:123; V:290
Lee Mansion (Virginia) see Arlington House, The Robert E. Lee Memorial
Lee Teng-hui (president of Taiwan)   C:271; T:9
Leeuwenhoek, Anton van (Dutch naturalist)   L:128; M:208a–208b
    advances in biology   B:201
    lenses, history of   L:141–42
    microbiology   M:277
    microscopes   M:286; O:179
    protozoans   P:495
    science, milestones in   S:71
    picture(s)   B:201; L:128; M:278
Leeward (away from the wind)   C:363
Leeward Islands (Caribbean island group)   C:113
Lefkosia (Cyprus) see Nicosia
Left Bank (of the Seine, Paris)   P:68
Left-handedness, handwriting problems of   H:24–25
Left wing (political group)   P:372
Legal holidays (in the United States)   H:164
Legalists (Chinese philosophers)   C:268
Legal profession see Lawyers
Legal tender (currency)   D:263; M:415 see also Paper money
Legato (Slurred notes) (in musical notation)   M:536, 539
Legend (life of a saint)   S:18c
Legend cycle (series of legends about one subject)   L:130
"Legend of Sleepy Hollow, The" (story by Washington Irving)   L:129
Legendre, Adrien Marie (French mathematician)   M:168
Legends   L:129–36 see also Folklore; Mythology
    Alfred and the cakes   A:179
    Appleseed, Johnny   A:333
    Archimedes and the golden crown   A:363
    Arthur, King   A:438–38c
    Australian Aborigines   A:498
    Chicago fire and Mrs. O'Leary's cow   C:220
    children's books, list of   C:243–44
    communication, history of   C:463
    compared to mythology   M:569
    dragons   D:295
    fairies   F:9–12
    Faust   F:72–73
    fire throughout history   F:142
    folklore, kinds of   F:307
    giants   G:201–3
    glassmaking, origin of   G:229
    Groundhog Day in February   F:74
    Holy Grail in early French literature   F:436; H:175
    Japanese legend of the Sun Goddess   J:40
    Loch Ness monster   L:281
    "The Pied Piper of Hamelin" (poem by Browning), excerpt from   B:413
    Robin Hood   L:134–36; R:251
    Roland and Oliver   L:131–34
    Romans and the Sabine women   R:310
    Romulus and Remus   R:309–10
    unicorns   U:30
    "Vanishing Hitchhiker, The"   L:131
    What happened to the princes in the Tower?   E:241
    picture(s)
        Devils Tower   V:382
Legends (Keys) (of maps)   M:96
    picture(s)   M:92, 93, 95
Léger, Fernand (French painter)   C:612; L:136
    picture(s)
        City, The   L:136
Legionnaires' disease (type of pneumonia)   D:198–99
Legion of Merit (American award)
    picture(s)   D:70

Legislation (lawmaking)   L:86
    California citizen proposals   C:29
    direct see Initiative, referendum, and recall
    how legislatures function   L:137
    president's legislative powers   P:450–51
    United States   U:163, 166–67, 168
Legislative branch (of the United States government)   U:163, 164, 168–69
Legislative waivers (in juvenile justice)   J:170
Legislatures   L:137; P:83–84 see also individual country and state articles for detailed information on national and state legislatures
    Kansas' Legislative Co-ordinating Council   K:185–86
    Nebraska's unicameral state legislature   N:91
    state legislatures   S:438
    United States, Congress of the   U:137–44
    Virginia's General Assembly is oldest legislature in America   V:355
Legnano, Battle of (1176)   H:178
Legs (of animals)
    beetles   B:124
    birds   B:220
    bones of the human leg   F:79; S:184
    centipedes and millipedes   C:168
    insects   I:230–31, 241
    picture(s)
        artificial   D:178
Legs (of triangles)   T:312
Leguía, Augusto (Peruvian dictator)   P:165
LeGuin, Ursula K. (American writer)   O:214–15 profile; S:79, 81 profile, 82
    picture(s)   S:81
Legumes (plants of the pea and bean family)   A:90
    cooking   C:543
    fertilizers   F:97
    food from plants   P:296
    food shopping   F:349
    nitrogen fixation   P:314
Leh (Kashmir)   K:198
Lehár, Franz (Hungarian composer)   M:553; O:166
    The Merry Widow (operetta)   O:168
Lehman, Herbert H. (American politician)   N:225
Lehman Caves National Monument (Nevada)   N:126
Lehmbruck, Wilhelm (German sculptor)   S:103
Lehr (cooling oven for glass)   G:234
Leib, Mani (Yiddish poet)   Y:361
Leibniz, Gottfried Wilhelm von (German philosopher)   C:293, 490; L:138; M:167; O:60
Leica cameras   P:214
Leicester Square (London, England)   L:294
Leichhardt, Wilhelm Ludwig (Prussian explorer)   A:516
Leiden (the Netherlands)   N:120c; P:344, 345
Leiden University (the Netherlands)   N:120
Leif Ericson (Norse sailor and explorer) see Ericson, Leif
Leino, Eino (Finnish poet)   S:58i
Leipzig (Germany)   G:156
Leipzig, Battle of (1813)   N:13
Leishmaniasis (disease)   V:284
Leisure activities see Games; Hobbies; How to; Indoor activities; Sports
Leitmotivs (melodic themes in music drama)   G:188; M:536; O:146
Lei-Tsu (Chinese empress) see Hsi-Ling-Shih
Leivick, H. (Yiddish author)   Y:361
Lekhanya, Justin (Lesotho political leader)   L:157
Leko, Peter (Hungarian chess champion)   C:212
Leland, Henry M. (American manufacturer)   A:543
Lely, Sir Peter (English painter)   E:259
Lem, Stanislaw (Polish writer)   S:82
Lemelin, Roger (Canadian author and journalist)   C:87; Q:15
    picture(s)   C:86
Lemercier, Jacques (French architect)   F:425; L:333
Lemieux, Mario (Canadian hockey player)   I:30–31 profile, 32
    picture(s)   I:31
Lemkin, Raphael (Polish-Jewish scholar)   G:96

Lemmings (rodents) **R:**277
Lemon (citrus fruit) **L:138–39**
LeMond, Greg (American bicyclist) **B:**177
Lemonnier, Camille (Belgian author) **B:**134
Lemon vine (plant) **C:**4
Lemoyne, Jean Baptiste (French founder of New Orleans) *see*
    Bienville, Jean Baptiste Lemoyne, Sieur de
Lemoyne, Pierre (Canadian naval commander and colonial
    governor) *see* Iberville, Pierre Lemoyne, Sieur d'
Lempa River (Central America) **E:**196
Lempira (Indian hero of Honduras) **H:**209
Lemurs (animals) **F:**83; **H:**128; **P:**456
    picture(s) **P:**455
Lena River (Russia) **R:**242, 243
Lendl, Ivan (Czech tennis player) **T:**97 *profile*
    picture(s) **T:**97
Lend-Lease Act (United States, 1941) **R:**326; **U:**195; **W:**295
L'Enfant, Pierre Charles (French army officer, engineer, and
    architect) **W:**36
L'Engle, Madeleine (American author) **C:**234 *profile*
Length (measurement) **W:**108–9, 110–12, 117
Lenin, Vladimir Ilich (Russian revolutionary leader) **L:**140;
    U:40, 41–42
    Communism **C:**473
    Leningrad (now Saint Petersburg) named for **S:**18b
    mausoleum in Moscow **M:**466–67
    Russian Revolution and Civil War **R:**371–72; **W:**289
    Stalin, warnings about **S:**419
    picture(s) **C:**472; **L:**140; **W:**272
        discarded statue **C:**472
        leading Bolshevik Revolution **E:**367; **R:**371
        May Day (1918) **U:**41
Leningrad (Russia) *see* Saint Petersburg
Lenni-Lenape (Indians of North America) *see* Delaware (Indians
    of North America)
Lennon, John (English musician and singer) **B:**108
    picture(s) **B:**108
Lenoir, Jean Joseph Étienne (French inventor) **A:**540; **I:**265,
    281
Le Nôtre, André (French landscape architect) **F:**394; **P:**72
Lenses **L:141–51**
    camera obscura **P:**210
    cameras **P:**199, 200, 202, 206–7, 213
    contact lenses **C:**535
    early use of **M:**286
    eye **B:**289; **E:**429, 430
    inventions **I:**280
    lighthouses **L:**228
    microscopes **M:**281–82, 284
    motion picture cameras **M:**479
    optical instruments **O:**178–82
    quartz crystals **Q:**7
    telescopes **T:**57, 58, 59, 60
Lent (pre-Easter period) **C:**116; **E:**43; **R:**154
Lenz, Siegfried (German author) **G:**182
Leo (constellation) **C:**529, 531; **Z:**387
Leo I, Saint (pope) **A:**490; **R:**292
Leo II, Saint (pope) **R:**292
Leo III, Saint (pope) **C:**290; **G:**158; **H:**176; **L:**151; **M:**290;
    R:288, 292
    picture(s) **H:**176
Leo IV, Saint (pope) **R:**292
Leo V (pope) **R:**292
Leo VI (pope) **R:**292
Leo VII (pope) **R:**292
Leo VIII (pope) **R:**292
Leo IX, Saint (pope) **R:**289, 292
Leo X (pope) **M:**202; **R:**158, 293; **T:**20–21
Leo XI (pope) **R:**293
Leo XII (pope) **R:**293
Leo XIII (pope) **L:**152; **R:**293, 294
León (Mexico) **M:**247
León (Nicaragua) **N:**246
León (Spain) **S:**376, 382
León, Fray Luis de (Spanish theologian and poet) **S:**388

León, Ponce de *see* Ponce de León
Leonard, Benny (American boxer) **B:**353
Leonard, Sugar Ray (American boxer) **B:**353 *profile*
Leonardo Bridge (Norway)
    picture(s) **N:**348
Leonardo da Vinci (Italian painter, architect, and inventor)
    I:396–97; **L:**152–54; **R:**159, 167
    aviation, history of **A:**559
    canals' miter gate invented by **C:**89
    Christianity and the Renaissance **C:**291
    contact lenses, idea of **C:**535
    drawing, history of **D:**317
    drawing of Vitruvian man **B:**204
    gears **G:**66
    helicopter, idea for a **H:**103
    Mona Lisa (painting) **L:**332
    painting, history of **P:**21
    parachute, idea for **P:**60
    Raphael influenced by Leonardo **R:**106
    scenery for court masques **D:**25
    picture(s)
        biology during Renaissance **B:**200
        Ginevra de' Benci (painting) **R:**168
        The Last Supper (painting) **A:**328
        Madonna of the Rocks (painting) **P:**21
        Mona Lisa (painting) **I:**397; **L:**153, 332
        Norwegian bridge based on his designs **N:**348
        plans for a glider **A:**560
        Self Portrait **L:**153
Leoncavallo, Ruggiero (Italian composer) **I:**412; **O:**160
Leonidas (Spartan king) **G:**343
Léonin (medieval French composer) **M:**296
Leonov, Aleksei Arkhipovich (Soviet cosmonaut) **A:**467;
    S:346 *profile*
Leopard (British warship) **W:**9
Leopardi, Giacomo (Italian poet) **I:**408
Leopards **L:155**
    cats, wild **C:**143–44, 145, 146
    snow leopard **E:**209
    picture(s) **C:**148; **L:**155
        dental checkup in zoo **Z:**393
        fur **C:**149
        stalking zebras and antelopes **B:**198
        taxidermy **T:**26
Leopold, Nathan (American murderer) **D:**38
Leopold I (king of Belgium) **B:**135
Leopold II (king of Belgium) **B:**135; **C:**502
Leopold III (king of Belgium) **B:**135; **W:**298
Leopold I (Holy Roman Emperor) **H:**2
Leopoldville (capital of Democratic Republic of Congo) *see*
    Kinshasa
Lepanto, Battle of (1571) **O:**260; **S:**157
Le Pen, Jean-Marie (French political figure) **F:**420
Lepers *see* Leprosy
Lepidoptera (scaly-winged insects) **B:**475
Lepidus, Marcus Amelius (Roman ruler) **A:**317, 495; **R:**316
Le Play, Frédéric (French economist) **S:**231
Lepper, Mark (American psychologist) **P:**510
Leprechauns (fairies) **F:**9
Le Prieur, Yves (French naval officer) **U:**27
Leprosy (Hansen's disease) **H:**51, 52, 60
Leptis Magna (Libya) **L:**189
Leptocephalus (eel larva) **E:**93, 94
Leptocyon (ancestor of dog family) **D:**240
Leptons (group of subatomic particles) **A:**489; **P:**232, 239
Lermontov, Mikhail (Russian poet) **R:**381
Lerner, Alan Jay (American lyricist) **M:**554
Lesage, Alain René (French novelist) **F:**440
Lesbians *see* Homosexuality
Lescot, Pierre (French architect) **F:**425; **L:**332
Lesh, Phil (American rock musician) **R:**262d
Lesotho **L:156–57**
    picture(s)
        flag **F:**234
        houses **L:**156

Less-developed countries *see* Developing countries and areas

Lesseps, Ferdinand de (French businessman)   **L:157; P:50; S:481**

Lesser Antilles (Caribbean island group)   **C:113** *see also* the names of islands in the group

Lesser apes   **A:325**

Lesser pandas *see* Red pandas

Lesser Sunda Islands (Indonesia)   **I:209**

Lessing, Doris (British writer)   **E:290**
   picture(s)   **E:290**

Lessing, Gotthold (German critic and fabulist)   **D:302; F:4; G:177**

Lesson plans (by teachers)   **T:37**

Let (in tennis)   **T:88**

Le Tellier, François Michel (French public official) *see* Louvois, Marquis de

Lethal injection (form of execution)   **C:104**

Lethbridge (Alberta)   **A:170**

"Let me win. But if I cannot win, let me be brave in the attempt" (motto of Special Olympics)   **S:394**

Leto (Latona) (Greek goddess)   **G:363**

Letsie III (king of Lesotho)   **L:157**

Letter, The (etching by Mary Cassatt)
   picture(s)   **E:326**

Letterman, David (American talk-show host and comedian)   **I:156–57** *profile*

Letterpress printing   **C:464; P:471, 472–74, 479**

Letters of the alphabet *see* Alphabet; individual letters

Letters patent (rights granted by early English kings)   **P:99**

Letter writing   **L:158–61**
   address, forms of   **A:21–22**
   autographs   **A:528**
   epistolary novels   **E:279; N:359**
   greeting cards   **G:375–76**
   letters to newspapers from their readers   **N:198**
   thank-you notes   **E:339**

Letting-out (of furs)   **F:503**

Lettuce   **V:289, 290**
   picture(s)   **C:26; L:112**

Lettuce coral
   picture(s)   **J:76**

Lëtzebuergesch (language) *see* Luxembourgisch

Leucippus (Greek philosopher)   **P:234**

Leukemia (disease)   **B:262; C:92, 94; D:195–96**

Leukocytes *see* White blood cells

Leukopenia (disease)   **B:262**

LeVasseur, Irma (Canadian doctor)   **Q:15**

Levassor, Émile (French engineer and auto racer)   **A:540**

Levator labii superioris alaeque nasi (muscle)   **M:520**

Le Vau, Louis (French architect)   **F:425; P:72**

Levees (to control floods)   **F:257; L:316; M:352; R:238**

Level (measuring tool) *see* Spirit level

Leven, Loch (lake, Scotland)
   picture(s)   **U:53**

Lever action repeaters (guns)   **G:422**

Lever House (New York City)   **A:375; U:136**
   picture(s)   **A:374**

Leverrier, Urbain (French astronomer)   **A:471; N:111**

Levers (simple machines)   **W:248–49**
   Australian Aborigines' use of   **A:7**

Lever tumbler locks   **L:282, 284**
   diagram(s)   **L:282**

Lévesque, René (Quebec separatist leader)   **Q:15, 17**

Levita, Elias (Yiddish author) *see* Bokher, Eli

Leviticus (book of the Old Testament)   **B:159**

Levittown (housing development, Long Island, New York)   **A:375–76**

Levulose (fruit sugar) *see* Fructose

Lewanika (tribal king of Barotseland)   **Z:378**

Lewes (Delaware)   **D:100**
   picture(s)   **D:88, 96**

Lewes, Battle of (1264)   **E:239; H:109**

Lewes, George Henry (English editor and writer)   **E:189–90**

Lewinsky, Monica (White House intern)   **C:368**

Lewis, Andrew (British colonel)   **W:138**

Lewis, C. Day (English poet) *see* Day Lewis, C.

Lewis, Carl (American runner and long jumper)   **O:106** *profile*, 113, 114, 116; **T:259** *profile*, 263
   picture(s)   **O:113; T:259**

Lewis, Ida (American lighthouse keeper)   **R:225** *profile*
   picture(s)   **R:225**

Lewis, John L. (American labor leader)   **L:16** *profile*, **162**
   picture(s)   **I:303; L:16**

Lewis, Lennox (British boxer)   **B:351**

Lewis, Meriwether (American explorer)   **M:428; T:82** *see also* Lewis and Clark expedition

Lewis, Percy Wyndham (English artist)   **E:263**

Lewis, Shari (American ventriloquist)   **P:548**

Lewis, Sinclair (American novelist)   **A:214b–215; L:162; N:361–62**
   picture(s)   **M:338**

Lewis, Vaughn (prime minister of Saint Lucia)   **S:18**

Lewis and Clark expedition   **E:408; L:163–64**
   assists U.S. competition for fur trade   **F:521**
   commemorative nickel   **C:400**
   Fort Clatsop National Memorial is site of winter encampment   **O:210**
   fur trade in Missouri   **M:379**
   Idaho   **I:56, 59**
   Montana   **M:439**
   Nebraska   **N:91**
   North Dakota   **N:333**
   Oregon   **O:215**
   overland trails and waterways   **O:271**
   Sacagawea   **S:2**
   South Dakota   **S:325**
   Washington   **W:26**
   map(s)   **L:163**
   picture(s)   **O:271; U:180**

Lewiston (Idaho)   **I:51, 53**

Lewiston (Maine)   **M:43, 48**

Lewitt, Sol (American artist)   **M:396b**

Lexicographers (dictionary makers)   **D:156, 157**

Lexicon Technicum (early English encyclopedia)   **E:207**

Lexington (Kentucky)   **K:217, 218, 221, 222**
   picture(s)   **K:218, 221**

Lexington (Massachusetts)   **M:144; R:198; U:177**
   picture(s)
   Revolutionary War   **R:199; U:176**

Lexington (Missouri)   **M:370**

Leyden (Netherlands) *see* Leiden

Leyte Gulf, Battle of (1944)   **W:313**
   picture(s)   **W:312**

Lhasa (capital of Tibet)   **T:190**

Lhasa apsos (dogs)   **D:247**
   picture(s)   **D:244**

Lha-Tshesangma (Tibetan religious figure)   **B:155a**

Lhotshampas (a people of Bhutan)   **B:155**

Liabilities (in bookkeeping)   **B:311**

Liability insurance *see* Insurance, liability

Lianja (epic of Democratic Republic of Congo)   **A:76c**

Liard River (Canada)   **B:402**

Libby, Willard (American chemist)   **A:357**

Libel (statement harmful to a person's reputation)
   case of John Peter Zenger   **Z:380**
   case of Oscar Wilde   **W:169**
   mass media regulations   **C:471**

Liberal-Democratic Party (in Japan)   **J:40**

Liberal Empire (France)   **N:14**

Liberalism   **U:121**

Liberal Party, British   **E:253; G:225; U:62**

Liberal Party, Canadian   **C:75; P:373**
   King, William Lyon Mackenzie   **K:252**
   Laurier, Sir Wilfrid   **L:82**
   Pearson, Lester B.   **P:116**
   Saint Laurent, Louis   **Q:15**
   Trudeau, Pierre   **T:322**
   Turner, John Napier   **T:354**

Liberation Day (in Italy)   **H:167**

Liberation Tigers of Tamil Eelam (Tamilese separatists in Sri
Lanka) S:416
Liberator, The (newspaper) A:6, 79g; S:195
picture(s) A:6b
Liberia L:165–68; P:152; S:195
map(s) L:165
picture(s)
boys playing soccer L:165
flag F:234
girl selling vegetables L:165
logging L:166
Monrovia L:167
woman sowing rice L:167
Liberius (pope) R:292
Libertarian Party (in the United States) P:372
"Liberty, Equality, Fraternity" (watchwords of French Revolution)
F:469
Liberty, Statue of L:169
picture(s) I:87; N:51; U:72, 205
Liberty Bell I:113; L:170
picture(s) L:170; P:127, 181
Liberty Bell Center (Philadelphia, Pennsylvania) L:170
Liberty Bonds
picture(s)
World War I poster W:277
Liberty dollars D:263
Liberty horses (in a circus) C:307
Liberty Island (New York Harbor) L:169
Liberty Leading the People (painting by Delacroix)
picture(s) F:429
Liberty of the press *see* Freedom of the press
Liberty Party (in the United States) A:6b; P:376
"Liberty Song" (by John Dickinson) N:22
Libeskind, Daniel (American architect) A:376
Libra (constellation) C:529; Z:387
Librarians L:179–81
Libraries L:171–86 *see also* Indexes and indexing; the
education section of country, province, and state
articles
automation of circulation systems A:532
Bibliothèque Nationale (Paris) P:69
books for the blind B:258
Carnegie, Andrew C:115
first circulating library in United States P:131
first county-supported library in America W:339
first free tax-supported public library in United States
N:155
genealogical research G:76c
history of L:171–75
how to use your library L:181–84, 186
librarians and what they do L:179–81
Library of Congress (Washington, D.C.) W:30
mass communication C:471
modern library services L:175–79
National Archives N:24
presidential *see* Presidential libraries
reference materials R:129
storytelling S:464
Sumerians built earliest B:318
Vatican Library V:281
picture(s)
Dublin, University of I:318
storytelling S:463
Library and Museum of the Performing Arts (Lincoln Center, New
York City) L:248
Library Association, The C:240
Library associations L:180–81
Library Company of Philadelphia L:175
Library Journal (periodical) L:181
Library of Congress (Washington, D.C.) L:174, 178; U:165;
W:30
books for the blind B:258
classification system L:183
genealogical resources G:76d
picture(s) W:33

Library of Parliament (Ottawa)
picture(s) L:179
Librations (motions of the moon) M:446
picture(s) M:447
Librettos (words of operas) M:552; O:140–41
Libreville (capital of Gabon) G:3
Libya L:187–90
Organization of Petroleum Exporting Countries O:222
Qaddafi, Muammar al- Q:2
World War II W:299, 301, 307
map(s) L:188
picture(s)
desert L:187
flag F:234
nomadic herders D:129
oil fields A:64; L:189
oil refinery S:7
people L:187
Sabrata L:190
Tripoli L:189
Libyan Desert (Africa) E:102; S:478
Lice (insects) H:262–63; V:284
picture(s) V:285
Licensed practical nurses (LPN's) N:418, 422
Licenses
amateur radio operators (hams) R:63
aviation careers A:570–71
cartoon characters licensed by manufacturers C:129
doctors D:238
driving D:327
hunting H:301
lawyers L:91
marriage licenses W:101
private utility companies P:520
radio broadcasting R:58
real estate broker R:113
teachers T:38
television stations T:68
Licensing Act (Great Britain, 1737) E:277
Lichens B:210; F:498; R:138
picture(s) A:147
Lichtenstein, Roy (American painter) P:31
Licinius (Roman emperor) C:528
Licklider, J.C.R. (American scientist) I:286
Licorice (plants) C:99
Lidar (optical radar system) R:38, 39
Liddell, Alice (for whom Lewis Carroll wrote *Alice's Adventures
in Wonderland*) C:119
Liddy, G. Gordon (American political figure) W:60 *profile*
Lie, Jonas (Norwegian writer) S:58i
Lie, Trygve (secretary-general of the United Nations) U:70
profile
picture(s) U:70
Liebermann, Max (German painter) I:105
Liebig, Baron Justus von (German chemist) F:98
Liechtenstein L:191–92
map(s) L:191
picture(s) L:191
flag F:234
Lied (plural: lieder) (German art song) C:351; G:186;
M:542–43
Lie detection E:204; L:193
Lies (not telling the truth) E:328; L:193, 194
Lieta, Maris (Soviet ballet dancer)
picture(s) B:30
Lieutenant governor (in Canadian government) C:78
Life L:195–211
adaptation *see* Adaptation
aging A:82–87
bacteria in the cycle of B:12
biological clocks L:203–4
biology is the study of living things B:195–204
blood is called the river of life B:259
carbon compounds C:106

cells are the basic units of life   **C:**159
cycles *see* Life cycles
death   **D:**51
Earth, history of   **E:**24–29
ecology   **E:**53–55
eggs and embryos   **E:**95–98
endangered species   **E:**208–11
energy and life   **E:**214–15
environment, problems of   **E:**299–306
evolution   **E:**372–79
food chains in *see* Food chains
fossil story of past life   **F:**383–88
genetics   **G:**77–91
hibernation   **H:**126–28
How many kinds of living things are there?   **K:**259
Is cloning a way to create new life?   **L:**210
kingdoms of living things   **K:**253–59
moon, life on   **C:**421; **M:**453–54
most forms could not exist in a vacuum   **V:**262
nature, study of   **N:**67–70
ocean environment   **O:**17, 18, 19–20, 23, 26–27, 29
origin of   **L:**209–11
photosynthesis in plants   **P:**219–21
plants necessary for all life   **P:**292, 294
reproduction   **R:**175–79
underwater exploration of life in the sea   **U:**25–26
virus is the simplest form   **D:**182
water is essential for living things   **W:**50–51
webs of   **L:**205
   table(s)
      Earth, history of   **E:**25
Life (magazine)   **M:**20
Life after death (religious belief) *see* Afterlife
Lifeboats (on ocean liners)   **O:**32, 33
Life cycles   **L:**196
   amphibians   **A:**223–24
   animal kingdom   **K:**255
   ants   **A:**321
   birds   **B:**228–39
   butterflies and moths   **B:**475–76
   cats, wild   **C:**144–47
   fish   **F:**194–98
   flowers   **F:**284–87
   fungi   **K:**257
   human beings   **H:**282
   mammals   **M:**67–70
   marsupials   **M:**114
   mosquitoes   **M:**471
   mosses   **M:**473
   plants   **K:**256; **P:**311–13
   picture(s)
      frog   **A:**223; **F:**478
      insects   **I:**232
Life expectancy *see* Life spans
Life insurance *see* Insurance, life
Life on other planets   **A:**476a–476b; **L:**211
   Europa (moon of Jupiter)   **J:**162
   Is there life on Mars?   **M:**109
   language created to communicate with possible
      extraterrestrial beings   **L:**40
   Mars   **M:**32; **P:**279; **S:**358
   radio-astronomy searches   **R:**70, 72
   SETI program   **S:**340c
   space exploration and travel   **S:**353–54
   space research and technology   **S:**362
   unidentified flying objects   **U:**31–32
Lifesaving *see* First aid; Safety
Life sciences (study of living things)   **E:**395–96, 397; **S:**66
Life spans (characteristic ages of death for people and animals)
      A:82–83, 86–87
   crocodilians   **C:**594
   dogs   **D:**255
   elephants   **E:**183
   highest and lowest countries, list of   **P:**388

horseshoe crab   **H:**245
increases in human life spans   **O:**98
insects   **I:**233–34
turtles   **T:**358
Life-support systems (for space exploration)   **S:**340h, 342–43
Liffey River (Ireland)   **I:**319; **R:**242–43
Lift (upward force opposing gravity)
   aerodynamics   **A:**38–39, 40, 41
   airplane flight   **A:**109, 115
   glider flight   **G:**237
   helicopter flight   **H:**104
   hydrofoil boats   **H:**315
   supersonic flight   **S:**501
Lifts *see* Elevators; Escalators; Hoisting and loading machinery
Ligaments (cords of tissue connecting bones)   **B:**278; **F:**160;
      P:226; **S:**183
Light   **L:**212–26 *see also* Bioluminescence; Color; Optical
      instruments; Sunlight
   biological clock, effects on   **B:**194
   bioluminescence (cold light)   **B:**205
   color   **C:**424–28; **R:**45
   constant speed: how shown by an interferometer
      R:140–41
   deep-sea fish, light organs of   **F:**183
   Earth receives light and heat from the sun   **E:**9
   effects in impressionistic painting   **F:**430; **M:**411
   energy   **E:**213
   fiber optics   **F:**106–7; **T:**48
   frequency in a gravitational field   **R:**144
   How do polarized sunglasses work?   **L:**222
   how light is measured   **L:**237
   Huygens and wave theory   **H:**310
   interior design considerations   **I:**259
   lasers   **L:**46a–46d
   lenses   **L:**141–51
   lidar (optical radar)   **R:**38
   lighting   **L:**230–38
   light waves, theories of   **R:**140
   magnetism and light   **M:**31
   meter, standard measure of the   **W:**110–11
   Michelson-Morley experiment   **R:**140–41
   mirage, cause of   **M:**341–42
   Newton's experiments with the spectrum   **N:**207
   ocean habitat zones   **O:**23
   optical instruments examine light   **O:**184–85
   phosphorescent paints   **P:**34
   photoelectricity   **P:**196–97
   photography   **P:**198–218
   photosynthesis   **P:**219–21
   physics   **P:**229–30, 235
   quasars   **Q:**8–9
   radiation   **R:**42, 46–47
   rainbows   **R:**98
   science, milestones in   **S:**73
   signals for communication   **C:**466
   solar cells   **B:**103c
   solar energy   **S:**239
   sun   **S:**488–97
   time and relativity theory   **T:**203–4
   underwater exploration   **U:**22
   X-rays and light rays   **X:**349
Light beers (with reduced alcohol and carbohydrates)   **B:**115
Light bulbs   **E:**150; **H:**93; **L:**234–35, 237
   picture(s)   **E:**145
Light-emitting diodes (LED's) (semiconductors)   **C:**370–71;
      T:276
Lighter-than-air craft *see* Airships; Balloons and ballooning
Light flyweight (in boxing)   **B:**351
Light heavyweight (in boxing)   **B:**351
Light horses   **H:**239–40
Lighthouse of the Pacific (nickname for the Izalco volcano)
      E:196
Lighthouses   **L:**227–29
   Apostle Islands (Wisconsin)   **W:**200

Lighthouses (cont.)
Fenwick Island (Delaware) **D**:96
Lewis, Ida **R**:225
navigational aid **N**:73
Pharos was a wonder of the ancient world **W**:219–20
Portland Head Light (Maine) **M**:44
Sandy Hook Light (New Jersey) **N**:172
picture(s)
Bass Harbor Head (Maine) **U**:77
Cape Hatteras **N**:307
Chesapeake Bay Maritime Museum Lighthouse
M:128
floating lighthouse with solar panels **P**:197
Lake Superior **M**:334
Montauk Point (New York) **N**:212
Portland Head Light (Maine) **M**:44
Wisconsin **W**:193
Lighting **L**:230–38
candles **C**:96
Edison's electric inventions **E**:72
electricity **E**:137–38, 150–51
how light is measured **L**:237
interior design **I**:259, 260, 261
kerosene lamps **K**:235
lighthouses and lightships **L**:227–29
neon and other noble gases **G**:61; **L**:224; **N**:105
photography **P**:207, 212
plays, stage lighting for **P**:337, 338
rules of good lighting **L**:237–38
tungsten filament in light bulbs **T**:332
picture(s)
neon and other noble gases **L**:224
Lighting designers (of plays) **T**:158
Light interference *see* Interference (of light)
Light meter **L**:237
Light microscopes *see* Optical microscopes
Light middleweight (in boxing) **B**:351
Lightning **T**:184, 185–87
ball lightning mistaken for UFO's **U**:32
Franklin's rod **F**:455
nitrogen in the air "fired" by lightning **N**:262
ozone produced by **O**:292
picture(s) **W**:79
Lightning bugs *see* Fireflies
Lightning rods **E**:138; **I**:281; **T**:187
Light rail systems **R**:81, 90
Lights, Feast of (Jewish holiday) *see* Hanukkah
Lightships **L**:229
Light therapy (in dermatology) **D**:124
Light verse **P**:353
Lightweight (in boxing) **B**:351
Light welterweight (in boxing) **B**:351
Light-year (unit of interstellar measurement) **A**:472; **S**:428;
T:204; **U**:211; **W**:117
Ligitan (island in Celebes Sea) **M**:59
Lignin (substance in wood) **P**:304; **W**:222, 227
Lignite (soft coal) **C**:388; **F**:488, 489; **N**:326
Lignum vitae (wood) **W**:227
Liguest, Pierre Laclède (French fur trader) *see* Laclède, Pierre
Ligurian Alps **A**:194d
Ligurians (people) **F**:404, 412; **G**:95; **I**:387
Ligurian Sea **O**:46
Lihue (Hawaii) **H**:50
Lilacs (flowers)
picture(s) **G**:36; **N**:151
Lilienthal, Otto (German aeronautical pioneer) **A**:561; **G**:237
picture(s) **A**:560
Lilies (flowers) **G**:46, 49; **V**:290
picture(s) **A**:133; **G**:37; **Q**:10a
Lilies of the valley (flowers) **G**:42
picture(s) **G**:44
Liliuokalani (queen of Hawaii) **H**:61 *profile*, 62
picture(s) **H**:61
Lille (France) **F**:410
Lilliput (imaginary country in *Gulliver's Travels*) **S**:530–32

Lilly, Bob (American football player)
picture(s) **F**:361
Lilongwe (ministerial and financial capital of Malawi) **M**:53
Lima (capital of Peru) **L**:239; **P**:163, 164; **S**:289, 293
picture(s) **L**:239; **P**:161; **S**:293
Lima beans (vegetables) **V**:289, 292
Limassol (Cyprus) **C**:617
Limbic system (structures in the brain) **B**:365
Limbourg brothers (Flemish painters) **D**:357; **F**:423
picture(s)
April (manuscript illustration) **D**:357
Limbus (a people of Nepal) **N**:107
Lime (calcium compound made from limestone) **R**:268
fertilizer **F**:96, 98
glass **G**:229
water purification **W**:57
Lime (citrus fruit) **L**:138–40
Limelight (motion picture, 1952) **C**:186
Limerick (Ireland) **I**:320, 323
Limericks **N**:274–75, 276; **P**:353
Limestone (Calcium carbonate) **G**:117; **R**:268
carbon **C**:106
Carlsbad Caverns **C**:155–56
cement made of **C**:165
gems result from impurities in **G**:71
harmful to home aquariums **F**:204
Indiana **I**:146, 151
lake basins, formation of **L**:27
marble **R**:271
shells of mollusks **S**:149
steelmaking, use in **I**:331
Limeys (nickname for British sailors) **L**:138
Limitations, statute of (law limiting period of time during which
legal actions may be taken) **L**:89
Limited duty officers (in the United States Navy) **U**:112
Limited nuclear war **N**:378
Limited Test Ban Treaty (1963) **C**:611; **F**:35
Limners (artists) **E**:258
Limoges (France) **E**:205; **F**:422
Limousin, Léonard (French artist) **E**:205
Limpets (mollusks) **M**:406; **S**:150
picture(s) **S**:149
Limpopo River (east central Africa) **Z**:382
Lin, Maya (American architect) **W**:32
Lincoln (capital of Nebraska) **N**:82, 86, 87, 89
picture(s) **N**:91
Lincoln, Abraham (16th president of the United States)
L:240–47; **P**:448
American literature **A**:211
amnesty for Confederates **A**:221
assassination as aftermath of Civil War **C**:347
Booth, John Wilkes **B**:335
Civil War **C**:336, 337, 340, 343, 347, 497
derringer used in his assassination **G**:418
Disney's Audio-Animatronic figure of **D**:216
Emancipation Proclamation **E**:200–201
Gettysburg Address **G**:191
Grant and Lincoln **G**:295
holiday on his birthday **H**:165
Illinois **I**:62, 70, 75
Indiana **I**:157
Johnson, Andrew, was vice president under **J**:117
Kentucky **K**:212, 220
quoted **Q**:22
Reconstruction Period anticipated **R**:116
Republican Party, rise of **P**:371
Thanksgiving Day proclamation **T**:154
Whitman's poems **P**:352–53; **W**:167
picture(s) **I**:75; **L**:240, 241, 244; **P**:447; **U**:186
at Antietam **L**:245
with family **L**:246
five-dollar bill **D**:261
Kentucky birthplace **K**:220
Lincoln-Douglas debates **C**:336; **L**:243

with McClellan **C:**340
Springfield home **L:**244
Lincoln, Mary Todd (wife of Abraham Lincoln) **F:**171; **L:**242
picture(s) **F:**171; **L:**246
Lincoln Boyhood National Memorial (Indiana) **I:**152
Lincoln Center for the Performing Arts (New York City) **J:**123;
L:248; **N:**230–31
Lincoln Continental (automobile)
picture(s) **A:**542
Lincoln County range wars (New Mexico, 1878–81) **N:**192,
193
Lincoln-Douglas debates **D:**288; **L:**243–44; **U:**185
picture(s) **C:**336
Lincoln Memorial (Washington, D.C.) **W:**32
picture(s) **L:**247; **S:**91; **W:**32
Lincoln National Forest (New Mexico) **N:**188
Lincoln Tunnel (New Jersey–New York) **N:**233
Lind, Jenny (Swedish singer) **B:**61
Linda Hall Library (Kansas City, Missouri) **L:**178
Lindbergh, Anne Spencer Morrow (American author) **L:**249
Lindbergh, Charles (American aviator) **L:**249 *see also* Aviation
aided Goddard's rocket research **G:**246
airmail pilot **P:**398
aviation history **A:**563
Charles A. Lindbergh House and Interpretive Center
(Minnesota) **M:**334
only civilian Medal of Honor winner **D:**71
picture(s) **L:**249
ticker-tape parade **U:**193
Lindegren, Erik (Swedish poet) **S:**58i
Linden (formerly **Mackenzie**) (Guyana) **G:**428
Linden (tree) *see* Basswood
Lindenwald (New York, home of Martin Van Buren)
picture(s) **V:**273
Lindgren, Astrid (Swedish author) **C:**239; **S:**528
Lindh, Anna (Swedish public official) **S:**529
Lindisfarne Gospels
picture(s) **I:**77
Lindros, Eric (Canadian hockey player) **I:**32
Lindsey, Benjamin Barr (American jurist) **C:**443 *profile*
Line (element in design) **D:**135
Lineage societies (whose members must have a certain
ancestry) **G:**76; **U:**121
Linear A (ancient script) **A:**237
Linear accelerators (atom smashers)
picture(s) **P:**238
Linear B (ancient script) **A:**237; **G:**353; **M:**562
Linear integrated circuits **T:**277
Linear motors **E:**152
Linear perspective (in drawing) **D:**313, 314
Linebacker (in football) **F:**358
Line defects (in crystals) *see* Dislocations
Line graphs **G:**311
Line illustrations **P:**470
Line Islands (in the central Pacific) **K:**265; **P:**9
Linen **F:**109
ancient Egyptians used for clothing **C:**374
textiles, history of **T:**143, 144
watercolor paper **W:**54
Linen-supply laundries **L:**82
Line of Demarcation **E:**405
Line officers (of the United States Navy) **U:**112–13
Line-powered clocks **C:**370
Line reflection (motion in transformation geometry) *see* Flip
Lines (for fishing) **F:**210, 214
Lines, geometric **G:**121
picture(s) **M:**169
Lines of force (electric and magnetic) **E:**140–41; **M:**29
picture(s) **M:**28
Line spectrum *see* Absorption spectrum
Lineup (batting order in baseball) **B:**80
Ling, Per Henrik (Swedish gymnast) **P:**223
Lingala language **C:**504
Lingonberries **G:**301
Lingua Cosmica (artificial language) **L:**40

Linguistic anthropology **A:**302–3, 304
Linguistics (study of languages) **A:**302–3
Linked hypertext documents (on the Internet) **I:**282
Linked verse (in Japanese poetry) **J:**52
Linking verbs **G:**289
Links (between World Wide Web documents) *see* Hyperlinks
Linnaeus, Carolus (Swedish botanist) **L:**250
biological classification **B:**202; **L:**207–9
botanical gardens **B:**342–43
nature, study of **N:**70
taxonomy **T:**27, 29
picture(s) **L:**250
Linné, Carl von (Swedish botanist) *see* Linnaeus, Carolus
Linocuts (linoleum prints) **L:**251
Linoleum-block printing **L:**251
picture(s) **L:**251
Linotype (typesetting machine) **T:**371
Linseed oil **I:**229; **L:**111; **O:**79, 81
Linsey-woolsey (home-woven cloth) **P:**255
Lint (cotton fiber) **F:**109
Lintel *see* Post and lintel construction
Linters (fibers of cottonseed) **C:**568
Linus, Saint (pope) **R:**292
Linz (Austria) **A:**521
Lion (constellation) *see* Leo
"Lion and the Mouse, The" (fable by Aesop) **F:**4
Lionfish **F:**201
Lion Gate (Mycenae, Greece)
picture(s) **G:**340; **S:**95
Lion King, The (animated cartoon) **M:**497
Lionni, Leo (Dutch-born American painter and children's
author) **C:**234 *profile*
Lions **L:**252
cats, wild **C:**144, 145, 146, 147, 148, 149–50
play **P:**334
vision **M:**67
picture(s) **A:**53; **C:**141, 144, 145, 146, 148; **L:**252
fur **C:**149
playing cubs **P:**334
in zoo **Z:**392
Lion's manes (jellyfish) **J:**76
Lip (part of the face)
muscle that curls the upper lip **M:**520
Lipase (digestive enzyme) **D:**164
Lipchitz, Jacques (American sculptor) **M:**391; **S:**104
Lipids (fatlike body compounds) **B:**187, 273, 295, 296;
L:199
diagram(s) **B:**297
Lipinski, Tara (American figure skater) **I:**45 *profile*
Liposomes (fat globules) **G:**89
Lippershey, Hans (Dutch eyeglass maker) **T:**60
Lippi, Fra Filippo (Italian painter) **I:**396
Lippmann, Walter (American editor and author) **J:**138 *profile*
Lippold, Richard (American sculptor) **S:**105
picture(s)
Encounter (sculpture) **D:**135
Lipreading *see* Speechreading
Lipstick (cosmetic) **C:**560
Liquefaction fractional distiller (for making liquid gases)
L:253
Liquefied natural gas (LNG) **N:**60
Indonesia is world's largest producer **I:**211
picture(s) **I:**210
Liquefied petroleum gas (LPG) **F:**488
Liquid air **G:**59
Liquid cooling systems (of engines) **A:**548
Liquid crystal display (L.C.D.) **C:**370, 371, 604; **W:**45
digital camera monitor screens **P:**203
television **T:**64
picture(s) **P:**205; **T:**67
Liquid crystals **C:**604
Liquid fuels **F:**487
coal liquefaction **C:**390
Goddard's rocket experiment with **G:**245–46

Liquid fuels (cont.)
  kerosene **K:**235
  liquid-propellant rockets **R:**257, 260
  missile fuels **M:**344–45
  new liquid fuels **P:**175
  petroleum **P:**173
Liquid gases L:253
  fluorocarbons **G:**61
  helium **H:**106
  hydrogen **H:**316
  liquids can exist in a range of temperatures **L:**254
  nitrogen **G:**59
  rocket fuels **R:**135, 259
  superfluidity **H:**92
Liquid lasers L:46b
Liquid measure W:115, 117
Liquid nitrogen N:262
Liquid oxygen (LOX) L:253
  Goddard's rocket experiment with **G:**245–46
  oxidation **O:**289
  oxidizer for rocket fuels **R:**260
  refrigeration **R:**135
Liquids L:254–55
  Archimedes' principle **A:**363
  astronauts: how they drink **A:**467
  defined **C:**204
  distillation process **D:**218–19
  floating and buoyancy **F:**250
  gases, liquefaction of **G:**59
  how heat changes matter **H:**89–92
  how to create layers of **E:**392
  hydraulic systems **H:**311–14
  lasers **L:**46b
  matter, states of **M:**172, 175
  osmosis **O:**239–41
  Pascal's Law **H:**311
  water **W:**47–57
Lisa, Manuel (American trader and explorer) **F:**521, 522
    profile; **N:**334 profile
Lisboa, Antonio Francisco (O Aleijadinho) (Brazilian sculptor)
    B:382; **L:**62
  picture(s)
    The Prophet Daniel **L:**62
Lisbon (capital of Portugal) **L:**256; **P:**393, 394
  picture(s) **C:**317; **L:**256; **P:**395
Lisping (speech disorder) **S:**397
Lissouba, Pascal (president of the Congo) **C:**506
Listening (one of the language arts) **L:**36
Listening posts (spies) **S:**407
Lister, Joseph (British doctor) **L:**257; **M:**208b; **S:**513
  picture(s) **M:**208b, 278
Lister's conchs (mollusks)
  picture(s) **S:**149
List making T:205
Liston, Sonny (American boxer) **A:**189; **B:**351
Liszt, Franz (Hungarian composer and pianist) **F:**447; **G:**187;
    L:257; **P:**242; **R:**304
  picture(s) **M:**543
Litanies (prayers) **E:**46
Litani River (Lebanon) **L:**120
Litchfield (Connecticut)
  picture(s) **C:**509
Liter (measure of volume) **W:**113
Literacy
  African education **A:**60
  developing lifelong readers **R:**111
  North America **N:**298
  Philippines has one of highest rates in Asia **P:**184
  tests required of immigrants **I:**91
Literary agents (for writers) **B:**324–25; **P:**524–25
Literary awards and medals see Awards, literary
Literary criticism E:288

Literature L:258–60 see also Africa, literature of; individual
    authors' articles, as Alcott, Louisa May; the literature of
    countries, as Germany, literature of
  Arabic literature **A:**341–42
  ballads **B:**24
  Bible **B:**156–67
  biography, autobiography, and biographical novel
    B:191–92
  children's see Children's literature
  Christmas literature **C:**299
  diaries and journals **D:**147–48
  drama **D:**297–307
  duels in **D:**350
  Egypt, ancient **E:**109
  essays **E:**321–22
  fables **F:**2–8
  fairies in **F:**12
  fairy tales **F:**19–32
  fiction **F:**113–16
  folklore **F:**304–12
  ghost stories **G:**200
  giants in **G:**203
  growth of national literature in Renaissance **R:**159–60
  Hispanic Americans **H:**147
  humanism **H:**284
  humor **H:**289–92
  literary terms, glossary of **L:**260
  magazine publishing **M:**19–20
  mythology **M:**568–77
  Nobel prizes **N:**265–66
  novels **N:**358–63
  oratory is thought of as spoken literature **O:**190
  poetry **P:**349–54
  Pulitzer Prizes **P:**533–38
  realism **R:**114
  romanticism **R:**303–4
  short stories **S:**161–65
Literature-based reading programs R:109
Literature for children see Children's literature
Litharge (compound of lead and oxygen) **L:**93
Lithium (element) **B:**103b; **E:**174; **M:**233
Lithography (printing technique) **G:**302, 308; **P:**402, 471,
    474–76
Lithosphere (soil and rocks of the ecosphere) **N:**63
Lithuania L:261–63
  disintegration of Soviet Union **C:**460
  independence **U:**44
  non-Slavic peoples in former Soviet Union **U:**34
  World War I **W:**290
  World War II **W:**296, 312
  picture(s)
    flag **F:**234
    Independence Day celebration **L:**263
    sheep in meadow **L:**262
    shrine **L:**261
Litigation (lawsuits initiated by lawyers) **A:**349; **L:**91
Litmus paper (for testing acidity or alkalinity) **S:**238
Litter (improperly disposed of waste materials) **P:**326
Litter (method of transportation) **T:**281
Litter boxes (for cats) **C:**140
Litters (groups of puppies born at the same time) **D:**251
Little, Frosty (American clown) **C:**310
Little, Malcolm (American civil rights leader) see Malcolm X
Little America (Byrd's Antarctic base) **B:**485
Little Bear (constellation) see Ursa Minor
Little Bighorn, Battle of (1876) **M:**428, 439, 440; **S:**325
Little Bighorn Battlefield National Monument (Montana) **M:**436
  picture(s) **M:**436
Little blue herons (wading birds) **A:**268; **H:**124
Little Blue Horse (painting by Franz Marc)
  picture(s) **G:**172
Little Brown Church in the Vale (Nashua, Iowa) **I:**298
Little Caesar (motion picture, 1930) **M:**491
Little Caesar (novel by Burnett) **M:**564
Little Colorado River (Arizona) **A:**395

Little Dog (constellation) *see* Canis Minor
Little Dorrit (novel by Dickens) **D:**151
Little Giant (nickname for Stephen A. Douglas) **D:**288
Little Havana (section of Miami, Florida)
    picture(s) **F:**265
Little House in the Big Woods (book by Laura Ingalls Wilder)
      W:170
    picture(s)
      Williams illustration **C:**245
Little House on the Prairie (book by Laura Ingalls Wilder)
    excerpt from **W:**171
Little House on the Prairie (television program) **W:**171
Little Ice Age (1640–1715) **S:**494
Little John (member of Robin Hood's band) **R:**251
Little Johnny Jones (musical by Cohan) **M:**553
Little League Baseball **B:**85; **L:264–67**
    international headquarters **P:**134
    Tee Ball **L:**266
"Little Match Girl, The" (story by Hans Christian Andersen)
    A:246
Little Mermaid (statue, Copenhagen, Denmark) **C:**551
    picture(s) **C:**552
Little Metropole (church, Athens) **B:**491
Little Moreton Hall (Cheshire, England)
    picture(s) **E:**258
Little Night Music, A (musical by Sondheim) **M:**554
Little Orphan Annie (game)
    picture(s) **G:**17
Little Pretty Pocket-Book (book by John Newbery) **C:**229
"Little Red Riding-Hood" (story) **F:29–32**
    picture(s)
      illustration by Gustave Doré **D:**286
Little Rhody (former nickname for Rhode Island) **R:**212
Little Rock (capital of Arkansas) **A:**406, 411, 413, 418, 419
    school desegregation **A:**79m, 79n; **S:**114
    picture(s) **A:**413
      school desegregation (1957) **A:**419
      State Capitol **A:**415
"Little Rose Tree, The" (poem by Rachel Field) **F:**124
Little Saint Bernard Pass (through the Alps) **A:**194d
Little Tear Gland That Says Tic-Tac (art by Max Ernst)
    picture(s) **M:**395
Little theaters (community theater groups) **D:**306
Little Tramp (character created by Charlie Chaplin) **C:**185,
    186
Little Turtle (Native American) **I:**156, 179 *profile*
Little Women (book by Louisa May Alcott) **C:**236
    excerpt from **A:**174–75
Liturgical drama *see* Religious drama
Liturgy
    Eastern Orthodox Churches **E:**45
    hymns **H:**321
    Protestant worship **P:**491
    Roman Catholic Church **R:**284
Livelihood support (for famine victims) **F:**45
Live oak (tree) **L:**317
    picture(s) **G:**133, 135
Liver **L:267–70**
    antibiotics may damage **A:**311
    digestive system **B:**281–82; **D:**163, 165
    energy use of liver cells **B:**297
    fish-liver oils **O:**79
    hepatitis affects the liver **H:**115; **V:**369
    living donors **O:**227
    sharks' livers help them stay afloat **S:**142
    diagram(s) **L:**268
    picture(s)
      color-enhanced view **L:**269
      healthy and diseased livers **L:**270
Live radio broadcasts (transmitted at the time of production)
    R:59, 60
Liverpool (England) **U:**49, 57, 59
Liverwort (plant) **P:**302
Livery (clothing in family colors) **G:**404; **H:**118

Livestock **L:271–73** *see also* Meat and meat packing; the
    agricultural section of continent, country, province, and
    state articles; the names of domestic animals
    agriculture, advancements in **F:**336
    Asia **A:**451
    Canada **C:**64
    cattle **C:**151–54; **D:**3–7
    cattle diseases in Britain **U:**56
    corn as feed **C:**558
    fairs and expositions **F:**13
    herded by dogs **D:**249, 256
    herding in Africa **A:**63
    llamas **L:**278
    pasture grasses and hay **G:**317
    railroad transportation **R:**84
    United States agriculture **U:**93
    veterinarians **V:**323
    picture(s)
      agricultural-fair prizewinner **F:**15
      early domestication **F:**336
Live television **T:**69
Living donors (of organs for transplant) **O:**227
Living fossils
    horseshoe crab **H:**245
    tuatara of New Zealand **N:**238–39
Living History Farms (near Des Moines, Iowa) **I:**298
Living history museums **M:**524
    Colonial Williamsburg (Virginia) **V:**354
    Jamestown Festival Park (Virginia) **V:**354
    Mystic Seaport (Connecticut) **C:**514
    Old Sturbridge Village (Massachusetts) **M:**144
    Plimoth Plantation (Massachusetts) **P:**347
    St. Mary's City (Maryland) **M:**128
    picture(s)
      Colonial Williamsburg (Virginia) **V:**347
      Mystic Seaport (Connecticut) **C:**509
      Olde Dover Days (Delaware) **D:**93
      Plimoth Plantation (Massachusetts) **M:**144
      Revolutionary War re-enactment **M:**144
      St. Mary's City (Maryland) **M:**128
Living standards *see* Standard of living
Livingston, Edward (American public official) **L:**274
Livingston, Philip (American merchant, 1686–1749) **L:**274
Livingston, Philip (American patriot, 1716–1778) **L:**274
Livingston, Robert (Scottish-American merchant, 1654–1728)
    L:273–74
Livingston, Robert (American merchant, 1708–1790) **L:**274
Livingston, Robert (Bob) (American public official, 1943–)
    L:274
Livingston, Robert R. (American patriot, 1746–1813) **F:**491;
    L:274, 330
    picture(s) **L:**273
Livingston, William (American political figure) **L:**274
Livingstone, David (Scottish missionary) **E:**412–13; **S:424**
    African exploration **A:**66
    Congo River **C:**507
    Malawi, exploration of **M:**53
    Zambia, history of **Z:**378
    picture(s) **S:**424
Livingston family (early American political leaders) **L:273–74**
Livius Andronicus, Lucius (Greek-born Roman poet and
    playwright) **L:**75
Livonia (historic region, Europe) **L:**81
Livy (Roman historian) **H:**151; **L:**76, **274**; **R:**159; **W:**258
Liyongo (African epic hero) **A:**76c
Lizardfish
    picture(s) **F:**188
Lizards **L:275–77**; **R:**180
    compared to snakes **S:**209
    "dinosaur" means "large lizard" **D:**167
    iguanas **I:**60
    leather, source of **L:**109
    Maori myth about origin **M:**574
    Why do chameleons change color? **L:**275

Lizards (cont.)
picture(s)
    forelimb **F:**80
Ljubljana (capital of Slovenia) **S:**203–4
picture(s) **S:**203
Llamas (hoofed mammals) **H:**220; **I:**108; **L:**273, **278**; **P:**163;
    S:283
picture(s) **A:**251; **B:**306; **G:**100; **L:**278; **P:**163; **S:**282
Llano Estacado (plateau, Texas–New Mexico) **N:**182; **T:**126,
    128
Llanos (grasslands of South America) **C:**404; **S:**277; **V:**296,
    297
picture(s) **C:**404
Llosa, Mario Vargas (Peruvian novelist) *see* Vargas Llosa, Mario
Lloyd, Harold (American actor and producer)
picture(s) **M:**489
Lloyd George, David (British statesman) **L:**279; **W:**290
picture(s) **W:**290
Lloyd's of London (insurance company) **I:**252
picture(s) **I:**252
Lloyd Webber, Andrew (English composer) **E:**293; **M:**555
Llywelyn (Welsh prince) **W:**4
LM *see* Lunar Module
LNG *see* Liquefied natural gas
Load (material carried by a river) **R:**236
Loaders (earth-moving machinery) **E:**32
Loading machinery *see* Hoisting and loading machinery
Loam (soil) **S:**235
Loans (in banking) **B:**57; **C:**582; **I:**255; **R:**113; **S:**454
Loa River (Chile) **C:**251
Lob (tennis stroke) **T:**92
Lobachevsky, Nikolai (Russian mathematician) **G:**128; **M:**168
Lobamba (Swaziland) **S:**521
Lobe-finned fish **F:**184–85, 188
Lobel, Arnold (American author and illustrator) **C:**234 *profile*
picture(s)
    illustration from *Frog and Toad Together* **C:**244
    illustration from *The Random House Book of Poetry for
      Children* **C:**240
Lobengula (king of the Ndebele) **Z:**383
Lobes (of the liver) **L:**267
Lobes (of the lungs) **L:**343
Loblolly pine trees
picture(s) **A:**133
Lobsterbacks (nickname for British soldiers) **R:**196
Lobsters (crustaceans) **C:**601, 602; **L:**279–**80**
    changes in the marketplace **F:**221
    fishing industry **F:**217
    glands control molting **G:**226
    Maine is foremost harvester **M:**45
    spiny lobsters' migration **H:**199
picture(s) **L:**280
    Maine **M:**43, 45
    peppermint lobster **O:**25
    spiny lobsters' migration **H:**199
    traps (pots) **P:**463
Lobules (of the liver) **L:**267–68
diagram(s) **L:**268
Local anesthetic **A:**255–56
Local-area network (LAN) (of computers) **C:**487
Local color (in literature) **S:**162
Local government *see* Counties; Municipal government; Towns
Local Group (of galaxies) **A:**474; **M:**309; **U:**216
Localized circulation (of the atmosphere) **W:**82
Local winds **W:**82
Locarno Conference (1925) **G:**162
Locations (natural settings for movies)
picture(s) **M:**483
Loch (Scottish for lake) *see* the names of lochs, as Ness, Loch
Loch Ness monster (legendary sea serpent) **L:**281; **S:**86;
    U:53
picture(s)
    famous 1934 photo now thought a hoax **L:**281
Locke, Alain (American publisher) **A:**215

Locke, John (English philosopher) **C:**293; **E:**297; **L:**281;
    P:506
picture(s) **P:**505
Lockerbie (Scotland) **airplane bombing** (1988) *see* Pan Am
    flight 103
Lockhorns, The (panel cartoon) **C:**129
Locking pliers (Vise grips) (tools) **T:**230
Lockjaw *see* Tetanus
Lockout (shutting down work by management) **L:**8, 10
Locks (of canals) **C:**88–89; **P:**49; **S:**15
picture(s) **E:**313; **M:**267; **P:**50
Locks (of guns) **G:**415
Locks and keys **L:**282–**84**
diagram(s) **L:**282, 283, 284
Locks at West Troy (painting by John Hill)
picture(s) **E:**313
Locomotion (steam locomotive) **R:**87, 88
Locomotion of animals *see* Animal locomotion
Locomotive cranes (machines) **H:**159c
Locomotives **L:**285–**88**; **R:**80–81, 85, 87–88
    diesel engines *see* Diesel locomotives
    first in U.S. built by Peter Cooper **C:**551
    railroads, model **R:**92
    transportation, history of **T:**285–86
    world's largest in Green Bay (Wisconsin) **W:**198
picture(s) **L:**286; **R:**80
Locust borer beetles
picture(s) **B:**123
Locusts (insects) **P:**286
Lodes (layers of rock) **G:**251
Lodestar *see* North Star
Lodestone (magnetic rock) **M:**28
Lodge, Henry Cabot (American statesman and writer) **U:**138
    profile; **W:**183
Lodges (of beavers) **B:**111–12
Lódz (Poland) **P:**361
Loeb, Richard (American murderer) **D:**38
Loess (sandy soil deposited by wind) **I:**292, 294; **M:**350;
    N:82; **S:**238
Loesser, Frank (American composer) **M:**554
Loewe, Frederick (American composer) **M:**554
Loewy, Raymond (French-born American industrial designer)
    I:215
Lofoten Islands (northwest of Norway) **I:**366; **N:**346
Log (apparatus to measure a ship's speed) **N:**73
Log (Logbook) (record kept by sailors) **N:**73
    Columbus' log **C:**445, 446
Logan (Utah) **U:**247, 251
Logan, John A. (American general) **H:**168
Logan, Mount (Canada) **C:**56; **Y:**370
Loganberries **G:**301
Logarithms (in mathematics) **M:**165
Log cabins **H:**187; **P:**251–52
    introduced to America by Swedes **C:**415
    similar wooden homes in Soviet villages **U:**35
picture(s) **H:**187; **W:**142
Loggerheads (turtles) **T:**357
Loggers *see* Lumberjacks
Logging *see* Lumber and lumbering
Logging trucks
picture(s) **T:**320
Logic (science of reasoning) **L:**289–**90** *see also* Probability
    aptitude test questions **T:**122–23
    Aristotle's key to knowledge **A:**387
    learning tool **L:**100
    logic puzzles **N:**392, 395
    mathematics **M:**159, 163, 169, 170
Logic gates (of microprocessors) **C:**487
Log lines (measure speed of ships) **K:**286
Logo (of a company) **C:**457
Logone River (Chad) **C:**180, 181; **L:**29
Loguen, Jermain (American abolitionist) **U:**16 *profile*
Logwood (tree) **D:**375

Lohengrin (opera by Wagner) **O:**155
  picture(s)
    poster for **M:**543
Lo'ichi (underwater volcanic island in Hawaii) **U:**82
Loihi (volcano, Hawaii) **H:**48
Loire River (France) **F:**408; **R:**243
Loki (Norse god) **N:**278, 279, 280, 281
Lollards (English religious group) **H:**109; **R:**130
Loma Mountains (Sierra Leone) **S:**172
Loma Prieta earthquake (1989)
  picture(s) **E:**36
Lombardi, Vince (American football coach) **F:**359
Lombards (Germanic tribe) **C:**188; **I:**388
Lomé (capital of Togo) **T:**217
Lomond, Loch (lake in Scotland) **L:**31; **S:**86; **U:**53, 54
  picture(s) **L:**24
Londinium (Roman town, now London, England) **L:**298
London (capital of the United Kingdom) **L:291–98;** **U:**59
  Cleopatra's Needle **O:**5
  economy **U:**54
  great fire of 1666 **F:**145
  libraries and museums **U:**49
  National Gallery **N:**35
  parks **P:**76
  people **U:**47
  police **P:**368
  population density **C:**312
  port **U:**57
  postal service **P:**396
  Shakespeare's London **S:**133
  Stock Exchange **S:**456
  theater **T:**160
  world's first electric subway **L:**287
  World War II **W:**299
  Wren, Christopher **W:**323
  map(s) **L:**292
  picture(s) **E:**232
    Big Ben **L:**293
    British Museum **L:**295
    changing of the guard **L:**293
    Doré illustration **I:**222
    Guildhall **G:**403
    Harrod's department store **L:**295
    houses of Parliament **U:**47
    London Eye ferris wheel **U:**59
    National Gallery **N:**35
    neighborhood shop **L:**294
    Piccadilly Circus **L:**294
    Saint Paul's Cathedral **B:**68
    Speaker's Corner **L:**298
    Thames River **R:**246
    Tower Bridge **L:**291
    Trafalgar Square **L:**293
    workers outside Stock Exchange **L:**296
    World War II damage **L:**298
London (Ontario) **O:**129, 134
London, Jack (American writer) **L:299–300**
  The Call of the Wild, excerpt from **L:**299–300
London, Tower of **L:**292; **U:**54
  boy prisoners in the tower **E:**242
  What happened to the princes in the Tower? **E:**241
  picture(s)
    White Tower **E:**256
London, Treaty of (1852) **C:**286
London, University of **L:**295
London Bridge (Arizona) **A:**400
London Bridge (England) **B:**401; **L:**297
"London Bridge Is Falling Down" (game song) **B:**401; **H:**34
London Company (business company to colonize America)
    J:22–23; **T:**168–70
London Eye (ferris wheel, London, England) **L:**298
London Piano School (group of English composers) **E:**293
Lones (Canadian Girl Guides who cannot attend regular
    meetings) **G:**218
Lone Star Republic **T:**108

Lone Star State (nickname for Texas) **T:**124, 125
Long, Crawford W. (American doctor) **A:**255
Long, Earl Kemp (American politician) **L:**300–301, 328
Long, Huey Pierce (American politician) **L:**300, 327 *profile,*
    328
  picture(s) **L:**300
Long, Jefferson (American politician)
  picture(s) **U:**143
Long, Richard (English artist) **E:**264
Long, Russell Billiu (American politician) **L:**301
Long, Stephen H. (American engineer) **C:**442; **N:**91; **O:**271
Longabaugh, Harry (American outlaw) *see* Sundance Kid
Longbow (in archery) **H:**292–93
  picture(s) **A:**360; **H:**293
Long-day plants **F:**287
Long Day's Journey into Night (play by Eugene O'Neill) **O:**122
Long Drive (of cattle over the Chisholm Trail) **O:**282
Long-eared owls **O:**284
"Longest Walk" (1978, to focus attention on Native American
    concerns) **A:**199
Longevity *see* Life spans
Long family (American politicians) **L:**300–301
Longfellow, Henry Wadsworth (American poet) **A:**209; **L:**301–2
  "The Arrow and the Song" **L:**302
  figures of speech **F:**122
  "Paul Revere's Ride," excerpt from **P:**350; **R:**192
  Wadsworth-Longfellow House (Portland, Maine) **M:**44
  picture(s) **L:**301
    Wadsworth-Longfellow House **M:**44
Longhaired cats **C:**139
Long hit (in field hockey) **F:**120
Longhorn cattle
  Chisholm Trail **O:**282
  cowboys **C:**577
  Kansas "cattle towns" **K:**189
  Texas **T:**124, 140
  Wichita Mountains Wildlife Refuge (Oklahoma) **O:**90
  picture(s) **O:**83
Long-horned beetles
  picture(s) **B:**126
Long horse (use in gymnastics) **G:**432
  picture(s) **G:**430
Longhouses (of the Iroquois Indians) **I:**175
  picture(s) **I:**176
Long Island (New York) **N:**212, 215
Long Island Sound (United States) **C:**508, 510
Longitude **L:77–78**
  international date line **I:**266
  maps and globes **M:**92, 94, 96
  navigation **N:**74
  time zones **T:**202–3
Longitudinal fibers (of muscle) **M:**520
Long jump (field event) **T:**257
  world records **T:**261
  picture(s) **T:**253
Longlining (fishing technique) **F:**219
  picture(s) **F:**220
Long March (in Chinese history) **M:**90
Long Parliament (English) **E:**245–46
Long period tides **T:**195
Long-playing records (LP's) **P:**195; **R:**123, 124
LOng RAnge Navigation *see* Loran
Longshan culture (in Chinese history) **P:**409
Longstreet, Augustus Baldwin (American humorist) **A:**212
Longstreet, James (Confederate army officer) **C:**345 *profile*
Long-tailed wood partridges (birds) **Q:**4a
Long-term-care facilities **N:**418
Long term memory **B:**367; **L:**101, 102–5
Long tom (for washing gold from sand) **G:**251
Long ton (measure of weight) **W:**115
Long Trail (hiking path, Vermont) **V:**314
Long-wall method (of developing coal mines) **C:**389
Long Walls (of ancient Athens) **A:**238
Longway sets (dance forms) *see* Contra dances
Longwood Gardens (Pennsylvania) **P:**134

Longwood Mansion (Natchez, Mississippi)
picture(s) **M:**358
Longworth, Alice Roosevelt (daughter of Theodore Roosevelt)
F:175
Lon Nol (Cambodian leader) **C:**38
Lonnrot, Elias (Finnish folklorist) **F:**312
Lon Po Po (book by Ed Young)
picture(s) **C:**243
Look Back in Anger (play by John Osborne) **O:**237
"Looking-Glass River" (poem by Robert Louis Stevenson)
S:450
Lookout Mountain (Colorado) **C:**438
picture(s) **C:**438
Lookout Mountain (Tennessee) **T:**82
picture(s) **T:**82
Lookout Mountain, Battle of (1863, Civil War) **C:**342
Looming (kind of mirage) **M:**342
Looms (for weaving textiles) **T:**142; **W:**97, 98b
how to make a simple loom **W:**98
Industrial Revolution improvements **I:**217–18
Jacquard's loom **A:**533
rug and carpet weaving **R:**353–54
picture(s)
silk weaving **S:**175
Loons (water birds)
picture(s) **B:**235; **M:**327; **O:**124
Loop, The (area of Chicago, Illinois) **C:**218
Looping (textile-making technique) **T:**142
picture(s) **T:**145
Loop knots **K:**288
Loos, Adolf (Austrian architect) **A:**374; **G:**172
Loose housing (for cattle) *see* Free-stall housing
Lope de Vega (Spanish dramatist and poet) *see* Vega Carpio,
Lope Félix de
López, Carlos Antonio (Paraguayan dictator) **P:**65
López, Francisco Solano (Paraguayan dictator) **P:**65
Lopez, Nancy (American golfer) **G:**258 *profile,* 261
picture(s) **G:**258
López de Mendoza, Íñigo (Spanish poet) *see* Santillana, Marquis
of
López Mateos, Adolfo (Mexican statesman) **M:**251
López Portillo, José (president of Mexico) **M:**251–52
Lops (rabbits with floppy ears) **R:**25
Loran (LOng-RAnge Navigation) **A:**119; **N:**76; **U:**125
Lorca, Federico García (Spanish poet and playwright) *see* García
Lorca, Federico
Lord Dunmore's War *see* Dunmore's War
Lord Mayor's Show (British spectacle) **U:**50
Lord of the Flies (novel by Golding) **F:**116
Lord of the Rings, The (film trilogy) **N:**240
Lord of the Rings, The (novels by J. R. R. Tolkien) **F:**12; **T:**220
Lords, House of (British Parliament) **E:**240; **P:**83; **U:**47–48,
61
picture(s) **U:**61
Lord's Prayer **L:**38; **P:**430, 431
Lords proprietors (in South Carolina history) **S:**308
Lord's Resistance Army (Ugandan rebel movement) **U:**7
Lord's Supper *see* Eucharist
Lorenz, Edward (American meteorologist) **M:**170
Lorenz, Konrad (Austrian naturalist) **L:**302
picture(s) **L:**302
Lorenzetti, Pietro and Ambrogio (Italian painters) **I:**394
Lorenzini, Carlo *see* Collodi, Carlo
Lorenzo the Magnificent (Italian statesman and art patron) *see*
Medici, Lorenzo de'
Lorenz's butterfly (mathematical pattern) *see* Strange attractor
Lories (birds)
picture(s) **P:**85
Lorises (animals related to monkeys) **P:**456; **S:**416
Lorrain, Claude (French painter) *see* Claude Lorrain
Lorraine (region of France) *see* Alsace-Lorraine
Los Alamos (New Mexico) **N:**185, 194
Los Angeles (California) **C:**27; **L:**303–8
Asian Americans **A:**457

influence of geography on the city's character **C:**319
major agricultural center **A:**94
Mexican Americans **H:**148
mural painting **H:**147
water supply **C:**23
map(s) **L:**304
picture(s) **C:**27; **G:**104; **L:**303
beach **L:**306
Beverly Hills Hotel **L:**307
Korean market **A:**459
University of California **U:**222
Los Angeles Lakers (basketball team) **B:**99
Los Angeles Ranges (California) **C:**20
Los Angeles Times (newspaper) **L:**308
Lost Colony, The (pageant) **N:**312; **P:**12
Lost colony of Virginia **N:**318; **T:**165–66
Lost Springs (Wyoming) **W:**334
Lost wax casting *see* Cire perdue
Lot (Biblical character) **A:**8–9
Lotions (cosmetics) **C:**560
Lots, Feast of *see* Purim
Lotteries, draft **D:**293
Lotus (water plant)
picture(s) **N:**67
Loudness (of sound) **S:**259
Loudspeakers (audio equipment) **H:**131, 133; **R:**54, 58;
S:267b
Louganis, Greg (American diver) **D:**229; **O:**106–7 *profile*
picture(s) **D:**229; **O:**107
Lou Gehrig's disease *see* Amyotrophic lateral sclerosis
Louis, Joe (American boxer) **A:**143 *profile*; **B:**351, 352, 353
profile
Louis, Saint *see* Louis IX (Saint Louis) (king of France)
Louis I (king of France) **C:**188; **L:**309
Louis II (king of France) **L:**309
Louis III (king of France) **L:**309
Louis IV (king of France) **L:**309
Louis V (king of France) **L:**309
Louis VI (king of France) **L:**309; **M:**290
Louis VII (king of France) **E:**126; **L:**309
Louis VIII (king of France) **L:**309
Louis IX (Saint Louis) (king of France) **F:**423; **L:**310; **M:**291
picture(s) **L:**309
Louis X (king of France) **L:**310
Louis XI (king of France) **F:**413; **L:**310
picture(s) **L:**310
Louis XII (king of France) **L:**310
Louis XIII (king of France) **F:**414; **L:**310–11, 333; **R:**231
picture(s) **L:**310
Louis XIV (king of France) **F:**414–15; **L:**312–13
Canada, history of **C:**80
danced in ballets **B:**25–26
fashion, influence on **C:**377
France, art and architecture of **F:**427
Huguenots **H:**279
Louisiana named after **L:**46
Louvre **L:**333
Versailles, Palace of **A:**372; **P:**72, 74
Why was Louis XIV called the Sun King? **L:**313
picture(s) **F:**415; **H:**7; **L:**312; **W:**267
Bernini's statue **B:**152
Louis XV (king of France) **F:**415; **L:**311
Du Barry, Madame **D:**342
picture(s)
dragon-shaped gem **J:**99
Louis XVI (king of France) **F:**415; **L:**311
Du Barry, Madame **D:**342
French Revolution **F:**467, 468, 469, 470 *profile*
Marie Antoinette **M:**103
picture(s) **F:**457; **L:**311
execution **F:**472; **W:**269
Louis XVII (king of France) **L:**311
Louis XVIII (king of France) **F:**417; **L:**311; **N:**13–14; **P:**74–75
Louis I (Louis the Great) (king of Hungary) **H:**298
Louis II (prince of Monaco) **M:**410

Louisbourg (fortress on Cape Breton Island, Canada)   **F:**463, 464; **N:**356, 357
Louise, Lake (Alberta)   **A:**165; **B:**46; **L:**31
Louis XV style (in furniture design)   **A:**315; **F:**511
  picture(s)   **F:**510
Louis XIV style (in furniture design)   **A:**315; **F:**510
Louisiana   **L:**314–28
  delta deposits from Mississippi River   **R:**236
  gumbo   **F:**333
  lakes   **L:**33
  law based on the Napoleonic Code   **L:**85
  Long family   **L:**300–301
  Louisiana World Exposition (1984)   **F:**17
  New Orleans   **N:**195–96
  pelican on state seal and flag   **P:**120
  map(s)   **L:**325
  picture(s)
    Baton Rouge   **L:**324
    cypress trees in bayou   **L:**315
    gambling casino   **L:**319
    Jungle Gardens   **L:**322
    Kisatchie National Forest   **L:**316
    Louisiana State University   **L:**319
    Mardi Gras   **L:**315
    New Orleans   **L:**318, 322; **N:**195, 196; **U:**99
    Oak Alley Plantation   **L:**322
    oil rig   **L:**321
    Shreveport   **L:**323
    shrimp industry   **L:**320
    sugarcane plantation   **L:**316
    tanker on Mississippi River   **L:**317
Louisiana Purchase (1803)   **L:**314, **329–30; U:**179
  commemorative nickel   **C:**400
  Jefferson, Thomas   **J:**70
  land laws and pioneer life   **P:**260
  Lewis and Clark expedition   **L:**163–64
  Louisiana, history of   **L:**327
  Monroe acted for Jefferson   **M:**424–25
  territorial expansion of the United States   **T:**105, 107
  westward movement   **W:**144
  map(s)   **L:**329
Louisiana Purchase Exposition (1904)   **F:**16; **S:**16
  iced tea, invention of   **T:**36
  jai alai introduced to United States   **J:**13
  Who invented the ice cream cone?   **I:**21
Louisiana State University   **L:**319
  picture(s)   **L:**319
Louis Napoleon *see* Napoleon III
Louis Philippe (Citizen King) (king of France)   **F:**417; **L:**311–12; **P:**75
Louis XVI style (in furniture design)   **A:**315
Louis the Fat *see* Louis VI (king of France)
Louis the Great *see* Louis I (Louis the Great) (king of Hungary)
Louis the Lion *see* Louis VIII (king of France)
Louis the Pious *see* Louis I (king of France)
Louis the Quarrelsome *see* Louis X (king of France)
Louis the Stammerer *see* Louis II (king of France)
Louis the Young *see* Louis VII (king of France)
Louisville (Kentucky)   **K:**217, 221, 222, 227
  picture(s)   **K:**213, 220
Louisville, University of (Kentucky)   **K:**217
Louisy, Allan (prime minister of Saint Lucia)   **S:**18
Lourenço Marques (Mozambique) *see* Maputo
Louse (insect) *see* Lice
Louvain, Catholic University of (Belgium)   **B:**131
L'Ouverture, Toussaint (liberator of Haiti) *see* Toussaint L'Ouverture
Louvois, Marquis de (François Michel Le Tellier) (French public official)   **L:**313
Louvre (art museum in Paris, France)   **L:**331–33; **M:**525, 528
  Paris   **P:**70, 73, 74, 75
  Pei, I. M.   **A:**376; **P:**118
  renovation begun under Francis I   **F:**425
  picture(s)   **L:**331, 332, 333; **M:**527
Love (in psychology)   **P:**509–10

Love (in tennis scoring)   **T:**89
Love, Mike (American rock musician)   **R:**262d
Love Canal area (Niagara Falls, New York)   **H:**72; **W:**65
Loveira, Carlos (Cuban novelist)   **C:**609
Lovejoy, Elijah Parish (American abolitionist)   **A:**6a *profile*
Lovelace, Augusta Ada Byron, Countess of (English mathematician)   **C:**490
Lovell, James Arthur, Jr. (American astronaut)   **S:**347 *profile,* 352
Love's Labour's Lost (play by Shakespeare)   **S:**137
"Love Song of J. Alfred Prufrock" (poem by T. S. Eliot)   **A:**214b
Low, Juliette Gordon (American founder of Girl Scouts of America)   **G:**215, 218
Löwchens (dogs)   **D:**247
Low Countries   **E:**349; **W:**296–97
Low-density lipids *see* LDL's
Lowell (Massachusetts)   **M:**144, 145
Lowell, James Russell (American author and diplomat)   **A:**209
  The Fountain (poem), excerpt from   **F:**393
Lowell, Percival (American astronomer)   **A:**471, 476 *profile;* **P:**341
  picture(s)   **A:**476
Lowell, Robert (American poet)   **A:**218; **L:**334
Lowell family (of Massachusetts)   **M:**150
Lower Canada   **C:**82, 83; **Q:**16, 17
Lower-case (Small) letters (of the alphabet)   **A:**194c
Lowest terms (of fractions)   **F:**398
Low explosives   **E:**420, 421
Low-fat milk   **D:**8
Low German (dialect of northern Germany)   **G:**174, 175
Low-grade ore   **M:**320, 324
Lowland tapirs (mammals)   **H:**218
Low-level languages (in computer programming)   **C:**483
Low-pressure areas (Lows) (in meteorology)   **W:**80–81, 82, 84, 85
  climate   **C:**363
  winds   **W:**186, 189
Low relief (in sculpture) *see* Bas-relief
Lowry, Lois (American author)   **C:**234 *profile*
LOX *see* Liquid oxygen
Loya jirga (Afghan grand council)   **A:**45
Loyalist House (Saint John, New Brunswick)   **N:**138e
Loyalists *see* Tories (Loyalists)
Loyalists, United Empire *see* United Empire Loyalists
Loyd, Sam (American puzzle maker)   **P:**553, 554
Loyola, Saint Ignatius (founder of the Jesuits)   **C:**293; **L:**334; **R:**291
  picture(s)   **R:**291
Lozenge (in heraldry)   **H:**118
Lozi (people of Africa)   **Z:**377
LPG *see* Liquefied petroleum gas
LPGA *see* Ladies Professional Golf Association
LPN's *see* Licensed practical nurses
LP's *see* Long-playing records
LSD (hallucinogenic drug)   **D:**331
Lualaba River *see* Congo River
Luanda (capital of Angola)   **A:**259, 260
  picture(s)   **A:**259
Luang Prabang (Laos)   **L:**42; **S:**334
Luba (a people of Africa)   **C:**499, 502
  picture(s)   **A:**72; **W:**228
Lubitsch, Ernst (German film director)   **M:**490
Lubrication and lubricants   **L:**335
  internal-combustion engines   **I:**265
  mineral oils   **O:**79
  petroleum, uses of   **P:**173–74
  silicones   **S:**173
Lubrication system (of an automobile)   **A:**546, 548
Lubumbashi (Democratic Republic of Congo)   **C:**502
Lucan (Roman poet)   **L:**76
Lucas (Kansas)   **K:**184
Lucas, George (American film producer and director)   **C:**32–33 *profile;* **M:**497
Lucas, Robert (American statesman)   **I:**303

Luce, Clare Boothe (American writer and political leader)
N:232 *profile*
Luce, Henry Robinson (American magazine publisher) J:138
profile; M:20; N:232 *profile*
picture(s) J:138
Luce-Cellar Act (United States, 1946) A:460
Lucerne, Lake of (Switzerland) L:31
Lucerne Festival (Switzerland) M:555
Lucia di Lammermoor (opera by Gaetano Donizetti) D:285;
O:155–56
picture(s) O:157
Lucian (Greek satirical writer) G:359
Luciano, Charles ("Lucky") (American mobster) O:224 *profile*
Lucid, Shannon W. (American astronaut) O:94 *profile;* S:349
picture(s) S:349
Luciferases (light-producing chemicals) B:205
Luciferins (chemicals that give off light in living things)
B:205
Lucilius (Roman poet) F:114
Lucius I, Saint (pope) R:292
Lucius II (pope) R:292
Lucius III (pope) R:293
Luck (unpredictable force that shapes events) S:503–4
Lucknow Pact (1916) J:109
Lucretius (Roman writer) G:107–8; L:75
Lucy, Saint S:18d *profile*
Ludendorff, Erich Friedrich Wilhelm (German general and
strategist) W:283, 284 *profile,* 289, 290
picture(s) W:277
Lue Gim Gong (American horticulturist) F:275 *profile*
Luffing (in sailing) S:11
diagram(s) S:10
Luftwaffe W:296, 298–99
Luganda (language) U:4
Luge racing (sport)
picture(s) O:109
Luggage, leather L:109, 110
Lukashenko, Aleksandr (president of Belarus) B:129
Luke, Saint B:165–66; S:18d *profile*
picture(s)
gospel book depiction I:77
Lulik (animist religion) T:207
Lullabies L:336–37
Lully, Jean-Baptiste (French composer) B:26, 70; F:445;
O:142
Lulu (opera by Alban Berg) B:145
Lumbar vertebrae (of the spine) S:183
Lumbee (Indians of North America) I:179
Lumber and lumbering L:338–42; W:222–27 *see also* the
industries and products section of country, province,
and state articles
Asia A:452
building materials B:433
furniture-making F:515
national forests, multiple use of N:30, 33, 34
Pennsylvania is a leading producer P:126, 132
plastic lumber P:327; R:125
plywood W:226–27
rain forests R:100
picture(s) F:376; L:338, 339, 340
Amazon Basin rain forest S:290
Arkansas E:57
British Columbia pulp mill B:405
Canada N:303
cutting methods L:341
elephant hauling teak log M:559
Georgia G:139
how a log is used L:341
Liberia L:166
logging truck T:320
logs at paper plant P:54
Montana M:434
mountain slope damage M:507
national forests, multiple use of N:32

Newfoundland and Labrador N:143
Ontario O:128
Oregon O:208
Sweden S:526
Washington W:21
wood-chopping contest F:14
Lumberjacks (lumber workers) L:339, 341
Lumière brothers (French inventors) M:487
Luminaria (candles in bags used as decorations)
picture(s) N:181
Luminosity (brightness of stars) A:473, 476
Luminous paints P:34
Lumumba, Patrice Emergy (Congolese nationalist leader)
C:503; M:383
Luna (Lunik) (series of Soviet spacecraft) M:447; S:359
Lunar calendar A:458; I:349; R:153; T:200
Lunar eclipses E:50, 51–52; M:448–49
diagram(s) E:51
picture(s) E:52
Lunar landing (July 20, 1969) *see* Apollo program—Apollo 11
Lunar module (LM) (of Apollo spacecraft) S:340g, 340h–340i
Lunar (Moon) probes S:357
Lunar Prospector (robotic spacecraft) M:454; S:354
Lunar rover S:347
Lunar seas (of moon's surface) M:450
Lunar tides (caused by the moon's gravitational pull) O:19
Luncheon of the Boating Party, The (painting by Renoir)
picture(s) I:103
Lund University (Sweden) S:524
Lundy's Lane, Battle of (1814) N:243
Lunenburg (Nova Scotia) N:352, 355, 356
Lunéville, Treaty of (1801) N:11
Lungfish F:184, 185, 192
Lungs (organs of breathing) B:282, 283; L:343–45
air pollution A:122, 123
asbestos can cause lung disease A:438c
asthma A:463; D:187
cancer C:93, 95
cardiovascular fitness P:225
cystic fibrosis D:191
effects of jogging and running on J:111
emphysema (disease) D:192
environmental diseases D:186
heart, function of the H:81
muscles that move the lungs L:344
pneumonia D:198–99
radon exposure and lung cancer G:61
smoking S:207
snakes with only one lung S:209
tuberculosis D:204; T:328–29
What is a yawn? L:345
diagram(s) L:343
Lunik III (Russian space probe) M:447
Lunt, Alfred (American actor) T:161 *profile*
Luo (a people of Africa) K:229
Luong, Tran Duc (president of Vietnam) V:334d
Lupercalia (Roman festival) V:266–67
Lupine (plant)
picture(s) P:293
Luque, Hernando de (Spanish priest) P:268
Lures (for fishing) F:209, 211, 213
animals use to catch prey A:281
Lusaka (capital of Zambia) Z:377
picture(s) Z:378
Lusitani (early people of Portugal) P:394
Lusitania (ocean liner) O:33; V:277; W:286
Luster (brightness) M:233, 314–15; P:114
Lusterware (ceramic pottery) I:359
picture(s) I:358
Lustre (Luster) (metallic glaze for pottery) P:411
Lüta (China) O:47
Lute (musical instrument) A:78; E:292
picture(s) M:547; S:469

Lute Player and Woman Playing the Harp (painting by Israel van Meckenem)
  picture(s) **D:**372
Lutetia (ancient city, now Paris, France) **P:**74
Lutetium (element) **E:**174
Luther, Martin (German leader of Protestant Reformation)
  C:292; **L:**346; **P:**492; **R:**130–31, 291
  Bible, translation of **B:**158
  demands for religious reforms divide Germany **G:**160
  German literature **G:**177
  hymn composer **H:**322
  influenced German language **G:**175
  introduced chorales into church music **G:**184
  picture(s) **L:**346; **P:**490; **R:**130
Lutheranism (religious belief) **P:**491, 492–93, 494;
  R:130–31
  established as Denmark's religion **C:**286
  New York, history of **C:**294
  Sweden **S:**523
Luthiers (makers of stringed instruments) **W:**232
  picture(s) **G:**405
Lutyens, Sir Edwin (English architect) **D:**263; **I:**139
Lützen, Battle of (1632) **T:**179
Lux (measure of light intensity) **L:**216, 237
Luxembourg **L:**347–48
  invasion by Hitler (1940) **W:**296
  Where and what are the Low Countries? **E:**349
  map(s) **L:**347
  picture(s)
    city of Luxembourg **L:**347
    flag **F:**234
Luxembourg (capital of Luxembourg) **L:**347
  picture(s) **L:**347
Luxembourg, Palais du (Paris) **F:**425
Luxembourg Gardens (Paris, France)
  picture(s) **G:**32
Luxembourgisch (language) **L:**347
Luxor (Egypt) **A:**365; **E:**103, 115, 116
Lu Xun (Chinese writer) **C:**279
Luzon (Philippines) **P:**183, 185, 187; **W:**313, 314
Lyallpur (Pakistan) *see* Faisalabad
Lyceum (Athens school founded by Aristotle) **A:**387
Lye (chemical) **O:**101 *see also* Sodium hydroxide
Lyell, Sir Charles (English geologist) **D:**40; **G:**110

Lying *see* Lies
Lyly, John (English writer) **E:**271; **Q:**22
Lyme disease **A:**287, 348; **T:**192; **V:**284–85
Lymph (fluid carried by the lymphatic system) **L:**349–50
Lymphadenopathy (swelling of lymph nodes) **L:**350
Lymphatic capillaries (of the lymphatic system) **L:**349, 350
Lymphatic system (of the human body) **C:**306; **L:**349–50
  infectious mononucleosis **D:**195
  swollen glands are not really glands **G:**228
  diagram(s) **L:**349
  picture(s) **I:**95
Lymphatic vessels (in the human body) **L:**268, 349, 350
Lymph nodes (of the lymphatic system) **L:**349–50
Lymphocytes (white blood cells) **B:**259–60, 261; **D:**195,
  203; **I:**96; **L:**350
Lymphoid tissue (in the human body) **L:**350
Lymphomas (cancers) **C:**92, 94; **L:**350
Lynch, Thomas, Jr. (American political figure) **A:**527
Lynchburg (Virginia) **V:**355
Lynching (hanging of an allegedly guilty person by a mob)
  African American history **A:**79h, 79j; **N:**25, 26
  violence and society **V:**344
  picture(s)
    New York City riots (1863) **A:**79g
Lyndon B. Johnson Library **T:**130
Lyndon B. Johnson Space Center (near Houston, Texas) **A:**466;
  H:271; **S:**339; **T:**132, 140
  picture(s) **T:**132
Lynn, Loretta (American singer and songwriter) **C:**573
Lynxes (wildcats) **A:**277; **C:**146
  picture(s) **A:**269
Lyocell fibers **F:**110, 112
Lyons (France) **F:**410
Lyra (constellation) **C:**531; **N:**96
Lyre (ancient instrument) **A:**78
  picture(s) **A:**237
Lyrical voice **V:**377
Lyric poems **G:**355–56; **L:**259; **O:**52; **P:**352–53; **R:**303
Lysergic acid diethylamide *see* LSD
Lysippus (Greek sculptor) **G:**350
Lys Offensive (World War I) **W:**289
Lysosome (cell structure) **B:**274
Lytic viruses **V:**365, 366–67
Lyttelton (New Zealand) **N:**240

PHOTO CREDITS

The following list credits the sources of photos used in THE NEW BOOK OF KNOWLEDGE. Credits are listed, by page, photo by photo—left to right, top to bottom. Wherever appropriate, the name of the photographer has been listed with the source, the two being separated by a dash. When two or more photos by different photographers appear on one page, their credits are separated by semicolons.

61 © Roberto Bunge—DDB Stock Photo; © Max & Bea Hunn—DDB Stock Photo.
62 © Robert Fried
63 Museo Nacional de Bellas Artes, Buenos Aires, Argentina
64 © Helen Marcus—Photo Researchers; Courtesy of the Marlborough Gallery; Courtesy of the Rachel Adler Gallery.
65 © Don Klein
66 The Granger Collection
67 The Granger Collection
68 © The Edward LaRocque Tinker Collection, Harry Ranson Humanities Research Center, University of Texas at Austin
69 © Bill Swersey—Liaison Agency
70 © Philippe Ledru—Corbis-Sygma; © Diane Walker—Liaison Agency; © Sophie Bassouls—Corbis-Sygma.
71 © Cameramann International Ltd.
72 © Fred Fehl
79 © Janis Miglavs—Image Source
80 © Janis Miglavs—Image Source
81 © Kimmo Raisanen—Lehtikuva Oy/SABA
83 The Granger Collection
84 © Joseph Sohm—ChromoSohm /Corbis; Scala/Art Resource.
85 The Granger Collection
86 © Al Cook—Photo Network
87 © Cary Wolinsky—Stock, Boston/PNI
88 © David Young-Wolff—Stone
91 © Victor Ramos—International Stock/Photo Network
92 © Michael Newman—PhotoEdit; © Robert E. Daemmrich—Stone.
95 United Nations
96 © Des Bartlett—Photo Researchers
97 © Liz Gilbert—Corbis-Sygma; © Corbis-Sygma.
109 © Bob Daemmrich—The Image Works; © White/Packert—The Image Bank/Getty Images; © John and Lisa Merrill—Danita Delimont, Agent.
110 Courtesy, Dr. Nicholas J. Cory
111 Courtesy, Dr. Nicholas J. Cory
112 © Gene Ahrens—Bruce Coleman Inc.; © David Overcash—Bruce Coleman Inc.; © Tom Tracy—Photo Network; © Karen McGougan—Bruce Coleman Inc.
114 © Jen & Des Bartlett—Bruce Coleman Inc.; © John S. Flannery—Bruce Coleman Inc.
115 © Bill Cardoni—Bruce Coleman Inc.; © John Shaw—Bruce Coleman Inc.
117 © Lee Rentz—Bruce Coleman Inc.; © Bruce Coleman Inc.; © Hubert Kranemann/OKAPIA—Photo Researchers.
118 © Robert and Linda Mitchell; © Michael P. Gadomski—Photo Researchers; © Michael P. Gadomski—Photo Researchers; © Gary Withey—Bruce Coleman Inc.
119 © Mahmoud Tawil—Sipa Press
120 © D. Williams—SuperStock
121 © Bill Foley—Woodfin Camp & Associates; © Karim Daher—Liaison Agency.
122 The Granger Collection
123 © Lena Kara—Sipa Press
124 © Marc Tulane—Rapho
125 Corbis-Bettmann
127 Archive Photos (all photos on page).
128 © Museum Boerhaave Leiden; © Dr. Jeremy Burgess/SPL/Photo Researchers.
134 The Granger Collection
136 Philadelphia Museum of Art: A. E. Gallatin Collection
139 © Buzzini; © Bruce Coleman Inc.
141 Minolta; Bushnell Optical Company—Division of Bausch & Lomb; American Optical; RCA Corporation; Edmund Scientific.
151 The Stapleton Collection/The Bridgeman Art Library
153 Scala, New York; Art Reference Bureau.
154 Courtesy IBM
155 © David Madison—Bruce Coleman Inc.; © John Giustina—The Wildlife Collection.
156 © John Moss—Photo Researchers
156b Culver Pictures; The Bettmann Archive; Culver Pictures.
158 Courtesy of Grolier Incorporated
165 ©Lineair—Peter Arnold, Inc.; © Heldur Netocny—Panos Pictures.
166 © Lisa Taylor—Panos Pictures
167 © Sean Sprague—Panos Pictures; © David Guttenfelder—AP/Wide World Photos.
169 © Adrienne Helitzer—Corbis-Sygma
170 © R. Glander—SuperStock
171 © Scala/Art Resource; The Granger Collection.

172 Culver Pictures
173 The Granger Collection; Scala/Art Resource.
174 © Rene Burri—Magnum Photos
175 © Bill Stanton—International Stock Photo
176 Reprinted by permission of the American Library Association; Reprinted by permission of the American Library Association; © Michal Heron—Monkmeyer Press.
177 © Donald Dietz—Stock, Boston; Reprinted by permission of the American Library Association.
178 © Topham—The Image Works
179 © R. Vroom—Miller Services
180 Reprinted by permission of the American Library Association; © Richard Hutchings—Photo Researchers.
181 Reprinted by permission of the American Library Association (all photos on page).
182 Reprinted by permission of the American Library Association
183 © Linda Triegel; © Pat Lanza Field—Bruce Coleman Inc.
186 © Richard Drew—AP/Wide World Photos; © Spencer Grant—PhotoEdit.
187 © O. Martel—Photo Researchers; © Voller Ernst—eStock Photo; © Frans Lemmens—The Image Bank/Getty Images.
189 © Jim Holland—Stock, Boston/PictureQuest; © Thomas Coex—AFP/Getty Images.
190 SIME s.a.s./eStock Photos; © Jacques Collet—AFP/Getty Images.
191 © Jose Fuste Raga/eStock
192 © Fritz Henle—Photo Researchers
193 © Brian Seed—Stone
212 © Craig Tuttle—The Stock Market
213 © David M. Dennis—Tom Stack & Associates
214 © Faith Bowlus—Photo Network; © Chris Cheadle—Stone.
218 © David Parker—Science Photo Library—Photo Researchers
220 © Thomas Eisner; © Thomas Eisner; © Blair Seitz—Photo Researchers.
221 © British Technical Films/Science Photo Library—Photo Researchers
223 © Ron Watts—First Light
224 © Martin Dohrn—Science Photo Library—Photo Researchers
226 © Chuck O'Rear—Woodfin Camp & Associates
228 © Grant Heilman Photography
229 U.S. Coast Guard
230 © Walter Bibikow—FPG International/Getty Images
237 © F. Robert Masini—Phototake
238 White Oak Design, Marblehead, Massachusetts
239 © Luis Rosendo/Taxi/Getty Images
240 The White House Collection, © copyright White House Historical Association; The Granger Collection; The Granger Collection.
241 The Bettmann Archive (all photos on page).
243 Henry Horner Lincoln Collection—Illinois State Historical Library
244 Henry Horner Lincoln Collection—Illinois State Historical Library; The Bettmann Archive.
245 The Granger Collection
246 The Granger Collection
247 The Granger Collection (all photos on page).
248 Michael Rougier—Life magazine, © Time, Inc.
249 United Press International
250 The Granger Collection
252 © Aragesco—Atlas Photo
254 © Sinclair Stammers/Science Photo Library—Photo Researchers
256 © Noboru Komine—Photo Researchers
258 © Yann Layma—Stone
261 © Sovfoto
262 © Sovfoto
263 © Peter Turnley—Black Star
264 Little League Baseball Inc.
265 © Alec Duncan—Taurus
266 © Jim Whitmer—Nawrocki Stock Photo
269 P. Motta/University La Sapienza, Rome/Science Photo Library—Photo Researchers; Lennart Nilsson—Bonnier Alba AB.
270 © Martin Rotker—Photo Researchers; © Biophoto Associates/Science Source/Photo Researchers.
271 © Paul Steel—The Stock Market; SuperStock.
272 © Miréille Vautier—Woodfin Camp & Associates; © Gianni Tortoli—Photo Researchers.
273 Brown Brothers
275 © Kevin Schafer—Stone; © Norbert Wu—The Stock Market.

276 © Stephen Dalton—Photo Researchers; © Belinda Wright—DRK Photo.
277 © Carol Christensen—New England Stock Photo; © Peter Ward—Bruce Coleman Inc.; © Stephen Dalton—Animals Animals.
278 © François Gohier—Photo Researchers
280 © Andrew J. Martinez—Photo Researchers
281 © Peter Marlow—Corbis-Sygma
283 Schlage Lock Company
285 © Tom Tracy—Photo Network
286 © Chris Rogers—The Stock Market
287 The Granger Collection; The Granger Collection; The Granger Collection; © Mike Del Vecchio.
288 © Porterfield-Chickering—Photo Researchers; © Mike McQueen—Stone.
289 Scala/Art Resource
291 © Will and Deni McIntyre—Photo Researchers
293 SuperStock; © Will and Deni McIntyre—Photo Researchers; © Bill Tice—Photo Network.
294 © Suzanne and Nick Geary—Stone; © Peter S. Ford.
295 © Adam Woolfitt—Woodfin Camp & Associates (all photos on page).
296 © Will and Deni McIntyre—Photo Researchers
297 © Josef Muench
298 © Michael Yamashita—Woodfin Camp & Associates; The Granger Collection.
299 Color Illustration Inc.; FPG International; © Robert Meyerriecks; © Stephanie Dinkins.
300 UPI/Corbis-Bettmann
301 The Granger Collection
302 Nina Leen—Life magazine, © Time Inc.
303 © John Post—Panoramic Images
305 SuperStock; © Alon Reininger—Unicorn Stock Photos.
306 © Joel Rogers—Stone
307 SuperStock
308 Brown Brothers; Regional History Collections/Department of Special Collections/University of California; © Eric Risberg—AP/Wide World Photos.
309 The Granger Collection
310 © Erich Lessing—Art Resource; Giraudon/Art Resource.
311 Giraudon/Art Resource
312 Giraudon/Art Resource
313 Mary Evans Picture Library
315 © Nathan Benn—Woodfin Camp & Associates; © Kunio Owaki—The Stock Market; Louisiana Office of Tourism.
316 Louisiana Office of Tourism; SuperStock.
317 © Cathlyn Melloan—Stone
318 © David Ball—Stone
319 © Jim Zietz/LSU Public Relations; © Jeff Greenberg—Unicorn Stock Photos.
320 © C. C. Lockwood—Bruce Coleman Inc.; © Robert McElroy—Woodfin Camp & Associates.
321 © Matt Bradley—Tom Stack & Associates
322 © Randy Wells—Stone; SuperStock; © Werner Bertsch—Bruce Coleman Inc.
323 © Garry D. McMichael—Photo Researchers
324 © John Elk—Stone
326 Corbis-Bettmann
327 Archive Photos; Bill Haber—AP/Wide World Photos.
328 The Granger Collection
329 © Art Siegel/Photography and Design—University of Pennsylvania; © Lennart Nilsson—Behold Man, Little, Brown and Company.
336 "Once: A Lullaby," Illustration © 1986 by Anita Lobel, by Permission William Morrow and Company; From The Lullaby Songbook, © 1986 Edited by Jane Yolen and Adam Stemple, reprint by permission Harcourt Brace Jovanovich, Inc.
337 From The Lullaby Songbook, © 1986 Edited by Jane Yolen and Adam Stemple, reprint by permission Harcourt Brace Jovanovich, Inc.
338 © Bruce Forster—Stone
339 © Richard Frishman—Stone; © Eric R. Berndt—Unicorn Stock Photos.
340 © Eric R. Berndt—Midwestock; © Ron Sanford—Stone; © John Blaustein—Woodfin Camp & Associates; © Tom Tracy—Photo Network.
342 © Pete Saloutos—The Stock Market
346 Scala/Art Resource
347 Courtesy, John B. Roney
350 © S. H. E. Kaufman & J. R. Golecki—Science Photo Library—Photo Researchers